Transact-SQL Programming

Transact-SQL Programming

Kevin Kline, Lee Gould, and Andrew Zanevsky

O'REILLY®

Beijing · Cambridge · Farnham · Köln · Paris · Sebastopol · Taipei · Tokyo

Transact-SQL Programming

by Kevin Kline, Lee Gould, and Andrew Zanevsky

Printed in the United States of America.

Published by O'Reilly & Associates, Inc., 101 Morris Street, Sebastopol, CA 95472.

Editor: Deborah Russell

Production Editor: Jeffrey Liggett

Printing History:

March 1999: First Edition.

This book is printed on acid-free paper with 85% recycled content, 15% post-consumer waste. O'Reilly & Associates is committed to using paper with the highest recycled content available consistent with high quality.

ISBN: 1-56592-401-0 [5/99]

Table of Contents

Foreword

I'm currently sitting at my desk imagining you, the potential reader of this book, wondering if you should invest in this excellent technical journal. If I just say "yes," you will think I'm some sales type. If I give you a long-winded analysis, you will think I'm an engineer. In fact, I'm somewhere in between. I was part of the original team that designed the Transact-SQL language in 1985 and built the architecture that is part of the Sybase and Microsoft databases you are using for your PC and Unix development. I was also the lead on the negotiating team that recruited Microsoft into the database cause in which Sybase so strongly believes—and in which you are investing part of your professional career. The language and the database principles it enables are every bit as important today as they were in the beginning.

Transact-SQL is the language of the PC database industry and the language that connects the Web to the data it needs. Collectively, Microsoft with SQL Server and Sybase with SQL Anywhere Studio and Adaptive Server hold the combined unit volume (measured in millions) for developers who want to be in the mainstream of the PC industry. In addition, most large enterprises invest in both NT and Unix, and the two share the Transact-SQL language as their common face to the developer. Until this book, there was nothing that gave you the details you needed to both optimize for and understand the differences between the Transact-SQL language for these two mainstream product lines.

A well-designed database should accomplish two goals. First, it should protect your data as a bank safe protects its contents—making sure that it is always there and available to whomever has a legitimate need to access it or store something new on it. Second, it should provide enough independence from the multiple applications that are accessing it so that significant changes can be made in the semantics of the data without requiring changes in the application itself. The absolute joy of experiencing these features for myself is something I'll never forget. I was developing the first course in Transact-SQL, had a distributed application running, and realized that I needed to change the semantics of the data. It took about 30 seconds to modify the behavior of a stored procedure in the database, and I didn't even have to restart the application! Transact-SQL gives you control over how data is accessed and changed. This book gives you the detailed information a developer needs to get the best value out of the language as well as the specific differences between the Microsoft and Sybase implementations.

The market for knowledgeable database developers has never been greater—nor has the usefulness of database products. Your knowledge of Transact-SQL, the leading language for the PC server industry, can be used for:

- A new category of applications for mobile computing in which a consolidated database is partitioned and replicated to mobile PCs
- A new generation of mobile "sub-PCs" inspired by devices like the PalmPilot, Windows-CE, and the Palm-sized PC
- Multidata source integration using Transact-SQL as a standard way to talk to a collection of different databases from different vendors
- High-performance, high-availability Unix enterprise servers

With so much going for Transact-SQL at the moment, it may seem ill-timed to ask what product will replace it. While predictions are always difficult, in my mind it will not be replaced as much as it will be integrated with new languages. My personal bet is on the integration of the Java object model (to extend what can be represented in a column) with the existing strength of Transact-SQL (the ability to manipulate data sets in a concise and data-independent way). Thus, the knowledge you gain for today's applications has a very long life.

Bob Epstein
Executive Vice-President
Sybase, Inc.

Preface

Many of the most exciting and innovative information systems in development or production today employ the Transact-SQL programming language. Transact-SQL is a powerful language used by developers and database administrators to extend procedural functionality to the SQL relational database language on database products supplied by Microsoft and Sybase.

This book teaches both the basics of SQL programming and the language-extending capabilities of Transact-SQL. It provides complete coverage of Transact-SQL, from the basics to the nitty-gritty details of the Microsoft and Sybase implementations of the language. It contains extensive examples of everything from the simplest query to complex, multistep operations. In addition to the examples in the book, you'll find many additional complete Transact-SQL programs and stored procedures on the companion CD-ROM.

Why Learn Transact-SQL?

Transact-SQL is a database programming language and SQL extension with enormous potential. Dialects of Transact-SQL are integral to several popular high-end relational database management systems—Microsoft SQL Server and Sybase Adaptive Server—and can also be found in the desktop database management system Sybase SQL Anywhere Studio. From the ubiquitous Windows NT Server installation to the glass-enclosed, high-end Unix data centers of Wall Street, Transact-SQL is a language you would do well to learn.

The Microsoft side of the equation alone shows some impressive numbers. In recent years, unit sales of Microsoft SQL Server have been increasing by 80 to 100% a year. Microsoft SQL Server's installed base now exceeds three million, and Microsoft expects the number of licenses to double over the next year. Although

Microsoft currently has only 15% of the overall database market (in comparison, Oracle has about 30% of that market), it has about 40% of the Windows NT market, and NT sales doubled last year (statistics from International Data Corporation, Dataquest, and *VARBusiness Magazine*). Developer interest is another good benchmark for the long-term prospects of a product; within a year, Microsoft expects to have 25,000 resellers, and another 25,000 end user database administrators, trained in the latest release, SQL Server 7.0, for a total price tag of $20 million.

Toss in the considerable market presence and growth of Sybase products from the Unix and Windows NT arena to Windows 95 and Windows 98, and you will discover another group of products where the Transact-SQL language is growing rapidly. Sybase's widely acclaimed Adaptive Server Enterprise on the high end, and SQL Anywhere Studio on the desktop, push the Transact-SQL language to even more users. Sybase has gone from a 1985 startup cofounded by Mark Hoffman and Bob Epstein in Bob's home to one of the top ten independent software houses of 1998, with revenues approaching $1 billion. Sybase, which is credited with popularizing the client/server application architecture, is known for its popular enterprise-level database products, middleware and gateway products, and development tools unit, PowerSoft. Sybase products are firmly entrenched in much of the Fortune 500.

What Does Transact-SQL Provide?

Transact-SQL, in the current versions offered by both Microsoft and Sybase, complies with current ANSI SQL-92 standards and with the Federal Information Processing Standards (FIPS 127-2) set by the National Institute for Standards and Technology. In the process of meeting federal government and industrial standards, Transact-SQL now provides database programmers with a broad range of tools that can create robust and full-featured programs.

Transact-SQL is used to implement many application functions, such as:

- Embedding important business rules into the database server through stored procedures, triggers, and table constraints
- Constructing powerful, standalone programs that enhance the functionality of a business application through scheduled tasks and command-line execution
- Building email-aware handling routines and applications that use them
- Connecting World Wide Web pages to a Microsoft or Sybase database management system

Although there are some minor variations between the Microsoft and Sybase implementations, Transact-SQL's abilities and features on both platforms include:

- A rich set of datatypes, including specialized datatypes for identifiers, timestamps, images, and long text fields
- Atomic-level transactions for Data Definition Language (DDL) commands and for Transact-SQL extensions like SELECT . . . INTO
- Fully programmable server objects like views, triggers, stored procedures, and batch command files; stored procedures and remote stored procedures are able to return entire data sets
- Local and global variables
- Conditional processing
- Multidirectional scrollable cursors
- Exception and error handling
- Temporary and persistent temporary tables
- Special aggregate operators such as ROLLUP and CUBE
- Full transaction control
- Trace flags to control server behavior
- System stored procedures that reduce the complexity of many operations, such as adding users or automatically generating HTML web pages

Audience for This Book

We wrote this book with both the novice programmer and the advanced Transact-SQL developer in mind. Everyone from the liberal arts major looking for a real job skill to the veteran database administrator (DBA) should find value in this book. We don't expect novices to necessarily know anything about the programming language, although you should know something about a good Windows text editor that will allow you to write programs. It would also help for you to have SQL Server installed either at work or at home. That way, you can test the programming concepts introduced in this book for yourself.

On the other hand, for veterans, we go into great detail on much of the minutiae of the Transact-SQL programming language. Even if you've already written many a Transact-SQL stored procedure, you'll still find material in this book that is new and interesting to you. Furthermore, we've included a number of stored procedures (found on the accompanying CD-ROM) that provide direct value to those who are running SQL Server in a development or production environment. In fact, we believe many of these stored procedures to be so valuable that some of you might buy this book solely for the Transact-SQL programs included with it. After all, some of these programs may save you 10 or 20 hours of work time.

Unlike many programming languages, Transact-SQL is used for many administrative functions, as well as for application programming. As a result, application programmers should find this text useful in teaching them how to perform operations against a Microsoft or Sybase database. These are high-end databases that frequently have a full-time database administrator. With this in mind, many of our examples are pertinent to both programmers and DBAs.

How to Use This Book

If you are unfamiliar with Transact-SQL, or even SQL, you can read this book from front to back. We've tried to organize it in a logical progression that provides clear and concise lessons about Transact-SQL. Those more skilled in Transact-SQL (or other SQL dialects) can simply read those chapters that are most interesting to them, as each chapter is largely self-contained. Some chapters are quite large and might take several days for you to plow through, while others are small and can be read in tens of minutes by the fast reader. In general, the book progresses from the foundation material to detailed discussions of specific aspects of Transact-SQL. Most readers will benefit by reading the book in order.

In writing this book, our intention has been to provide you with a comprehensive resource for Transact-SQL programming. Too many people have to learn programming languages through trial and error. We'll try to spare you. This book will show you the basic building blocks of Transact-SQL, coupled with useful and complete examples. As with many programming languages, Transact-SQL offers you many different ways to meet a set of programming requirements. It's our intention to show you those best practices with Transact-SQL that will help you skirt the "trial" stages of learning, minimizing your exposure to "error" and putting you that much closer to writing productive Transact-SQL programs.

To make our lessons a bit easier, we've used the ubiquitous "pubs" database, which is available with every installation of Microsoft SQL Server and Sybase Adaptive Server. The pubs database is designed to store the information of a fictional publishing and book distribution firm. If you don't know anything about pubs, see Chapter 2, *Database Analysis and Design*.

About the Contents

This book is divided into five major sections:

Part I, *The Basics: Programming in Transact-SQL*
: Chapters 1 through 5 show you the foundation of Transact-SQL. This part provides some background information about the origins of SQL Server and Transact-SQL, as well as relational database theory. It also delves into the

basics of good database design and programming, plus widely recognized and elegant programming styles. This part illustrates the SQL statements used to query and modify data, plus those that create database objects. Also discussed are several fundamental concepts, like reserved words and keywords, server character sets and sort orders, and Transact-SQL object identifiers.

Part II, *The Building Blocks: Transact-SQL Language Elements*

Chapters 6 through 11 describe the basic Transact-SQL programming components: constants, variables, conditional processing and control-of-flow statements, cursors, error handling, temporary structures, and transaction management. After reading this part, you should understand how the complex business requirements of your applications could be assembled using the various building-block components of Transact-SQL. The main emphasis of this part is how, when, and where to best apply each given programming construct.

Part III, *Functions and Extensions*

Chapters 12 and 13 illustrate the functions and extensions to SQL and the Transact-SQL language that are available in Microsoft and Sybase database management systems. In Chapter 12, you will learn about the multitude of functions that manipulate and transform data, obtain system information, compare data, and perform many other workhorse operations. Chapter 13 reveals the query and reporting capabilities offered by the CASE, COMPUTE, CUBE, and ROLLUP commands. A key determinant of effective and efficient Transact-SQL programming is how well you utilize the capabilities provided by these functions and extensions. You certainly don't want to spend several hours reinventing a programmatic function that is already built into the Transact-SQL programming language!

Part IV, *Programming Transact-SQL Objects*

Chapters 14 through 17 delve into specific tips and techniques for constructing well-designed Transact-SQL objects: stored procedures, triggers, and views. This part also brings to light much useful information about system and extended stored procedures provided by the database vendors. Perhaps more than any other aspect of code development, your design for Transact-SQL objects will pay off in terms of application development time, maintainability, and effectiveness.

Part V, *Performance Tuning and Optimization*

Chapters 18 through 21 tell you how to polish, manage, and optimize your Transact-SQL programs. This part contains detailed tips, tricks, and traps for improved SQL coding. Other topics include testing and debugging code and code maintenance. All of these issues are critical to the success of multiuser systems and multideveloper projects.

Part V, Appendixes

The appendixes to this book provide additional information about the system tables and catalogs used in Microsoft SQL Server and Sybase Adaptive Server and the new and exciting changes to Transact-SQL found in Microsoft SQL Server Version 7.0.

About the Examples

This book contains a multitude of examples—multiline programs that will help you appreciate the full potential of Transact-SQL. We wanted to provide you with information that transcends the vendor-provided documentation to reveal not only the use of particular features but also how they can be best utilized. We've tried to make our examples relevant to both developers and database administrators, both initiates and gurus of the language. Much of the material will provide you with real-world examples of real-world problems. We've also attempted to show you procedures and processes for writing efficient and maintainable code.

In general, whenever we show a query in this book, we'll follow it with the result set produced by the program.

Whenever possible, it's a good idea to read through the book with an open connection to SQL Server, trying examples as you read. The best way to learn any programming language is to work with it. We heartily recommend that you do so, if at all possible.

When you look at a syntax example, remember the coding conventions used to distinguish elements of the command; see "Conventions Used in This Book."

Conventions Used in This Book

The following conventions are used in this book:

`constant width`
: Represents display text, error messages, examples, and in-text references to syntax models.

`constant width bold`
: Occasionally used for emphasis in sample output.

lowercase
: Represents @ variables, @@ variables, and user-defined names.

lowercase italic
: Represents ep_, sp_, and xp_ functions, Unix commands, and Unix filenames. Also used for the first occurrence of important terms.

UPPERCASE
: Represents constraints, datatypes, functions (except for ep_, sp_, and xp_ functions), keywords, options/specifiers, reserved words, and Transact-SQL commands.

UPPERCASE ITALIC
: Represents Windows NT commands and filenames.

`{braces}`
: In code, items shown in braces are required; type only the information in the braces, not the braces themselves.

`[brackets]`
: In code, items shown in brackets are optional; type only the information in the brackets, not the brackets themselves.

`(parentheses)`
: In code, indicates that you can repeat the previous syntax item.

`-- (double dash)`
: In code, represents the beginning of a comment line. It is there to provide you with information about the program but is not executed with the other code.

`/* and */`
: In code, delimits multiple-line comments.

`| (pipe)`
: In code, indicates an "or" choice for a single item within the brackets or braces. If a list of items appears in brackets or braces, select only one item.

Indicates a tip, suggestion, or general note. For example, we'll tell you if you need to use a particular SQL Server version or if an operation requries certain privileges.

Indicates a warning or caution. For example, we'll tell you if SQL Server does not behave as you'd expect or if a particular operation has a negative impact on performance.

Environment

The database management systems that utilize Transact-SQL (Microsoft SQL Server, Sybase Adaptive Server, Sybase SQL Anywhere, and Sybase Adaptive Server IQ) can run under several different operating systems. The following table shows the operating systems and the database management systems (DBMSs) that run on them:

Operating System	DBMS
Windows NT	Microsoft SQL Server 6.5 and Sybase Adaptive Server Enterprise (ASE), Sybase Adaptive Server Anywhere (ASA), Sybase Adaptive Server IQ
Windows 95, 98	Microsoft SQL Server 7.0, Sybase Adaptive Server Anywhere
Windows 3.1 and DOS	Sybase Adaptive Server Anywhere
Unix (different flavors)	Sybase Adaptive Server Enterprise, Sybase Adaptive Server IQ

Windows NT is the only operating system supported by all Transact-SQL environments. Furthermore, Windows NT is probably the most popular environment for the development of Transact-SQL programs. As a result, this book is written from a Windows NT, Intel-based hardware perspective. Some of the examples shown in this book focus on the features available through this operating system. However, if you use a different system, this shouldn't be a problem, since only the simplest operating-system features (like *DIR* commands) are referred to in the book.

At the time we're completing this book, Microsoft is just starting to ship SQL Server 7.0, and Sybase is starting to ship Sybase Adaptive Server Enterprise (ASE) 11.9. Most customers are still using earlier versions and probably will continue to do so for some time. As a result, we've elected to have the bulk of this book focus on the versions actually being used in the field—Microsoft SQL Server 6.5 and ASE 11.5. The vast majority of Transact-SQL syntax is identical from version to version. We've noted the most important differences in the appropriate sections of the text. For Microsoft SQL Server, we've also included an appendix (Appendix B, *What's New for Transact-SQL in Microsoft SQL Server 7.0*) that summarizes the differences that affect Transact-SQL.

The examples in this book and on the accompanying CD-ROM have generally been designed for Micrsoft SQL Server 6.5 and ASE 11.5. Many more are designed for SQL Server 7.0. Version compatibility is described with each example or sample program.

In some cases, examples are skewed to take advantage of a specific feature offered in either Microsoft's or Sybase's implementation of Transact-SQL. In that case, the example is introduced so that you'll know under which implementation it will run most effectively. However, unless otherwise mentioned, all examples will work fine under both Sybase and Microsoft implementations.

The Name of the Game

Unlike other SQL extensions, such as the PL/SQL extension offered by Oracle Corporation, Transact-SQL is widely known both by its full name and by its abbreviated name, T-SQL. (In this book, for consistency, we always use the full name.) In contrast, it's rather unusual to see anyone refer to PL/SQL by its full name, which is Procedural Language/SQL.

Similarly, Sybase and Microsoft have made some efforts to differentiate their products. A good starting place for that is with new and different names. As a result, Sybase now calls its flagship database management system the Sybase Adaptive Server. You may see us refer to "SQL Server" at various places throughout the text, but rest assured that the functionality also describes the Sybase Adaptive Server, unless otherwise noted.

About the CD-ROM

The CD-ROM accompanying this book contains many examples of Transact-SQL code, mostly in the form of several dozen stored procedures. These can save you countless hours of programming time by performing such useful functions as:

- Automating DBCC checks on databases being dumped
- Providing an improved way of viewing the code of Transact-SQL objects, like views, stored procedures, and triggers
- Supplying a method for quickly searching the source code for an occurence of any given variable, object name, or other string of text

In addition to the code examples, the CD-ROM contains a number of complete software packages, including an evaluation version of Microsoft SQL Server 7.0. In addition, you'll find evaluation copies of Embarcadero's RapidSQL and Sylvain-Faust International's SQL-Programmer, both Transact-SQL debuggers that can help you perform a number of workbench activities while building complex Transact-SQL programs. Just like C++ or VB debuggers, these tools can help you improve efficiency and reduce programming problems.

Refer to the *README* file on the CD-ROM for detailed descriptions of the contents of the CD-ROM. The *README* file contains important information about system compatibility, as well as hardware and sofware requirements needed to run the trial software.

We've made many of the code examples included on the CD-ROM available on the O'Reilly web site as well. See "Comments and Questions." The web site also provides links to the latest versions of the free evaluation software included with the CD-ROM. We recommend that you investigate these links to ensure that you have the most recent versions available.

Comments and Questions

Please address comments and questions concerning this book to the publisher:

O'Reilly & Associates, Inc.
101 Morris Street
Sebastopol, CA 95472
800-998-9938 (in the U.S. or Canada)
707-829-0515 (international or local)
707-829-0104 (fax)

You can also send us messages electronically. For corrections and amplifications for this book, as well as for copies of many of the examples found in the book, check out:

http://www.oreilly.com/catalog/wintrnssql

See the ads in the book for information about all of O'Reilly & Associates' online services.

Acknowledgments

Before each author takes a few moments at the podium to thank those close to him, we, as a team, would specifically like to thank a few special individuals at O'Reilly and Associates. First, we all owe a huge debt of gratitude to Debby Russell, our editor. Debby, you're the best. We now know why O'Reilly puts little animals on the covers of their books; you're shepherd, lion tamer, horse trainer, cattle driver, and trail boss. Thank you for such excellent work. Thanks for your patience, insight, and talent. You've helped make this book what it is. Also, a special word of thanks to Steve Abrams. Steve, the many hours you logged on this project are much appreciated. And of course, we owe much to Tim O'Reilly. Thanks for taking a bet on this book.

We also owe a debt to our fine technical reviewers. To Eoin Woods, Troy Christensen, and Bob Pierce, we owe a hearty thanks. Your contributions have greatly improved the accuracy, readability, and value of this tome. We also would like to thank Lynda Davis, Dale Qualls, and Mike Drexler. You've provided significant insight and direction.

To Bob Epstein, the designer of SQL Server and founder of Sybase, thank you for being so willing to help out on this book. It's not often that mere mortals are able to breathe the same air as a luminary such as yourself. Your vision has helped make Transact-SQL one of the most popular procedural extensions to SQL available today, and we are grateful for your endorsement of our work on Transact-SQL.

We are very grateful to several people and organizations for providing evaluation copies of software for inclusion on the CD-ROM that accompanies this book: Amy Stuhlberg, Marketing Manager and Developer Relations, Microsoft; Tom Kreyche, SQL Server Marketing, Microsoft; Coleen Weeks, Vice-President, Sales and Marketing, Embarcadero Technologies; and Karen Pallister, Manager, Marketing Programs, Sylvain Faust International. Thanks too to Baya Pavliashvili who helped make the CD-ROM.

From Kevin

These acknowledgments are for those who had a hand in this project and in my life in general. If you're not one of those people, feel free to read on—but at your own risk. You'd think that taking a moment to acknowledge people is easy. But it's not. Think for a moment. How do you properly convey the significance of how much a person means to you in a few terse turns of phrase? A poet could do better, so I'll just put it out there, roughhewn, and hope you get the gist.

First, let me thank my colleagues, Andrew and Lee. You two are just fabulous—resourceful, talented, and knowledgeable. It is an honor to work with individuals of your caliber. Thank you so much for joining in on the book, taking the bull by the horns, and turning out such a fine product. Also, I must make mention of the significant contribution of Terry Murphy on the material for views. Terry, you, my friend, are the cavalry who came over the hill! Thanks for pulling my fat outta the fire when the deadlines loomed near.

Kelly—witty, wise, and strong. At the end of an arduous day, there's no reward greater than your loving embrace. Thank you for your support and care. Dylan! You had to spend some time alone on your favorite computer games and I know it felt like a sacrifice. But consider it practice time. Now that I'm back, you'll spend many a night disintegrating the old man in Virtual Combat. Thank you, Emily, for giving up those bedtime stories and evenings in my lap. The stars that shine at night couldn't equal the twinkle in your eyes. Your mischievous and hilarious pranks fill me with a joy and mirth that cannot be equaled!

My brother Dan, do you have even a hint of how much you shaped my life? In countless ways, you set the bar always a notch higher for me, and then showed me how to leap. I still want to be like you when I grow up. Dad, thanks for putting the technology in me. It's made my life prosperous. Mom, thanks for putting the arts in me. It's made my life rich. And thanks to both of you for putting love into me. It's made me who I am.

To all the crew at Deloitte & Touche LLP Practice Service Center. I've never worked with a more exceptional group of individuals. In fact, I'm spoiled now. I keep thinking that everybody should be as smart and talented as you. Jeff Bogard, Joe Terry, Evelyn Hutchison, Dwayne Seiber, Lynda Davis, and Anthony Santini—thanks for letting me chew on your ears when the stress levels got too high. Your friendship is a treasure to me.

I'd also like to give a special thanks to Doug Watts, Office Managing Partner of the Practice Service Center, and Doug Greenleaf, Chief Information Officer for Deloitte & Touche LLP, for your blessings on this project. Your leadership has helped make Deloitte the star that others navigate by. I feel immense pride to be a part of this team.

And lastly, a tip of the hat to Liz Kennedy, Pat Burns, and Beverly Meeler for helping me forge my latent database skills into a useful tool way back in the early days. Finally, to Doctors Gerberding, Satterfield, and Shipman. You were the teachers who made a difference.

From Lee

To my parents Sylvia and Ray Gould: without your love, encouragement, and wisdom I would not be where I am today. You have guided me perpetually, and knowing that you are always there gives me the strength to succeed, even if it has to be on a telephone across the continent. My brother and his wife—Paul and Sally Gould: you are my family and are always there for me. Paul, you will always be my Iron Man training partner regardless of where we live.

For Kevin Kline and Andrew Zanevsky, my teammates in this project: your constant source of inspiration, wit, and talent are what helped drive me through this entire process. In spite of our geographical dispersion, I felt you were both at my side every single step of the way. Your ever-present dedication and pride in your work have kept me going when I would have usually given up.

To Sally Perrow: your warmth, wisdom, love, and deep friendship could always be relied upon and continues to be a constant source of strength for me. Your perpetual support, encouragement, and ready ear have proved that you can be next to me even when you are a continent away.

A special thanks to Peter Steyn from CCSC, who was willing to take a chance with me and bring me over from South Africa; and to Sid Amster from ETCI, who has always been there, providing a good dose of wit and cynicism, and who introduced me to Sybase, Inc.

Lisa Alter, without a doubt, you have probably had the hardest job that anyone could ever have; you have had to both manage and mentor me over the last three years. My heartfelt thanks go not only to you but also to your family, Jason and Ross, as well.

To Karen Watterson, who got my writing career off the ground and introduced me to Kevin and Andrew: your talent as an editor has both forged and helped refine my writing style. Your technical skill, diversity, and interest have been invaluable and will always be a guide.

To my dear friends Karin Williams, Dana Spanger, and David Berger: having friends like you, where the friendship has no bounds, has been the greatest gift a friend could ask for. We have shared so much of our lives together and have learned so much from each other, and I will be forever thankful that we all share such a wonderful friendship with each other.

To my many other peers and advisers at Sybase, Inc., not the least of whom are Frances Thomas, Denise McCutchen, and Judy Podell, the unknown faces of sps_consult, and the staff at Engineering who either fielded my questions or provided encouragement along the way.

To all of my friends, family, and advisors around the world—among them Dr. Elizabeth King Williams; Dr. Ulrike Schultz; Janet and Jorge Cortez; David and Karen Zahler; Cantor Claire; Alan and Lael Rebecca Franco; Lori Nichols; Gita, Stanley, Melanie, and Justin Redfearn; Eric, Gina, and Clare Pienaar; Shelley and David Lurie; Jay Ionson and Frank Kassteen; Gert and Marayna Odendaal; Ella, Jerry, and Hana Da Silva. You all nourished my soul and in some cases my stomach with both good food and wine and could always be counted on to provide constant companionship, interest, understanding, and advice during the writing of this book.

I have lived on three continents now, in England, South Africa, and America. Without doubt, I would like to acknowledge all the friends and family whom I have not mentioned already and who live in all of those countries and have helped and continue to help me in life. A special thank you goes to my adopted country, America, for giving me the opportunity to fly "Higher than an Eagle."

From Andrew

First, I would like to thank my wife, Katrin, for the most wonderful relationship of love, friendship, and unconditional support. Being a SQL Server DBA herself, she was my first editor and technical advisor. She has also written some of the system stored procedures included on the CD-ROM accompanying the book.

I thank my parents for teaching me to think, to learn, to set new goals, and to achieve them. I only wish that we weren't separated by eight-hour belts and could meet more often.

My coauthors Kevin and Lee have been fantastic teammates. Not many people can survive as much criticism as we had to give one another when cross-reviewing one another's chapters. I thank them for their patience, for their deep knowledge, for correcting my mistakes, for jokes, and for words of support when we were all tired.

I have had so many excellent teachers in my life who gave students their hearts and minds. I particularly thank the professors and staff of the Belarus State University of Informatics and Radioelectronics, who taught me programming and defined my career.

My friend Boris Goldberg offered me his help when I needed it most—during my first year in the United States—and I am extremely grateful for that.

Boris Zibitsker, President of BEZ Systems, Inc., and Ella Zibitsker, Director of Computer Systems Institute, were my first employers in the United States and sponsored my application to become a U.S. resident. Their vast knowledge and tremendous experience have always been of great value to me.

I owe my writing career to Karen Watterson, an independent consultant, author of several books, and the editor of *Microsoft SQL Server Professional* and *Visual Basic Developer* (Pinnacle Publishing). She offered me a monthly column in her newsletter back in 1995, and we have worked together ever since. Her constant encouragement and guidance have helped me immensely in developing writing skills and shaping my style.

I thank all my clients who trusted me with administering or developing for their SQL Servers. I have had the pleasure of working with many wonderful people—technical specialists and managers. I learned from you, my friends and colleagues.

Finally, I want to thank the United States from the bottom of my heart. This country has welcomed me and has given me every opportunity to succeed professionally and personally. I am honored to live here.

I

The Basics: Programming in Transact-SQL

Part I provides the foundations of Transact-SQL. If you read only Part I, you will come away with a good understanding of the origins of SQL Server and Transact-SQL, as well as some of the basics of relational database theory and some basic database design concepts. You will learn the SQL statements used to query and modify data, as well as those that create database objects. Finally, you will review basic conventions of Transact-SQL coding, including best practices for formatting your Transact-SQL programs.

Part I contains these chapters:

- Chapter 1, *Introduction to Transact-SQL*
- Chapter 2, *Database Analysis and Design*
- Chapter 3, *SQL Primer*
- Chapter 4, *Transact-SQL Fundamentals*
- Chapter 5, *Format and Style*

In this chapter:

- *SQL and the Introduction of Transact-SQL*
- *The Relational Database Model*
- *Normalization*
- *Row Processing Versus Set Processing*
- *The History of SQL Server*
- *What Is Transact-SQL?*
- *Summary*

1

Introduction to Transact-SQL

Transact-SQL, an extension to the SQL database programming language, is a powerful language offering many features—a wide variety of datatypes, temporary objects, system and extended stored procedures, scrollable cursors, conditional processing, transaction control, exception and error handling, and much more. We'll introduce those features later in this chapter in the section "What is Transact-SQL?" Before getting to Transact-SQL specifics, however, we'll provide some background information that will help you get a feel for the overall database environment in which Transact-SQL operates. After we explain the basic differences between ANSI SQL and Transact-SQL, we'll jump back to more generalized topics. We'll cover the genesis of the relational database model and its impact on SQL programming languages. We'll talk a bit about normalizing data and introduce you to the idea of row-processing and set-processing information technology. We'll spend a little time talking about the history of SQL Server in general. Finally, we'll introduce many of the features of the Transact-SQL programming language itself.

SQL and the Introduction of Transact-SQL

SQL, on which Transact-SQL is based, started life in the mid-1970s as an IBM product called SEQUEL. SEQUEL stood for Structured English Query Language. After a permutation or two and some legal problems, IBM changed the name to SQL—the *Structured Query Language*. The language was designed to provide a standard method for accessing data in a relational database. Ironically, although IBM introduced SQL, Oracle was the first to bring a SQL-using product to market.

Today, many different relational database systems utilize SQL as the primary means for accessing and manipulating data. When the American National Standards Institute (ANSI) published a standard for the SQL language in 1989, they set a universal standard to which database vendors could adhere. Later, in 1992, ANSI released an update to the SQL standard, known as SQL-92. The standards helped formalize many of the behaviors and syntax structures of SQL. The ANSI standard covered lots of important details concerning the querying and manipulation of data. The syntax was formalized for many commands; some of these are SELECT, INSERT, UPDATE, DELETE, CREATE, and DROP.

Unfortunately, the standards didn't address every facet of programming for a relational database. To meet the needs of their own user communities, database vendors began to extend the SQL language with capabilities that enhanced the basic functionality of SQL. The Transact-SQL language was introduced by Sybase to answer user requirements for programming extensions to SQL—extensions enabling conditional processing, error handling, declared variables, row processing, and numerous other functions. Even some of the simplest operations, like creating an index or performing a conditional operation, are extensions to the SQL language.

Furthermore, many relational database products had been on the market for some time before a standard of any kind had been published. As a result, many developers began to implement their own extensions to the SQL language. In most cases, these extensions to SQL were incompatible from vendor to vendor. A program written in Oracle's dialect of SQL, for example, wouldn't run properly under Sybase or DB2 and vice versa unless it contained only the simplest ANSI-standard SQL statements.

The Relational Database Model

These days, relational database management systems (RDBMSs) like SQL Server and Sybase are the primary engines of information systems everywhere—particularly distributed client/server computing systems. Though RDBMSs are now common enough to trip over, it wasn't always that way. Not too long ago, you would probably trip over hierarchical database systems or network database systems or COBOL (heck, that *still* happens). Here's a quick-and-dirty definition for a *relational database*: a system whose users view data as a collection of tables related to one another through common data values.

Perhaps you are interested in more than a quick-and-dirty definition? Here goes. The whole basis for the relational model follows this train of thought: data is stored in *tables*, which are composed of *rows* and *columns*. Tables of independent data can be linked, or *related*, to one another if all have columns of data that represent the same data value, called *keys*. This concept is so common as to seem trivial; however, it was not so long ago that achieving and programming a system capable of sustaining the relational model was considered a long shot with limited usefulness.

Relational data theory was first proposed by E. F. Codd in his 1970 paper to the ACM entitled "A Relational Model of Data for Large Shared Data Banks." Soon after, Codd clarified his position in the 1974 paper to the Texas Conference on Computing Systems entitled "The Relational Approach to Data Base Management: An Overview." It was in this paper that Codd proposed the now legendary 12 Principles of Relational Databases. If a vendor's database product didn't meet Codd's 12-item litmus test, then it was not a member of the club. The good news is that rules do not apply to applications development; rather, these rules determine whether the database engine itself can be considered truly "relational." Nowadays, most RDBMSs—including both Microsoft and Sybase variants of SQL Server—pass the test.

There is some debate about why relational database systems won out over hierarchical and network database systems, but the following reasons seem self-evident:

- The relational high-level language interface is much simpler to learn and more intuitive than with nonrelational databases (you are, after all, reading *this* book as opposed to one on Xbase).
- Relational databases provide efficient and intuitive data structures that easily accommodate ad hoc queries. From phone books to hotel registries, relational databases (of a sort) are second nature to most people.
- Relational databases provide powerful integrity controls such as check constraints and referential integrity—thus providing higher-quality data.
- The RDBMS vendors combined slick marketing and adept hardware positioning to gain a market and mindshare advantage.

One of the key risks you face when developing relational databases is their simplicity. They're just so *easy*. It is no chore to slap together a set of tables and columns for a database. Even assigning relationships between tables is not a big deal. The whole process of database creation can be accomplished so easily that many developers entirely skip the distinct and separate process of *database design*. There are literally volumes of work written about proper relational database design, which is beyond the scope of this text. But there are a few key concepts you must understand fully if you're going to leverage the power of relational databases and, hence, Transact-SQL. Prominent among them are the concept of normalization and the drastic difference in the set-processing behavior preferred by SQL Server versus the row-processing behavior of popular rapid application development (RAD) tools.

Codd's Rules for a Truly Relational Database System

Are you curious about Codd's 12 Principles of Relational Databases? Don't be ashamed that you don't know them by heart; few on the SQL Server's development staff do, and no one on the marketing staff does. However, the few folks who *do* know these principles by heart treat them like religious doctrine and likely would be mortified by their "lightweight" treatment here:

1. Information is represented logically in tables.
2. Data must be logically accessible by table, primary key, and column.
3. Null values must be uniformly treated as "missing information," not as empty strings, blanks, or zeros.
4. Metadata (data about the database) must be stored in the database just as regular data is.
5. A single language must be able to define data, views, integrity constraints, authorization, transactions, and data manipulation.
6. Views must show the updates of their base tables and vice versa.
7. A single operation must be able to retrieve, insert, update, or delete data.
8. Batch and end user operations are logically separate from physical storage and access methods.
9. Batch and end user operations can change the database schema without having to re-create it or applications built upon it.
10. Integrity constraints must be available and stored in the metadata, not in an application program.
11. The data manipulation language of the relational system should not care where or how the physical data is distributed and should not require alteration if the physical data is centralized or distributed.
12. Any row processing done in the system must obey the same integrity rules and constraints that set-processing operations do.

Transact-SQL and the SQL Server database management system accomplish all of these functions.

Normalization

There is an old urban legend that claims the term *normalization* entered the database design lexicon thanks to the late President Richard Nixon. It seems that the researchers developing relational theory in the early 1970s were searching for a term to describe the process of properly defining database tables and their relationships to one another. Coincidentally, the news media were full of stories about President Nixon "normalizing" the relationship between the United States and the People's Republic of China. Somewhere, over someone's head, a lightbulb went off and the term was introduced into the computer world. Don't bet any money on this story, but we have it on good authority from a friend of a friend that this is true.

So what is normalization used for? Normalization is a design technique that enables database designers and programmers to develop table structures that minimize programming problems. As we discuss normalization, we'll show you each set of problems that a particular kind of normalization helps negate.

The process of normalization is characterized by levels of adherence called *normal form.* If a table design conforms only to the lowest level of normalization, it is said to be in *First Normal Form,* which is abbreviated as 1NF. If a table design conforms to the next higher level, it is in *Second Normal Form* (2NF), and so on. It is uncommon and probably never necessary to take a table design beyond *Third Normal Form* (3NF). In fact, in some cases, it is actually advantageous in terms of performance to *denormalize* a table from a higher normal form back to a lower normal form, like from 3NF to 2NF. It is also important to remember that normalizing tables is not full database design; rather, it is an important step in the analysis process. (The database design process is described briefly in Chapter 2, *Database Analysis and Design.*)

Assume that we are keeping a database that contains information about all of our circus animals. (What do you mean you don't own any circus animals? Well, some of you have kids, so that's pretty close.)

Unnormalized.

The data, when completely unnormalized, looks like this:

```
Circus_Info Table, Unnormalized
1.  animal_nbr (the primary key)
2.  animal_name
3.  tent_nbr
4.  tent_name
5.  tent_location
6.  trick_nbr1
7.  trick_name1
8.  trick_learned_at1
9.  trick_skill_level1
10. trick_nbr2...(and on through 16)
11. trick_name2...(and on through 16)
12. trick_learned_at2...(and on through 16)
13. trick_skill_level2...(and on through 16)
```

In this example, the animal_nbr column (in boldface) is our primary key, or the value that uniquely identifies each row. This is an *unnormalized* structure. But why go to the trouble of normalizing it? Well, otherwise, there would be a number of logical anomalies to deal with. In fact, there would be logic faults whenever you attempted insert, delete, or update operations on this table. (Similar problems are resolved each time you apply a higher level of normalization.) The reason there are so many problems with this table design is that much of the data is redundant and does not wholly depend on the key of the table (animal_nbr). These are the main problems:

Insert problem
: Suppose that a chimpanzee has been acquired and has to be added to the table. It would be impossible to add the new chimp without also adding a trick. Conversely, a new trick couldn't be added to the database without also assigning the trick to a circus animal, which might not reflect the actual business rule.

Delete problem
: What happens if a trick is deleted from the table? Unfortunately, important data about a circus animal would also be deleted. The situation also falters when an animal is deleted. This erases information about a trick that may still be used by the circus.

Update problem
: Updates in the unnormalized table could cause actions on multiple records. Great care must be taken to properly identify the appropriate record when making a change.

First Normal Form (1NF)

To put this in *First Normal Form* (1NF), we must eliminate repeating groups. That means that any subgroups of data that appear within the record should be split into separate tables. In this case, we have at least two major repeating groups to split. Thus, our unnormalized structure becomes two tables in 1NF:

```
Circus_Animals Table in 1NF
1.  animal_nbr  (the primary key)
2.  animal_name
3.  tent_nbr
4.  tent_name
5.  tent_location

Tricks Table in 1NF
1.  animal_nbr (the concatenated key)
2.  trick_nbr  (the concatenated key)
3.  trick_name
4.  trick_learned_at
5.  trick_skill_level
```

Now that our tables are in 1NF, we have the obvious advantage of reduced space consumption. Plus, an animal that only knows a few tricks doesn't use up the space allotted for 16 tricks in the unnormalized table. On the flip side, the animal can also know more than 16 tricks. Also note that in the Tricks table, the key had to be expanded to include both animal_nbr and trick_nbr. Concatenated keys are often the byproduct of the normalization process.

Second Normal Form (2NF)

Let's take our 1NF circus tables to *Second Normal Form* (2NF) by eliminating partial dependencies. Say what? A *partial dependency* is a fancy word for data that doesn't depend on the primary key of the table to uniquely identify it. For example, the trick name appears in every animal record, but the trick_nbr should be sufficient since we've already got the name in the Tricks table.

So this 1NF table:

```
Tricks Table
1.  animal_nbr
2.  trick_nbr
3.  trick_name
4.  trick_learned_at
5.  trick_skill_level
```

becomes these 2NF tables:

```
Tricks Table
1.  trick_nbr
2.  trick_nam

Animal_Tricks Table
1.  animal_nbr
2.  trick_nbr
3.  trick_learned_at
4.  trick_skill_level

Animal Table in 2NF
1.  animal_nbr
2.  animal_name
3.  tent_nbr
4.  tent_name
5.  tent_location
```

Unfortunately 2NF, like 1NF, has its own logical faults when attempting data manipulation:

Insert problem

Assume that we want to create a new record to represent a tiger assigned to the "Big Cats" tent. It's impossible to create an additional tiger record for the Animal table without first creating a new tent. This is due to the fact the tent_nbr column has a transitive dependency to the animal_nbr column, which more uniquely identifies its information than does the tent_nbr column.

Delete problem

Deleting a particular animal might result in the loss of an entire tent, even though you still want to retain information about that tent. For example, deleting the sole ostrich in the circus completely removes all traces of the "Big Birds" tent, since you only have one of these large birds.

Update problem

Tent information is redundant in the Animal table, so any change to tent information require a search of the entire table to locate the records needing alteration. Plus, the number of the records requiring the update may vary over time.

An additional step of normalization is needed to eliminate these logic faults. This added step converts a 2NF table into a 3NF table.

Third Normal Form (3NF)

To take this motley crew of tables to *Third Normal Form* (3NF), we must now take 2NF tables and eliminate all transitive (i.e., hidden) dependencies. In other words, every column that isn't a part of the key must depend on the key for its informational value. Non-key columns should have no informational value if they are separated from the key of a 3NF table. Remember that the term "eliminate" doesn't mean "delete." Instead, it means to split into separate tables.

Our tables in 3NF would now look like this:

```
Tricks Table (unchanged, it was already 3NF!)
1.  trick_nbr
2.  trick_name

Animal_Tricks Table (unchanged, it was already 3NF!)
1.  animal_nbr
2.  trick_nbr
3.  trick_learned_at
4.  trick_skill_level
```

The Animal table becomes two new 3NF tables:

```
Animal_Lodging Table in 3NF
1.  animal_nbr
2.  animal_name
3.  tent_nbr

Tents Table in 3NF
1.  tent_nbr
2.  tent_name
3.  tent_location
```

2NF and 3NF are all about the relationship between non-key and key fields. A 3NF table should provide a single-value fact about the key and should use the whole key (if concatenated), and nothing but the key, to derive its uniqueness.

By the time you get to 2NF, the columns all depend on the primary key for their identity. However, the columns may have such a distinction from other columns in the table that they should be split out into a separate table. In the Animal_Lodging table, the tent_nbr still appears as a non-key column in the table, even though it is the primary key of the Tents table. Thus, tent_nbr is a foreign key within the animal_Lodging table. Using tent_nbr as a foreign key, we are able to join the data together from the two separate tables to form a single data set.

Remember, normalizing data means eliminating redundant information from a table and organizing the data so that future changes to the table are easier. A table is in First Normal Form (1NF) when each field contains the smallest meaningful data and the table contains no repeating fields. Second Normal Form (2NF) refers only to tables with a multiple-field primary key. Each non-key field should relate to all of the fields making up the primary key. Third Normal Form (3NF) refers only to tables with a single-key field and requires that each non-key field be a direct description of the primary key field.

The steps described here are merely guidelines that help you design a set of stable table structures.

Denormalization

You've just read all about how and why to normalize tables. Designing table structures to 3NF reduces data redundancy and provides clean, logical table structures. But now we're going to tell you all the reasons to *denormalize* tables. Odd as this might sound, denormalization is not diametrically opposed to normalization (although some purists might testify otherwise).

The main benefit of denormalization is improved performance, although simplified data retrieval and manipulation are sometimes lesser benefits. Both of these benefits are rendered through the reduction in the number of joins needed for the proper functionality of your application. *Joins* (described in Chapter 3, *SQL Primer*) merge the data of two related tables into a single result set, presenting a denormalized view of the data. Joins, however, are rather time consuming and utilize a lot of CPU cycles. So, to reduce the expense of joins, many developers preempt what would otherwise be a very common join with a denormalized table. The table is now exposed to the vulnerabilities inherent in its lower normal form, but

Beyond 3NF?

There are additional steps in normalization used to solve other specific logic faults in table design; however, they are seldom practical in the use of non-academic applications. Read on for a quick glimpse of normal forms beyond 3NF:

Boyce-Codd Normal Form (BCNF)
: Ensures that absolutely no hidden dependencies exist by splitting off tables if *determinate* columns exist in a 3NF table. A determinate is a column on which some other column is fully functionally dependent. This would be akin to splitting the store_dept table into two tables: one called store_dept, which contains only store_nbr and dept_id, and the other called dept_name, which contains only dept_id and dept_name.

Fourth Normal Form (4NF)
: Compensates for multivalued dependencies in a three-column table (of A, B, and C), where columns A and B have a well-defined relationship, columns A and C have a well-defined relationship, but columns B and C are completely independent.

Fifth Normal Form (5NF)
: Almost a purely academic exercise, SNF reduces offset joins and projection dependencies that cause spurious results, hence called Join-Projection Normal Form.

Domain-Key Normal Form (DK/NF)
: Introduced by Donald Fagin back in 1981, it solves most insertion and deletion logic faults and provides generic definitions of deriving normal forms. However, no methodology or standardized algorithm exists for deriving DK/NF.

considerable time is saved because the application no longer has to join multiple tables together in a temporary workspace. Denormalization can also save processing time that might have been spent on the creation of summary reports.

The first thing you need to remember about denormalization is that you must thoroughly understand the needs and behavior of the data. There are some other tips to keep in mind when considering denormalizing tables:

- Denormalization means that more storage space will be needed for the redundant data.
- Redundant data usually speeds up queries but can slow down updates since multiple instances of the data item must be altered.

- Denormalized tables can introduce logic faults that must be compensated for in the application code.
- Maintaining integrity can be more difficult with redundant data.
- Denormalization yields the best improvements on tables that are frequently queried, such as validation tables or reporting tables. Tables in which records are frequently inserted, updated, and deleted are less viable candidates for denormalization.

Denormalization is generally regarded as a tuning method of last resort by the purists. On the other hand, many database administrators feel that it is perfectly natural to denormalize a frequently-used eight-way join to create a simpler three-way join, for example. Denormalization is usually accomplished by adding columns and foreign keys from other tables into the denormalized table or by adding aggregate columns to the denormalized table. If every query issued against a given table commonly has to join to columns from one or more other tables, you're looking at a candidate for denormalization.

Row Processing Versus Set Processing

One of the first things an experienced third-generation language (3GL) programmer must do when learning Transact-SQL (or any SQL variant, for that matter) is toss all her programming techniques and tricks out the window. Yes, you must unlearn much of what made you a star 3GL programmer to become a star database programmer. Procedural 3GLs, like FORTRAN, COBOL, or BASIC, perform their data operations in a manner that is quite contrary to effective Transact-SQL programming. That is because the basis of 3GL data manipulation requires the programmer to actually tell the program exactly how to treat the data, one record at a time. Since the 3GL program cycles down through a list of records, performing its logic on one record after the other, this style of programming is frequently called *row-processing* or *declarative programming.* Using this style of programming in Transact-SQL programs does to SQL Server what a parade does to traffic—slows things down.

On the other side of the equation, programs written for SQL-based RDBMSs prefer to operate in logical *sets* of data. Unlike the row-processing style, you tell SQL Server only *what* you want for the data, not *how* each individual piece of data should be handled. Sometimes you will see *set processing* referred to as *procedural processing,* since you code only what you want, as in "Give me all employees in the southern region who earn more than $70,000 per year."

To use an analogy, assume that you want to buy a long list of automobile parts for the 1970 Oldsmobile 442 convertible you're restoring (well, that's the car I'd want to restore). You go to the first parts store on your list. There you have to pull out a shopping cart and wheel it up and down every single aisle searching for the parts you want. Furthermore, when you find a part you need, you have to take it out of the shipping crate and, later, you have to barscan it and bag it yourself. That is what row processing is like. To compare set processing in the analogy, you take the same list to another store, where you hand it to a clerk at a receiving window. The clerk disappears behind the window, presumably to fetch your parts. Why's it taking so long? Is he having a talk at the water cooler or getting your parts? You really can't tell, because you can't see past the partition, but soon enough he returns with all your parts, packaged up and ready to go. It seems that the clerk has been gone a long time. But, in reality, the clerk got your list ready much faster than you would have at the first store, because he was able to skip all the aisles that didn't have the parts you wanted. It's very similar with set processing.

The History of SQL Server

SQL Server, like many things related to SQL, is a story of diversity. At one time, both Sybase and Microsoft had virtually the same product. Today, the two products are growing increasingly divergent. In fact, Sybase now calls their implementation of the product Sybase Adaptive Server Enterprise. For purposes of simplicity, in this book we refer to both Microsoft and Sybase implementations as SQL Server.

Today, major differences in the two implementations are largely a result of their most popular operating system and hardware platforms. Sybase Adaptive Server Enterprise is deployable on many operating systems, including Windows NT and stalwart Unix platforms. Adaptive Server has many features that leverage Very Large Database (VLDB) and multithreading capabilities. Sybase carries the Transact-SQL language uniformly throughout their product line. So, you're just as likely to see Transact-SQL programs on the powerful and mobile Sybase SQL Adaptive Server Anywhere (formerly known as SQL Anywhere) running on Windows 95 and Windows 98 computers. Going to the high end of the spectrum for online analytical processing (OLAP) and data warehouses, Sybase Adaptive Server IQ utilizes Transact-SQL for programmatic needs and, in fact, utilizes the same parser as Sybase Adaptive Server. Conversely, Microsoft has focused on ease of use and administration, as well as tightly integrating the product with other no-cost features like replication and alert forwarding. In any event, all of these database platforms provide their respective user groups with efficient and effective database management tools.

Today, there's a good deal of discussion about encapsulating Java as the primary SQL programming extension for not only Sybase and Microsoft but also for competitors like Oracle. Even with this alternative looming in the distance, Transact-SQL will enjoy many years of active support and augmentation by the vendors. Even if you know or are learning Java, you'll still have to know Transact-SQL to excel on either Sybase or Microsoft database platforms. Heck, the backward-compatibility issues alone are enough to ensure that Transact-SQL will have many, many more years of coding ahead.

But that's the present and future. Maybe you want to know about how things got to be the way they are? By reading this section, you are actually making an admission that many programmers and analysts are loath to: history is interesting or perhaps even *enjoyable*. This is not actually a sign of weakness as some might attest. With tongue planted firmly in cheek, please read on. Table 1-1 shows the evolution of both Microsoft and Sybase's versions of SQL Server.

Table 1-1. The Evolution of SQL Server

Time	Event
1987	Microsoft and Sybase announce a technology and marketing partnership. Microsoft gets exclusive rights to market Sybase's DataServer product on OS/2 and all Microsoft-developed operating systems. Sybase gets royalties and added credibility in the Unix and VMS markets. Sybase ships its first commercial DBMS product, called DataServer, for Sun workstations running Unix.
1988	Microsoft and Ashton-Tate announce a marketing partnership. Microsoft can't put a dent in dBase's tremendous market presence. Ashton-Tate wants access to Sybase's powerful multiuser database management technology, which ships this year. Microsoft forms a three-way alliance.
1989	Ashton-Tate/Microsoft SQL Server Version 1.0 ships.
1990	Ashton-Tate dBase IV was floundering. Microsoft wanted to beef up its offerings for the new OS/2 LAN Manager product. Microsoft and Ashton-Tate quit the partnership. "Microsoft SQL Server" Version 1.1 ships by summer with support for Windows 3.0.
1991	A proliferation of Windows 3.0 front-end tools spurs the growth of Microsoft SQL Server. Later that year Microsoft and Sybase amend their contract to allow Microsoft to make actual bug fixes—all under Sybase supervision. IBM and Microsoft call off their OS/2 partnership with Microsoft to focus on Windows. Sybase surpasses $100 million in revenue and goes public on NASDAQ.
1992	Microsoft and Sybase SQL Server 4.2 ships. Microsoft diverts its attention away from OS/2 and into Windows NT. Microsoft SQL Server for Windows NT later ships its beta release while Sybase ships its much-vaunted System 10.
1993	Microsoft Windows NT 3.1 ships, closely followed by Microsoft SQL Server. By 1994, Sybase SQL Server System 10 and Microsoft SQL Server were competing unabashedly as the two formally ended their partnership.
1995	Microsoft SQL Server 6.0, a very significant release, ships in June. Sybase ships the highly lauded, technically potent Sybase SQL Server 11. Sybase and PowerSoft merge to form the seventh largest independent software house.
1996	Microsoft SQL Server 6.5 goes into production. Sybase Adaptive Server Enterprise 11.5 production ships.
1997	Microsoft SQL Server 7.0 beta ships. Sybase ships the production version of Adaptive Server Enterprise 11.5.
1998	Sybase Adaptive Server Anywhere 6.0 ships in the summer, while the Adaptive Server Enterprise 11.9.2 production release goes out the door in September. Microsoft SQL Server 7.0 ships release to manufacturing copy late in the year.

What Is Transact-SQL?

The name Transact-SQL isn't exactly self-explanatory, but it does imply the idea of "transactional" extensions to the SQL database programming language. Transact-SQL isn't a standalone product. You can't use it to write applications in the same way you could with C++ or Java. Instead, Transact-SQL is the main enabler of programmatic functionality within the relational databases provided by Microsoft and Sybase. Transact-SQL is very closely integrated with SQL while adding programming capabilities not already standardized within the SQL database programming language. At the same time Transact-SQL extends SQL, it also integrates seamlessly with it.

In the following sections, we'll show you some of the capabilities of Transact-SQL, along with some rudimentary examples. Don't worry if the examples don't immediately make sense to you. After a little study, you'll see that these are relatively simple sets of code.

Here's an example of a stored procedure in which Transact-SQL statements and SQL statements are combined to provide useful functionality. The following little program allows you to selectively delete old information from the sales table of the pubs database (we'll explain this database in Chapter 2) based on the order_id. The business rule being applied here is "Don't allow a delete from the sales table unless the data is more than two years old." Sounds like a simple proposition, doesn't it? But it's not all that simple. Implementing a sensible business rule like that in a Microsoft or Sybase database requires the combination of both SQL and Transact-SQL statements:

```
CREATE PROCEDURE purge_sales
    @order_id VARCHAR(20) = NULL
AS
IF @order_id IS NULL
    RAISERROR 50001 "Error! Please supply transaction order number."
ELSE
    DELETE temp_sales
    -- The datediff function tells us if the order date in the ord_date value
    -- is more than 2 years older than the current date stored in getdate().
    WHERE  ord_num  = @order_id
      AND  DATEDIFF(year, ord_date, GETDATE()) > 2
GO
```

Our simple task was to allow a user to purge records more than two years old from the sales table based on the ord_id stored in the table. To accomplish this task, we had to utilize the Transact-SQL components of an IF . . . ELSE construct, variables, the DATEDIFF and GETDATE functions, and finally a RAISERROR statement for error handling. To finish things off, we added a bit of commentary (as all good programmers should) using Transact-SQL extensions to explain what the heck we're doing. At the same time, we had to combine those commands with a basic SQL DELETE statement. This synergy of SQL and Transact-SQL enables you to implement powerful applications and information systems.

Programming Concepts

When you write a program in a third-generation language (3GL) and even most other fourth-generation languages (4GLs), you're looking at a whole other animal. While programs in third-generation and fourth-generation languages can be entirely self-contained, Transact-SQL programs in a sense are merely extensions of the database environment.

To explain more fully, programming in Transact-SQL is a blend of several distinct, yet integrated, components. Let's say that you're about to begin developing a new application. You'll probably start out with a period of design and analysis in which you'll map out what the database will (probably) look like. You'll build your development database using declarative SQL statements or perhaps a visual data-modeling tool. You might later implement a set of complex business rules on your database tables through triggers coded in Transact-SQL. From there, you might create reports and business processing modules that support the user interface through stored procedures coded in Transact-SQL.

Meanwhile, another group of programmers may have begun building the graphic user interface via a client/server or web application development tool. They might utilize a technology that connects their Java-based application to your database backend. When the frontend graphical user interface performs certain transactions, they may actually call the stored procedures you've coded and stored on the server, or their application may initiate transactions that fire triggers on some of the database tables.

This hodgepodge of technologies and programming environments may seem daunting at first. For some developers who have grown up in the structured world of third-generation languages like FORTRAN or COBOL, the comfortable and proven methodologies are no longer 100% effective. At the other end of the spectrum, novice developers may drift about without any structure, cranking out report after report and screen after screen without giving a second thought to documentation, maintainability, or code reusability. The truth is that no matter what background you come from, you must adjust to the different types and techniques of coding you'll face when developing a new application. For what this blend of technologies introduces in terms of challenge, it adds even more in terms of flexibility and power.

The kernel features of Transact-SQL are described in the following sections.

A Wide Variety of Datatypes for Variables and Constants

Transact-SQL lets you declare and then utilize local variables and constants within a Transact-SQL object. These variables and constants must be of a datatype known to the database, like VARCHAR or INT. Special-purpose datatypes exist within Transact-SQL to provide a special functionality. For example, the IDENTITY datatype is used to store an automatically increasing numeric counter within the column of a given table. TIMESTAMP is another special-purpose Transact-SQL datatype that is used to stamp each record of a given table with a unique marker.

Additionally, you can construct your own special-purpose user-defined datatypes on top of an existing system datatype. These user-defined datatypes enable you to constrain the use of, or data stored within, a variable or constant of your special datatype.

Present in Sybase Adaptive Server and new to Microsoft SQL Server Version 7.0 are several new Unicode datatypes, including NCHAR, NVARCHAR, and NTEXT. These new datatypes allow data storage that is independent of the local language character set. Other new datatypes found in Microsoft SQL Server 7.0 include the UNIQUEIDENTIFIER, which uniquely distinguishes each row in a table even across multiple servers, and the CURSOR datatype, which facilitates the use of cursors within a Transact-SQL program.

Programmer-Defined Temporary Objects

Transact-SQL provides several useful temporary objects that endure only as long as the current session. These temporary objects include tables and stored procedures. The objects are stored in the tempdb database and can be used for short-term applications that need exist only while a user is connected or a system operation is executing. Temporary tables can have all the trimmings of their more permanent counterparts, including indexes, constraints, and triggers. Temporary tables are very useful as a sort of "holding tank" where data can be massaged and manipulated into a more useful format. In some cases, temporary tables are used to simulate the functionality of an array found in a third-generation language.

Here's an example of the definition of a temporary table that also populates the temporary table with data:

```
SELECT *
INTO   #temp_titles
FROM   titles
WHERE  NOT EXISTS
       (SELECT * FROM sales WHERE title_ID = titles.title_ID)
```

Using the speedy SELECT . . . INTO syntax enables you to quickly create and populate a temporary (or permanent) table with data. There are good and bad times to use the SELECT . . . INTO statement. Temporary tables are designated by a single pound sign (#) as a prefix. They are usable only by the user or process that created them. Global temporary tables are designated by double pound signs (##). Global temporary tables are available to all users or processes as long as the creating user or process remains connected to the database server.

Specialized Functions and Global Variables

Unlike local variables, which are declared by the programmer in the body of a Transact-SQL program, global variables and functions are provided by Microsoft and Sybase to augment your programming toolset. Global variables enable you to immediately retrieve a particular piece of system information. For example, the global variable @@connections allows you to see how many connections have been attempted since the last time the server was started. The global variable @@error shows the last error number generated within the current user's session (or a 0 if the last command was successful).

Functions, on the other hand, allow you shortcuts to manipulate and manage data. There are a large number of functions to choose from, but they fall into these basic categories:

Aggregate functions
: Aggregate functions compute a single value result, such as the sum or average value of a given column in a table.

Conversion functions
: There are a few versatile functions within Transact-SQL that allow you to convert data from one datatype to another or to reformat data.

Date functions
: Date functions manipulate DATETIME and SMALLDATETIME values.

Mathematical functions
: These functions provide statistical, trigonometric, logarithmic, and exponential capabilities when manipulating numbers.

String functions
: A number of string functions allow you to analyze and modify CHAR, VARCHAR, and, in some cases, TEXT columns and variables.

System (niladic) functions
: System functions allow you to retrieve information from system tables and parameters. In this usage, they are somewhat like global variables. Some system functions also provide a way to perform logical comparison of data.

Text and image functions
Manipulation of TEXT and IMAGE data differs from other types, because they have several usage restrictions. Transact-SQL provides several specialized functions to support the use and manipulation of these datatypes.

System and Extended Stored Procedures

In addition to the wide variety of system functions and global variables, Microsoft and Sybase supply system stored procedures and extended stored procedures, which provide ready-made programs and/or powerful extensions to Transact-SQL. Here are some examples of system and extended stored procedures:

sp_adduser
A system stored procedure that allows you to add a new user to a database

sp_help
A system stored procedure that shows detailed information about a wide variety of database objects

sp_lock
A system stored procedure that details the locking by user and system processes within the database server

sp_who
A system stored procedure that shows what user and system processes are active within the database server

xp_cmdshell
An extended stored procedure that allows you to execute any operating-system command-line executable

You might, for example, use the *xp_cmdshell* extended stored procedure to ensure that a necessary file exists before performing a data load operation.

Control-of-Flow Operations

Transact-SQL provides procedural extensions to SQL that provide several different control-of-flow structures:

- Conditional processing with IF . . . ELSE
- Iterative processing with WHILE
- Branching control with GOTO
- Delay control with WAITFOR

Conditional processing with the IF . . . ELSE construct allows your Transact-SQL program to make choices. You can nest your IF . . . ELSE conditionals as deep as you'd like. The IF . . . ELSE construct requires the use of a BEGIN . . . END block if more than one SQL or Transact-SQL command is dependent upon the condition. The result of this coding constraint is a structured, block orientation. Here's an example of an IF . . . ELSE statement:

```
-- Simple Boolean comparison with ELSE clause.
IF (suser_name() = 'sa')
    PRINT 'Congratulations. You are SA on this system.'
ELSE
    PRINT 'You are not the SA on this system.'
```

The Transact-SQL WHILE extension provides iterative controls that allow a single block of Transact-SQL code to be repeated. You can even nest loops within other loops. In the simple example that follows, an output line is constructed and printed 12 times, once for each month. This example shows what a WHILE loop looks like:

```
DECLARE @month INT, @full_date VARCHAR(30), @line VARCHAR(255)
SELECT  @month=0

WHILE @month <= 12
BEGIN
    -- increment a variable for the month
    SELECT  @month      = @month + 1

    -- build a variable for the full date
    SELECT  @full_date = RTRIM(CONVERT(CHAR(2), @month)) + '/01/99'

    -- build the output line
    SELECT  @line       = 'Processing for date: ' + @full_date

    -- print the output line
    PRINT @line
END
```

You have some other useful control-of-flow statements in the GOTO command and the WAITFOR command. GOTO transfers control from one executable statement to another labeled section in the current Transact-SQL program. The WAITFOR command provides Transact-SQL programs with delay controls. Here's a Transact-SQL program that illustrates both commands:

```
-- The line with the colon at the end is a GOTO label.
start_of_routine:

-- Let's check today's date.
IF GETDATE() > 'Jan 1 1999 12:00 AM'
BEGIN
    PRINT 'Ending'
    GOTO end_of_routine
END

ELSE
```

```
BEGIN
    PRINT 'Waiting'
    -- The WAITFOR DELAY command will make the program wait 1 hour.
    WAITFOR DELAY '01:00:00'
    GOTO start_of_routine
END

end_of_routine:
```

Row-Based Operations Using Cursors

As we discussed earlier, one of the most potent features of relational database management systems is their ability to process data in sets of records rather than on a row-by-row basis. Set-based processing is very fast, but it is limiting in that you cannot selectively modify a single record within a given result set. Transact-SQL has extended this set-based functionality to row-based operations using *cursors*.

Cursors allow you a high degree of control over the manipulation of data within your database. In a sense, a cursor is a SELECT statement that steps through its result set one record at a time. To properly use a cursor, you must declare, open, fetch from, and close a cursor. In many cases, you also should deallocate the cursor. Interestingly, you can use a cursor to scroll forward or backward through a result set. You also can set a cursor to step through a table one record at a time or to skip along several records per step.

The following example shows you all the steps needed to properly utilize a cursor:

```
-- declare the cursor
DECLARE titles_cursor CURSOR
FOR
SELECT title_id
FROM   titles

-- declare the variables that will hold values retrieved by the cursor
DECLARE @title_id CHAR(6)

-- fetch the next set of values retrieved by the cursor
FETCH titles_cursor INTO @title_id

SELECT @title AS 'Name of book'

-- close and deallocate the cursor
CLOSE titles_cursor
DEALLOCATE CURSOR titles_cursor
```

Error Handling

Transact-SQL allows you to detect the occurrence of errors in the course of executing a program. Errors in Transact-SQL fall into three categories: informational, warning, and fatal.

- Informational errors output a message but do not cause the program to abort.
- Warning messages output an error message and abort the currently executing SQL or Transact-SQL statement but do not abort the entire program or Transact-SQL batch.
- Fatal errors are baaaad. They send an error message and a notification to the operating system error log. Furthermore, fatal errors terminate the Transact-SQL program where the error occurred.

Transact-SQL uses a linear code model for error handling. So, if you don't check for a particular level or type of error, Transact-SQL will not provide any special response to it. For that reason, it is very important for you to properly check and evaluate error conditions throughout the execution of your Transact-SQL programs.

The following Transact-SQL block checks to see if certain data exists within the database. If the data doesn't exist, then an ad hoc error message is raised:

```
IF EXISTS (SELECT * FROM authors WHERE au_fname = 'Elmer'
    AND au_lname 'Fudd')
    PRINT "Happy Hunting, it's duck season!"
ELSE RAISERROR('Warning! Duck hunting widout a wicense!',16,1)
```

Both Microsoft and Sybase also provide you with the ability to add your own user-defined error messages into the system error message table, sysmessages. This capability allows you to define a set of error messages specifically for your application and embed them in the database, rather than solely within the Transact-SQL program logic.

Transact-SQL Objects and Transaction Control

One of the key features of Microsoft SQL Server and Sybase Adaptive Server is the ability to store Transact-SQL objects (triggers, views, and stored procedures) within the database itself. These blocks of Transact-SQL code can then be invoked by any user or system session that has adequate privileges to perform the task. In fact, both Sybase and Microsoft support the use of remote procedure calls (RPCs), allowing a single local server to invoke a stored procedure on a remote server. Through Transact-SQL objects, the database becomes a repository for both application code and data. Transact-SQL objects are stored in their own memory area, the procedure cache, within the database's memory space.

At a more elemental level, transactions can be closely controlled and monitored in a Transact-SQL program using the global variables @@transtate and @@trancount. A *transaction* is a SQL or Transact-SQL statement that produces a measurable unit of work by retrieving, inserting, deleting, or modifying data. You can allow Transact-SQL to use implicit transactions, or you can explicitly define a transaction using the BEGIN TRAN, COMMIT TRAN, and ROLLBACK TRAN statements. By properly gauging and constructing your transactions, you can greatly reduce or even eliminate the possibility of blocks in an application supporting multiple concurrent connections.

Tracing and Debugging

A wide variety of tracing and debugging features are supplied by Transact-SQL using the DBCC and SET commands. In addition to providing tracing and debugging capabilities, these commands allow you to control server behavior, monitor performance, and alter the session environment and behavior.

The DBCC command offers functions that fall into several general categories:

Database consistency checks
: Commands like DBCC NEWALLOC and DBCC UPDATEUSAGE check a given database for inconsistencies in the data and, in some cases, take remedial action.

Database and server configuration
: In dire straits, you can use DBCC command to drop or shrink databases.

Debugging
: Common debugging applications for the DBCC command include controlling tracing functions and examining the input and output buffer of various system and user sessions on the database server.

Performance tuning and monitoring
: A wide variety of DBCC commands allow you to monitor the behavior and performance of the server. Other commands enable you to pin tables into memory, rebuild indexes, reestablish fillfactors, or display the selectivity and value of a given index.

Conversely, the SET command enables you to mandate specific behaviors for a given session or user connection. You can use the SET command to enable or disable certain ANSI standards, determine deadlock resolution preference, and perform a wide range of other functionalities.

Special Aggregate Operators

Transact-SQL, under Microsoft SQL Server, has grown to support new aggregate operators, such as ROLLUP and CUBE, that are specifically optimized for very large databases, such as those found in data marts and data warehouses.

CUBE and ROLLUP are optional operators of the GROUP BY clause of a SELECT statement. A SELECT query using GROUP BY WITH CUBE returns all rows that it would return without the CUBE switch. In addition, it produces summary rows for every possible combination of GROUP BY keys. A query using WITH ROLLUP returns just a subset of the rows produced by WITH CUBE. ROLLUP is useful in computing running sums and running averages. Unlike CUBE, which computes aggregates for any possible combination of keys of GROUP BY, ROLLUP is sensitive to the order of items in the GROUP BY.

Here's an example of a SELECT statement and result set with a SUM aggregation and a simple GROUP BY clause:

```
SELECT   type, pub_id, SUM(ytd_sales)
FROM     titles
GROUP BY type, pub_id
```

The query returns this result set:

```
type         pub_id Sum
------------ ------ -----------
business     0736   18722
business     1389   12066
mod_cook     0877   24278
popular_comp 1389   12875
psychology   0736   9564
psychology   0877   375
trad_cook    0877   19566
UNDECIDED    0877   (null)
```

Yet if we add one simple CUBE operator, we get this:

```
SELECT   type, pub_id, SUM(ytd_sales)
FROM     titles
GROUP BY type, pub_id
WITH CUBE
```

The result set now contains extra rows with the type of NULL per pub_id and a grand total of all titles sold:

```
type         pub_id Sum
------------ ------ -----------
business     0736   18722
business     1389   12066
business     (null) 30788
mod_cook     0877   24278
mod_cook     (null) 24278
popular_comp 1389   12875
popular_comp (null) 12875
psychology   0736   9564
psychology   0877   375
psychology   (null) 9939
trad_cook    0877   19566
trad_cook    (null) 19566
UNDECIDED    0877   (null)
UNDECIDED    (null) (null)
(null)       (null) 97446
```

```
(null)       0736   28286
(null)       0877   44219
(null)       1389   24941
```

Finally, if we switch to the ROLLUP functions (CUBE and ROLLUP are mutually exclusive), we get this:

```
SELECT   type, pub_id, SUM(ytd_sales)
FROM     titles
GROUP BY type, pub_id
WITH ROLLUP
```

returning this result set:

```
type         pub_id Sum
------------ ------ -----------
business     0736   18722
business     1389   12066
business     (null) 30788
mod_cook     0877   24278
mod_cook     (null) 24278
popular_comp 1389   12875
popular_comp (null) 12875
psychology   0736   9564
psychology   0877   375
psychology   (null) 9939
trad_cook    0877   19566
trad_cook    (null) 19566
UNDECIDED    0877   (null)
UNDECIDED    (null) (null)
(null)       (null) 97446
```

All of these features, and many more, are described in the following chapters of this book. Enjoy!

Summary

This chapter examined mostly background information about Transact-SQL. It described relational databases in general and looked specifically at how Transact-SQL got to be the way it is today. Specific points to remember:

- Transact-SQL in light of the ANSI standard for SQL—how they are similar and how they differ.
- The relational database model, how it got started, and why it took root and prospered.
- Benefits and techniques for normalization and the uses for denormalization.

- Important concepts about the differences in row and set (a.k.a., declarative versus procedural) processing; *if you remember anything in this chapter, remember the difference in row versus set processing*.
- The history of the SQL Server database engine, including details about both Microsoft and Sybase development efforts with the product.
- The basic features and capabilities of Transact-SQL.

2

Database Analysis and Design

Transact-SQL is no more intelligent than the myriad other programming languages that abound today. The intelligence of a programming language lies not in its flexibility, but rather in its ability to enable you (the programmer or designer) to reproduce your business requirements on a computer.

In this chapter we take a step back from the language itself and look at the analysis and design phases of an application—these are the foundation for every application. There have been significant strides in this area, and now there are a number of tools available on the market to help you in the analysis and design phase.

The Need for Adequate Analysis and Design

There have been many evolutions in the computer industry, not the least of which are in the area of systems analysis and design. Systems analysis deals with the understanding of the process or system we are trying to model in a computer system. This in itself is not radical, since from the beginning of time we have been compelled to improve the efficiency with which we work (probably so we can spend more time eating, drinking, partying, and sleeping!).

We design databases to store information, which we use to determine any number of things, be it the manufacturing cost of an item, the location of our market, or the address of the local pizza parlor. As the programmer accessing the database, your concern is being able to find the information you are looking for in a timely manner. In this book, we look at numerous ways in which you can retrieve data in a database in the most efficient way possible. In this chapter, however, we look at how you would make sure the information you are ultimately looking for is in the database to begin with.

The Systems Life Cycle

The traditional systems life cycle is made up of five major milestones: analysis, design, code, test, and implementation. The life cycle should not be seen as a serial process, however, because prior steps may need to be revisited in order to move forward. The life cycle model is illustrated in Figure 2-1.

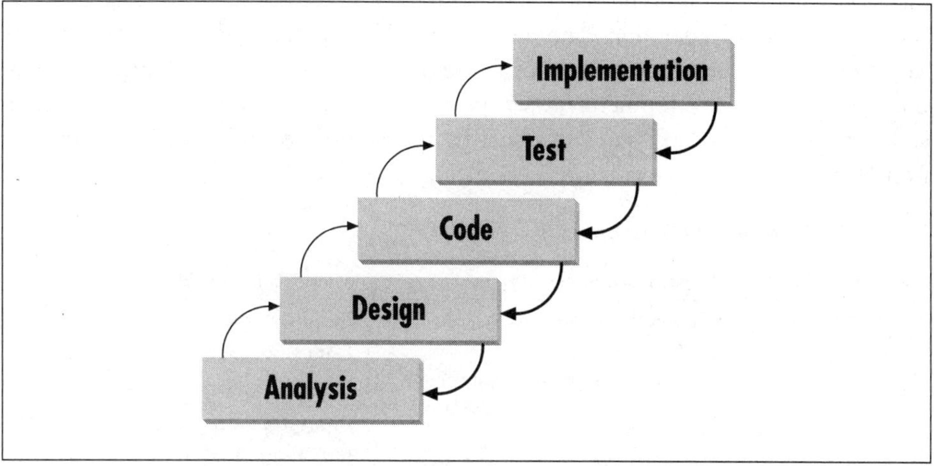

Figure 2-1. Life cycle model

These are the milestones:

Analysis
: The requirements for the system are identified and documented.

Design
: A model is developed that will satisfy the individual requirements identified in the analysis phase.

Code
: The actual design is implemented using a programming language like Transact-SQL and usually some form of frontend language like Visual Basic or PowerBuilder.

Test
: The system or processes are validated to ensure that they conform to the system requirements. Testing need not occur only after coding has been completed. In many cases, it is as important to test the application's assumptions with the users prior to implementation either by walking through the paper system and applying different scenarios to it or by building a prototype and testing that with the users. Many applications fail because testing is left until it is too late in the development process to effectively fix significant logic errors. Testing often results in a revision of work completed in previous steps.

Implementation

Once you have verified that the system is working correctly, it usually goes into production, that state in which users start to get really demanding and set unrealistic expectations for you to meet.

Each milestone builds on the results of the milestone that precedes it and determines the probability of success in the milestones that succeed it. Further, each milestone sits at a different level and addresses a slightly different angle of the problem under consideration. The life cycle itself is iterative, and it is often necessary to modify work completed in prior steps in order to include changes that are uncovered as the development project proceeds. Table 2-1 summarizes each milestone, the questions answered during that milestone, and the major deliverables from it.

Table 2-1. Milestones in the Systems Life Cycle

Milestone	Questions Answered	Major Deliverables
Analysis	What is the proposed system meant to do? Why is the proposed system meant to do what has been proposed?	Requirements document Data flow diagrams Data dictionary Entity relationship diagrams Functional hierarchy
Design	How are the requirements going to be implemented? Is this a client-centric application or is this a server-centric application?	Data flow diagrams Logical database design Physical database design Program specifications
Code	When is this program going to be finished? Why did you code it like this? Who will take responsibility for implementing the requirements?	Database program code (DDL) Middleware code (e.g., replication scripts) Frontend program (GUI) code
Test	Do we know what to test and how we are going to test it ? Does the program meet the requirements in terms of functionality and speed? Does the program introduce new problems elsewhere in the system?	Functional test plan Working database Working programs

Table 2-1. Milestones in the Systems Life Cycle (continued)

Milestone	Questions Answered	Major Deliverables
Implementation	How do we roll this out (especially if this is a distributed application and needs to be implemented at numerous offices)? What is the best method to support this application? How do we maintain this system? How will upgrades be implemented?	Happy users Late nights and weekend work Gray hair and ulcers

Each of these milestones is characterized by a series of deliverables that need to be produced and agreed upon in order to proceed successfully to the next phase. In this chapter we deal with the first two phases: analysis and design; the rest of this book deals with the final three phases: code, test, and implementation.

Overview of Analysis

Analysis, as its name implies, is a process that is followed to determine the requirements of a system. To make this determination, the analyst is required to break down the system into its component parts. The analysis process defines the proposed system in sufficient detail to enable the designer to implement the infrastructure layer necessary to build the system. The analyst answers the question of what the system is required to do by identifying what is currently being done. The analyst also may be required to answer why the system should perform in a certain fashion, since it is fairly common to use the results of the analysis phase for cost justification.

Analysis is as much an art as it is a science. However, there are several tasks we can perform during analysis that, when combined, may not guarantee success but will at least reduce the chance of failure:

- Applying a method
- Understanding clearly the problem domain
- Verifying the users' requirements
- Understanding what is going to be done with the analysis results

Applying a Method

Throughout this book, we have chosen to use the term "method" in lieu of the more commonly used term "methodology." If you are more used to the latter term, you can consider it synonymous, at least in this book.

A number of methods have been developed to help us in our quest, such as:

- Structured Systems Analysis and Design, developed by Yourdon and Constantine
- Data Flow Diagramming, developed by Gane and Sarson
- Information Engineering, developed by James Martin
- Joint Application Development, developed by IBM

These methods provide a variety of tools in the form of diagrams, templates, questions, and procedures. When followed, these methods can assist the analyst in uncovering all the salient information about the system being modeled. In many cases, the results of one method serve as the input into the next method.

For example, in the case of data flow diagrams, one of the outputs is a data dictionary. This data dictionary serves as an input into the relational database design or, for that matter, an object-oriented design method in which the data will (we hope) be normalized into an efficient database design.

A method may be either very generalized or highly detailed. A generalized method serves as a guide that the analyst will use as required to assist in the analysis process. A highly detailed method acts as a methodical plan that the analyst will be required to follow in a lemming-like fashion until completion, whereupon the analysis phase will have miraculously been completed. This is not to say that analysis done in a highly detailed fashion will not work; rather, analysis depends more upon the consummate skill of the person performing the analysis than on the tools used to perform the process.

Understanding the Problem Domain

Successful analysis relies less on our understanding of technology and more on our understanding of what it is we are trying to model. At the end of the day, it doesn't matter if we have the latest technology to store our data if we don't have a clue what it is we are going to do with it! Because of this, many analysts specialize in a particular area such as finance or manufacturing. The greater the depth of understanding they have in a particular domain, the less likely they are to forget to ask about a critical part in the system being modeled. To a certain extent, the way the questions are posed by the analyst (such as open-ended or free-format versus close-ended) can help eliminate large gaps in the system.

Because the analyst is usually charged with improving the existing process as well, having knowledge about different ways in which similar problems have been solved can enable an analyst to introduce innovative ideas into the analysis phase. This is very important, since even if a suggestion is not followed, it may serve as a catalyst in an area that otherwise would have remained unexplored.

Assuming that the analyst has at least a logical understanding of the problem being modeled, the next step is to validate what the user is asking to be done.

Verifying Users' Requirements

James Martin, a prolific writer on system methods, once wrote, "A user doesn't know what they want until they get it, and then they are not even sure if that is what they wanted!" This may sound familiar to many of you. The more users you speak to in the course of your analysis, the better the chance your analysis process will be complete. Doing so will not only help you learn more about the content but also will help you build a more realistic (rather than idealized) view of the proposed system being built.

This is not to say that users should be classed as pathological liars, but that a single view of a system tends by its very nature to be one-sided. No solution that affects a group of individuals is a solution based solely on a single point of view.

Most methods encourage discussion groups with users who, working together, can help define the requirements specification. Different methods encourage different ways this goal can be achieved—for example, walkthroughs, discussion groups, interviews, and so on.

Utilizing the Analysis Results

Once the analysis process has been successfully completed, the outputs will invariably go into some form of design process that may or may not be performed by the same person. Having a clear idea of what somebody is going to do with the results of your investigation and knowing how to formulate your results in a clear and concise way goes a long way toward facilitating the next stage in the process.

Today it is quite common for a prototype to be built during the analysis stage. A prototype is usually built using a rapid application development (RAD) tool that allows the person building the prototype to present the basic system functions in a quasi-working system using a screen layout similar to the proposed end product. Using a prototype, the user can validate that the analysis process has correctly captured the business processes the system is meant to perform and can also get a sense of how the system will work. Often, a prototype will spur many changes to the proposed system.

One of the problems in analysis is the large body of documentation that seems to be produced. Documentation is not necessarily a bad thing; it just needs to be tempered and produced in quantities appropriate to the task at hand. Many projects get bogged down on the semantic details of an issue and the format of presentation while ignoring the real issues that are meant to be addressed in the document to begin with. Whenever possible, follow the "Keep It Simple, Stupid (KISS)" principle. Remember that the documents you are producing here are not likely to be entered into a literary competition, and your high school English teacher is not going to critique you, either!

A practical approach to this problem is to prepare standard templates that can be used repeatedly for different projects. Maintaining a consistent format that has been prepared previously can save valuable time when it comes to preparing the final deliverables.

Once the analysis process has been completed, the results of the analysis process need to be presented to the user community. The users will typically review the document and, after adding any necessary comments and revisions, will agree to the document. If you are really lucky, they may even sign off on it! After some form of agreement has been reached, you'll be able to move on to the next major milestone in the systems life cycle—design.

Overview of Design

Design is concerned with finding an efficient solution to an identified problem. During the design phase, you'll finalize decisions about the technology platform, the database product, and the chosen development tools. Since these decisions impose limits on the proposed system, the designer is faced with the challenge of finding an innovative and efficient solution. This solution must work against a backdrop of real constraints that have been described in the analysis phase deliverables.

In many respects, design is about juggling a series of trade-offs into an optimal configuration. As with analysis, there are certain tasks we can perform to minimize the possibility of failure. Unfortunately, there is always an element of risk in any project, but if analysis has been thorough, and if competent designers are performing this phase of the life cycle, the risk is minimal.

These are the basic design tasks:

- Applying a design method
- Getting a sense of the amount of data and the user load the system will need to manage
- Understanding the technology that will be used
- Redesigning an existing system or developing a new design

Applying a Design Method

It is equally important to select an appropriate method for design. Many organizations have a preference about what sort of design method is used, although in some cases, you may be lucky enough to be able to define a method of your choosing. Design methods are similar to coding standards; you need to have them but you need to temper their implementation with common sense. For a fuller discussion of coding standards, refer to Chapter 5, *Format and Style*.

Current design methods cover some of the following topics:

- Distributed processing versus centralized processing
- Mainframe versus client/server, intranet, or Internet-based application
- Object-oriented databases versus relational databases
- Structured systems design versus object-oriented design
- Unix versus Windows NT

Each of these methods is designed to encourage heated debates since each has its own merits. However, sometimes one approach is more appropriate than another for a particular environment. As the designer, your responsibility is to weigh the relative merits of each approach and decide which one is more appropriate for the particular system being designed. Each organization has a different set of operating conditions. Therefore, a design strategy that proves successful in one organization may not necessarily be successful in another. Always bear in mind the unique conditions of the organization when you evaluate different methods.

As a designer, you need to be aware of the major principles that underlie each of these individual approaches and determine which of the approaches (or combination) is more appropriate to your particular scenario. Your decision will invariably be swayed in a particular direction as a result of the information you gather from the other design tasks.

Getting a Sense of the Amount of Data

Data is the foundation of every system. For a system to have a purpose, it must take in inputs of some form or another and produce a series of outputs. The data in a system may be stored in a database or, heaven forbid, in a flat file. The amount of data the system is responsible for and the processing to be performed on this data determine the appropriate database to use. Even with a flexible budget, you can still have overkill, which may serve to inhibit performance for your particular environment.

Understanding your data volume is critical when it comes to designing a database and configuring it for optimal performance. Knowing this information before you begin the design process enables you to consider a more appropriate implementation strategy once you get to a physical design.

It is also critical to be aware of the volume of users who are going to be using this system. Very few systems are designed for single users. A database design may need to be modified if there are large numbers of users who consistently access the same data, since this may cause problems like blocking and user contention. Chapter 11, *Transactions and Locking*, discusses these issues in detail.

Numbers Matter

One site we know of purchased the latest Unix server, which failed to give them adequate performance. The problem was that this server was designed to give the same response regardless of the number of users on it. Unfortunately for them, they only ever had 10 users. Worse still, the server could not be reconfigured to give better performance for this particular case.

Understanding the Technology

Many organizations have preferred vendors who supply their hardware and software, and these vendors cannot be changed. During the design phase, you need to identify what technology infrastructure is already in place. Upper management usually chooses these vendors, which means that you will have to implement a permutation of a familiar theme that has been previously implemented.

Technology changes rapidly, and one of the biggest issues that usually has to be addressed here is making a purchasing decision for a solution that may not actually exist for a long period of time. This happens when the development phase may take years to complete. One of the approaches that has been adopted in many organizations is the use of a prototype solution. Typically, a scaled-down version of the final solution is implemented using only key components of the eventual system. In following this type of approach, it is possible to do a proof of concept that can (if successful) engender the support required to get the budget approval needed for this particular project.

It is highly unlikely that you will need to have everything from a technology infrastructure standpoint before you can begin the development phase. Often, it is possible to grow your technology requirements in tandem with your implementation schedule; a multiphased implementation schedule is not uncommon in systems development.

Analysis and design are critical steps in any systems life cycle. Numerous studies have proven that the cost of change increases exponentially as you step through each stage in the traditional life cycle. A change you identify and implement in the analysis phase could save you hundreds or even thousands of dollars over finding it out in the coding stage.

All too often, analysis and design are left by the wayside and regarded as costly and unnecessary. But in reality, a well-designed system is not an unreachable goal. There are many systems in every organization that are living examples of this.

Redesigning an Existing System or Developing a New Design

Designing a new system is a lot easier than retrofitting an existing system into a new design. Often, a system will already exist, and the new system that is being developed will be required to utilize components of the existing system (for better or for worse). As a system designer, during the design process you need to identify what has to remain and what can go. Based on these decisions, you can determine how you integrate these components without compromising your design.

Before you begin your design process, take an inventory of what components are in the current system and what components are going to need to stay. Prioritize these components as critical, probable, and not sure. After you have completed this inventory, you will have two basic paths you can follow based on this inventory:

- Design your new system as if the checklist didn't exist; then, once you have a perfect design, focus on how you incorporate these components into your new design.
- Design your new system, taking those components into consideration and designing your system around them.

As you can see, regardless of the approach you take, compromise will be the order of the day. Somewhere in between these two paths is where the best road actually lies (since you can often ignore things you originally thought you couldn't). There are always going to be cases where you have to include something you would rather not. As a designer, knowing what you have to work with gives you a better chance of being able to integrate successfully than ignoring the whole situation and hoping the problem will go away.

Putting It Together with CASE Technology

Computer Aided Software Engineering (CASE) technology is a category of software tools specifically designed to store on a computer some of the information captured during the analysis and design phases. This information can then be used to generate the underlying database, its myriad of objects, and, in some cases, parts of the eventual application as well. Using a computer to record this information makes it simpler to maintain the model through its numerous revisions and also makes it less time-consuming when using the CASE tool to generate code.

Elements of a CASE Tool

CASE tools are designed to provide aid during the different phases in the systems life cycle. Many CASE tools are broken down into different modules; each module focuses on a particular phase. In general, CASE tools will provide support for some of the following:

- Process modeling using data flow diagrams
- Entity relationship diagrams/logical database design
- Physical database design
- Flow charts
- Code generators

When vendors supply multiple modules in their CASE tool suites, the modules are usually capable of interacting with one another and can share common data.

When you are selecting a CASE tool for your organization, be very sure to review the features provided by each of the products to determine whether they will satisfy your requirements.

Important things to consider when selecting a CASE tool include the following:

- Can the CASE tool generate Data Definition Language (DDL) for your organization's databases?
- Does the CASE tool allow you to reverse-engineer using Open Data Base Connectivity (ODBC)?
- Can the CASE tool allow multiple users to use and share a single model?
- Can the CASE tool generate reports besides the basic diagrams?
- Does the CASE tool allow you to modify an existing database easily?
- Does the CASE tool support the method your organization follows?
- Can you buy the modules to the tool separately?
- Can the CASE tool be used to generate source code for your applications?
- Can you modify the default code the CASE tool generates?
- Does the CASE tool support data warehouse requirements?

The CASE Market Today

The CASE tool market has grown significantly since its humble beginnings. There are now numerous excellent products on the market. Those of you who are looking at purchasing a CASE tool for your organization can use any of the following forums as a starting point to identifying a CASE tool that meets your corporation's needs:

- The World Wide Web
- Computer trade shows like DBExpo
- Colleagues and friends who may have had exposure to a CASE tool
- Your database vendor; they may have a tool that complements their database offering

In the next section we'll show how a CASE tool can help us prepare some of the diagrams that aid in performing the analysis and design phases of the systems life cycle.

A CASE Study: The pubs Database

As we mentioned in the Preface, we've elected to use the pubs database* as the basis for many of the sample programs we present in this book. In keeping with

* The pubs database contains imaginary data and doesn't represent any actual publishers or bookstores.

this theme, the analysis and design discussion presented here deals with hypothetical questions and requirements that needed to be satisfied in order to create the pubs database to begin with. Remember: this is a hypthetical case, although we hope it helps you understand the process.

Analysis

Bonanza Books, Inc., asked Musketeer Consultants to perform an analysis of their existing operations. This analysis will then be used to produce a new database design that they plan on implementing on a Windows NT SQL Server, although the database itself has not yet been agreed upon. Bonanza further requested Musketeer to prepare a requirements specification and data flow diagram as part of the analysis phase.

Musketeer elected to use the Gane and Sarson Data Flow Diagramming technique to represent the data flow diagrams. The requirements specifications were prepared using a combination of existing methods as well as Musketeer's internal method.

Musketeer chose to use two of their in-house analysts, Eric and Karin, who have several years of experience in the publications industry, to perform the analysis phase.

Musketeer follows an internal standard for deliverables to maintain a consistent look and feel for all their documents. These documents are familiar to all employees of Musketeer. Musketeer requires all of its analysts to have regular meetings with the design teams to ensure that all the information they require is included in the final deliverables for the analysis phase.

After several weeks of political intrigue and interdepartmental fighting, the following documents were prepared:

- Requirements document
- Data flow diagram

Requirements document

The requirements document is shown in the upcoming sidebar, "Requirements Document for Bonanza Books, Inc."

Requirements Document for Bonanza Books, Inc., by Musketeer Consultants Eric and Karin—September 1999

1. Problem definition

Bonanza Books, Inc., requires a system to track the following key aspects of their purchasing and distribution process:

1.1 Publishers—All publishers who provide the titles that Bonanza Books distributes to its retail outlet chain

1.2 Titles—Detailed information about the titles stocked by Bonanza Books

1.3 Stores—Information about the location and purchasing behavior of their retail chain of booksellers

1.4 Sales—Information about the quantities and order details for every store that purchases goods from Bonanza Books

1.5 Authors—Information on the titles written by an author and any royalties associated with a particular title

1.6 Employees—Basic information about each of their employees, as well as a job description for their current job

2. Analysis goals

Bonanza Books would like to use the information contained in their database to help develop an accurate model of their stores' buying behaviors. They also wish to track the return on investment they get with each individual author so they can better track investment costs for the books they publish, the life span of a book, and the specialty areas that seem to enjoy the biggest return on investment. Since Bonanza Books is looking at increasing the range of books they sell, they are looking to strategically determine the best areas in which to develop.

3. Contributing parties

The following company departments were involved in the preparation of this document:

3.1 Distribution—Provided information about how the store purchases were tracked, as well as all information relating to process flow from requisition to distribution

3.2 Financial—Provided information about the way royalties are calculated for their authors and how royalties are tracked and paid

3.3. Human Resources—Provided information about the job categories in Bonanza Books and how employees are allocated to a particular job category

3.4 Technology—Provided information about the existing and proposed technology infrastructure within Bonanza Books

4. Existing system

Bonanza Books currently has a computer system to perform their purchases and sales order processing. They do not currently track information about the authors in any existing computer system since that is presently performed as a manual process by the accounts department. Human Resources uses Microsoft Word to store their employee details. Bonanza Books would like to convert at least this financial year's data into the new computer system so they can reconcile their books at the end of the year.

5. Requirements

Requirements are summarized below:

5.1 Author

Currently there is no author who is also an employee of Bonanza Books. Author information needs to be kept in order to prepare annual tax forms for the royalty payments made to the authors.

Bonanza Books currently signs a formal book contract with their authors only after their proposals have been accepted. However, in order for the HR department to prepare a contract if the book proposal is accepted, the author's details need to be captured in the computer system. The following information needs to be tracked about the author's personal details: last name, first name, phone number, address, city, state, Zip Code, and a contract indicator. All of Bonanza Books' authors live within the USA. Each author needs to have a unique identifier.

5.2 Author titles

An author may publish more than one book. Each book is subject to an advance and some form of royalty percentage, calculated as a percentage of gross sales (currently 12.5%). Since royalties are paid in arrears, the publication date is used to determine the start date for the calculation of the period. Currently, there are three royalty payments per annum. Each title needs to have a unique identifier.

Although royalties are currently calculated at a fixed rate, Bonanza Books would like to be able to calculate royalties using a variable rate schedule.

In order to perform better statistical analysis of their sales, Bonanza would like to classify each of their titles. They also would like to keep the current financial year's sales quantity, along with the published price for the book. Comments are sometimes kept on each of the books. Titles may be published by other publishers, and this needs to be stored for each title.

5.3 Publishers

Bonanza Books would like to be able to use their publishers' logos in some of their in-store advertising campaigns. They would like to keep this information in their database if possible. They need to track the following information about their publishers: name, city, state, and country. Not all of the publishers whose books they sell are from the USA. Each publisher needs to have a unique identifier.

5.4 Stores

Bonanza Books supplies titles to all of their affiliated bookstores. Each store has a unique identifier, and information about the store's physical location needs to be kept, since this is where deliveries are sent. Store information that needs to be kept includes: name, address, city, state, and Zip Code. Currently, all their stores are in the USA. Each store is entitled to a discount rate based on the quantity of books bought. Volume sales have a variable discount rate associated with them.

5.5 Sales

Sales are tracked at an individual book level. An order number is assigned to each book that is sold. Information on the order includes: order date, sales quantity, payment terms, and store details, as well as the title information. All order numbers are unique.

5.6 Employees

Bonanza Books would like to track their employees who act in a customer support role with their publishers. Each employee is assigned only one publisher to work with since the "products" are the individual publishing houses. The following information needs to be kept about the employees: first name, last name, job type, job level, and hire date. A unique identifier needs to be created for each employee.

5.7 Jobs

Many of the employees can share a common job role; therefore, in order to track promotions and determine the impact of a grade change on an employee, a job description, as well as minimum grade and maximum grade, needs to be kept. Each job should have a unique identifier.

Data flow diagram

The data flow diagram (DFD) in Figure 2-2 was drawn to represent the requirements findings. In order to understand this DFD, we need to introduce the basic building blocks used to prepare this document.

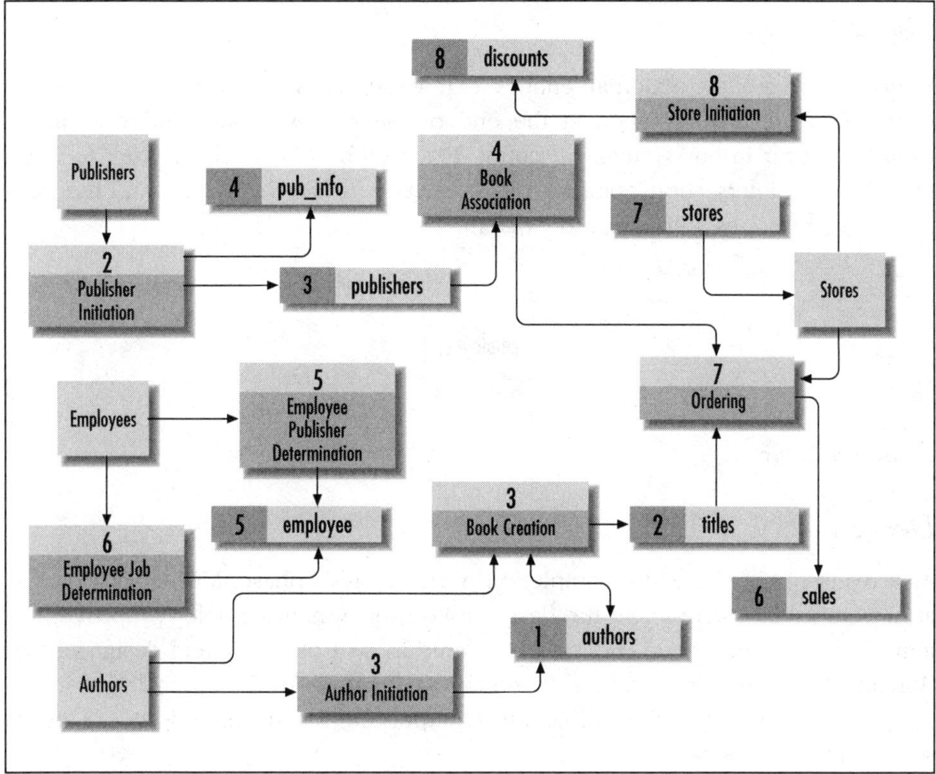

Figure 2-2. Data flow diagram

Data store. A data store (Figure 2-3) contains the data in the system and usually feeds a process of some sort. The data stores will form the basis of the tables in the database that is eventually designed.

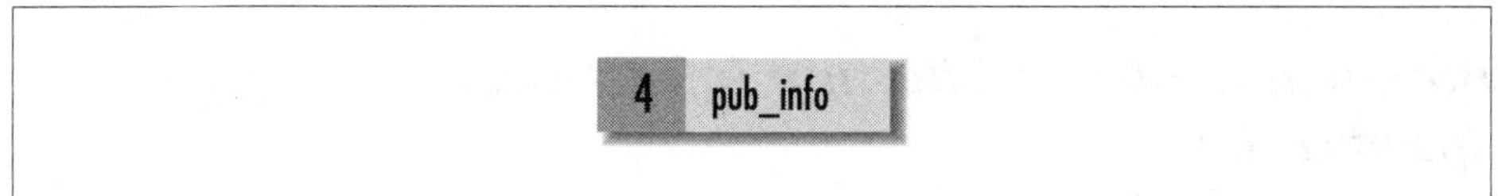

Figure 2-3. Data store

Process. A process (Figure 2-4) performs an operation of some sort—for example, adds a user. The processes become the functions of the system that is being designed and usually map to a program, procedure, system, or function.

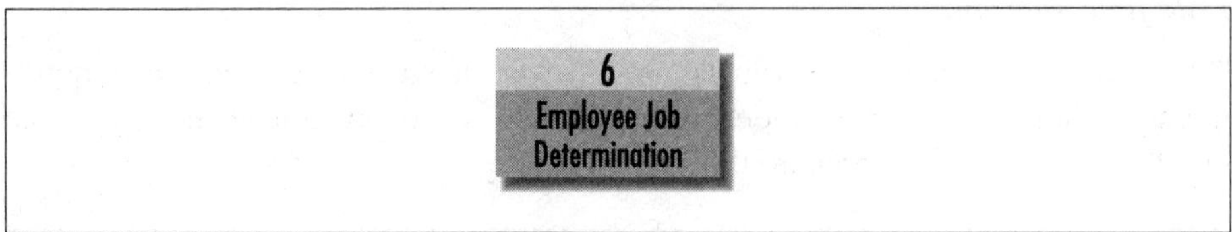

Figure 2-4. Process

Entity. These are the external entities that either cause a process to begin or expect to receive information at the end of the process. The employee causes events to occur in our system. An entity (Figure 2-5) is included in order to identify where an intersection point or trigger exists between the system and the people or organizations who affect the system.

Figure 2-5. Entity

Design

As a result of the successful completion of the analysis phase, Musketeer Consultants were asked to complete the design phase for Bonanza Books' proposed system. The following documents were prepared as part of the system design phase. Bonanza Books required that a fully functional database design be included in the design document, as well as all necessary supporting documentation to ensure its successful implementation:

Bonanza Books database specification
: This document should describe in detail the proposed database for this system.

Architecture infrastructure specification
: This document should describe in detail the necessary architectural infrastructure required to implement this system.

Bonanza Books Architecture Infrastructure Specification

The architecture infrastructure specification is shown in upcoming sidebar, "Architecture Infrastructure for Bonanza Books, Inc."

Architecture Infrastructure for Bonanza Books, Inc., by Musketeer Consultants Eric and Karin—November 1999

Overview to the proposed architecture infrastructure

The following architecture infrastructure is based on the discussions held with all interested parties from the analysis phase to the present. The infrastructure presented is proven in the field and has been found to be highly reliable. The technology cost of this solution is reasonable, which is a consideration since Bonanza Books will need to perform extensive hardware upgrades to their entire infrastructure as a result of this new system.

Part of this infrastructure covers the software architecture and covers standards that will need to be followed during the application development in order to ensure that the user experiences a consistent look and feel to the system.

Hardware

Two Baileys C5000 dual 330MHz CPU server machines will be purchased with 256MB on-board RAM. Each machine will have 10GB RAID storage devices connected to a Wheezy Mark II SCSI controller card. Two Speedy network cards will be installed on each machine. Each machine will also have a CD-ROM and an additional 4GB internal hard-drive. Each machine will have a color VGA monitor.

The fileservers will run Microsoft NT 4.0.

One of these machines will be used for the new file server, and the other one will be used for the database server.

Twenty Baileys C100 200MHz CPU workstation machines with 64MB on-board RAM, 2GB internal disk drives, a network card and a VGA monitor will be purchased. These machines will run Microsoft Windows 98.

Two Clear-Not-Fuzzy laser printers will be purchased.

A Smart-Technology scanner will be purchased.

A 56Kb modem will be installed.

Network

A speedy 10Mb LAN network will be installed, since all users of the system are located within a single building. The network will be broken into two segments to maintain adequate performance levels for the entire user community.

Microsoft Network will be used for LAN connectivity.

Relational database management system

The most recent version of SQL Server for NT will be used since Bonanza Books wants to provide its salespeople with distributed mobile databases sometime in the near future. Once this becomes a requirement, the current technology offerings will be evaluated to determine an appropriate product.

Software architecture guidelines

The application interface will use standard windowing methods—for example, file save, window modality, cursor events, key events, and printing. A single application menu will be developed for the application and, during a login process, appropriate menu items will either be made available or unavailable based on the users' privileges. Each window will have the same basic tool set assigned to it (Open, Save, Print, Cancel). Buttons, messages, and fields will be placed in a consistent manner on the screen using the same basic fonts (type and size).

Development tools

Microsoft Visual Basic will be used to develop the proposed system. The standard toolset provided with SQL Server will be used for all additional development tools (e.g., ISQL and BCP).

Productivity tools

Microsoft Office will be purchased for all the workstations.

Implementation schedule

Implementation has been broken down into two stages: Phase I and Phase II delivery. The implementation schedule is broken down as follows:

Phase I—Key deliverables—The editing department

- Authors
- Titles
- Publishers

Phase II—Key deliverables—The administration department

- Stores
- Sales
- Employees

The preceding implementation schedule will allow Bonanza Books to modify their processes in an orderly fashion and enable them to provide their staff with the necessary training required to use the new hardware infrastructure. Since the Sales system will be implemented in the second phase, this will enable Bonanza Books to close their books and transfer only balances to the new system.

Bonanza Books Database Specification

The Bonanza Books database layout is detailed in Tables 2-2 and 2-3.

Table 2-2. Entity List

Name	Label
authors	This table holds all the authors' key details.
discounts	This table contains the discount schedule given to each store.
employee	This table contains the employee details.
jobs	This table contains the job and grade details.
pub_info	This table contains the publishers' marketing information.
publishers	This table contains the publishers' details.
roysched	This table contains the royalty schedule breakdown for each author.
sales	This table contains the orders by store.
stores	This table contains the store details.
titleauthor	This table contains the titles belonging to each author.
titles	This tables contains all the details about the titles stocked.

Table 2-3. Data Dictionary

Name	Type	Label
address	VA40	This is the address information for the author.
advance	MN	This is the advance amount given to an author (such as $300.00).
au_fname	VA20	This is the author's first name.
au_id	VA11	This is the author's unique identifier.
au_lname	VA40	This is the author's last name.
au_ord	BT	This is an indicator for each title associated with the author.
city	VA20	This is the city in which the publisher resides.
contract	BL	This indicator shows whether a contract has been signed: (1) if it has, (0) if it hasn't.
country	VA30	This is the country in which the publisher resides.
discount	DC4,2	This is the actual discount rate given to the store for a particular volume of sales (such as 5.33%).
discounttype	VA40	This describes the type of discount that has been given.
emp_id	A9	This is the employee's unique identifier.
fname	VA20	This is the first name of the employee.
highqty	SI	This is the upper limit for a particular discount before a higher discount is given.
hirange	I	This is the upper limit of royalty payments, since royalties are subject to an annual maximum.
hire_date	DT	This is the date the employee was hired.
job_desc	VA50	This is a brief description of the job.
job_id	NO	This is the unique identifier given to the job.
job_lvl	BT	This is the grade of a particular job.
lname	VA30	This is the last name of the employee.
logo	PIC	This is the logo of the publisher.
lorange	I	This is the minimum payout schedule for the royalties.
lowqty	SI	This is the lowest order quantity required in order to qualify for a particular discount rate.
max_lvl	BT	This is the maximum level indicator.
min_lvl	BT	This is the minimum level indicator.
minit	A1	This indicator reflects whether the employee record has been validated by HR.
notes	VA200	These are any notes that need to be stored for the titles.
ord_date	DT	This is the date on which the order was placed.
ord_num	VA20	This is the order number given to the order.
payterms	VA12	These are the payment terms for this order.
phone	A12	This is the author's telephone number (Note: this is confidential information).

Table 2-3. Data Dictionary (continued)

Name	Type	Label
pr_info	TXT	This is a free-form field, which can contain any notes relating to this publisher.
price	MN	This is the current sales price for this title.
pub_id	A4	This is the unique identifier given to the publisher.
pub_name	VA40	This is the name of the publisher.
pubdate	DT	This is the first date on which the title was published.
qty	SI	This is the quantity of books ordered.
royalty	I	This is the amount of the royalty that has been paid out for a particular title.
royaltyper	I	This is the quantity of royalty payments per year.
state	A2	This is the state in which the person/entity resides.
stor_address	VA40	This is the address of the store.
stor_id	A4	This is the store identifier, which is unique.
stor_name	VA40	This is the name of the store.
title	VA80	This is the title of the book.
title_id	VA6	This is the unique identifier given to the book.
type	A12	This is the book's primary classification (such as cookery).
ytd_sales	I	This is this financial year's sales volume.
zip	A5	This is the Zip Code of the person/entity.

The Physical Database Model

Figure 2-6 shows the physical database model developed by Musketeer Consultants.

Next Steps

The proposed architecture and database need to be signed off on in order for the necessary purchasing and development work to begin.

The actual system processes that will be required to support this database will be detailed in the system processes design document. Once the processes have been agreed to, it will be possible to begin development on the system.

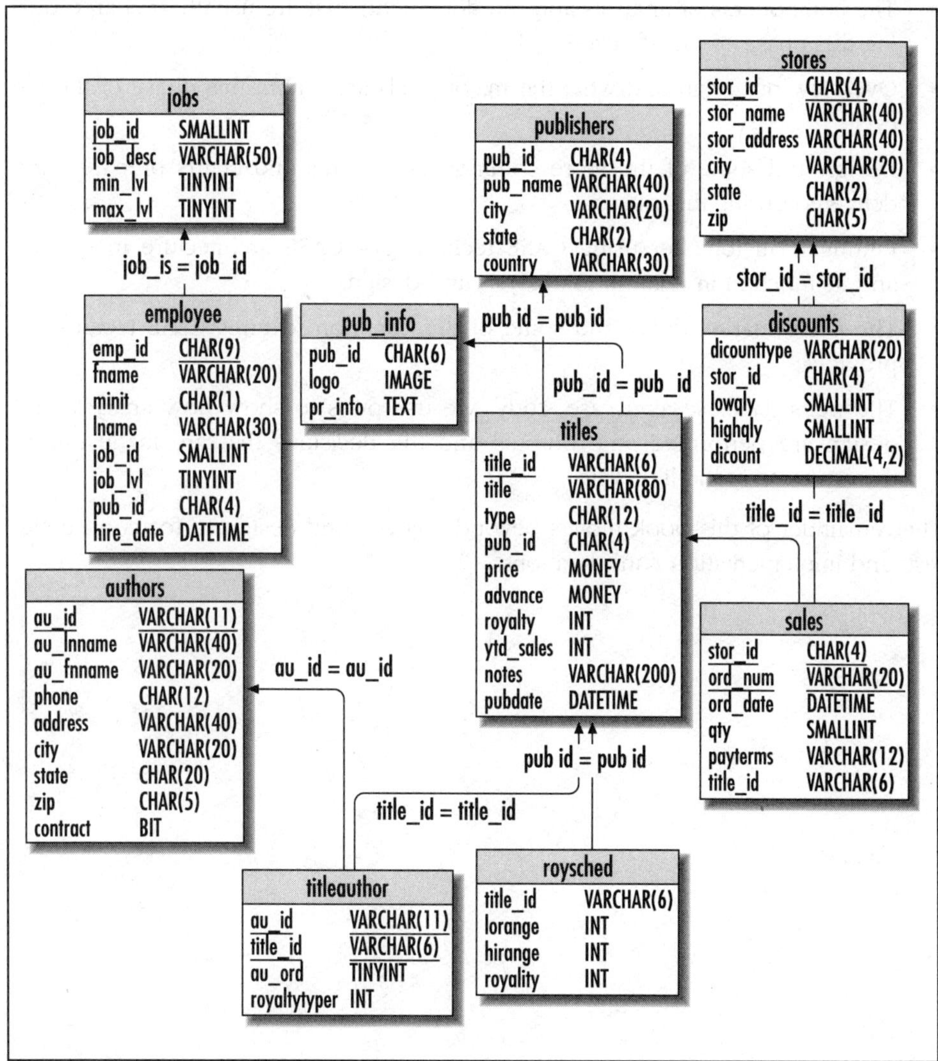

Figure 2-6. Physical data model

Summary

In this chapter we've briefly covered analysis and design: what they are, what the goals are for each phase, and what the major deliverables are for each phase. Major points to remember:

- The need for adequate analysis and design.
- The systems life cycle.
- Overview of analysis and its purpose in the life cycle.

- The components of analysis and the documents that are usually prepared during this phase of the life cycle.
- Overview of design and what the major goals are within this phase of the life cycle.
- Design and some of the more common documents and charts prepared and delivered during this phase.
- Putting it all together using CASE technology—CASE architecture in general and its function in relation to analysis and design.
- The CASE market today and some of the common features CASE technology provides.
- The pubs database as a case study; we use pubs to show how analysis and design are performed—the outputs and the decisions that are made during these phases in the life cycle.

The remainder of this book moves beyond analysis and design to focus on code, test, and implementation considerations.

In this chapter:
- *SQL Versus Transact-SQL*
- *Data Definition Language*
- *Data Manipulation Language*
- *Summary*

3
SQL Primer

Before you can write the thousand-line, miraculously potent Transact-SQL programs that you always dreamt of (or perhaps had nightmares over), you first must have a thorough understanding of the SQL (Structured Query Language) that forms the backbone of most SQL Server-based code. SQL provides the basis for all interactions with the SQL Server RDBMS—data creation, retrieval, modification, and deletion. SQL in itself is no small fish to fry. If you're completely new to SQL, you'd probably get a lot of benefit from studying SQL in depth. This chapter provides you with the information you need to become familiar with, if not expert at, the basics of SQL as it is implemented in the SQL Server RDBMS. Be warned! This chapter goes fast; we're giving you a quick tour of a large amount of material.

If you really don't know the first thing about SQL, you might want to look for a complete volume on the language. Since SQL commands a great deal of shelf space unto itself at the bookstore, you will have many books from which to choose.

SQL Versus Transact-SQL

What's the difference between SQL and Transact-SQL? We touched on that difference in Chapter 1, *Introduction to Transact-SQL*. The main thing to remember is that SQL is the foundation on which Transact-SQL is built. SQL provides the basis for most of the user-database interface. SQL is divided into three subsets:

- Data Manipulation Language (DML)
- Data Definition Language (DDL)
- Data Control Language (DCL)

DML provides specific commands that handle data, like SELECT, INSERT, UPDATE, and DELETE. DDL contains commands that handle the accessibility and manipulation of database objects (e.g., tables and views), including commands like CREATE and DROP. DCL contains permission-related commands like GRANT and REVOKE. (Don't be distressed if the commands we mention here are unfamiliar. DML and DDL are described in this chapter; DCL is described in Chapter 14, *Stored Procedures and Modular Design.*)

All three of these languages are largely industry-standard. So, if you learn how to query data using the SQL SELECT command, this knowledge is likely to transfer readily to many other relational databases, such as Oracle or Informix.

All of the examples shown in this chapter are based on the pubs database, commonly found in every SQL Server installation, which we introduced in Chapter 2, *Database Analysis and Design*. If your server doesn't have pubs, you can install it by running the *INSTPUBS.SQL* script included in the *INSTALL* directory under the SQL Server root directory. (The directory varies depending on which version and vendor of SQL Server you are using.)

While SQL is industry-standard, Transact-SQL contains a number of enhancements specific to SQL Server, such as conditional processing, variables, error handling, and temporary tables (also known as hash tables). You won't find Transact-SQL commands in other relational databases, although it is likely that other vendors have included some proprietary enhancements of their own that do the same thing.

Data Definition Language

Data Definition Language, or DDL, is composed of three major commands:

CREATE
DROP
ALTER

You use DDL statements to create most of the database objects used to store and manage data in a SQL Server database. For example, you can both CREATE and DROP defaults, indexes, procedures, rules, tables, triggers, views, and even databases. Once created, the only database object that allows the ALTER command is the table.

Technically, the SELECT . . . INTO command and the TRUNCATE TABLE command are considered DDL statements. However, because of their functional similarities, these two commands are included in the sections on SELECT and DELETE, respectively.

This section describes those DDL commands associated with the construction and management of tables, as well as their associated dependent objects: constraints, defaults, indexes (briefly), and rules. Procedures, triggers, and views are described in later chapters (Chapters 14, 15, and 16, respectively). The GRANT and REVOKE statements are described in Chapter 14, *Stored Procedures and Modular Design*.

Managing Tables

Since the table is the storage place for most data in a database, you will have to know the ins and outs of creating and managing tables. You can use the nifty little GUI tools included with SQL Server's management tools to create every table you'll ever use, but any DBA worth two cents will tell you that you need to know the commands *and use them*. Among the old-timers of the relational database world, there is the popular argument that the GUI tools can make you lazy (just as my grandfather used to grumble that TV was the root of all teenage sloth and rebelliousness).

However, this is only partially true, because in many instances the GUI tools make *more* work for you. Case in point: when using only GUI tools to create the tables, how many times will you have to create those tables when the boss decides to roll the application to 12 new sites? At least 12 times over, and the opportunity for spelling and transposition errors stagger the mind if you type as well as most application developers (at least the ones we know). There are numerous other situations in which knowing the code is of critical importance. What if the server experiences a corrupt hard disk that hampers or disables the use of the GUI? It's happened to us. Or what if you want to write a stored procedure that creates a new table? You can't use the GUI inside a stored procedure. The solution is to code all of your table management into scripts. And in order to do that, you have to learn the code.

CREATE TABLE: Creating Tables

The syntax for the CREATE TABLE statement on Microsoft and Sybase looks like this:

Microsoft	Sybase

`CREATE TABLE [database.[owner].]`
`    table_name`
`(`
`{column_name datatype(length)`
`properties [col_constraint [,]`
`    col_constraint]}`
`[[,] {column2_name... |`
`    table_constraint}]`
`[[,] {column3_name... |`
`    table2_constraint}...]`
`)`
`[ON segment_name}`
	`CREATE TABLE [database.[owner].]`
	`    table_name`
	`(`
	`{column_name datatype(length)`
	`properties [col_constraint [,]`
	`    col_constraint]}`
	`[[,] {column2_name... |`
	`    table_constraint}]`
	`[[,] {column3_name... |`
	`    table2_constraint}...]`
	`)`
	`[WITH max_rows_per_page = n]`
	`[ON segment_name]`

There are a few rules about the number and row length of tables you'll need to take into account when creating a new table:

- SQL Server allows up to 2 billion tables per database.
- Up to 250 columns are allowed for a single table, adding up to a total width of 1,962 bytes.
- SQL Server will create a table containing VARCHAR or VARBINARY columns with a width greater than 1,962 (with a warning message), but SQL Server will barf (ah, that is, produce an error) when an update or insert causes the row length to exceed 1,962 bytes.
- Tables are created in the currently open database unless a different database (where you have table creation privileges) is explicitly defined.
- The Sybase option WITH `max_rows_per_page` allows you to explicitly tell SQL Server how many records you'd like it to store on a 2K data page.
- You may specify the "segment" where the table, constraint, or index will be created. Segments aren't really pertinent to a discussion of Transact-SQL; it's more of a database administration topic. If you want to learn more about segments (and you have to be a glutton for punishment if you do), please refer to the vendor documentation.

Creating a simple table

Let's assume that we now want to create a new table in the pubs database called distributors. (If you are using a user ID other than SA to create a table, CREATE TABLE permissions must be explicitly granted to that user ID.) In this exercise, we'll use the simplest form of the CREATE TABLE statement, specifying only the `column_names`, `datatypes`, and `properties`:

```
CREATE TABLE distributors
    (dist_id        CHAR(4)      NOT NULL,
     dist_name      VARCHAR(40) NULL,
     dist_address1 VARCHAR(40) NULL,
     dist_address2 VARCHAR(40) NULL,
     city           VARCHAR(20) NULL,
     state          CHAR(2)      NULL,
     zip            CHAR(5)      NULL,
     phone          CHAR(12)     NULL,
     sales_rep      empid        NULL)
```

The table created by this statement is about as simple as they get. We've created a nine-column table. Each new record of the table requires, at a minimum, only a dist_id; all other columns are optional. The table has no indexes or defined primary key, no column defaults, not even any check constraints. In its current shape, this table is just a raw heap for data.

NULL and NOT NULL

The only extra coding we performed in this statement was the inclusion of the NULL keyword. The two most common column properties are the NULL and NOT NULL keywords. They simply indicate if data is optional or required, respectively, in the given column. SQL Server defaults a column to NOT NULL if no property is specified. However, our advice is to get in the habit of doing it anyway. That's because SQL Server currently defaults to a non-ANSI standard; the ANSI standard requires columns to default to a NULL property.

Microsoft SQL Server can be forced to use the ANSI standard of setting columns to NULL as a default by using the command:

```
sp_dboption 'pubs','ANSI null default',TRUE
```

where you can replace "pubs" with the name of your own database.

Dropping a table

The creation of the distributors table worked out just fine, but what if we want to add a few features to the table? Since no data has yet been added to the table, we can simply drop the table and re-create it using a more complex incarnation of the CREATE TABLE statement. We'll describe how to drop a table later on in the section "DROP TABLE: Dropping a Table."

sp_depends sometimes forgets about dependencies when objects are dropped and then re-created. Refer to Chapter 19, *Code Maintenance in SQL Server*, for more details on this stored procedure. For a more functional procedure, use the stored procedure *sp_grep* enclosed on the accompanying CD-ROM. *sp_grep* searches for an occurrence of a text string or a combination of text strings in the source code of all objects and reports object names. It may report some objects that have the text string in a comment (which is not a real dependency), but it won't miss existing dependencies as *sp_depends* sometimes does.

IDENTITY columns

We've already seen the NULL and NOT NULL column properties. Another property, IDENTITY, provides a monotonically increasing counter generated by the system. On Microsoft, only NOT NULL columns of datatypes TINYINT, SMALLINT, INT, NUMERIC, and DECIMAL may be used as IDENTITY columns, and only one may exist in the entire table. Sybase requires that IDENTITY columns be numeric with a scale of 0. Also, you use the IDENTITY property in lieu of a NULL or NOT NULL property, though it still treats the column as NOT NULL. Identities may be declared as primary keys or index columns, but they cannot be bound by a default value.

In Microsoft SQL Server, identities are specified along with a *seed* value and an *increment* value. The seed value determines the value of the identity when the very first record is inserted into the table. All subsequent records are inserted at a value equal to the last identity plus the increment value. Both values default to 1 if none is specified in the CREATE TABLE statement. To create a table with an IDENTITY column, use this command syntax:

```
CREATE TABLE databasename.owner.tablename
    (column_name datatype(length) IDENTITY[(seed, increment)]...)
```

For example, the following code creates a temporary table with an identity counter that starts at the number 20 and increases by 10 with every new record inserted into the table:

```
CREATE TABLE temp_sales_tally
    (sales_id     INT    NOT NULL IDENTITY(20, 10),
     sales_rep    empid NOT NULL,
     total_sales money NULL)
```

Sybase does things a little differently. With Sybase, all you need to do in the CREATE TABLE command is specify that the column is an IDENTITY column, as shown in the following example:

```
CREATE TABLE temp_sales_tally
    (sales_id     NUMERIC(5,0) IDENTITY,
     sales_rep    empid NOT NULL,
     total_sales money NULL)
```

Sybase allows control over the seed and increment values of IDENTITY columns by using the "auto identity" database option and the "size of auto identity" configuration parameter. If you want to include an IDENTITY column in a nonunique index, you must set the identity in the "nonunique index" database option.

Table and column constraints

You can apply all kinds of nifty constraints to a table in a single CREATE TABLE statement. Certain types of constraints apply to the table as a whole; more specifically, only one—for example, a primary key—may exist for an entire table. On the other hand, other types of constraints—such as foreign keys, of which up to 31 can be defined for a single table—can exist aplenty in a table.

Another difference between table and column constraints is where in the CREATE TABLE statement they appear. Table constraints appear at the end of the statement, after all columns have been defined. Column constraints, on the other hand, appear immediately after the column definition. Note that column-level and table-level constraints perform their functions in exactly the same way; they are merely defined at different levels of the CREATE TABLE command, in much the same way that waiters and salad bars are both methods of getting food to your face (except that you must leave waiters a better tip).

You can explicitly name table constraints, or you can allow SQL Server to provide a system-generated name for them. It's a good idea to apply a comprehensible name to any constraints you create on a table, since that name will appear in any error message generated by the constraint (i.e., that means no silly names along the lines of pk_doofus_dingleberry, either!).

Give names to new constraints. If you do not, SQL Server assigns them automatically. You may be unhappy about its choice when you need to drop a constraint and have to type a name like FK_new_title_au_id_511012C4.

Table 3-1 summarizes each type of constraint:

Table 3-1. Table and Column Constraints

Constraint	Comments
PRIMARY KEY	This constraint enforces uniqueness and data integrity for each row of a table based upon one or more columns. All columns participating in a PRIMARY KEY constraint must possess the NOT NULL property. A primary key creates a unique index on the specified column(s), which can be dropped only when the table or primary key constraint is dropped. PRIMARY KEY constraints can be CLUSTERED (the default) or NONCLUSTERED, and only one may exist for a given table. Alternate primary keys can be implemented with added UNIQUE constraints. Primary keys may be table- or column-level, but multicolumn primary keys must always be defined at the table level.
FOREIGN KEY	This constraint provides referential integrity by comparing values in the specified columns against values in the referenced tables and columns. The columns of the local table must exactly match the datatype and length of the columns in the referenced table and must be NOT NULL. The referenced table must exist in the same database, must not be a temporary table, and must have columns that possess either a PRIMARY KEY constraint or a UNIQUE constraint. The absolute upper limit for foreign keys on a single table is 31, though using this many is probably indicative of an overly complex table design. FOREIGN KEY constraints, unlike PRIMARY KEY constraints, do not automatically create an associated index. If you're bothering to create foreign keys, you should also create an index on the same columns using the CREATE INDEX command. SELECT or REFERENCE permissions must be granted on the referenced columns. Foreign keys may be table- or column-level, but multicolumn keys must always be defined at the table level.

Table 3-1. Table and Column Constraints (continued)

Constraint	Comments
UNIQUE	Like the PRIMARY KEY constraint, this constraint enforces uniqueness and data integrity for each record in a table based upon the columns specified. Unlike the PRIMARY KEY constraint, the columns composing a UNIQUE constraint may contain null values (though it doesn't take a rocket scientist to see that this is not advisable in most cases). Only one row in the table can possess null values in a unique key. A table can contain any number of UNIQUE constraints. SQL Server automatically creates a unique index to go along with the UNIQUE constraints, which can be CLUSTERED or NONCLUSTERED (the default). The unique index created with the UNIQUE constraints can be removed only by dropping the constraint itself or the table.
DEFAULT	This constraint tells SQL Server a value to use for a column when none is supplied in an INSERT statement. The column may not be a TIMESTAMP or IDENTITY column. Defaults may be literals (explicitly defined numbers or characters), functions, niladic functions, or NULL. Niladic functions are system-supplied values like CURRENT_USER, SERVERNAME, and DATABASE_NAME. DEFAULT constraints are dropped when the table is dropped, but you can also use the CREATE DEFAULT statement to independently create column-based defaults. Defaults may be table- or column-level.
CHECK	This constraint limits the possible values that can be entered into the columns of a table. Multiple CHECK constraints may exist for a single column, but only one can be defined on a column in any given CREATE TABLE statement. Hence, each column may have multiple conditions in a single statement. The CHECK constraint must be a Boolean expression (read: no subqueries!). CHECK constraints act the same as rules (see the discussion of CREATE RULE later in this chapter), with the exception of automatically binding to the referenced column. All restrictions are evaluated when multiple checks and/or rules exist. CHECK constraints are column-level.
CHECK [NOT FOR REPLICATION]	On Microsoft SQL server only, you may turn off CHECK constraints for data that is recorded in the database via replication using the clause NOT FOR REPLICATION. (A discussion of replication is beyond the scope of this book.)

Whenever constraints are added through the CREATE TABLE statement, please be aware that they do not go into effect until the CREATE TABLE transaction is complete. Thus, if you've got a CREATE TABLE statement and an INSERT statement for that same table grouped into one transaction, none of the constraints will take effect on the record as it is inserted. Any time one of these constraints is violated, the command will be aborted and any transactions in the command will be rolled back (or committed, if possible).

Creating a constrained table

We've decided to revamp the distributors table by dropping and re-creating it. This time around, we are going to add more features (or, more accurately, more constraints) to the table, including a primary key, a foreign key, default values for columns, and check constraints. Each time, we'll demonstrate the various table and column-level constraint syntax.

Creating a PRIMARY KEY constraint. The specific code fragment for creating a primary key on a table looks like this:

Microsoft	Sybase

`[CONSTRAINT constraint_name]`
`PRIMARY KEY`
`[CLUSTERED | NONCLUSTERED]`
`(column_name [..., column16_name])`
`[WITH FILLFACTOR = n]`
`[ON segment_name]`
	`[CONSTRAINT constraint_name]`
	`PRIMARY KEY`
	`[CLUSTERED | NONCLUSTERED]`
	`(column_name [..., column16_name])`
	`[WITH FILLFACTOR = n] |`
	`    [WITH MAX_ROWS_PER_PAGE = n]`
	`[ON segment_name]`

This generic code includes the options for creating both table- and column-level PRIMARY KEY constraints. The following examples show how to create them:

```
-- Creating a column-level constraint
CREATE TABLE distributors
    (dist_id        CHAR(4)      PRIMARY KEY NONCLUSTERED,
     dist_name      VARCHAR(40) NULL,
     dist_address1 VARCHAR(40) NULL,
     dist_address2 VARCHAR(40) NULL,
     city           VARCHAR(20) NULL,
     state          CHAR(2)      NULL,
     zip            CHAR(5)      NULL,
     phone          CHAR(12)     NULL,
     sales_rep      empid        NULL)
GO

-- Creating a table-level constraint
CREATE TABLE distributors
    (dist_id        CHAR(4)      NOT NULL,
     dist_name      VARCHAR(40) NULL,
     dist_address1 VARCHAR(40) NULL,
     dist_address2 VARCHAR(40) NULL,
     city           VARCHAR(20) NULL,
     state          CHAR(2)      NULL,
     zip            CHAR(5)      NULL,
     phone          CHAR(12)     NULL,
     sales_rep      empid        NULL,
    CONSTRAINT      pk_dist_id  PRIMARY KEY NONCLUSTERED
                   (dist_id)
    WITH FILLFACTOR = 70)
GO
```

By using the column-level constraint in the first set of code, we have to rely on several system-generated values. The system will generate its own name for the primary key, as well as its own fillfactor. Fillfactor is the percent amount of free space that SQL Server will leave on each new 2K page. There are a number of optimization and tuning reasons for establishing a fillfactor, discussed in more detail later in the "Creating Indexes" section. Sybase supports the use of either the MAX_ROWS_PER_PAGE or FILLFACTOR keyword. MAX_ROWS_PER_PAGE allows you to specify a specific maximum number of rows allowed on a single 2K page of data. When using the table-level constraint, we have the freedom to specify all aspects of the new primary key.

A comma is required after the last column definition and before the first constraint. Commas also are required between multiple constraints on a single CREATE TABLE command.

The only ways to drop a primary key, once created, are to drop the entire table or to drop the constraint using the ALTER TABLE . . . DROP CONSTRAINT command.

Creating a FOREIGN KEY constraint. The FOREIGN KEY constraint is used to cross-check the values in one or more columns of the local table with values that exist in a primary key or uniquely constrained columns of other tables. The general syntax for the constraint is shown here:

```
[CONSTRAINT constraint_name
[FOREIGN KEY
(column_name [..., column16_name])]
REFERENCES [owner.]ref_table [(ref_column [..., ref_column16]]
[NOT FOR REPLICATION])]
```

As with the code for primary keys, this generic syntax is adaptable to both column-level and table-level FOREIGN KEY constraints. Note that column-level and table-level constraints perform their functions in exactly the same way. They are merely defined at different levels of the CREATE TABLE command. The following code creates a single-column foreign key on the sales_rep column referencing the empid column of the employee table:

```
-- Creating a column-level constraint
CREATE TABLE distributors
    (dist_id        CHAR(4)       PRIMARY KEY NONCLUSTERED,
     dist_name      VARCHAR(40) NULL,
     dist_address1 VARCHAR(40) NULL,
     dist_address2 VARCHAR(40) NULL,
     city           VARCHAR(20) NULL,
     state          CHAR(2)       NULL,
     zip            CHAR(5)       NULL,
     phone          CHAR(12)      NULL,
```

```
    sales_rep       empid        NOT NULL REFERENCES employee(empid))
GO

-- Creating a table-level constraint
CREATE TABLE distributors
   (dist_id          CHAR(4)        NOT NULL,
    dist_name        VARCHAR(40)    NULL,
    dist_address1    VARCHAR(40)    NULL,
    dist_address2    VARCHAR(40)    NULL,
    city             VARCHAR(20)    NULL,
    state            CHAR(2)        NULL,
    zip              CHAR(5)        NULL,
    phone            CHAR(12)       NULL,
    sales_rep        empid          NULL,
   CONSTRAINT        pk_dist_id     PRIMARY KEY NONCLUSTERED
                    (dist_id)
      WITH FILLFACTOR = 70,
   CONSTRAINT        fk_emp_id      FOREIGN KEY (sales_rep)
      REFERENCES employee(emp_id))
GO
```

When the table-level constraint is used, we are given the option of supplying an actual foreign key name. Note that the column in our local table does not have the same name as the column in the target value. The columns must be of the same datatypes and lengths, and of course their values should be logically related. The table-level FOREIGN KEY constraint *must* be used when defining multiple-column foreign keys.

The column-level constraint provides the benefits of being "quick and dirty." We don't even have to specify the keyword FOREIGN KEY to create a column-level constraint.

Remember that, at this point, our distributors table has a foreign key on the sales_rep column, but no index on that column. FOREIGN KEY constraints, unlike PRIMARY KEY and UNIQUE constraints, do not automatically generate subsidiary indexes. The next logical step here would be to issue a CREATE INDEX statement that adds an index to the sales_rep column.

Creating a UNIQUE constraint. UNIQUE constraints force every value in the constrained column to be unique, allowing up to one record to have a null value in the process. These columns are often alternate keys to the table's primary key. The command structure to add a UNIQUE constraint is shown here:

Microsoft	Sybase
[CONSTRAINT constraint_name] UNIQUE [CLUSTERED | NONCLUSTERED] (column_name [..., column16_name]) [WITH FILLFACTOR = n] [ON segment_name]	[CONSTRAINT constraint_name] UNIQUE [CLUSTERED | NONCLUSTERED] (column_name [..., column16_name]) [WITH FILLFACTOR = n] | [WITH MAX_ROWS_PER_PAGE = n] [ON segment_name]

Because we want to limit the number of distributors we do business with, our system analysts came up with the bright idea of limiting our distributors to only one per Zip Code. We also want to allow one (and only one) record to have a null Zip Code. Furthermore, the table is to be physically written to disk (i.e., CLUSTERED) in Zip Code order. This functionality can be implemented easily enough using a UNIQUE constraint.

```
-- Creating a column-level constraint
CREATE TABLE distributors
    (dist_id        CHAR(4)       PRIMARY KEY NONCLUSTERED,
     dist_name      VARCHAR(40)   NULL,
     dist_address1  VARCHAR(40)   NULL,
     dist_address2  VARCHAR(40)   NULL,
     city           VARCHAR(20)   NULL,
     state          CHAR(2)       NULL,
     zip            CHAR(5)       NULL UNIQUE CLUSTERED,
     phone          CHAR(12)      NULL,
     sales_rep      empid         NOT NULL REFERENCES employee(empid))
GO

-- Creating a table-level constraint
CREATE TABLE distributors
    (dist_id        CHAR(4)       NOT NULL,
     dist_name      VARCHAR(40)   NULL,
     dist_address1  VARCHAR(40)   NULL,
     dist_address2  VARCHAR(40)   NULL,
     city           VARCHAR(20)   NULL,
     state          CHAR(2)       NULL,
     zip            CHAR(5)       NULL,
     phone          CHAR(12)      NULL,
     sales_rep      empid         NULL,
    CONSTRAINT      pk_dist_id    PRIMARY KEY NONCLUSTERED
                   (dist_id)
        WITH FILLFACTOR = 70,
    CONSTRAINT      fk_emp_id     FOREIGN KEY (sales_rep)
        REFERENCES employee(emp_id),
    CONSTRAINT      unq_zip       UNIQUE CLUSTERED (zip)
        WITH FILLFACTOR = 20)
GO
```

The table-level default allows us to define an explicit constraint name for the UNIQUE constraint; we also can add a fillfactor to the subsidiary index that SQL Server creates with the constraint. If you don't want to be bothered with such things, the column-level constraint provides a quick and easy alternative. If we later need to drop the UNIQUE constraint index, we'd have to either drop the whole table (yucky!) or drop the UNIQUE constraint via the ALTER TABLE command.

Creating DEFAULT constraints. Default constraints supply a value that is used in INSERT and UPDATE statements when no other value is specified. Defaults are often used to insert literal values, such as explicitly defined character strings or numeric values. Defaults might also contain functions, like GETDATE(), which must be enclosed in parentheses, or niladic functions (that is, system-supplied values like USER or SERVERNAME), which should not be enclosed in quotes. The syntax for defaults looks like this:

```
[CONSTRAINT constraint_name]
DEFAULT {constant_expression | niladic-function | NULL}
[FOR column_name]
```

You also can add DEFAULT constraints to columns that possess other constraints, such as primary or foreign keys. In this example, we'll add a default to both the sales_rep column (which already has a foreign key) and to the state column, since much of our business originates in the state of California:

```
-- Creating a column-level DEFAULT constraint
CREATE TABLE distributors
    (dist_id        CHAR(4)      PRIMARY KEY NONCLUSTERED,
     dist_name      VARCHAR(40)  NULL,
     dist_address1  VARCHAR(40)  NULL,
     dist_address2  VARCHAR(40)  NULL,
     city           VARCHAR(20)  NULL,
     state          CHAR(2)      NULL CONSTRAINT def_st DEFAULT ("CA"),
     zip            CHAR(5)      NULL UNIQUE CLUSTERED,
     phone          CHAR(12)     NULL,
     sales_rep      empid        NOT NULL DEFAULT USER
                                     REFERENCES employee(emp_id))
GO
```

The default on the sales_rep column inserts the value of the niladic function USER (a system-generated value) if no value is supplied on an INSERT or UPDATE statement. Remember, though, that it also has a foreign key on the emp_id column of the employee table, so the USER value must also exist in the employee table for a successful default value to be saved in this column.

Creating CHECK constraints. CHECK constraints are pretty cool. How's that for a sweeping generalization? To be more specific, CHECK constraints allow explicit control over a wide variety of values entered into a given column. Although CHECK constraints exert overhead on INSERT and UPDATE statements, they have the potential to take processing out of client applications and centralize a great deal of system logic on the server. CHECK constraints differ somewhat between Microsoft and Sybase:

Microsoft	Sybase

`[CONSTRAINT CONSTRAINT_name]`
`CHECK [NOT FOR REPLICATION]`
`(expression)`
	`[CONSTRAINT CONSTRAINT_name]`
	`CHECK (expression)`

The major difference between the two implementations is that Microsoft SQL Server allows you to disable the CHECK constraint on any transaction that originates from replication using the NOT FOR REPLICATION keyphrase.

CHECK constraints are limited to Boolean operations (like =, >=, <=, or <>) although they may include some of SQL Server's specialized operands, such as IN or LIKE, and they may be appended to one another (for a single column) using AND or OR clauses.

The following example adds a CHECK constraint to the dist_id and zip columns. The Zip Code must fall into the normal ranges for postal Zip Codes, while the dist_id values are allowed to contain either four alphabetic characters or two alphabetic plus two numeric characters:

```
-- Creating column-level CHECK constraints
CREATE TABLE distributors
     (dist_id        CHAR(4)      CONSTRAINT pk_dist_id PRIMARY KEY NONCLUSTERED
                                  CONSTRAINT ck_dist_id CHECK
                                      (dist_id LIKE '[A-Z][A-Z][A-Z][A-Z]' OR
                                       dist_id LIKE '[A-Z][A-Z][0-9][0-9]'),
      dist_name      VARCHAR(40)  NULL,
      dist_address1  VARCHAR(40)  NULL,
      dist_address2  VARCHAR(40)  NULL,
      city           VARCHAR(20)  NULL,
      state          CHAR(2)      NULL CONSTRAINT def_st DEFAULT ("CA"),
      zip            CHAR(5)      NULL CONSTRAINT unq_dist_zip UNIQUE CLUSTERED
                                  CONSTRAINT ck_dist_zip CHECK
                                      (zip LIKE '[0-9][0-9][0-9][0-9][0-9]'),
      phone          CHAR(12)     NULL,
      sales_rep      empid        NOT NULL DEFAULT USER
                                      REFERENCES employee(emp id))
GO
```

Getting Information About a Table

Now that we've finally finished with the creation of the distributors table, we can query SQL Server for a summary report on the table using the *sp_help* system stored procedure. The stored procedure returns a significant amount of information (some say it's overkill) about all columns, constraints, indexes, and other dependent objects built upon a given table (whose name is specified as an argument).

To find out how much space a particular table consumes, use the *sp_spaceused* system stored procedure. It will tell you how much space is currently in use and how much is set aside for any given table. For more detail on both of these stored procedures, refer to Chapter 17, *System and Extended Stored Procedures.*

CREATE DEFAULTS and CREATE RULE: Creating Defaults and Rules Separately from Tables

Just as you are able to create DEFAULT and CHECK constraints as a table is being created, you can create and "bind" acceptable default values or CHECK-type constraints called *rules* after the table is created. The required commands are CREATE DEFAULT and CREATE RULE, respectively.

You'll almost always want to use table and column constraints to accomplish this functionality, since multiple conditions can be defined for any given column using the CREATE TABLE command. However, CREATE DEFAULT does provide some added value in that the default command can be reused on many different columns.

The basis syntax for CREATE DEFAULT is:

```
CREATE DEFAULT [owner.] default_name
AS constant_expression
```

The next step in creating a separately defined default or rule is to bind it to a column in a particular table. You can bind defaults using the *sp_bindefault* system stored procedure for this function. To bind a rule, use the *sp_bindrule* system stored procedure.

The following example shows how to create a default and then bind it:

```
-- Creates a default of 'CA' for columns showing the state postal address
CREATE DEFAULT state_dflt AS "CA"
GO

-- Binds the specified default, the first value, to the table and column in
-- the second value, in quotes.
SP_BINDEFAULT state_dflt, 'distributors.state'
GO
```

A column with a default can still have a null value if an INSERT or UPDATE statement explicitly adds one to the column. The default will apply its value when no value is specified or when the DEFAULT keyword is specified in the INSERT or UPDATE statement. Defaults can be bound to columns or to user-defined datatypes. You can append the keyword FUTUREONLY to the *sp_bindefault* system stored procedure to indicate that the default should be applied only to new columns, not to existing ones. FUTUREONLY can be used only on user-defined datatypes.

Defaults must match the datatype of the column; however, default values that are too long for the column will be used and truncated to the length of the column. And, of course, the default also must agree with any CHECK constraint or rule on the column. You must unbind a default using *sp_unbindefault* before you can drop it using DROP DEFAULT.

The basic syntax for CREATE RULE is:

```
CREATE RULE [owner.] rule_name
AS condition_expression
```

CREATE RULE is limited in that only one rule may be applied to a column. Rules can also be applied to user-defined datatypes. This example shows how to create and bind a rule:

```
-- Creates several sample rules.  The @item is the variable used to check
-- against values found in the table and column.
CREATE RULE range_sample
    AS          @range >= 100000
    AND         @range <= 990000
GO

CREATE RULE list_sample
    AS          @list       IN ('CA','OR','WA','AZ')
GO

-- Binds the specified rules.  The first value is the rule (by name) and the
-- second value is the table and column that the rule is bound to.
sp_bindrule range_sample, 'distributors.sales_rep'
GO

sp_bindrule list_sample, 'distributors.state', FUTUREONLY
GO
```

As you may have noticed, CREATE RULE cannot be executed in a batch with any other SQL statements. It's a loner! Rules cannot be bound to TEXT, IMAGE, or TIMESTAMP columns. With both rules and defaults, SQL Server does not return an error if you have bound a constraint improperly to a table (such as a character to a numeric column). That's because the constraint is evaluated when an INSERT or UPDATE executes against the constrained column, not at bind time. Although you can add a rule to a column that already has one, the old rule will be overridden. So too will a rule bound to a column that has a user-defined datatype with a bound rule. You must unbind a rule using *sp_unbindefault* before dropping it with DROP RULE.

DROP TABLE: Dropping a Table

The DROP TABLE command allows you to drop one or many tables in a single command. There aren't a lot of rules to remember about dropping a table, except these:

- You must have permissions to drop the table as a normal user, a DBO, or an SA.
- Constraints, indexes, and triggers go down the tubes with a table when it is dropped. Defaults and rules become unbound. Re-creating the table will not restore the bindings.

- Tables referenced by a FOREIGN KEY constraint cannot be dropped without first dropping the referring foreign key.

The command for dropping a table looks like this:

```
DROP TABLE [[database].owner_name.]table_name
    [,[[database].owner_name.]table_name]
```

You can drop multiple tables in one statement as long as their names are separated by commas. The command assumes that you wish to drop a table in the local database unless you specify another database or a table owner. Here's an example of dropping multiple tables with one command:

```
DROP TABLE pubs.dbo.distributors,
   new_sales,
   pubs..sales_analysis
GO
```

Dropping a table, much like dropping a long-time dating partner, can have lasting repercussions. When you drop the table, any indexes or keys associated with the table also are dropped. However, any views or stored procedures built upon the table will continue to exist, *and will fail when anyone tries to use them*, until they are either corrected or until they too are dropped.

When dropping a table that has been around for a while, it's a good idea to check for any objects that might depend on it and thus be dramatically affected by its absence. You can use the system stored procedure *sp_depends* to find out what other database objects depend on a table that might be dropped. To find out what depends on the authors table in the pubs database, you would use this command:

```
sp_depends authors
```

Results:

```
In the current database the specified object is referenced by the following:
name                                    type
--------------------------------------- ----------------
dbo.reptq2                              stored procedure
dbo.titleview                           view

(1 row(s) affected)
```

ALTER TABLE: Altering an Existing Table

SQL Server allows you to make modifications to a table without dropping it. Unfortunately, altering a table does have its limitations. You can use the ALTER TABLE statement to:

- Add new columns to an existing table
- Add new constraints to an existing column or table

- Disable foreign key constraints (Microsoft only)
- Defer constraints during replication
- Disable (or enable) constraints without dropping them (Microsoft only)

Would you like to drop a column from a table, but still keep the rest of the table intact? Sorry, but the ALTER TABLE command does not allow that functionality.

The syntax for the ALTER TABLE command is shown here:

Microsoft

```
ALTER TABLE [database.[owner.]]
      table_name
[WITH {CHECK | NOCHECK}]
     {{CHECK | NOCHECK} CONSTRAINT
     {constraint_name | ALL} |
[ADD {column_name datatype(length)
properties
     [constraints] | [[, ]
         table_constraint]}
     [, { column_name datatype(length)
      properties
     [constraints |
      next_table_constraint}]...] |
     [DROP CONSTRAINT]
      constraint_name [,
      constraint_name2]...]}
```

Sybase

```
ALTER TABLE [database.[owner].]
     table_name
{ADD column_name datatype
[DEFAULT {constant_expression |
     user| NULL}]
{[{IDENTITY | NULL}]
| [[CONSTRAINT constraint_name]
   {{UNIQUE | primary key}
     [CLUSTERED | NONCLUSTERED]
     [WITH {FILLFACTOR |
          MAX_ROWS_PER_PAGE} = x]
          [ON segment_name]
     | REFERENCES [[database.owner.]
          ref_table
          [(ref_column)]
     | CHECK (search_condition)}]}...
  {[,next_column]}...
| ADD {[CONSTRAINT constraint_name]
   {UNIQUE | PRIMARY KEY}
     [CLUSTURED | NONCLUSTERED}
     (column_name [{,column_name}...])
     [WITH {FILLFACTOR |
          MAX_ROWS_PER_PAGE} = x]
          [ON segment_name]
  | FOREIGN KEY (column_name
       [{,column_name}...])
       REFERENCES [[database.]owner.]
          ref_table
          [(ref_column
               [{,ref_column}...])]
  | CHECK (search_condition)}
| DROP CONSTRAINT constraint_name
| REPLACE column_name
  DEFAULT {constant_expression |
       user| NULL}
| PARTITION number_of_partitions
| UNPARTITION}
```

On Microsoft, the WITH NOCHECK subclauses allow you to add new FOREIGN KEY and CHECK constraints to a table and column without verifying that existing data meets the constraints. The WITH CHECK option is the default when adding new FOREIGN KEY or CHECK constraints and may be omitted.

On Microsoft, the CHECK CONSTRAINT and NOCHECK CONSTRAINT elements enable and disable a specific FOREIGN KEY or CHECK constraint. You can leave out the name of a specific constraint and enter the keyword ALL to enable or disable all the FOREIGN KEY and CHECK constraints. Any UNIQUE or PRIMARY KEY constraints continue to function normally. You'll get an error if you attempt to enable or disable a constraint that doesn't exist or when the ALL keyword shows no constraints on a given table.

The ADD subclause works in a way that's similar to the body of the CREATE TABLE statement. You can create new columns and any properties or constraints associated with them, as well as table-level constraints, just as you would when using the CREATE TABLE command. Any new columns added to the table must have the NULL property.

The DROP CONSTRAINT clause allows you to drop a table-level constraint or a named column-level constraint. You cannot drop a column. Note that Microsoft allows you to drop multiple constraints at one time, while Sybase allows only one constraint to be dropped at a time.

An optional specifier for Sybase ASE is PARTION or UNPARTITION, which is used to specify multiple database page chains for a given table. When this option is enabled, Sybase will allow you to perform concurrent inserts onto the table. A positive integer number >= 2 must be specified. When partitions are used, an additional control page is created for each partition. This means you need to ensure that you have both adequate memory and disk space prior to adding partitions. If you select UNPARTITION, then these multiple page chains are disabled.

Sybase also allows the REPLACE option. This option allows you to replace the defaults for a single column with another set of values. As with a regular default value, the value can be a literal, a system function, a user-defined expression, or NULL.

The following example adds a table-level FOREIGN KEY constraint to the sales table:

```
ALTER TABLE sales
ADD CONSTRAINT fk_sales_title_id FOREIGN KEY (title_id)
    REFERENCES titles(title_id)
GO
```

In this example, we disable a constraint without removing it. We then reenable the constraint:

```
ALTER TABLE authors
NOCHECK CONSTRAINT CK__authors__au_id
GO

ALTER TABLE authors
CHECK CONSTRAINT CK__authors__au_id
GO
```

Here we add an all-new column to the authors table, complete with dependent constraints:

```
ALTER TABLE authors
ADD contract_date SMALLDATETIME    NULL    DEFAULT GETDATE()
    CONSTRAINT ck_cont_date
    CHECK (contract_date BETWEEN 'Jan 01 1995' AND 'Oct 31 1999')
GO
```

Later on, we find out that we didn't like that new constraint and need to drop it (aren't we fickle?):

```
ALTER TABLE authors
DROP CONSTRAINT ck_cont_date
GO
```

Using Indexes with Tables

Tables are well suited for the purpose of holding data. But if you want really fast data retrieval on a table of any measurable size, you need indexes. Indexes provide speedy access to specific rows of a table based upon the values stored in specific columns. On the other hand, indexes can actually slow down certain types of operations (specifically, INSERT, UPDATE, and DELETE statements). That's because every time a record is inserted or deleted in a table, a similar entry must be made in the indexes built on that table.

It's often a good idea to place indexes on the columns of tables that are frequently used as search conditions, particularly if the table is queried frequently.

SQL Server utilizes two main types of indexes and one subtype:

Nonclustered indexes
: The columns of this type of index are logically ordered for quick access. Each index entry is assigned a pointer that directs the query processor to the actual physical location of the entire record. If you don't specify what type of index to create, a nonclustered index will be created. Although we can't imagine why you'd need so many, you can create up to 248 nonclustered indexes on any single table.

Clustered indexes
: The columns of this type of index are physically ordered on the storage media. Only one clustered index can exist on a table, since a table can be written to disk in only one order. Clustered indexes are usually faster than nonclustered indexes and should be created before any nonclustered indexes. Creating a clustered index will automatically cause all nonclustered indexes to be re-created as well.

The Down-and-Dirty Details

In SQL Server, indexes are composed of 2-kilobyte pages formed into "branching-tree" (or just plain B-tree) structures. (Tables that have no indexes, clustered or otherwise, are said to be in a *heap* structure.) The starting page of an index record records pointers within the table, which in turn can point to other pages with more specific pointers to the data. This branching can cascade many layers deep until the data is finally reached. The 2K pages used to store the branching information are called *node pages*. The final layer is called the *leaf layer*. On a clustered index, the leaf layer is where the data resides, but on a nonclustered index, the leaf layer is still one layer away from the data. Sounds to us as if this terminology could use a good gas-powered leaf blower and a garden rake!

Whenever an index must expand, it does so in blocks of eight 2K pages, also known as an *extent*. SQL Server allocates a new extent each time the most recently created extent fills up. The system stored procedure *sp_spaceused* can help you find out how much space is allocated and how much is used by a table and its indexes.

SQL Server maintains information about the usefulness of the index on a single 2K *distribution page*. The distribution page maintains statistics about the usefulness of that specific index. As the data is added, altered, and deleted from a table, the index statistics slowly grow stale. You should regularly refresh the index statistics on a table that sustains heavy transaction processing or in situations in which the index is created on an empty table, using the command UPDATE STATISTICS.

Creating indexes can be a space hog. Whenever you create a clustered index, plan on having at least 125% more space on hand than is currently consumed by the raw data. That's because the old, unsorted data is rewritten in sorted order, and then the old data is deleted.

Unique and nonunique indexes

Unique indexes may be used with either clustered or nonclustered indexes. (If you don't declare an index as unique, then—guess what—it's nonunique and allows duplicate values.) A unique index tells SQL Server that each new record entered into the table must have a unique value in the indexed column(s). Null is an allowable value if the column is nullable. If an attempt is made to enter a nonunique value into the index, the entire statement is canceled and an error is raised, even if only one row in a multirow statement is at fault. You can't create a unique index on a table whose columns already contain nonunique values.

Creating Indexes

We've told you a little bit about indexes, but how do you create them? Indexes are created using the CREATE INDEX statement (although certain kinds of indexes can be created along with a PRIMARY KEY table constraint). Here's the general syntax for the CREATE INDEX statement:

Microsoft	Sybase

CREATE [UNIQUE] [CLUSTERED |
NONCLUSTERED] INDEX index_name
ON [[database.]owner.]table_name
    (column_name [, column_name]...)
[WITH
    [FILLFACTOR = fillfactor,]
    [[,] IGNORE_DUP_KEY]
    [[,] SORTED_DATA |
        SORTED_DATA_REORG]
    [[,] IGNORE_DUP_ROW |
        ALLOW_DUP_ROW]]
    [[,] PAD_INDEX]
[ON segment_name]
	CREATE [UNIQUE] [CLUSTERED |
	NONCLUSTERED] INDEX index_name
	ON [[database.]owner.]table_name
	    (column_name [, column_name]...)
	[WITH
	    [FILLFACTOR |
	        MAX_ROWS_PER_PAGE} = x]
	    [[,] IGNORE_DUP_KEY]
	    [[,] SORTED_DATA]
	    [[,] IGNORE_DUP_ROW |
	        ALLOW_DUP_ROW]]
	[ON segment_name]

Only the owner of a table may create indexes on it. When you create an index, you must first specify its type (CLUSTERED or NONCLUSTERED) and whether it is UNIQUE. Once that is done, you must give it a name of 30 characters or less. The name must be unique for the table, but doesn't have to be unique for the database. Then you tell SQL Server what table and column(s) the index is built upon. Any column may be a candidate, except for those of BIT, TEXT, or IMAGE datatypes. (There are some general rules for picking likely candidate columns to index, which are covered in Chapter 20, *Transact-SQL Optimization and Tuning.*)

Here's an example of creating a simple, nonclustered index on the pub_id column of the titles table:

```
CREATE INDEX pub_id ON titles(pub_id)
GO
```

Indexes built upon multiple columns are known as *composite indexes* or *concatenated indexes.* When you build a composite index, the columns must appear inside parentheses after the table name in the exact sort-priority order you desire. Up to 16 columns may be used in a composite index, and the columns in the index may not exceed 256 bytes in length. Here's a slightly more complex CREATE INDEX statement. In this, we'll create a concatenated, unique, clustered index on several columns in the sales table:

```
CREATE UNIQUE CLUSTERED INDEX unq_cl_sales
    ON sales(stor_id, ord_num, title_id)
GO
```

In this example, the sales table will be physically sorted first by stor_id. Where stor_id values are equal, the rows will be sorted by ord_num. And on those few records where the stor_id and ord_num are duplicated, the row will be sorted by title_id.

The previous paragraph describes the elements required to build an index. You may also attach additional options to the index that allow you greater control over the behavior and functionality of the index. Here are the details on the available options:

FILLFACTOR

This setting, with allowable values from 0 to 100, tells SQL Server how full to make each index page. The setting is not always needed, since it's mostly a performance tuning feature, unless the table already has data. In that case, it's useful for reducing future page splits. For example, FILLFACTOR = 50 tells SQL Server to fill each index page only 50% before creating a new index page (if you're building a clustered index, then the data pages are also only 50% full). Then, as new records are inserted, the system doesn't have to spend any time allocating new pages for the new rows since there's room enough on the existing pages. SQL Server doesn't maintain fillfactors, so you may have to rebuild indexes from time to time if you want to maintain the percentage of free space. Now, as it turns out, the sales table is going to incur a lot of transaction processing. So we've decided to add a fillfactor of 50% to the data pages of the sales table. Here's what our command should look like:

```
CREATE UNIQUE CLUSTERED INDEX unq_cl_sales
    ON sales(stor_id, ord_num, title id)
WITH FILLFACTOR = 50
GO
```

IGNORE_DUP_KEY

This setting tells SQL Server to allow the entry of duplicate keys into a unique index on an INSERT or UPDATE that affects multiple rows. Normally, SQL Server will issue a warning and fail to insert or update duplicate rows. However, with this setting in place, SQL Server ignores duplicate rows after the first row, allowing the subsequent rows to be inserted or updated. You can't create a unique index on a column that already has duplicate values. This setting is mostly used to temporarily disable a UNIQUE index constraint for a batch routine that will enter many duplicate values and will be cleaned up later.

Be careful: this usage can cause problems on UPDATE that result in lost records because some updates are actually processed as a DELETE followed by an INSERT. For example, if you go to update author Wagner to Bach, but Bach already exists, you'll wind up with one Bach and zero Wagners because the first record was essentially deleted without a substitute record properly inserted in its stead.

Here's an example. We want to add a unique, nonclustered index on the stores table that will ignore INSERT or UPDATE statements that attempt to insert a duplicate key:

```
CREATE UNIQUE NONCLUSTERED INDEX stor_ids ON stores(stor_id)
WITH IGNORE_DUP_KEY
GO
```

IGNORE_DUP_ROW | ALLOW_DUP_ROW

These mutually exclusive options may be used only on nonunique clustered indexes and make no measurable difference on nonunique, nonclustered indexes. If neither option is set on a table containing duplicate rows, both the CREATE INDEX and INSERT statements will fail. If the ALLOW_DUP_ROW option is set on a table containing duplicate rows, both the CREATE INDEX and INSERT statements will succeed. If the IGNORE_DUP_ROW option is set on a table containing duplicate rows, the CREATE INDEX statement will succeed, but the duplicate rows will be deleted and an error message will be returned. Any attempt to insert duplicate rows will result in the duplicates being deleted.

MAX_ROWS_PER_PAGE

This setting, usable only on Sybase installations, allows you to specify the total number of rows on the data page and leaf level pages, rather than a percentage of the page as specified by the FILLFACTOR setting. It is mutually exclusive of the fillfactor. It may have values ranging from 0 to 256 for tables and clustered indexes. Nonclustered indexes have an upper limit governed only by the total number of rows one of its data pages can actually hold.

PAD_INDEX

This option forces the fillfactor setting onto both index and data pages of a table. This is a useful tuning approach for a heavily indexed table that also sees a lot of INSERT, UPDATE, and DELETE transactions. Even with this setting in place, an index page will never have fewer than two records on it. If we want to force the fillfactor of the sales table not only to the data pages but also to the index leaf pages, we might issue this command:

```
CREATE UNIQUE CLUSTERED INDEX unq_cl_sales
    ON sales(stor_id, ord_num, title_id)
WITH FILLFACTOR = 50,
PAD_INDEX
GO
```

SORTED_DATA

This option tells SQL Server that the table is already sorted in the order called for by the clustered index. This command is faster than actually building (or rebuilding) the clustered index because it checks only the sort order; it does not move any data around or rebuild nonclustered indexes.

SORTED_DATA_REORG

This option is similar to SORTED_DATA, except that the data is physically reorganized. This is good for re-establishing fillfactors (that is, defragmenting a table).

Finally, you have the option of specifying a specific *segment* where you'd like to place the index. Segments were once a popular method of manually performing load balancing on older and slower hard disk subsystems. With the advent of redundant arrays of inexpensive disks (RAID) technology, few DBAs or developers continue to use segments. In fact, the vendors are not planning to support segments much longer. We highly recommend that you stay away from segments. If you need to use or support segments, please refer to the vendor documentation.

Getting Information on Indexes

Getting information about indexes on a specific table is a snap with the system stored procedures *sp_helpindex* and *sp_help*. Both system stored procedures make checks on the sysindexes system table to find out what indexes exist on a given table.

The *sp_helpindex* procedure will report on up to eight indexes on a given table. Here's a sample of the output from *sp_helpindex* as run against the titles table (*sp_help* produces the same output about indexes, although it includes a lot more information about other structures within and related to the specific table):

```
sp_helpindex titles
```

Results:

```
index_name       index_description                                  index_keys
---------------- -------------------------------------------------- ----------
UPKCL_titleidind clustered, unique, primary key located on default title_id
titleind         nonclustered located on default                    title

(1 row(s) affected)
```

DROP INDEX: Dropping Indexes

It's a piece of cake to drop an index. When you drop an index, you immediately regain all the space it previously consumed. You can drop an index only in the current database. The general syntax of the command is shown here:

Microsoft	Sybase

`DROP INDEX [owner.]`
`    table_name.index_name`
`[, [owner.]table_name.index_name...]`
	`DROP INDEX table_name.index_name`
	`[, table_name.index_name...]`

You cannot drop indexes on system tables or indexes created as a part of a constraint (i.e., those created with a CREATE TABLE or ALTER TABLE statement). On Microsoft, the database owner may need to specify the name of the owner of the table to properly drop the index. For example:

```
DROP INDEX titles.pub_id
GO
```

Data Manipulation Language

Data Manipulation Language, or DML for short, is a subset of SQL that encompasses the commands used to create, manipulate, and delete data within a relational database. In general, any database that uses SQL can use the DML commands discussed here. So the good news is that if you learn DML for SQL Server, that knowledge can also be applied to other SQL-based RDBMS. The bad news is that almost all of the vendors have implemented some degree of variation, even in the basic SQL commands, if for no other reason than they do not *want* to be completely identical in their SQL implementations.

This section covers the major DML statements:

SELECT
INSERT
DELETE
TRUNCATE
UPDATE

It also describes the READTEXT, UPDATETEXT, and WRITETEXT statements used to handle TEXT and IMAGE data.

SELECT: Retrieving Data

The logical place to start learning about SQL is with the process of retrieving existing data from the database: the SELECT command. Instead of using the term "select" to denote the act of retrieving data from the database, we more commonly call this a *query*. The data retrieved by a query is commonly called the *result set* or simply the *results*. The SELECT statement is important not only for the obvious reason that you use it for data retrieval, but also because it forms the basis for powerful variants of the other DML commands—INSERT, DELETE, and UPDATE—as you will soon see. The SELECT command follows this syntax:

Microsoft	Sybase

`SELECT [ALL | DISTINCT] select_item1,`
`    select_item2, select_item3, ...`
`    [INTO new_table_name]`
`[FROM tablename [alias] [,...,`
`    tablename16 [alias16]] [hint]]`
`    {tablename CROSS JOIN tablename |`
`    tablename [join type]`
`JOIN tablename`
`    ON search_conditions}`
`[WHERE clause]`
`[GROUP BY clause]`
`[HAVING clause]`
`[ORDER BY clause]`
`[COMPUTE clause]`
`[FOR BROWSE]]`
	`SELECT [ALL | DISTINCT] select_item1,`
	`    select_item2, select_item3, ...`
	`    [INTO new_table_name]`
	`[FROM tablename [alias] [,...,`
	`    tablename16 [alias16]] [hint]]`
	`    {tablename CROSS JOIN tablename |`
	`    tablename [join type]`
	`JOIN tablename`
	`    ON search_conditions}`
	`[WHERE clause]`
	`[GROUP BY clause]`
	`[HAVING clause]`
	`[ORDER BY clause]`
	`[COMPUTE clause]`
	`[FOR {READ ONLY | UPDATE [OF list_of_`
	`    columns]}]`
	`[AT ISOLATION {READ UNCOMMITTED | READ`
	`    COMMITTED | SERIALIZABLE}]`
	`[FOR BROWSE]]`

As you can tell, there's a lot to the SELECT command. Each separate line of the preceding command constitutes a *clause* of the SELECT command. Thus, when discussing a DML statement, we refer to the FROM clause, the WHERE clause, the ORDER BY clause, or perhaps the GROUP BY clause. The important thing to remember at this point, though, is that you don't need every clause to make a valid SELECT statement. In fact, all you really need to retrieve data are the SELECT and FROM clauses, as you'll soon see.

The order of the clauses, as shown in the preceding syntax example, is significant. Each clause must appear in the correct order. For example, the ORDER BY clause must appear after the WHERE clause or else the query will fail.

Each of these clauses has different rules governing the way it is used and how it affects the general behavior of the query. In the following sections we'll discuss the clauses of a query in the order in which they must appear.

The FOR BROWSE clause is used only in DB-Library applications and not in direct queries against the database. The FOR BROWSE clause allows a table to be browsed in an application under the following circumstances:

- The table must include a column defined with the TIMESTAMP datatype.
- The table must have a unique index.
- The FOR BROWSE statement is the last clause in the SELECT statement.
- The query does not use the UNION operator or the HOLDLOCK optimizer hint.

The COMPUTE clause is discussed in Chapter 13, *CASE Expressions and Transact-SQL Extensions*. Optimizer hints, shown in the syntax example, are explained in Chapter 20, *Transact-SQL Optimization and Tuning*.

The most basic form of a query must have a select item list and a FROM clause. This two components tell SQL Server *what* data you want to retrieve (the list) and *where* to get it (the FROM clause). The simplest type of query and its results might look like this:

```
SELECT   au_lname,
         au_fname,
         phone
FROM     authors
```

Results:

```
au_lname                                 au_fname             phone
---------------------------------------- -------------------- ------------
White                                    Johnson              408 496-7223
Green                                    Marjorie             415 986-7020
Carson                                   Cheryl               415 548-7723
...<some data deleted for brevity>...
McBadden                                 Heather              707 448-4982
Ringer                                   Anne                 801 826-0752
Ringer                                   Albert               801 826-0752
```

Not much to it, is there? The query simply returns the last name, first name, and phone number for every record stored in the authors table of the pubs database. This query doesn't have any of the neat bells and whistles possible with a query, like aliases, sorted results, or a filtered result set. We'll introduce those techniques in the next few sections. We'll also look at each of the clauses of the SELECT statement in detail, and we'll go into a little extra detail on the topics of subqueries and joins.

The select item list

The first component of a query is the select item list. The select item list basically contains all the bits and pieces of information you want to retrieve from the server. Many different types of elements can appear in the select item list. In the example shown earlier, only data values from the authors table were retrieved, but you also can retrieve literal strings, aggregate functions, or mathematical calculations. You can even execute a subquery in the select item list!

Notice the select item list shown here:

```
SELECT [ALL | DISTINCT] select_item1, select_item2, select_item3, ...
```

The first keywords after the SELECT command itself are ALL and DISTINCT. These keywords are purely optional, hence the brackets surrounding them. The ALL keyword is the default if neither keyword is supplied (that's why you'll almost never see it used), and it tells SQL Server to retrieve all rows in the result set of the query. DISTINCT, on the other hand, is quite a powerful option. DISTINCT tells

SQL Server to retrieve only *unique* rows in a result set. Thus, if the authors table contained two records, one for Abraham M. Bennet and one for Abraham Q. Bennet, a default query for author names with a last name of Bennet would return two records, but a DISTINCT query on the same criteria would return only one.

There are several other rules for what can and cannot appear in the select item list. They are detailed here:

- Most commonly, list out all the columns desired using a comma between each one.
- An asterisk, * , serves as shorthand to retrieve all of the columns in every table shown in the FROM clause as they were listed in the CREATE TABLE statement.

It's a bad idea to use SELECT * in any form of reusable server code, such as a trigger, view, or stored procedure. If the base tables of a query are ever dropped and re-created with columns in a different order or if columns are unexpectedly added to the table, your code could fail or behave unexpectedly.

- Add in column aliases to replace the default column headings used in the results. Use the format `alias = column` or `column alias`. This is especially useful when a column heading is too cryptic to be readily understood. Aliases can be up to 30 characters long in newer versions of Microsoft SQL Server but only 20 characters long for current releases of Sybase. For example:

```
-- alias format
SELECT " author's last name" = au_lname
FROM   authors

-- alternative alias format
SELECT au_lname " author's last name"
FROM   authors
```

- Local and global variables may appear as a select list item. They should be treated just as columns are.

Comments may be dispersed throughout any SQL or Transact-SQL statement by using either the double-dash (--) or the slash-asterisk (/* . . . */). The double-dash tells SQL Server to ignore any text that follows the double-dash until the end of the line. The slash-asterisk tells SQL Server to ignore any text within the slash-asterisk and inverse slash-asterisk.

- The table name must (at times) be appended to the select list item if it is a column in a query from multiple tables. You must prefix the table name to the column in queries drawing data from multiple tables that contain identical column names. Technically, you do not need to apply the table name to any column not in *both* tables; however, it's commonly considered good technique to do so anyway. For example, both the jobs and the employee table contain the job_id column:

```
SELECT   employee.emp_id,
         employee.fname,
         employee.lname,
         jobs.job_desc
FROM     employee,
         jobs
WHERE    employee.job_id = jobs.job_id
ORDER BY employee.fname,
         employee.lname
```

- The database name and owner name must also be prefixed to the select list item if it is a column extracted from a database other than the one in which the query is run. If the other database is owned by another username, then that name must be included in the column reference. For example, assume that this example query is run in the pubs database and that some associated data is retrieved from the sales_summary table in the sales database (there isn't an actual sales database; this is just an example):

```
SELECT   employee.emp_id,
         sales.salesadmin.sales_summary.total_amt
         -- the database, username, table, and then column name must be
         --     listed!
FROM     employee,
         sales.salesadmin.sales_summary
WHERE    employee.emp_id = sales.salesadmin.sales_summary.emp_id
ORDER BY employee.emp_id
```

If the owner of the other database is the DBO, then the select list item can be shortened to `databasename..tablename.column_name`.

- A Transact-SQL query nested inside the main query using parentheses may be used as a select list item if and only if it retrieves a single value. For example:

```
SELECT e.emp_id,
       (SELECT MAX(hire_date) FROM employee) = "Max_Hire_Date"
FROM   employee
```

- Literal expressions may be used as select list items. To concatenate select list items together, use the plus (+) sign. Literals are particularly useful for constructing queries based on the system tables that build queries for you. For instance, suppose you wanted to know the number of records in all of the user tables in the pubs database. The following query builds a result set that may then be executed again to find out how many records exist in each user table:

```
SELECT   'SELECT COUNT(*) FROM ' + name
FROM     sysobjects
WHERE    type = 'U'
ORDER BY name
```

  Results:

```
SELECT COUNT(*) FROM authors
SELECT COUNT(*) FROM discounts
SELECT COUNT(*) FROM employee
SELECT COUNT(*) FROM jobs
SELECT COUNT(*) FROM non_mgr_emp
SELECT COUNT(*) FROM pub_info
SELECT COUNT(*) FROM publishers
SELECT COUNT(*) FROM roysched
SELECT COUNT(*) FROM sales
SELECT COUNT(*) FROM stores
SELECT COUNT(*) FROM temp_employee
SELECT COUNT(*) FROM titleauthor
SELECT COUNT(*) FROM titles
```

- Variables are also assigned a value as a select list item using the syntax `@variable = value`. Here's a set of examples. In the first, we extract the date and time of the most recent sale in the sales table into a variable. In the second, we assign a literal value to a set of variables (one date, one numeric, and one character variable):

```
-- Declaring our first variable
DECLARE @datetime_container DATETIME

-- Assigning the variable a value using a subquery
SELECT @datetime_container = (SELECT MAX(ord_date) FROM sales)

-- Declaring variables for our next example
DECLARE @date_string SMALLDATETIME,
    @num_string      INT,
    @char_string     VARCHAR(30)

-- Assigning literal values to the variables
SELECT @date_string = 'July 16 1999',
    @num_string     = 1900,
    @char_string    = 'Jeenkies!  A clue!'
```

- Mathematics calculations can be entered as a select list item. For example:

  ```
  SELECT 2 + 2
  ```

  Results:

  ```
  4
  ```

- You don't have to remember the IDENTITY column of a table when performing any DML statement. Instead, you can use the IDENTITYCOL keyword on Microsoft SQL Server and the SYB_IDENTITY keyword on Sybase Adaptive Server. So, if you were retrieving data from the jobs table (where the job_id column is an IDENTITY), you could issue this command on Microsoft SQL Server:

  ```
  SELECT IDENTITYCOL,
      job_desc
  FROM jobs
  WHERE job_desc like '%edit%'
  ```

The FROM clause

For years, the FROM clause served two purposes: to list the tables where a query got its data (with commas separating table names) and to assign an alias for long table names, making coding lengthy queries a lot easier. With the implementation of some of the latest ANSI SQL standards, though, we can now use the FROM clause to control all of our join behavior. Joins can be pretty tough to understand, so we'll spend a little extra time on those. With SQL Server, the FROM clause is also where bold and enterprising programmers place *optimizer hints.* Optimizer hints are a non–ANSI-standard method for overriding SQL Server's default query-processing behavior. We'll explore the topic of hints in depth in Chapter 20.

Queries in SQL Server can access up to 16 total tables at one time (32 for Microsoft SQL Server Version 7.0). This 16-table maximum includes not only the FROM clause of the main query but also the FROM clauses in any subqueries or views used in the main query. Thus, a view built on a 4-table join adds a count of 4 table references to the 16-table maximum of a single query. Sybase has the further limitation of allowing a maximum of 12 temporary worktables in the query. Worktables are temporary tables automatically generated by SQL Server to join tables, filter out DISTINCT records, sort records based on ORDER BY or GROUP BY clauses, and so on.

Table aliases in the FROM clause. There are plenty of databases out there with very *long* table names. And why not? SQL Server allows table names of up to 32 characters in length, which means that database designers can now give database tables truly meaningful names instead of hyperabbreviated (and unintelligible) names. But long table names do not generate cheers of joy from the ranks of hard-at-work database programmers. That's because queries with more than one table must have special handling for the select list items: you must qualify each mutual column name with the name of the table it comes from. SQL Server has fortunately made this process much easier by allowing programmers to *alias* a table name to a short mnemonic.

You can assign an alias in the FROM clause by two means: by typing the table name, a space, and the alias; or by typing the tablename, the AS keyword, and the alias. The following example illustrates each of these techniques. An example of a query that extracts data from multiple tables might have a FROM and WHERE clause and might look like this:

```
SELECT   e.emp_id,
         e.fname,
         e.lname,
         j.job_desc
FROM     employee e,
         jobs AS j
WHERE    e.job_id = j.job_id
ORDER BY e.fname,
         e.lname
```

Once you have assigned an alias in a query, be sure to use it exclusively for table references within that query. Do *not* mix references of the full table name and the alias in a query.

This query retrieves the emp_id, the first name, and the last name of each employee stored in the employee table and *joins* the job_id of the employee, which is a code number, with the full job description found in the jobs table. In the next section we'll delve into the topic of joins.

Joining data found in distinct tables. Any database application built on even a mildly normalized design is going to have many, many queries that contain joins. It is just part of the territory that comes with relational databases. In older versions of SQL Server, the join operation was performed in the WHERE clause, as shown in the previous example. In the latest version, ANSI SQL-92 standards have taken root and now allow the join to be performed in an entirely different way—in the FROM clause of the query. These join methods are known as the *old style* and the *ANSI style* of joins, respectively. We'll show you both ways to perform a join in this section, but first, some more about joins.

To retrieve joined data from two or more tables, the tables must first share a meaningful relationship (shouldn't we all?). Most of the time, these relationships are defined while the database is being designed and may be explicitly codified within SQL Server using FOREIGN KEY constraints. On the other hand, you don't have to define a foreign key for two tables to be related as logical entities. In any event, the tables to be joined must possess a column, or columns, that share a common set of values that allow the tables to be meaningfully linked. This column, or columns, is called the *join key* or *common key*. Most of the time, the join key will be the primary key of one table and a foreign key in another table.

Joins do not require that the common key columns have the same column name in each table, only that the *data* in the columns share a common set of values and be of the same datatype. So if the employee table had a column called employment_code and the jobs tables had a column containing the exact same values in a column called job_status, the join would still be possible in a Transact-SQL query.

In the pubs database, both the employee table and the jobs table contain a job_id column. Thus, job_id is the common key between the employee and jobs tables. Figure 3-1 shows these tables and how the server merges together the data from the tables sharing the common key.

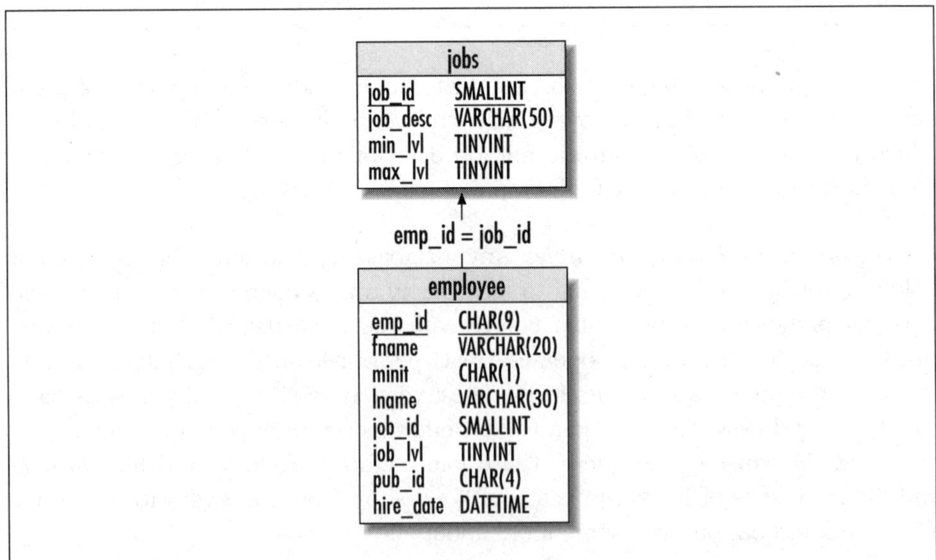

Figure 3-1. An example of a join

The figure shows the old style for performing a join. Under this style of coding, the join conditions are specified in the WHERE clause. Although performing joins in the WHERE clause is called the old style, it is still far more common than the ANSI style, despite the benefits of the ANSI style. Since many SQL programmers learned under the old style, that is still the way they like to do it. And you can bet that RDBMS vendors will continue to support it for some time to come.

When writing joins in the old style, it is common practice to list the join as the first element of the WHERE clause and have all other search conditions follow after. This is simply an issue of style. It doesn't impact performance. *Never* mix old-style and ANSI-style joins in the same query.

ANSI-style joins have the marked benefit of setting aside the join into its own clause, instead of sharing space with other search conditions under the WHERE clause. And after you get used to reading ANSI-style joins, they seem to have a stronger intuitive meaning, particularly when performing special types of joins called *outer joins.* (Outer joins will be explained soon.)

To perform the same query using an ANSI-style join in the FROM clause, list the first table, the keyword JOIN, then the name of the table to be joined. Then, after specifying the second table name, include the keyword ON and the join condition you would have used in the old-style query. Here is the original query in ANSI style:

```
SELECT   e.emp_id,
         e.fname,
         e.lname,
         j.job_desc
FROM     employee e
JOIN     jobs     j ON e.job_id = j.job_id
ORDER BY e.fname,
         e.lname
```

There are some important conditions to remember when performing joins, and they have a dramatic effect on the result set of your queries. Consider these scenarios: what happens if you leave off the join conditions entirely? If you want to see every job description in the database but know that some of the job descriptions aren't filled at the moment, what will the query retrieve? What if a new employee has not received a job title yet? Will she appear in the result set? These questions are answered by the use of *join types* in the ANSI style and the equals-asterisk ('=*') combination in the old style. Table 3-2 shows how to control this behavior in joins:

Table 3-2. JOIN Types

Join Type	Description	Example

CROSS JOIN	The complete cross product of two tables. For each record in the first table, all the records in the second table are joined, creating a *huge* result set. Has the same effect as leaving off the join condition—also known as a *Cartesian product.*	`-- old style`
		`SELECT e.emp_id,`
		`       e.fname,`
		`       e.lname,`
		`       j.job_desc`
		`FROM   employee e,`
		`       jobs j`
		
		`-- ANSI style`
		`SELECT e.emp_id,`
		`       e.fname,`
		`       e.lname,`
		`       j.job_desc`
		`FROM   employee e`
		`CROSS JOIN jobs j`

INNER JOIN	Specifies that unmatched rows in either table of the join should be discarded. If no join type is explicitly defined in the ANSI style, this is the default.	`-- old style`
		`SELECT e.emp_id,`
		`       e.fname,`
		`       e.lname,`
		`       j.job_desc`
		`FROM   employee e,`
		`       jobs j`
		`WHERE  e.job_id = j.job_id`
		
		`-- ANSI style`
		`SELECT e.emp_id,`
		`       e.fname,`
		`       e.lname,`
		`       j.job_desc`
		`FROM   employee e`
		`JOIN   jobs j ON`
		`       e.job_id = j.job_id`

LEFT JOINS	Specifies that all records from the table on the left side of the join statement be returned. If a record from the left table has no matching record in the table on the right side of the join, it will still be returned. Columns from the right table will return null values. (In this case, all employees will be returned whether or not they have a job description.)	`-- old style`
		`SELECT e.emp_id,`
		`       e.fname,`
		`       e.lname,`
		`       j.job_desc`
		`FROM   employee e,`
		`       jobs j`
		`WHERE  e.job_id *= j.job_id`
		
		`-- ANSI style`
		`SELECT e.emp_id,`
		`       e.fname,`
		`       e.lname,`
		`       j.job_desc`
		`FROM   employee e`
		`LEFT JOIN jobs j ON`
		`       e.job_id = j.job_id`

Table 3-2. JOIN Types (continued)

Join Type	Description	Example

RIGHT JOIN	Specifies that all records from the table on the right side of the join statement be returned, even if the table on the left has no matching record. Columns from the left table will return null values. (In the example, all records in the jobs table will be returned with or without a matching record in the employee table.)	`-- old style`
		`SELECT e.emp_id,`
		`       e.fname,`
		`       e.lname,`
		`       j.job_desc`
		`FROM   employee e,`
		`       jobs j`
		`WHERE  e.job_id =* j.job_id`
		
		`-- ANSI style`
		`SELECT e.emp_id,`
		`       e.fname,`
		`       e.lname,`
		`       j.job_desc`
		`FROM   employee e`
		`RIGHT JOIN jobs j ON`
		`       e.job_id = j.job_id`

FULL JOIN	Specifies that all rows from either table be returned, regardless of matching records in the other table. The result set will show null values where no data exists in the join.	`-- old style does not support`
		`-- this function`
		
		`-- ANSI style`
		`SELECT e.emp_id,`
		`       e.fname,`
		`       e.lname,`
		`       j.job_desc`
		`FROM   employee e`
		`FULL JOIN jobs j ON`
		`       e.job_id = j.job_id`

As Table 3-2 demonstrates, joins in the ANSI style are actually easier to understand than the old style, since you can look at the query and clearly see which table is on the left in a left join or which table is on the right in a right join. Using the old style, it's a little tougher to remember on which side of the equals sign the asterisk must go. As it stands, you're going to have to learn both methods. There's so much existing code written in the old style, you'll have to learn how to use it to leverage older code. On the other hand, vendors are threatening to one day stop support of the older style, so it's advisable to become proficient in the ANSI method as well. If you're going to use the old style to write new programs, just remember to put the asterisk on the side where *all* records should be returned.

The syntax to perform a similar query with multipart keys and multiple tables joined together is largely an extension of the same technique:

```
--old-style query with multiple tables
SELECT   a.au_lname,
         a.au_fname,
         t2.title
FROM     authors a,
         titleauthor t1,
         titles t2
WHERE    a.au_id      = t1.au_id
    AND  t1.title_id = t2.title_id
ORDER BY t2.title
```

```
-- ANSI-style query with multiple tables
SELECT   a.au_lname,
         a.au_fname,
         t2.title
FROM     authors a
    JOIN titleauthor t1 ON a.au_id     = t1.au_id
    JOIN titles      t2 ON t1.title_id = t2.title_id
ORDER BY t2.title
```

The join conditions for a query with a multipart key look like this:

```
--old-style query with multipart key
SELECT   s1.store_id,
         s1.title_id,
         s2.qty
FROM     sales s1,
         sales_projections s2
WHERE    s1.store_id = s2.store_id
    AND  s1.title_id = s2.title_id
ORDER BY s1.store_id, s2.title_id

-- ANSI-style query with multipart key
SELECT   s1.store_id,
         s1.title_id,
         s2.qty
FROM     sales s1
    JOIN sales_projections s2 ON s1.store_id = s2.store_id
        AND s1.title_id = s2.title_id
ORDER BY s1.store_id, s2.title_id
```

The WHERE clause

You've already seen the WHERE clause get quite a workout when used to construct join conditions. The WHERE clause is an extremely potent component of the SELECT statement. It is also pretty darn complex, considering all the possible variations and permutations. The WHERE clause provides most of the search conditions that cull unwanted data from the query; the remaining search conditions are satisfied by the HAVING clause (this clause will be explained soon). A poorly-written WHERE clause can ruin an otherwise beautiful SELECT statement, so it behooves all SQL programmers to know it inside and out. Here's an example of a typical query and its multipart WHERE clause:

```
SELECT   a.au_lname,
         a.au_fname,
         t2.title,
         convert(char,t2.pubdate)
FROM     authors a
    JOIN titleauthor t1 ON a.au_id = t1.au_id
    JOIN titles t2 ON t1.title_id = t2.title_id
WHERE    (t2.type = 'business' OR t2.type = 'popular_comp')
    AND  t2.advance > $5500
ORDER BY t2.title
```

Did you notice the placement of parentheses around some of the elements of the WHERE clause? Just as in the old algebra classes, parentheses affect the priority of the elements in the WHERE clause. To summarize, parentheses scream "Use me first!" to SQL Server. With the parentheses in place, this query will retrieve all rows for books where the author received an advance greater than $5,500 and that are about either business or popular computing. If no parentheses were used, the query would retrieve all business titles, plus any popular computing title with an advance greater than $5,500. Very different indeed!

There are many more specific capabilities of the WHERE clause than are illustrated in the examples. Table 3-3 helps provide a quick rundown of the common capabilities of the WHERE clause.

Table 3-3. Search Conditions Using the WHERE Clause

<table>
<tr><th>Search Condition Shorthand</th><th>Syntax and Example</th><th>Usage and Description</th></tr>
<tr><td>Simple Boolean check</td><td><code>WHERE [NOT] expression comparison_
operator expression</code>

<code>SELECT au_id
FROM   authors
WHERE au_id = '172-32-1176'</code>

<code>SELECT au_id
FROM   authors
WHERE au_lname NOT LIKE 'John%'</code></td><td>When comparing expressions, you can use the operators <, >, <>, >=, <= , and =. There are also a number of special comparison operators, such as LIKE, described later.
The keyword NOT checks for the inverse of any Boolean check based on the regular operators <, >, <>, >=, <=, and =, plus special operators such as LIKE, NULL, BETWEEN, IN, EXISTS, ANY, and ALL.</td></tr>
<tr><td>Multiple search conditions</td><td><code>WHERE [NOT] expression comparison_
operator expression
{AND | OR}
expression comparison_operator
expression</code>

<code>SELECT au_id
FROM   authors
WHERE au_id = '172-32-1176'
AND   au_lname = 'White'</code></td><td>AND merges multiple conditions and returns results when both conditions are true. AND takes priority over other operators. Parentheses in the WHERE clause further affect the priority of operators.
OR merges multiple conditions and returns results when either condition is true. OR takes priority after AND.</td></tr>
</table>

Table 3-3. Search Conditions Using the WHERE Clause (continued)

Search Condition Shorthand	Syntax and Example	Usage and Description

NULL check	`WHERE [NOT] column_name IS [NOT] NULL`
	
	`SELECT *`
	`FROM   titles`
	`WHERE  price IS NULL`
		IS NULL and IS NOT NULL tell SQL Server to check for null values (or all values except null values).

JOIN check	`WHERE [NOT] column_name [*]=[*] column_name`
	
	`SELECT a.au_lname,`
	`       a.au_fname,`
	`       t2.title`
	`FROM  authors a,`
	`      titleauthor t1,`
	`      titles t2`
	`WHERE a.au_id = t1.au_id`
	`AND t1.title_id = t2.title_id`
	`ORDER BY t2.title`
		JOIN checks can be performed by evaluating the common key between two or more tables. Outer joins are accomplished by adding the asterisk to the side where all records should be retrieved. Refer to the previous section on joins for more information.

LIKE check	`WHERE [NOT] column_name [NOT] LIKE 'match_string'`
	
	`/* get any phone number starting with 415 */`
	`SELECT * FROM authors`
	`WHERE phone LIKE '415%'`
		LIKE tells SQL Server to use pattern matching on the string in quotes. Remember that leading and trailing blanks are significant! LIKE with a wildcard character works on DATETIME, CHAR, and VARCHAR data, though you can't search seconds or milliseconds in a DATETIME with LIKE. The wildcard symbols are detailed in Table 3-4.

EXISTence check	`WHERE [NOT] EXISTS (subquery)`
	
	`SELECT p1.pub_name`
	`FROM publishers p1`
	`WHERE EXISTS`
	`    (SELECT *`
	`    FROM titles t1`
	`    WHERE pub_id =p1.pub_id`
	`    AND type =`
	`    'psychology')`
		EXISTS is always used in conjunction with a subquery. But rather than returning data, the subquery is a Boolean test of whether the data exists. The example will return all publishers of psychology books.

BETWEEN range check	`WHERE [NOT] expression [NOT] BETWEEN expression AND expression`
	
	`SELECT *`
	`FROM titles`
	`WHERE ytd_sales BETWEEN 4000 AND 9000`
		BETWEEN performs an inclusive range check. It is the same as: `WHERE (expression >= x AND expression <= y)`

Table 3-3. Search Conditions Using the WHERE Clause (continued)

Search Condition Shorthand	Syntax and Example	Usage and Description

IN range check	WHERE [NOT] expression [NOT] IN
	(value_list | subquery)
	
	SELECT *
	FROM stores
	WHERE state IN ('WA','IL','NY')
	
	SELECT *
	FROM stores
	WHERE stor_id IN
	  (SELECT stor_id
	  FROM sales
	  WHERE ord_date LIKE
	  'Oct%')
		IN returns a result set that matches any of a list of values or returns a result set of the outer query whose value matches those values returned by a subquery. The value_list or subquery should be enclosed in parentheses. It's a good idea to limit the value_list to 16 or fewer items (some older versions of SQL Server abort with more than 16 list items).

ANY | ALL range check	WHERE [NOT] expression comparison_
	operator
	{[ANY | SOME] | ALL} (subquery)
	
	-- to duplicate the functionality
	-- of IN
	SELECT au_lname,
	       au_fname
	FROM authors
	WHERE city = ANY
	    (SELECT city
	     FROM publishers)
	
	-- to duplicate the functionality of
	-- NOT IN
	SELECT au_lname,
	       au_fname
	FROM authors
	WHERE city <> ALL
	    (SELECT city
	     FROM publishers)
	
	/* to find the titles that got an
	advance larger than the minimum
	advance amount paid New Moon Books*/
	SELECT title
	FROM titles
	WHERE advance > ANY
	    (SELECT advance
	     FROM publishers,
	      titles
	     WHERE titles.pub_id =
	       publishers.pub_id
	     AND pub_name = 'New
	       Moon Books')
		ALL and ANY are always used with a subquery and a comparison operator: <, >, <>, >=, or <=.
		A query of the ALL type evaluates to either TRUE or FALSE when *all* values retrieved by the subquery match the value in the WHERE (or HAVING) clause, or when the subquery returns no rows of the outer statement.
		ANY, synonymous with ANSI-standard SOME, works the same as ALL except that it evaluates to TRUE when *any* value retrieved in the subquery satisfies the comparison predicate in the WHERE clause of the outer statement. ANY and SOME have the same functionality as EXISTS.

As mentioned in the previous table, you can use wildcard characters to augment your search options, especially with the LIKE operator. Table 3-4 describes these wildcard operators.

Table 3-4. Wildcard Operators

Operator	Example	Description

%	`/* get any city with ...ville... in its name. */`
	
	`WHERE city like '%ville%'`
		Matches any string. (Kind of like the * in DOS operations. Remember DOS?)

[ ]	`/* get any author with a last name like Carson, Carsen, Karson, or Karsen. */`
	
	`WHERE au_lname LIKE '[CK]ars[eo]n'`
		Matches any value in the specified set, as in [abc], or any range, as in [k–n].

[^]	`/* get any author with a last name that ends in arson or arsen BUT NOT Larsen or Larson. */`
	
	`WHERE au_lname LIKE '[A-Z^L]ars[eo]n'`
		Matches any characters not in the specified set or range.

_	`/* get any author with a first name such as Sheryl or Cheryl. */`
	
	`WHERE au_fname LIKE '_heryl'`
		Matches any single character.

SQL Server's default *sort order* can make a big difference in the result sets retrieved by a query. Installations with a sort order of dictionary-order, case-insensitive (the default and also the most common sort order) make no differentiation between Smith, smith, and SMITH. But servers using dictionary-order, case-sensitive, or binary sort order would find the values Smith, smith, and SMITH to be unequal.

Aggregates: GROUP BY and HAVING clauses

The GROUP BY clause and the HAVING clause are needed only in queries that utilize *aggregate functions.* Queries using aggregate functions are able to provide many types of summary information. Aggregate functions are discussed in greater detail in Chapter 12, *Functions.* The common SQL Server aggregate functions are listed here:

AVG
: Returns the average of all non-null values in the specified column(s)

COUNT
: Counts the occurrence of all non-null values in the specified column(s)

COUNT DISTINCT
: Counts the occurrence of all unique, non-null values in the specified column(s)

COUNT(*)
: Counts every record in the table

MAX
: Returns the highest non-null value in the specified column(s)

MIN
: Returns the lowest non-null value in the specified column(s)

SUM
: Totals all non-null values in the specified column(s)

The aggregate functions are limited to certain datatypes. Only COUNT and COUNT DISTINCT can be used on a column of any datatype. MIN and MAX can operate on numeric columns (of any type), as well as date and character columns. The SUM and AVG functions may operate only on numeric columns, including DECIMAL, FLOAT, INTEGER, MONEY, NUMERIC, REAL, SMALLINT, SMALLMONEY, and TINYINT datatypes.

If you ever need to perform aggregate functions on columns containing null values, use the ISNULL() function to assign a value to the null columns.

Aggregate functions work beautifully as the sole result in queries. When executed alone, the aggregates return a *scalar aggregate* value, meaning that they return a single value without the use of a GROUP BY clause. For example:

```
SELECT AVG(price)
FROM titles
```

Results:

```
14.77
```

Queries that return both regular column values and aggregate functions are commonly called *vector aggregates*. Vector aggregates use the GROUP BY clause and return one or many rows. There are a few rules to follow when using GROUP BY:

- Specify GROUP BY in the proper clause order, after the WHERE clause and before the ORDER BY clause.
- Include all nonaggregate columns in the GROUP BY clause.
- Do not use a column alias in the GROUP BY clause, though table aliases are OK.

Suppose you wanted to know how many employees occupy each type of job within the firm:

```
SELECT   j.job_desc "Job Description",
         COUNT(e.job_id) "Nbr in Job"
FROM     employee e
```

```
    JOIN jobs j ON e.job_id = j.job_id
GROUP BY j.job_desc
```

Results:

```
Job Description                                    Nbr in Job
-------------------------------------------------- -----------
Acquisitions Manager                               4
Business Operations Manager                        1
Chief Executive Officer                            1
Chief Financial Officer                            1
Designer                                           3
Editor                                             3
Managing Editor                                    4
Marketing Manager                                  4
Operations Manager                                 4
Productions Manager                                4
Public Relations Manager                           4
Publisher                                          7
Sales Representative                               3
```

You can add search conditions to the query result set by augmenting the GROUP BY clause with a HAVING clause. The big benefit of the HAVING clause is that it doesn't affect the rows used to calculate the aggregates; it affects only the rows returned by the query. HAVING works very much like the WHERE clause. You can use all of the search conditions described in Table 3-3 with the HAVING clause, just as you can with the WHERE clause.

At a fundamental level, this is a very different kind of processing from that offered by the WHERE clause. Whereas SQL Server uses the WHERE clause to filter out rows that will not be returned in the result set (and thus improves performance by allowing SQL Server's optimizer to use the best indexes), the HAVING clause *provides no performance benefit and often exacts an overhead toll.* This performance cost is due to the fact that SQL Server must build a temporary table with every GROUP BY statement; then it must cull out every record meeting the criteria of the HAVING clause. This warning is not designed to dissuade you from using the HAVING clause. In fact, many queries could not be properly accomplished without it—for example, to find out which job most people in the firm are performing:

```
SELECT   j.job_desc "Job Description",
         COUNT(e.job_id) "Nbr in Job"
FROM     employee e
    JOIN jobs j ON e.job_id = j.job_id
GROUP BY j.job_desc
HAVING   count(e.job_id) > 3
```

Results:

```
Job Description                                    Nbr in Job
-------------------------------------------------- -----------
Acquisitions Manager                               4
Managing Editor                                    4
```

```
Marketing Manager                            4
Operations Manager                           4
Productions Manager                          4
Public Relations Manager                     4
Publisher                                    7
```

As an aside, it's a little-known fact that a HAVING clause may be used in a SELECT statement without a GROUP BY clause. For example, the following query is perfectly valid:

```
SELECT SUM(ytd_sales) AS "Total Sales"
FROM   titles
HAVING SUM(ytd_sales) > 10000
```

Look, ma, no GROUP BY clause! This query will work on SQL Server. (Of course, what good this query does is another matter altogether.)

Assembling a Result Set: Order of Operations

Remember that SQL Server follows this order for assembling the result set returned by a query:

1. SQL Server parses the query to ensure that the syntax is correct.
2. The query is checked against index statistics, and a query plan is constructed.
3. All rows are assembled that meet the criteria specified in the WHERE clause.
4. Temporary tables are assembled for each GROUP BY or ORDER BY statement (unless there is a clustered index on the ORDER BY columns). SQL Server might also create additional worktables in an attempt to optimize the query if the query is extremely complicated, uses subqueries, or joins tables without good indexes. In the case of GROUP BY, the worktable is populated with aggregated rows (one per group).
5. After the worktables are populated, they are filtered according to the HAVING clause conditions such that rows not meeting these conditions are deleted from the worktable.
6. Rows in the worktable are sorted according to the parameters in the ORDER BY clause.
7. Any processing specified in a COMPUTE statement is executed against the remaining data.
8. The result set is returned to the client.

Current versions of Sybase still allow the exclusion of non-aggregate columns in the GROUP BY clause. Microsoft started enforcing the ANSI syntax in Version 6.0.

In Sybase, you can write this query (which wouldn't be allowed by Microsoft):

```
SELECT column1, column2, MAX(column3)
    FROM foo GROUP BY column1
```

There is one practical application for this syntax—selecting all columns of duplicate rows. Suppose that you have a table in which some rows have duplicate keys in `column1`. The following query returns all columns containing duplicate values in `column1`:

```
SELECT * FROM foo GROUP BY column1 HAVING COUNT(*) > 1
```

On Microsoft SQL Server, you'd have to do something like this:

```
SELECT column1 INTO #dups FROM foo GROUP BY column1
HAVING COUNT(*) > 1

SELECT * FROM foo, #dups
    WHERE foo.column1 = #dups.column1
```

The ORDER BY clause

The simple act of sorting a result set is accomplished with the ORDER BY clause, in accordance with SQL Server's *sort order* chosen during installation. (Chapter 4, *Transact-SQL Fundamentals,* describes the sort order choices.) The result sets may be sorted in either ascending (ASC) or descending (DESC) order, although not both in the same query. If you do not specify ASC or DESC, SQL Server defaults to ASC. Up to 16 columns can be specified in the ORDER BY clause. You cannot ORDER BY TEXT columns, IMAGE columns, subqueries, aggregates, or constant expressions.

Examine the query below:

```
SELECT   e.emp_id "Emp ID",
         rtrim(e.fname) + " " + rtrim(e.lname) "Name",
         j.job_desc "Job Desc"
FROM     employee e,
         jobs AS j
WHERE    e.job_id = j.job_id
    AND  j.job_desc = 'Acquisitions Manager'
ORDER BY e.fname DESC,
         e.lname DESC
```

Results:

```
Emp ID    Name                           Job Desc
--------- ------------------------------ --------------------
M-R38834F Martine Rancé                  Acquisitions Manager
MAS70474F Margaret Smith                 Acquisitions Manager
```

```
KJJ92907F Karla Jablonski                   Acquisitions Manager
GHT50241M Gary Thomas                       Acquisitions Manager
```

Multiple columns in the ORDER BY clause are nested within the preceding column of the clause. What does that mean in English? For the preceding example, that means that all the authors are sorted by first name; after all the first names are sorted; the last names are then sorted in descending order where the first names are equal; and so on until the entire clause is resolved.

You can use the *ordinal position* of a select list item as shorthand in the ORDER BY clause. That is, if you want to order the result set by the second, first, and then the third column in the select item list, you can simply say ORDER BY 2,1,3. This technique has some benefits and some disadvantages. The main benefits are (surprise!) it's a lot faster to type, and aggregates and constant expressions that are long and drawn out can be referenced using simple ordinal positions. The main drawback is that if you change the select list items at all, say by adding or removing a column from the query, you'll probably have to rewrite the ORDER BY clause, too. The following example illustrates an ORDER BY using ordinal positions:

```
SELECT   au_fname "First Name",
         SUBSTRING(au_lname,1,20) "Last Name",
         phone "Phone"
FROM     authors
WHERE    au_lname BETWEEN 'Dull' AND 'Smith'
ORDER BY 2 DESC, 1, 3
```

Results:

```
First Name           Last Name            Phone
-------------------- -------------------- ------------
Meander              Smith                913 843-0462
Albert               Ringer               801 826-0752
...<some lines deleted for brevity>...
Marjorie             Green                415 986-7020
Ann                  Dull                 415 836-7128
```

This query retrieves the first name, last name, and phone number of each author with a last name equal to or between Dull and Smith. After the result set is pared down to meet the search conditions, the result set is sorted by the authors' last names in descending order; where the authors' last names are equal, the authors' first names are sorted in ascending order (since no order was specified). And if any authors happened to have the same first and last name, they'd be sorted by phone number in ascending order.

If no ORDER BY clause is specified, SQL Server returns the data according to the clustered index of the table queried. If there is no clustered index, SQL Server may return the result set according to any other index used in the query. If absolutely no indexes exist on the table, SQL Server returns the data in whatever order it was inserted into the table.

SELECT . . . INTO

The SELECT . . . INTO feature is a somewhat controversial command option found only in SQL Server. You won't find it in competing database products because it is strictly Transact-SQL in origin and not in compliance with the ANSI standards. The SELECT . . . INTO command quickly copies the rows and columns queried from other table(s) into a new temporary or permanent table using a nonlogged operation. Only the SA or the DBO may SELECT . . . INTO a permanent table; other users may only SELECT . . . INTO temporary tables, provided that the database has the SELECT INTO/BULKCOPY option turned on.

To find out if the SELECT INTO/BULKCOPY option is enabled in the pubs database, type:

```
sp_helpdb 'pubs'
```

To engage the SELECT INTO/BULKCOPY option in the pubs database, type the

```
command: sp_dboption 'pubs', 'select into', TRUE
```

Do *not* apply this database option without the approval of your DBA. It has far-reaching implications for database recoverability.

In this example, we create a table called non_mgr_employees using SELECT . . . INTO. The table contains the emp_id, first name, and last name of each nonmanager from the employee table joined with their job descriptions taken from the jobs table:

```
SELECT   e.emp_id "emp_id",
         convert(char(25),rtrim(e.fname) + " " + rtrim(e.lname)) "name",
         substring(j.job_desc,1,30) "job_desc"
INTO     non_mgr_employee
FROM     employee e
    JOIN jobs AS j ON e.job_id = j.job_id
WHERE    j.job_desc NOT LIKE '%MANAG%'
ORDER BY 2,3,1
```

Results:

```
(18 row(s) affected)
```

To see what this data created, we perform a simple query:

```
SELECT   emp_id,
         name,
         job_desc
FROM     non_mgr_emp
ORDER BY 3,2,1
```

Results:

```
emp_id    name                      job_desc
--------- ------------------------- ------------------------------
PTC11962M Philip Cramer             Chief Executive Officer
F-C16315M Francisco Chang           Chief Financial Officer
ENL44273F Elizabeth Lincoln         Designer
KFJ64308F Karin Josephs             Designer
PSA89086M Pedro Afonso              Designer
H-B39728F Helen Bennett             Editor
HAS54740M Howard Snyder             Editor
Y-L77953M Yoshi Latimer             Editor
CFH28514M Carlos Hern dez           Publisher
JYL26161F Janine Labrune            Publisher
LAL21447M Laurence Lebihan          Publisher
MJP25939M Maria Pontes              Publisher
PXH22250M Paul Henriot              Publisher
RBM23061F Rita Müller               Publisher
SKO22412M Sven Ottlieb              Publisher
CGS88322F Carine Schmitt            Sales Representative
PMA42628M Paolo Accorti             Sales Representative
TPO55093M Timothy O'Rourke          Sales Representative
```

Many hardworking, "in-the-trenches" DBAs and database programmers like to use SELECT . . . INTO on their development database servers because it provides a remarkably easy and fast way to create new tables and move data around (provided that the database option SELECT INTO/BULKCOPY is enabled). Because SELECT . . . INTO is not logged, huge amounts of data can be moved from one table to another brand-new permanent table without filling up the database's transaction log.

On the other hand, there are some valid reasons why the more academically minded literally *despise* the SELECT . . . INTO command:

- SELECT . . . INTO provides a means of creating tables without logging the insertion of new records. (However, a record is logged in the system tables that a new table was created.)
- SELECT . . . INTO enables the insertion of data into a table without logging those transactions either.
- This command should *not* be used in a production environment, but somebody always seems to do it anyway.
- SELECT . . . INTO is not allowed to appear in an explicit transaction.
- After running this command, you must first perform a full database backup before any transaction log backups can run.

SELECT . . . INTO locks the system tables of the local database and, if you're creating a temporary table, of the tempdb database. While the system tables are locked, no one else can create objects in the same database.

It turns nasty when someone creates a large temporary table with SELECT . . . INTO because the transaction locks the system tables and prevents all other users from creating new objects in the database until the command has completed. If SELECT . . . INTO is creating a temporary table, then everyone on the server is likely to be affected since even a simple query uses tempdb to build worktables.

Our endorsement of the SELECT . . . INTO statement is only for development environments that are monitored by a knowledgeable DBA. It also should be used only to create small tables that take no longer than a few seconds.

SELECT . . . INTO can be used in stored procedures to quickly create a temporary table that substitutes for a large multitable join or by developers who want to create several versions of a table for testing purposes. The INSERT . . . SELECT command should often be used instead of SELECT . . . INTO, especially if the stored procedure is going to be used in a production system. However, INSERT . . . SELECT (discussed in the next section) logs all transactions; it can be slower and requires that the target table already exist.

There are a few rules to remember when using a SELECT . . . INTO statement to create a new table with an IDENTITY property. A column with an IDENTITY property creates a system-generated, monotonically increasing value. Normally, a new table will inherit an IDENTITY column from the original table, unless one of the following conditions is true:

- The SELECT statement contains a join, GROUP BY, aggregate function, or union.
- The IDENTITY column is selected more than once.
- The IDENTITY column is part of an expression or derived value.

If none of these conditions prove to be true, the new table inherits the IDENTITY just as the original table has it defined. Otherwise, the new table is created, but the IDENTITY column is converted to a NOT NULL column and is treated as an otherwise-normal column.

INSERT: Creating Data

The INSERT statement is used to add rows of data to a table or view. After many late nights, staring blurry-eyed at a computer monitor, I might have preferred a command like CRAM or SHOVE to populate a table with data. But the ANSI committee chose a less emotionally charged verb—INSERT.

In SQL Server, INSERT adds data to a table in three distinct ways:

1. The INSERT . . . VALUES method can be used to add a single row of data into a table.
2. The INSERT . . . SELECT method can be used to add multiple rows of data into a table.
3. This is *really* cool for Microsoft users! The INSERT . . . EXECUTE method allows you to take the results of a local or remote stored procedure and load them directly into a table.

The basic syntax of the INSERT command looks like this:

Microsoft	Sybase

`INSERT [INTO] [[database_name.]owner.]`
`{table_name | view_name}`
`[(column_list)]`
`{[DEFAULT] VALUES | list_of_values |`
`SELECT_statement |`
`EXECUTE_stored_procedure}`
	`INSERT [INTO] [[database_name.]owner.]`
	`{table_name | view_name}`
	`[(column_list)]`
	`{[list_of_values | SELECT_statement]}`

INTO is an optional keyword. The `database_name` may be left off when inserting into the local database, but it must be specified when inserting into another specific database. The `owner` also can be left off, unless the local or specified database is owned by another user. You can leave off the `database_name` and `owner` if you are just inserting data into a table within the local database. The `table_name` or `view_name` is an existing table or view in the local or specified database. The `column_list` is one or more columns where the data will be stored, enclosed in parentheses and separated by commas. The columns can be in any order, but the inserted data must be in the same order as the `column_list`. You can leave off the `column_list`, but all columns that are defined for the table are then assumed to exist among the inserted data.

The DEFAULT VALUES keywords tell Microsoft SQL Server to insert a new record composed entirely of the default values assigned to the table. If a column does not have a default value, NULL will be inserted. If a NOT NULL column does not have a default, the INSERT . . . DEFAULT VALUES will fail. This method is mutually exclusive from the `list_of_values`, `SELECT_statement`, and `EXECUTE_stored_procedure` method of storing records. You can mix this method with the others.

`list_of_values`, `SELECT_statement`, and `EXECUTE_stored_procedure` are discussed in the next three sections. We'll discuss and illustrate each of these methods for using INSERT based on the general syntax shown previously. We'll also go over a few general rules for the command.

INSERT . . . VALUES

The INSERT . . . VALUES statement is used to add a single row of data to a table using literal values supplied in the SQL string. Consider this example:

```
INSERT INTO authors
     (au_id,
      au_lname,
      au_fname,
      phone,
      address,
      city,
      state,
      zip,
      contract )
VALUES
     ('111-11-1111',
     'Rabbit',
     'Jessica',
     DEFAULT,
     '1717 Main St',
     NULL,
     'CA',
     '90675',
     1)
```

In this example, we insert a new row in the authors table for the author Jessica Rabbit (va-va-voom!). Every column is assigned a specific, literal value except the phone column, which is assigned the default value. DEFAULT values are assigned to a column with the CREATE TABLE statement, or later on using the ALTER TABLE . . . ADD CONSTRAINT command.

When inserting a value into *every* column of a table, SQL allows you to leave off the column list if you list the values in the natural order in which the columns were defined. So the preceding example could actually look like this:

```
INSERT INTO authors
VALUES
     ('111-11-1111',
     'Rabbit',
     'Jessica',
     DEFAULT,
     '1717 Main St',
     NULL,
     'CA',
     '90675',
     1)
```

There might be times when an INSERT is executed against a table in which every column has a DEFAULT assigned to it. In those circumstances, the INSERT statement is allowed to insert only the default values via the command:

```
INSERT INTO tablename DEFAULT VALUES
```

Partial INSERT. If you want to insert data into only a few columns of the table, you *must specify both the* `column_list` *and the values*, as in the next example:

```
INSERT authors (au_id,          au_lname, au_fname,  phone,   contract)
VALUES         ('111-11-1111', 'Rabbit', 'Jessica', DEFAULT, 1)
```

In this example, we use an alternate notation for the INSERT statement. This notation is fairly common and has the benefit of showing you each column and the corresponding value to be inserted. The INTO keyword is optional, so we leave it off in this example. In this example, we inserted data into only the columns defined as NOT NULL. The authors table contains four columns that are allowed to contain null values. When you insert values for some, but not all, of the columns in a table, one of three things will happen:

- A DEFAULT value will be inserted, if one is defined for the column or for the user-defined datatype on which the column is based.
- A value of null will be inserted into the column if it allows nulls.
- The insert will fail with the following error message because one or more of the columns are NOT NULL:

  ```
  Msg 233, Level 16, State 2
  The column %% in table %% may not be null.
  ```

INSERT into tables with IDENTITY or TIMESTAMP. Special column constraints such as IDENTITY and TIMESTAMP datatypes dictate slightly different behavior in the INSERT statement. With these two datatypes, you are *not* supposed to supply a value, since SQL Server will do that automatically. When inserting into tables with these datatypes, simply leave these columns off of the `column_list`. If, for some reason, you must explicitly enter a value for IDENTITY or TIMESTAMP columns, just use the DEFAULT keyword in the values list.

You can enable the insertion of specific values to an IDENTITY column by issuing the command:

```
SET IDENTITY_INSERT tablename ON
```

before the INSERT statement. This can introduce data integrity errors, though, since SQL Server does not influence the uniqueness or ensure that no gap exists between the inserted value and the other identity values. This option is most typically used when you need to move data from one table to another but want to keep the same identity values. You'd set this option ON and then perform the operation. The option is enabled for the current user only during his current session.

INSERT . . . SELECT

The INSERT statement combined with a nested SELECT statement allows you to quickly populate a table with multiple rows. When using INSERT . . . SELECT between two tables, be sure that the tables possess compatible datatypes and structures; although you can often compensate for incompatibilities in the SELECT statement. To make things even easier, if columns in both tables are identical in order and datatype in their respective CREATE TABLE statements, you do not need to specify a `column_list` in either the INSERT or SELECT statement.

INSERT . . . SELECT between identically structured tables. Let's start with the simplest form of the INSERT . . . SELECT command: selecting data from a source table that is virtually identical to the target table. This example adds a new row to the temp_titles table for every row existing in the titles table:

```
INSERT temp_titles
SELECT *
FROM titles
```

Because the tables temp_titles and titles are essentially copies of the same table, with an identical column structure and order, there is no need to specify the `column_list` in either the INSERT or SELECT portion of the command. Of course, if you want only a subset of the data from the titles table, you could append a WHERE clause to the SELECT statement. Using this method to fill a table with data has two benefits over the SELECT . . . INTO command. First, the entire operation is logged, thus providing stronger backup and recovery options. Second, INSERT may be used with preexisting tables already containing data; SELECT . . . INTO must create the target table.

INSERT . . . SELECT between dissimilarly structured tables. There may be times when you wish to move data between two tables that are dissimilar in the arrangement of columns and datatypes. When you need to achieve this sort of functionality, you must perform any needed datatype conversions in the SELECT statement.

Assume that the publishing company using the pubs database just acquired another publishing company. We want to incorporate all of their sales data into our sales table. (You can also assume that any referential integrity issues, such as new store records, are already taken care of.) In the following example, our sales table is described on the left compared to the new company's sales table on the right:

```
sales                                     new_sales
stor_id    CHAR(4)       NOT NULL   store_nbr         INT        NOT NULL
ord_num    VARCHAR(20)   NOT NULL   terms             CHAR(15)   NOT NULL
ord_date   DATETIME      NOT NULL   salesperson_nbr   INT        NOT NULL
qty        SMALLINT      NOT NULL   order_nbr         INT        NOT NULL
payterms   VARCHAR(12)   NOT NULL   order_date        CHAR(8)    NOT NULL
```

```
title_id   tid            NOT NULL   title_nbr         INT        NOT NULL
                                     quantity          SMALLINT   NOT NULL
```

As you can see, quite a few of the columns differ between the two tables. To properly insert records from the new_sales table into the sales table, the nested SELECT statement must make the necessary translations. And since the sales table contains no nullable columns, a value must be provided for every column on every row to be inserted. The INSERT statement might look like this:

```
INSERT sales
    (stor_id,
    ord_num,
    ord_date,
    qty,
    payterms,
    title_id)
SELECT
    CONVERT(CHAR(4),store_nbr),
    CONVERT(VARCHAR(20),order_nbr),
    CONVERT(DATETIME, order_date),     -- new_sales.order_date in
    --      format 'dd/mm/yy'
    quantity,
    SUBSTRING(payment_terms,1,12),
    CONVERT(CHAR,title_nbr)
FROM new_sales
WHERE order_date >= '01/01/96'         -- retrieve only the newer records
```

In this case, we had to use the CONVERT function to translate incompatible datatypes between the two tables. And in one instance, with the `payment_terms` column, we actually had to restrict the size of the data retrieved from the new_sales table. Finally, we added the WHERE clause to ensure that we retrieved only records of a somewhat recent date.

Inserting a string of spaces or an empty string ('') into a VARCHAR column adds only a single space to the column. On the other hand, CHAR columns are right-padded with spaces until the column is full.

INSERT . . . EXECUTE

The INSERT . . . EXECUTE command (you can specify EXEC in place of EXECUTE) is a powerful new function added in Microsoft SQL Server 6.5 that tells SQL Server to store the result set returned by a dynamic Transact-SQL statement, a system stored procedure, a user stored procedure, a remote procedure call (RPC), or an extended stored procedure into a local table.

The result set returned by the stored procedure is stored in the table, but there are limitations. The results of DBCC statements, RAISERROR statements, PRINT statements, and FETCH statements cannot be stored in a local table using INSERT . . . EXECUTE. The table storing the result set must already exist, and the regular rules for INSERT statements apply. Thus, a stored procedure that produces a TINYINT result set cannot be stored in a column defined as CHAR, and so forth.

The INSERT . . . EXECUTE command provides an added level of power when using RPCs. You can execute a remote stored procedure on any server recorded in the sysservers table and then record the results in a table on the local server. This technique could be used in any number of applications, such as lightweight replication schemes, polling tools, monitoring tools, and so on.

The number of columns in the local table must match the datatype and number of columns returned in the result set of the stored procedure. So you should have a thorough understanding of both the table where the data will be stored and the result set of the stored procedure that will populate it to properly perform an INSERT . . . EXECUTE statement.

The exact syntax for the INSERT . . . EXECUTE statement follows:

```
INSERT [INTO] {table_name | view_name}
    [(column_list)]
EXEC[UTE] { procedure_name }
    [[@parameter_name=] {value [OUTPUT] | DEFAULT}
    [, [@parameter_name =] {value [OUTPUT] | DEFAULT}]...]
```

INSERT . . . EXEC with an extended stored procedure. Assume for a moment that we need a Transact-SQL program to copy a file from one server to another from within SQL Server. The Transact-SQL program also must perform error checking to tell the end user if the copy succeeded or failed. You can do this interactively by executing the *xp_cmdshell* extended stored procedure and checking the results for the literal string "1 file(s) copied" or "file not found", the Windows NT system messages indicating success or failure. Here's a Transact-SQL batch that does this:

```
CREATE TABLE #ins_exec_container
  (column1 VARCHAR(100) NOT NULL)
GO

INSERT INTO #ins_exec_container
EXEC master..xp_cmdshell
    "copy \\CHAMPAGNE\c_share\data\download\emp01.fmt C:\data\load\emp01.fmt"
GO

SELECT *
FROM #ins_exec_container
GO
```

Results:

```
----------------------------
       1 file(s) copied
```

At this point, it would be very easy to take this code and modify it for use in a stored procedure. You could add a variable to flag the success or failure of the file copy and, based on the flag, raise an error or send email to the DBA indicating the status of the operation. This sort of stored procedure is rather advanced, so if you're interested in using or modifying its code, look on the accompanying CD-ROM for a file called *copy_winnt_file.sp.*

INSERT . . . EXEC with a system stored procedure or user stored procedure. You can also store the output of system stored procedures such as *sp_lock* or *sp_who.* You might want to poll a troubled server every 15 minutes with an RPC of *sp_lock* to establish the general locking trend information on that server. Here's a Transact-SQL batch that does something like that:

```
-- drop the table, if it already exists
DROP TABLE dbo.sp_lock_history
GO

-- create the table to hold sp_lock output
CREATE TABLE dbo.sp_lock_history (
    spid     SMALLINT      NOT NULL ,
    locktype VARCHAR(30)   NOT NULL ,
    table_id INT           NOT NULL ,
    page     INT           NOT NULL ,
    dbname   VARCHAR(30)   NOT NULL
)
GO

-- execute sp_lock on a remote server
INSERT INTO sp_lock_history
EXECUTE SAVIGNON.master..sp_lock
GO

-- just to see what's in there
SELECT *
FROM   sp_lock_history
GO
```

Results:

```
spid   locktype                       table_id    page        dbname
------ ------------------------------ ----------- ----------- ----------
20     Sh_intent                      1136007078  0           PUBS
20     Sh_page                        1136007078  33628       PUBS
38     Sh_intent                      1746105261  0           master
38     Ex_intent                      1008006622  0           billables
38     Ex_extent                      0           368         tempdb
39     Sh_intent                      1136007078  0           PUBS
```

```
39      Sh_page                         1136007078  33628       PUBS
50      Sh_intent                       1136007078  0           PUBS
50      Sh_page                         1136007078  33628       PUBS
51      Sh_intent                       1136007078  0           PUBS
51      Sh_page                         1136007078  33628       PUBS

(11 row(s) affected)
```

You can use this same technique to store data from your own stored procedures. Since the system stored procedures provide ready examples, we used one of them here.

You could allow the RPC to accumulate data throughout the business day, then review the results. You'd have plenty of information to change your locking strategy by revealing things like too many table locks or excessive locks on a single page of data.

DELETE and TRUNCATE: Removing Data

Removing rows from a SQL Server table is a cinch with the DELETE statement. In fact, it is so easy that you need to exercise great care when issuing this command. This is the basic syntax for both Microsoft and Sybase:

```
DELETE [FROM] {table_name | view_name}
[WHERE clause | CURRENT OF cursor_name]
```

You will almost never want to issue a DELETE statement without a WHERE clause, since doing so will result in deleting *all* rows from the affected table. There are a couple of reasons why this can be bad:

- You may not want all rows deleted from a table. Ouch!
- The DELETE statement logs every record deleted. You may be in danger of filling up the transaction log when deleting from very large tables. Adding a WHERE clause will reduce the transaction into manageably sized pieces.

You can delete from only one table in a single DELETE statement; you can, however, use a join in a subquery of the WHERE clause to determine exactly which rows in the table get deleted. Similarly, you can delete from a view that references only one underlying table, whether or not the view references all of the columns in the underlying table. Another thing to keep in mind about DELETE is that although DELETE removes all rows in a table, it does not reset any IDENTITY column back to its seed (or starting) number. Any new rows added to the table will pick up where the IDENTITY left off before the DELETE was issued.

Here's a typical DELETE statement:

```
DELETE FROM new_sales
WHERE stor_id IN
    (SELECT stor_id
    FROM sales)
```

Results:

```
(21 row(s) affected)
```

SQL Server also contains a Transact-SQL extension (some people might call it "a non-ANSI-compliant version") of the DELETE statement that lets you add an additional FROM statement, making correlated subquery search criteria (that is, a WHERE containing a SELECT statement) much easier. What does that mean? Examine the following example:

```
-- ANSI style
DELETE FROM sales
WHERE stor_id IN
    (SELECT  s1.stor_id
     FROM    sales s1,
             stores s2
     WHERE   s1.stor_id  = s2.stor_id
        AND  s1.payterms = 'ON invoice')
```

Results:

```
(4 row(s) affected)
```

Now consider:

```
-- Transact-SQL style
DELETE   sales
    FROM stores s2
WHERE    sales.stor_id  = s2.stor_id
    AND  sales.payterms = 'ON invoice'
```

Results:

```
(4 row(s) affected)
```

The Transact-SQL style avoids building search criteria in lengthy subqueries that join a result set from multiple tables. You can reference multiple tables in the second FROM clause to build very complex search criteria. You can even use an ANSI-style JOIN clause in the FROM clause, as in:

```
DELETE FROM  sales
    FROM     stores s2
        JOIN sales on sales.stor_id  = s2.stor_id
    WHERE    sales.payterms = 'ON invoice'
```

Results:

```
(4 row(s) affected)
```

Even so, the additional FROM clause affects only the number and types of rows deleted from the sole table referenced in the DELETE statement. It will not enable deletion from more than one table in a single command.

Only one variation is allowed in the WHERE clause of a DELETE statement: the WHERE CURRENT OF cursor_name. This option tells SQL Server that, when used in combination with a cursor, it should delete only the single record where the cursor is currently positioned.

There may be instances in which all you want to accomplish is to empty out the entire contents of a table. If this is the case, you'd be best served by issuing a TRUNCATE TABLE command. Although this command is technically a DDL command, TRUNCATE TABLE works much like a DELETE, with two notable exceptions. First, it erases every row in the table while leaving the table structure intact. There is no way to limit the scope of the TRUNCATE command. Second, TRUNCATE TABLE does not log the transaction, so it is extremely fast. On the other hand, it is not recoverable.

Whenever you perform numerous or very large INSERT, UPDATE, or DELETE statements against a table, you'd be well advised to perform an UPDATE STATISTICS command on that table. Transactions that alter the amount or kinds of data in a table also affect the indexes SQL Server uses to answer queries. If you do not keep the indexes updated via the UPDATE STATISTICS command, response time will slowly decline to a crawl. On our heavily used production systems, we use UPDATE STATISTICS on a nightly basis.

The syntax for TRUNCATE is very simple since there are very few options:

```
TRUNCATE TABLE [[database.]owner.]table_name
```

TRUNCATE TABLE also has one other benefit over DELETE; it basically resets an IDENTITY counter to zero (or whatever number at which the counter was specified to begin counting). TRUNCATE does not affect indexes, triggers, defaults, defined constraints, or any other database objects associated with the table being truncated. Remember that since TRUNCATE is not logged, it will not cause any trigger—including delete triggers—to fire. As with other nonlogged operations, TRUNCATE can also have an impact on transaction log dumps and recoverability.

Here's what the command to clean out the titles table looks like:

```
TRUNCATE TABLE titles
```

Results:

```
This command did not return data, and it did not return any rows
```

Although the results may look odd, this is SQL Server's way of saying "OK, I did what you asked." This result set is returned for most commands that do not impact actual *rows* of data. If a command does have an impact on rows of data in a table, SQL Server will reply with the more common result of "(x row(s) affected)."

You cannot use TRUNCATE on a table with a foreign key, like that found on the authors table. The command simply fails, as shown here:

```
TRUNCATE TABLE authors
```

Results:

```
Msg 4712, Level 16, State 1
Cannot truncate table 'authors' because it is being referenced by a foreign
key constraint.
```

UPDATE: Modifying Data

In some ways, an UPDATE statement is to the SQL Server world what cars are to the average driver. How's that again? Well, many people think of a car in terms of what it provides, transportation, without giving a second thought to the countless complexities under the hood. The UPDATE statement is similar. It's a simple command that enables you to alter the data stored in existing records, but what goes on behind the scenes can be very complex at times.

The syntax for UPDATE looks like this:

```
UPDATE {table_name | view_name}
SET {column_name | variable_name} = {DEFAULT | expression} ,
    . . .
[FROM {table_name1 | view_name1} ,
    . . .
[WHERE clause | CURRENT OF cursor_name]
```

As with the DELETE statement, you will seldom issue an UPDATE command without a WHERE clause, and for the same reasons:

- The UPDATE will affect every row in the entire table.
- The UPDATE will generate at least one transaction for every row in the table, potentially filling up the transaction log when performing the update on a very large table.

Generally, you'll want to issue a SELECT command using the same WHERE clause before you issue the actual UPDATE (or INSERT or DELETE) command. This will enable you to check all the rows in the result set before saving any data into the database. Whatever rows are returned by the SELECT will be modified by the UPDATE.

A basic UPDATE statement looks like this:

```
UPDATE titles
SET    type  = 'pers_comp',
```

```
       price = (price * 1.15)
WHERE  type  = 'popular_com'
```

Results:

```
(3 row(s) affected)
```

This query will update all the popular com titles by increasing their price by 15% and altering their type to pers comp. So our fictional publishing company can now open up a business computing line that will challenge the likes of, well, any other big publishing companies besides O'Reilly & Associates.

You can use the Transact-SQL extension of the FROM clause, also available with the DELETE statement, in an UPDATE statement. Using a FROM clause in an UPDATE statement isn't exactly an ANSI-compliant command, but it does have its benefits. Chief among the benefits are much easier multitable joins. Here's a sample of table joins using both syntaxes:

```
-- ANSI style
UPDATE titles
SET    pubdate = GETDATE()
WHERE  title_id IN
    (SELECT title_id
     FROM   titleauthor
     WHERE  au_id IN
         (SELECT au_id
          FROM   authors
          WHERE  au_lname = 'White'))
```

Results:

```
(1 row(s) affected)
```

Now consider:

```
-- Transact-SQL style
UPDATE  titles
SET     pubdate = GETDATE()
FROM    authors a,
        titleauthor t2
WHERE   a.au_id       = t2.au_id
    AND t2.title_id = titles.title_id
    AND a.au_lname  = 'White'
```

Results:

```
(1 row(s) affected)
```

In each example UPDATE, all we know for sure is that there is only one title by author White and that the record must have its publication date set to the current date and time. To perform the update using the Transact-SQL style is simply a matter of a three-table join between authors, titles, and titleauthor. But to perform the same operation using ANSI-compliant code, we must first find the au_id in the author table and pass that up to the titleauthor table, where we must find the title_id, which we must then pass up to the main UPDATE statement.

Here's an important point to remember when performing updates: always perform as many elements of the update as possible in a single transaction. That is, if you are changing three columns on a given table, alter all three columns in one statement, rather than in three separate statements. Doing so has the obvious performance impact of reducing three transactions to one.

UPDATE statements can be executed only against a single table at a time, or against views that reference only one underlying table. As with any DML statement, you can use the IDENTITYCOL keyword on Microsoft or the SYB_IDENTITY on Sybase in the WHERE clause as a catchall in place of the actual column_name of the IDENTITY column, as in WHERE IDENTITYCOL = 10010.

As with the DELETE statement, the only variation allowed in the WHERE clause of an UPDATE statement is the clause:

```
WHERE CURRENT OF cursor_name
```

This option tells SQL Server that, when used in combination with a cursor, it should update only the single record where the cursor is currently positioned.

Manipulating TEXT and IMAGE Fields

Columns of the TEXT and IMAGE datatype are a special case in SQL Server. They cannot be manipulated by normal means. That's because TEXT and IMAGE fields are a little bit deceptive. A normal column datatype, such as VARCHAR(255), stores data on the 2K data page along with all the other columns of its table. TEXT and IMAGE data, conversely, consists of a *pointer* on the first data page that links the table's record to the first 2K data page of the TEXT/IMAGE field. In effect, TEXT and IMAGE data looks as if it's a part of the record, but it's really stored elsewhere in the database. Figure 3-2 gives a graphic representation of regular data pages versus TEXT and IMAGE data pages.

As described, SQL Server stores TEXT and IMAGE data as a linked list, necessitating a lot of extra overhead in keeping all those pointers consistent. Another side effect of the linked list structure of TEXT and IMAGE fields is restrictions on usage. To summarize, TEXT and IMAGE columns have these characteristics:

- They cannot be used as local variables.
- They cannot be used in an index.

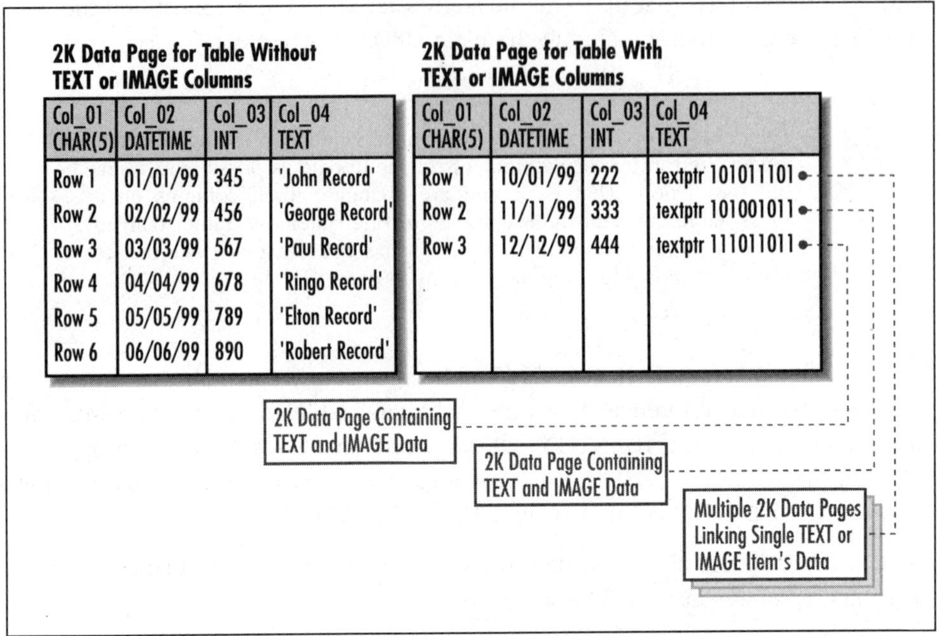

Figure 3-2. Data storage on a regular data page and on a TEXT or IMAGE data page

- They cannot be used in ORDER BY, COMPUTE, or GROUP BY clauses.
- IMAGE fields cannot be addressed in a WHERE clause, although TEXT fields can, but only with the LIKE operator and with some built-in functions, such as PATINDEX, DATALENGTH, and those that work with text pointers.
- When a TEXT field is queried in a SELECT statement, only a partial result is returned, as defined by the SET TEXTSIZE command.

The READTEXT command is more effective when reading a full TEXT field. Instead of using the regular DML commands INSERT and UPDATE, use the Transact-SQL commands WRITETEXT and UPDATETEXT, respectively.

Chapter 6, *Datatypes and Variables,* contains more discussion about TEXT and IMAGE fields.

TEXT and IMAGE functions

Whenever you work with TEXT and IMAGE fields, you'll find the TEXTPTR and TEXTVALID functions to be invaluable. Refer to Chapter 12 for more information about the use and functionality of these functions, which are used to manipulate TEXT and IMAGE fields.

The READTEXT command

To read a TEXT or IMAGE field, use the READTEXT command:

Microsoft	Sybase

`READTEXT [[database.]owner.]`
`table_name.column_name`
`text_pointer offset size [HOLDLOCK]`
	`READTEXT [[database.]owner.]`
	`table_name.column_name`
	`text_pointer offset size [HOLDLOCK]`
	`[USING {BYTES | CHARS | CHARACTERS}]`
	`[AT ISOLATION {READ UNCOMMITTED |`
	`READ COMMITTED | SERIALIZABLE}]`

You must include both the table name and the column name. You must also include the `text_pointer` value, which can be found with the function TEXTPTR. You can include the function directly within the READTEXT command or store the output of the TEXTPTR in a local variable. You can use the OFFSET value to skip a number of bytes before reading the field. By specifying a value for the SIZE parameter, a specific number of bytes can be read. A SIZE of 0 will read 4K of data, unless it is superseded by the SET TEXTSIZE command if @@textsize is less than the value for the SIZE parameter. (You can look up the TEXTSIZE value using the @@textsize global variable.) HOLDLOCK is the only allowable hint with READTEXT.

Sybase's version of the command offers all the features that Microsoft's does, but it also has some added options. The USING option allows the command to interpret offset and size as bytes or as characters (either CHARS or CHARACTERS will work). This setting doesn't work on IMAGE columns. The AT ISOLATION option allows you to specify an isolation level of 0, 1, or 3 for the query. Chapter 11, *Transactions and Locking,* has a detailed discussion of isolation levels. The default isolation level of 1 (read committed) is sufficient for most applications.

For example, to select the pr_info column in the pub_info table, specify the following:

```
-- declare a local variable to store the pointer
DECLARE @pointervalue VARBINARY(16)

-- find and assign the value of the pointer
SELECT @pointervalue = TEXTPTR(pr_info)
FROM   pub_info
WHERE  pub_id = '1389'

-- show the value of the TEXT field
READTEXT pub_info.pr_info @pointervalue 50 25
```

Results:

```
pr_info
-----------------------------------------------------------------------------
publisher1389inthepu
```

Notice that the read began at an offset of the 50th digit and continued for the next 25 digits of data.

The UPDATETEXT command

The UPDATETEXT command is used to replace, delete, or insert data into a TEXT or IMAGE field. UPDATETEXT is fairly flexible in that it enables changes to any portion of the field. The general syntax for the command, which is supported only by Microsoft, is shown here:

```
UPDATETEXT [[database.]owner.]table_name.column_name
    text_ptr {NULL | insert_offset} {NULL | delete_length} [WITH LOG]
    [data_string | [{[database.]owner.]table_name.source_column_name
    source_text_ptr}]
```

As with the READTEXT command, the table and column names come first, followed by the text pointer value. These values represent the column and text pointer value to be updated. Every UPDATETEXT command must have these first two parameters. Once those are in place, the parameters that follow depend on the operation to be performed:

- When replacing data, include a non-null `insert_offset` value, a nonzero `delete_length`, and the data to be inserted.
- When deleting data, include a non-null `insert_offset` value and a nonzero `delete_length` only. Do not include new data to be inserted.
- When inserting new data, set the desired `insert_offset` needed to position the data properly, a `delete_length` of zero, and the data to be inserted.

The `insert_offset` and `delete_length` are tricky parameters. The `insert_offset` is the number of bytes (starting at zero) to skip before UPDATETEXT inserts new data. If any data exists in the field, it will be shifted to the right to make room for the new data. A null `insert_offset` will append any new data to the end of existing data, while a zero will insert the data at the beginning of the existing data value. Similarly, `delete_length` is the number of bytes (starting at `insert_offset`) to *delete* from the TEXT or IMAGE field. Be careful with this parameter, because a value of null will delete all data starting at the `insert_offset` position to the end of the field. A value of zero tells UPDATETEXT not to delete any data.

UPDATETEXT operations can be logged using the WITH LOG keywords. This option allows recoverability and provides greater flexibility when writing explicit transactions. Of course, using this option can quickly fill up the transaction log, particularly if the transaction log is small or if many records are altered by the operation. An UPDATETEXT operation must have the database option "select into/bulkcopy" set on when not using the WITH LOG option.

Finally, the command accepts either a **data_string** or the value of another field as the inserted data. The **data_string**, which will be inserted at the **insert_offset** position, can be a single CHAR, VARCHAR, BINARY, VARBINARY, TEXT, or IMAGE string. By substituting a **table_name** and **source_column_name**, data of any of the previously mentioned datatypes can be inserted into the TEXT or IMAGE field. Instead of a **data_string**, you can insert the value stored in another **table_name** and **source_column_name**, as long as the source data is one of the previously mentioned datatypes. If the **source_column** is a TEXT or IMAGE field, be sure to include the **source_text_pointer** value (retrievable with the TEXTPTR function).

This example finds the text pointer and stores it in the local variable @pointervalue. Then, it alters the value stored in the sysarticles.filter_clause TEXT column:

```
-- declare a local variable to store the pointer
DECLARE @pointervalue VARBINARY(16)

-- find and assign the value of the pointer
SELECT @pointervalue = TEXTPTR(pr_info)
FROM   pub_info
WHERE  pub_id = '1389'

-- alter the value of the TEXT field
UPDATETEXT pub_info.pr_info @pointervalue 8 10 WITH LOG '-ABCDEFGHI-'

-- now show what has changed
READTEXT pub_info.pr_info @pointervalue 1 25
go
```

Results:

```
pr_info
-------------------------------------------------------------------------------
his is -ABCDEFGHI-t data
```

The value of the column filter_clause has now been modified as a logged transaction to include the string -ABCDEFGHI-.

The WRITETEXT command

The WRITETEXT command enables Transact-SQL programmers to perform non-logged inserts to a TEXT or IMAGE field, completely overwriting any contents currently stored in the field. Up to about 120K of data can be inserted by this command. A default WRITETEXT command is not logged to avoid filling the transaction log. Since TEXT and IMAGE fields are so large (2K at a minimum), they can quickly pack a transaction log. The command syntax is the same for Microsoft and Sybase:

```
WRITETEXT [[database.]owner.]table_name.column_name
    text_pointer [WITH LOG] data_string
```

As expected, the first parameter required by the command is the name of the table and column that are subjected to the write operation. (Database and owner name are optional.) Next, the `text_pointer` value (retrievable with the TEXTPTR function) must be specified. The optional WITH LOG keywords can be added to the command to improve recoverability and transaction handling. (Use this option with caution because it can fill up the transaction log so quickly.) The nonlogged features of WRITETEXT can be used only in a database with the option "select into/bulkcopy" set ON. If you attempt to use the nonlogged version of the command when "select into/bulkcopy" is not enabled, you get this response:

```
Msg 7130, Level 16, State 3
UPDATETEXT with no log is not valid at this time. Use sp_dboption to set the
'select into/bulk copy' option on for database pubs.
```

The WRITETEXT command must be used only on previously initialized TEXT and IMAGE columns. TEXT and IMAGE columns are initialized by inserting actual data into the column or by updating the column with a data value or a NULL value. Refer to Chapter 6 for more information on TEXT and IMAGE fields.

This example finds the text pointer and stores it in the local variable @pointervalue. Then, it overwrites the value stored in the pub_info.pr_info TEXT column with a new value.

```
-- declare a local variable to store the pointer
DECLARE @pointervalue VARBINARY(16)

-- find and assign the value of the pointer
SELECT @pointervalue = TEXTPTR(pr_info)
FROM   pub_info
WHERE  pub_id = '1389'

-- alter the value of the TEXT field
UPDATETEXT pub_info.pr_info @pointervalue 'Now is the time for all good
    citizens to come to the aid of their party'

-- now show what has changed
READTEXT pub_info.pr_info @pointervalue 1 25
GO
```

Results:

```
pr_info
------------------------------------------------------------------------------
ow is the time for all go
```

To read the whole value of the column pr_info, the READTEXT offset should be 0 and the size should be about 75.

When using the WRITETEXT or UPDATETEXT commands without the WITH LOG option, you are prevented from performing the DUMP TRANSACTION command. That's because the "select into/bulkcopy" option must be enabled. As long as it is enabled, it prevents any subsequent attempt to dump the transaction log until the full database dump has occurred.

Summary

This chapter introduced the most important commands in SQL, which you will use to build full-featured Transact-SQL programs. SQL commands in the Data Definition Language (DDL) include the following:

- The CREATE TABLE, ALTER TABLE, and DROP TABLE statements, which give you ways to manage tables
- The CREATE DEFAULTS, CREATE RULE, and CREATE INDEX statements, which give you ways to manage defaults, rules, and indexes
- Other commands and system stored procedures, such as *sp_help*, that manage or return information about tables

SQL commands in the Data Manipulation Language (DML), along with their Transact-SQL variants, include the following:

- The SELECT statement for retrieving data
- The SELECT . . . INTO statement (Transact-SQL variant) for creating temporary and permanent tables
- The INSERT statement for adding data to a table
- The INSERT . . . EXECUTE statement (Transact-SQL variant) for inserting data derived from a stored procedure
- The DELETE and TRUNCATE TABLE statements for erasing data
- The UPDATE statement for altering existing data

We also discussed the Transact-SQL commands needed to read, write, and update data stored in TEXT and IMAGE columns; these include READTEXT, WRITETEXT, and UPDATETEXT.

4

Transact-SQL Fundamentals

Before you begin the actual process of writing Transact-SQL programs, you need to acquire a bit of background knowledge. Nobody will ask you to quote book, chapter, and verse about the fundamentals we describe in this chapter, but knowing these fundamentals can make a big difference in the Transact-SQL programs you write later on. This chapter explains how the character set and sort order of a server affect processing and commonly used objects in a database. It also covers the use of identifiers, delimiting blocks of code, code "batches," reserved words and keywords to avoid when naming objects, and the main command-line interface into SQL Server.

Server Character Sets

A character set is a collection of the 256 characters used by the server to represent the data therein. The basic 128 characters make up the standard uppercase and lowercase letters found in all character sets, while the 128 extended characters are specific to each set. Your results can be quite unpredictable if a server and client have different characters sets or if two servers sharing data have different character sets. Because character sets are often created for a specific foreign language market, you also may hear them referred to as *language sets.* This discussion focuses only on those character sets that are common in the United States.

There are three primary character sets in SQL Server and lots of regional or foreign-language-specific sets. The three main sets are the ANSI ISO 8859 set (the default), the multilingual set (Code page 850), and the U.S. English set (Code page 437). For installation purposes, the default sort order is by far the fastest, requiring only 5 to 10 minutes for installation. The other character sets can take upward of 30 minutes. The most common character sets are defined as follows:

ISO 8859-1 (ANSI or Latin1)
: This is the default character set. We recommend that you use this one unless there are some very special circumstances. Its main benefits are quick installation and compatibility with the ANSI characters used in Microsoft operating systems like Windows, Windows 95, and Windows NT. This character set is also the most compatible set for Unix and VMS environments.

Multilingual (Code Page 850)
: This character set includes the characters common to most of the languages of Europe and the Americas. This character set is best used when you have lots of MS-DOS-based clients that use the extended character set.

U.S. English (Code Page 437)
: This is probably (though not always) one you should stay away from in favor of the highly compatible multilingual character set. Although it's very commonly used in the United States, there are two good reasons to avoid it. First, any self-respecting Brit or European will tell you that American English is butchery of the language. Second, this character set includes many graphic characters that cannot be stored in the database.

It is critical that the DBA staff set up the server character set right the first time; otherwise, they'll have to jump through flaming, razor-blade-laden hoops to straighten out the mistake. To install a new character set, the DBA will have to: (1) extract all data from important databases using BCP -c, (2) reinstall SQL Server with the proper character set, (3) rebuild the databases, (4) import all data using BCP -c, and (5) kiss a good night's sleep goodbye.

Server Sort Orders

Sort orders, like character sets, are chosen when SQL Server is installed. And like character sets, they're a bear to change once set. Sort orders determine the order in which SQL Server collates the result set of a query. Sort order also has a big impact on which records meet the search criteria of a query. In SQL terms, sort orders make a major difference in the function of ORDER BY and GROUP BY clauses of a SQL statement, as well as in the WHERE, HAVING, and DISTINCT clauses.

There are many sort orders available in SQL Server, and they have a noticeable impact on performance and on the development of applications. The examples in this book are based on the sort order known as dictionary-order, case-insensitive. This is by far the easiest way to develop systems and the most natural (i.e., most humanlike) way to sort and compare data. The dictionary-order, case-insensitive sort order outnumbers other installations of sort orders by about four to one. Unless you have an overriding reason to do otherwise, you should stick with it.

Another sort order you might see is binary order. Binary order is the fastest sort order in SQL Server and the most machinelike in behavior. It also returns significantly different data from that returned by a server using dictionary-order, case-insensitive. Table 4-1 summarizes the available sort orders.

Table 4-1. Sort Orders

ID	Name	Filename	Overhead[a]	Notes
30, 40, 50	Binary order	CP437BIN.437, CP850BIN.850, ISO_1BIN.ISO		When comparing values, only characters with an identical ID (0 through 255) in the character set evaluate as equal. Sorting behaves similarly, with the lowest character ID being sorted first. In binary, XYZ would precede abc since they appear earlier in the character set.
31, 41, 51	Dictionary order, case-sensitive	DICTION.437, DICTION.850, DICTION.ISO	20%	When comparing values, uppercase and lowercase characters of the same letter are not equal to each other or to any accented variant. When sorting, uppercase comes first, then lowercase, followed by accented uppercase, and finally accented lowercase.
32, 42, 52	Dictionary order, case-insensitive	NOCASE.437, NOCASE.850, NOCASE.ISO	20%	This is the default sort order. When comparing values, uppercase and lowercase characters of the same letter are equal, but accented variants of the letter are not. When sorting, uppercase and lowercase letters may appear in any order, though unaccented characters are sorted before accented characters.

Table 4-1. Sort Orders (continued)

ID	Name	Filename	Overhead[a]	Notes
33, 43, 53	Dictionary order, case-insensitive, uppercase preference	NOCASEPR.437, NOCASEPR.850, NOCASEPR.ISO	20%	Uppercase and lowercase letters are equal in comparisons, but uppercase letters are sorted first in a result set. Characters with accent marks do not equal those without marks. Thus, Jose = jose but Jose != José. Uppercase unmarked are sorted before lowercase unmarked, followed by uppercase marked, then lowercase marked. Characters are sorted as they appear in the character set; for example, A is sorted in this order: A, a, à, á, â, Ä, ä, Å, å.
34, 44, 54	Dictionary order, case-insensitive, accent-insensitive	NOACCENT.437, NOCASE34.850, NOACCENT.ISO	35%	When comparing, uppercase, lowercase, and diacritical characters all evaluate as equal, e.g., A = a = à = á = â = Ä = ä = Å = å. When sorting, unmarked characters appear before accented characters.
49	Strict compatibility with Version 1.*x* case-insensitive databases			Uses dictionary-order, case-insensitive for the first 128 characters in the set and binary sort order for the remaining 128 characters. This offers no benefit over the other sort orders except strict compatibility with Version 1.x databases. We're not going to discuss this sort order here because anyone using a version this old isn't reading new books either.
55	Alternate dictionary order, case-sensitive	ALTDICT.850	>20%	Same as the primary sort order of the same type, with a few exceptions. *Ø* and *ø* sort at the end of the set. *Ñ* and *N* sort distinctly. Plus, all uppercase variants are sorted before any lowercase variants, e.g., A, À, Á, Ä, a, à, á, ä.

Table 4-1. Sort Orders (continued)

ID	Name	Filename	Overhead[a]	Notes
56	Alternate dictionary order, case-insensitive, uppercase preference	ALTNOCSP.850	>20%	Same as the primary sort order of the same type, with a few exceptions. *Ø* and *ø* sort at the end of the set. *Ñ* and *N* sort distinctly.
57	Alternate dictionary order, case-insensitive, accent-insensitive	ALTNOACC.850	>35%	Same as the primary sort order of the same type, with a few exceptions. *Ø* and *ø* sort at the end of the set. *Ñ* and *N* sort distinctly.
58 ...	Specific language sort-orders, such as the Scandinavian dictionary order, case-insensitive, uppercase preference	SCANNOCP.850 . . .	>35%	Same as the primary sort order of the same type, except extended characters (like *Ø*, *Å*, *Ä*, and ...) are sorted after *Z*.

[a] Approximate cost of this sort order compared to the binary sort order

You can compensate for some differences in sort order when coding a Transact-SQL program. For example, you can use the UPPER or LOWER functions to evaluate the character values in a column as all uppercase or all lowercase. So a table on a server with a sort order of dictionary-order, case-sensitive that contains the values Smith, smith, and smiTH would fail to return any data with this command:

```
SELECT fname,
    lname
FROM employees
WHERE lname = 'SMITH'
ORDER BY lname,
    fname
```

The preceding command would fail because there is no occurrence of all uppercase SMITH, even though there are occurrences of it with different variations in uppercase and lowercase. To compensate, you could issue this query:

```
SELECT fname,
    lname
FROM employees
WHERE UPPER(lname) = 'SMITH'
ORDER BY lname,
    fname
```

With this query, the UPPER function translates all character values in the lname column to their uppercase equivalents. Thus, every instance of the expression smith, regardless of its current case, is translated into SMITH. Note too that functions like UPPER suppress the use of any index on the column where they are active if used in a WHERE clause. Chapter 20, *Transact-SQL Optimization and Tuning,* covers these behaviors in detail.

Identifiers

It doesn't take a rocket scientist to figure this one out. Identifiers are the user- or system-defined names for server objects—things like databases, tables, views, columns, indexes, keys, triggers, stored procedures, constraints, and so on. When issuing the command that creates a server object, you usually must specify a name for that new object (table and column constraints are the only exceptions). Here are the rules for naming server objects:

- The identifier can be no longer than 30 characters in length.
- The identifier may contain numbers, characters, and symbols.
- The identifier must begin with a letter or the underscore (_) symbol. The starting symbols @ or # have special significance to SQL Server.
    - — The at sign (@) is used by SQL Server to identify local variables. A double-at sign (@@) designates a global system variable.
    - — The pound mark (#) is used by SQL Server to identify a temporary table or stored procedure. A double-pound mark (##) indicates that the object is a global temporary object. Temporary server objects are restricted in length to 20 characters on Microsoft SQL Server v6.x and 12 characters on Sybase and older versions of MS SQL Server. This restriction includes the hash marks, because SQL Server appends an internally generated suffix to the object.
- The second character of the identifier must be a letter, a number, or the symbol #, $, or _.
- Identifiers may not contain spaces or other special characters; however, *quoted identifiers* do allow these characters. Quoted identifiers are discussed later in this chapter.
- Most identifiers must be unique for each owner within a given database. A table (or view, stored procedure, etc.) must have a unique name for each owner within its database. The only exceptions to this rule are columns and indexes. Column and index names need be unique only within the table that contains them. So, three different tables might contain a zip_code column and an index called ndx_zip_cd, but only one such column or index is allowed within each table. Database names, on the other hand, have to be unique on a given server.

Fully Qualified Identifiers

There are times when a Transact-SQL program will need to access objects in other databases or objects owned by other users. In order to access these objects, we must use *fully qualified identifiers.* The full qualifier for any object besides a column is the database name and owner's name. In the case of a column, the table or view name must follow the owner's name to fully qualify it. Between each level of qualification, a single period should be present in this syntax:

```
[[database_name.]owner_name.]object_name[.column_name]
```

For example, the following identifier references the *byroyalty* stored procedure in the master database owned by the developer auser.

```
pubs.dbo.byroyalty
```

Each object in brackets in the syntax example, [database_name.], for example, indicates that the qualifier is optional. If you leave off the qualifier, the database defaults to the current database, and the owner defaults to the current user. When referencing an intermediate qualifier, such as [owner_name.], you still have to include the period. So, to reference an object owned by the default user, specify:

```
[database_name.].object_name
```

To illustrate, when a stored procedure is executed under the SA account, which is treated as the DBO (current database owner) in all databases, the owner is not needed. It could be referenced in this way:

```
pubs..byroyalty
```

When referencing remote stored procedures, you also must qualify the procedure with the servername:

```
remote_server_name.database_name.owner_name.procedure_name
```

such as:

```
SAUVIGNON.msdb..sp_helptask
```

You can use the shorthand term DBO to reference an object owned by the current database owner, rather than using the actual username of the database owner. So, if you wished to access the byroyalty object owned by the user developer in the pubs database, and developer was the DBO, you could reference the object in this way:

```
pubs.dbo.byroyalty
```

Any time you reference an object without fully qualifying it, SQL Server will attempt to find the object within the current database under the current user account. If SQL Server cannot find the object, it will attempt to locate it under the

DBO's ownership. If the DBO has granted the proper permissions, you will be able to access the object. If not, the object is inaccessible to you.

System stored procedures, designated by the prefix *sp_*, can be referenced in any database without the need for specifying the database name. Many system stored procedures can be executed only by the DBO of a given database or the SA (system administrator role) (due to the potentially destructive power of some system stored procedures). Other system stored procedures may be executed by any user with the EXECUTE privilege assigned in the master database.

Quoted Identifiers

The rules for normal identifiers will apply to most properly designed database applications. However, developers occasionally set their hearts on an object name that defies common sense. In those circumstances in which an object name requires unusual characters, like spaces, or in which the name is a reserved word or keyword (detailed later in this chapter), you can use a *quoted identifier* of up to 30 characters in length. Quoted identifiers, which must be contained within double-quote marks, can contain just about any character allowed in the character set except double-quote marks. Quoted identifiers may even contain reserved words, keywords, database terms, or other restricted words. (This is *strongly* discouraged!) When referenced in a Transact-SQL command of any kind, the quoted identifier must always appear within the double quotes.

Quoted identifiers may not be fully supported by third-party tools.

The ability to use quoted identifiers can be controlled at the session level by using the command SET QUOTED_IDENTIFIER. Quoted identifiers are allowed only while this setting is ON. With SET QUOTED_IDENTIFIER enabled, quoted identifiers are not evaluated or checked against reserved words or keywords. With the option disabled, quoted identifiers must otherwise conform to the rules of normal identifiers. In fact, with the option disabled, any quoted identifier containing a keyword that was created at an earlier date cannot even be referenced without producing an error.

Foundation Units

There are a number of components that make up a block of Transact-SQL code. In this section, we'll discuss several kinds of components, or foundation units, that are universal to most types of Transact-SQL code. We've already discussed the very important topic of identifiers, as well as the basics of character sets and sort orders. This section covers the use of literals, statement delimiters, operators, reserved words, and keywords.

Literals

Transact-SQL judge literals as any explicit numeric, character, string, date, or Boolean value that is not an identifier. SQL Server allows a variety of literal values in Transact-SQL programs. SQL Server allows literal values for most of the numeric, character, and date datatypes. For example, SQL Server numeric datatypes include (among others) INTEGER, REAL, and MONEY. Thus, numeric literals could look like these:

```
30
-117
+883.3338
-6.66
$70000
2E5
7E-3
```

As you can see, SQL Server will allow signed or unsigned numerals, in scientific or normal notation. And since SQL Server has a MONEY datatype, you can even include a dollar sign. SQL Server does not allow other symbols in numeric literals (besides 0 1 2 3 4 5 6 7 8 9 + - $. E e), so don't include any commas in there. SQL Server interprets a comma in a numeric literal as a list item separator. Observe:

```
SELECT 3,000
GO
```

Results:

```
----------- -----------
3           0

(1 row(s) affected)
```

Character and string literals must always be enclosed by single quotes (' ') in a Transact-SQL program, though you can use double quotes (" ") as well. As long as the literal is opened and closed with the same delimiter, SQL Server allows both kinds. The only difference between character and string literals is that a character literal contains only a single character, while a string literal contains lots of them. Character and string literals aren't restricted to just the alphabet. In fact, any printable character in the server character set can be represented as a literal. All of the following are character or string literals:

```
'1998'
'$70,000 + 14000'
```

```
'There once was a man from Nantucket,'
'Oct 28, 1966'
```

All of these examples are in fact compatible with the CHAR and VARCHAR datatypes. Don't confuse the string literal '1998' with the numeric literal 1998. String literals are associated with CHAR and VARCHAR datatypes and cannot be used in arithmetic operations. On the other hand, SQL Server does perform automatic conversion of string literals when compared against DATETIME and SMALLDATETIME datatypes. Notice the successful completion of this Transact-SQL statement:

```
SELECT  *
FROM    sales
WHERE   qty       > 20
    AND (ord_date = '09/14/94'
    OR   ord_date = 'September 14, 1994')
GO
```

Results:

```
stor_id ord_num        ord_date                 qty    payterms    title_id
------- -------------- ------------------------ ------ ----------- ----------
7131    N914014        Sep 14 1994 12:00AM      25     Net 30      MC3021
```

Even though the string literals were in completely different formats, SQL Server automatically converted them to the DATETIME datatype.

What if you want to represent a single quote in a string literal? That could be tough, since the single quote itself is used to delimit the string. SQL Server allows two methods of achieving this function. First, you can use double quotes (yes, or even double-double-quote marks) each time a single quote should appear. This example should give you the idea:

```
SELECT 'Where''s the beef?'
GO
```

Results:

```
-----------------
Where's the beef?

(1 row(s) affected)
```

SQL Server provides the same functionality by allowing nesting of both the single-quote and double-quote marks as string delimiters in a single statement. The only rule to remember when using this method is that single-quote and/or double-quote marks must be properly matched with a mated delimiter. For example:

```
SELECT 'So he said "Who''s Le Petomaine?"!'
```

Results:

```
--------------------------------
So he said "Who's Le Petomaine?"!

(1 row(s) affected)
```

In this example, single quotes serve as the outer delimiters, while double-quote marks serve only as a string value, and the double quote is used to show a single quote in the string. You could just have easily used double-quote marks as the delimiters and single quotes within the string literal.

The only string literal you must be careful of is the *empty string*. The empty string, represented as (‘’) or (“”), is not considered a null value by CHAR or VARCHAR datatypes. For comparison operations, variables, or column data, the empty string is considered a single space.

Delimiters and Operators

Delimiters are those symbols within the character set that have special significance to SQL Server. SQL Server uses delimiters to judge the order or hierarchy of processes and list items. *Operators* are those delimiters used to judge values in comparison operations, including symbols commonly used for arithmetic or mathematic operations. Table 4-2 lists the delimiters and operators allowed by SQL Server:

Table 4-2. SQL Server Delimiters and Operators

Symbol	Usage
+	Addition operator; also concatenation operator
-	Subtraction operator; also a range indicator in CHECK constraints
*	Multiplication operator
\	Division operator
=	Equality operator
<> !=	Inequality operators
<	Less-than operator
>	Greater-than operator
<=	Less-than or equal-to operator
>=	Greater-than or equal-to operator
(	Expression or hierarchy delimiter
)	Expression or hierarchy delimiter
%	Wildcard attribute indicator
,	List item separator

Table 4-2. SQL Server Delimiters and Operators (continued)

Symbol	Usage
@	Local variable indicator
@@	Global variable indicator
.	Identifier qualifier separator
‘’ “”	Character string indicators
“”	Quoted identifier indicators
--	Single-line comment delimiter
/*	Beginning multiline comment delimiter
*/	Ending multiline comment indicator

It's good practice not to use any delimiter or operator symbol as an object name. In many cases, attempting to create an object containing a delimiter symbol will fail outright, as in the following example:

```
CREATE TABLE temp*storage
 (column1 CHAR(5))
```

Results:

```
Msg 156, Level 15, State 1
Incorrect syntax near the keyword 'temp'.
```

However, there are cases in which you can slide through an object name with one of the delimiter symbols in the mix. Our advice is to avoid this practice altogether. Chapter 5, *Format and Style,* has detailed recommendations for such coding practices.

Bitwise operators

A special subset of operators performs mathematical operations between integer values by translating the integer parameters into a binary representation. These special operators are known as *bitwise operators*. The bitwise operators have the effect of translating an integer value into a binary representation, then evaluating it according to the function of the operator. The operators are listed in Table 4-3.

Table 4-3. Bitwise Operators

Symbol	Usage
&	Bitwise AND operator; requires two operands; use only with INT, TINYINT, or SMALLINT columns
^	Bitwise OR operator; requires two operands; use only with INT, TINYINT, or SMALLINT columns

Table 4-3. Bitwise Operators (continued)

Symbol	Usage
|	Bitwise exclusive OR operator; requires two operands; use only with INT, TINYINT, or SMALLINT columns
~	Bitwise NOT operator; use with only one operand; use only with INT, TINY-INT, or SMALLINT columns

Operator precedence

A pecking order is applied when operators are combined in a single expression or command. SQL Server's internal operator precedence determines which comparisons or computations are performed first; precedence has a big impact on the values generated by many types of calculations. Here's the basic operator precedence:

1. Primary grouping: ()
2. Bitwise: ~
3. Multiplicative: * / %
4. Other: + - ^ & |
5. NOT
6. AND
7. OR

If the only operators in an expression are equal, SQL Server evaluates them in order from left to right. Parentheses alter the order of execution for any other expression, starting with the most deeply nested expression.

Reserved Words and Keywords

Just as certain symbols have special meaning and functionality within SQL Server, there are also a number of words and phrases that have special significance. In SQL Server *keywords* are words whose meaning are so closely tied to the operation of the RDBMS that they cannot be used for any other purpose. For example, you could not use the word SELECT as a table name. (Using quoted identifiers will let you get by with naming objects after reserved words and keywords, but this is *strongly* discouraged.) *Reserved words*, on the other hand, do not have special significance now, but they probably will in a future release. Thus, they are reserved for future use and should not be used as an object name.

Table 4-4 lists all SQL Server keywords. After reviewing this table, you can see that most keywords are words used in a Transact-SQL or SQL command.

In this table, boldface keywords are Microsoft only; underlined are Sybase only; all others are currently held in common between Microsoft and Sybase.

Table 4-4. SQL Server Keywords

ACTIVATION	ADD	ALL
ALTER	AND	ANY
ARITH_OVERFLOW	AS	ASC
AT	AUTHORIZATION	AVG
BEGIN	BETWEEN	BREAK
BROWSE	BULK	BY
CASCADE	CASE	CHAR_CONVERT
CHECK	CHECKPOINT	CLOSE
CLUSTERED	**COALESCE**	COMMIT
COMMITTED	COMPUTE	CONFIRM
CONSTRAINT	CONSUMERS	CONTINUE
CONTROLROW	CONVERT	COUNT
CREATE	CURRENT	**CURRENT_DATE**
CURRENT_TIME	**CURRENT_TIMESTAMP**	**CURRENT_USER**
CURSOR	DATABASE	DBCC
DEALLOCATE	DECLARE	DEFAULT
DELETE	DESC	DISK
DISTINCT	DOUBLE	DROP
DUMMY	DUMP	ELSE
END	ENDTRAN	ERRLVL
ERRORDATA	ERROREXIT	ESCAPE
EXCEPT	EXCLUSIVE	EXEC
EXECUTE	EXISTS	EXIT
EXTERNAL	FETCH	FILLFACTOR
FLOPPY	FOR	FOREIGN
FROM	GOTO	GRANT
GROUP	HAVING	HOLDLOCK
IDENTITY	IDENTITY_INSERT	IDENTITY_START
IDENTITYCOL	IF	IN
INDEX	**INSENSITIVE**	INSERT
INTERSECT	INTO	IS
ISOLATION	KEY	KILL

Table 4-4. SQL Server Keywords (continued)

LEVEL	LIKE	LINENO
LOAD	MAX	MAX_ROWS_PER_PAGE
MEMBERSHIP	MIN	MIRROR
MIRROREXIT	NATIONAL	**NOCHECK**
NOHOLDLOCK	NONCLUSTERED	NOT
NULL	**NULLIF**	NUMERIC_TRANSACTION
OF	OFF	OFFSETS
ON	ONCE	ONLINE
ONLY	OPEN	OPTION
OR	ORDER	OVER
PARTITION	PASSWD	PERM
PERMANENT	**PIPE**	PLAN
PRECISION	PREPARE	PRIMARY
PRINT	PRIVILEGES	PROC
PROCEDURE	PROCESSEXIT	PROXY
PUBLIC	RAISERROR	READ
READTEXT	RECONFIGURE	REFERENCES
REPEATABLE	REPLACE	**REPLICATION**
RETURN	REVOKE	ROLE
ROLLBACK	ROWCOUNT	RULE
SAVE	SCHEMA	**SCROLL**
SELECT	**SERIALIZABLE**	SESSION
SESSION_USER	SET	SETUSER
SHARED	SHUTDOWN	SOME
STATISTICS	STATISTICS	STRIPE
SUM	SYB_IDENTITY	SYB_RESTREE
SYSTEM_USER	TABLE	**TAPE**
TEMP	TEMPORARY	TEXTSIZE
THEN	TO	TRAN
TRANSACTION	TRIGGER	TRUNCATE
TSEQUAL	**UNCOMMITTED**	UNION
UNIQUE	UNPARTITION	UPDATE
UPDATETEXT	USE	USER
USER_OPTION	USING	VALUES
VARYING	VIEW	WAITFOR
WHEN	WHERE	WHILE
WITH	WORK	WRITETEXT

Reserved words, unlike keywords, are not always words used in Transact-SQL or SQL commands. Most reserved words are words commonly associated with database technology, but they may or may not have an explicit link to commands in SQL Server. For example, the word "cascade" may not have a lot of significance to you, but the database term CASCADE is used to describe triggers that allow their action, such as a delete or update, to "flow down," or cascade, to any child tables. Cascading triggers are not currently available in SQL Server, but they are available in competitors' database products, so you can bet it's only a matter of time until SQL Server has them. Microsoft and Sybase want you to know about reserved words as you are designing your current applications, so you won't encounter them as keywords at some later revision. Table 4-5 lists all the reserved words currently found in SQL Server:

Table 4-5. SQL Server Reserved Words

ABSOLUTE	ACTION	ALLOCATE
ARE	ASSERTION	AT
AUTHORIZATION	BOTH	CASCADE
CASCADED	CAST	CATALOG
CHAR_LENGTH	CHARACTER	CHARACTER_LENGTH
COLLATE	COLLATION	COLUMN
CONNECT	CONNECTION	CONSTRAINTS
CORRESPONDING	DATE	DAY
DEFERRABLE	DEFERRED	DESCRIBE
DESCRIPTOR	DIAGNOSTICS	DISCONNECT
DOMAIN	END_EXEC	ESCAPE
EXCEPTION	EXPIREDATE	EXTERNAL
EXTRACT	FALSE	FILE
FIRST	FULL	GET
GLOBAL	HOUR	IMMEDIATE
INITIALLY	INNER	INPUT
INTERVAL	JOIN	LAST
LEADING	LEFT	LOCAL
MATCH	MINUTE	MONTH
NAMES	NATIONAL	NATURAL
NCHAR	NEXT	NO
OCTET_LENGTH	OUTER	OUTPUT
OVERLAPS	PAD	PARTIAL
POSITION	PRESERVE	PRIOR
PRIVILEGES	RELATIVE	RESTRICT
RETAINDAYS	RIGHT	ROWS

Table 4-5. SQL Server Reserved Words (continued)

SCHEMA	SECOND	SESSION
SIZE	SPACE	SQLSTATE
TIME	TIMESTAMP	TIMEZONE_HOUR
TIMEZONE_MINUTE	TRAILING	TRANSLATE
TRANSLATION	TRUE	UNKNOWN
USAGE	USING	VALUE
VOLUME	WORK	WRITE
YEAR	ZONE	

Checking for keywords and reserved words

Microsoft SQL Server contains a utility in the *\MSSQL\BINN* or *\SQLxx\BINN* directory that can check your database for upgrade compatibility and the existence of keywords and reserved words. For Versions 4.2x and 6.0 of Microsoft SQL Server, this utility was called *CHKUPG.EXE*. For Versions 6.5 and 7.0 of Microsoft SQL Server, this utility is called *CHKUPG65.EXE* and *CHKUPG70.EXE*, respectively. Although the names of the executables are a little different, they work exactly the same way. The syntax for the command follows:

```
chkupg.. /Uusername /Ppassword /Sserver_name /opath_and_filename_of_output
```

For example:

```
chkupg70 /Usa /P /SCHAMPAGNE /oC:\MSSQL\LOG\CHKUPG.OUT
```

This command would check the CHAMPAGNE server using the SA account. By leaving the /P parameter blank, the program will prompt you for the password. The switches *are* case-sensitive. The output file will be dumped to the path and the filename listed with the /o parameter. You must then review the output file using a text editor. The output file is a report showing the database status, that all necessary comments exist in the syscomments table, and that no keyword or reserved word conflicts exist in the server. The presence of keywords and reserved words in a server you are about to upgrade will not halt the upgrade process.

You can accomplish similar functionality in Sybase implementations using the system stored procedure *sp_checkreswords*. This system stored procedure is called as a part of the upgrade process and will alert you of any naming transgressions.

Executing Transact-SQL

There are two primary methods of executing Transact-SQL commands that ship with SQL Server, one through the GUI and one from the command line. There are a whole bunch of third-party products that enable you to execute Transact-SQL commands against a SQL Server database, but none of those are discussed here. The vendors each ship graphic user interfaces such as SQL Enterprise Manager and ISQL/W (it stands for Interactive SQL for Windows, get it?) from Microsoft and SQL Advantage by Sybase. The command-line interface for both vendors is known simply as ISQL. ISQL is very similar for Microsoft and Sybase implementations, but there are some differences, explained in this section.

You can use ISQL as both an online and offline method of executing Transact-SQL statements. Now that the vendors ship easy and effective GUI-based tools, ISQL is used less often for online processing and more often to execute Transact-SQL programs as part of batch routines and scheduled tasks.

ISQL Command-Line Interface

When executing commands using ISQL, the commands are submitted as either an interactive session or an offline session that SQL Server processes and, when requested, returns a result set. In many cases, ISQL commands can be grouped into script files, also known as command files. Thus, you can use ISQL to execute a long and involved Transact-SQL program containing many, many commands. By adding a few switches when executing the command file, you could even capture normal output to one file and error messages to another file. The ISQL command-line interface has a wide variety of command switches to affect how the query interacts with the server as well as the behavior of the SQL or Transact-SQL program itself.

Online or offline command execution

ISQL allows you to execute Transact-SQL commands online as you type them. However, with the growing popularity of the GUI tools, fewer and fewer people, especially those new to the product, are using ISQL for online transactions. It's much more common to find people using ISQL to execute a script offline, as part of a scheduled task or in an operating system batch file. In this scenario, all the user needs to do is write her Transact-SQL program to an operating system file (using a tool like Notepad or vi). From there, the script executed with ISQL is called by the scheduled task or batch file.

Originally, the ISQL command-line interface was virtually identical for both Microsoft and Sybase implementations of the product, but they have diverged significantly over time. The command-line switches for each implementation are explained separately in the following sections.

Microsoft ISQL command-line switches

The syntax for Microsoft's version of the ISQL command-line interface looks like:

```
isql [/a packet_size] [/c command_terminator] [/d database_name] [/e] [/E]
    [h header_space] [/H workstation_name] [/i input_file] [/L]
    [/m error_level] [/n] [/o output_file] [/p] [/P password] [/q "query"]
    [/Q "query"] [/r {0 | 1}] [/s column_separator] [/S server_name]
    [/t timeout] /U login_id [/w page_width] [/?]
```

The case-sensitive switches for the ISQL command-line interface are listed here:

/a Enables you to specify a different network packet size for the ISQL session. For example, Windows NT–based networks prefer a network packet size of 4,096 bytes, but SPX/IPX-based networks prefer a network packet size of 512 bytes. The default in most cases is 8,192 bytes but will drop to 512 bytes if the request (default or otherwise) cannot be granted. Large packet sizes can speed performance when the SQL statement or result sets are very large.

/c Specifies a command terminator other than the default GO statement, such as Oracle's semicolon (;). To work properly in ISQL, the command terminator must be on a line by itself, followed by a carriage return. The command terminator can be almost anything except a SQL Server reserved word, keyword, operator, or delimiter.

/d Starts the session in the named database. This switch is equivalent to issuing a USE *database* statement when ISQL is started.

/e Echoes input.

/E Uses a trusted connection instead of standard security.

/h Dictates the number of records to print before repeating the column headings. By default, headings are printed only once for a given result set. You can turn headers off by issuing the string /h-1 (no space!).

/H Allows you to specify a workstation name that will be used in the dynamic system table sysprocesses and in the SQL Enterprise Manager Current Activity window. The current workstation name is assumed as the default.

/i Indicates the path and name of a file that should be processed. This file contains a batch of Transact-SQL commands. This switch may be substituted with the input-pipe symbol or, more commonly, the less-than symbol (<).

/L Tells ISQL to display a report showing the locally configured servers and the names of the servers broadcasting on the network.

/m Allows you to display error messages as they occur during the processing of the query. You set the value equal to the error level for which messages should be displayed. ISQL will then return the message number, state, and error level of the specified level or greater. Any error message below the specified level is ignored. You can use the string /m-1 (no spaces!) to display *all* messages, even those pesky informational messages.

/n Turns off numbering and the prompt symbol (>) from input lines.

/o Indicates the path and name of a file that will receive the output from the batch of Transact-SQL commands processed in this session. This switch may be substituted with the output-pipe symbol or, more commonly, the greater-than symbol (>). To append ISQL output to the end of an existing file, rather than overwrite as the > symbol does, you can use the double-pipe symbol (>>). You can also prefix the pipe or double-pipe marks with a 1 and 2 (1>, 2>, 1>> , and 2>>, respectively) to cause the standard output to differentiate between regular output (1) and errors from ISQL itself (2). This usage enables you to save ISQL errors, which are not normally preserved, to a separate file.

/p Prints out performance statistics.

/P Is the case-sensitive password for a given user login ID. If you do not include this switch, ISQL will prompt you to provide the password. When used as the last switch in the command line without a value, ISQL assumes a null password. To evaluate /P as a null password in the middle of a string of switches, leave two spaces after the /P switch (before the next switch).

/q Executes a single query when ISQL starts, although the session remains active after the completion of the statement. The query should be enclosed in double-quote marks and should not include a GO statement at the end. Use single-quote marks around anything embedded in the SQL query. You can use enviroment variables (%variable or %variable%) with this option. In the following example, all data in the sysdevices table is retrieved:

```
SET table = sysdevices
    isql /q "Select * from %table%"
```

/Q Executes a single query, then ends the ISQL session. Otherwise, it functions the same as the /q switch.

/r Is the "redirect" switch. You use this switch to redirect output to the stderr device. You may specify a value of 0 or 1. If you specify 0 (or nothing), only severity 17 (or higher) error messages will be displayed. By specifying 1, all message output, such as that generated by PRINT statements, will be redirected.

/s Sets the column-separator character to a value other than the default of blank. You can even use delimiters or operands, but these special characters must be preceded with a backslash (\).

/S Tells ISQL to which server to connect. If you leave this switch off, ISQL assumes a connection to the local machine.

/t Specifies the number of seconds before an ISQL command times out. By default, a command runs indefinitely, although login attempts will time out in eight seconds.

/U Is the SQL Server user login ID. It is case-sensitive.

/w Sets the page width for output to a value other than the 80-character default. Output that exceeds the page width is wrapped onto multiple lines.

/? Provides help in the form of a report on ISQL syntax and switches.

Sybase ISQL command-line switches

The Sybase version of the ISQL command-line interface works in essentially the same fashion as the Microsoft version; however, the command-line switches are different. Sybase ISQL also has a few keywords that may be used within an ISQL script. These special commands include RESET (clears the query buffer), QUIT or EXIT (exits ISQL), and !! (executes an operating system command). The basic syntax follows:

```
isql [-a display_charset] [-A packet_size] [-c command_terminator]
    [-d database_name] [-e] [-E editor.exe] [-F] [-h header_space]
    [-H workstation _name] [-i input_file] [-I interface_file]
    [-J client_charset] [-K keytab_file] [-l login_timeout] [/L]
    [-m error_level] [-n] [-o output_file] [-p] [-P password] [-q "query"]
    [-Q "query"] [/r {0 | 1}] [-R remote_server_principal]
    [-s column_separator] [/S server_name] [-t timeout] -U login_id [-v]
    [-V security_options] [-w page_width] [-Y] [-z language]
    [-Z security-mechanism] [/?]
```

The case-sensitive switches for the ISQL command-line interface are:

-a Allows the display of character sets on the terminal that are different from the machine running ISQL. Used in conjunction with -J, it identifies the character set translation file (*.xlt* file) required for character set conversion. Used without -J only when the client character set is the same as the default character set.

-A Enables you to specify a different network packet size for the ISQL session. Same as Microsoft's /a.

-b Turns off column headers from output.

-c Specifies a command terminator other than the default GO statement.

-D Starts the session in the named database. Equivalent to issuing a USE database statement when ISQL is started.

-e Echoes input.

-E Specifies a text editor other than the default editor.

-F Enables the FIPS flag, identifying any nonstandard SQL commands sent.

-h Dictates the number of records to print before repeating the column headings. By default, headings are printed only once for a given result set. You can turn headers off by issuing the string /h-1 (no space!).

-H Allows you to specify a workstation name that will be used in the dynamic system table sysprocesses.

-i Indicates the path and name of a file that contains a batch of Transact-SQL commands that should be processed. This switch may be substituted with the input-pipe symbol or, more commonly, the less-than symbol (<). The file is governed by the normal rules of Transact-SQL programming and should contain its own command terminators.

-I Specifies the path and name of the interfaces file to search when connecting to Adaptive Server. If -I is not specified, ISQL looks for the default interfaces file, *SQL.INI* for Windows platforms.

-J Specifies the character set to use on the client workstation. -J establishes a filter to convert input between client_charset and the Adaptive Server character set. -J with no arguments sets the value to NULL and disables conversion, while omitting -J sets the character set to the default used by the server.

-K Specifies the path and name of a keytab_file for DCE network-based security services. It contains the security key for the username specified with the -U option. If omitted, the ISQL user must be logged into DCE with the same username as shown with the -U switch.

-l Specifies the maximum timeout value allowed for users connecting to the server.

-m Allows you to display error messages as they occur during the processing of the query. You set the value equal to the error level for which messages should be displayed. ISQL will then return the message number, state, and error level of the specified level or greater. Any error message below the specified level is ignored. You can use the string /m-1 (no spaces!) to display *all* messages, even those pesky informational messages.

-n Turns off numbering and the prompt symbol (>) from input lines.

-o Indicates the path and name of a file that will receive the output from the batch of Transact-SQL commands processed in this session. This switch may be substituted with the output-pipe symbol or, more commonly, the greater-than symbol (>). To append ISQL output to the end of an existing file, rather than overwrite as the > symbol does, you can use the double-pipe symbol (>>). You can also prefix the pipe or double-pipe marks with a 1 and 2 (1>, 2>, 1>>, and 2>>, respectively) to cause the standard output to differentiate between regular output (1) and errors from ISQL itself (2). This usage enables you to save ISQL errors, which are not normally preserved, to a separate file.

-p Prints out performance statistics.

-P Is the case-sensitive password for a given user login ID. If you do not include this switch, ISQL will prompt you to provide the password. When used as the last switch in the command line without a value, ISQL assumes a null password. To evaluate -P as a null password in the middle of a string of switches, leave two spaces after the -P switch (before the next switch).

-R Specifies the principal name for the server. By default, the server's principal name and network name match. The -R option must be used when the names are different.

-s Sets the column-separator character to a value other than the default of blank. You can even use delimiters or operands, but these special characters must be preceded with a backslash (\).

-S Tells ISQL to which server to connect. If you leave this switch off, ISQL assumes a connection to the local machine.

-t Specifies the number of seconds before an ISQL command times out. By default, a command runs indefinitely, although login attempts will time out in 60 seconds. This affects commands issued from within ISQL, not the connection time.

-U Is the SQL Server user login ID. It is case-sensitive.

-v Prints version and copyright information.

-V Specifies network-based user authentication, where the user must log into the network security system before running ISQL. Users must supply their network username with the -U switch; any password supplied with the -P option is switched. Additional security services can be specified by adding one or several of the following key-letters:

c Enables data confidentiality service

i Enables data integrity service

m Enables mutual authentication for connection establishment

o Enables data origin stamping service

q Enables out-of-sequence detection

r Enables data replay detection

-w Sets the page width for output to a value other than the 80-character default. Output that exceeds the page width is wrapped onto multiple lines.

-X Initiates client-side password encryption to the server. When the client indicates that encryption is desired, the server sends an encryption key to the client, which is then used for authentication.

-Y Initiates the use of chain transactions.

-z Displays an alternate language for ISQL prompts and messages.

-Z Specifies a security mechanism for network-based security services.

The GO Statement

Although this section and the following sections are last in this chapter, they are probably the two most important concepts presented here.

GO is one of the most frequently used, but least understood, keywords in the Transact-SQL lexicon. The GO command is used to mark the end of a batch of Transact-SQL statements in both Transact-SQL programs and in various online tools. The unusual thing about GO is that it is used only by the SQL Server utilities. The utilities use GO to distinguish the end of the current batch of Transact-SQL commands. Once GO is found, the preceding batch is sent to the server, where it is parsed and compiled into a single execution plan. Thus, the current batch of Transact-SQL statements contains all commands entered since the last GO or since the session was started.

However, its creators do not consider GO a Transact-SQL command. It's a statement accepted only by the utilities, not by SQL Server. For example, applications that send Transact-SQL statements to SQL Server using ODBC or OLE-DB do not use GO to mark the end of a batch. In fact, the GO statement is not actually transmitted to the server; instead, the vendor utilities use GO to mark the end of the batch, and then they send only the batch itself to the server.

Syntactically, GO is a bit of an odd bird, too. It must always be the first word to appear on the line, and in older SQL Server utilities, even preceding and trailing spaces weren't allowed. Most of the newer versions of the GUI tools allow you to place comments after the GO command, but many of the interfaces require that the line be completed with a carriage return. In any case, no other Transact-SQL commands are allowed on the same line. The newer vendor tools will place an implied GO at the end of any batch sent to the server without a GO, but older versions required an explicit GO statement, or else the entire batch was not sent to the server. In these older versions, any statements after the last GO were ignored!

Many of the rules about batches are governed by how and where GO commands are placed in the batch. For example, a variable cannot be declared in one batch and then referenced in another. Also, you cannot place GO in the middle of a stored procedure; it ends the CREATE PROCEDURE statement, and commands after GO are considered a separate batch. This is a mistake frequently made by people who are new to Transact-SQL. These rules are detailed in the next section, but for almost all Transact-SQL batches, where you place the GO command marks where one batch ends and the next begins.

Transact-SQL Batches

A batch is a very important concept in SQL Server. As with Grandma working in the kitchen on a batch of cookies, there are certain rules governing the behavior of a batch. In my Grandma's case, that rule was "no touching the cookie dough until the cooking is done." A pretty tough rule, if you ask me.

In the case of SQL Server, a *batch* is a set of SQL and Transact-SQL statements submitted for execution together as a group. No chocolate chips, though. The most ready identifier of a batch is the keyword GO terminating the Transact-SQL batch. A batch can be a block of code in the SQL Enterprise Manager, the text following the /q or /Q switch in an ISQL command, or the entire text of a file used with the ISQL /i command. Do not confuse the term "batch" with the term "script." A *script*, or command file, is a file containing many batches submitted to SQL Server as a single grouping. Batches provide the benefit of compiling only once for the whole set of commands.

The following code illustrates three Transact-SQL batches in a single script:

```
USE pubs
GO

CREATE TABLE sales_analysis
    (qty       INT      NOT NULL,
     title_id CHAR(6) NOT NULL)
GO

INSERT sales_analysis
    SELECT   sum(qty),
             title_id
    FROM     sales
    GROUP BY title_id

SELECT * FROM sales_analysis
GO
```

A batch is compiled only once as a complete block of code. It is most often terminated by a single end-of-batch delimiter, usually a GO statement. Because of this, there are many restrictions on both batch size and content. Those restrictions are detailed here:

- If there's an error in the batch, none of the statements within the batch will execute.
- If the database name and database owner of an object are not explicitly stated, then unqualified objects are parsed under the current database and owner context.

- Stored procedures can be called by name only if they're the first item in the batch. Otherwise, they must be preceded by the EXECUTE command.
- Multiple batches can be included in a single script if each batch is separated by a GO statement followed by a carriage return.
- Maximum batch size cannot exceed 128K in Microsoft or 64K in Sybase. Since SQL Server must also compile an execution plan for the batch, the actual limit for a given batch is somewhat less than the upper values of 128K and 64K, respectively.
- Some variations of the SET command take effect only at the end of a batch; others take effect immediately. For example, SET ROWCOUNT, SET NOCOUNT, and SET ARITHIGNORE (and others) take effect immediately. SET SHOWPLAN, SET NOEXEC, and others take effect at the end of the batch. It is best practice to issue any SET commands first, in their own batch, followed by any other batches.
- Some commands must be issued in a batch by themselves. These commands include: CREATE DEFAULT, CREATE PROCEDURE, CREATE RULE, CREATE TRIGGER, and CREATE VIEW. Other commands, like CREATE TABLE, aren't restricted in this fashion, but usually should be written as the sole command in their batch.
- You cannot issue a DDL command, such as CREATE, ALTER, or DROP, and reference the subject of the DDL command in the same batch. This precludes activities like:
  - — Dropping a table, then re-creating it in a single batch
  - — Dropping (or creating) an object, then referencing it anywhere in the same batch
  - — Altering a table by adding a new column, then inserting data into the new column in the same batch
  - — Binding a rule or check constraint to a table and then requiring those rules or checks to enforce data integrity in a same batch

  Temporary objects are exempted from most of these rules.

Although it may seem trivial, SQL Server batches have been known to fail if the final GO statement in the batch is not followed by a carriage return!

Summary

This chapter introduced many of the fundamental concepts you will need to know to become a solid Transact-SQL programmer. Major points covered in this chapter include:

- Server character sets, which determine the full set of characters and symbols used by SQL Server, and server sort orders, which determine the way in which SQL Server sorts query result sets and compares values
- Identifiers, which name the user- and system-generated objects on a given server
- Literals
- Delimiters, reserved words and keywords, and operators, the symbols and words that SQL Server has invested with special meaning
- ISQL, the command-line method for interacting with SQL Server
- Transact-SQL batches and the GO command

5

Format and Style

There are probably more different coding styles than there are programmers in the world. Why? Each programmer uses more than one style throughout his career, depending on the programming language, tools, company standards, and personal preferences that change over time. Diversity itself is not an issue as long as others easily understand your style. There is no one canon for everyone to follow. However, certain commonsense rules and common practice govern how your code should be formatted.

This chapter discusses the main elements of a good coding style. We have also tried to consistently use the same style in all code examples throughout the book. You will find examples of Transact-SQL command formatting in almost every chapter.

Why Bother?

The importance of a good coding style and program formatting may not be that obvious when you are *writing* your code. But step on the other side and try to *read* someone else's program. Do you have to stop several times on every page and search for additional information scattered throughout various technical manuals? Has some critical information been lost when the original programmers left the project? Does your patience wear thin when you attempt to decrypt a particularly twisted programming trick? Too bad—the original author was probably very proud of it but forgot to comment. Do you want to know who the last person was to touch this program and what she changed? Can you find this information in the code? You know poor style when you see it.

Most authors don't intend to complicate program maintenance. There may be a few people who do that in an attempt to guarantee their job security. But most of us just don't have enough time to care about documentation and good coding style. Programmers are rewarded for completing tasks and not for making them easier for someone else years later. The details of the algorithm are too fresh in the author's mind, and exotic programming tricks are very clear to the person who wrote them. So why bother commenting, right? Moreover, it's much easier to type in all lowercase, not caring about elegant positioning and extra blanks.

There is no real incentive for programmers to produce code that is easy to maintain. Coding style is one of those "protect the environment" types of issues. You have to care about future generations (in this case, the programmers who will inherit your code). You need to be a conscientious person to spend extra time creating programs that are easy to maintain.

Most companies realize that the moral dilemma may be too hard for some. They consequently enforce coding style standards. Some companies become so concerned with programming style guidelines that at some point standardization work becomes completely detached from any practical tasks. It continues flying on its own, sucking up resources and not returning expected results. It may be quietly ignored or even hated by the very programmers it is supposed to benefit. The solution to this problem lies in finding a reasonable balance of uniformity and freedom. Any constitution has to be accepted by the members of the society it governs before they will conform to it. Similarly, programmers have to adopt a coding style voluntarily. Otherwise, it has a very slim chance of being followed.

Consistency in code produced by different teams on different projects makes it easier to maintain when programmers move from one group to another. The larger a particular project and the longer its expected life cycle, the more critical good style will be. More people will work with the same piece of code, more eyes will browse through its lines, and more minds will puzzle over a cryptic variable name or an unexplained algorithm.

What Is a Good Coding Style?

This section describes the most important aspects of a good coding style.

Self-Documenting Program

An ideal program contains enough information for a programmer to support it without additional documents. All the critical facts about the algorithm, possible input parameters, special conditions and requirements of use, and revision history are either obvious from the code or embedded in comments.

Granted, development and support documentation is necessary for any serious piece of code. What happens a few years after an application is born? The original developers may not be around to answer technical questions or make new modifications. Certain details of specifications, algorithms, and programming techniques may be forgotten over time. Moreover, even the author may not recognize his own program a year after writing it. Thus, documentation appreciates in value over time. But the reality is that programmers do not like writing documentation, and nobody enjoys reading technical documentation.

When a document is separate from a program, reading the code requires that you go back and forth between the two. It is the same as reading a book in a foreign language with a dictionary. It takes away the fun of reading and bores you too fast. Who said that work should be fun? Well, at least it should not be unnecessarily boring, or programmers will seek more exciting tasks elsewhere.

We are not suggesting that you eliminate documents. Any program with complicated algorithms and business logic needs a manual. But try to implant the basic facts (an abstract of the document if you wish) in the body of your program. Format the code to simplify reading and provide sufficient comments supplementing the lines of code.

Efficient Typing

Quick entry of the code is the least important factor of a good style. However, it is too often the dominating principle for programmers to choose how they write. Typing efficiency in itself is good. But consider: how long does it take to enter a program compared to other phases of its life? Optimizing something that may take 1% of the whole programming effort is not worth it.

```
its ez 2 type all txt in lwrcase abbreviate AMAP and never use shft key or
punctuation some people on 'net r doing that in order 2 type faster making it
hard for z rest 2 read
```

Your typing speed decreases when you have to think about whether you should press and hold the Shift key. Then while you are holding it down, you can type with only one hand. Some people prefer to use Caps Lock, but others (like us) always forget to turn it off and then have to retype part of the text.

Of course, if you write a one-time ad hoc query, you can ignore any standard and use the style that helps you type faster. But if you are writing a program that will serve its users for several years, do not allow typing performance considerations to obscure your view.

It takes a little extra effort to use UPPERCASE or Mixed_Case_And_Underscores and to spend additional time explaining your code in comments. But someone who deals with your creation later on may thank you for doing a good job. Are we being too idealistic?

Diversity of Styles

Each person has her own preferences in dress, food, hobbies, friends, and many other things. Programming format is another area where each one of us knows what is best. As we started writing the chapters of this book, we decided to agree first on the elements of programming style. Naturally, we wanted our code examples to look consistent throughout the book. Even among the three of us, we had different preferences on things like uppercase/lowercase use for Transact-SQL keywords and user object names, indenting BEGIN/END blocks, and naming conventions for stored procedures, triggers, and indexes. Imagine what happens on a large project with many programmers writing code!

Consistency

Being *consistent* in coding style and formatting is more important than choosing a particular style. You can standardize almost every style element in several reasonably good ways.

No matter how good your chosen style may be, there is always someone with different preferences. It is often a matter of experience from a previous project. Adjusting to a standard is not a major effort. It just requires understanding that it is important for the success of the project in the long run. Once members of a programming team accept the main reason behind enforcing certain guidelines, they usually adapt quickly.

Companies should create a set of no-nonsense rules and guidelines for all projects in the same operating environment and ask teams to adhere to them. This makes it easier for people transitioning between projects to read code written by others.

Preexisting Standards

Your choice of each particular style option may be influenced by several preexisting standards:

"Legacy" standards
: The company may have developed these for a different programming language and may now impose them on Transact-SQL code for the sake of interplatform consistency.

CASE tools
: Some of these tools allow configuring style options to a degree, but most are inflexible and generate code in a certain format. If this style is reasonably good, then you may simply follow it in manually written objects. It makes CASE-generated programs consistent with handwritten code. It is, however, too time-consuming to manually reformat CASE programs just because they do not conform to your chosen style. It may be better to compromise and keep CASE code intact while using a different standard for human programmers.

"De facto" standards
: These standards arise when previous programmers on your project have used a certain style they liked. If the amount of such existing code is significant and the style is reasonable, it may be best to adopt it as the standard for all future development. Otherwise, you need to choose a different style and implement it for all new objects. Rewriting existing objects to comply with the new style is usually hard to justify. We recommend that you keep the old code unchanged and apply the new style only to new objects and to those that you need to modify significantly for other reasons.

Prevailing industry standards
: You may want to use what is commonly adopted by others. It helps newcomers in your team to adjust quickly because most style elements are already familiar to them. Do not use exotic style elements. Try to follow standards that you see in books, vendor technical documentation, and other projects.

Sometimes legacy standards or outdated tools may impose unnecessary restrictions on your Transact-SQL code. One of us used to work for a company that employed a mainframe-based data dictionary system to maintain table, view, and column names for DB2, DS/SQL, Microsoft SQL Server, and Oracle. It limited the length of user-defined names to 18 characters. As a result, SQL Server identifiers had to be shorter than allowed by Transact-SQL. That forced aggressive abbreviations and in some cases made programs less readable.

What Should Be Standardized?

There are only a few style items that should be subject to standardization:

- Case of keywords and user-defined names
- Naming conventions: standard abbreviations, object name prefixes and suffixes
- Error handling
- Use of indents, space characters, commas, and blank lines
- Formatting of DDL and DML statements
- Formatting of transaction blocks and procedural blocks
- Comments: header, revision history, and program body comments

The rest of this chapter shows you the most popular options for each style element. If you need to develop a coding style standard for your company or just want to choose your own style—remember that you have choices.

Don't Overkill

A coding standard should not become overkill. This is one type of regulation that does not have to be religiously followed. Occasional violations do not cause a bug in the program; they may just slow down future support. So instead of strict rules, it is better to adopt guidelines. In some cases, programmers should even be allowed to choose from a set of formatting options.

An unnecessarily restrictive coding standard costs more than it saves. The soul of a standard involves making the code easier to maintain. No-exceptions-allowed policies that require indents, blanks, and comment formatting to conform to a rigid standard alienates programmers. Developers deserve some freedom in choosing their programming style.

If some object has been coded in a completely different style, it may be wise to leave it as is until modifications become necessary. Remember that formatting is important for maintenance. Some programs have never been changed since their creation. Maybe an object that violates every standard you've adopted isn't ever going to be modified anyway. Why bother reformatting it? But once you decide that it has to be altered for any reason, you may as well reformat it and make it compliant with the current standard.

One of us once worked on a project in which coding standards were observed religiously. Programmers were sent back to modify their stored procedures when they dared to use a tab instead of eight spaces for indents. Tabs were banned in case someone used a different editor. Peer code reviews lasted for hours to nail down every case of improperly indented BEGIN/END blocks, incorrect order of header line comments, or use of two column names on one line of a SELECT. The company hired almost 100 people to work on the project. Granted, standards were important, but they took a very high toll on programmers' productive time. Guess what? The project ran way over the budget and got scrapped. All this wonderfully formatted code has been thrown away. Don't let the same thing happen to your work!

Case of Keywords and User-Defined Names

Transact-SQL reserved words and keywords can be coded in uppercase, lowercase, or mixed case. Good style requires that you choose a case and apply it consistently in all programs.

User-defined elements are names of user databases, objects (tables, views, stored procedures, triggers, defaults, rules, indexes, constraints), table columns, and global and local variables. On a SQL Server with case-insensitive sort order, you have the flexibility to code any user-defined name in any case. But this flexibility may lead to a mess when the same object is referred to in a different case. For example, on a server with a case-insensitive sort order, the names authors, Authors, and AUTHORS all refer to the same table name. On a case-sensitive server, these names would refer to different objects. Some discipline is required from a programmer on a case-insensitive server to code user-defined names consistently in the same case.

Table 5-1 shows the various case choices for SQL keywords and reserved words.

Table 5-1. Case Choices for Transact-SQL Keywords and Reserved Words

Case	Example	Comments
lowercase	`select @@rowcount`	Very popular because it is the fastest to type. It is also the style used in most system stored procedures. It is a good choice when user-defined elements are all uppercase.
Capitalized	`Select @@Rowcount`	Rarely used.

Table 5-1. Case Choices for Transact-SQL Keywords and Reserved Words (continued)

Case	Example	Comments
MixedCase	`Select @@RowCount`	Rarely used.
UPPERCASE	`SELECT @@ROWCOUNT`	This is probably the most popular style in books on SQL programming and standards adopted by many corporations. It makes keywords easy to identify, provided that lowercase or mixed case is adopted for user-defined names.

Use system-defined names (e.g., master, *sp_who*, sysobjects) exactly as they appear in the database—that is, in lowercase. Original names should be preserved even if your server is set up as case-insensitive. It makes your code portable between different servers.

Table 5-2 shows the various case choices for user-defined names.

Table 5-2. Case Choices for User-Defined Names

Case	Example	Comments

lowercasewithout underscores	`titleauthors`
	`@booklimitprice`
	`@ioperformance`
	`casetoolslist`
		We recommend against using this style. It is much harder to read than the next one.

lowercase_with_ underscores	`title_authors`
	`@book_limit_price`
	`@i_o_performance`
	`case_tools_list`
		Very popular among programmers, in books, and in vendor manuals. Also used in system stored procedures and in the pubs sample database.

MixedCaseWithout Underscores	`TitleAuthors`
	`@BookLimitPrice`
	`@IOPerformance`
	`CASEToolsList`
		This style is widely used in GUI development languages and is popular. Names that contain an abbreviation or a one-character element are at a disadvantage, as demonstrated by the last two examples. An all-capital element is inseparable from the next word in the name and may be confusing at times.

Mixed_Case_With_ Underscores	`Title_Authors`
	`@Book_Limit_Price`
	`@I_O_Performance`
	`CASE_Tools_List`
		This style is easier to read than the previous one and is popular. The price is a more frequent use of the Shift key.

UPPERCASE_ WITH_UNDER-SCORES	`TITLE_AUTHORS`
	`@BOOK_LIMIT_PRICE`
	`@I_O_PERFORMANCE`
	`CASE_TOOLS_LIST`
		This style makes sense when lowercase is used for keywords.

Table 5-3 shows the most popular combinations of case selection for keywords and user-defined names.

Table 5-3. Choosing the Right Case Mix for Keywords and User-Defined Names

Keywords and Reserved Words	User-Defined Names	Examples	Comments
lowercase	lowercase_with_underscores	`select * from title_authors` `select @cd_rom = 1`	Programmers like this style because it is easy to type. However, it is often difficult to tell user-defined names from keywords.
lowercase	Mixed_Case_With_Underscores	`select * from Title_Authors` `select @CD_ROM = 1`	This style is easy to type and read. Programs resemble normal nontechnical text more than any other style does.
UPPERCASE	lowercase_with_underscores	`SELECT * FROM title_authors` `SELECT @cd_rom = 1`	This style makes all keywords stand out. It is widely adopted in the industry and used in many books and technical documentation. This is also the style that we have chosen for this book.[a]
UPPERCASE	Mixed_Case_With_Underscores	`SELECT * FROM Title_Authors` `SELECT @CD_ROM = 1`	This style makes keywords stand out. Use of all-uppercase abbreviations in names may represent a problem. It makes them look like keywords, as demonstrated by the @cd_rom variable name in the example.[a]

[a] When your code contains a lot of keywords, then uppercase becomes predominant and slows down reading. ALL-CAPS TEXT IS USUALLY EVEN LESS COMPREHENSIBLE than the proverbial fine print. The latter is just more difficult to notice on the back of a promotional brochure. When lowercase prevails in your code, there is more whitespace between the lines. It simplifies reading.

Enforcing consistent case is less critical for names of local variables than it is for permanent object names, because local variable names are important only within a particular object.

Naming Conventions and Abbreviations

The length of user-defined names is limited. Current versions of Microsoft SQL Server and Sybase allow names of up to 30 characters. Names of temporary tables should be even shorter—20 characters on Microsoft SQL Server 6.x and 12 characters on Sybase and older versions of Microsoft SQL Server.* These limitations may force you to abbreviate certain words in a user-defined name. Abbreviations are in order and are commonly used in many companies. It is critical that once an abbreviation is introduced, it be used consistently throughout all programs. There should be one and only one abbreviation for each word, and the word itself should not be spelled completely in names if it has an abbreviation. Sometimes it is proper to abbreviate several words or a phrase.

As we discussed in Chapter 4, *Transact-SQL Fundamentals*, Transact-SQL has a list of reserved words that may not be used as user-defined object names. There is also a list of keywords that are not yet reserved but may become reserved in the future. Vendors recommend that you not use them either, because future versions of Transact-SQL may restrict them and force you to modify your code. This has already happened in the past when both Microsoft and Sybase departed from SQL Server 4.x and made many new words reserved for the sake of ANSI standards compliance.

Try to use shorter names as long as they are not too cryptic. It helps to reduce the size of the program code, so it reads faster. It also makes lines shorter and helps avoid excessive line wrapping. Shorter names may be used for more "transitory" objects that exist only within the context of your stored procedure or trigger—names of temporary tables and their columns, temporary stored procedures, and user-defined variables. Parameters of stored procedures are a different story, because they may be used in other objects by name.

What to Avoid in User-Defined Names

The following list demonstrates typical mistakes in object naming in examples from standard SQL Server databases:

Confusing abbreviations

Example: pubs means publications, but may be confused with a beer-drinking establishment . . . especially after a hard day at work!

Commemorating your company name in the database name

Examples: msdb (Microsoft SQL Server only)—this database is used to store information about scheduled tasks and has nothing specific to do with Microsoft; sybsystemprocs (Sybase only)—the syb prefix (which apparently means Sybase) does not make the name easier to remember and does not further clarify the purpose of the database.

* It is still possible to create a temporary table with a name of up to 30 characters, but certain limitations apply.

Using db prefix or suffix in database names

It must be obvious from the context that it is a database name. Examples: msdb (Microsoft SQL Server only), tempdb.

Using all-lowercase names without underscores

Examples: column names used in pubs tables: lorange, highqty, roysched.

Using inconsistent abbreviations for the same word

Examples: the word "low" is abbreviated in column name lorange and spelled completely in lowqty.

Using unclear abbreviations

Example: column pr_info in table pub_info—abbreviation pr could be misinterpreted in several ways because many words begin with pr.

Using quoted identifiers

This configurable option in SQL Server (introduced in Chapter 4) allows you to use user-defined names that contain space characters, special characters, or start with a digit. While this option gives you extra flexibility in choosing names, it is not supported by most third-party software and your code may not port to any other system without additional work. When this option is enabled, quoted identifiers have to be enclosed in double quotes, and string constants should be enclosed only in single quotes to avoid being confused with identifiers. It sometimes makes the code very confusing.

Best abbreviations are those that are commonsense and widely used in technical and general literature, such as ID for identification, QTY for quantity, MAX for maximum, YTD for year-to-date, SSN for social security number, TEL for telephone, and so on. Choose intuitive abbreviations. Do not be too aggressive in cutting words. For example, AMT is a better choice for amount than AM, PROD is better for product than PR. Make sure an abbreviation is not related to a particular context. For example, NO may be a good abbreviation for the word number in ACCT_NO. But it is confusing in FLAG_NO where it may be misinterpreted as a flag indicating false. Once you abbreviate a word, do it the same way in all objects regardless of the context.

Do not use the full word that already has an abbreviation. For example, if you abbreviate the word quantity as qty, then you should not create a column called quantity along with another one called high_qty.

Do not use all 30 characters allowed by SQL Server for table names. If you are going to use a special suffix or prefix for indexes, triggers, and constraints associated with a table, then the table name needs to be shorter than 30 to allow space for the suffix/prefix. Choose the maximum length based on the standard for prefixes and suffixes discussed in the next section.

If you introduce abbreviations, you need to maintain a data dictionary. Some CASE tools will do that for you. If you do not use one, then you may just create a table on your SQL Server to maintain abbreviations:

```
CREATE TABLE abbreviations (
    abbreviation         CHAR(30)      NOT NULL,
    full_word_or_phrase  VARCHAR(255)  NOT NULL
)
```

If you have built a database full of objects and used underscores to separate words in user-defined names, you can use the stored procedure *sp_object_name_words* included on the CD-ROM that accompanies this book. It reviews all words and abbreviations you have already used in your identifiers. It extracts information from system tables in the current database. Run it in your user databases to see if you have redundant, inconsistent, or confusing abbreviations.

Prefixes and Suffixes

Many developers use special prefixes and suffixes to indicate object type, application area, or relation to another object in a database. Some prefixes and suffixes are justified, and some are unnecessary. System stored procedures in SQL Server have names starting with a standard prefix of "sp." Most system tables have a name prefix of "sys."

Table 5-4 shows various choices for prefixes and suffixes.

Table 5-4. Use of Prefixes and Suffixes in User-Defined Names

Prefix or Suffix	Example	Comment
Prefix or suffix in all object names to indicate object type	Prefix `t_` in all table names, prefix `v_` in all view names, prefix `up_` in all user stored procedure names.	We do not recommend this. It is true that the object type is obvious from the context. Table and view use is almost the same semantically, so you cannot tell the object type from the context. But we make no exception for views. If you ever convert them into tables, then the name prefix indicating that the object is a view would have to change to indicate a table. This calls for the revision of all programs that reference the object.
Prefix or suffix in all column or variable names to indicate datatype	Prefix `i` for all integer columns or variables, prefix `c` for character, prefix `d` for datetime.	GUI developers may find this style very familiar. It helps the programmer avoid mistakes when comparing or converting datatypes.

Table 5-4. Use of Prefixes and Suffixes in User-Defined Names (continued)

Prefix or Suffix	Example	Comment
Prefix or suffix in an index name to indicate index type	Index name contains suffixes like _pk to indicate a primary key, _unq to indicate a unique index, and _cl to indicate a clustered index.	This helps read optimizer hints referring to index names in the code. If an index definition ever changes, this style requires you to alter the index name accordingly. This causes the extra work of finding and correcting every reference to the index in all your Transact-SQL programs.
Prefix or suffix in a trigger name to indicate trigger type	Trigger name is formed as the underlying table with a suffix _ti for trigger on insert, _tu on update, or _td on delete.	This allows you to quickly select all trigger names related to one table from sysobjects by executing: SELECT name FROM sysobjects WHERE name like '<table_name>t%' Table names have to be shorter than 30 characters in order to leave room for a suffix.
Prefix indicating application name	All stored procedures for accounting application have a prefix of ac_, human resources have hr_, etc.	This makes sense when objects for different applications share the same database. It is not justified if all user objects in a database would have the same prefix as a result.
Prefix indicating application area	All reporting stored procedures have a prefix of rp_, all batch processing procedures have a prefix or bat_, all staging tables used for data loads have a prefix of stg_, etc.	This helps to quickly select names of all objects in a particular subject area.
Suffix in stored procedure names to indicate action type	Stored procedure name is formed of a table name with a suffix _sel for select, _upd for update, etc.	This is fine for stored procedures that perform a single operation on a table but does not work for complex ones.
Prefix in all quasi-temporary objects (permanent objects you do not intend to keep for a long time)	All "temporary" objects in databases other than tempdb begin with tmp.	This is a good idea, because such objects are easy to identify when you do your database "housekeeping" and cleaning.
Standard prefix for all temporary object names in addition to # or ##	All temporary table names begin with #temp_.	Do not use this. "#" already indicates the temporary nature of the object, and an additional prefix is unnecessary. Another problem is that object names in tempdb should not exceed 12 characters for Sybase and 20 characters for Microsoft SQL Server. The additional prefix takes away several more precious positions.

One of us used to consult with a client who dragged a mainframe-born standard onto SQL Server stored procedure names. Every name had to begin with a three-character prefix that defined an application. This prefix was the same for all stored procedures on the project, even though they did not share the database with any other application. The fourth and fifth characters could be used for a business function description (from a standard list of a couple dozen such functions). The sixth character was left to the programmer's discretion. The seventh described an action on data (retrieve, add, modify, etc.), and the eighth was a hardcoded A. Needless to say, it was impossible to tell the purpose of a stored procedure without opening the code and looking at the comments.

Index Names

SQL Server doesn't require you to make index names unique in a database, but it is better not to use the same index name on two or more tables. Good index names are important if you use optimizer hints because then they actually appear in the code. Give indexes descriptive names reflecting the column name or the composite key description. Index type may be reflected in a prefix or suffix.

Database Names

There are usually so few databases on a SQL Server compared to the number of objects that databases deserve special descriptive names.

The best database name is the name or acronym of the application it serves. One of our colleagues once suggested picking database names from the official list of future hurricane names. It would be difficult to link such names to application names, but it sure would be fun. Imagine a conversation at the coffee machine in your corporate office:

Q: What happened to Hugo last night?

A: We tried restoring it from a backup, but then *George* got corrupt again and we had to fix it.

If you are still wondering, this idea did not fly in a corporate environment.

Standard Error Handling

It is important to standardize the way errors and exceptions are handled in Transact-SQL code. You need to consider the following error-processing aspects in terms of good coding standards:

- Transact-SQL commands that may cause runtime errors requiring special handling
- Standard methods of error processing
- Samples of error-handling code

As a rule of thumb, you should test every INSERT, UPDATE, and DELETE command for errors. They may cause errors that do not interrupt your program unless you handle them programmatically. Examples of such errors are key and constraint violations and deadlocks. This topic is covered in detail in Chapter 9, *Error Handling*. You will also find error-handling code samples there.

Program exceptions are not limited to Transact-SQL error messages. In any application you will also find a number of logical conditions based on business rules that require special processing.

There are quite a few ways to handle errors:

- Print error message with the PRINT or SELECT command.
- Exit a stored procedure with a special RETURN code indicating an error to the calling procedure or Transact-SQL batch.
- Use the RAISERROR command to report the error in the output, the SQL Server ERRORLOG, or the NT event log.
- Use the *xp_logevent* extended stored procedure to record the error in the NT event log.
- Store error information in a user table.
- Use other methods of recording errors in user-defined objects or files.

All of these commands are explained elsewhere in the book (see Chapters 3, 9, 14, and 17).

Style Odds and Ends

This section summarizes a variety of style recommendations not discussed elsewhere.

Editors and Word Processors

Editors and word processors that you use to develop Transact-SQL code influence your formatting. If they support different fonts, make sure that you choose a non-proportional font such as `Courier New`. It helps preserve indentation when the same code is viewed in a different editor. If you choose a word processor to enter Transact-SQL programs, you have to suppress all "intelligence" it provides, such as automatic capitalization of the first word in a sentence, conversion to lowercase or uppercase, automatic spelling correction, "smart" quotes, and so forth. These functions are designed to simplify normal text typing rather than program code entry.

Indents and Tabs

Indentation of code lines in accordance with the hierarchy of algorithm steps is one of the major elements of program formatting. You may choose several space characters as your indent step, or you may use a Tab character. Tabs certainly save keystrokes during code entry. But make sure that they indent to the 8th, 16th, 24th, and so on, positions in different editors used in your company. If they use some other indentation (especially one tied to a distance from the left side of the sheet, rather than the number of characters), your code will look different in text editors such as Windows' Notepad, Wordpad, and others.

In this book, we use four space characters as the standard indent step in our code examples. We could not use Tab characters because we have used a word processor, and our tabs would not line up the same way in a plain text editor. However, you are free to choose your own style. If you select four spaces for your standard indent, you will also be able to use the Tab character when you need to skip two indent steps.

Indents should be used to shift nested lines of code to the right. Indent inner statements of WHILE loops, BEGIN/END blocks, IF/ELSE constructs, continuations of wrapped long lines, and other appropriate statements. Indents also help to format multiline DDL and DML statements to simplify reading.

Use extra levels of indentation for nested blocks, as in the following example:

```
WHILE <condition1>
BEGIN
    <statements>
    IF <condition2>
    BEGIN
        <statements>
        WHILE <condition3>
        BEGIN
            <statements>
        END
    END
    <statements>
END
```

Blank Lines and Space Characters

Use blank lines around multiline commands and blocks of code that relate to one step of the algorithm.

Use whitespace (blank, tab, or line break) to separate each element of a Transact-SQL line: keyword, reserved word, object name, variable, parenthesis, operation sign, and so on. Whitespace simplifies navigation through the code by "next word tabbing" (standard Ctrl-RightArrow and Ctrl-LeftArrow in Windows) and usually makes it more readable.

The following style is not recommended:

```
SELECT discount=str(discount,5,2)+'%' FROM discounts WHERE lowqty=100
```

Use extra space characters and line breaks to show each element and ease code navigation with "hot" keys:

```
SELECT  discount = str( discount, 5, 2 ) + '%'
FROM    discounts
WHERE   lowqty = 100
```

Commas

In most styles, commas immediately follow the previous word. Some programmers choose to use commas in front of an element in a multiline list as in the example in Table 5-5.

Table 5-5. Positioning of Commas

Commas Before an Element	Commas After an Element

<pre>SELECT a.state
       ,a.stor_name
       ,c.title
       ,b.qty
FROM   stores a
       ,sales b
       ,titles c
WHERE   a.stor_id = b.stor_id
    AND b.title_id = c.title_id
    AND b.ord_date = '06/15/1992'</pre>
	<pre>SELECT a.state,
	        a.stor_name,
	        c.title,
	        b.qty
	FROM stores a,
	        sales b,
	        titles c
	WHERE a.stor_id = b.stor_id
	    AND b.title_id = c.title_id
	    AND b.ord_date = '06/15/1992'</pre>

The positioning of commas shown in the left column of Table 5-5 is consistent with the use of AND/OR in the WHERE clause. Indeed, ANDs in the example precede each condition in the same way that commas precede each column name in the SELECT clause and table name in the FROM clause. All commas are also aligned nicely. However, this is different from the way commas are placed in almost any other technical document or work of literature—right after the word rather than before it. Formatting of the same query shown in the right column of Table 5-5 is more conventional.

Quotes

Transact-SQL allows you to use either single or double quotes to indicate literal strings. The choice of using one or another is entirely yours. It is easier to type single quotes because they do not require using the Shift key. You may still want to use double quotes on those occasions when your string contains a single quote inside. But you may also repeat a quote twice if the same one is used to surround the literal.

Literal strings cannot be enclosed in double quotes if you use the quoted identifiers option.

Wrapping Long Lines

Even if you consistently use a separate line for each list element, you still have to wrap lines sometimes. Line length should be defined by the capabilities of the word processors or code editors used by all developers on the project. You have to settle for "the least common denominator"—a line length that will fit on any screen with any editor. Scrolling the screen to the right in order to see the tail of a long line significantly slows down reading. Wrapped lines should be indented against the beginning one.

You may choose to ignore this guideline when it improves reading. It may also be necessary to make an exception when you have a long literal string (e.g., in a PRINT statement that has to print a line wider than your screen).

Formatting DML and DDL Statements

DML and DDL statements typically consist of multiple clauses and multiple list elements, such as lists of columns, values, object names, and conditions. They usually do not fit into one line on the screen and have to be formatted in multiple lines.

Formatting DML Statements

SELECT, INSERT, UPDATE, and DELETE statements consist of several clauses. There are many ways to format them. Some of the most popular ones are shown in Table 5-6.

Table 5-6. SELECT Statement Formatting

<table>
<tr><th>Style</th><th>Example</th><th>Comments</th></tr>
<tr><td>Each clause is indented compared to the command itself.</td><td><pre>
SELECT a.state,
        a.stor_name,
        c.title,
        b.qty
    FROM stores a,
         sales b,
         titles c
    WHERE   a.stor_id = b.stor_id
        AND b.title_id = c.title_id
        AND b.ord_date = '06/15/1992'
    ORDER BY a.state
</pre></td><td>This is a popular style, but it shifts your code to the right and alignment of elements is not as good as the next one.</td></tr>
<tr><td>All clauses are lined up at the same position. Multiple conditions within a WHERE clause are indented by four space characters.</td><td><pre>
SELECT a.state,
        a.stor_name,
        c.title,
        b.qty
FROM   stores a,
        sales b,
        titles c
WHERE   a.stor_id = b.stor_id
    AND b.title_id = c.title_id
    AND b.ord_date = '06/15/1992'
ORDER BY a.state
</pre></td><td>This is the style we recommend. We have used it for the code examples in this book.</td></tr>
<tr><td>Same as preceding, but conditions within WHERE are not indented.</td><td><pre>
SELECT a.state,
        a.stor_name,
        c.title,
        b.qty
FROM   stores a,
        sales b,
        titles c
WHERE   a.stor_id = b.stor_id
AND   b.title_id = c.title_id
AND   b.ord_date = '06/15/1992'
ORDER BY a.state
</pre></td><td>This style may save you a few characters during typing, but we favor indenting ANDs and ORs as in the previous style.</td></tr>
<tr><td>All clause words are lined up at the right position, while all clause elements are lined up at the left. This style leaves the same number of blanks separating the end of each clause word from elements.</td><td><pre>
  SELECT a.state,
         a.stor_name,
         c.title,
         b.qty
    FROM stores a,
         sales b,
         titles c
   WHERE a.stor_id = b.stor_id
     AND b.title_id = c.title_id
     AND b.ord_date = '06/15/1992'
ORDER BY a.state
</pre></td><td>This style has some aesthetic elegance but requires extra effort when formatting lines. It is not very widespread. Use at your own discretion.</td></tr>
</table>

Use aliases for table names. An alias should resemble the table name but still be short. One or two characters should normally suffice for an alias. Longer ones defeat the purpose of using them. Table 5-7 summarizes the uses of table names aliases.

You may set your preferred style to use full table names, but you cannot completely evade aliases. They are necessary when a table is self-joined or otherwise participates in the query several times.

Table 5-7. Use of Table Name Aliases

Style	Example	Comments

Aliases are assigned alphabetically.	`SELECT   a.state,`
	`         a.stor_name,`
	`         c.title,`
	`         b.qty`
	`FROM     stores a,`
	`         sales  b,`
	`         titles c`
	`WHERE    a.stor_id  = b.stor_id`
	`AND      b.title_id = c.title_id`
	`AND      b.ord_date = '06/15/1992'`
	`ORDER BY a.state`
		This style is simple enough to follow and provides the shortest alias possible, but it may be a little difficult to read when several tables are involved, because the reader has to look up table names in the FROM clause for aliases.

Aliases are very short table name abbreviations.	`SELECT   st.state,`
	`         st.stor_name,`
	`         t.title,`
	`         sal.qty`
	`FROM     stores st,`
	`         sales  sal,`
	`         titles t`
	`WHERE    st.stor_id    = sal.stor_id`
	`AND      sal.title_id = t.title_id`
	`AND      sal.ord_date = '06/15/1992'`
	`ORDER BY st.state`
		Aliases may be a little longer than one character, because some tables in the query may begin with the same first letter. It takes a few more keystrokes when the code is entered but makes it more readable.

No aliases used.	`SELECT   stores.state,`
	`         stores.stor_name,`
	`         titles.title,`
	`         sales.qty`
	`FROM     stores,`
	`         sales,`
	`         titles`
	`WHERE    stores.stor_id = sales.stor_id`
	`AND      sales.title_id = titles.title_id`
	`AND      sales.ord_date = '06/15/1992'`
	`ORDER BY stores.state`
		The table name is obvious in each referenced column. The code takes longer to enter than when aliases are used. In some cases, this style will be more difficult to read because table names may be long and a reader will have to browse through more text.

UPDATE and DELETE statement formatting is very similar to SELECT statement formatting. An example of an UPDATE is shown here:

```
UPDATE  stores
SET     stor_name = upper( stor_name )
WHERE   stor_id like '7%'
    AND state   = 'WA'
```

In most cases, it is better to place each element of a list (e.g., a list of columns in a SELECT clause) on a separate line. It usually takes more lines and makes the overall code longer but easier to read. Some exceptions (illustrated in the next few examples) may be in order for very short queries.

The following example shows the formatting of a short SELECT statement. Here, standard formatting requires a separate line for each clause:

```
SELECT  stor_name
FROM    stores
ORDER BY 1
```

A reasonable deviation from the standard allows putting the whole command into one line, if the programmer desires:

```
SELECT stor_name FROM stores ORDER BY 1
```

In the next example of a short INSERT statement, standard formatting requires formatting the INSERT on multiple lines:

```
INSERT  discounts (
    discounttype,
    stor_id,
    discount
)
VALUES (
    'Holiday Sale',
    NULL,
    10
)
```

But if you put the same command in two lines, it becomes easier to match values and columns:

```
INSERT  discounts ( discounttype,   stor_id, discount )
VALUES            ( 'Holiday Sale', NULL,    10       )
```

Note the extra blanks added to align each value right under the corresponding column name.

The exceptions we've shown here should be left to the programmer's discretion and neither restricted nor recommended in a coding style standard.

Formatting DDL Statements

DDL statements are best formatted with each element on a separate line. An example of a CREATE TABLE statement is shown in Table 5-8.

Table 5-8. CREATE TABLE Statement Formatting

Style	Example	Comments

CREATE TABLE statement formatted by Microsoft SQL Enterprise Manager	`CREATE TABLE dbo.authors (`
	`au_id id NOT NULL ,`
	`au_lname varchar (40) NOT NULL ,`
	`au_fname varchar (20) NOT NULL ,`
	`phone char (12) NOT NULL ,`
	`address varchar (40) NULL ,`
	`city varchar (20) NULL ,`
	`state char (2) NULL ,`
	`zip char (5) NULL ,`
	`contract bit NOT NULL`
	`)`
		Column definitions may be difficult to read.

Column-aligned formatting	`CREATE TABLE dbo.authors (`
	`au_id    id          NOT NULL ,`
	`au_lname varchar(40) NOT NULL ,`
	`au_fname varchar(20) NOT NULL ,`
	`phone    char(12)    NOT NULL ,`
	`address  varchar(40) NULL ,`
	`city     varchar(20) NULL ,`
	`state    char(2)     NULL ,`
	`zip      char(5)     NULL ,`
	`contract bit         NOT NULL`
	`)`
		Datatypes and NULL/ NOT NULL properties are aligned and are easier to read.

SQL Server does not preserve the original author's DDL statement formatting for permanent tables, unlike the code of stored procedures, triggers, and views. Therefore, CREATE TABLE statement formatting is important only when it appears in a stored procedure or in case you maintain original DDL files for your objects. Otherwise, a DDL statement may be treated as an ad hoc query for which formatting is not important.

Formatting Transaction Blocks and Procedural Blocks

Transaction blocks and procedural blocks are series of Transact-SQL commands that represent one or more macrosteps of a program.

Formatting Transaction Blocks

Your coding style may define whether the transaction-control statements BEGIN, COMMIT, COMMIT, ROLLBACK, and SAVE TRANSACTION require any special indentation. On the one hand, they do not denote a procedural block, and indentation may seem superfluous. On the other hand, indentation helps to locate the beginning and end of a transaction block. We recommend that you avoid indenting inner statements in a transaction, because doing so may conflict with indentation of procedural blocks.

In the following example, the transaction block does not need indentation:

```
BEGIN TRAN correct_qty

UPDATE  sales
SET     qty = qty + 10
WHERE   stor_id  = '7131'
    AND ord_num  = 'P3087a'
    AND title_id = 'PS3333'

UPDATE  titles
SET     ytd_sales = ytd_sales + 10
WHERE   title_id  = 'PS3333'

IF @@ERROR = 0
BEGIN
    COMMIT TRAN correct_qty
END
ELSE
BEGIN
    ROLLBACK TRAN correct_qty
    PRINT 'Transaction failed'
END
```

The commands between BEGIN TRAN and COMMIT TRAN are not indented. This example illustrates that it is difficult to reconcile indentation between transaction and procedural blocks.

Transact-SQL allows the naming of each transaction. It is easier to locate the beginning and end of a named transaction than of an unnamed one. Transaction names also leave a trace in the transaction log and some third-party DBA tools such as Platinum Technologies' Log Analyzer may retrieve this information if necessary (visit Platinum Technology's web site for more details).

Formatting Procedural Blocks

Procedural blocks should always be indented in order to show the hierarchy of algorithm steps. Whether you use a single or a compound statement (enclosed in BEGIN...END), block indentation dramatically simplifies reading. There are several ways to position a BEGIN...END block, as shown in Table 5-9.

We use the BEGIN . . . END construct even when there is only one statement in the block. Transact-SQL syntax allows you to use a single statement after WHILE,

Table 5-9. Formatting of a Compound Block (BEGIN/END)

Style	Example	Comments

BEGIN/END are positioned under the corresponding WHILE, IF, or ELSE statement.	`WHILE <condition>`
	`BEGIN`
	    `<multiple lines of code>`
	`END`
	`IF <condition>`
	`BEGIN`
	    `<a single line of code>`
	`END`
	`ELSE IF <condition>`
	`BEGIN`
	    `<multiple lines of code>`
	`END`
	`ELSE BEGIN`
	    `<multiple lines of code>`
	`END`
		A very popular style. END is easy to match against the corresponding BEGIN.

BEGIN/END block is indented against the WHILE, IF, or ELSE and statements within BEGIN/END are also indented.	`WHILE <condition>`
	    `BEGIN`
	        `<multiple lines of code>`
	    `END`
	`IF <condition>`
	    `BEGIN`
	        `<a single line of code>`
	    `END`
	`ELSE IF <condition>`
	    `BEGIN`
	        `<multiple lines of code>`
	    `END`
	`ELSE`
	    `BEGIN`
	        `<multiple lines of code>`
	    `END`
		An extra indent compared to the previous style does not simplify reading.

BEGIN is placed in the same line with WHILE, IF, or ELSE; END is aligned under the corresponding WHILE, IF, or ELSE, rather than BEGIN.	`WHILE <condition> BEGIN`
	    `<multiple lines of code>`
	    `END`
	`IF <condition> BEGIN`
	    `<a single line of code>`
	`END`
	`ELSE IF <condition> BEGIN`
	    `<multiple lines of code>`
	`END`
	`ELSE BEGIN`
	    `<multiple lines of code>`
	    `END`
		This style is easy to read and saves you one line of total program length every time you use it. END becomes an operand that closes every WHILE, IF, or ELSE. It especially makes sense if you consistently use BEGIN/END after WHILE, IF, and ELSE, regardless of how many lines are included in the block.

IF, or ELSE. But it frequently causes errors when the code is modified and extra statements are inserted between the condition and the immediately following line.

Do not use BEGIN . . . END to surround all lines of code within a stored procedure or trigger. It is semantically unnecessary and does not help in reading the code, as shown in Table 5-10.

Table 5-10. Using BEGIN . . . END Around All Stored Procedure Statements Is Unnecessary

Not Recommended	Recommended

`CREATE PROCEDURE example`
`AS`
`BEGIN`
`    <stored procedure code>`
`END`
`GO`
	`CREATE PROCEDURE example`
	`AS`
	`<stored procedure code>`
	`GO`

Commenting Your Code

Comments are important in practically any computer language. Program body comments explain rules, algorithms, and other details not obvious from the code. Header comments explain the purpose of the program and special execution conditions and provide revision history information.

Transact-SQL provides two different ways to introduce comments. The "old" comment style is to enclose any portion of the program in /* and */ tags. It may be one or several lines or just a part of one line.

The new style (not supported in SQL Server 4.x) is to use a double-dash "--" to indicate that the remainder of the line is a comment. It is easier to type and does not look as heavy in the code as the /* . . . */ style. But if you need to introduce several lines of comment or want to temporarily comment out a block of code, then /* . . . */ tags are easier to enter. Double-dash tags have to be repeated at the beginning of every commented line.

Double-dashes are good for the "remainder of the line" comments.

It would be unwise to standardize one comment style or another. What information is commented is more important than which tags indicate a comment.

Program Body Comments

Comments should explain the algorithm if it is not obvious from the code itself. Use business description and process explanation comments. Avoid commenting on the obvious. Table 5-11 shows various commenting styles for the program body.

Table 5-11. Use of Comments

<table>
<tr><th>Not Recommended</th><th>Recommended</th></tr>
<tr><td><pre>-- report error 99999 and return
RAISERROR 99999 "System error"
RETURN -1</pre></td><td>No comment is necessary at all—the purpose of the code is obvious.</td></tr>
<tr><td><pre>-- set rowcount to 100 and delete
-- rows of roysched in a loop
SET ROWCOUNT 100
WHILE 1=1
BEGIN
    DELETE roysched
    -- if rowcount=0 break
    IF @@ROWCOUNT = 0 BREAK
END</pre></td><td><pre>-- delete all roysched rows
-- in small batches to avoid
-- overflowing transaction log
SET ROWCOUNT 100
WHILE 1=1
BEGIN
    -- delete up to 100 rows
    DELETE roysched
    -- stop when the table is empty
    IF @@ROWCOUNT = 0 BREAK
END</pre></td></tr>
</table>

Header Comments

Header comments should explain the purpose of the program, rules, restrictions, and implications of use, and should include history and revision information. Locate header comments in your stored procedure or trigger CREATE statement right after the CREATE line. Then such comments are kept in the syscomments system table together with the object source code and may be reverse-engineered with the whole object code. If you separate a header comment from CREATE with a GO, then it is not kept in the database. Some SQL Server experts argue that removing comments from the code helps reduce the size of the syscomments table and improves the performance. We believe that this is not a good approach. Performance improvements are marginal, while code maintenance may be complicated when comments are not stored in your SQL Server.

The exact format of the header comment should be chosen by the development team. We offer you several ideas on what to put and what not to put in the header. The following example speaks for itself:

```
CREATE PROC sale_price_adjustment
--------------------------------------------------
-- Purpose: Adjust single title sale price for one
--          store, given discount percent.
-- Revision History:
--------------------------------------------------
-- Version 1.00  W.A.Mozart   12/05/1791
-- Original version
--------------------------------------------------
-- Version 1.01  A.Salieri    07/05/1825
-- Added error control, modified discounts handling
--------------------------------------------------
    @stor_id  CHAR(4),        -- store having a sale
    @title_id VARCHAR(6),     -- title to go on sale
    @dicount  DECIMAL(4,2)    -- discount percent
AS
<stored procedure statements>
```

The CREATE PROCEDURE statement has a structure that is partially self-documenting. This example illustrates that it is unnecessary to include the object name in the header comment, since it appears in the CREATE statement. The input parameters section in the comment is also redundant because you can embed comments explaining each parameter right in its declaration in the CREATE statement.

Some corporate standards also require that programmers include in the header comment such sections as:

- Return codes
- Error codes and messages
- Referenced objects

They may be justified in some situations but usually just create extra work for programmers. We recommend making these sections optional. Once you introduce them, you have to keep their contents current. Every change in the program requires a review of the header comment for possible modifications. If you do not always update header comment information, it is better to drop such sections entirely.

A detailed header is more important in long procedures (multiple pages of code). It practically becomes an abstract of the procedure.

If you use a version-control system to maintain your code, the format of header comments may be dictated by the package you use. Does your project involve thousands of stored procedures and triggers? Use a version-control system to stop the programming chaos and versioning confusion.

Summary

A good and consistent coding style demonstrates a programmer's professionalism. It helps reduce the development and maintenance costs of a program. All the style guidelines offered in this chapter may be summarized in the following set of criteria defining a well-written program:

- Choose lowercase, uppercase, or mixed case for keywords and for programmer-defined names. If you work in a team, make this a part of the coding standard. Use it consistently.
- If you use abbreviations, make them meaningful and easy to understand for an outsider. Standardize abbreviations so that the same word is always abbreviated the same way.
- Include error-handling code in all programs. Certain conditions may cause a runtime error and result in a failure of a single command, but the program may continue.

- Use of indents, spaces, tabs, blank lines, and proper line wrapping makes your program easy to read and understand.
- Format DDL and DML statements in a consistent way. Use indentation to show clauses of SQL commands and branches of IF and WHILE commands, as well as CASE expressions.
- Use header comments in every program to explain its purpose, document the programmer's name, date of creation, dates and reasons for modifications, and include additional important details. Use comments in the body of the program to explain the algorithm, highlight major steps, and document changes.

II

The Building Blocks: Transact-SQL Language Elements

Part II describes the Transact-SQL building blocks that allow you to use more advanced programming techniques. The chapters within this part will help you understand how data is categorized into datatypes and how you can declare and use variables. Chapter 1 introduced the differences between row processing and set processing; in this part, you'll learn how to perform row-based operations in the set-processing world of SQL Server. We'll describe conditional processing, error handling, and temporary structures. We'll also discuss transactions and locking, key issues for multiuser information systems.

Part II contains these chapters:

- Chapter 6, *Datatypes and Variables*
- Chapter 7, *Conditional Processing*
- Chapter 8, *Row Processing with Cursors*
- Chapter 9, *Error Handling*
- Chapter 10, *Temporary Objects*
- Chapter 11, *Transactions and Locking*

In this chapter:

- *Datatypes*
- *User-Defined Datatypes*
- *Processing Nulls*
- *Variables*
- *Parameters*
- *Summary*

6

Datatypes and Variables

Datatypes and variables are to the novice database programmer what road signs and traffic lights are to the 16-year-old driving student: intriguing, but mostly an annoyance that obstructs the most fun part of the process. In the case of this once-16-year-old driving student, the best part was stomping the accelerator as hard as possible for as long as possible. Many developers have that same mindset: spew code at full speed without languishing on the details. However, failing to learn the intricacies of datatypes and variables can cause a variety of problems, from slow performance to the dreaded program crash. In this chapter, we'll ease off the accelerator pedal to discuss topics relating to the characteristics of data: system- and user-defined datatypes, nulls, local and global variables, and parameters.

Datatypes

Datatypes are used to define the main characteristics of a specific data element, typically the columns of a table, parameters of a stored procedure, or variables in a Transact-SQL program.

SQL Server provides a wide variety of system datatypes. System datatypes are categorized into groups based on the type of data stored within the datatype. There are 10 basic categories of system datatypes in SQL Server, as described in Table 6-1. We'll cover each category and system datatype in some detail in the following sections.

Table 6-1. System Datatypes

Category	Datatype	Allowable Synonym
Binary	BINARY[(length)]	
	VARBINARY[(length)]	BINARY VARYING

Table 6-1. System Datatypes (continued)

Category	Datatype	Allowable Synonym
Character	CHAR[(length)]	CHARACTER
	VARCHAR[(length)]	CHARACTER VARYING
Date/time	DATETIME	
	SMALLDATETIME	
Exact numeric	DECIMAL[(precision[, scale])]	DEC
		NUMERIC
Approximate numeric	FLOAT[(length)]	DOUBLE PRECISION
	REAL	
Integer	INT	INTEGER
	SMALLINT	
	TINYINT	
Monetary	MONEY	
	SMALLMONEY	
Special	BIT	
	TIMESTAMP	
Text and image	TEXT	
	IMAGE	

It is pretty rare to find the synonym of a datatype used. The vast majority of applications reference datatypes by their regular names. In general, we recommend that you stick to the regular usage of the datatype, unless you are providing maintenance support on an older system that already contains synonyms or if you really want to be "different."

Binary Datatypes

The BINARY and VARBINARY datatypes are used to store exact bit patterns. A binary string may consist of up to 255 bytes. Each byte is represented by a two-position hexadecimal number, 00 through FF. The whole binary string value should be prefixed with 0x, so the pair FF would be entered as 0xFF. When you specify the length of a binary column, every base-16 pair counts as one increment of length. Thus, a length of 10 could hold 10 base-16 pairs.

These datatypes should not be used to store hexadecimal data, since any conversions or calculations of hex numbers stored in binary fields can be erroneous.

The BINARY(length) datatype always stores the fully specified length. If you don't specify a length, SQL Server assumes a length of 1. Use this datatype only on columns (or variables) that will be consistently similar in length. Don't store a 10-character bit pattern in a BINARY(20) because SQL Server will always pad the remaining 10 bytes, consuming unused space. On the other hand, data that is too long for a binary column is truncated.

If you attempt to create a BINARY column that allows NULL, SQL Server will automatically make it VARBINARY. It does not support nullable fixed-length BINARY. Since BINARY columns have a fixed storage length, they're a little faster to access than VARBINARY columns.

The VARBINARY(length) datatype is a variable-length datatype that stores only the actual length of the data being entered. VARBINARY columns are best used to store bit patterns that vary in size or are frequently null. Data stored to a VARBINARY column is not padded to the column length, although data that exceeds the length of the column is truncated.

Character Datatypes

The character datatypes are used to store strings in any combination of letters, numbers, and symbols. Character data must be enclosed in single or double quotes, such as 'Joe' or "Wabbit season?!" The only exceptions to this rule are null values, which should be specified as the NULL keyword in INSERT or UPDATE statements. An empty string (basically, one quote right after the other, as in '') inserts a single blank space in a column of a character datatype. Character datatypes can range from 1 to 255 characters in length, with 1 as the default if you do not specify any length.

Remember that character data containing numbers (such as 90210) are not equal to numeric data of the same number. Numerals stored as character data must be converted to a numeric datatype before they can be used in calculations or compared directly to numeric data.

The CHAR(length) datatype always stores the fully specified length, regardless of how long a CHAR value is. Any empty space in a CHAR column is right-padded with spaces. CHAR is useful for columns containing data that is consistently similar in size and never NULL.

If you attempt to create a CHAR column that allows NULL, SQL Server will automatically make it VARCHAR. It does not support nullable fixed-length CHAR columns. CHAR columns are a little faster for SQL Server to access than a VARCHAR column because they have less overhead than a VARCHAR column.

The VARCHAR(length) datatype can have a maximum length of 255, but always stores only the data value entered without adding any trailing spaces. VARCHAR is useful for data that is widely variable in length or might contain NULL values. Columns of this datatype exact a slight overhead in both storage and access speed but are extremely useful due to their flexibility. The vast majority of all character data is stored in VARCHAR columns.

A Pronunciation Guide

There's a bit of controversy surrounding exactly how you pronounce the CHAR and VARCHAR datatypes. For most people, it's simply a matter of personal preference. For others, this is matter of fanatical devotion.

Here are your options:

The "Rhymes with Care" denomination
: The datatypes are pronounced "care" and "vare-care." People of this camp generally believe that the datatypes are abbreviations of the full terms "character" and "variable-character" and should thus be pronounced in this way.

The "Rhymes with Char" denomination
: These individuals prefer to say "char" (as in "charcoal") and "var-char." That's how it's written, isn't it?

The "Rhymes with Car" denomination
: This group, probably originating in the Detroit "Motown" area of the country, interprete these datatypes with a bias toward "car." In their opinion, the datatypes are properly spoken as "car" and "var-car."

The Agnostics
: These folks don't really know how to pronounce it. They're open to the full phonetic experience. Sometimes it comes out "var-char," sometimes "var-car," and sometimes the heretical "var-chair." Watch out for this kind.

Data that is too long for a given character column is right-trimmed. When entering strings shorter than the length of the character column, NOT NULL CHAR columns are always padded with spaces until the column is full; nullable CHAR and VARCHAR columns are not padded with spaces.

Date/Time Datatypes

Date and time data is most effectively stored in alphanumeric strings with a DATETIME or SMALLDATETIME datatype. Like character data, date/time data must be enclosed in single or double quotes. SQL Server does not pay attention to the case of the date/time values, and spaces may appear freely between the various date parts. By default, SQL Server will display a date/time field in the format:

```
mon dd yyyy hh:mmAM
```

SQL Server will interject several default values if you omit any portion of a DATETIME or SMALLDATETIME value. Omitting the date will result in a default of January 1, 1900, while omitting the time will result in a value of 12:00:00:000AM (if that precision is needed). If a month is given without a date, the first day of the month is returned.

The DATETIME datatype is a higher precision storage format. DATETIME consumes 8 bytes of storage space, 4 bytes for date and 4 bytes for the milliseconds past midnight. This datatype can store dates between January 1, 1753, and December 31, 9999. All values outside this range are rejected. Although this datatype stores milliseconds, it does so only to an accuracy of one three-hundredths of a second (3.33 milliseconds).

The SMALLDATETIME datatype is less precise than DATETIME but requires only 4 bytes of storage space. You may use any date between January 1, 1900, and June 6, 2079, with accuracy up to the minute.

Date formats

SQL Server recognizes many different formats for date and time. Table 6-2 shows you the date formats SQL Server allows.

Table 6-2. Date Formats in SQL Server

Style	Format	Format with Century	Style Number (Regular / Century)
Default	mon dd yyyy hh:miAM (or PM)		0 / 100
USA1	mm/dd/yy	mm/dd/yyyy	1 / 101

Table 6-2. Date Formats in SQL Server (continued)

Style	Format	Format with Century	Style Number (Regular / Century)
ANSI	yy.mm.dd	yyyy.mm.dd	2 / 102
British/French	dd/mm/yy	dd/mm/yyyy	3 / 103
German	dd.mm.yy	dd.mm.yyyy	4 / 104
Italian	dd-mm-yy	dd-mm-yyyy	5 / 105
Alternate1	dd mon yy	dd mon yyyy	6 / 106
Alternate2	mon dd, yy	mon dd, yyyy	7 / 107
Alternate3	month dd, yy	month dd, yyyy	8 / 108
Time	hh:mm:ss		9 /109
Default milli-seconds	mon dd yyyy hh:mi:ss:mmmAM (or PM)		10 / 110
USA2	mm-dd-yy	mm-dd-yyyy	11 / 111
JAPAN	yy/mm/dd	yyyy/mm/dd	12 / 112
ISO	yymmdd	yyyymmdd	13 / 113
Europe default milliseconds	dd mon yyyy hh:mm:ss:mmm(24h)		14 / 114
USA Military Time	hh:mi:ss:mmm(24h)		15 / 115

Notice that styles 0 and 100, 9 and 109, and 13 and 113 always display in century format.

The character set of the server makes a difference in how SQL Server interprets the default format for date/time data. Servers with US_English as the character set always return a default date format of mdy. You can further control the default format of dates using the SET DATEFORMAT command. SET commands are discussed in Chapters 20 and 21.

If you opt for the two-digit year, SQL Server interpretes values under 50 as the year 20xx, while values greater than or equal to 50 are interpreted as the year 19xx. Thus, Aug 25, 13 would be interpreted as in the year 2013, while August 25, 69 would be interpreted as in the year 1969.

Numeric date formats

Most of the time, you'll enter dates as a mix of alphabetic, symbolic, and numeric characters. However, there may be times when you will use dates that are strictly numerals without any alphabetic characters or symbols like slash, comma, or period. You'll hardly ever find all-numeric dates inside SQL Server. Instead, all-numeric date formats are most commonly encountered when importing data from another system, like a mainframe. In these situations, six- and eight-digit strings are always interpreted as ymd, with month and day always two digits long. A four-digit string is always assumed to be a four-digit year with a date of January 1.

Don't use numeric date formats inside SQL Server. Numeric date formats are mostly the domain of import utilities like BCP. INSERT or UPDATE statements that use numeric formats for date columns will fail.

For example, the numeric string 102866 would be interpreted as October 28, 1966 in a date field. Similarly, the numeric string 06051991 would be interpreted as June 5, 1991. The numeric string 1976 would be interpreted as January 1, 1976. Strings like 779555 or 125 are out of range and will produce an error when attempting to insert them into a SQL Server table.

Time formats

Time values, like date values, must be enclosed in single or double quotes. Hours may be in 12- or 24-hour time. When using 12-hour time, the A.M. and P.M. may be applied. SQL Server does not care whether they are shown uppercase or lowercase. Valid time formats could be any of the following:

```
18:31
18:31:20:999
18:31:20.9
6pm
6 PM
06:31:20:999PM
```

The precision separators for time formats are usually colons, although you can use a colon or a period to separate milliseconds. The period has special significance for milliseconds, though. If only a single digit follows the period in the millisecond date part, then that digit represents tenths of a second, two digits represent hundredths, and three digits represent thousandths. Using a colon to precede milliseconds tells SQL Server to always interpret the value, even single or double digits, as milliseconds.

Other rules for dates

There are a few other important rules to remember when using date/time values in queries and Transact-SQL programs.

- DATETIME values carry precision to the millisecond. Use the LIKE function to query on DATETIME columns when you are interested only in the month, day, and year. For example, the WHERE clause `WHERE hire_date = May 5, 1994` will return only those records that have a time of 12:00:00.000AM, but the clause `WHERE hire_date LIKE May 5, 1994%` will return all records with that month, day, and year. There is a performance trade-off: the LIKE function forces SQL Server to abandon any index that might exist on the DATETIME column.
- When using LIKE to search for a single-digit month, place two spaces between the month and day. Otherwise, you may get unexpected results. For example, if you search using the clause `LIKE %July 1%` (with only one space), you'll get all records with dates between July 10 and July 19, but not July 1. By placing the second blank space between the month and the day, you ensure that records with a date of July 1 (and any time value) are returned.
- The anomalies described in the previous item also apply to single-digit hour values in DATETIME and SMALLDATETIME fields.

Exact Numeric Datatypes

Although SQL Server has two precision numeric datatypes, DECIMAL and NUMERIC, they function exactly the same way. (The only reason they are both present in SQL Server is for ANSI compatibility.) Both datatypes can store values to the left and right of the decimal point with great precision. Values can range from 10^{38} - 1 through -10^{38} - 1. Storage ranges from 2 to 17 bytes, depending upon the exact precision of the data element.

When specifying exact numeric datatypes, you have the option of also specifying a precision and scale—DECIMAL[(precision[,scale])]. Precision is used to specify the maximum length of the number (excluding the negative sign), while scale specifies the maximum length of the number to the right of the decimal point. Scale cannot be greater than precision. To illustrate this, assume that you have a table with a DECIMAL(5,2) column. The maximum allowable value for this field is 999. 99 and the minimum is -999.99. Any attempt to place a value outside of this boundary will result in an error.

Storing Exact Numeric Data

Here's a quick chart for determining the storage space required for a numeric column:

Precision	Bytes of Storage
1–2	2
3–4	3
5–7	4
8–9	5
10–12	6
13–14	7

Precision	Bytes of Storage
15–16	8
17–19	9
20–21	10
22–24	11
25–26	12

Precision	Bytes of Storage
27–28	13
29–31	14
32–33	15
34–36	16
37–38	17

If you do not specify a precision or scale, these values default to 18 and 0, respectively. Precision may range from 1 to 38, although 28 is the maximum value usually supported by SQL Server due to frontend constraints. Scale may range from 0 to whatever the precision is.

You can enable precisions greater than 28 digits in length by starting SQL Server with the /p parameter. Refer to the SQL Server database administration documentation for details.

Approximate Numeric Datatypes

Approximate numeric datatypes (FLOAT and REALl) are used to store fractional numeric values with limitations in accuracy. Many floating-point values (such as .3, .6, and .7) cannot be accurately represented, so SQL Server rounds them up as needed. All values stored within approximate numeric datatypes are guaranteed to be accurate, but slight variations in floating-point values can result from the rounding schemes. Since floating-point values are tough to quantify accurately, it's a good idea to avoid using them in any sort of search criteria (WHERE or HAVING). Aside from the intrinsic approximation of these datatypes, they work normally with all arithmetic operations except modulo.

The FLOAT datatype, specified as FLOAT(length), can hold positive and negative floating-point numbers with a maximum 15-digit precision. Although you can specify a float length of 1 to 15, the default is 15. This enables a range of values from positive 2.23E-308 through 1.79E-308, zero, and (negative) -2.23E-308 through -1.79E-308. Floats are frequently used in scientific notation. Float values always consume 8 bytes of storage space.

The REAL datatype, specified as REAL(length), is essentially a float with a more limited range of values. REAL is limited to a 7-digit maximum precision. Its allowable range of values encompasses 1.1E-38 through 3.40E-38, zero, and (negative) -1.18E-38 through -3.40E-38. Its storage requirements are 4 bytes per REAL value. It is otherwise identical to FLOAT.

Integer Datatypes

Integer data is among the most common form of numeric data encountered in SQL Server. Integer datatypes are used to store whole numbers. Allowable integer datatypes include INT, SMALLINT, and TINYINT. The INT datatype can accommodate values ranging from -2,147,483,647 to 2,147,483,647; consuming 4 bytes of storage. The SMALLINT datatype allows values ranging from -32,768 to 32,767 and takes up 2 bytes of space. Finally, the TINYINT datatype is a cute little critter that allows values of 0 through 255. It takes only 1 byte of space.

Monetary Datatypes

The monetary datatypes of MONEY and SMALLMONEY are used to handle (surprise!) United States currency. You can use these datatypes to store any currency you like, but they do not provide any monetary conversion functionality. Monetary data is rounded up to the nearest cent when displayed by SQL Server. When referencing monetary data, always preface the value with a dollar symbol. Any positive or negative signs should appear between the dollar sign and the numeric value. Otherwise, SQL Server will treat the value as a numeric datatype with a scale of 4. Despite the fact that *you* are supposed to reference monetary data with a dollar sign, SQL Server does not extend the same courtesy, returning data without the dollar sign. Modulo is the only arithmetic operation that doesn't work with monetary datatypes.

The storage size of the MONEY datatype is 8 bytes and the datatype allows values from -922,337,203,685,477.5807 to +922,337,203,685,477.5807—obviously enough storage capacity to track any bank account we'll ever see! For smaller ranges of values, use the SMALLMONEY datatype. SMALLMONEY has a storage size of 4 bytes and allows values from -214,748.3647 to +214,748.3647. SMALLMONEY values are rounded up two places when displayed. Both datatypes store data with an accuracy of one ten-thousandth of a monetary unit.

SQL Server exhibits inconsistent behavior when dealing with monetary datatypes. SQL Server displays monetary datatypes in the American comma-delimited format with a comma after every third numeral, as in $123,456,789.10. On the other hand, SQL Server does *not* allow commas when inserting values into monetary columns. That's because SQL Server evaluates a comma as the end of one value and the start of another. If you attempt to insert a monetary value with the commas, you'll get this message:

```
Msg 213, Level 16, State 5
Insert error: column name or number of supplied values
does not match table definition.
```

Special Datatypes

The BIT and TIMESTAMP datatypes provide special functionality for SQL Server applications.

The BIT datatype holds 1 or 0 and is typically used only for true/false and yes/no types of data. BIT datatypes cannot be NULL and can't have an index built on them. You can insert any integer into a BIT field, but SQL Server will convert any nonzero value to 1. SQL Server packs up to 8 bit columns into one byte. If you have only one bit column, it will take the whole byte. The unique offset position of a BIT column is tracked in the syscolumns..status column.

Since the BIT type does not allow nulls, you cannot alter a table and add a BIT type column. You can only use this type at table creation time.

The TIMESTAMP datatype is a unique variation on a BINARY(8) column. Although the name might make you think of a DATETIME column, TIMESTAMP has no relationship with dates or time. It is actually a unique, monotonically increasing value that is automatically generated every time a record is inserted or updated in a table. INSERT and UPDATE statements should not make direct reference to this column. SQL Server will automatically handle this column. Only one TIMESTAMP column is allowed per table.

You can create a default BINARY(8) timestamp column by simply adding a column named timestamp to the table. SQL Server will handle all the details. You can, on the other hand, create a column called timestamp and give a specific datatype. Of course, it will not receive the automatic updates as it normally would. Timestamps can be NULL or NOT NULL. The net result of making a TIMESTAMP nullable is to alter its base datatype to VARBINARY(8).

Text and Image Datatypes

TEXT and IMAGE data are character strings or binary large objects (BLOBs) managed as a linked list of 2K data pages. The linked lists make it appear as if the data were stored in the table record. In actuality, only a 16-bit pointer is physically stored with the record. Elsewhere, a 2K data page is initialized to hold the text or image data. If the record is created with an INSERT statement containing a NULL value for the text/image field, the data element is not initialized and the 2K of space is saved.

When initialized, TEXT and IMAGE values are never less than a full 2K. It's advisable to insert NULL into these columns until they can be fully populated with data, because even 1 byte of data in a TEXT and IMAGE column will use at least 2K of storage. Each 2K page of data expends 112 bytes of overhead to maintain the linked lists. However, any update on a row containing a TEXT or IMAGE column will initialize the pointer and consume 2K of storage regardless of whether the TEXT or IMAGE column was directly addressed by the update. Large text or image objects can span many, many 2K data pages. Because they can span so many pages, TEXT and IMAGE columns are not defined with an explicit length, and they automatically allow NULL values.

TEXT can contain as much as 2,147,483,647 bytes of data. TEXT has some of the characteristics of a VARCHAR column:

- It must be enclosed in single or double quotes when inserted into the table.
- It can be searched in a WHERE clause with LIKE and wildcard symbols.
- It can be retrieved in a query (according to the value set by SET TEXTSIZE).

TEXT can be explicitly converted to CHAR or VARCHAR, up to the 255-character limit of those datatypes.

The IMAGE is named after the data it most frequently stores—graphic files in the GIF or JPEG format. IMAGE, like TEXT, can also contain as much as 2,147,483,647 bytes of data. It can be explicitly converted with a CONVERT statement to BINARY or VARBINARY, up to the 255-character limit of those datatypes. IMAGE cannot be used as a variable or a parameter. IMAGE values inserted into a table must be prefixed with 0x in an INSERT statement. Interestingly, SQL Server does not accept IMAGE values with an odd number of characters when greater than 255 bytes in length. When the value is odd numbered and less than 255 bytes in length, SQL Server pads the value with a leading zero, making 0xababa into 0x0ababa.

TEXT and IMAGE columns cannot be used as local variables; in an index; or in ORDER BY, COMPUTE, or GROUP BY clauses.

TEXT and IMAGE may be used in only a limited number of functions: PATINDEX, DATALENGTH, TEXTPTR, TEXTVALID, and CHAR_LENGTH (only for TEXT datatypes on Sybase servers).

IMAGE data cannot be addressed in a WHERE clause. TEXT data can be addressed in a WHERE clause, but only with the LIKE operator.

Once a text or image column has been initialized with an INSERT or UPDATE statement, its full value can be retrieved using the READTEXT command (as opposed to the partial contents of the column with a regular SELECT statement). The WRITETEXT command enables the insertion or replacement of TEXT and IMAGE data, while the UPDATETEXT command allows TEXT and IMAGE data to be modified. You can use the UPDATE statement to set a TEXT or IMAGE column to NULL, thereby reclaiming all the space it had previously used (except for the first 2K page). To completely clean out the space consumed by a TEXT or IMAGE value, drop the offending record, then reinsert all of its data except the TEXT/IMAGE data.

User-Defined Datatypes

SQL Server enables the creation of *user-defined datatypes*. User-defined datatypes are constructed over an underlying system datatype, with possible rules and/or defaults bound to it.

Let's illustrate user-defined datatypes with a mini-case study: assume that we want to store an employee's social security number (SSN) as the primary key for each record in the employee table. (Be forewarned: this isn't exactly how they do it in the pubs database.)

- Since SSNs are 9-digit strings of integer numbers, we could create a column called emp_id with a datatype of INT or SMALLINT. Using an INT for such a number has one big problem: INT does not retain leading zeros. Thus, an employee with an SSN of 0012-34-567 would be stored as 1234567 in an INT column instead of 001234567—a clear error. So we must choose a CHAR(9) or VARCHAR(9) datatype so that we can retain all leading zeros. In this case, CHAR is superior to VARCHAR for two reasons. First, the column will always contain a 9-digit string (so we don't need the variable aspect of a VARCHAR column). And second, the column is the primary key of the table and thus NOT NULL. These behaviors play into the strengths of the CHAR datatype.

- We can now create our own user-defined datatype called empid as a CHAR(9) field using the system stored procedure *sp_addtype*:

```
EXEC sp_ADDTYPE empid, 'char(9)', 'NOT NULL'
```

- We've created our user-defined datatype, picking CHAR(9) for our datatype. But CHAR allows any alphabetic or symbolic character to be stored, while we only want the values 0 through 9 to occupy any portion of the string. To further constrain the allowable values in the datatype empid, we can create a rule to allow only numeric values and bind it to the datatype:

```
CREATE RULE check_emp_id
@value LIKE '[0-9][0-9][0-9][0-9][0-9][0-9][0-9][0-9][0-9]'
GO

sp_BINDRULE check_emp_id, empid
GO
```

- Now that we have created our unique datatype and bound all necessary rules and defaults to it, we may safely use it as a datatype in CREATE TABLE statements, in ALTER TABLE . . . ADD COLUMN statements, in variables, and in stored procedure parameters.

To create a user-defined datatype, we make use of the *sp_addtype* system stored procedure. This procedure creates a user-defined datatype by adding a descriptive record to the systypes system table. The syntax for *sp_addtype* follows:

```
sp_ADDTYPE user_datatype_name, system_datatype [,nullability]
```

The syntax is fairly simple: the command followed by the name for the new datatype, the name and length of the base-level system datatype (like CHAR(5) or TINYINT) enclosed in quotes, and the NULL or NOT NULL status. For example, here is an *sp_addtype* command used in the case study:

```
EXEC sp_ADDTYPE empid, 'char(9)', 'NOT NULL'
```

You do not have to enclose the system datatype in quotes if it does not contain spaces or special symbols, as in the case of BIT, DATETIME, or INT. In the case of commonly used datatypes that make use of the special symbols for parentheses like CHAR(x), VARCHAR(x), or DEC(x), you must enclose the system datatype in quotes. It is good programming practice to always enclose the system datatype in quotes and to always declare the nullability of your new datatype. Although you do not have to declare the nullability of the new datatype, it will default to the current default nullability, usually NOT NULL. It is also important to remember that the nullability of a user-defined datatype can be overridden by the specification of the datatype in the CREATE TABLE or ALTER TABLE command.

Dropping a user-defined datatype is an even easier command than the one that creates it. Just follow this syntax:

```
sp_DROPTYPE user_datatype_name
```

The only restriction on using *sp_droptype* is that a user-defined datatype cannot be dropped if a table or other database object references it. You must first drop any database objects that reference the user-defined datatype before dropping the user datatype itself.

Processing Nulls

Many people who are new to relational database technology tend to think of null as zero or blank. In fact, null is neither of these. In the relational database world, null literally means that the value is unknown or indeterminant. (This question alone, whether null should be considered unknown *or* indeterminate, has provoked countless volumes of academic argument.) This differentiation enables a database designer to distinguish between those entries that represent a deliberately placed zero or blank and those where the data is either not recorded in the system or where a null has been explicitly entered.

For an example of this semantic difference, consider the royalty payment of an author in the pubs..roysched table. A null royalty does not mean that we authors are working for free (though heaven knows it sometimes feels like it); instead, a null royalty indicates that the fee is not known or perhaps not yet determined.

One side effect of the indeterminate nature of a null value is that it cannot be used in a calculation or a comparison. Here are a few brief, but very important, rules to remember about columns that contain null values:

- You cannot insert a null value into a column defined as NOT NULL unless the column has a default value bound to it.
- Null values are not equal to each other. It's a frequent mistake to compare two columns that contain null and expect the null values to match. (You can search for NULL in a WHERE clause or a Boolean expression using phrases like value IS NULL, value IS NOT NULL, value = NULL, or value <> NULL.)
- A column containing a null value is ignored in the calculation of aggregate values like AVG, SUM, or MAX.
- Columns used in a GROUP BY clause will contain a separate entry for null values.
- Joins between a table that contain records and a table that does not are governed by the rules for outer joins. Refer to Chapter 3, *SQL Primer*, for details on outer joins.

Variables

Variables are user-defined objects that hold programmatically assigned values for a limited period of time, unlike the columns of a table, which are designed to store data indefinitely. Variables are like the columns of a table in that they must be assigned a datatype. Variables fall into one of two categories: local and global. Local variables are created with a DECLARE statement, assigned a value with a SELECT statement, and then used within the session or Transact-SQL program in which they were created. Local variables are easy to identify because they are prefixed with a single at sign (@). Global variables, on the other hand, are predefined system values that are useful for a wide variety of situations. Global variables are designated with a double at sign (@@).

Local Variables

Local variables are used within a Transact-SQL program, such as a stored procedure or script. A local variable must be declared in the body of the Transact-SQL program before it can be assigned any value. The syntax for the DECLARE statement is shown here:

```
DECLARE @variable_name datatype(length[,precision])]
        [, @variable_name datatype(length[,precision])]...]
```

Declaring local variables

It is good programming practice to create all of your variables early in the program in a declaration block. Many programmers also include a quick comment explaining what each variable is used for. This is especially good advice when the variable's purpose is not self-evident. Although the syntax for DECLARE allows multiple variable declarations at one time, some programmers prefer to declare each variable separately. Notice the code example taken from the system stored procedure *sp_spaceused*:

```
DECLARE @id       INT              -- The object id of @objname.
DECLARE @type     SMALLINT         -- The object type.
DECLARE @pages    INT              -- Working variable for size calc.
DECLARE @dbname   VARCHAR(30)
DECLARE @dbsize   DEC(15,0)
```

The preceding code fragment is essentially the same as the next one:

```
DECLARE @id       INT,              -- The object id of @objname.
        @type     SMALLINT,         -- The object type.
        @pages    INT,              -- Working variable for size calc.
        @dbname   VARCHAR(30),
        @dbsize   DEC(15,0)
```

Or even a single line of code:

```
DECLARE @id INT, @type SMALLINT,@pages INT, @dbname VARCHAR(30), @dbsize
DEC(15,0)
```

Declaring multiple variables in one DECLARE is a little better from a performance point of view. But the difference is slight because DECLARE takes only milliseconds anyway.

There are a few simple rules when declaring a variable. First, the first character of the name *must* be the at symbol (@). Second, the name can be no longer than 29 alphanumeric characters but must otherwise conform to the rules of identifiers (see Chapter 4 for more information). Finally, the variable may be any datatype except TEXT or IMAGE.

Assigning a value to a local variable

Assigning a value to a variable is commonly accomplished using a specialized SELECT statement. The syntax is:

```
SELECT @variable_name1 = [expression1 | (SELECT expression1 FROM...)]
    [, @variable_name2 = [expression2 | (SELECT expression2 FROM...)...]
[FROM...]
```

You can use a SELECT statement to assign values to multiple variables at one time.

In SQL Server, you may use this alternate syntax to assign values returned by a stored procedure:

```
EXEC @variable_name1 = stored procedure result
```

Often, you'll simply assign a constant value appropriate for the variable and its datatype, whether it be 12344, Antonio Vivaldi, or Aug 25, 1969. Variables can also store a value returned by a SELECT statement. The query should normally return only one value and should never return any data other than that needed by the variable. If a query fails to assign a value to a variable, perhaps because the query returned more than one value, the variable will retain the last value assigned to it. The following examples illustrate assigning values to a variable:

```
-- A simple batch to declare a variable and assign a value to it.
SET NOCOUNT ON

DECLARE @loc_id CHAR(5)

-- Part 1: Initializing the variable with a constant
SELECT @loc_id = '00000'
PRINT  '---> Initial value <---'
PRINT  @loc_id
PRINT  ' '

-- Part 2: Assigning a single value from a query
SELECT @loc_id = (SELECT MAX(zip) FROM authors)
```

```
PRINT  '---> single SELECT assignment <---'
PRINT  @loc_id
PRINT  ' '

-- Part 3: A failed value assignment
SELECT @loc_id = MAX(zip) FROM authors WHERE zip > '99000'
PRINT  '---> a failed SELECT assignment <---'
PRINT  @loc_id
PRINT  ' '

-- Part 4: Assigning a known NULL
SELECT @loc_id = (SELECT ISNULL(MAX(zip),'NOVAL') FROM authors WHERE zip >
'99000')
PRINT  '---> no records returned in SELECT assignment <---'
PRINT  @loc_id
PRINT  ' '

-- Part 5: Assigning a the last value from a multi-row result set
SELECT @loc_id = zip FROM authors
PRINT  '---> multi-value SELECT assignment <---'
PRINT  @loc_id

GO
```

Results:

```
---> Initial value <---
00000

---> single SELECT assignment <---
97330

---> a failed SELECT assignment <---


---> no records returned in SELECT assignment <---
NOVAL

---> multi-value SELECT assignment <---
84152
```

The result of each code fragment is explained here:

Part 1 (initial value)
: This is a simple assignment of a constant value to a variable. Nothing fancy here.

Part 2 (single SELECT assignment)
: This bit of code searches the authors table for the single highest Zip Code (97330) and assigns that value to the variable. Again, there is nothing fancy about this section of code.

Part 3 (failed SELECT assignment)

The query that assigned a value was chosen specifically because it would not return any records. When the SELECT statement returns no rows, the variable is assigned a NULL value.

Part 4 (known NULL)

You can use the ISNULL function to provide a default value on a SELECT assignment.

Part 5 (last value)

The SELECT statement may return more than one value, but SQL Server will assign only the last value returned by the query to the variable. In this example, the SELECT assigns the value of the last Zip Code returned by the query, 84152. If you had used a subquery to assign the value, as in `SELECT @loc_id = (SELECT zip FROM authors)`, the assignment would have failed outright. It's a good idea to use a straight SELECT to assign a value to a variable, as shown in Part 5, rather than to use a subquery.

Using local variables in SQL statements

Local variables are most often used in stored procedures or Transact-SQL batches, like a script or a command file. Local variables, in and of themselves, can be used as a substitute for only a constant value. Variables cannot be directly used in place of a database object, like a table or view, or in place of a keyword. Notice in the following example that such a Transact-SQL command fails:

```
SET NOCOUNT ON

-- A variable representing a database object
DECLARE @table_name varchar(30)

SELECT  @table_name = 'authors'

SELECT  *
FROM    @table_name
WHERE   zip = '97330'

GO
```

Results:

```
Msg 170, Level 15, State 1
Line 8: Incorrect syntax near '@table_name'.
```

The reason variables fail in this way is that the values they represent are resolved at compile time. SQL Server looks at the SELECT statement and cannot complete it because @table_name has no meaning to it. You can accomplish this same functionality in Microsoft SQL Server, though, by using the EXECUTE statement. (The

Sybase Version 11.5 stored procedure *sp_remotesql* can be used to mimic Microsoft's *EXEC()* function.) The following example shows how:

```
SET NOCOUNT ON

-- A variable representing a database object executed with EXEC.
DECLARE @table_name varchar(30)

SELECT  @table_name = 'sales'

EXEC ("SELECT  *
       FROM " + @table_name + "
       WHERE title_id = 'BU1032'")

GO
```

Results:

```
stor_id ord_num         ord_date                 qty   payterms     title_id
------- --------------- ------------------------ ----- ------------ ---------
6380    6871            Sep 14 1994 12:00AM      5     Net 60       BU1032
8042    423LL930        Sep 14 1994 12:00AM      10    ON invoice   BU1032
```

Since SQL Server compiles the EXEC statement at runtime instead of compile time, SQL Server concatenates the EXEC statement as it is run. It determines that the sales table does indeed exist and that the rest of the query, like the WHERE statement, is acceptable.

Global Variables

Global variables are predefined variables maintained by SQL Server. Global variables have two at symbols (@@) preceding their names. Although you can create a variable with a double at sign, you cannot create a global variable. It is simply treated as a local variable by SQL Server. Many global variables are reported in the system stored procedure *sp_monitor*, but you can also use them in Transact-SQL programs of your own design. Global variables are available to all users, not just SA.

You can access the value of a global variable through a simple SELECT statement. For example, to discover the current session's SPID and the servername, you'd issue this query:

```
SELECT @@spid, @@servername
```

Results:

```
------ ------------------------------
14     SAVIGNON

(1 row(s) affected)
```

There are oodles of global variables. Table 6-3 contains a list of both Microsoft and Sybase SQL Server's global variables:

Table 6-3. Global Variables in SQL Server

Global Variable Name	Vendor Support	Description
@@char_convert	Sybase	Displays a 1 if character set conversion is in effect and 0 if not.
@@client_csid	Sybase	Displays the most recently used client character set ID or -1 if the client character set hasn't been initialized.
@@client_csname	Sybase	Displays the most recently used client character set name or NULL if the client character set hasn't been initialized.
@@connections	MS, Sybase	The number of logins attempted since SQL Server was last started.
@@cpu_busy	MS, Sybase	Officially, this is the number of timeticks the CPU has devoted to SQL Server since it was last started. However, the inside word is that this variable reflects the number of timeticks during which the server performed logical (or cache) I/O activity. In a sense, this indirectly reflects CPU activity.
@@curread	Sybase	Returns the sensitivity label telling which database objects the current session is allowed to read. The current session can only read tables or databases with a sensitivity label less than the value returned by @@curread.
@@curwrite	Sybase	Returns the sensitivity label telling the level of data the current session is allowed to write. Also establishes the sensitivity label of all databases and tables created during the session. Also sets the sensitivity level for all table rows written, except when in over_range mode.
@@cursor_rows	MS	The number of qualifying rows returned in the most recently opened cursor in a specfic users session. Values include: 0—indicating the most recently opened cursor is closed, deallocated, or no cursor has been opened N—indicating the number of rows returned by a fully populated cursor -N—indicating the number of rows in the current keyset of an asynchronously generated cursor

Table 6-3. Global Variables in SQL Server (continued)

Global Variable Name	Vendor Support	Description
@@data_high	Sybase	The special reserved label Data High, the label that supersedes all other labels in the system. Retrievable only when the @@curread is equal to Data High.
@@data_low	Sybase	The special reserved label Data Low, the label that is superseded by all other labels in the system.
@@datefirst	MS	The current value of the SET DATEFIRST parameter, indicating the first day of each week. A value of 1 means Monday, 2 means Tuesday, all the way through 7 meaning Sunday. The U.S.-English default is Sunday, the first day of the week.
@@dbts	MS	Microsoft documentation says this is the value of the current TIMESTAMP datatype for the current database. However, it is more appropriately described as marking a timestamp each time the database is changed, but not actually maintaining the value of the special TIMESTAMP datatype.
@@error	MS, Sybase	Shows the last error number generated within the current user's session, or 0 if the last command was successful. @@error is frequently used within control-of-flow statements to perform error handling.
@@fetch_status	MS	The status of a cursor FETCH command: 0 indicates the fetch is successful -1 indicates failure or the row was beyond result sets -2 indicates the row fetched is missing
@@identity	MS, Sybase	The last value inserted into an identity column for a specific user session. The value is updated at every INSERT, SELECT . . . INTO, or bulk copy operation. INSERT statements that affect a table that has no IDENTITY columns update @@identity to NULL. This value is not rolled back if the affecting operation fails.
@@idle	MS, Sybase	The number of timeticks that SQL Server has been idle since it was last started.
@@io_busy	MS, Sybase	The number of timeticks that SQL Server has devoted to physical input/output operations since it was last started.

Table 6-3. Global Variables in SQL Server (continued)

Global Variable Name	Vendor Support	Description
@@isolation	Sybase	The current isolation level of the Transact-SQL program (0, 1, or 3).
@@langid	MS, Sybase	The local language ID used in the current user session, specified in the system table syslanguages.langid.
@@language	MS, Sybase	The local language used in the current user session, specified in the system table syslanguages.name.
@@maxcharlen	Sybase	The maximum length (in bytes) for multibyte characters in the default character set.
@@maxread	Sybase	The maximum level at which reads are allowed for the current user session.
@@maxwrite	Sybase	The maximum level at which writes are allowed for the current user session.
@@max_connections	MS, Sybase	The maximum number of simultaneous connections supported by the current computer environment of SQL Server, but not necessarily the number currently configured.
@@max_precision	MS	The level of precision used in DECIMAL and NUMERIC datatypes. The default is a maximum precision of 28, although that can be exceeded by starting SQL Server with the /p paramenter.
@@microsoftversion	MS	An internal tracking number used by the coots in Redmond (Microsoft, if you couldn't tell by the name of the variable). If you really want to know the version number, use @@version.
@@minwrite	Sybase	The minimum level that the current user session can write to database objects.
@@ncharsize	Sybase	The average length (in bytes) of a national character.
@@nestlevel	MS, Sybase	The nesting level of the current operation, initially 0. Incremented every time a stored procedure calls another stored procedure within the current user session. If the maximum value of 16 is ever exceeded, the transaction is terminated.
@@omni_version	Sybase	The date and version of the loaded Component Integration Services.
@@options	MS	The current values of query-processing SET options for a given user process.

Table 6-3. Global Variables in SQL Server (continued)

Global Variable Name	Vendor Support	Description
@@os_session_label	Sybase	The label assigned to the current user session when logged onto the client operating system.
@@pack_received	MS, Sybase	The number of input packets read by SQL Server since it was last started.
@@pack_sent	MS, Sybase	The number of output packets written by SQL Server since it was last started.
@@packet_errors	MS, Sybase	The number of errors that occurred while SQL Server was sending or receiving packets since it was last started.
@@parallel_degree	Sybase	The current maximum parallel degree setting.
@@procid	MS, Sybase	The stored procedure ID of the stored procedure currently executing in the user's session.
@@remserver	MS	The servername of a remote server accessed during the user's current session.
@@rowcount	MS, Sybase	The number of rows affected by the last operation, or 0 if the operation does not affect rows, like an IF statement.
@@scan_parallel_degree	Sybase	The current maximum parallel degree setting for nonclustered index scans.
@@servername	MS, Sybase	The name of the SQL Server installation.
@@servicename	MS	Currently, the same as @@servername, but future versions will show the name of a running service.
@@spid	MS, Sybase	The server process ID of the current process, as stored in the system table sysprocesses.spid.
@@sqlstatus	Sybase	Similar to Microsoft's @@fetch_status. @@sqlstatus shows the status information about the last fetch statement of the current user session. Values include: 0—fetch completed successfully 1—fetch caused an error 2—no more data in the result set A status value of 2 occurs when the current cursor position is on the last row of the result set when a fetch command is issued.
@@textcolid	Sybase	The column ID of the column referenced by @@textptr.
@@textdbid	Sybase	The database ID of the database holding the column referenced by @@textptr.

Table 6-3. Global Variables in SQL Server (continued)

Global Variable Name	Vendor Support	Description
@@textobjid	Sybase	The object ID of an object containing a column referenced by @@textptr.
@@textptr	Sybase	The text pointer ID of the last TEXT or IMAGE column inserted or updated by an operation (distinct and separate from the TEXTPTR function).
@@textsize	MS, Sybase	The size of an IMAGE or TEXT file in the current session displayed by a SELECT statement. This value can be reset using the SET TEXTSIZE command. The default is 4K.
@@texttx	Sybase	The text timestamp of a column referenced by @@textptr.
@@thresh_hysteresis	Sybase	No, not hysteria; the decrease in 2K data pages allowed before activating a threshold.
@@timeticks	MS, Sybase	The number of microseconds per tick, depending on the computer. Usually 1/32 second or 31.25 milliseconds.
@@total_errors	MS, Sybase	The number of errors that have occurred during read or write operations since SQL Server was last started.
@@total_read	MS, Sybase	The total number of noncache disk reads since SQL Server was last started.
@@total_write	MS, Sybase	The total number of disk writes since SQL Server was last started.
@@tranchain	Sybase	The current transaction mode, either 1 for chained or 0 for unchained.
@@trancount	MS, Sybase	The number of currently active transactions in the current user's session.
@@transtate	Sybase	The current state of a transaction after it executes in the current user session. Similar to @@error, except that @@transtate is not cleared for each batch. Its value is changed only by execution errors, not by syntax or compile errors. Values include: 0—transaction in progress (a transaction is in effect, previous statement successful) 1—transaction succeeded and committed 2—previous statement aborted, no effect on current transaction 3—transaction aborted and rolled back

Table 6-3. Global Variables in SQL Server (continued)

Global Variable Name	Vendor Support	Description
@@update_mode	Sybase	The current update mode. Values include: standard—only mode available to single-level user, allowing user to write only rows whose sensitivity label is equal to the user's curwrite session label reclassify—allows multilevel user to alter sensitivity level of data rows whose levels are between the user's minwrite and maxwrite session labels over_range—allows a multilevel user to alter sensitivity level of data rows without changing the original sensitivity label Refer to the *Sybase Security Features User's Guide* for more information.
@@version	MS, Sybase	The date, version number, and processor type for the current installation of SQL Server.

As the source code between Microsoft and Sybase has become more distinct over time, new global variables have been introduced that are supported by only one vendor. For example, the @@maxread, @@maxwrite, and @@update_mode global variables introduced by Sybase are used to support Sybase's more demanding security model.

Global variables that report time do so in timetick increments. A timetick is equivalent to 1/32 second or 31.25 milliseconds. Global variables can be queried directly as followed:

```
SELECT @@total_read, @@total_write, @@io_busy
```

Results:

```
----------- ----------- -----------
1209767     315797      19683

(1 row(s) affected)
```

The value of a global variable also can be stored in a local variable. Observe:

```
DECLARE @reads varchar(20)
SELECT  @reads = convert(varchar,@@total_read)
PRINT   @reads
GO
```

Results:

```
(1 row(s) affected)

1209767
```

Parameters

Parameters are a special subtype of a local variable used to pass values into and out of stored procedures. Since they are variables of a type, they must follow the rules of local variables, with these exceptions: they are declared differently, they may have a default, and they last only for the duration of the stored procedure. Parameters are specified in a CREATE PROCEDURE statement (also discussed in Chapter 14, *Stored Procedures and Modular Design*). This is the general syntax for declaring parameters:

```
CREATE PROCedure procedure_name
    [(@parameter_name1   datatype[,
    @parameter_name2    datatype = default_value]...
   [@parameter_name255 datatype OUTPUT])]
AS sql_statements
```

The parentheses around the parameters are optional. Like a local variable, a parameter is prefixed by a single at symbol (@). Up to 255 parameters may be declared for a single stored procedure. The stored procedure will fail if it is executed without a value for each parameter, unless the parameters have a default value. Conversely, the parameter exists only in the context of the called stored procedure, so many different stored procedures can have a parameter of the same name and datatype. As with local variables, parameters can substitute only for constant values. They cannot substitute for database object names (like tables) or keywords, unless used with the EXECUTE statement (see the earlier section, "Using local variables in SQL statements"). When specifying the datatype of a parameter, any datatype except IMAGE is OK. It's sometimes a bad idea to use the TEXT datatype for a parameter, since it's really, *really* big and it cannot be used with an OUTPUT parameter anyway. In general, you'd be better off passing CHAR or VARCHAR parameters unless you have a specific need to pass a TEXT parameter.

When specifying OUTPUT parameters, you may shorten the keyword to OUT.

Using Parameters

Here are several examples of procedures with parameters. We'll start with a very simple one and move to some more complex examples.

First, let's examine a simple stored procedure that selects all titles of a specific type, based on the value of an input parameter.

```
CREATE PROCEDURE titles_by_type
    @type varchar(20)
AS

SELECT title
FROM   titles
WHERE type = @type

GO
```

When executed, the stored procedure will retrieve all titles of a particular type:

```
Titles_by_type 'business'
```

Results:

```
title
--------------------------------------------------------------------------------
The Busy Executive's Database Guide
Cooking with Computers: Surreptitious Balance Sheets
You Can Combat Computer Stress!
Straight Talk About Computers

(4 row(s) affected)
```

In the next example, we'll illustrate a more complex stored procedure and the use of explicit parameter ordering. The stored procedure, called *nt_dir*, will perform a regular Windows NT *DIR* command and show the date and time on the server. This stored procedure accepts two parameters: a string for the path_and_filename and a Y/N flag telling whcther you want to see the date and time. Both parameters have a default value.

Here's what the stored procedure looks like:

```
CREATE PROCEDURE nt_dir
    @path_and_filename varchar(40) = 'C:\',
    @datetime_flag     char(1)     = 'N'
AS

-- Joe S. Bach, 10/15/97, A simple stored procedure to show the directory
-- of the Windows NT server where SQL Server is installed.

SET NOCOUNT ON       -- a good performance tuning trick

DECLARE @cmdshell_line varchar(55)  -- used to build the full NT dir command
```

```
-- let's build the command-line to perform a "dir" on the specified directory
SELECT  @cmdshell_line = "xp_cmdshell 'dir " + @path_and_filename + "'"

-- if they want the time and date, give it
IF @datetime_flag = 'Y'
   PRINT 'Date and Time is:'
   SELECT getdate()

-- execute the command that will retrieve the "dir" result set
EXEC  (@cmdshell_line)
GO
```

You could execute this procedure without any parameter values, thus invoking the defaults, or you could provide values of your own—something like:

```
nt_dir 'C:\MSSQL\LOG', 'Y'
```

This method of executing the stored procedure uses *implicit parameter ordering*. Implicit parameter ordering is used when you know the exact order of the parameter values. The problem with implicit parameter ordering, particularly with stored procedures that have a lot of parameters, is that you must get the values in the correct order and you must not skip any values. SQL Server only knows to link each value provided to each parameter in cardinal order.

The best way to skip or alter the order of parameters is to use *explicit parameter ordering*. Explicit parameter ordering is accomplished during the call to the stored procedure by naming each parameter and its value explicitly. In this manner, you can completely rearrange the order of the parameters or skip any parameters you desire. Do not mix parameter ordering methods within a single stored procedure call. For example:

```
nt_dir @datetime_flag ='Y', @path_and_filename = 'C:\MSSQL\LOG'
```

The results, depending on the contents of your directory, might look like this:

```
Date and Time is:
---------------------------
Oct 15 1997 10:45AM

output
------------------------------------------------------------------------------
 Volume in drive C has no label.
 Volume Serial Number is A8F3-9E02
(null)
 Directory of c:\mssql\log
(null)
10/09/97  08:39a        <DIR>              .
10/09/97  08:39a        <DIR>              ..
10/15/97  10:06a               111,253 ERRORLOG
10/09/97  08:14a                64,892 ERRORLOG.1
10/07/97  05:06p                 7,461 ERRORLOG.2
10/07/97  04:36p               463,164 ERRORLOG.3
```

```
09/22/97  08:09a              382,799 ERRORLOG.4
09/12/97  09:05a              241,048 ERRORLOG.5
09/04/97  09:03a            1,040,345 ERRORLOG.6
10/09/97  08:39a            1,847,745 SQLEXEC.OUT
12/27/97  03:07p                6,263 sqlexec.txt
               11 File(s)       4,164,970 bytes
                            2,019,827,712 bytes free
```

Both a parameter value and its default can contain SQL Server wildcard characters like %, _, [ ], and ^ when used in conjunction with LIKE inside the procedure. For example, we could make a slight adjustment to the Titles_by_type stored procedure and retrieve all titles of type mod_cook and trad_cook using the percent (%) wildcard symbol.

First, we'll alter the code of the stored procedure:

```
CREATE PROCEDURE titles_by_type
    @type varchar(20)
AS

SELECT title
FROM   titles
WHERE type LIKE @type      -- changed the '=' to 'LIKE'

GO
```

Now, we'll call the stored procedure, looking for all titles whose type contains the string %cook%:

```
Titles_by_type '%cook%'
```

Results:

```
title
--------------------------------------------------------------------------------
Silicon Valley Gastronomic Treats
The Gourmet Microwave
Onions, Leeks, and Garlic: Cooking Secrets of the Mediterranean
Fifty Years in Buckingham Palace Kitchens
Sushi, Anyone?

(5 row(s) affected)
```

OUTPUT Parameters

Now you might be asking yourself "Gee, parameters are great with user interaction, but what if I want to bounce them around between a few nested stored procedures?" If you are asking yourself that, you're way ahead of the game because that's covered in Chapter 14 ad nauseum. However, you've hit upon the importance of the OUTPUT keyword when joined to a stored procedure. OUTPUT is designed to do precisely that—return a parameter to a calling stored procedure, which can then be used in its processing.

When designating an output parameter, all you have to do is add the OUTPUT (or just OUT for short) keyword at the end of the parameter description. To then "catch" the output parameter in the calling stored procedure, you must use the EXECUTE command with an OUTPUT parameter. The difference here is that the OUTPUT parameter in the parent procedure is the place where the OUTPUT parameter from the child procedure is stored.

This example should help clear things up. We have two stored procedures: parent and child. Their names have nothing to do with parents and children. It merely indicates which is the calling and called procedure, respectively. Parent and child are extremely simple, merely adding two values, but they can help give you an idea of how values are passed between two stored procedures:

```
CREATE PROCEDURE child
  @add1  int = 0,
  @add2  int = 0,
  @total INT OUTPUT
AS

-- the SET string provides a slight performance gain for stored procedures
SET NOCOUNT ON

IF @add1 = 0 AND @add2 = 0

    BEGIN
        SELECT @total = 0
        RETURN -100
    END

SELECT @total = @add1 + @add2

RETURN 0

GO
```

When creating child and parent stored procedures, it's a good idea to create the child first. The reason for this is that SQL Server will issue a warning that the dependent child object is missing, although it will create the parent stored procedure. It's cleaner to create the dependent first. In SQL Server, the egg comes before the chicken.

```
CREATE PROCEDURE parent

AS

-- the SET string provides a slight performance gain for stored procedures
SET NOCOUNT ON

DECLARE @get_total     int,      -- stores output parameter from child proc
        @return_status int       -- stores return code from child proc
```

```
EXEC @return_status = child 12345, 44, @get_total OUTPUT

-- other Transact-SQL code might go here to manipulate value returned from --
-- child proc

SELECT @return_status AS "Return Status",
       @get_total     AS "Total"
GO
```

If you execute the parent procedure, your results look like this:

```
Return Status Total
------------- -----------
0             12389
```

Of course, if you wanted, you could pass the child any integers you wanted from the parent and get entirely different results.

Summary

This chapter is all about datatypes and how they are used: in tables, as variables in Transact-SQL programs, and as parameters passing data in and out of stored procedures. We've discussed the minutiae of all of the allowable datatypes in SQL Server. In addition, we've looked at:

- The creation of user-defined datatypes
- The important topic of NULL values and how they affect processing
- The declaration, assignment, and use of local variables, along with the specifics of the system-generated and maintained global variables
- The use of parameters in stored procedures, including an introduction to nested procedures through the use of OUTPUT parameters

In this chapter:

7

Conditional Processing

Every programming language provides methods for controlling the flow of command execution throughout its programs. With Transact-SQL, the default processing order is the exact order in which the commands are recorded in a given Transact-SQL block, script, or stored procedure. However, many operations require that we perform data processing nonsequentially. SQL Server has provided a number of constructs that enable our programs to have exact control of flow, performing operations only when and where we choose.

This chapter discusses each of the following control-of-flow statements used in Transact-SQL:

BEGIN . . . END
IF . . . ELSE
GOTO
WAITFOR
WHILE
RETURN

Some other commands provide a certain degree of control of flow, but these commands are discussed elsewhere in the book:

CASE
DECLARE
EXECUTE
ISNULL
PRINT
RAISERROR

BEGIN . . . END Constructs

The simplest control-of-flow construct is BEGIN . . . END. BEGIN . . . END defines a *statement block* within a Transact-SQL program. A statement block is an entire bunch of SQL and Transact-SQL statements grouped into one unit, allowing SQL Server to process the entire logical group of statements at once. BEGIN . . . END blocks are very useful in enhancing the readibility of code and grouping code into functional modules. In a limited way, blocks are to Transact-SQL programs what parentheses are to arithmetic operations—they help group operations. BEGIN . . . END blocks also have a pronounced effect on how Transact-SQL commands—especially IF and WHILE statements (described in the next section)—are processed.

The syntax is very simple:

```
BEGIN
   {Transact-SQL_statements}
END
```

Any SQL statement in and of itself may appear within the confines of a BEGIN . . . END block, although some Transact-SQL statements should not be blocked together. For example, CREATE RULE and INSERT should not be combined in a single block, at least not if you want the rule to work. Here are some other quick rules to remember about commands within a BEGIN . . . END block:

- CREATE DEFAULT, CREATE PROCEDURE, CREATE RULE, CREATE TRIGGER, and CREATE VIEW statements must be submitted one at a time. They cannot appear with other statements in a BEGIN . . . END block.
- The *sp_bindrule* and *sp_bindefault* system stored procedures cannot be used to bind rules, checks, or defaults to columns in the same batch as an INSERT statement that uses the rule, check, or default.
- Dropping an object and then referencing or re-creating it in the same block is prohibited.
- Adding new columns and then referencing the new columns in the same block is prohibited.
- SET statement changes take effect only at the end of the batch. It's a good idea to issue these commands by themselves.

BEGIN . . . END blocks may be nested an unlimited number of times.

BEGIN . . . END blocks are often paired with IF statements and WHILE statements. That's because IF and WHILE commands allow only *one* Transact-SQL command or block to follow the command. Enclosing multiple Transact-SQL statements in a BEGIN . . . END block tells SQL Server to think of the whole batch of commands as a single unit, thus enabling the IF or WHILE to function properly.

Even though a BEGIN . . . END block is not always necessary, it's often a good idea to include one anyway to provide logical bookends or markers around code. Even one line of code can benefit from a BEGIN . . . END block wrapper. BEGIN . . . END blocks do not cost anything in terms of performance, and they can help avoid readability problems and occasional logic errors.

IF Constructs

Using Transact-SQL's conditional function, IF, you will be able to implement requirements such as the following:

- If monthly sales exceed 200 units, then grant a $3,000 bonus to the sales staff.
- If monthly sales range between 100 and 199 units, then grant a $1,500 bonus to the sales staff.
- If monthly sales range between 10 and 99 units, then grant a $500 bonus to the sales staff.
- If monthly sales are under 10 units, invoke the alert-management stored procedure.

The IF . . . ELSE Transact-SQL construct allows you to define alternate operations (like the preceding examples) based on the results of a Boolean operation. When the Boolean comparison is true, the Transact-SQL statement or block immediately following the IF statement is executed. When the Boolean comparison is NULL, SQL Server acts as if the condition is proved false. (You can use the ISNULL function to specify a default value in the event of a NULL value.) The full syntax of IF . . . ELSE looks like this:

```
IF Boolean_comparison [...AND Boolean_comparison...]
 [...OR Boolean_comparison...]
    {Transact-SQL statement | BEGIN...END block}
[ELSE
    {Transact-SQL statement | BEGIN...END block}]
```

Boolean comparisons will usually be a simple true/false Boolean evaluation. You can also use a SELECT statement in the Boolean comparison.

Simple IF and BEGIN . . . END

Unlike many other SQL extensions, Transact-SQL does not use IF . . . THEN constructs because the THEN functionality is always implied. When the IF condition is true, SQL Server executes one subsequent Transact-SQL statement or BEGIN . . . END block found before an ELSE or GO keyword. When the condition is false or null, SQL Server skips the immediately subsequent Transact-SQL statement for the next sequential Transact-SQL statement or BEGIN . . . END block. The simplest form of an IF statement contains no ELSE clause:

```
-- Simple Boolean comparison.
IF (suser_id() = 1)
    PRINT 'Congratulations. You are the SA on this system.'
```

In this example, we check to see if the current user session is the SA or some other user by checking the system function SUSER_ID(). If SUSER_ID() returns a value of 1, the current session is owned by the SA; otherwise, it's owned by another user. When the SA is the user, then the PRINT statement is executed. The construct does not test for any other conditions. Use this construct when you do not need to test for the inverse Boolean value or any alternative conditions.

You can test a comparison and provide a course of action when the comparison fails by adding an ELSE clause to the structure. For example:

```
-- Simple Boolean comparison with ELSE clause.
IF (suser_id() = 1)
    PRINT 'Congratulations. You are the SA on this system.'
ELSE
    PRINT 'You are not the SA on this system.'
```

You can use the alternative technique of testing a Boolean condition based upon the results of a SELECT statement. For example:

```
-- A Boolean comparison using a SELECT statement.
IF (SELECT COUNT(SPID) FROM  master.dbo.sysprocesses WHERE  suid <> 1) > 0
    PRINT 'SA is not the only active user.'
```

In this example, we count every SPID (an ID that tracks active processes within SQL Server) that is not equal to '1'. (1 is the SPID reserved for SA and system processes.) If the SELECT statement finds any SPIDs other than the SA's, a PRINT command is executed. But executing a PRINT command is very simple. What if you need to accomplish some complex functionality based on an IF statement?

When executing multiple Transact-SQL statements based on the IF, the subsequent Transact-SQL statements should be enclosed in a BEGIN . . . END block. This example code fragment checks to see if the variable for the author's last name (@au_lname) is Fudd. If true, the program inserts two new records into the titles table for our burgeoning author:

```
-- check to see if the current user is the SA
IF @au_lname = 'Fudd'
BEGIN
   INSERT INTO titles
   VALUES ('FD1711', 'Zen and the Art of Wabbit Hunting', 'psychology',
          '1389', $20.00, $8000.00, 10, 0, 'Find true personal contentment
          in hunting small, helpless woodland creatures.', '06/12/99')
```

```
    INSERT INTO titles
    VALUES ('FDU1032', 'The ACME Shopping Experience', 'business','1389',
            $19.99, $5000.00, 10, 0, 'Common-sense business tips for those in
            need of ACME products. Illustrated.', '07/16/99')
END
```

The idea here is that multiple operations specific to an IF statement should be enclosed in a BEGIN . . . END block to ensure that they are executed only when the IF condition is true. If the INSERT commands were not enclosed in the BEGIN . . . END block, then the second INSERT command would be executed no matter what the results of the IF statement were. However, inside the BEGIN . . . END block, the whole block is executed only when the IF condition proves true.

Testing Multiple Boolean Comparisons (IF...AND and IF...OR)

SQL Server allows the combination of multiple Boolean tests in a single IF statement using the AND and OR keywords. We call these *multitest IF statements* for short. For example:

```
-- declare variables
DECLARE @ytd_sales INT,
        @type      VARCHAR(30)

-- assign a value to the variables
SELECT  @ytd_sales = ytd_sales,
        @type      = type
FROM    titles
WHERE   title_id = ' FD1711'

-- test the variables
IF @ytd_sales > 4000 AND @type = 'psychology'
    PRINT 'Strong selling psych title'
ELSE
    PRINT 'Weak selling psych title'
```

Results:

```
Strong selling psych title
```

In this example, the AND keyword requires that both Boolean conditions prove TRUE for the first action to be executed. If either Boolean condition proved FALSE, then the ELSE clause would execute. There is no specific limit on the number of Boolean conditions allowed in a multitest IF statement, but reason dictates that no more than a few should be used at any given time. If you find that you must test for many different conditions, you should probably rethink the program logic before using a multitest IF statement with many conditions.

Performance note: All Boolean conditions in a multitest IF statement are tested, even if an earlier condition has already proved FALSE. This can be especially expensive in a multitest IF statement that uses SELECT subqueries, because all the subqueries will be executed. Depending on the circumstances, it may be preferable to use a nested IF statement. The section titled "Nested IF . . . ELSE Statements" contains an example.

Another approach to the multitest IF statement is available through the OR keyword. Although OR is available, we do not generally recommend its use. Whenever possible, you should use nested IF statements instead. There may be a rare scenario in which a multitest IF statement using an OR keyword is useful. An IF . . . OR statement might look like this:

```
DECLARE @job INT

SELECT  @job = job_id
FROM    employee
WHERE   emp_id = 'MGK44605M'

IF (@job = 2) OR (@job = 3) OR (@job = 4)
    PRINT 'Upper management'
ELSE
    PRINT 'Not upper management'
```

Results:

```
Not upper management
```

For an IF . . . OR statement, only one of the Boolean conditions of the IF clause needs to be TRUE for it to execute. However, when all Boolean conditions of the IF statement are FALSE, then the ELSE clause will be executed. IF . . . OR statements have performance costs similar to IF . . . AND statements because every condition must be tested.

IF...EXISTS Conditions

Similar to the plain IF, the IF . . . EXISTS construct enables you to check the existence of a value. After all, sometimes you don't need to know what a value is; you only need to know that the value exists. For example, you might want to know if a given database object exists in the database. Here's the basic syntax:

```
IF [NOT] EXISTS (SELECT_statement)
...Transact-SQL commands...
```

Unlike other types of IF statements, the conditions are tested in the SELECT statement rather than in a Boolean condition. Basically, the SELECT statement is considered true if it returns any records. The SELECT statement is considered false if it returns no records. As shown in the syntax, you also can test for the nonexistence of an object or value by adding the optional NOT keyword.

IF . . . EXISTS often performs better than a regular IF . . . SELECT Boolean statement, especially in a situation in which you're not looking for a single specific value.

To illustrate this concept, we've included an elaborate example stored procedure called *calculate_db_space* on the accompanying CD-ROM, and it can calculate the space used and available on a given database. This stored procedure checks for the existence and nonexistence of objects within the database using the IF . . . EXISTS construct. Here's a simple example that shows the idea:

```
IF EXISTS (SELECT * FROM titles WHERE title_id IN ('FD1711','FD1032'))
BEGIN
   UPDATE titles SET ytd_sales = 1700
   WHERE  title_id = 'FD1711'

   UPDATE titles SET ytd_sales = 3000
   WHERE  title_id = 'FD1032'
END
```

This example tests for the existence of two values in the titles table. If the values don't exist, then no UPDATE operations are performed. If they do exist, our fine author Fudd has his ytd_sales numbers updated.

It would be easy enough to alter this code to test for the existence of database objects using IF . . . EXISTS. In this case, you'd simply change your SELECT statement to search for a given object name and/or type.

IF . . . ELSE Conditions

Often, you must implement dual requirements based on a single value. You know the drill; if the Boolean comparison has value A, then do operation X; if the Boolean comparison has some other value, then do operation Y.

Let's take our previous examples regarding our author Fudd a step further. If we've already got the two records in the titles table for Fudd, then we have to increase his ytd_sales. But if we don't have those records in the table in the first place, we must insert them. The Transact-SQL code for this requirement might look like:

```
IF EXISTS (SELECT * FROM titles WHERE title_id IN ('FD1711','FD1032'))
BEGIN
   UPDATE titles SET ytd_sales = 1700
   WHERE  title_id = 'FD1711'
```

```
   UPDATE titles SET ytd_sales = 3000
   WHERE  title_id = 'FD1032'
END
ELSE
BEGIN
   INSERT INTO titles
   VALUES ('FD1711', 'Zen and the Art of Wabbit Hunting', 'psychology',
          '1389',$20.00, $8000.00, 10, 1700, 'Find true personal contentment
          in hunting small, helpless woodland creatures.', '06/12/99')

   INSERT INTO titles
   VALUSE ('FDU1032', 'The ACME Shopping Experience', 'business','1389',
          $19.99, $5000.00, 10, 3000, 'Common-sense business tips for those
          in need of ACME products. Illustrated.', '07/16/99')
END
```

Using this construct, when the Boolean condition is TRUE (one of the title_ids exists), then the BEGIN . . . END block found immediately after the Boolean condition and before the ELSE clause is executed.

There is nothing to prevent you from putting the IF and BEGIN keywords onto a single line:

```
IF EXISTS (SELECT * FROM titles WHERE title_id IN ('FD1711','FD1032')) BEGIN
   SELECT...
```

In fact, some Transact-SQL gurus prefer to smash the BEGIN clause onto the same line as the IF. (You would have to place the SELECT on a new line, however.)

Nested IF . . . ELSE Statements

IF . . . ELSE statements may be nested any number of times. The IF and ELSE clauses may be nested any number of times. Of course, where you place the subordinate IF clause will have a direct impact on how the code is processed. When the IF condition evaluates to TRUE, any subsequent Transact-SQL statements found before the ELSE (or GO) will be executed. On the other hand, when the IF condition turns out to be FALSE or NULL, then processing will skip to the next ELSE statement or even to the next valid Transact-SQL statement. The general format for this programming construct of IF is:

```
IF Boolean_comparison1

   IF Boolean_comparison2
      ...Transact-SQL statement1...
   ELSE

      IF Boolean_comparison3
         ...Transact-SQL statement2...
      ELSE
         ...Transact-SQL statement3...
```

```
ELSE
    ...Transact-SQL statement4...
```

Although it may not be explicit from the syntax example, nested IF statements may appear after either the IF or the ELSE clause. Nested IF statements are usually required only when implementing complex business requirements. However, our recommendation is to use them cautiously since they can be very difficult to debug and understand, even if you provide outstanding commentary throughout the code. Any time nesting takes you more than three levels deep, it is advisable to reconsider the entire logical approach. Many times, you may find that a method easier than complex nested structures will present itself.

The major benefit gained by using a nested IF statement is deferred evaluation. That is, the inner conditions are never checked unless the outer condition is evaluated as true. This can provide especially noticeable dividends when the evaluation of a condition is resource-intensive (i.e., takes up a lot of CPU or I/O resources). By using an inner nested IF statement, you can effectively delay the most expensive evaluation until after all other conditions are proved true.

This example shows how nesting an IF statement can save you some CPU cycles:

```
-- Poor coding structure.  Should use a nested IF statement.
IF (suser_id() = 1) AND EXISTS
    (SELECT * FROM pubs..sysobjects WHERE  id = OBJECT_ID('titles'))
    PRINT 'Table "titles" already exists.'
ELSE
    PRINT 'Table "titles" does not exists or not SA.'
```

The simple comparison of the SUSER_ID system variable to a literal value takes up considerably fewer resources than the EXISTS clause, since the EXISTS clause must query the database. You could defer the expense of the EXISTS clause to only those situations in which the Boolean test of SUSER_ID is already known to be true:

```
-- Better structure using a nested IF statement.
IF (suser_id() = 1)
    IF EXISTS (SELECT * FROM   sysobjects WHERE  id = OBJECT_ID('titles'))
        PRINT 'Stored procedure "titles" already exists.'
    ELSE
        PRINT 'Stored procedure "titles" does not exists.'
ELSE
    PRINT 'Not SA.'
```

Not only is the expense of the EXISTS clause's query postponed, but the program now has a better message interface. In the earlier nonnested IF statement, only one message was returned when the ELSE clause executed. Thus, the message had to be the general-purpose message "Table titles does not exist, or Not SA." After switching to the nested IF statement, the general-purpose message could be broken out into two specific messages. One message now says "Not SA" and the other says "Table titles does not exist."

IF NOT . . . ELSE

SQL Server also allows you to search for the inverse of a condition with the IF NOT . . . ELSE statement. The syntax is essentially the same as a regular IF . . . ELSE statement, except that the NOT keyword must immediately follow the IF keyword and must immediately precede the condition to be tested, as shown here:

```
IF NOT Boolean_comparison
    {Transact-SQL statement | BEGIN...END block}
[ELSE
    {Transact-SQL statement | BEGIN...END block}]
```

For example:

```
-- declare the variable
DECLARE @weekday INT

-- assign a value to the variable. Sunday = 1 and Saturday = 7
SELECT @weekday = DATEPART(weekday, GETDATE())

-- test the condition
IF NOT (@weekday IN (1,7))
    PRINT 'Open for business, Monday through Friday.'
ELSE
    PRINT 'Closed for the weekend.'
```

This little routine assigns the day of the week to the variable @weekday. Sunday starts the week with a value of 1, while Saturday ends the week with a value of 7. Based on the value of the variable, the IF NOT statement prints a different message on business days from the one it prints on weekend days.

GOTO Branching and Error Handling

The GOTO keyword provides branching capabilities within a Transact-SQL program. GOTO unconditionally diverts the stream of execution to another section of the Transact-SQL program. Branching was a common and popular programming technique with many older file-oriented programming languages, but you don't see this technique used as often in Transact-SQL programs today. GOTO is a little tricky because it has two separate but equally important parts: the GOTO command and the GOTO label. The general format for a GOTO statement is:

```
GOTO label_name
```

where the `label_name` is the name of the exact point in the Transact-SQL programming where GOTO will unconditionally branch. The GOTO label must follow this format:

```
label_name:
```

The colon *must* follow the name.

GOTO, in its most useful implementation, may be used to branch to an error-handling section of code at the end of the Transact-SQL program. (There's a stored procedure on the CD-ROM called *returned_merchandise* that provides an elaborate example of using GOTO statements.) Here's a simple example that illustrates this concept:

```
IF @inventory_level <= 100 GOTO step2

IF @inventory_level BETWEEN 99 and 21
BEGIN
   EXECUTE order_books @title_id
   step2
END

IF @inventory_level >=  20 GOTO dangerously_low_inv

step2:
   ...<some more code here>...

dangerously_low_inv:
   EXECUTE order_books @title_id
   RAISERROR('This item may have been backordered!',16,1)
   step2
```

In this example, we're checking the inventory levels of a given book to see if we can complete an order. If the inventory level is 100 or more, then, hey, no problem, go to step2, where the order will be processed. If the inventory level is between 99 and 21, then order some more books; then process the order. If the inventory level is 20 or fewer, then we might not have enough on hand to complete the order, so order more books and warn the order taker of a possible back order before entering the order.

WAITFOR Construct

Sometimes a Transact-SQL program needs to pause for a moment or two (despite the constant griping from end users that "it's not *fast* enough!"). If this is ever a requirement, WAITFOR meets the need. WAITFOR will pause for a specified time, a time interval, or even a specified event before triggering the execution of the Transact-SQL statement, block, stored procedure, or transaction. Scenarios in which this might be useful include pausing a stored procedure to reduce locking contention or queuing all transactions of a special type to execute at a predefined time (don't forget that the transactions will still hold locks until they are either committed or rolled back). The general syntax for the command is shown here:

Microsoft	Sybase
`WAITFOR {DELAY 'hh:mm[:ss[:mmm]]' | TIME 'hh:mm[:ss[:mmm]]'}`	`WAITFOR {DELAY 'hh:mm[:ss[:mmm]]' | TIME 'hh:mm[:ss[:mmm]]' | ERROREXIT | PROCESSEXIT | MIRROREXIT }`

In Microsoft SQL Server, there are two available options when using this command: specifying how long to wait with DELAY and specifying when to execute with TIME. Here's a little more detail on the difference in these two versions of the command.

WAITFOR DELAY

WAITFOR DELAY tells SQL Server to wait a specified period of time. When SQL Server encounters WAITFOR DELAY, it immediately pauses operation of the Transact-SQL program. It does not move to the next command in the Transact-SQL program until the specified period of time has elapsed. Once the specified interval has elapsed, SQL Server resumes execution of the Transact-SQL program, starting with the command immediately after the WAITFOR DELAY command.

To force a Transact-SQL program to wait for three seconds, the syntax would be:

```
WAITFOR DELAY '00:00:03'
```

To force a Transact-SQL program to wait for 12 hours and 30 minutes, the syntax would be:

```
WAITFOR DELAY '12:30'
```

The WAITFOR command can also be used to trigger an event. This functionality is achieved by pairing the WAITFOR command with a WHILE loop. The WHILE loop checks for the existence of the triggering event. In this example, the loop checks for a new row in the table ##new_orders every minute until the count exceeds 0. As long as the count is 0, the WAITFOR command will cause the loop to wait one minute before checking again. Once the count exceeds 0, the next statement is executed. Here is the syntax:

```
WHILE (SELECT COUNT(*) FROM ##new_orders) = 0 WAITFOR DELAY '00:01:00'
```

WAITFOR TIME

WAITFOR TIME tells SQL Server to wait until a specified time of day. When SQL Server encounters WAITFOR TIME, it immediately pauses operation of the Transact-SQL program until the next occurrence of the specified time within a 24-hour interval. Once the specified time has been reached, SQL Server resumes execution of the Transact-SQL program starting with the command immediately after the WAITFOR TIME command.

To force a Transact-SQL program to wait until the next occurrence of 3:00 A.M., the syntax would be:

```
WAITFOR TIME '03:00'
```

To force a Transact-SQL program to wait until the next occurrence of 11:59:28:012 P.M., the syntax would be:

```
WAITFOR TIME '23:59:28:012'
```

You can also use a WHILE loop and the WAITFOR TIME command to wait for a specific event to occur. But this is not a good programming technique since it could cause long-running lock and blocking problems.

The maximum delay is 23:59:59.998 hours. When specifying milliseconds, remember that SQL Server rounds up to the third millisecond. Thus, 01:00:00:002 rounds up to 01:00:00:003 and 23:59:59:999 rounds to 00:00:00:000, translating to zero time instead of 24 hours. With either DELAY or TIME, the time must be in a format acceptable to SQL Server. The time setting does not accept dates; that's why there's a 24-hour limit on WAITFOR. A local variable can be substituted for the time string. Remember, the quotes are required.

Don't put a WAITFOR command inside a transaction. All locks issued by the transaction are held for the duration of the WAITFOR command, blocking any other transactions needing access to the locked data.

Any connection that uses WAITFOR is effectively locked up until the specified time or event has occurred. The process is given a status of waiting by SQL Server and can be released (prior to normal execution) only by killing the connection.

Sybase Extensions

Sybase allows the use of several additional options with the WAITFOR command not found on Microsoft SQL Server: ERROREXIT, PROCESSEXIT, and MIRROREXIT. Each of these options is mutually exclusive of the others and of the options TIME and DELAY. Here's a brief discussion of what they're used for:

ERROREXIT
: Tells Sybase Adaptive Server to wait until the system or user process terminates abnormally

PROCESSEXIT
: Tells Sybase Adaptive Server to wait until the system or user process terminates for any reason

MIRROREXIT
: Tells Sybase Adaptive Server to wait for a mirror failure (often used with DB-Library calls)

These options are used mostly for stored procedures or Transact-SQL scripts that control and call other stored procedures or scripts. For example:

```
BEGIN
WAITFOR ERROREXIT
RAISERROR 50000 "Subprocedure Process exited abnormally!"
END
```

This fragment of Transact-SQL code will wait for any process to exit abnormally. After an abnormal termination has occurred, Sybase Adaptive Server will raise an error message as shown.

WHILE Loops

Loops are an iterative control structure that allow the same code to execute repeatedly. SQL Server enables looping through the general-purpose WHILE statement. (Other languages also offer looping through FOR loops and DO loops; SQL Server does not.) WHILE loops in SQL Server function by setting a Boolean condition for the repeated execution of a Transact-SQL statement or block. The statements will execute repeatedly until the Boolean condition is no longer true or until the loop is intentionally disrupted with the BREAK command. Once a WHILE loop is terminated, processing passes to the next valid Transact-SQL statement that follows the loop. The CONTINUE command can be used to pass control to the top of the WHILE loop, skipping any Transact-SQL statements between the CONTINUE command and the end of the loop.

The syntax for a WHILE loop looks like this:

```
WHILE Boolean_condition
   {Transact-SQL_statement | statement_block}
    { . . . may contain multiple CONTINUE and/or BREAK statements}
```

The Boolean condition can evaluate two variables, a variable and a literal, or even a SELECT statement. If you use a SELECT statement in the Boolean condition, it must be enclosed in parentheses.

WHILE loops have an *implied* structure like that of IF . . . ELSE structures. The WHILE statement initializes the structure; the body of the structure is assumed to be the next valid Transact-SQL statement or block of statements enclosed in a BEGIN . . . END block. The following sections illustrate this concept.

An Infinite Loop

There may be situations in which you wish to create a loop that will execute an infinite number of times or until a programmatic event executes the BREAK command (or until the whole session is terminated with a KILL command).

Here's an example of an *infinite loop*:

```
WHILE 1=1     -- this Boolean condition always true, so loop will never end!
BEGIN
   WAITFOR '012:00:00'
   IF (SELECT getdate() ) BETWEEN 'March 1 1999' and 'June 1 1999'
      PRINT 'At wast! Wabbit Season!!!"
END
```

In this example, the WHILE loop is truly an infinite loop. As long as SQL Server is running, the loop will continue to execute. The loop is infinite because its Boolean condition is always true; 1 will always equal 1. You could have just as easily used A = A or 942386 = 942386. As long as the Boolean condition is always true, the loop will cycle infinitely.

In this example, the loop first pauses for 12 hours, then it checks the system date. If the system date is between the start and end date of rabbit season, a message is printed. The loop then repeats on a 12-hour interval. There is no BREAK clause, so this loop will never terminate.

A Simple Loop and the BREAK Command

Infinite loops are occasionally useful, but most programs don't need a loop that never ends. It's more likely that you'll need a loop that has an ending point, sometimes an *unknown* one. To achieve this end, we'll use a structure called a *simple loop*. A simple loop is (simply) an infinite loop that contains a conditional BREAK clause. The BREAK clause is usable only within a loop. BREAK tells SQL Server to immediately exit the loop. Execution of the Transact-SQL program will resume at the first command following the WHILE loop.

Simple loops offer a couple of benefits: first, the executable statements within the loop are certain to execute at least one time; and second, the exact number of iterations of the loop doesn't have to be known. Here's an example of a simple loop with a BREAK statement:

```
WHILE 1=1     -- this Boolean condition always true, so loop will never end!
BEGIN
   WAITFOR '012:00:00'
   IF (SELECT getdate() ) BETWEEN 'March 1 1999' and 'June 1 1999'
   BEGIN
      PRINT 'At wast! Wabbit Season!!!"
      BREAK
   END
END
```

We've altered our earlier example to include a BREAK command. Now we still have no idea how many times the loop will have to execute before it's finally rabbit season. But the program now has a conditional escape.

It's a good idea to place the BREAK command at the end of the statement block. That way, you can be sure that all program logic has been properly processed before exiting the loop. When BREAK is executed, any Transact-SQL commands following it are skipped. Processing continues with the first valid Transact-SQL command outside of the loop (usually the first command after the END clause of the BEGIN . . . END block).

Here's an example of a somewhat more complex WHILE loop. Normally, we'd shift this more complex example to the CD-ROM; however, this one teaches a lot of useful tricks. Imagine that your Transact-SQL program will be given a list of names (of accounts, clients, employees, or whatever) with only a comma delimiting each one. The names might also have spaces (none or many) between each one. Each name must have a specific action applied to it. You do not know in advance how many names will be supplied. How can you parse out a single long line into a set of actions on each individual item? This bit of code shows you how:

```
SET NOCOUNT ON

DECLARE @sample_list    VARCHAR(250)  -- the list of input names
DECLARE @parsing_list   VARCHAR(250)  -- manipulates the input list
DECLARE @recipient      VARCHAR(30)   -- the individual author extracted
                                      --   from the list
DECLARE @find_comma     INT           -- locates the ordinal position of
                                      --   each comma
DECLARE @output_line    VARCHAR(250)  -- the final output

-- the sample list is taken from the authors table
SELECT @sample_list    = "Reginald Blotchet-Halls, Innes del Castillo,
Charlene Locksley,Akiko Yokomoto,    Michael O'Leary"

SELECT @parsing_list   = @sample_list

WHILE  @parsing_list  IS NOT NULL
BEGIN
    -- the PATINDEX function finds the occurrence of any character, a comma
    --   in this case
    SELECT @find_comma        = PATINDEX('%,%',@parsing_list)
    IF     @find_comma       <> 0
    BEGIN
        -- the list is paired down up to the first comma and reevaluated
        SELECT @recipient     = SUBSTRING(@parsing_list,1,(@find_comma-1))
        SELECT @parsing_list = LTRIM (SUBSTRING(@parsing_list,
                                   (@find_comma+1),250))
        PRINT  @recipient
        CONTINUE
    END
    ELSE
    BEGIN
        -- this block finds the last value
        SELECT @recipient     = @parsing_list
        SELECT @parsing_list = null
```

```
            PRINT   @recipient
            BREAK
        END
    END
```

Results:

```
Reginald Blotchet-Halls
Innes del Castillo
Charlene Locksley
Akiko Yokomoto
Michael O'Leary
```

The loop searches for each instance of a comma using the PATINDEX function. Once it finds a comma, it extracts the text prior to the comma into the @recipient variable and the text after the comma into the @parsing_list variable. If the @parsing_list variable is not null, it repeats the process until there are no longer any values in the @parsing_list variable. You could easily adapt this code into a stored procedure that, for each name in the list, prints a report, sends an email, calls a stored procedure, or does whatever is needed.

Nested Loops and CONTINUE

WHILE loops can be nested many levels deep. (The exact number of levels is dependent on the configuration of the server.) When using nested loops, be careful with BREAK statements. In nested loops, the innermost BREAK exits to the next outermost loop, not all the way out. Any Transact-SQL statements following the end of the innermost loop are executed first; then the next outermost loop restarts. You can easily exit all the way out of an nested loop from the innermost loop using the GOTO command.

In some cases, you might want to restart a loop that has already begun processing. You can do this from within a loop using the CONTINUE command. CONTINUE has no use outside of a loop and will, in fact, generate a compile error when used outside a loop. The CONTINUE command causes processing to bounce up to the top of the WHILE loop and reevaluate the Boolean condition. Processing then continues as usual: if the condition is true, the loop continues as usual. If the Boolean condition is false, the loop exits normally.

In the following example, we construct a nested loop in the pubs database. The Transact-SQL program compiles a report of units sold by month and year based on an inner loop that cycles through the years 1992 through 1994, while an outer loop cycles through the months of the year. Although this problem could also be solved with cursors or with the CASE expression, we'll use it to illustrate nested WHILE loops:

```
-- turn off unnecessary output
SET NOCOUNT ON
```

```
-- declare the necessary variables
DECLARE @year SMALLINT, @month TINYINT, @line VARCHAR(80),
DECLARE @monthly_sales SMALLINT

-- print the report header
PRINT '
     Monthly Sales

Month  1992  1993  1994
----- ----- ----- -----'

-- initialize the outer loop variable
SELECT @month = 0
WHILE @month < 12
BEGIN
    -- increment the month variable and initialize the inner loop variable
    SELECT  @month = @month + 1,
            @year  = 1991
    -- build the month portion of the output string
    SELECT  @line  = ' ' + SUBSTRING(
                'JanFebMarAprMayJunJulAugSepOctNovDec',
                @month * 3 - 2, 3 ) + ' '
    -- begin the inner loop
    WHILE @year < 1994
    BEGIN
        -- increment the year variable
        SELECT  @year = @year + 1

        -- calculate the unit sales
        SELECT  @monthly_sales = ISNULL( SUM( qty ), 0 )
        FROM    sales
        WHERE   DATEPART( year,  ord_date ) = @year
            AND DATEPART( month, ord_date ) = @month

        IF @@ROWCOUNT = 0 SELECT @monthly_sales = 0

        -- build the output line
        SELECT  @line = @line + ' ' + STR( @monthly_sales, 5 )
    END
    -- print the output line
    PRINT @line
END
```

Results:

```
     Monthly Sales

Month  1992  1993  1994
----- ----- ----- -----
 Jan      0     0     0
 Feb      0    35     0
 Mar      0    25     0
 Apr      0     0     0
 May      0   165     0
 Jun     80     0     0
```

```
Jul     0    0    0
Aug     0    0    0
Sep     0    0  163
Oct     0   15    0
Nov     0    0    0
Dec     0   10    0
```

The Transact-SQL program compiles a report of units sold each month during the years 1992 through 1994. An outer loop determines which month is evaluated while an inner loop cycles through each year, calculating the unit sales.

Terminating a Loop

There is only one way to start a loop. Unfortunately, there are lots of ways to get out of a loop and several of them are bad, bad, bad! Here are a few of the better ways to terminate or exit from a loop:

- Programmatically force the condition of the WHILE loop to be met within the loop itself. On its next cycle, the loop will gracefully terminate.
- Use the BREAK command to terminate the loop. In some cases, you'll have to issue many BREAK commands to exit through each level of a nested loop.
- Use the GOTO statement to hop completely out of a loop to another point in the Transact-SQL program. This is especially useful in a controlled environment where GOTO is used only to, say, exit to an error-handling section of the program. (As an aside, structured programming purists advocate *never* using a GOTO statement!)
- Use the RETURN command, which exits immediately and irrevocably from a procedure or query. This command is generally not recommended unless you wish to completely exit the Transact-SQL program from within a loop. It's kind of like a fighter pilot hitting the EJECT button to escape a burning fighter jet.

RETURN Statement

The RETURN statement is SQL Server's equivalent of the barroom bouncer. It is used to immediately and completely halt processing of the batch, query, or procedure. Transact-SQL statements that follow RETURN are not executed. Do not pass GO, do not collect $200. Unlike the BREAK command, which can be used only in loops, RETURN can be used anywhere in a Transact-SQL program. Inside of stored procedures, RETURN has the added functionality of returning a status code indicating the state of processing at the time RETURN was executed. The syntax for the command follows:

```
RETURN [([integer])]
```

When used in a Transact-SQL program other than a stored procedure, the integer should not be used. For example:

```
BEGIN TRANSACTION
   INSERT INTO titles
   VALUES ('FD1711', 'Zen and the Art of Wabbit Hunting', 'psychology',
           '1389',$20.00, $8000.00, 10, 1700, 'Find true personal contentment
           in hunting small, helpless woodland creatures.', '06/12/99')

   INSERT INTO titles
   VALUSE ('FDU1032', 'The ACME Shopping Experience', 'business','1389',
           $19.99, $5000.00, 10, 3000, 'Common-sense business tips for those
           in need of ACME products. Illustrated.', '07/16/99')

    SELECT @err_status = @@error

    IF @@err_status <> 0
        BEGIN
            ROLLBACK TRANSACTION
            RETURN
        END
    ELSE
        COMMIT TRANSACTION
END
```

In this case, the Transact-SQL batch attempts to update a record. If an error occurs during the processing, then the transaction is to be rolled back and the batch aborted. If no errors are encountered, then the transaction is to be committed.

SQL Server has predefined status codes between -99 and 0. The current status codes 0 through -14 are described in Table 7-1, while -15 through -99 are reserved for future use. You can use a status code of your own choosing, but it must not conflict with the reserved status codes used by SQL Server. If you do not assign a status code to the RETURN (integer), SQL Server will assign a value for you.

Table 7-1. SQL Server Predefined Status Codes

Status Code	Meaning
0	Procedure executed successfully.
-1	Object is missing.
-2	Datatype error occurred.
-3	Process chosen as deadlock victim.
-4	Permission error occurred.
-5	Syntax error occurred.
-6	Miscellaneous user error occurred.
-7	Resource error occurred (such as out of space or locks).
-8	Nonfatal internal error encountered.
-9	System limit reached.

Table 7-1. SQL Server Predefined Status Codes (continued)

Status Code	Meaning
-10	Fatal internal inconsistency occurred.
-11	Fatal internal inconsistency occurred.
-12	Table or index is corrupt.
-13	Database is corrupt.
-14	Hardware error occurred.

Stored procedures that end with the RETURN command can pass their status codes back to the Transact-SQL program that called them through a variation of the EXECUTE command. The EXECUTE command must be used to call the stored procedure and must follow the exact format:

```
EXEC[UTE] @return_status = stored_procedure_name
```

The variable name used for @return_status can be any valid variable identifier. The return status is of the INT datatype and defaults to zero if no value is provided. Even when a stored procedure terminates without the benefit of a RETURN command, it assumes a return status equal to RETURN 0.

Summary

Chapter 7 discussed the conditional processing and control-of-flow commands available within Transact-SQL, including:

- IF . . . ELSE structures, which allow you to implement program requirements based on the results of a Boolean operation. Transact-SQL programs of any complexity will require heavy use of IF . . . ELSE structures, so learn them by heart.
- BEGIN . . . END blocks, a set of commands used to group a block of Transact-SQL commands into a single unit of code.
- GOTO, a command that unconditionally diverts the stream of execution to another section within the Transact-SQL program.
- WAITFOR, a statement that tells a Transact-SQL program to wait for an interval or a specified time of day.
- WHILE loops, a powerful structure in Transact-SQL, that allow the same block of code to be executed repeatedly.
- The RETURN statement, which completely and immediately halts Transact-SQL processing in the query, batch, stored procedure, or trigger in which it was executed.

8

Row Processing with Cursors

In this chapter:

Cursor processing is an important element of Transact-SQL programming. A cursor allows you to process the rows of a certain result set one at a time. This is useful when necessary operations cannot occur within a single query. Cursors allow you to define a set of rows and then move within this set, performing operations on individual rows. Old versions of Transact-SQL did not support cursors on the database server level, although the SQL Server API (DB-Library) and ODBC provided cursor functions. The API implementation was less efficient. It required the whole result set to be retrieved and stored in the client machine's memory before cursor processing could begin. Server-based cursors are more versatile, allowing powerful manipulations on rows and flexible browsing options, such as moving forward or backward in the result set or even skipping to a row by number.

Many programmers like cursor processing, because it is so similar to the way most algorithms are described. A typical loop in a program written in a 3GL says: "take the first record, apply this action to it, then take the next record, and continue until all done." Cursor processing allows you to code algorithms exactly as they are specified. Compare this to set processing, which is the heart and soul of relational database programming. You write a query that describes an action and then you command your database: "go do it for every record that qualifies." You do not have to code loops and exit conditions—the RDBMS does it for you. Cursors may be relatively new in Transact-SQL, but in fact they preserve a coding methodology that was formed back in the 1950s.

The catch of cursor processing is a severe performance penalty compared to set processing. For this reason, a good rule of thumb is to avoid cursors in your programs as much as possible. But we do not suggest that you remove them from your Transact-SQL programming palette completely. There are certain tasks for which cursors are very useful. For example, you may need to call a stored procedure for every row of a result set or perform a set of commands that cannot be implemented via set processing. Another likely application area is the processing of a relatively small number of rows. Typically, a few dozen cursor iterations do not kill the response time. One more task for cursors is the batch job processing of very large data sets, in which performance is a lesser concern than overflowing a transaction log or locking a large table. Cursors reduce locking to one or a few pages and allow dumping of the transaction log while the batch job is in progress. Knowing the strengths and weaknesses of cursors will allow you to apply them where they work best.

Microsoft and Sybase implementation of cursors is quite different in several important areas. As appropriate, we'll compare differences in syntax and behavior in both vendors' versions.

Cursor Fundamentals

Every cursor has a life cycle consisting of predefined stages:

1. First, a cursor needs to be declared with a DECLARE CURSOR statement. It defines a SELECT statement on one or more tables or views.
2. Then, the cursor may be opened when necessary with an OPEN statement. At this point, the RDBMS performs the SELECT statement but does not return any data yet.
3. Next, the FETCH CURSOR command allows you to retrieve rows one at a time. Depending on cursor type, you may be able to move back and forth in the set of rows and update or delete retrieved rows.
4. When your program decides it is done with all rows that need processing, it closes the cursor with, you guessed it, a CLOSE command.
5. At this point, the cursor has another chance to reincarnate. If your program requires, you may reopen the cursor and fetch rows again. This is often done when the SELECT statement used to declare the cursor depends on some variables and you want a new data set for different variable values. Reopening a cursor may also give you a different data set if your process or other users have changed the data in underlying tables. Unlike cats, cursors may be granted more than nine lives. You can close and reopen them as many times as you need.

6. When your program has had enough, it destroys the cursor with a DEALLOCATE command. Now you can allocate another one under the same name if you wish. If you create a cursor inside a stored procedure, it does not disappear when the procedure ends. It exists in your process until you explicitly close and deallocate it. SQL Server, however, automatically destroys all cursors when their creator processes terminate.

Your program may have multiple cursors allocated and open at the same time. Each cursor should have a unique name within your SQL Server session. Other users can use the same name for their own cursors. Cursors belong to their creator only and may not be shared between server processes. Another process may declare and use the same cursor if it needs access to the same data set.

Declaring a Cursor

Every cursor is associated with a SELECT statement that defines a set of rows. Cursors are declared by the same command that creates local variables—DECLARE, but with a different syntax, as shown in Table 8-1.

Table 8-1. Declare Cursor Syntax

Microsoft	Sybase

`DECLARE cursor_name`
`[INSENSITIVE] [SCROLL] CURSOR`
`FOR select_statement`
`[FOR {READ ONLY`
`| UPDATE [OF column_list]}]`
	`DECLARE cursor_name`
	`CURSOR`
	`FOR select_statement`
	`[FOR {READ ONLY`
	`| UPDATE [OF column_list]}]`

In this syntax, `cursor_name` is the name of the cursor being defined; the name must be a valid Transact-SQL identifier.

The keyword INSENSITIVE is supported only by Microsoft. It makes the cursor "insensitive" to any changes in the underlying tables. When you open such a cursor, it creates a temporary copy of the data and works with it until closed. Other users can make changes to the real data without any effect on your cursor. INSENSITIVE cursors cannot be used for updates. SQL Server automatically makes a cursor INSENSITIVE if one or more tables defined in the `select_statement` do not have a unique index.

INSENSITIVE cursors may have serious performance implications. Creating a temporary copy of all the rows defined by a cursor may take a long time and a lot of space in tempdb. Use this option only if you want to protect the data set defined by the cursor from modifications made by other processes.

Microsoft SQL Server automatically makes the cursor INSENSITIVE if one or more of the following is true. Watch out for these conditions to avoid inadvertent creation of an insensitive cursor and the associated performance penalty:

- The `select_statement` contains the keywords DISTINCT, UNION, GROUP BY, or HAVING.
- There is no unique index on one or more of the underlying tables.
- There is an outer join in the `select_statement`.
- The select items list contains a constant.

The keyword SCROLL (supported only by Microsoft) specifies that you can use any possible method of fetching data via this cursor. We will discuss the FETCH command later in this chapter.

The `select_statement` is a regular SELECT statement, with some limitations, which defines a set of rows. Cursors do not allow the keywords COMPUTE, COMPUTE BY, FOR BROWSE, and INTO within their `select_statement`.

The READ ONLY option prevents your program from updating any row within the cursor data set. By default, updates are allowed, provided that the `select_statement` does not contain one or more of the following:

- Aggregate function
- Join
- Subquery
- UNION operator
- DISTINCT keyword
- GROUP BY clause

If you do not intend to update rows accessed via the cursor, it may be better to define it with the READ ONLY option. It makes the code easier to read and protects you from inadvertently coding an update.

UPDATE [OF `column_list`] specifies columns that may be updated via the cursor. OF `column_list` limits modifications to the listed columns only; otherwise, any column may be updated. It makes it easier for someone reading the code to understand which columns may be updated. However, if the list contains a lot of columns, it may make your program unnecessarily bulky. One more benefit is that you protect columns not included in the UPDATE OF list from inadvertent updates in your own code.

In this first example, the following cursor provides access to all titles. By default it permits updates on any column:

```
DECLARE titles_cursor CURSOR
FOR
SELECT title_id, title, type, pub_id, price
FROM   titles
```

The next example for Microsoft SQL Server is a cursor that may be used to read information about sales. It makes a temporary copy of all data when opened and does not reflect any data changes made by other users while it is in use:

```
DECLARE browse_orders INSENSITIVE CURSOR
FOR
SELECT  UPPER( st.stor_name ) 'store',
        UPPER( ti.title ) 'title',
        sa.ord_num,
        sa.ord_date,
        sa.qty,
        sa.payterms
FROM    sales sa, stores st, titles ti
WHERE   sa.stor_id  = st.stor_id
    AND sa.title_id = ti.title_id
FOR READ ONLY
```

The following statement declares a Microsoft SQL Server cursor that can be used to fetch complete store records and move in the result set in any direction:

```
DECLARE scroll_stores SCROLL CURSOR
FOR
SELECT * FROM stores
```

Syntactically correct DECLARE CURSOR statements do not produce any output. They only prepare a cursor and do not execute the actual SELECT statement used in the DECLARE command. Data retrieval is done by other commands discussed in the following sections.

Opening a Cursor

Declared cursors may be opened with the following command:

```
OPEN cursor_name
```

If the cursor is defined as INSENSITIVE (Microsoft only), a temporary table is created at this time. It contains all rows of the result set in the order defined in the DECLARE CURSOR statement. This data is not affected by subsequent updates, inserts, and deletes performed by other users on underlying tables. You may consider it a snapshot of data in time.

For cursors other than INSENSITIVE, SQL Server still creates a temporary data set that contains keys to all qualifying rows. Depending on the number of affected rows, this process may take a long time and require significant space in the tempdb database. (Later in this chapter we will discuss a related issue of asynchronous keysets and their performance impact.)

For example, we can open the cursors we declared in the previous section as follows:

```
OPEN titles_cursor
OPEN browse_orders
OPEN scroll_stores
```

This command returns no result, but it impacts some global variables. On Sybase SQL Server you can use variable @@rowcount, which contains the number of rows in the data set. This variable is affected by many other commands and changes as soon as you execute the next one. Therefore, you have to check it immediately after OPEN. Microsoft SQL Server provides a different global variable for the same purpose—@@cursor_rows. It also reports how many rows qualify for the last opened cursor:

```
SELECT @@CURSOR_ROWS
```

The value is positive when SQL Server already knows exactly how many rows there are in the data set. It is zero if there are no rows in the set or if the last opened cursor is already closed or deallocated. The value may also be negative in case the keyset is being populated asynchronously (see the next section) and SQL Server has not yet finished this process. While SQL Server populates the keyset, it keeps changing the value of @@cursor_rows. Once the keyset is fully populated, the value becomes positive and reflects the exact number of rows that qualify for the cursor.

When we check the value of @@cursor_rows after opening the browse_orders cursor on Microsoft SQL Server, it returns the following:

```
-----------
21

(1 row(s) affected)
```

Asynchronous Keysets

As we explained in the previous section, SQL Server creates a temporary table containing keys to all rows defined by the cursor. This happens when you open a cursor that is not insensitive. If you are going to browse through millions of rows via this cursor, the process of populating a temporary table may be a time-consuming operation. If SQL Server put your program on hold until the temporary table is populated, it could be disastrous to its performance. In order to optimize this process, SQL Server may choose to populate the temporary keyset *asynchronously*. This means that it automatically opens a separate thread and uses it to populate the keyset. At the same time, your process can start using what has already been populated right away. The asynchronous process will typically run faster than your program processing rows and will be done with more keys by the time you need them.

Microsoft SQL Server decides when to use asynchronous keysets depending on the SQL Server configuration parameter "*cursor threshold*." This parameter is an advanced configuration option; to be able to see it, you may need to execute the following commands:

```
sp_configure 'show advanced options', 1
GO
RECONFIGURE WITH OVERRIDE
GO
```

Then you can query the configuration value:

```
sp_configure 'cursor threshold'
```

The result depends on your configuration. If you have not changed default settings, the command returns:

```
name                 minimum     maximum     config_value run_value
-------------------- ----------- ----------- ------------ ----------
cursor threshold     -1          2147483647  -1           -1
```

The setting of -1 tells SQL Server to generate all keysets synchronously. A zero value makes all keysets asynchronous. Positive values establish a threshold that defines when to generate an asynchronous keyset. When you open a cursor, the optimizer estimates the number of rows that may qualify for the result set. If this estimated number exceeds the configured cursor threshold, SQL Server generates an asynchronous keyset; otherwise, it generates a synchronous keyset.

Configuring this parameter may require some research. The optimal setting depends on your hardware configuration, operating system, SQL Server version, and application characteristics. *Synchronous keysets* are faster to build, but your program has to wait until the whole keyset is built before it may begin scrolling through the data set. Asynchronous ones take extra time to build, but allow almost instant access to the first rows. They improve perceived response time for users, even though they require extra resources. As the last result set demonstrates, the default configuration value is -1, which means only synchronous keysets. You may want to change this default to a reasonably high value, such as 1,000. But do not take this number as a rule of thumb. You have to test different settings in your own environment and measure the performance of those transactions that utilize cursors.

Fetching Data

Fetching rows means retrieving them, one at a time, via a cursor. The FETCH command allows you to select data from columns defined by the cursor and store it in local variables. It also defines which row to access. A cursor defines a consecutive set of rows. The most typical way to process these rows is to start from the first row and read, one by one, until you reach the end of the data set. Some programs may require that you occasionally move backward to those rows that have already been processed. It may also be necessary to skip several rows at a time or move to a row by its absolute position in the data set. The syntax of the FETCH command is shown in Table 8-2.

Table 8-2. FETCH Syntax

Microsoft	Sybase
`FETCH [ [NEXT | PRIOR | FIRST | LAST | ABSOLUTE n | RELATIVE n] FROM] cursor_name [INTO @local_variable1, @ local_variable2, . . . ]`	`FETCH cursor_name [INTO @local_variable1, @ local_variable2, . . . ]`

Microsoft provides substantially more options with a FETCH command; these are explained in Table 8-3. NEXT is the most common one and is used by default. All other options are available only with SCROLL cursors. If an option is specified after FETCH, then the FROM keyword is also required.

Table 8-3. FETCH Command Options on Microsoft SQL Server

Option	Which Row Is Retrieved
NEXT	If this is the first FETCH command for the cursor, then the first row is fetched; otherwise, the next row after the last one is fetched. NEXT is used by default when no option is specified.
PRIOR	The previous row in the set.
FIRST	The very first row of the set.
LAST	The very last row of the set.
ABSOLUTE n	If n is positive, then the nth row of the set (that has the nth absolute position (number) from the beginning of the set) is fetched. If n is negative, then SQL Server counts rows from the end of the set and returns the nth row from the bottom.
RELATIVE n	For a positive n, the nth row moving forward after the currently fetched row is fetched. If n is negative, then the nth row going backward from the currently fetched row is fetched.

The INTO list specifies the list of variables in which you want to store the columns of the row. The number and datatype of variables in the INTO list should be the same as the number and datatype of the columns specified in the DECLARE CURSOR statement. Implicit datatype conversion is not supported here. Types must match precisely, although you can use CHAR/VARCHAR and BINARY/VARBINARY interchangeably. You can also fetch columns into variables with higher length. For example, a CHAR(12) column can be stored in a CHAR(40) variable. But you cannot fetch a MONEY column into an INT variable or CHAR(80) into CHAR(72). FETCH stores columns in variables in the same order in which they appear in the DECLARE CURSOR command. If you omit the INTO list, FETCH acts as a SELECT statement for a single row.

The FETCH command returns nothing when the specified row does not exist in the result set. For example, when you have reached the end of the set and attempt to fetch the next row or request a nonexistent absolute row number, FETCH does not fail, but brings no data back. If you fetch into variables, they do not change their values. How do you tell when there is nothing else to process?

Microsoft and Sybase maintain special global variables to check the status of the last FETCH command. On Microsoft SQL Server, use @@fetch_status, and on Sybase, use @@sqlstatus. A global variable has a value in the context of your session and is changed every time you fetch a row. Table 8-4 provides information about the values of these variables depending on FETCH results.

Table 8-4. Global Variables Describing FETCH Status

Microsoft @@fetch_status		**Sybase @@sqlstats**	
Value	**Description**	**Value**	**Description**
0	Successful FETCH.	0	Successful FETCH.
-1	The cursor has reached the end of the data set or the specified row does not exist.	2	The cursor has reached the end of the data set.
-2	The row has been deleted or its key has been updated after you opened the cursor.	1	FETCH resulted in an error.

Your program should analyze the @@fetch_status variable after every FETCH command to determine if it has succeeded and you can proceed to using fetched results.

Sybase provides a special SET command not supported by Microsoft that allows you to control how many rows are returned by a FETCH command:

```
SET CURSOR ROWS number FOR cursor_name
```

The initial number setting for any new cursor is 1, but you may set it higher when necessary. When this option is used, a FETCH command without an INTO variables list returns a specified number of rows, provided that the data set has that many. It may not be one-row-at-a-time processing after all!

In the following examples, we use cursors that we have declared and opened earlier in this chapter.

Example 1. Retrieve a row from titles_cursor. For a cursor that has just been opened, the following command returns the first row of the result set. Without an INTO list of variables, it produces results as a single-row SELECT.

```
FETCH titles_cursor
```

Results:

```
title_id title                                 type         pub_id price
-------- ------------------------------------- ------------ ------ ------
BU1032   The Busy Executive's Database Guide   business     1389   19.99

(1 row(s) affected)
```

Example 2. Sybase SQL Server allows you to retrieve more than one row via a cursor:

```
SET CURSOR ROWS 4 FOR titles_cursor
FETCH titles_cursor
```

Results:

```
title_id title                                     type     pub_id price
-------- ----------------------------------------- -------- ------ -----
BU1032   The Busy Executive's Database Guide       business 1389   19.99
BU1111   Cooking with Computers: Surreptitiouss... business 1389   11.95
BU2075   You Can Combat Computer Stress!           business 0736   2.99
BU7832   Straight Talk About Computers             business 1389   19.99

(4 row(s) affected)
```

Example 3 (Microsoft only). We declared cursor titles_cursor without the SCROLL option. Therefore, it permits only forward movement from the first to the last row. SQL Server produces an error message if we attempt to fetch a row identified by its absolute or relative location in the result set:

```
FETCH FIRST FROM titles_cursor
```

Results:

```
Msg 16911, Level 16, State 1
fetch: The fetch type FETCH_FIRST cannot be used with forward only cursors
```

Example 4. We fetch columns into variables via the same cursor. Even if we are not interested in all columns of the row, we have to create variables and fetch each one of them. The following code gets a row of the result set and shows title and price.

```
DECLARE @title_id CHAR(6),
        @title    VARCHAR(80),
        @type     CHAR(12),
        @pub_id   CHAR(4),
        @price    MONEY
FETCH titles_cursor INTO @title_id, @title, @type, @pub_id, @price
SELECT @title, @price
```

Results:

```
(0 row(s) affected)


------------------------------------------------------------ --------
Cooking with Computers: Surreptitious Balance Sheets           11.95

(1 row(s) affected)
```

Example 5 (Microsoft only). We declared a cursor, scroll_stores, with the SCROLL option. It allows jumping between the rows of the result set as our program requires. The following code selects the last row, then the third, then the fifth from the end, and then it skips three rows forward (to the second row from the end), and finally gets one next row (which happens to be the last row of the result set). The program may not make a lot of business sense, but it allows us to demonstrate different cursor positioning options.

```
SET NOCOUNT ON
FETCH LAST FROM scroll_stores
FETCH ABSOLUTE 3 FROM scroll_stores
FETCH ABSOLUTE -5 FROM scroll_stores
FETCH RELATIVE 3 FROM scroll_stores
FETCH NEXT FROM scroll_stores
```

Results:

```
stor_id stor_name            stor_address       city       state zip
------- -------------------- ------------------ ---------- ----- -----
8042    Bookbeat             679 Carson St.     Portland   OR    89076
stor_id stor_name            stor_address       city       state zip
------- -------------------- ------------------ ---------- ----- -----
7067    News & Brews         577 First St.      Los Gatos  CA    96745
stor_id stor_name            stor_address       city       state zip
------- -------------------- ------------------ ---------- ----- -----
7066    Barnum's             567 Pasadena Ave.  Tustin     CA    92789
stor_id stor_name            stor_address       city       state zip
------- -------------------- ------------------ ---------- ----- -----
7896    Fricative Bookshop   89 Madison St.     Fremont    CA    90019
stor_id stor_name            stor_address       city       state zip
------- -------------------- ------------------ ---------- ----- -----
8042    Bookbeat             679 Carson St.     Portland   OR    89076
```

Example 6 (Microsoft only). This demonstrates what happens with the @@fetch_status global variable as we move through the rows. The following code fetches the last row of the result set, then attempts to fetch one more row after the last, and then tries to fetch nonexistent row number 1,000:

```
SET NOCOUNT ON
FETCH LAST FROM scroll_stores
SELECT @@FETCH_STATUS 'Fetch Status'
FETCH NEXT FROM scroll_stores
SELECT @@FETCH_STATUS 'Fetch Status'
FETCH ABSOLUTE 1000 FROM scroll_stores
SELECT @@FETCH_STATUS 'Fetch Status'
```

Results:

```
stor_id stor_name   stor_address    city       state zip
------- ----------- --------------- ---------- ----- -----
8042    Bookbeat    679 Carson St.  Portland   OR    89076
Fetch Status
------------
0
stor_id stor_name   stor_address    city       state zip
------- ----------- --------------- ---------- ----- -----
Fetch Status
------------
-1
stor_id stor_name   stor_address    city       state zip
------- ----------- --------------- ---------- ----- -----
Fetch Status
------------
-1
```

Closing and Deallocating a Cursor

The CLOSE command closes a previously opened cursor. The syntax is:

```
CLOSE cursor_name
```

This command does not completely destroy the cursor; it only discards the current result set. You may reopen the cursor with the OPEN command. At this point, it creates a new keyset using current data and you may start browsing rows from the beginning. You may use coupled CLOSE and OPEN commands to restart reading rows of a cursor even if nothing has changed in the data. For example, you cannot go back to the first row of a forward-scrolling cursor titles_cursor, but the following commands let you fetch the first row again:

```
CLOSE titles_cursor
OPEN  titles_cursor
```

They return no output if the cursor name is valid.

If you no longer need a cursor, you can drop it with the DEALLOCATE command. The syntax is shown in Table 8-5.

Table 8-5. DEALLOCATE Cursor Syntax

Microsoft	Sybase
cursor_name	DEALLOCATE CURSOR cursor_name

For example, if you are done using the browse_orders cursor, you may discard it with the following command on Microsoft SQL Server:

```
DEALLOCATE browse_orders
```

No output is returned if the cursor exists. Once deallocated, a cursor cannot be re-opened until you declare it again.

When you use a cursor inside a stored procedure, you have to explicitly close and deallocate it before exiting, unless you intend to keep using the same cursor in your session. If you do not destroy a cursor, it remains active and does not allow you to again execute the same stored procedure or another one that may use the same cursor name. Cursors in this respect are different from variables and local temporary stored procedures that disappear once the stored procedure that created them finishes. If you have several RETURN statements in the stored procedure, then you have to close and deallocate all cursors before each and every RETURN.

Working with Cursors

By default, cursors allow updating and deleting rows of the result set. If you want to prevent such modifications, you may declare cursors as READ ONLY. UPDATE and DELETE statements provide a special WHERE clause syntax that tells SQL Server that the context of the query is the row most recently fetched via the specified cursor. The UPDATE syntax is the following:

```
UPDATE table_name
SET column1 = expression1 [, column2 = expression2 [, ...] ]
WHERE CURRENT OF cursor_name
```

The same syntax of the WHERE clause can be used in DELETE statements:

```
DELETE [FROM] table_name
WHERE CURRENT OF cursor_name
```

As your program moves through the rows of a cursor data set, it may need to modify or delete some of them. UPDATE and DELETE statements with the WHERE CURRENT OF clause affect only one row—the last one fetched. Once you or another user updates a row of the result set, your program cannot update or delete it again via the cursor until you close and reopen it.

Updating and Deleting with Cursors

In the following example, we use the previously declared and opened cursor titles_cursor to manipulate a record in the titles table. The script can be executed on Microsoft or Sybase SQL Server but returns different results. It performs the following actions:

1. Inserts a new title record.
2. Closes the cursor titles_cursor that we opened in previous examples.
3. Opens the cursor again to include the new inserted row in the result set.
4. Fetches one row, which happens to be the one that we inserted in step 1 (this is because in this example we used a title_id that placed it at the top of the table).
5. Updates the fetched row.
6. Tries to update the row one more time. On Microsoft SQL Server, the second update of the same record fails. Sybase allows you to update the same row again.
7. Attempts to delete the row. This operation also fails on Microsoft SQL Server because the row has been updated and the keyset is no longer current. Sybase allows the delete.
8. Closes and reopens the cursor.
9. Fetches the same first row once again.
10. Deletes the row. This time DELETE succeeds on Microsoft SQL Server, because we have reopened the cursor and the keyset is current. It also works on Sybase.

```
-- This script assumes that cursor titles_cursor has already been
-- declared and opened. You can find necessary DECLARE and OPEN commands
-- earlier in this chapter.
-- step 1
INSERT titles VALUES (
    'AB3000',
    'Cooking with SQL Server',
    'mod_cook',
    '0736',
    99.99,
    75000,
    40,
    360000,
    'A guide to preparing just about any meals with SQL Server',
    '01/01/2000'
)

DECLARE @title_id CHAR(6),
        @title    VARCHAR(80),
        @type     CHAR(12),
        @pub_id   CHAR(4),
        @price    MONEY
```

```
-- step 2
-- we have used this cursor in previous examples, so let's
-- close and reopen it to start from the first record again.
CLOSE titles_cursor

-- step 3
OPEN titles_cursor

-- step 4
FETCH titles_cursor INTO @title_id, @title, @type, @pub_id, @price
SELECT @title, @price

IF @title_id = 'AB3000'
BEGIN
    -- step 5
    PRINT 'Updating once...'
    UPDATE titles SET ytd_sales = 400000 WHERE CURRENT OF titles_cursor
    -- step 6
    PRINT 'Updating again...'
    UPDATE titles SET ytd_sales = 420000 WHERE CURRENT OF titles_cursor
    -- step 7
    PRINT 'Trying to delete...'
    DELETE titles WHERE CURRENT OF titles_cursor
    -- step 8
    CLOSE titles_cursor
    OPEN titles_cursor
    -- step 9
    FETCH titles_cursor INTO @title_id, @title, @type, @pub_id, @price
    -- step 10
    PRINT 'Trying to delete once again...'
    IF @title_id = 'AB3000' DELETE titles WHERE CURRENT OF titles_cursor
END
```

Results:

Microsoft SQL Server 6.5	Sybase Adaptive Server 11.5
(0 row(s) affected) (1 row(c) affected) (0 row(s) affected) ------------------------ ------ Cooking with SQL Server 99.99 (1 row(s) affected) Updating once . . . (1 row(s) affected) Updating again . . . Msg 16934, Level 16, State 1 Optimistic concurrency check failed, the row was modified outside of this cursor (0 row(s) affected) Trying to delete . . . Msg 16934, Level 16, State 1 Optimistic concurrency check failed, the row was modified outside of this cursor (0 row(s) affected) (0 row(s) affected) Trying to delete once again . . . (1 row(s) affected)	(1 row(s) affected) - ----- Cooking with SQL Server 99.99 (1 row affected) Updating once . . . (1 row affected) Updating again . . . (1 row affected) Trying to delete . . . (1 row affected) (1 row affected) Trying to delete once again . . . (1 row affected)

Transaction Log Considerations

Cursors used for the update and deletion of rows allow flexible management of the database transaction log. Only one row is affected at a time, and SQL Server has a chance to dump the transaction log as needed while cursor processing scrolls through a large data set. Compare this to a single-query UPDATE or DELETE that writes a lot of information into the transaction log and may overflow it. When a database runs out of transaction log space, many users—not just your job—may be affected. Cursor processing may be slower but better suited for huge data modification jobs.

"Everything on Sale" Task

Cursors are typically used inside loops that scroll through a result set and apply the same algorithm to each row. The following program provides an example of this technique. It discounts all computer-related titles by 25%. It defines "computer-related" as all titles of type popular_comp, and those with the word "computer" in the title. The program discounts all other titles by 10%. Titles with year-to-date sales exceeding 10,000 are excluded from the preceding discounts and are discounted by 5% only.

Due to differences in Sybase and Microsoft versions of Transact-SQL, the same code cannot work for both products. The following program is for Microsoft SQL Server. You have to modify three lines, as described in our comments, in order to make it Sybase-compliant.

```
PRINT '*** titles data before processing:'
SELECT  title, type, ytd_sales, price FROM titles
GO
SET NOCOUNT ON
GO
DECLARE discount_titles CURSOR
FOR
SELECT  title, type, ytd_sales
FROM    titles
GO
DECLARE @title      VARCHAR(80),
        @type       CHAR(12),
        @ytd_sales  INT,
        @adjustment NUMERIC(2,2),
        @counter    INT

SELECT  @counter = 0

OPEN discount_titles

-- get the first row
FETCH discount_titles INTO @title, @type, @ytd_sales
```

```
-- For SYBASE: Replace @@FETCH_STATUS in the following line with @@SQLSTATUS
WHILE @@FETCH_STATUS = 0
BEGIN
    IF @ytd_sales > 10000
        SELECT @adjustment = 0.95
    ELSE IF @type = 'popular_comp' OR LOWER( @title ) LIKE '%computer%'
        SELECT @adjustment = 0.75
    ELSE
        SELECT @adjustment = 0.9

    UPDATE  titles
    SET     price = price * @adjustment
    WHERE   CURRENT OF discount_titles

    SELECT  @counter = @counter + 1
    -- get the next row
    FETCH discount_titles INTO @title, @type, @ytd_sales
END

-- For SYBASE: Replace "@@FETCH_STATUS = -1"
-- in the following line with "@@SQLSTATUS = 2"
IF @@FETCH_STATUS = -1 SELECT @counter, 'titles discounted'
ELSE SELECT 'Processing interrupted due to a fetch failure after
discounting',
            @counter, 'titles'

CLOSE discount_titles
GO
-- For SYBASE: Insert the word "CURSOR" after "DEALLOCATE"
-- in the next line
DEALLOCATE discount_titles
GO
SET NOCOUNT OFF
GO
PRINT '*** titles data after processing:'
SELECT  title, type, ytd_sales, price FROM titles
GO
```

Results:

```
*** titles data before processing:
title                                         type         ytd_sales price
--------------------------------------------- ------------ --------- ------
The Busy Executive's Database Guide           business     4095      19.99
Cooking with Computers: Surreptitious Balance business     3876      11.95
You Can Combat Computer Stress!               business     18722     2.99
Straight Talk About Computers                 business     4095      19.99
Silicon Valley Gastronomic Treats             mod_cook     2032      19.99
The Gourmet Microwave                         mod_cook     22246     2.99
The Psychology of Computer Cooking            UNDECIDED    (null)    (null)
But Is It User Friendly?                      popular_comp 8780      22.95
Secrets of Silicon Valley                     popular_comp 4095      20.00
Net Etiquette                                 popular_comp (null)    (null)
Computer Phobic AND Non-Phobic Individuals: B psychology   375       21.59
Is Anger the Enemy?                           psychology   2045      10.95
```

```
Life Without Fear                               psychology   111       7.00
Prolonged Data Deprivation: Four Case Studies psychology   4072      19.99
Emotional Security: A New Algorithm             psychology   3336      7.99
Onions, Leeks, and Garlic: Cooking Secrets of trad_cook    375       20.95
Fifty Years in Buckingham Palace Kitchens       trad_cook    15096     11.95
Sushi, Anyone?                                  trad_cook    4095      14.99

(18 row(s) affected)


----------- -----------------
18          titles discounted


*** titles data after processing:
title                                           type         ytd_sales price
----------------------------------------------- ------------ --------- ------
The Busy Executive's Database Guide             business     4095      17.99
Cooking with Computers: Surreptitious Balance business     3876      8.96
You Can Combat Computer Stress!                 business     18722     2.84
Straight Talk About Computers                   business     4095      14.99
Silicon Valley Gastronomic Treats               mod_cook     2032      17.99
The Gourmet Microwave                           mod_cook     22246     2.84
The Psychology of Computer Cooking              UNDECIDED    (null)    (null)
But Is It User Friendly?                        popular_comp 8780      17.21
Secrets of Silicon Valley                       popular_comp 4095      15.00
Net Etiquette                                   popular_comp (null)    (null)
Computer Phobic AND Non-Phobic Individuals: B psychology   375       16.19
Is Anger the Enemy?                             psychology   2045      9.86
Life Without Fear                               psychology   111       6.30
Prolonged Data Deprivation: Four Case Studies psychology   4072      17.99
Emotional Security: A New Algorithm             psychology   3336      7.19
Onions, Leeks, and Garlic: Cooking Secrets of trad_cook    375       18.86
Fifty Years in Buckingham Palace Kitchens       trad_cook    15096     11.35
Sushi, Anyone?                                  trad_cook    4095      13.49

(18 row(s) affected)
```

The same task is programmed using CASE expressions in Chapter 13, *CASE Expressions and Transact-SQL Extensions.* Review and compare these two solutions. The code in Chapter 13 is shorter. It is also more efficient, but on a small data set the difference in performance is negligible. Many programs that utilize cursor processing can be rewritten using different techniques.

Performance Issues for Cursors

The best optimization technique for cursors is not to use them. Relational database management systems (RDBMSs) in general, and SQL Server in particular, are optimized for set processing. Cursor-processing support is a successor to older programming techniques and 3GL algorithmic approaches.

Let's consider several tasks and demonstrate how each one can be implemented with and without cursors. In order to get meaningful performance measurements, we need a test program that takes at least several seconds. That is why we chose not to work with tiny pubs tables in these examples and instead used the system tables syscomments and sysobjects, which have more rows.

Performance on a Table-Scanning Cursor

The simplest example comparing the performance of cursor and set processing is a table scan. Suppose that you have a task that requires reading every row of a table to compute the final result. For example, we can calculate the total length of source code of all objects stored in master..syscomments. The text column contains lines of source code. We need to apply the DATALENGTH() function to every value and sum them up.

Here is a Microsoft SQL Server script that uses a cursor. In order to use it on Sybase, modify two lines as described in our comments.

```
SET NOCOUNT ON
GO
DECLARE code_scan CURSOR
FOR
SELECT DATALENGTH( text ) FROM master..syscomments
GO
DECLARE @total INT, @text_length INT
SELECT  @total = 0

OPEN code_scan

FETCH code_scan INTO @text_length

-- For SYBASE: Replace @@FETCH_STATUS in the following line with @@SQLSTATUS
WHILE @@FETCH_STATUS = 0
BEGIN
    SELECT  @total = @total + @text_length
    FETCH code_scan INTO @text_length
END

CLOSE code_scan
SELECT  'Total code length =', @total
GO
-- For SYBASE: Insert the word "CURSOR" after "DEALLOCATE"
-- in the next line
DEALLOCATE code_scan
GO
```

This is very similar to how the algorithm would be implemented in a program reading a flat file. The next piece of code is a single relational query computing the same results:

```
SELECT  'Total code length =', SUM( DATALENGTH( text ) )
FROM    master..syscomments
```

Results produced by both scripts are the same (the number may vary on your server):

```
------------------- -----------
Total code length = 1074836
```

In our tests, the second query was approximately 2.5 times faster than the first one. In some cases, a program with cursors may be 50 to 100 times slower than an equivalent one utilizing set processing and producing the same result. The reason is that RDBMSs are optimized to process queries. When you execute a SELECT statement, SQL Server scans several rows on the same data page at the price of a single I/O operation. It may use the read-ahead technique, and it makes better use of indexes. A cursor makes some of these performance-boosting advantages unavailable.

Finding an Object by String

In this example, we offer you a solution for a very practical task. In a database containing many objects, you may want to search for every stored procedure that references a specific column name, a comment line with your name embedded in it, or some other string. This is somewhat similar to the Windows NT command *FIND* or *FINDSTR,* which searches files for a given string or combination of strings. In Unix, the same is done with the *grep* command.

In order to search for all objects containing a string, we can scan the syscomments database. It contains the source code of all objects. An exception is objects created with the ENCRYPTION option in Microsoft SQL Server. We also assume that you are not using a trick of deleting syscomments rows directly in order to hide your trade secrets embedded into the program! Every stored procedure, view, trigger, rule, and default may have one or more rows in syscomments. Column text contains the source code split into pieces not larger than 255 characters. This presents a challenge, because the string we are searching for may be split between two sequential rows in syscomments if it starts in one and "wraps" to the next. We can use cursor processing to handle this:

```
CREATE PROC find_string
-- Purpose: Search for objects that contain given @string in their source
-- Note:    Microsoft SQL Server Transact-SQL syntax code.
--          See comments to modify 2 lines for Sybase compliance.
    @string VARCHAR(80)
```

```
AS

SET NOCOUNT ON

DECLARE @id             INT,
        @previous_id    INT,
        @text           VARCHAR(255),
        @previous_text  VARCHAR(255),
        @skip_this_id   INT

-- create a temporary table that will be populated with found object names
CREATE TABLE #found ( name VARCHAR(30) )

-- object_seach cursor will be used to scan table syscomments
DECLARE object_search CURSOR
FOR
SELECT id, text FROM syscomments

OPEN object_search

SELECT  @skip_this_id = 0, @previous_id = 0, @previous_text = NULL
FETCH object_search INTO @id, @text

-- For SYBASE: Replace @@FETCH_STATUS in the following line with @@SQLSTATUS
WHILE @@FETCH_STATUS = 0
BEGIN
    -- the following condition may be true if this object
    -- has already been added to the list of found ones
    IF @id != @skip_this_id
    BEGIN
        -- check if this line is a continuation of the same object text
        IF @id = @previous_id
        BEGIN
            -- check for @string in the tail of the previous line
            -- concatenated with the head of the current one;
            -- if it is present then add object name to the list of found
            IF CHARINDEX( @string, @previous_text +
                                   SUBSTRING( @text, 1, 80 ) ) > 0
            BEGIN
                INSERT #found VALUES ( OBJECT_NAME( @id ) )
                -- set the variable to skip the remainder of this
                -- object's text; scanning it isn't necessary since
                -- we have already determined that it qualifies
                SELECT @skip_this_id = @id
            END
        END
        IF @skip_this_id != @id
        BEGIN
            -- check for @string in the current line;
            -- if it is present then add object name to the list of found
            IF CHARINDEX( @string, @text ) > 0
            BEGIN
                INSERT #found VALUES ( OBJECT_NAME( @id ) )
                -- set the variable to skip the remainder of this
```

```
                    -- object's text; scanning it isn't necessary since
                    -- we have already determined that it qualifies
                    SELECT @skip_this_id = @id
                END
            END
        END
        -- preserve the last 80 characters of the current line
        -- in case the searched string begins at the end of the
        -- current one and continues in the next
        SELECT @previous_id = @id, @previous_text = RIGHT( @text, 80 )
        -- get the next row
        FETCH object_search INTO @id, @text
    END

    CLOSE object_search
    -- For SYBASE: Insert the word "CURSOR" after "DEALLOCATE"
    -- in the next line
    DEALLOCATE object_search

    -- produce the list of all found object names
    SELECT name FROM #found ORDER BY 1
    DROP TABLE #found
    GO
```

This stored procedure searches for a string of up to 80 characters in the source code of all objects in the current database and returns the list of object names. For example, if you decide to change the column name title_id and want to find every object that may be affected, execute the following:

```
find_string 'title_id'
```

Results:

```
name
------------------------------
reptq1
reptq2
reptq3
titleview
```

This procedure is a nice programming exercise in cursor processing. But it may be more efficiently implemented as follows:

```
CREATE PROC find_string2
-- Purpose: Search for objects that contain given @string
-- in their source code
    @string VARCHAR(80)
AS

SET NOCOUNT ON

SELECT  OBJECT_NAME( id )
FROM    syscomments
WHERE   CHARINDEX( @string, text ) > 0
```

```
UNION
-- check for 'wrapped' strings
SELECT  OBJECT_NAME( a.id )
FROM    syscomments a, syscomments b
WHERE   a.id = b.id
    AND a.colid + 1 = b.colid
    AND CHARINDEX( @string, RIGHT( a.text, 80 ) +
        SUBSTRING( b.text, 1, 80 ) ) > 0
GO
```

This second procedure is shorter. In our tests, find_string was about 10% slower than find_string2 even though the first procedure makes only one pass through the table (cursor scroll), while the second one makes two table scans plus a join with the same table. Both procedures return the same results given the same argument. This comparison once again demonstrates that cursors are inherently slower than relational queries.

A more sophisticated version of this procedure is included on the accompanying CD-ROM. It is called *sp_grep* (after the Unix *grep* command). It allows searching for a single string as well as a combination of them, such as "find all objects containing string A or string B and string C, but not string D." You may be surprised how often it will come handy in your SQL Server programming work.

Getting Help on All Tables

For a change, let's show you an example in which cursor processing is indeed necessary and efficient. It executes system stored procedure *sp_help* for every user table found in pubs.

```
DECLARE user_tables CURSOR
FOR
SELECT name FROM sysobjects WHERE type = 'U'
GO
SET NOCOUNT ON

DECLARE @name VARCHAR(30)

OPEN user_tables
FETCH user_tables INTO @name

-- For SYBASE: Replace @@FETCH_STATUS in the following line with @@SQLSTATUS
WHILE @@FETCH_STATUS = 0
BEGIN
    SELECT REPLICATE( '*', 30 ) + ' ' + @name + ' ' + REPLICATE( '*', 30 )
    EXEC sp_help @name
    FETCH user_tables INTO @name
END

CLOSE user_tables
GO
-- For SYBASE: Insert the word "CURSOR" after "DEALLOCATE"
```

```
-- in the next line
DEALLOCATE user_tables
GO
```

Results contain output of *sp_help* for every user table, which includes table structure, as well as information about table indexes, constraints, and keys. Could this be done without cursors? In fact, the answer is yes, although the solution does not use set processing either. Here is another version of the same program that generates the same output, but without a cursor. It creates a temporary table to hold all rows that need to be processed and discards them one by one. This solution is not better or more efficient than the one with cursors, but the technique may be useful in some applications. It is impractical on large data sets, because a temporary table may require too much space. But you may consider it in case you already have a table with a data set and you can delete rows as you process them:

```
SET NOCOUNT ON

DECLARE @name VARCHAR(30), @count INT

CREATE TABLE #user_tables ( name VARCHAR(30) )

INSERT #user_tables SELECT name FROM sysobjects WHERE type = 'U'
SELECT @count = @@rowcount

WHILE @count > 0
BEGIN
    SET ROWCOUNT 1
    SELECT @count = @count - 1, @name = name FROM #user_tables
    DELETE #user_tables  -- only the first row is deleted
    SET ROWCOUNT 0
    SELECT  REPLICATE( '*', 30 ) + ' ' + @name + ' ' + REPLICATE( '*', 30 )
    EXEC sp_help @name
END

DROP TABLE #user_tables
```

Locks Imposed by a Cursor

One of the useful features of cursors is their granular locking. A cursor locks only one or a few table pages at a time, unless you surround a cursor-processing loop with BEGIN TRANSACTION and COMMIT TRANSACTION commands. This narrow scope of locking may be key when your process has to share a table with concurrent users. It allows your job to peacefully coexist with others. Suppose that you have two versions of the same program. One utilizes cursors and the other is a single query. Both return the same result. The first version is slow but never locks more than one table page. The second one is several times faster but locks the whole table. In such a case, you may choose a slower program, with cursors, that does not monopolize the whole table. These considerations are especially critical in online transaction-processing systems (OLTPs) in which you also need to occasionally execute long-running batch jobs. When you use cursor processing for batch programs, you may slow them down compared to set processing, but you improve the performance of more critical online transactions and thus avoid negative impact on users.

Summary

This chapter discussed server-side cursor processing in Transact-SQL. A cursor allows your program to define a set of table rows and then move through this set and process one row at a time. SQL Server also supports client-side cursors that are outside the scope of this book. Note the following:

- A cursor is created with the DECLARE . . . CURSOR command, which uses a SELECT statement to define rows for cursor processing. It also specifies cursor options READ ONLY and UPDATE OF columns. Microsoft supports the additional DECLARE CURSOR options INSENSITIVE and SCROLL.
- Declared cursors may be opened with the OPEN command. You cannot access data via a cursor until it is opened.
- Some types of cursors may result in the creation of asynchronous keysets. This type of keyset is a virtual copy of cursor data that makes your results immune to ongoing updates by other users. Asynchronous keysets may be necessary depending on your algorithm, but have performance implications that you need to carefully consider.
- After opening a cursor, you can browse through its rows using FETCH commands. The most typical FETCH command retrieves the next sequential rows from the data set. Microsoft SQL Server allows moving to a row specified by its absolute position in the data set or a position relative to the currently fetched row, as well as to the first or last row of the data set.
- The data set of an open cursor may be discarded with a CLOSE command, after which you may OPEN it again and get a fresh data set. A cursor is destroyed with a DEALLOCATE command or when your session ends.
- Special global variables assist you in programming cursor processing. They differ between vendor implementations. Microsoft uses the variables @@cursor_rows and @@fetch_status to show the number of rows in an open cursor and the status of the last FETCH command. Sybase uses @@rowcount and @@sqlstatus for the same purpose. Sybase's SET CURSOR ROWS command specifies the number of rows returned by a FETCH from a cursor and may be used to retrieve more than one row at a time.

- Cursors are very often a performance drag. Programs using cursors may be several times slower than those using set processing to obtain the same result. We recommend that you limit cursor processing to those tasks in which it is efficient. Good applications for cursors are those in which you have a relatively small data set (e.g., several dozen rows) or need to process each record by a stored procedure or a set of commands that cannot be implemented in one query. Cursors usually do not lock the whole table, but only one or a few data pages, in order to optimize a cursor performance check if it uses asynchronous keysets. This is an option that may be configured and controlled programmatically. It defines whether SQL Server has to finish creating the whole data set before you can start processing it or whether you can start working with the first rows while the rest of them are being prepared.

9

Error Handling

In this chapter:

There are three basic categories of end users. The first category is the intellectual type. They get the idea of a Transact-SQL program with very little formal education or training. A real gem among stones. Then you have the middle tier of end users. These folks can be trusted to succeed at most types of applications, provided they have an adequate amount of training and documentation. And, finally, we have the knuckle-dragging Neanderthals. This type sleeps through training and uses the documentation as a placemat for their meal. They are most dangerous to the application when near a computer that is actually turned on. Fortunately, Transact-SQL provides us with several methods of reacting to situations and end user input that cause errors in a program's behavior.

Code Processing and Error Handling: Basic Concepts

Transact-SQL uses a serial processing model for executing statements and handling errors. That means that a Transact-SQL program executes each command one after the other, as these commands appear in the Transact-SQL code. Remember that output for a Transact-SQL batch program is piped after the execution of each GO statement, but the output from a stored procedure is piped to the output device only when the entire program is completed.

Transact-SQL groups errors into two basic categories: *systemic* and *programmatic*. This chapter focuses on programmatic errors. A systemic error occurs when a Transact-SQL program encounters a deficiency or unexpected condition with a system resource. For example, if your program encountered insufficient space in tempdb to process a large query, this is a systemic error. On the other side of the coin, programmatic errors occur when your Transact-SQL program encounters a logic or behavioral error during processing. An infinite loop or a user-provided input that is out of range are both examples of programmatic errors.

When a system error is encountered, such as the database or transaction log running out of space, the current Transact-SQL statement is terminated. (In one unusual circumstance on Sybase servers, when a transaction log has exceeded the last-chance threshold, the Transact-SQL statement is suspended rather than terminated.) Programmatic errors, on the other hand, often continue unchecked. The idea with error handling in a Transact-SQL program is to anticipate and code routines to manage all foreseeable problems. That doesn't mean that you need to write a huge error-handling block of code that will catch every imaginable error. Instead, you need to perform a little analysis and attempt to compensate for the two or three most likely error scenarios.

In addition to the techniques discussed in this chapter, there are a number of other techniques available in Transact-SQL for handling errors. Other techniques include:

- Capturing a return status from a stored procedure (see the RETURN command in Chapter 7, *Conditional Processing*)
- Defining customized return values from a stored procedure (see Chapter 14, *Stored Procedures and Modular Design*)
- Passing parameters from a called stored procedure to its calling stored procedure (see Chapter 14)

Displaying an Error Message with PRINT

Assume that you're writing a Transact-SQL program in which the end user is allowed to provide some input. If the end user provides input values that are out of line with the acceptable limits, you can return a simple message to the end user using the PRINT statement. The PRINT statement only serves to return a message to the client and has no other special functionality. Again, the idea with displaying errors is that you have to anticipate the possibility of such an error arising and provide an alternative set of actions to take when faced with such an error. Otherwise, your program will have to accept the server's default handling of such an error, which usually means trouble.

The simplest way to return to the client a message of your own design is through the PRINT statement. The PRINT statement has somewhat divergent syntax between Microsoft and Sybase, as shown here:

Microsoft	Sybase
`PRINT {'your text message'	@local_variable	@@global_variable}`	`PRINT {'your text message'	@local_variable	@@global_variable	[,argument_list]}`

The most common usage is a simple text message, hardcoded by the developer. The message can be 255 bytes long in Microsoft and Sybase Transact-SQL programs, although the total combination of text message, local variables, and global variables can be 512 bytes long in a Sybase Transact-SQL program. Here's an example of a code fragment showing simple text messages:

```
IF EXISTS (SELECT * FROM authors WHERE au_fname = 'Elmer'
    AND au_lname = 'Fudd')
    PRINT 'Duck Season!'
ELSE PRINT 'Wabbit Season!'
```

When using local and global variables, the datatype of the variables must be CHAR or VARCHAR. The variables also have to be declared within the same batch or procedure as the PRINT statement. Long messages that contain variables can be strung together using concatenation. Here's an example code fragment of a concatenated PRINT string showing the starting and ending times of a given Transact-SQL program:

```
DECLARE @output_line VARCHAR(255) -- a variable that holds the output for
display
SELECT  @output_line = 'Program started at: ' + CONVERT(char(19), GETDATE())
PRINT   ' '                          -- just a blank line
PRINT   @output_line

< . . . other Transact-SQL code . . . >

SELECT  @output_line = 'Program ended at: ' + RTRIM(CONVERT(char(30),
    GETDATE()
PRINT   ' '                          -- another blank line
PRINT   @output_line
```

A cool feature of Sybase's implementation of the PRINT statement is the use of *placeholders*. Placeholders, in the format %nn!, allow you to automatically concatenate the value of each respective local variable contained in the argument list into the placeholder contained in the text message. Placeholders are especially useful for multilanguage applications, where the order of words in a message might need to vary. (Microsoft has this feature in RAISERROR, but not PRINT.) Here's a Sybase example with a single placeholder:

```
DECLARE @placeholder1  VARCHAR(30)
SELECT  @placeholder1 = au_lname FROM authors WHERE au_lname = 'Smith'
```

```
-- A simple SELECT to retrieve one value
PRINT "I think we have %1! here", @placeholder1
```

Results:

```
I think we have Smith here.
```

Here's a more complex example using two placeholders:

```
-- declare the placeholder variables and assign a value to them
DECLARE @tabname VARCHAR(30), @usrname VARCHAR(30)
SELECT  @tabname = 'ACME Incorporated',
        @usrname = 'Anthony'

PRINT "The account '%1!' is represented by the salesperson '%2!'.",
        @tabname, @usrname
```

Results:

```
The account 'ACME Incorporated' is represented by the salesperson 'Anthony'.
```

Placeholders are available in the RAISERROR command in both Microsoft and Sybase implementations.

Raising an Error with RAISERROR

You've seen how to display a simple error message (or any message for that matter) to the client using the PRINT statement. But what if you need more functionality? Use the RAISERROR statement.

RAISERROR is like the PRINT statement on anabolic steroids. Like the PRINT statement, RAISERROR does return a message to the client, but it also does a lot more. The message sent to the client can be a developer-defined message as with PRINT, or it can be an error message as stored in the sysmessages system table. RAISERROR always sets the value for @@error to that of the current error message or optionally to 0 for low-severity level messages. Plus, it can optionally place an error message in the SQL Server and Windows NT error logs. (Later on, we show you how to dynamically scan the error logs for specific messages.) As with PRINT, there are a few minor syntactical differences between the vendors:

Microsoft	Sybase
`RAISERROR ({error_number | 'your text message'}, severity, state [,argument_list]) [WITH LOG | NOWAIT | SETERROR]`	`RAISERROR error_number [{'your text message' | @local_variable}] [, argument_list] [WITH error_data | restricted_select_list]`

A Microsoft-specific error message might look like this:

```
IF EXISTS (SELECT * FROM authors WHERE au_fname = 'Elmer'
    AND au_lname = 'Fudd')
    PRINT 'Happy Hunting, it's duck season!'
ELSE RAISERROR('Warning! Duck hunting dewing wabbitt season!',18,1) WITH LOG
```

The previous message is an error coded by a developer. The RAISERROR statement doesn't specify a specific error message. Instead, the developer has coded some ad hoc text, a severity level, and a state. The error message will automatically be raised with the error number of 50,000. You might wish to raise an error that already exists in the sysmessages table. In that case, the command would look something like this:

```
RAISERROR (7216, 18, 10, @remote_srv)
```

This command specifically references the error number, the severity, and the state of the error number and passes the error message the required variable to display a meaningful message. A vendor-neutral error message would look like this:

```
IF EXISTS (SELECT * FROM authors WHERE au_fname = 'Elmer'
    AND au_lname = 'Fudd')
    PRINT 'Happy Hunting, it's duck season!'
ELSE RAISERROR 50000 'Warning! Duck hunting dewing wabbitt season!'
```

To enable a RAISERROR message that works equally well on both Microsoft and Sybase, you must display the command in this format: `RAISERROR 50000 'text message'`. Other variations on the command are not allowable, unless you are willing to lose the ability to run on both platforms.

When you use the `error_number` on Microsoft, system-defined error numbers should be less than 50,000, while user-defined error messages equal or exceed 50,000. (We'll say more about adding and removing user-defined error messages later.) If you don't include an `error_number` value, SQL Server defaults the `error_number` to 50,000. The value of the `error_number` used in RAISERROR is also assigned to the @@error global variable.

The `error_number` on Sybase behaves a bit differently. In this case, errors must exceed 17,000. For errors 17,000 through 19,999, Sybase retrieves the error messages from master..sysmessages when the message text is empty or missing. For errors numbered 20,000 or more, Sybase will pull the message text from the local sysmessages table when the message text is missing or empty.

Ad Hoc Errors

You can raise an *ad hoc error message* in your Transact-SQL code. An ad hoc error message is one in which you assign the error text, severity level, and state but allow the error message to use the default error code of 50000. For example, an ad hoc error message in Microsoft SQL Server might look like this:

```
RAISERROR ('Warning! No duck hunting dewing wabbitt season!',16,2)
```

The message text can be up to 255 characters long, with some clever formatting tricks available on the Microsoft SQL Server platform. For those of you familiar with the *printf* function available in C, RAISERROR offers some similar functionality. (More details about this capability are provided in the later paragraphs detailing argument-list placeholders.)

The value for `severity` (detailed in Table 9-1) can be 0 through 25 on Microsoft SQL Server. (Sybase forces all ad hoc error messages to severity level 16.)

Severity levels 0 through 18 are considered to be of a more informational nature and can be used by any user. Errors of levels 13 through 17 are severe enough to abort the currently processing statement or command, but not enough to terminate the entire batch or program. Severity levels greater than 18 (levels 19 through 25) are considered "fatal" and can be raised only by the SA and only with the WITH LOG option. All fatal errors suspend the current task that caused the error, and errors of severity level 20 or greater disconnect the client after sending the error message and logging it to the event log. If your organization has a database administrator (DBA), you should inform him whenever a fatal error occurs.

For those of you who are familiar with the Windows NT Event Viewer, you can force the *severity icons* shown in the Event Viewer when raising a SQL Server error message to the Windows NT event log. The Windows NT Event Viewer has three severity icons: informational (an *I*), warning (an exclamation point), and error (a stop sign). These icons correlate to a RAISERROR severity level of less than 16, 16, and greater than 16, respectively.

The value for `state`, used only with Microsoft error messages, can be any value from 1 through 127. Don't bother using a negative value for `state`, since it will default to 1. `State` represents an invocation state of the error that has meaning only for specific error messages. In general, it has no effect on the behavior of RAISERROR, especially on ad hoc error messages. For example, Sybase uses `state` with a few transaction-related error messages offering information about whether the transaction committed or rolled back. We recommend that you leave this value at 1, unless your research into a specific error message indicates that another `state` is needed.

The use of an optional `argument_list` provides some interesting flexibility in creating error messages. The argument_list contains parameters used to substitute for variables defined in the message text (or in the corresponding message ID). You can have up to 20 arguments of the INT, CHAR, VARCHAR, BINARY, and VARBINARY datatypes.

Table 9-1. Error Severity Levels

Severity Level	Vendor Description	Notes	Stress Level
00–01	Miscellaneous System Information	This is a purely informational message about system activities. Most messages that tell you an event succeeded, like a new user being successfully created, are severity level 0. Severity level 1 is only used to relay DBCC (Database Consistency Checker) messages and a few other miscellaneous events.	*Nonexistent.*
02–06	Reserved	You won't get a message of this severity level, since they're being saved for later releases of the product.	*Nonexistent.*
07	Notification: Status Information	Another informational message that identifies when tasks or operations are started, stopped, paused, etc.	*Huh?*
08	Notification: User Intervention Required	This severity level is used to distinguish situations in which an operation or process requires a user's response.	*Measures .001 on the Richter scale.*
09	User Defined	Error messages of severity level 09 are reserved for user-defined messages stored in sysmessages or user-defined ad hoc messages. Many developer-defined messages are severity level 9.	*Minor.*
10	Information	Another one of those informational severity levels. Severity level 10 messages are most often used for cursors, DBCC commands, the status of DUMP and LOAD commands, and other DBA-ish activities.	*Isn't that special?*
11	Specified Database Object Not Found	This severity level is commonly encountered during development when objects are frequently dropped, altered, or renamed. This covers every type of database object from tables, devices, and databases to remote servers and scheduled tasks.	*Why didn't you tell me you renamed the table from EH01_14A to Employee?*
12	Currently unused		
13	User Transaction Syntax Errors	This severity level indicates that a transaction has been improperly coded, usually that a BEGIN TRAN was not properly paired with a COMMIT or ROLLBACK.	*Furrowed brows.*
14	Insufficient Permissions	The current user ID doesn't have the necessary permissions to access an object or data. This includes users attempting to access an object they don't have permissions to, as well as constraint violations, database recovery messages, and the results of the KILL command.	*You're probably frowning at this point.*

Table 9-1. Error Severity Levels (continued)

Severity Level	Vendor Description	Notes	Stress Level
15	Syntax Error in SQL Statement	Encountered mostly during development, this severity level includes most messages you get when you write bad Transact-SQL code. *If you're getting a lot of these, you haven't studied this book well enough!* It's also encountered when a script written for an older version of SQL Server is run on a newer version that doesn't support the old syntax.	*Try, try again.*
16	Miscellaneous User Error	This could be any one of many different errors determined by the actions of an end user. Datatype conversion and object usage messages are the most common type of error at this severity level. This is a favorite severity level for developer-coded error messages. It includes more messages than any of the other datatypes.	*D'oh!*
17	Insufficient Resources	Sometimes SQL Server can run short on internal system resources like allocation units, log space, locks, hush puppies, or corn dogs. Well, not really on those last two. When the server runs short on important internal resources, bad things happen, as documented by a severity 17 message. Also, the process that caused the shortage is usually aborted.	*Cripes!*
18	Nonfatal Internal Error	This severity level is another that is commonly used in developer-coded error messages. Most commonly, severity level 18 messages deal with connecting to a remote server and sorting queries.	*Don't grimace so intensely...*
19	SQL Server Fatal Error in Resource	Some nonconfigurable limit in SQL Server has been breached, like too many tables or databases in a query, insufficient memory, not enough locks available, etc. This kind of error is rare and should be brought to the attention of your DBA or primary support provider.	*Slightly perturbed. Might find you saying "Darn, I'll try to reconnect."*
20	SQL Server Fatal Error in Current Process	An individual statement has encountered a problem, but the server itself and its component database are OK. These are usually transaction-related problems such as sort problems or name resolution for a specific database object.	*Annoyed, as in "Shucks, gotta rekey all that data."*

Table 9-1. Error Severity Levels (continued)

Severity Level	Vendor Description	Notes	Stress Level
21	SQL Server Fatal Error in Database (dbid) Processes	An error has arisen that affects all processes in the current database, though damage to the database is unlikely. Severity level 21 includes funky errors like buffering, allocation, and locking problems.	*You're irritated, and so's everybody else. "Ohmygawd, hope nobody was in the database!"*
22	SQL Server Fatal Error Table Integrity Suspect	The table or index specified in the message is damaged. DBCC checks and/or restarting the server can help with this sort of problem. Also, deleting and rebuilding the erroneous object can fix the problem. Severity level 22 errors are often related to TEXT or IMAGE columns, as well as allocation and system table problems.	*Anxious concern. For example, "Whaddya mean the employee payroll table is corrupt!!"*
23	SQL Server Fatal Error: Database Integrity Suspect	An error message of this level means that an entire database is suspect due to hardware or software problems. DBCC checks and/or restarting the server can fix the problem. Database dump problems are the most common cause of a level 23 error.	*Sweating bullets. If it's your fault, you might be saying "Hello, is this the employment agency?"*
24	Hardware Error	Some kind of media failure has occurred that might necessitate a reload of the database or even a call to the hardware vendor. These are almost always I/O errors, whether from cache or from disk.	*As a software developer, you feel concern. "The bad news is that it's a hardware problem. The good news is that it's a hardware problem. Hope they have a backup!"*
25	Internal System Error	Internal system errors like a page chain corruption cause this sort of error. Quite rare.	*Angst. "Yikes, start a level 3 diagnostic, lieutenant!"*

Here's an example of an error message that shows exactly what error occurred and at what time:

```
IF @@ERROR <> 0
RAISERROR('Warning! Command encountered error %i at %i secs',
        18,1, @sql_error, @time) WITH LOG
```

Microsoft allows the `argument_list` placeholder as a percent sign (%) plus any alphanumeric character. Sybase requires the placeholder to follow the format of a percent sign (%) plus a numeric value from 1 to 20, plus an exclamation point. If more than one placeholder is needed, then each subsequent placeholder should increment one value higher. The preceding example would look slightly different for Sybase:

```
IF @@ERROR <> 0
RAISERROR('Warning! Command encountered error %1! at %2! secs',
        18,1, @sql_error, @time) WITH LOG
```

Here, the placeholder %1! is used to designate the first argument value, %2! is used to designate the second argument value, and so on. Skipping numbers between the placeholders, like going from %1! to %3!, will cause an error. This is extremely useful because Sybase supports multilingual applications that have differing grammatical rules. You can now construct multiple RAISERROR statements for each language or character set by merely reordering the placeholders. For example, some Romance languages prefer the adjective before the predicate. Without this feature, French or Italian readers might be reading a translation that says "An error severe has occurred," although it would look perfectly normal to an English-speaking user.

You can duplicate placeholder functions found in the PRINTF statement common to C programs in the RAISERROR message string. The syntax for this more elaborate placeholder is:

```
% [[flag] [width] [precision] [{h | l}]] type
```

As before, the percent sign (%) designates a placeholder. The flag value indicates the spacing and justification of the value. Flag values include the following:

- *(minus)*
: Left-justifies the value within the given width. Precedes the value with a minus if it is a signed type.

+ *(plus)*
: No effect on justification. Precedes the value with a plus sign (+) if it is a signed type.

0 *(zero)*
: Pads the value with zeros until the minimum width is reached. This flag is ignored if an integer type is used (like i, u, x, X, o, or d) or when flag 0 and - are paired.

(number)
: This flag is used to designate hexadecimal codes in a message string. Any nonzero value held in the field is displayed with a 0, 0x, or 0X when used in conjunction with o, x, or X types. Otherwise, the number (#) flag is ignored.

' ' (blank)
: The blank flag pads the output value of the field with spaces if the value is signed and positive. It is ignored on placeholders that use the plus (+) flag.

The width predicate defines the minimum width of the placeholder. The precision predicate determines the maximum length of the output field or the minimum number of digits printed for integer types. An asterisk (*) may be substituted for the width or precision, allowing the argument to specify its value. The predicate {h | l} type is paired with an identifier showing the datatype of the output field. The lowercase *h* identifies short integers and the lowercase *L* (not the number 1) identifies long integers:

d or I
: Signed integer

O
: Unsigned octal

P
: Pointer

S
: String

U
: Unsigned integer

x or X
: Unsigned hexadecimal

As you can see (if your eyes aren't blurry and watering from this complicated mess), certain types are not supported. Unsupported types include float, double-character and single-character types.

Now that all of the rules have been laid out, perhaps an example can help demystify this usage:

```
--This is just a code fragment
SELECT @totamt = 9798.6, @mon = 'June'
RAISERROR( "Total Price = %d8.2   Month Due: %s",@ totamt, @mon )
```

This statement formats a default error with an integer totamt value with length of 8, precision of 2, substitutes it in place of the placeholder %d8.2, and substitutes the string mon in place of %s. Then the error is raised based on the values provided.

The RAISERROR command also gives you a few options that you can leverage for more potent error-handling solutions. Options include:

WITH LOG
: (Microsoft) Writes an entry for the error in the Windows NT event log and in the SQL Server error log. It's required for errors of severity level 19 or higher.

It can be used only by the SA. (All users can use RAISERROR, but only the SA can use it with the WITH LOG option.)

NOWAIT
(Microsoft) Sends an immediate message to the client.

SETERROR
(Microsoft) Revalues @@error to the message ID (or 50,000) regardless of the severity level. Usually, only fatal errors (severity levels greater than 18) revalue the @@error global variable to the message ID. Messages of severity levels 1 through 10 set @@error to 0.

ERROR_DATA
(Sybase) Provides extended error data for Client-Library programs.

restricted_select_list
(Sybase) The regular entries used to define columns in a SELECT command are allowed here, including the syb_identity keyword instead of a specific identity column, functions and aggregates, aliases on columns, and so on.

Raise Only Errors

There's a common programming rule of thumb that states "raise errors only when errors occur." That means use error-handling calls only when an error has occurred. But what happens when you want the functionality of RAISERROR (like writing a message to the event log) when there's been no error?

In this case, Transact-SQL has made it a little easier by including the extended stored procedure *xp_logevent*. *xp_logevent* allows you to add an entry to the Windows NT event log of a user-defined error without actually raising a SQL Server error. Its only advantage over RAISERROR is that it does not send an alert to the client and does not set the value of @@error. The basic syntax for *xp_logevent* is similar to that of RAISERROR:

```
xp_logevent error_number, message_string, [severity]
```

The `error_number` must be greater than 50,000, since only user-defined error messages can be raised in this way. The `message_string` may be any string up to 255 characters in length. This string is recorded in the SQL Server log file and/or the Windows NT Event Viewer. Unlike RAISERROR, the severity is one of three nonnumeric values: informational, warning, or error. If no value is provided for severity, informational is used by default. For example, the following code logs a message in the Windows NT event log:

```
DECLARE @season  VARCHAR(30), @message VARCHAR(255)
SELECT  @season = 'Duck',
    @message = 'It is now ' + UPPER(@season) + '! Happy Hunting!"
EXEC xp_logevent 60000, @message, informational
```

Finding Error Conditions with Global Variables

Many of the errors your Transact-SQL program could encounter are foreseeable. Testing should reveal any programmatic or logical errors in your application. The addition of a few carefully placed RAISERROR statements can make the program bullet-proof against end user mistakes, such as providing invalid parameter values.

There are, however, a whole slew of errors that you cannot see or predict. Can you anticipate if a hardware I/O problem will occur during the execution of your program? You can't predict such events, but you can protect against some of them using @@error.

The @@error global variable is an integer datatype variable that specifies the last error number generated by the system during the current connection or process. In this role, the @@error global variable can be used to check the success or failure of the most recently executed statement. Unlike our paychecks, the magic number for @@error is 0—meaning the last statement executed successfully. If @@error equals any other value besides 0, you've got a problem. Any time a regular SQL Server error message is encountered, @@error will contain the value of that error. (Some catastrophic errors will crash the server without the polite manners of providing a value to @@error.) Thus, if your program attempted to perform an INSERT on a table that would duplicate the primary key values, @@error would be populated with the value 2627 (system error message 2627 is commonly known as the "Violation of PRIMARY KEY constraint" error).

In the following example, the code fragment is taken from a stored procedure that attempts to insert some data into a temporary table:

```
-- Builds and populates the temporary table
CREATE TABLE #author_payments(
    au_id          VARCHAR(11) NOT NULL,
    au_lname       VARCHAR(40) NOT NULL,
    au_fname       VARCHAR(20) NOT NULL,
    total_advance DEC(10,2) NOT NULL)

BEGIN TRAN
INSERT INTO #author_payments
SELECT a.au_id,
       au_lname,
       au_fname,
       SUM(advance)"Total Advance"
FROM   authors a,
       titleauthor ta,
       titles t
WHERE  a.au_id       = ta.au_id
   AND ta.title_id = t.title_id
GROUP BY a1.au_id,
```

```
    au_lname,
    au_fname

IF @@error <> 0           -- check for the possibility of errors
BEGIN
    ROLLBACK TRAN         -- undo the transaction if an error occurred
    RETURN -1             -- RETURN can only be used inside of a stored
                          --   procedure
END
ELSE
    COMMIT TRAN
```

As the fragment of the stored procedure shows, you combine control-of-flow language with the @@error global variable to produce the sort of error handling you want.

There are several statements that need to be checked for errors. You should usually check for @@error <> 0 after every INSERT, DELETE, UPDATE, and SELECT . . . INTO. There's no need to check @@error after SELECT statements. If SELECT ever fails, it always terminates the whole procedure and does not allow the next command to execute. For that reason, never check for errors after SELECT. Furthermore, it also doesn't make much sense to check @@error after non-DML commands or dynamic SQL (that is, EXECUTE) statements.

But what if you want to provide some fancy-schmancy handling beyond that provided by simple control-of-flow processing? The next section addresses this topic.

Handling Errors with GOTO

There are two basic approaches to handling errors in Transact-SQL programs. The first approach uses @@error along with control-of-flow language to properly handle an error. The second approach builds error-handling routines through a modular programming technique via the GOTO statement (described in Chapter 7, *Conditional Processing*). Detractors of this technique, and there are many, refer to this kind of programming as *spaghetti code*, because the code can quickly become a tangled and incomprehensible mess if you don't manage it well. We'll look at the second approach in greater detail here, since the first approach was discussed in the previous section "Finding Error Conditions with Global Variables."

The advantage to using a modular approach to error handling is that you have to write an error-handling routine only one time. You can check for the occurrence of the error many times and simply route processing to the error-handling block when and if the error occurs. If the same kind of error can occur in several different statements of your Transact-SQL program, you need to write only one error-handling block that is invoked whenever the error is encountered. This is an important advantage because Transact-SQL is a serially processed language. Commands are executed one after the other. So if you want to handle an error at all, you have to do it right after it is detected. Even when a statement within the program encounters an error, processing will usually pass to the next command, even if it should actually abort the whole program.

There is a downside to using the GOTO statement to handle errors. Not only must you provide code that branches out to the error-handling module, in some circumstances you need to provide code that will branch you back to the source code. This sort of back-and-forth looping can quickly result in *spaghetti code*. You must provide Transact-SQL programs with the logic to gracefully terminate when needed. You must also make your programs easy to read and make sure that their logic can be followed from start to completion for every type of error handling introduced.

Creating Specialized Error Messages

Ta-da! You have the power to create your own error messages. This simply means that you can save your own error messages in the master..sysmessages table and retrieve them at a later date using the RAISERROR command. Thus, you can write error messages specifically tailored for your application(s) and access them from any application connecting to the server. SQL Server provides this functionality through the system stored procedure *sp_addmessage*. The basic syntax for the system stored procedure is:

```
sp_addmessage message_id, severity, 'text of message'
     [,language [,{true | false} [,REPLACE]]]
```

A simple example might look like this:

```
sp_addmessage 50001, 16, 'Please re-execute with a more appropriate value.'
```

When you execute the system stored procedure, the `message_id` must be an integer unique to the sysmessages table. The message may be assigned a severity of 1 through 25 (refer to Table 9-1), but only the SA can create messages of severity 19 through 25. The text of the message may be any alphanumeric sequence enclosed in single quote marks, up to the 255 characters. You can optionally specify the language in which the message is written (English is the default). You may also force an automatic entry into the Windows NT event log and the SQL Server error log whenever the error is raised by specifying the `true` option. A new error message in sysmessages can still be written to the Windows NT event log by using RAISERROR . . . WITH LOG.

If you ever need to overwrite a preexisting error message with a new message text or severity level, use the REPLACE option.

Once you've created a new error message, you can raise it just as you would any other error message.

Finding Error Messages in Operating System Files

You've already seen how to raise an error within your Transact-SQL program so it writes to the SQL Server error log. Error log files are also produced using ISQL with the /o switch. There are often situations in which you need to examine this type of system event log, such as a troubleshooting or alert-forwarding application. For these cases, Windows NT has provided us with a utility, *FINDSTR.EXE*, that enables this sort of activity. (The *grep* command offers a similar functionality on Unix platforms.)

Of course, this functionality is off the beaten path for a book on Transact-SQL, but if you ever have to write an application that reviews DBCC . . . WITH INFOMSGS output or need to regularly check on the SQL Server error log, you'll be glad you know this little tidbit. *FINDSTR* is a powerful pattern-searching utility, and because it's a command-line executable, you can embed it in batch files or Transact-SQL programs. It's kind of like a SELECT . . . WHERE statement for ASCII system files.

There are two basic approaches to using *FINDSTR*:

1. Tell it the explicit character strings to find.
2. Tell it to find all character strings except a specific string.

Under the first approach, you specify a string or list of strings *FINDSTR* will match. If you want it to search for many strings, use a file containing a list of all searchable strings. In the following example, our Transact-SQL batch will search all log files in the specified directory, looking for any string shown in the file *find_string.txt*. However, you could easily modify this routine to search the output file from a Transact-SQL batch program, a BCP load program, or other applications by simply changing the path and name of the files to be searched. The output from the routine will be piped to an output file *find_string.out*.

```
EXEC master..xp_cmdshell 'findstr /i /g:find_string.txt
     c:\mssql\log\errorlog*.* > find_string.out'
```

Our input file, *find_string.txt*, contains the following search strings:

```
msg 604
msg 640
msg 2504
```

So if any of the log files in *C:\MSSQL\LOG* contain an error 604, 640, or 2504, they'll be piped to *find_string.out*.

A good general error-searching pattern is based on severity levels. If SQL Server encounters an error with a severity level of 16 or higher, you probably have a rather severe problem. Thus, you could search for such errors using an input file that contains "level 16" . . . "level 25."

You can turn *FINDSTR* on its head by providing an input file listing only those strings you *don't* want to find. You add this functionality by adding the /v switch. For example:

```
EXEC master..xp_cmdshell 'findstr /v /i /g:find_string.txt c:\mssql\log\
    errorlog*.* > find_string.out'
```

As with the regular string search, the input file, *find_string.txt*, contains the following main search criteria. However, because we've added the /v switch to find all strings except those specified, the file *find_string.txt* should contain only those strings that we don't want retrieved.

You can even use the pipe function to keep one set of inclusive search conditions and exclude a subsequent set of unwanted strings. For example:

```
EXEC master..xp_cmdshell 'findstr /i /g:include.txt errorlog*.* |
    findstr /v/i /g:exclude.txt > err.out'
```

In this case, the file *include.txt* tells the routine which error strings to look for. The result set is then parsed a second time, looking for strings to exclude based on the contents of the file *exclude.txt*. The final results are stored in the file *err.out*. One of the cool features of this utility is that you can actually nest it several levels deep, each higher-level command piping the results down to the next search criteria.

Summary

Transact-SQL programs typically encounter two types of errors: programmatic (also called logic errors) and systemic errors. In either situation, you can add code to your Transact-SQL program that will detect, report, and handle errors. Here are some of the ways to handle errors:

- The PRINT command is sometimes used to report on low-level, low-severity errors or logic faults, particularly if the program need not terminate.
- The RAISERROR statement can be used to report a problem, but also to log an error message to the Windows NT event log and to the SQL Server error log. RAISERROR can be used to report on standard system errors, described in the system table master..sysmessages, or on ad hoc error messages provided by the developer.
- System errors (and some programmatic errors) are usually detected by checking the global variable @@error.

- Once an error is detected, you can add code to handle the problem immediately or to GOTO an error-handling block of code.
- Furthermore, you can add new messages to master..sysmessages by using the system stored procedure *sp_addmessage.*
- Finally, we tossed in a few tips on how to search operating system files within a Transact-SQL program in case you're looking for error messages in an output file, audit trail file, or the SQL Server error logs.

10

Temporary Objects

In this chapter:

- *Creating and Manipulating Temporary Objects*
- *The tempdb Database*
- *Classes of Temporary Objects*
- *Query Optimization with Temporary Tables*
- *Management of the tempdb Database*
- *Summary*

Database transactions often consist of a series of steps forming the final result set. It is not always possible to produce the result in one query. To deal with this problem, programmers need some temporary storage area where they can place intermediate data. Transact-SQL does not offer the arrays supported by most 3GL languages, but temporary tables are similar to and, in some ways, even better than arrays. If Transact-SQL coding is part of your job responsibility, chances are that you are using temporary tables and other types of temporary objects quite often. Temporary objects are a feature of Sybase and Microsoft SQL Server that are available in very few other systems.

Temporary tables also come in handy in query performance optimization. If SQL Server chokes on a 10-table join, it may be best to split the query into several steps, joining fewer tables and storing results in a temporary table. We will illustrate this technique with examples later in this chapter.

Despite all the benefits of temporary objects, we have to warn you against overusing them. Try to produce results in a single query without creating an intermediate temporary table, unless it hurts program performance. Temporary tables take space in the common shared database—tempdb. A single stored procedure that creates a huge temporary object may overflow this database. Subsequently, SQL Server terminates other processes attempting to use tempdb and causes trouble for many users. Efficient Transact-SQL programming techniques discussed in other chapters often may eliminate the need to create temporary objects.

In this chapter, we classify all temporary structures into several classes that differ by longevity of objects and who can access them. Each class may allow different types of objects—tables, stored procedures, views, rules, and defaults. Local temporary tables are arguably the most popular kind of temporary structures.

Creating and Manipulating Temporary Objects

We'll start our discussion with an example of a local temporary table. Later in this chapter, we'll dive into the intricacies of different classes and types of temporary objects.

You can use the same DDL statements to create temporary objects as you do to create permanent ones. The easiest object for any user to create is a local temporary object. By Transact-SQL naming convention, a local temporary object is created if the first character of the object name is #.

```
CREATE TABLE #titles (
    au_lname VARCHAR(40) NOT NULL,
    au_fname VARCHAR(20) NOT NULL,
    title    VARCHAR(80) NOT NULL,
    pub_name VARCHAR(40) NULL,
    price    MONEY       NULL
)
```

Once you have created a temporary table, you can manipulate it the same way you can any permanent table. The next several queries demonstrate that you can use regular DML statements with temporary tables:

```
INSERT  #titles (   au_lname,   au_fname,   title,   pub_name,   price )
SELECT              a.au_lname, a.au_fname, t.title, p.pub_name, t.price
FROM    titleauthor ta, authors a, titles t, publishers p
WHERE   ta.au_ord   = 1
    AND ta.title_id = t.title_id
    AND ta.au_id    = a.au_id
    AND t.pub_id   *= p.pub_id

DELETE  #titles WHERE price < 20

UPDATE  #titles SET price = price * 0.85

SELECT  au_lname, title, pub_name, price
FROM    #titles
WHERE   price IS NOT NULL

DROP TABLE #titles
```

Results:

```
(17 row(s) affected)

(12 row(s) affected)

(4 row(s) affected)
```

```
au_lname title                     pub_name             price
-------- ------------------------- -------------------- ------
Carson   But Is It User Friendly?  Algodata Infosystems 19.51
Dull     Secrets of Silicon Valley Algodata Infosystems 17.00
Karsen   Computer Phobic AND Non-P Binnet & Hardley     18.35
Panteley Onions, Leeks, and Garlic Binnet & Hardley     17.81

(4 row(s) affected)
```

Microsoft SQL Server allows you to create local temporary stored procedures. For example:

```
CREATE PROCEDURE #books_of_type
    @type CHAR(20)
AS
SELECT  title, price
FROM    titles
WHERE   type = @type
GO
```

We'll explain how you can create other classes of temporary objects when we discuss each one of them in detail.

The tempdb Database

Creating database tables is a DBA's prerogative—unless, of course, you have SQL Server installed on your home PC, where you are the Ultimate Ruler and Emperor of all the databases. Developers in a corporate environment typically write stored procedures or embed Transact-SQL queries into their frontend code. The DBA creates tables and indexes. But most developers secretly desire full control of the database and unrestrained permission to create and drop objects without asking someone else. Their wish may never be granted in full, but they do have these powers in one database—tempdb.

The tempdb database is a system database automatically created on SQL Server at installation time. It cannot be dropped. This database is shared by all users working on the server. It is used to hold temporary objects, such as tables, stored procedures, and views. These objects are considered temporary because their life is short by SQL Server standards. AllMS of them disappear when SQL Server is shut down. When it restarts, SQL Server re-creates tempdb from the *model* database and does not remember any temporary objects from its previous life. Most temporary objects disappear even sooner—when their parent session ends or even when the stored procedure that has spawned them finishes. SQL Server also likes to create its own objects in tempdb—worktables that it builds dynamically in order to optimize complex queries. They may be very expensive to build (take a lot of time and I/O power) but go away quietly once the query is complete.

The default size of the tempdb database is the same as it was on the first version of SQL server more than 10 years ago—2 MB. What was once a lot of memory is not sufficient by today's standards. You need to increase the size of tempdb even if you run SQL Server on your home PC. Sizing it correctly is part of the DBA's art. It depends on the number of concurrent users, application specifics, and the size of your databases and large tables. You can start by making tempdb equal to 25% of the size of your largest database and increase it later if it proves insufficient. Some applications, especially transaction-processing ones, may get by with tempdb sized for as little as 5% of the size of the largest database. Decision-support applications typically require more temporary space to build and sort large result sets.

The default 2 MB segment of tempdb is located on the master device. It is not a good idea to expand tempdb on the master device even if it has spare room. Create a new SQL Server device to hold tempdb extensions and then expand the database on this new device. You may use either GUI administration tools supplied by your vendor or the Transact-SQL commands DISK INIT and ALTER DATABASE.

Avoid creating permanent tables in user databases to hold temporary results. If all work with a temporary table is encapsulated in one stored procedure or within one Transact-SQL batch, it is best to use tempdb for this purpose. The main benefit is that tempdb is self-cleaning while user databases are not. If your stored procedure that created a permanent object terminates for any reason, then you create a maintenance problem for DBAs who have to clean your orphan tables. You don't want to antagonize your DBA, do you?

Classes of Temporary Objects

Table 10-1 shows the classes of objects that can be found in tempdb. We'll discuss each class in more detail in later sections.

Table 10-1. Classes of Objects in tempdb

Class of Temporary Objects	Vendor	Name Prefix	Who Has Access	When Dropped
Local tables	Both	#	Creator only	When explicitly dropped by the creator, when the parent session ends (if created in a batch), or when the stored procedure that created the object finishes (if created in a stored procedure).

Table 10-1. Classes of Objects in tempdb (continued)

Class of Temporary Objects	Vendor	Name Prefix	Who Has Access	When Dropped
Local stored procedures	Micro-soft only	#	Creator only	Same as preceding.
Global tables, stored pro-cedures, views	Micro-soft only	##	Any user	When explicitly dropped by any user or when the parent session ends. If some other process is using the object when the parent session ends, then its life is extended until this usage stops.
"Persistent" temporary objects	Both	No spe-cial prefix	Any user	When explicitly dropped or when SQL Server is shut down.
Model objects	Both	No spe-cial prefix	Any user	When explicitly dropped or when SQL Server is shut down. Reincar-nated from the model database every time SQL Server is restarted.
Worktables	Both	Inter-nal names assign ed by SQL Server	Used by SQL Server internally; users can-not access	Discarded by SQL Server when the query that caused creation of the worktable completes. Cannot be explicitly dropped by a user.

Local Temporary Objects

The ability to create local temporary tables has been in SQL Server from the day it was born. Recent versions of Microsoft SQL Server have added the ability to create temporary stored procedures. Interestingly, you also can execute CREATE VIEW, CREATE RULE, and CREATE DEFAULT statements producing local temporary views, rules, and defaults. No error is reported at the time of creation, but any attempt to use these objects fails. We believe that this capability is a "feature."

Local temporary objects also are sometimes referred to as "private" because they belong to a single SQL Server session—the one that created them. What happens if several users attempt to create a local temporary table under the same name at the same time? This is often the case when some frequently executed stored procedure needs a temporary table. Every session that executes this procedure will demand a new private object under the same name. SQL Server guarantees that there is no conflict by appending automatically generated suffixes to local temporary object names. Each session gets a different suffix, so they in fact use different object names. You do not normally need to know what suffix is assigned to your private tables and stored procedures. Your programs can still refer to such objects by the names you gave them at birth.

Let's create a small temporary table to demonstrate what happens with its name:

```
CREATE TABLE #my_titles (
    title VARCHAR(80) NOT NULL,
    price MONEY       NOT NULL
)
```

This command creates a temporary table in database tempdb. Let's now search the system catalog table, sysobjects, which contains information about each object:

```
SELECT name 'in current db:'
FROM sysobjects
WHERE name LIKE '#my_titles%'

SELECT name 'in tempdb:'
FROM tempdb..sysobjects
WHERE name LIKE '#my_titles%'
```

Results:

```
in current db:
------------------------------

(0 row(s) affected)

in tempdb:
------------------------------
#my_titles__________0000000001

(1 row(s) affected)
```

The results confirm that the object is created not in your current database but in tempdb. We also see the suffix appended to our object name. What if another user does the same? You can open one more connection to the SQL Server (another query window or one more ISQL sessions) and execute the same CREATE TABLE and SELECT statements as the preceding. Now the results of the SELECT statement show two #my_titles objects in tempdb:

```
in tempdb:
------------------------------
#my_titles__________0000000001
#my_titles__________0000000002
```

Each local temporary object belongs to one, and only one, session that has created it. Even if you log in with the same user ID, you still will not be able to access local temporary objects that you create in your other sessions. You cannot refer to your own or somebody else's local temporary object by its nam with a suffix. The following query executed from your second session attempts to access a private object of the first session and fails:

```
select * from #my_titles__________0000000001
```

Results:

```
Msg 229, Level 14, State 2
SELECT permission denied on object #my_titles__________0000000001, database
tempdb, owner dbo
```

For all practical purposes, local temporary tables with the same name created by different sessions have nothing in common. They may have a completely different structure. Another session could even create a local temporary stored procedure under the same name as our local temporary table.

To ensure that a suffix can be added to the name, SQL Server limits the name length of local temporary objects. The maximum (including the mandatory # character) is 20 characters for Microsoft SQL Server and 12 characters for Sybase and old Microsoft versions. Microsoft reports a compile-time error when you use a name longer than 20 characters. Sybase allows you to use names longer than 12 characters but trims them to 12 and appends a suffix.

Do not use local temporary objects with names longer than 12 characters on Sybase SQL Server. The CREATE statement does not fail, but if you attempt to create another object with a similar name, which has the same first 12 characters, it fails at runtime. For example, the names #title_author_address and #title_author_phone translate to the same actual name consisting of "#title_autho" plus the same suffix.

In the next example, we use a temporary table to store and manipulate intermediate results:

```
CREATE TABLE #city_state (
    city  VARCHAR(20) NOT NULL,
    state CHAR(2)     NOT NULL
)

INSERT  #city_state ( city, state )
SELECT  DISTINCT      city, state
FROM    authors

INSERT  #city_state ( city,        state )
VALUES              ( 'New York', 'NY'  )

DELETE  #city_state
WHERE   state = 'UT'
```

```
SELECT  p.*
FROM    #city_state c, publishers p
WHERE   p.state = c.state
    AND p.city  = c.city

DROP TABLE #city_state
```

Results:

```
(16 row(s) affected)

(1 row(s) affected)

(1 row(s) affected)

pub_id pub_name                 city         state country
------ ------------------------ ------------ ----- ------------
1389   Algodata Infosystems     Berkeley     CA    USA
9952   Scootney Books           New York     NY    USA

(2 row(s) affected)
```

This example demonstrates that you can perform the same operations on a temporary object that you can on a permanent one.

You can create indexes on local temporary objects as needed. The index name does not need any special prefix. All rules and limitations on indexes are the same as for permanent objects. Indexes may be very important in optimizing access to large temporary tables. Here are some examples of index creation statements for the table #my_titles introduced earlier:

```
CREATE UNIQUE CLUSTERED INDEX name_key ON #my_titles ( title )
CREATE INDEX price_key ON #my_titles ( price )
```

Global Temporary Objects (Microsoft Only)

Global temporary objects differ from local ones in several ways. First, and most obvious, their names begin with two # characters. All users may share them, so they are also sometimes called *public temporary objects*. Only one global temporary object may be created under the same name. SQL Server does not add any suffix to the name as in the case of local objects. You can create global temporary tables, stored procedures, views, rules, and defaults. Compare this to local temporary objects that allow only tables and procedures. Global temporary rules and defaults may be bound only to columns of temporary tables.

Creating global temporary objects is as easy as creating local ones. You can use the same DDL statements. The ## name prefix tells SQL Server that you want a global temporary object, and it creates one in the tempdb database. For example:

```
CREATE TABLE ##states (
    state CHAR(2) NOT NULL,
```

```
        name  VARCHAR(30) NOT NULL
    )
```

As with the local temporary tables, global ones allow indexes. Index names do not require any special prefix. For example:

```
CREATE UNIQUE INDEX state_key on ##states ( state )
```

Global temporary objects exist for as long as their creator session is alive. In some cases, they may get an extension on their life. This happens if somebody is using the object when its creator session ends. The object in use cannot be dropped until it is released.

Figure 10-1 provides an example of a global temporary object's life span. User A creates a global temporary table called ##X, and then another table called ##Y. He populates ##Y with a lot of data. User B starts a long-running SELECT from table ##Y. User A disconnects from SQL Server. Table ##X is automatically dropped, but table ##Y is in use so it continues to exist. SQL Server waits for user B to finish her SELECT and only then drops table ##Y.

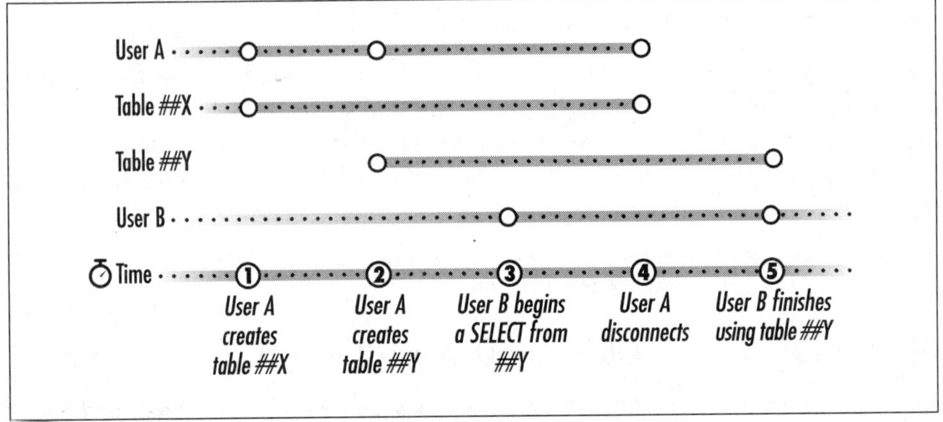

Figure 10-1. Life of global temporary objects

Global temporary objects are very useful in applications that establish several connections to SQL Server and need to share the same set of objects. They are also useful when you need to execute a dynamic SQL query referring to a temporary object you create in the static portion of the code. Dynamic SQL runs as a separate session and does not share local temporary objects. Global temporary objects come to the rescue here.

When you create a long-running program, consider using a global temporary table to reflect the job's status. For example, it could contain a step number of the algorithm or the count of processed records if the global temporary table is executing cursor processing. It allows you to monitor what the program is doing from another session without disturbing it. This is impossible with local temporary tables.

Another practical example is sending email via the extended stored procedure *xp_sendmail*. One of the options is to send results of a query to recipients. You can dynamically create a global temporary table, populate it with some information you want to send, and then call *xp_sendmail* as follows:

```
-- Create a message-holder table
CREATE TABLE ##email ( text_line VARCHAR(255) )
-- Create the 1st line of the message
INSERT ##email VALUES ( 'Top three best selling business titles:' )
-- Add 3 more message lines - best selling titles
SET ROWCOUNT 3
INSERT ##email SELECT title FROM titles ORDER BY ytd_sales DESC
SET ROWCOUNT 0
DECLARE @qry VARCHAR(255)
SELECT  @qry = 'SELECT text_line FROM ##email'
-- Send an email consisting of results produced by the query above.
-- Message holder must be a permanent table or a global temporary one because
-- xp_sendmail cannot access local temporary objects created in your session.
EXEC master.dbo.xp_sendmail 'Grieg, Edward',
                            @query = @qry,
                            @no_header = 'TRUE'
DROP TABLE ##email
```

The benefit of global temporary objects—the fact that multiple users may share them—may backfire if several sessions attempt to create the same global object. Only the first one will succeed. Therefore, you cannot use a global temporary object in a stored procedure that may be concurrently executed by multiple users. Another potential problem is the dependency of global temporary objects on their creators. You cannot create a global object for everyone to use and then disconnect. If you want an object to stay, you need to use "persistent" temporary objects (we'll discuss these later on).

A workaround for the situation when you need a "personal" global temporary object is to generate a unique name for an object and create it through dynamic Transact-SQL in Microsoft SQL Server. On the accompanying CD-ROM is a stored procedure, *sp_rand_global_temp_name*, that generates random names not used by any other global temporary object.

Global temporary views and stored procedures may be very useful if some users need short-term access to certain data or want to perform a specific function that will never be needed again. In these cases, you can create temporary objects instead of bothering with permanent ones. For example, you could create a global temporary view that would allow users to see all titles with the name of the primary author and price:

```
CREATE VIEW ##title_author
AS
SELECT  ti.title, au.au_fname, au.au_lname, ti.price
FROM    authors au, titles ti, titleauthor ta
WHERE   au.au_id    = ta.au_id
    AND ti.title_id = ta.title_id
    AND ta.au_ord   = 1
GO
```

This view is available to all users for as long as you keep your session active. Notice that even though the view is placed in tempdb, it refers to tables in the pubs database that were current at the moment of view creation.

Persistent Temporary Objects

The name *persistent temporary objects* may sound self-contradictory. We have to warn you that this is not an official term used by vendors to describe the type of objects that we are about to discuss. We use this term to highlight the much more persistent nature of these temporary objects compared to global and local ones.

We have already said that tempdb is a special database. It is completely rebuilt from the model database every time SQL Server starts. But while SQL Server is up and running, you can use tempdb like any other database. You can create objects in it without a # prefix: stored procedures, tables, views, triggers, constraints, indexes, rules, and defaults. These objects have no dependency on the creator process. They will stay in tempdb after the session that created them terminates. They may be shared, just as global temporary objects may be.

You may have problems with permissions to create persistent objects if you do not have DBO authority in tempdb. Every user is a member of the public group. You do not need to add users to tempdb, but if you want them to have permissions to create persistent temporary objects, then the SA should explicitly grant these rights to public with the following command executed from the tempdb database:

```
GRANT CREATE TABLE, CREATE VIEW, CREATE PROCEDURE, CREATE DEFAULT,
    CREATE RULE
    TO public
```

The catch is that this command is in effect only until SQL Server is restarted, at which point tempdb is rebuilt again. In order to make these permissions permanent, you have to set them in the model database. Beware that this action also affects every new user database created on the server. If you want to restrict permissions to create objects in new databases, you can manually revoke unnecessary permissions after creating a database.

Persistent objects created by users without DBO privileges in tempdb are owned by the guest user.

Here is an example of a persistent temporary table:

```
CREATE TABLE tempdb..bestsellers (
    title_id   char(6)     NOT NULL,
    title      varchar(80) NOT NULL,
    price      money       NULL,
    ytd_sales  int         NOT NULL
)
```

Index creation of persistent temporary objects is the same as on local and global ones.

Creating persistent temporary stored procedures, views, rules, and defaults is less convenient than creating tables. You have to switch to the tempdb database before issuing a CREATE statement. If your procedure or view refers to objects in a user database, then you need to prefix them with the database and owner name. The same applies to triggers and constraints on persistent temporary tables. Here are some examples:

```
USE tempdb
GO
CREATE PROCEDURE title_publisher
    @title_id char(6)
AS
SELECT  p.pub_name, p.city, p.state, p.country
FROM    pubs.dbo.titles     t,
        pubs.dbo.publishers p
WHERE   t.title_id = @title_id
    AND t.pub_id   = p.pub_id
GO

USE tempdb
GO
CREATE VIEW cooking_titles
AS
SELECT title, price
FROM   pubs.dbo.titles
WHERE  type LIKE '%cook%'
GO
```

```
USE tempdb
GO
CREATE TRIGGER bestsellers_ins
ON bestsellers
FOR INSERT
AS
-- Prevent insertion of records with invalid title_id
IF @@rowcount <> (
    SELECT  COUNT(*)
    FROM    pubs..titles t, inserted i
    WHERE   t.title_id = i.title_id )
BEGIN
    ROLLBACK TRAN
    PRINT 'Invalid title_id. Nothing inserted.'
END
GO
```

Model Temporary Objects

The model database is used as a prototype for any new database created on SQL Server. It contains a "vanilla" set of objects that are automatically created in every new database. There is a default set of system tables in the model database created at SQL Server installation. You can also add your own custom-built objects.

Even though the model database is usually discussed in association with new databases, the most frequent use of it is in spawning tempdb. Every time SQL Server restarts, the model database is used to rebuild tempdb. Every object you place in model in addition to the standard system objects will be created in tempdb as well. So you can use model as a template for persistent temporary objects. Keep in mind that the same objects will be placed in every new user database you create.

This type of temporary object is somewhat exotic and has limited practical use. If you need persistent temporary objects, you may as well create them in auto execution (a.k.a. startup) stored procedures that you can schedule to automatically fire every time SQL Server starts. See Chapter 14, *Stored Procedures and Modular Design,* for instructions on how to create auto execution stored procedures.

Worktables

A *worktable* (sometimes called *work table*) is a special kind of a system temporary table, which SQL Server creates automatically in some cases. SQL Server users have no direct control over worktables. You cannot create them, drop them, or select from them. In many cases, you do not even know when they are created and what their names are. Nevertheless, you need to understand why they are created and how to limit their negative impact on performance. Worktables are created by SQL Server to resolve certain types of queries. They are usually like red flags indicating performance problems with your queries. SQL Server creates them in several cases:

- For all queries with GROUP BY.
- For queries with ORDER BY unless there is a good index on the key used for ORDER BY. The optimizer favors clustered indexes and most likely will avoid creating a worktable if one exists. Nonclustered indexes may be also used, but the optimizer decides on a case-by-case basis if using the index is more costly than creating a worktable.
- For queries that use DISTINCT, unless there is a good index. The same rules for choosing an index apply as in the previous case.
- For queries that do not have a good execution plan in the optimizer's educated opinion. The optimizer often struggles to resolve a query that has no selective indexes or join conditions or that has huge subqueries. When it fails to find a good plan, its last resort is to create a worktable. This desperate measure often causes even more pain, because SQL Server may unexpectedly run out of tempdb or spend a long time populating and indexing worktables.

When you review SHOWPLAN output for a query and see the "Worktable created for REFORMATTING" message, it most likely spells trouble. This query needs more work. Review existing indexes and join conditions to determine what is wrong.

Before we illustrate worktables with some examples, we need to turn on the special SQL Server options that will allow us to see the query execution plan. You may set these options once, execute all example queries, and then turn them off. These options will affect only your own session. They are explained in more detail in Chapter 21, *Debugging Transact-SQL Programs*. For now, just trust us that the following two commands force SQL Server to show the execution plans for every query and turn off the actual execution of queries, since we are interested only in the query plan and not the results. We use boldface to emphasize the word *worktable* in all examples.

These are the options:

```
SET SHOWPLAN ON
GO
SET NOEXEC ON
GO
```

If you prefer to use the GUI, you could achieve the same results in Microsoft SEM or ISQL/W by going to *"Query | Set Options . . . "* and then checking the *"No Execute"* and *"Show Query Plan"* checkboxes. Similar options are available in Sybase's SQL Advantage interface.

Once you have set the options, execute the following queries to review query plans using worktables.

Example 1

A query with GROUP BY always creates a worktable:

```
SELECT   type, SUM( ytd_sales )
FROM     titles
GROUP BY type
```

Query execution plan:

<table>
<tr><th>Microsoft</th><th>Sybase</th></tr>
<tr><td><pre>STEP 1
The type of query is SELECT
(into a worktable)
GROUP BY
Vector Aggregate
FROM TABLE
titles
Nested iteration
Table Scan
TO TABLE
Worktable 1
STEP 2
The type of query is SELECT
FROM TABLE
Worktable 1
Nested iteration
Table Scan</pre></td><td><pre>QUERY PLAN FOR STATEMENT 1 (at line 1).
    STEP 1
        The type of query is SELECT
        (into Worktable1).
        GROUP BY
        Evaluate Grouped SUM OR AVERAGE
        AGGREGATE.

        FROM TABLE
            titles
        Nested iteration.
        Table Scan.
        Ascending scan.
        Positioning at start of table.
        Using I/O Size 2 Kbytes.
        With LRU Buffer Replacement Strategy.
        TO TABLE
            Worktable1.

    STEP 2
        The type of query is SELECT.

        FROM TABLE
            Worktable1.
        Nested iteration.
        Table Scan.
        Ascending scan.
        Positioning at start of table.
        Using I/O Size 2 Kbytes.
         With MRU Buffer Replacement Strategy.</pre></td></tr>
</table>

Example 2

A query with ORDER BY creates a worktable if there is no good index on the key used for ordering:

```
SELECT   ytd_sales, title
FROM     titles
ORDER BY ytd_sales
```

Query execution plan:

<table>
<tr><th>Microsoft</th><th>Sybase</th></tr>
<tr><td><pre>STEP 1
The type of query is INSERT
The update mode is direct
Worktable created for ORDER BY
FROM TABLE
titles
Nested iteration
Table Scan
TO TABLE
Worktable 1
STEP 2
The type of query is SELECT
This step involves sorting
FROM TABLE
Worktable 1
Using GETSORTED Table Scan</pre></td><td><pre>QUERY PLAN FOR STATEMENT 1 (at line 1).

    STEP 1
        The type of query is INSERT.
        The update mode is direct.
        Worktable1 created for ORDER BY.

        FROM TABLE
            titles
        Nested iteration.
        Table Scan.
        Ascending scan.
        Positioning at start of table.
        Using I/O Size 2 Kbytes.
        With LRU Buffer Replacement Strategy.
        TO TABLE
            Worktable1.

    STEP 2
        The type of query is SELECT.
        This step involves sorting.

        FROM TABLE
            Worktable1.
        Using GETSORTED
        Table Scan.
        Ascending scan.
        Positioning at start of table.
        Using I/O Size 2 Kbytes.
        With MRU Buffer Replacement Strategy.</pre></td></tr>
</table>

Example 3

A query using DISTINCT creates a worktable if there is no good index on the columns under DISTINCT:

```
SELECT  distinct pub_id
FROM    titles
```

Query execution plan:

<table>
<tr><th>Microsoft</th><th>Sybase</th></tr>
<tr><td><pre>STEP 1
The type of query is INSERT
The update mode is direct
Worktable created for DISTINCT
FROM TABLE
titles
Nested iteration
Table Scan
TO TABLE
Worktable 1
STEP 2
The type of query is SELECT
This step involves sorting
FROM TABLE
Worktable 1
Using GETSORTED Table Scan</pre></td><td><pre>QUERY PLAN FOR STATEMENT 1 (at line 1).

    STEP 1
        The type of query is INSERT.
        The update mode is direct.
        Worktable1 created for DISTINCT.

        FROM TABLE
            titles
        Nested iteration.
        Table Scan.
        Ascending scan.
        Positioning at start of table.
        Using I/O Size 2 Kbytes.
        With LRU Buffer Replacement Strategy.
        TO TABLE
            Worktable1.

    STEP 2
        The type of query is SELECT.
        This step involves sorting.

        FROM TABLE
            Worktable1.
        Using GETSORTED
        Table Scan.
        Ascending scan.
        Positioning at start of table.
        Using I/O Size 2 Kbytes.
        With MRU Buffer Replacement Strategy.</pre></td></tr>
</table>

Example 4

A query joining two large tables on a key that is not indexed in either table creates worktables. This example is a purposely inefficient query that we wrote to demonstrate how the optimizer penalizes programmers for not caring about proper indexes. We will discuss query optimization in much more detail in Chapter 20, *Transact-SQL Optimization and Tuning,* and show you how such queries could be improved. In this example, we queried different tables on Microsoft SQL Server and Sybase.

<table>
<tr><th>Microsoft</th><th>Sybase</th></tr>
<tr><td><pre>SELECT OBJECT_NAME(p.id)
FROM   pubs..syscomments p,
        master..syscomments m
WHERE   p.text = m.text</pre></td><td><pre>SELECT OBJECT_NAME(p.id)
FROM   pubs..syscomments p,
        sybsystemprocs..syscomments m
WHERE   p.text = m.text</pre></td></tr>
</table>

<table>
<tr><th>Microsoft</th><th>Sybase</th></tr>
<tr><td><pre>
STEP 1
The type of query is INSERT
The update mode is direct
Worktable created
for REFORMATTING
FROM TABLE
master..syscomments
Nested iteration
Table Scan
TO TABLE
Worktable 1
STEP 2
The type of query is INSERT
The update mode is direct
Worktable created
for REFORMATTING
FROM TABLE
pubs..syscomments
Nested iteration
Table Scan
TO TABLE
Worktable 2
STEP 3
The type of query is SELECT
FROM TABLE
Worktable 2
Nested iteration
Table Scan
FROM TABLE
Worktable 1
Nested iteration
Using Clustered Index
</pre></td><td><pre>
QUERY PLAN FOR STATEMENT 1 (at line 1).

    STEP 1
        The type of query is INSERT.
        The update mode is direct.
        Worktable1 created for REFORMATTING.

        FROM TABLE
            pubs..syscomments p
        Nested iteration.
        Table Scan.
        Ascending scan.
        Positioning at start of table.
        Using I/O Size 2 Kbytes.
        With LRU Buffer Replacement Strategy.
        TO TABLE
            Worktable1.

    STEP 2
        The type of query is SELECT.

        FROM TABLE
            sybsystemprocs..syscomments m
        Nested iteration.
        Table Scan.
        Ascending scan.
        Positioning at start of table.
        Using I/O Size 2 Kbytes.
        With LRU Buffer Replacement Strategy.

        FROM TABLE
            Worktable1.
        Nested iteration.
        Using Clustered Index.
        Ascending scan.
        Positioning by key.
        Using I/O Size 2 Kbytes.
        With LRU Buffer Replacement Strategy.
</pre></td></tr>
</table>

A good rule of thumb is to avoid worktables as much as possible. If you need to use GROUP BY, then you have no choice, but in other cases you may consider using additional indexes or alternative ways to obtain the same result.

Do not use DISTINCT "just in case." It penalizes your query performance. Use it only to eliminate duplicate rows where they may possibly appear.

Do not use ORDER BY if the query has a DISTINCT or GROUP BY on the same set of items, because they have the side effect of ordering rows.

Once you finish executing sample queries, don't forget to turn off the session options:

```
SET NOEXEC OFF
GO
```

```
SET SHOWPLAN OFF
GO
```

You also can use the GUI, as explained earlier, and uncheck the same options you checked before executing the sample transactions.

Query Optimization with Temporary Tables

Temporary tables are frequently used to split complicated join queries into several manageable steps. The number of queries executed by such transactions increases along with the number of lines of code, but the resulting program may sometimes be many times faster than a single query. It is difficult to find such an example on the relatively small pubs database. Still, the following code demonstrates the technique.

Here is the original query:

```
SELECT  au.au_lname, ti.title, pu.pub_name, st.stor_name, sa.qty
FROM    titleauthor ta,
        authors     au,
        titles      ti,
        publishers  pu,
        stores      st,
        sales       sa
WHERE   ta.title_id = ti.title_id
    AND ta.au_id    = au.au_id
    AND ti.pub_id   = pu.pub_id
    AND sa.title_id = ti.title_id
    AND st.stor_id  = sa.stor_id
```

One of the ways to split the original query into two steps is shown here:

```
CREATE TABLE #titleauthor (
    au_lname VARCHAR(40) NOT NULL,
    title    VARCHAR(80) NOT NULL,
    title_id CHAR(6)     NOT NULL,
    pub_id   CHAR(4)     NOT NULL
)

INSERT  #titleauthor
SELECT  au.au_lname, ti.title, ti.title_id, ti.pub_id
FROM    titleauthor ta,
        authors     au,
        titles      ti
WHERE   ta.title_id = ti.title_id
    AND ta.au_id    = au.au_id

SELECT  x.au_lname, x.title, pu.pub_name, st.stor_name, sa.qty
FROM    #titleauthor x,
        publishers  pu,
```

```
         stores      st,
         sales       sa
WHERE    x.pub_id    = pu.pub_id
     AND x.title_id  = sa.title_id
     AND st.stor_id  = sa.stor_id
```

This script creates a temporary table to store intermediate results. It joins three tables of the six joined in the original query and saves the result in the temporary table. Two columns—title_id and pub_id—are kept in the temporary table to allow a subsequent join with the remaining three tables. The next step selects results from a join of the temporary table with the rest of the original ones. Therefore, we have replaced one six-table join with one three-table join inserted into the fourth table and a four-table join. The results of this program are the same as those returned by the original query. We don't show them here because they are not important to understanding the technique.

The benefits of using this approach may not be obvious or may even appear questionable when tables contain few rows. However, on large tables and multitable joins, you should find this technique very useful. When you need to optimize a query, you have to carefully evaluate several possible ways to program the same function. This typically requires displaying the query execution plan and executing your code on realistic test data sets. You need to estimate and compare the price of every solution in disk and cache I/O operations. In many cases, you will find that two or more small steps require significantly less I/O than one huge query.

SQL Server allows the use of up to 16 tables in one query. If you need to join more, you have to use intermediate temporary tables and break your query into several steps. Moreover, the SQL Server optimizer does not guarantee a good plan on joins of more than four tables on Microsoft SQL Server and more than six tables on Sybase. Therefore, you may need to break even a five-table join into several steps using temporary tables. This may cost extra development time and result in a longer program, but performance improvements are in many cases outstanding.

Management of the tempdb Database

The tempdb database is shared by all users. With sharing come some etiquette requirements, so your temporary objects do not impede the work of others. One important limitation is the space allocated to tempdb by the DBA. The default size is 2 MB, but practically every seriously used SQL Server must have a bigger tempdb.

Programmers have to ensure that their temporary objects do not grow so large that they take most of the tempdb space or, worse yet, overflow it. When you overflow tempdb, you impact every session on the server that needs space in tempdb. Several important transactions may be aborted due to one person's negligence. If you expect your stored procedure or batch program to place significant amounts of data in tempdb, make estimates first and compare your requirements to the available tempdb space. If your procedure may be concurrently executed by several users and creates a large local temporary table, you have to multiply the temporary space requirements of a single transaction by the maximum number of concurrent sessions.

SQL Server keeps a transaction log in tempdb the same way it does in any other database. But it cannot be backed up because of the transient nature of tempdb. Restoring this database does not make sense, since it is rebuilt fresh every time SQL Server restarts. The transaction log in tempdb is always truncated on checkpoint, regardless of whether you activate this database option. It may still grow very large if you execute a statement affecting many rows of a temporary table.

Do not use SELECT . . . INTO to create temporary tables, unless you are certain that it will take no time to execute. SELECT . . . INTO is dangerous in any database, because it locks system catalog tables and prevents other users from creating objects in the same database. But it may be devastating if you lock tempdb for all users. What happens when you execute a SELECT . . . INTO that takes several hours to execute? Nobody else is able to create a temporary object until your query is done. If this happens, you may find yourself surrounded by not-too-friendly coworkers discussing the quickest way to terminate your transaction.

One more aspect of tempdb space management is the decision about whether to use the *"tempdb in RAM"* option. This is a Microsoft SQL Server configuration parameter that defines how many megabytes of tempdb should reside in RAM. This is done in order to optimize the performance of temporary objects. Many transactions may create temporary tables or cause the creation of worktables. If you place tempdb in RAM, access to these temporary objects becomes much faster compared with dealing with objects on disk. But there is a flip side to this coin. The amount of RAM is limited. Dedicating memory to tempdb reduces the size of the data cache. This takes a toll on transactions in user databases that could take advantage of a larger data cache. In most environments, it is best *not* to place tempdb in RAM. The most recently used pages, including those of temporary tables, will be found in the data cache anyway. SQL Server will give cache space to objects that need it regardless of whether they are temporary tables or permanent ones. If you want to consider this option, you need to thoroughly investigate it and evaluate which applications running on the server will be positively or negatively affected.

In fact, the "tempdb in RAM" option is so frequently misused and its benefits are so hard to justify that Microsoft has decided to discontinue it in SQL Server 7.0.

Sybase provides an option of creating named data caches in RAM. They can be assigned to any database, including tempdb. You can use named data caches for critical tables. This technique optimizes performance on selected tables, but takes memory away from "not-so-privileged" objects. As with the Microsoft option, it requires thorough analysis.

Summary

This chapter discussed the use of temporary objects. Temporary tables, stored procedures, and other objects are created in the tempdb database shared by all users on SQL Server. Some notes about temporary objects:

- Temporary tables provide a convenient way to store transient data used and discarded within a short period of time. They also are useful in optimizing complex queries.
- Regular DDL and DML statements can be used to manipulate temporary objects with respect to permissions. The names of local temporary objects always begin with #; global temporary objects begin with ##. This naming standard allows SQL Server to recognize when you want to create a temporary object.
- The tempdb database always exists on any SQL Server. All users share it, and all temporary objects are created in this database.
- Our classification of objects in tempdb includes local, global, persistent, model, and worktable temporary objects. The most frequently used types of temporary objects are local and global temporary tables. Local temporary tables are privately owned and used by their creator, while all users may share global ones. Local temporary tables and stored procedures are automatically discarded when the session that created them ends. If they are created in a stored procedure, then they are destroyed at the end of the stored procedure. Global temporary tables, stored procedures, and views are destroyed when their creator session ends but may exist longer if some other session continues using them.

- Temporary objects may be used to optimize performance. You may find it more efficient to split a large query into several steps, storing intermediate results in a temporary table. SQL Server sometimes creates worktables in tempdb in an attempt to build a reasonable execution plan for complex queries. This often presents a performance problem. Creation of worktables is not directly controlled by users but may often be avoided by rewriting and optimizing queries or creating proper indexes on tables. Avoid using the SELECT . . . INTO command to create temporary tables with multiple rows. This command locks system tables in tempdb and halts every other user attempting to create temporary objects.
- The default size of the tempdb database is only 2 MB. It should be expanded for almost any serious system. Users should be careful not to overflow tempdb with their own objects because doing so affects the work of others.

In this chapter:
- *About Transactions*
- *Locking*
- *Transactions and the Database*
- *Summary*

11

Transactions and Locking

You buy a candy bar on the home leg of the daily commute. That's a transaction. You flag down a taxi. That too is a transaction. And when you pay the cabby, you've completed yet another transaction. And when you get home, you immediately call the Psychic Hotline. Hey, another (somewhat questionable) transaction. Our lives—the epitome of capitalist decadence—are filled with transactions. It's the same way in a database application (only there are fewer calls to the Psychic Hotline).

A simple definition for a *transaction* in SQL Server is "the act of selecting, inserting, updating, or deleting data within a database." But this definition doesn't properly convey the crucial role transactions play in database applications. Transaction processing affects the performance of a database application more strongly than just about any other consideration (except the initial database design). An information system with carefully conceived transactions can easily scale from a handful of users to hundreds of users without significant modification or degradation in performance. On the other hand, poorly formulated transactions can needlessly consume server resources, lock important sections of the database, and even block the execution of other transactions.

Transactions are the process by which data is deposited into the database. At the start of this chapter, we'll spend some time analyzing the impact of transactions on the transaction log and the database where transactions take place.

Hand in hand with transactions is the topic of *locking*. Any time SQL Server processes a transaction, certain resources within the database must be locked in order to complete the transaction. Locking ensures that many users may access the same record or records within a database without disrupting the consistency and integrity of the data.

About Transactions

SQL Server automatically handles the way most transactions occur within a Transact-SQL program through *implicit* transactions. However, there are many instances in which you'll need to override SQL Server's default handling with *explicit* instructions of your own. The types of transactions issued by your application will directly affect how resources are locked on the server.

In this section, we'll discuss the following topics:

- Writing a transaction
- Implicit and explicit transactions
- Error-checking transactions
- Named transactions
- Savepoints in transactions
- Nesting transactions

Writing Transactions

Transact-SQL contains four commands that are used to write an explicit database transaction: BEGIN, COMMIT, ROLLBACK, and SAVE.

The BEGIN TRAN command marks the starting boundary of a new transaction. As the syntax points out, you can apply a name to a specific transaction.

```
BEGIN TRAN[SACTION] [transaction_name]
```

COMMIT TRAN saves the results of the transaction. COMMIT TRAN is used when the transaction completes successfully and the changes need to be made permanent:

```
COMMIT TRAN[SACTION]
```

ROLLBACK TRAN is used when the transaction is unsuccessful and the operation must be undone. ROLLBACK TRAN completely rolls back all pending transactions.

If you've issued a SAVE TRAN as follows, you can roll back to a *savepoint* rather than undo the entire transaction:

```
ROLLBACK TRAN[SACTION] [transaction_name | savepoint_name]
SAVE TRAN[SACTION] savepoint_name
```

Transactions can be divided into logical breakpoints using the SAVE TRAN command. If you decide to use savepoints, they must be explicitly named. This command does not save any portion of the transaction to the database as a COMMIT does. Instead, SAVE TRAN places a marker in the transaction that enables a transaction to be *partially* rolled back.

All of these individual statements may not make much sense as solitary components. You'll see examples of increasingly more complex transactions throughout the chapter, but to give you a quick glimpse of what a transaction might look like, consider this example sans savepoints:

```
BEGIN TRAN -- initializes a transaction

-- the transaction itself
INSERT INTO sales
VALUES('7896','JR3435','Oct 28 1997',25,'Net 60','BU7832')

-- some error-handling in the event of a failure
IF @@ERROR <> 0
BEGIN
    -- raises an error in the Windows NT event log and skips to the end
    RAISERROR 50000 'Insert of sales record failed'
    ROLLBACK TRAN
    GOTO end_of_batch
END

-- the transaction is committed if no errors are detected
    COMMIT TRAN

-- the GOTO label that enables the batch to skip to the end without
--     committing
end_of_batch:
```

Implicit Transactions

Consider a simple, unbounded transaction that might occur in the pubs database. (A transaction is *unbounded* when it is not enclosed in a BEGIN TRAN . . . COMMIT TRAN statement.) When a sale occurs, a new record must be added to the sales table and the ytd_sales column of the titles table must be updated. The transaction could be written as:

```
INSERT INTO sales
VALUES('7896','JR3435','Oct 28 1997',25,'Net 60','BU7832')

UPDATE titles
SET    ytd_sales = (ytd_sales + 25)
WHERE  title_id  = 'BU7832'
```

Here, the net effect of the two statements is the following: insert a new sales record into the sales table and update the ytd_sales column for that book title in the titles table. What is not immediately evident is that each command is an *implicit transaction.* Any time SQL Server sees an unbound DML statement, it treats the command as one atomic transaction. That means that SQL Server interprets the preceding code more like the following (implied commands are shown in brackets):

```
-- the angle brackets, < >, designate implied commands
<BEGIN TRAN>

INSERT INTO sales
VALUES('7896','JR3435','Oct 28 1997',25,'Net 60','BU7832')

<COMMIT TRAN>

<BEGIN TRAN>

UPDATE titles
SET    ytd_sales = (ytd_sales + 25)
WHERE  title_id  = 'BU7832'

<COMMIT TRAN>
```

The ACID Test

In SQL Server (and most relational databases), a transaction is a command that inserts, updates, or deletes data; one record or one thousand records may be affected by the operation. References to Dr. Timothy Leary aside, the acronym ***ACID*** is often used to describe the properties of a transaction. Here's what the letters of the acronym mean:

A *for Atomic*
: The transaction has an *all or nothing* characteristic. When successful, the data is permanently recorded. When unsuccessful, all effects of the transaction are reversed.

C *for Consistent*
: Data within the transaction is unaffected until the process is complete. This keeps the actions of users from interfering with one another's uncommitted data when work is in progress.

I *for Isolated*
: Isolated transactions don't affect other transactions in process. Isolated transactions impose no change in behavior on other incomplete transactions that affect the same data.

D *for Durable*
: The transaction can complete despite a system failure or rollback and undo all changes if interrupted by a system failure. SQL Server maintains transaction durability through the recovery process. The recovery process is invoked when the server starts, rolling back all uncommitted transactions found in the transaction log and rolling forward all transactions that were committed but had not been flushed from cached data pages to disk prior to server shutdown.

Explicit Transactions

Many times, the implicit transaction handling of SQL Server is a good thing. However, what would happen if some error occurred between the completion of the first transaction and the start of the second transaction? In that case, the first transaction might succeed while the second transaction might fail, or never start. Then the underlying tables would be out of balance, and the usefulness of the database would be compromised. Risks such as these can be minimized by using an *explicit, bounded transaction,* as shown here:

```
BEGIN TRAN

INSERT INTO sales
VALUES('7896','JR3435','Oct 28 1997',25,'Net 60','BU7832')

UPDATE titles
SET    ytd_sales = (ytd_sales + 25)
WHERE  title_id  = 'BU7832'

COMMIT TRAN
```

Using this code, the pair of commands will be treated as *one* transaction with the addition of the BEGIN TRAN . . . COMMIT TRAN transaction control statements. Either both work and are committed to the database, or neither works and the transaction is "rolled back."

Always check that you have paired every explicit BEGIN TRAN statement with a COMMIT TRAN. Be careful! Stored procedures and triggers *will* compile with unpaired BEGIN TRAN statements. They will fail later at execution time or cause failures in other procedures.

Error-Checking Transactions

Error checking in a transaction is especially important in programs that may not have direct human supervision. Error checking is facilitated through the global variable @@error. SQL Server automatically maintains the @@error value based on the status of the current operation. The rule of thumb is this: if @@error is anything other than 0, you've got a problem. (Refer to Chapter 6, *Datatypes and Variables,* for more details about @@error.) Typical errors that are captured by @@error include duplicate entries on a primary key or unique index, datatype mismatches, or a full transaction log. (Chapter 9, *Error Handling,* has lots of information about the exact meaning of @@error codes.) Unlike other programming languages that halt processing when an error arises, Transact-SQL generally continues to execute statements after the error. Here's an example of how you can incorporate error checking into a transaction:

```
BEGIN TRAN
    INSERT INTO sales
    VALUES('7896','JR3435','Oct 28 1997',25,'Net 60','BU7832')
    -- undo the operation and quit the program if there are any errors
    IF @@ERROR <> 0
    BEGIN
    -- the RAISERROR syntax shown is compatible with both Sybase and
    --      Microsoft
          RAISERROR 50000 'Insert of sales record failed'
          ROLLBACK TRAN
        GOTO end_of_batch
    END

    UPDATE titles
    SET    ytd_sales = ytd_sales + 25
    WHERE  title_id  = 'BU7832'
    -- undo the operation and quit the program if there are any errors
    IF @@ERROR <> 0
    BEGIN
        RAISERROR 50000 'Update of sales record failed'
        ROLLBACK TRAN
        GOTO end_of_batch
    END
COMMIT TRAN

-- if an error is encountered, skip all the way to this point
end_of_batch:
```

This block of code is a single transaction, despite the fact that it affects multiple records. The execution of the error-handling code is handled serially, just as in all Transact-SQL programs. Once an error is detected, the error-checking code will write an error to the SQL Server error log, roll back the transaction, and then skip to the end of the program. This type of error-checking code is effective for database errors like inadequate permissions or data-integrity errors (like no corresponding record in the titles table). Error-checking code of the kind shown previously does not affect hardware failures, which are handled by SQL Server's *recovery* process. For hardware failures, the recovery process initializes on server restart, rolling back all uncommitted transactions found in the transaction log and rolling forward all transactions that were committed but had not been flushed from cached data pages to disk prior to server shutdown.

Named Transactions

SQL Server allows you to further refine explicit transactions by specifying a *name* for any given transaction. The name of the transaction must appear immediately after the BEGIN TRAN statement. For example:

```
BEGIN TRAN  new_sales
    INSERT INTO sales
    VALUES('7896','JR3435','Oct 28 1997',25,'Net 60','BU7832')
```

```
    -- undo the operation and quit the program if there are any errors
    IF @@ERROR <> 0
    BEGIN
        -- the RAISERROR syntax is compatible with both Sybase and Microsoft
        RAISERROR 50000 'Insert of sales record failed'
        ROLLBACK TRAN new_sales
        GOTO end_of_batch
    END

    UPDATE titles
    SET    ytd_sales = ytd_sales + 25
    WHERE  title_id  = 'BU7832'
    -- undo the operation and quit the program if there are any errors
    IF @@ERROR <> 0
    BEGIN
        RAISERROR 50000 'Update of sales record failed'
        ROLLBACK TRAN new_sales
        GOTO end_of_batch
    END
COMMIT TRAN new_sales

-- if an error is encountered, skip all the way to this point
end_of_batch:
```

The transaction name is required only after the BEGIN TRAN statement. It is optional with the COMMIT TRAN or ROLLBACK TRAN statement. Named transactions do not provide much additional benefit besides adding a bit of self-documentation to the program code.

The biggest logic errors you may ever encounter are programs that pause a transaction pending user input. That is, the program initiates a transaction and, without committing the transaction, displays a dialog box asking "Save Changes to the database?" You can bet that sooner or later a user goes to lunch without answering the dialog box, locking important database resources for who knows how long. That's because locks issued in a transaction prevent any other user from accessing the same data. A good way to avoid this problem is to avoid initiating transactions at the frontend. Instead, transactions can be limited to stored procedures and Transact-SQL batches on the backend that do not require user interaction to complete successfully.

Savepoints in Transactions

Transactions can be divided into logical breakpoints using the SAVE TRAN command. The main benefit provided by the SAVE TRAN command is that transactions may be partially rolled back to a unique savepoint marker using the ROLLBACK TRAN command. When the command:

```
ROLLBACK TRAN savepoint_name
```

is executed, SQL Server rolls the transaction back to the appropriate savepoint, then continues processing at the next valid Transact-SQL command following the ROLLBACK TRAN statement. Finally, the transaction must be concluded with a COMMIT TRAN statement, even when rolled back to a savepoint. As an example, we could add savepoints to our new_sales transaction as follows:

```
BEGIN TRAN  new_sales
    INSERT INTO sales
    VALUES('7896','JR3435','Oct 28 1997',25,'Net 60','BU7832')

    IF @@ERROR <> 0
    BEGIN
        -- there's no point in continuing if the first transaction fails
        -- the RAISERROR syntax is compatible with both Sybase and Microsoft
        RAISERROR 50000 'Insert of sales record failed'
        ROLLBACK TRAN new_sales
        GOTO end_of_batch
    END

    INSERT INTO sales
    VALUES('7131','N914177','Jan 9 1998',25,'Net 30','MC3021')

    -- undo the operation and quit the program if there are any errors
    IF @@ERROR <> 0
    BEGIN
        RAISERROR 50000 'Insert of sales record failed'
        ROLLBACK TRAN new_sales
        GOTO end_of_batch
    END

    -- the save point is issued after some work has successfully completed
    SAVE TRAN new_sales_part_1

    UPDATE titles
    SET    ytd_sales = ytd_sales + 25
    WHERE  title_id  IN ('BU7832', 'MC3021')

    IF @@ERROR <> 0
    BEGIN
        RAISERROR 50000 'Insert of sales record failed'
        COMMIT TRAN new_sales
        GOTO end_of_batch
    END

    UPDATE titles
    SET    ytd_sales = ytd_sales + 25
    WHERE  title_id  = 'MC3021'

    -- undo the operation and rollback to the SAVE TRAN new_sales_part_1 if
    -- there are any errors
    IF @@ERROR <> 0
    BEGIN
        RAISERROR 50000 'Update of sales record failed'
```

```
        ROLLBACK TRAN new_sales_part_1
    END

COMMIT TRAN new_sales

PRINT 'New sales transaction completed without error'

-- if an error is encountered, skip all the way to this point
end_of_batch:
```

Savepoints should be issued only when the program has accomplished a measurable amount of work. In our example, the savepoint new_sales_part_1 is issued only after the INSERT statements succeed. We don't want to lose those INSERT statements if the UPDATE statements fail. Instead, we want to retry the UPDATE statements. Thus, the combination of SAVE TRAN and ROLLBACK TRAN serve effectively as control-of-flow statements only within the context of the larger transaction.

SQL Server does not reject duplicate savepoint names within a single transaction. However, SQL Server will use only the first occurrence of the savepoint name when executing a rollback, possibly rolling back more than you intended. Be careful!

Nesting Transactions

Nesting transactions within a single Transact-SQL program is usually a bad idea. Generally speaking, nested transactions provide few benefits and many dangers. The danger with nested transactions is that ROLLBACK and COMMIT affect all pending transactions for a given user session. (Other less common problems with nested transactions are discussed shortly.) Most Transact-SQL programmers heed the warning (as you should!) and do not code nested transactions within a single Transact-SQL program. The danger typically arises when a stored procedure opens a transaction, then invokes another stored procedure that opens a new transaction without first closing the open transaction.

You might think that by naming a stored procedure you can skirt the dangers of nested transactions by naming inner nested transactions differently from the outer transaction, then committing each of them specifically. This just isn't true.

The problem is that SQL Server maintains the name of only the outermost transaction. Rollbacks to any transaction name other than the outermost transaction will fail. COMMIT statements, on the other hand, do not fail. But they do act erratically; they commit all open transactions when executed, even if they are paired with named transactions.

To help alleviate the potential problem of nested transactions, Sybase and Microsoft SQL Server maintain the global variable @@trancount to tell you how many open transactions exist in the current user session. The value of @@trancount is incremented or decremented according to the transaction control statement used on it, as shown in Table 11-1.

Table 11-1. @@trancount Modifiers

Transaction Control Statement	Effect on @@trancount
BEGIN TRAN	Increased by 1
COMMIT TRAN	Decreased by 1
ROLLBACK TRAN	Reset to 0
ROLLBACK TRAN savepoint_name	No effect
SAVE TRAN	No effect

Data cannot be committed to the database until @@trancount equals 0. Exclusive locks are not released until @@trancount equals 0, but shared ones are released as soon as SELECT finishes (unless you override the default behavior with optimizer hints). You can easily add code to your Transact-SQL program to check on the status of @@trancount. Thus, @@trancount can be quite useful for checking the status of long-running transactions or for transactions that might be spawned from a stored procedure.

Tracking @@trancount can be particularly important when invoking a stored procedure while a transaction is already open. Stored procedures that may be called while other transactions are open should be aware of the current transaction nesting level, or else the calling stored procedure must be able to intelligently react to the return code of the spawned stored procedure. It's generally easier to code the appropriate behavior in the subordinate program. Here is an update of the new_sales transaction batch that takes transaction nesting into account:

```
IF @@trancount = 0

BEGIN TRAN  new_sales
    INSERT INTO sales
    VALUES('7896','JR3435','Oct 28 1997',25,'Net 60','BU7832')

    IF @@ERROR <> 0
    BEGIN
        -- there's no point in continuing if the first transaction fails
        -- the RAISERROR syntax is compatible with both Sybase and Microsoft
        RAISERROR 50000 'Insert of sales record failed'
        ROLLBACK TRAN new_sales
        GOTO end_of_batch
    END

    INSERT INTO sales
    VALUES('7131','N914177','Jan 9 1998',25,'Net 30','MC3021')
```

```
    -- undo the operation and quit the program if there are any errors
    IF @@ERROR <> 0
    BEGIN
        RAISERROR 50000 'Insert of sales record failed'
        ROLLBACK TRAN new_sales
        GOTO end_of_batch
    END

    -- the save point is issued after some work has successfully completed
    SAVE TRAN new_sales_part_1

    UPDATE titles
    SET    ytd_sales = ytd_sales + 25
    WHERE  title_id  IN ('BU7832', 'MC3021')

    IF @@ERROR <> 0
    BEGIN
        RAISERROR 50000 'Insert of sales record failed'
        COMMIT TRAN new_sales
        GOTO end_of_batch
    END

    UPDATE titles
    SET    ytd_sales = ytd_sales + 25
    WHERE  title_id  = 'MC3021'

    -- undo the operation and roll back to the SAVE TRAN new_sales_part_1 if
    -- there are any errors
    IF @@ERROR <> 0
    BEGIN
        RAISERROR 50000 'Update of sales record failed'
        ROLLBACK TRAN new_sales_part_1
    END

IF @@trancount = 0
BEGIN
    COMMIT TRAN new_sales
    PRINT 'New sales transaction completed without error'
    GOTO end_of_batch
END

IF @@trancount > 0
BEGIN
    RAISERROR 50000 'Nested transaction.  Skipping to end of the batch.'
    GOTO end_of_batch
END

-- if an error is encountered, skip all the way to this point
end_of_batch:
```

Now the transaction is aware of the current nesting level. If the transaction is nested, it will abort the new_sales transaction rather than begin a new transaction. Once the steps of the transaction have completed, the entire transaction is committed.

Sybase SQL Server also has an additional global variable to assist with nested transactions called @@transtate. @@transtate can be queried in the same way as @@trancount; however, @@transtate will return only one of the four values shown in Table 11-2.

Table 11-2. @@transtate Values

Transtate Value	Description
0	The previous statement was completed successfully, although an explicit or implicit transaction is still in progress.
1	The transaction completed and committed all changes.
2	The previous statement was aborted, although there was no effect on the transaction.
3	The transaction aborted and rolled back all changes.

Transaction Tips

Keep these tips in mind when dealing with SQL Server transactions:

- Performance is enhanced when transactions are kept as short as possible. Short (in terms of time) and quick (in terms of CPU cycles) transactions lock fewer system resources and reduce concurrence problems. To make transactions shorter and quicker, commit transactions as frequently as possible without violating any data-integrity rules of the application.
- Avoid grouping many operations into a single transaction batch whenever appropriate.
- You may wish to allow the frontend application to fetch a portion of the rows needed for a query or transaction. When returning small portions of data, you *minimize* the locked area. Compare this to one long-running SELECT that imposes long-lasting locks on many pages or even a table lock that causes blocks. And many times, all of the data in a large query may not even be needed! Consider an application that fetches the first 20 rows on the screen and allows the user to decide whether to fetch the next 20 rows or to quit. No locks are held while the user is thinking. Just make sure that you retrieve the data to the screen using SELECT statements (which only issue shared locks), then execute the data-modification statement separately. This will help minimize locking problems.
- Don't build the client application in a way that allows the end users to define the WHERE clause of queries or reports. Users will frequently leave these fields blank or enter a wildcard, forcing a long-running query. (As an optimization hint, many client applications require the end user to at least enter the first letter in a search field.)

- SQL Server performs transaction processing a little differently for triggers. SQL Server considers triggers to be implied transactions, so all transactions within a trigger act as if they were nested one layer deep. The reason they are already nested one layer is because triggers are considered a component of the transaction that invoked them (whether that be INSERT, UPDATE, or DELETE). Even though the trigger seems like a distinct transaction, SQL Server doesn't treat it like one. Thus, if the invoking transaction is rolled back, so is the trigger. On the flip side, if a trigger is rolled back, so is the transaction that fired it. (For a complete discussion of triggers, refer to Chapter 15, *Triggers and Constraints.*)
- Transaction control statements, like COMMIT or ROLLBACK, do not span servers during the execution of remote procedure calls (RPCs) or distributed transactions. Transactions must be administered locally within the RPC with their own explicit transaction control statements. (There are exceptions when using the statement BEGIN DISTRIBUTED TRANSACTION, but that is beyond the scope of this book.)
- Local variables declared within the context of a transaction cannot bridge batches terminated with GO statements. The variable must be declared again, and it must have a value reassigned for each batch.
- Although SQL Server does allow other commands besides DML statements within a transaction, some commands fail within an explicit transaction. We recommend that you avoid encapsulating any of the following commands within an explicit transaction:
  — ALTER DATABASE
  — DISK INIT
  — DUMP TRANSACTION
  — LOAD DATABASE
  — LOAD TRANSACTION
  — RECONFIGURE
  — UPDATE STATISTICS
  — Any system stored procedure that alters the master database

Locking

Locks have been used for lots of interesting things throughout the ages: locking chastity belts, keeping criminals out of your place, keeping criminals in their place, and locking myself out of my car come readily to mind. In relational database technology, locks have a special meaning. Whenever a transaction is initiated, SQL

Server automatically locks the required records so that only one user can modify the data at a time. When a record is locked by a user's transaction, all other users must wait for the first transaction to complete. SQL Server uses different kinds of locks to complete different kinds of transactions. It's important that you have a good understanding of locks and locking behavior so that your Transact-SQL program does not needlessly lock resources, preventing other users from completing their work.

An Example of Locking

To illustrate the huge importance of locking in a multiuser database application, let's look at an example based on the pubs database. In this example, our sales agents are recording books sale through an order entry application. Inventory levels are tracked in a hypothetical table called inventory, a summary value of year-to-date sales is updated for each book title in the titles table, and a new sales detail record is created when each order is submitted. A complete operational process follows this path:

1. Initiate a new sales ticket by first checking the number of items ordered.
2. Check to see if there are enough of the items in inventory to cover the order.
3. Reduce inventory if enough of the product exists; otherwise, roll back.
4. Insert a new detail record in the sales table.
5. Update the summary sales information in the titles table.

All five steps make up one complete unit of work—in simpler terms, they are a single transaction. If any one step fails, then the whole process should be aborted. Only if all steps succeed should the data-entry operation be committed to the database. SQL Server's locking routines ensure this behavior. By locking all the data used to complete this operation, SQL Server can ensure that no other users are attempting to modify the same data at the same time. Consider how this order entry system might work in an application that does not lock the data:

1. Evelyn initiates a sales ticket for 30 copies of *Secrets of Silicon Valley*. She presses the "Check Inventory" button.
2. Joe kicks off a sale for 25 copies of the same book at the same time.
3. Evelyn sees that 35 copies of the book are currently in stock, so she tells the customer that the books are on order as she prepares to deduct the 30 copies from inventory.
4. Joe checks the inventory status and sees that more than enough are in stock. He too prepares to deduct his order quantity of 25 from inventory.

The bad news is that without locking, both sales will go through. That means that inventory will be quite out of sync (35 - 30 - 25 = -20 books in inventory). Systems that do not lock data are subject to all sorts of insertion, deletion, and modification anomalies like this.

The good news is that SQL Server's default behavior does not allow nonlocking transactions. (Check out the discussion of isolation levels under the SET command later in this chapter for more information on how to change SQL Server's default locking behavior.) In the example scenario, as Evelyn begins to execute the sales order, SQL Server is be told to place exclusive locks on the data needed to complete the transaction. At the moment Joe attempts to initiate his transaction, he is placed in a queue, lasting just a few milliseconds or seconds, until Evelyn completes her work. Once Evelyn's transaction has completed, the resources are released to Joe—who then finds out that there aren't enough units of the book in stock to complete the order. Time for Joe to back-order the book for his client.

Observing Locks and User Sessions

SQL Server provides several tools for evaluating the locking behavior of transactions. You'll use the system stored procedure *sp_lock* to observe the locks in an application. The system stored procedure *sp_who* enables you to quickly check up on user and system processes within SQL Server. And the Microsoft command DBCC INPUTBUFFER allows you to retrieve detailed information about a specific user process.

Observing locks in SQL Server

Old hands at SQL Server can predict with some accuracy the locking behavior of a given transaction. But if you're new to SQL Server or you're coding a new or difficult transaction, you might want to observe the actual locking behavior of SQL Server as your transaction executes. The system stored procedure *sp_lock* will report on all locks held in SQL Server. You can retrieve a report on up to two system process IDs (or SPIDs) by issuing the command:

```
sp_lock [spid [, spid]].
```

The sp_lock procedure, including the difference between Microsoft and Sybase, is discussed in gruesome detail in Chapter 17, *System and Extended Stored Procedures*. This example uses Microsoft's version. With this command (*sp_lock* without any arguments), we can find all the locks opened in SQL Server during the execution of the new_sales transaction:

```
BEGIN TRAN  new_sales
    INSERT INTO sales
    VALUES('7896','JR3435','Oct 28 1997',25,'Net 60','BU7832')
    -- undo the operation and quit the program if there are any errors
    IF @@ERROR <> 0
        BEGIN
```

```
            RAISERROR ('Insert of SALES record failed.',16,-1)
            ROLLBACK TRAN new_sales
            RETURN
        END

    UPDATE titles
    SET    ytd_sales = (ytd_sales + 25)
    WHERE  title_id  = 'BU7832'
    -- undo the operation and quit the program if there are any errors
    IF @@ERROR <> 0
        BEGIN
            RAISERROR ('Update of TITLES record failed.',16,-1)
            ROLLBACK TRAN new_sales
            RETURN
        END

    EXEC sp_lock
 -- to view all current table and pages locks via the master..syslocks table.
COMMIT TRAN new_sales
```

Results:

```
(1 row(s) affected)

(1 row(s) affected)

spid   locktype                             table_id    page        dbname
------ ----------------------------------- ----------- ----------- ----------
210    Sh_intent                            2103678542  0           master
210    Ex_intent                            192003715   0           pubs
210    Ex_page                              192003715   400         pubs
210    Sh_intent                            192003715   0           pubs
210    Update_page                          192003715   400         pubs
210    Sh_intent                            368004342   0           pubs
210    Ex_intent                            416004513   0           pubs
210    Ex_page                              416004513   592         pubs
210    Ex_page                              416004513   616         pubs
210    Ex_extent                            0           368         tempdb
```

If you prefer, you can use the command:

```
sp_lock [spid1[, spid2]]
```

to zero the report in on the locks of up to two specific SPIDs. *sp_lock* returns a report showing the SPID (or process ID) holding the lock, the type of lock, the object ID of the table where the lock was held, the exact data page(s) locked, and the database where the lock was held. Here's a more detailed explanation of each element of the report:

SPID

The system process ID that identifies every distinct SQL Server connection or process. End users might actually have many connections, and thus many SPIDs, on a SQL Server database.

LOCKTYPE

This is a two-part designator. The portion of the string preceding the underscore character indicates one of three basic types of locks: shared, exclusive, or update. The portion of the string following the underscore character tells the amount of data held by the lock. This might include an intent lock (explained later in this chapter), row, 2K page, extent (eight 2K pages) or table lock.

TABLE_ID

The unique object_id SQL Server creates for every new object within a database (including tables). This value is stored in the sysobjects table of every database. There are two easy ways to find out which table holds a given object_id, as shown here:

```
USE pubs
GO

SELECT object_name(416004513)
GO

SELECT name
FROM   sysobjects
WHERE  id = 416004513
GO
Results:
------------------------------
sales

name
------------------------------
sales
```

PAGE

This column will show a nonzero numeric value when a specific 2K data page is locked. This allows you to hone in on a specific area of a table where contention may be occurring. If the column shows a zero, then a table lock is indicated.

DBNAME

The name of the database where the lock is occurring.

Observing user sessions

Observing system and user activity on SQL Server is made easy using the *sp_who* system stored procedure. Chapter 17 has lots more information on *sp_who*.

To find out who is active on SQL Server at any given moment or to find out the specific SPID of a process, you can use *sp_who*. The basic syntax for *sp_who* is shown here:

```
sp_who [login_name | 'spid' | active]
```

You can narrow the result set of *sp_who* by specifying a login name, a SPID, or the keyword ACTIVE. The ACTIVE keyword returns all processes that are not idle or sleeping. By default, *sp_who* reports on all the current system processes, including blocked processes, as shown here:

```
spid status   loginame  hostname    blk dbname     cmd
---- -------  --------- ----------- --- ---------- ----------------
1    sleeping sa                    0   master     MIRROR HANDLER
2    sleeping sa                    0   master     LAZY WRITER
3    sleeping sa                    0   master     CHECKPOINT SLEEP
4    sleeping sa                    0   master     RA MANAGER
10   sleeping sso       WKSTN9501   0   master     AWAITING COMMAND
11   sleeping sa        CHAMPAGNE   0   master     AWAITING COMMAND
12   sleeping sa        CHAMPAGNE   0   master     AWAITING COMMAND
13   sleeping sa        CHAMPAGNE   0   master     AWAITING COMMAND
14   sleeping probe     SQL PerfMon 0   master     AWAITING COMMAND
15   runnable Evelyn    WKSTN9534   0   pubs       UPDATE
16   sleeping sso       WKSTN9501   0   pubs       AWAITING COMMAND
17   sleeping sso       WKSTN9501   0   pubs       AWAITING COMMAND
18   runnable Joe       WKSTN9577   15  pubs       INSERT
19   sleeping sa        CHAMPAGNE   0   distributi AWAITING COMMAND
20   sleeping sa        CHAMPAGNE   0   distributi AWAITING COMMAND
```

sp_who will always show four sleeping system processes: Mirror Handler, Lazy Writer, Checkpoint Sleep, and the Read-Ahead (RA) Manager. These are normal background processes for SQL Server that cannot (and should not) be killed. All other SPIDs shown by *sp_who* are either user-invoked or application-invoked processes. In this example, spid 19 and 20 are replication processes, while spid 14 is used by SQL Performance Monitor. Sybase has more system processes: Housekeeper, Network Handler, Deadlock Tune, Mirror Handler, Shutdown Handler, and Checkpoint Sleep. All the other processes are actual users. In one case, the user process spid 18 is blocked by spid 15 (as shown in the "blk" column). Here's a quick-and-dirty explanation of each column in the report (Chapter 17 has details on all the variations between Sybase and Microsoft, and there are a few):

SPID
: The system process ID that identifies every distinct SQL Server connection or process.

STATUS
: User and system processes may be "runnable" or "sleeping," meaning they are either working or idle, respectively. This column is somewhat misleading, since it reports status only for the exact millisecond the command was executed. A process that was sleeping .01 seconds ago may be churning away at this very moment.

LOGINAME
: Indicates the SQL Server login name under which the process is running.

HOSTNAME
This is usually the name of the computer where the processes were executed. Some processes internal to SQL Server will have a distinct hostname. And some applications will have a specifically coded hostname value.

BLK
Perhaps the most important piece of information in the report, BLK tells the SPID of any other process that is blocking that SPID. In the preceding example, spid 18 is blocked by spid 15.

DBNAME
The name of the database where the SPID is active.

CMD
The (very) general command being executed by the SPID.

Getting details about specific processes in Microsoft SQL Server

sp_who tells you only the main type of activity a user or system process is executing, such as SELECT, INSERT, or UPDATE. But *sp_who* does not tell you the details of the process, like which table is being queried. On Microsoft SQL Server, you can quickly discover the specifics of a process using the command DBCC INPUTBUFFER. This command will reveal the last (yes, I said last) 255 characters of the last command executed by a specific process. If the process doesn't have an input stream (like some system processes), the command will return the following message:

```
The specified SPID does not process input/output data streams.
DBCC execution completed. If DBCC printed error messages, see your System
Administrator.
```

The exact syntax of the command looks like this:

```
DBCC INPUTBUFFER (spid)
```

For example, to find out the exact command that spid 15 (from the *sp_who* report shown earlier) is executing, you would execute this command:

```
DBCC INPUTBUFFER (15)
GO
```

Results:

```
INPUT BUFFER
-------------------------------------------------------------------------------
UPDATE  sales
SET     terms    = 'Net 30'
WHERE   terms    = 'Net 60'
    AND stor_id = '7896'

DBCC execution completed. If DBCC printed error messages, see your System
Administrator.
```

Types of Locks

SQL Server uses one of four types of locks to complete a transaction. Once SQL Server has determined whether the transaction will merely read data or will update it, the locks are issued. Locking occurs not only on the data pages of a table, but also on its index pages. So remember, any time a record is inserted, updated, or deleted in a table, an index page may be altered too. Table 11-3 shows some information about the four types of locks in order of least restrictive to most restrictive lock.

Table 11-3. SQL Server Lock Types

Lock Type	Description
Intent	This is the least restrictive type of lock. As the name implies, intent locks show the future intentions of the lock manager for a given transaction. SQL Server uses intent locks to queue exclusive locks on a data resource, thus ensuring that multiple exclusive locks will be placed on the data in the order the transactions were initiated. Intent locks are further divided into intent shared locks, which indicate that the process intends to take out a shared lock on a given data resource, and intent exclusive locks, which indicate that the process intends to grab an exclusive lock on a given data resource. Intent locks are also used by SQL Server's lock manager to determine when to escalate a transaction from a page or extent lock up to a full table lock.
Shared	Shared locks are used for transactions that do not change data, such as SELECT statements. Other read-only processes can access the same data concurrently without being blocked by other shared locks. No one can write data to a page held by a shared lock.
Update	Update locks are issued just prior to the modification of existing data in a table. (They are also used for inserts into a table with a clustered key.) Update locks operate in two steps. First, the update lock is issued against the data resource (other users can still read this data); then the update lock is escalated to an exclusive lock to complete the modification of the data.
Exclusive	This is the most restrictive type of lock. Exclusive locks are issued when data is modified through UPDATE, INSERT, or DELETE statements. Exclusive locks prohibit all access to the data being locked, including simple reads. Exclusive locks are usually the culprits behind any blocking or deadlocking problems in the application. You should attempt to limit the time exclusive locks are open as much as possible, since they completely lock data until the locking transaction has completed.

A standard application has to contend with many processes and activities simultaneously. As a result, a wide variety of lock types might be issued at any given moment. Table 11-4 shows you which lock types are compatible with one another. This information can help you structure an application to avoid transactions that invoke incompatible locks. The table demonstrates, for example, that allowing numerous exclusive locks in your application during the peak reporting period would be a bad move, because those users pulling reports would have to wait for the exclusive locks to be released.

Table 11-4. Lock Compatibility

	Shared	Update	Exclusive	Insert_page	Link_page
Intent exclusive	X	X	X	X	X
Intent shared	OK	OK	OK	X	X
Shared	OK	OK	X	X	X
Update	OK	X	X	X	X
Exclusive	X	X	X	X	X
Shared with intent exclusive	OK	X	X	X	X
Insert_page (Microsoft only)	X	X	X	OK	X
Link_page (Microsoft only)	X	X	X	X	X
Demand (Sybase only)	X	X	X	X	X

Insert row-level locking (IRL) on Microsoft servers

When Microsoft SQL Server is running insert row-level locking (IRL), there are additional types of locks to be aware of: insert_page and link_page locks. Insert_page locks are compatible only with other insert_page locks. So, non-INSERT transactions treat insert_page like a page lock, while other INSERT statements treat it as a insert_page lock. Link_page locks are used whenever a table is about to be completely filled. In that case, the insert_page lock is escalated to a link_page lock so that a new 2K data page can be allocated and linked. Any subsequent insert_page locks are blocked until the link_page lock is released.

Demand locking on Sybase servers

Sybase has a nifty little internal lock, known as a demand lock, that you won't see using lock-monitoring tools like *sp_lock*. However, you'll notice the beneficial effect of demand locks. These locks are invoked by SQL Server to indicate that the next write transaction in the queue gets the data resource, preventing any new shared locks from stepping ahead in the queue—as in, "I demand to see the manager!" Demand locks prevent a situation in which read transactions with overlapping shared locks monopolize a data resource so that write transactions have to wait indefinitely for its exclusive lock. If a write transaction has to wait on several different read transactions, SQL Server will invoke a demand lock on behalf of the waiting transaction. Once the last read transaction finishes and releases its shared lock, the write transaction can sneak in under an exclusive lock and do its business.

Scope of Locking

The scope of a lock simply means the amount of data held by a single lock. This is also known as *granularity*. Locking in a relational database is resource-intensive. Highly granular locks can help reduce concurrency issues but can incur greater overhead. In SQL Server, each lock consumes the same amount of overhead no matter what its granularity. So, to conserve system resources, SQL Server attempts to balance its lock strategy between low-cost, high-granularity locks and high-concurrency, low-granularity locks. What does this mean? High-granularity locks (say a table lock or extent lock) are great on locking resources but lousy for concurrency. After all, how many users can modify a table when every transaction against the table holds a table lock? Only one at a time. On the other hand, if every transaction is granted a single row-level lock, many users can work concurrently on the same table, but the server must have enough processing power to accommodate the substantial overhead of thousands of simultaneous locks.

The following list describes the scope of the data a lock can hold:

Row
: In Microsoft SQL Server 6.5, row-level locking is available only on insert transactions. (Sybase SQL Server 11.0 and earlier versions do not have any form of row-level locking, although it can be simulated using the max_rows_per_page option under CREATE INDEX.) Insert row-level locking (IRL) is useful in reducing contention on a 2K data page where many transactions are waiting to perform an insert. When using IRL, you may notice two new lock types in use: insert_page and link_page. Link_page locks are used to acquire an insert_page lock. Insert_page locks hold a whole 2K data page. Only another insert_page lock may access a page held by an insert_page lock. Full row-level locking is available in Microsoft SQL Server 7.0 and Sybase Adaptive Server 11.9. Both Microsoft SQL Server Version 7.0 and Sybase Adaptive Server 11.9 have added full row-level locking. Although this adds greater locking granularity, all of the information presented in this chapter is still accurate, since all the other locking scopes are still used.

Page
: Page locks are the most frequently used form of locking in both Sybase and Microsoft SQL Server databases. Page locks acquire a 2K data page or index page at a time. When overhead is subtracted out, a 2K page can store 1,962 bytes of data. Most of the time, a single page lock will hold many records. As an example, the entire contents of the authors table (24 records) fits on a single 2K page. Any transaction that acquires an exclusive page lock on the authors table will actually lock the whole table! Large transactions often acquire locks on many pages before escalating to a table lock.

Extent
: Extent locks are used only when deallocating or allocating additional space for a table. This might be due to creating a new index, a new worktable being created in tempdb, or a transaction inserting so many rows into a table that

more space must be allocated for the table. An extent is a contiguous group of eight 2K data pages or index pages. Extent locks typically occur during CREATE transactions, DROP transactions, or INSERT transactions that require the creation of new data or index pages.

Table

Transactions that affect more than half of the data in a table are often escalated to a table lock. In this case, an entire table, including all data and indexes, is locked. Some transactions start out using page locks. If the transaction requires much of the table to complete, and there aren't any other transactions on the table competing for locks, a table lock will be granted. Other situations, like an unrestricted UPDATE that attempts to alter all records of a table, may cause SQL Server to go straight for a table lock. If other transactions are holding locks on the table, the table lock would be de-escalated to a multitude of page locks. Table locks are often encountered when a new index is created on a table, on full table scans, or when a transaction has exceeded the page lock escalation threshold setting for the server.

Locking Problems

The two most common locking problems in SQL Server are blocks and deadlocks. These problems afflict even the best-designed database applications but are much more common in databases with poor table design, indexing, or query construction. A good database design and frontend application will preempt most foreseeable locking problems. If you encounter locking problems, it's often a good idea to look for improvements in the database design and/or frontend application. Locking problems also tend to appear only after large numbers of users begin to log in to the database. A carefully executed test plan that simulates the work of multiple concurrent users can help reveal a database or application design that is vulnerable to locking problems.

Single-user and read-only databases don't incur locks because there are no concurrency issues.

Blocking is a situation in which a transaction holds an exclusive lock, causing other transactions to queue, waiting for the locks to be released. There are both short blocks that go by in a wink and long blocks that raise everyone's dander. In a long-lasting block, as the transactions pile up, later transactions are able to acquire some but not all of the locks they need. So, these later transactions in turn create new blocks. Even multiple transactions by the same user, if issued at different times, can block one another. In some cases, unabated blocking can bring the whole server to a standstill.

Deadlock is a subset of blocking. When deadlock occurrs, two transactions block each other. Neither one can complete until the other releases its locks, but neither will release its locks until it commits or rolls back its transaction. On the bright side, SQL Server automatically detects deadlocks. On the dark side, SQL Server automatically rolls back one of the deadlocked transactions.

Blocked transactions

Blocked transactions must wait for another, earlier transaction to release its locks on a resource. There are a number of scenarios in which this might occur due to the index design, server setup, or transaction coding. We'll examine a few frequently encountered blocking scenarios in the following sections.

The "page congestion" scenario. The order entry system that records sales for the pubs database is protected by a security table. Each sales clerk must sign into the system at the start of the business day, but lately the login process is taking forever. Monitoring the server reveals nothing more than a normal number of exclusive page locks on the security table. What's the holdup?

In many cases like this, the design of the table, and especially the table's indexes, may be to blame. The first thing you should notice is that the login transaction places a shared lock on the security table and an exclusive lock on the security_audit table. Unfortunately, we cannot change the exclusive lock to a shared lock because corporate policy requires an audit trail each time a clerk logs in. And since we're writing the audit record to the security table, we'll always get an exclusive lock. But there's another element to the problem—page locks.

In the case of the security table, a large number of records appears on a single 2K data page. Aha! That means any time a sales clerk logs in, all the other sales clerks who are recorded on the same data page of the security_audit table are also locked. There are two ways to reduce the number of records on a 2K page of data:

- Reduce the fillfactor setting on the tables' clustered index. (On Sybase, you could use the even better max_rows_per_page index setting.) Fewer records are stored on a 2K data page when the fillfactor setting is set lower, thus leading to a lower chance of blocking. Unfortunately, fillfactors are not maintained by SQL Server. So the only way to maintain the fillfactor on a table is to occasionally drop and re-create the clustered index. (Refer to the section on CREATE INDEX in Chapter 3 for more information and caveats about the process.)
- Artificially increase the size of a record so that fewer records fit on a 2K data page. This technique is known as *row padding*. You can effectively pad a row,

so that only one record exists per page, by adding dummy columns that contain only blank spaces. Each row must be padded out to at least 1,005 bytes to retain only one record per page. (Don't forget that nullable and variable-length columns might reduce the total length of the record.) Although purists of relational theory would be offended by this idea, sometimes that's the only way to reduce the number of records on a page.

The lock escalation scenario. A developer writes a SQL Server application on a small test server. When the coding is complete, multiuser testing reveals that the rapidly growing SALES table is subject to frequent table locks. What's causing the entire SALES table to be locked by a single transaction?

The answer may be in a server setting known as *lock escalation*. Lock escalation settings (described in the sidebar) tell SQL Server how many page locks a connection should be granted before attempting to escalate to a table lock. By default, SQL Server has a default lock escalation setting of only 200! That's less than 400K of data. If you experience frequent, unexplained table locks, then you should increase the lock escalation setting. (You may need to coordinate any such changes with the DBA because it affects all databases on the server, not just yours.)

The "hot spot" scenario. An older mainframe system has been migrated to SQL Server recently. Now blocking occurs when many users attempt to insert data into the billing table. What could be happening?

SQL Server's page-locking strategy is susceptible to *hot spots*. (It's not what you're thinking.) A hot spot occurs when many users compete for an exclusive lock on the final 2K page of a table, usually due to a monotonically increasing clustered index (such as those created by an IDENTITY property). A table is susceptible to hot spots if:

- It has a clustered index built on a monotonically increasing key.
- It has no clustered indexes.

You can easily solve the problem of hot spots by altering whichever condition is most prevalent. For example, if the table has a clustered index built on the incremental key, move the clustered index onto another one or more columns of the table. If the table doesn't have a clustered index, add one. If, even after altering the hot spot condition, you continue to experience blocking on a Microsoft SQL Server installation, you can implement insert row-level locking (IRL). IRL was designed specifically to combat hot spot scenarios but also can help with other blocking problems on INSERT transactions. You should coordinate the implementation of IRL on a given table with the local DBA.

The bad transaction scenario. The marketing department is complaining of an unusually long wait while their biweekly sales report generates. An investigation

Lock Escalation

SQL Server contains several system configuration settings that affect how and when the lock manager escalates from page locks to table locks. These settings are typically controlled and set by the DBA, but they significantly affect how your transactions (and the transactions of all users) will behave. *Lock escalation* (or LE for short) is a term meaning the point at which SQL Server's lock manager decides that moving from a bunch of page locks to a single table lock will improve general system throughput. If you haven't caught the drift yet, SQL Server, not you, decides when and how locks are implemented. (You can get around this limitation using optimizer hints, discussed later in this chapter.)

First of all, there's the locks configuration parameter, which establishes the total number of locks supported by the entire server, including page, table, and extent locks. It's important to set this value high enough to service all page lock requests of your application. If SQL Server ever has requests for more locks than are currently available under this setting, any command that was in process (but ran out of locks) is terminated and rolled back. For small applications, the default value of 5,000 may be enough. A decent rule of thumb is to set this value at least as high as your largest table that sustains heavy transaction processing. Thus, an application whose largest OLTP table is 80,000 2K pages might also have a locks value of 80,000 or more. One thing to remember is that 32 bytes of memory are reserved for each lock configured for SQL Server. This takes away from memory available to SQL Server and can inhibit overall system performance if set unnecessarily high.

The LE threshold maximum setting is the maximum number of 2K pages SQL Server will lock before attempting to escalate to a table lock on a Microsoft server. This setting is usually a low, low 200. That means that any time a transaction tries to lock 200 or more pages of data, SQL Server will attempt to escalate the transaction to a table lock. You will probably want to increase this setting. A quick rule for this setting is to set this value to one-third or one-half your largest OLTP table. In Sybase, this setting is called lock promotion HWM (as in high-water mark).

The LE threshold minimum setting is the minimum number of page locks required before SQL Server will attempt to escalate to a table lock on a Microsoft server. Again, the SQL Server default for this setting is a very low 10. That means that, at a minimum, only 10 page locks are needed on a table before SQL Server will attempt to gain a table lock. This setting is useful in preventing the escalation to a table lock on the smaller tables of your database where the threshold minimum is reached quickly. You'll want to set this value higher than the number of pages in any small, frequently accessed tables. In Sybase, this setting is called lock promotion LWM (as in low-water mark).

—Continued—

> The LE threshold percent setting provides you with a means of escalating tables based on the percentage of the table locked on a Microsoft server. It's zero by default, since SQL Server opts to use the LE threshold maximum setting as its default. If LE threshold percent and LE threshold maximum are both set, then LE threshold percent is superseded by the LE threshold maximum setting. On Sybase, this setting is called lock promotion PCT (as in percent).
>
> Sybase also has the very cool capability of setting lock escalation at the table level. Sybase provides a system stored procedure called *sp_sysmon* that allows you to see how many times and what types of lock escalations occur on the server. Microsoft only allows you to set lock escalation for the entire server, although you can modify that behavior using session-level settings and optimizer hints.

reveals that the report queries are stuck waiting for locks to be released on the titles table (and not the sales table where you might've guessed the problem was). More research reveals that the main transaction code in the sales application issues a blank update on the titles table to recalculate all ytd_sales values—every time a sale is completed! That means the entire titles table is exclusively locked every time a sale goes through. A disaster waiting in the wings!

Obviously, the solution is to revamp the transaction. It could be altered so that the ytd_sales value is recalculated only for those few book titles involved in the sale. Or the update could be removed entirely from the sales transaction and merged into the marketing report generation program or placed into a separate piece of code altogether.

The "zombie process" scenario. A development team is creating a new SQL Server application. The code is still rough but is progressing nicely. However, whenever a developer on the team reboots their client workstation, their SQL Server session and SPID do not die. Instead, they continue to exist on the server, locking (and blocking) database resources. This problem has both a short-term and long-term resolution.

The short-term solution is to simply find the developer's session and kill it. Literally! You can kill the runaway process with the *sp_who* system stored procedure. Once you've found the spid, you can kill it using the KILL command. The exact command to kill spid 15 would be:

```
KILL 15
```

That's it!

Sometimes, these runaway processes don't respond to the KILL command. These kinds of processes are called *zombie processes* because they just won't die (yuk-

yuk-yuk). Zombie processes are almost always caused by an ungraceful disconnection between the client and the server (most often, it's a three-finger salute by the user). The solution to zombie processes is detailed in the long-term solution described next.

The long-term solution might involve SQL Server's *thread pooling*. By default, SQL Server provides 255 threads to process user and system sessions. Each user or system session gets its own thread until SQL Server runs out of threads. SQL Server then piggybacks any new user or system sessions onto other preexisting threads. The problem of zombie processes arises in situations in which a process dies or disconnects while piggybacked on a currently active thread used by another process. As long as the other process is active on the same thread as the zombie process, the zombie will not die (sounds melodramatic, doesn't it?). You can help alleviate the problem of zombie processes by increasing the SQL Server configuration parameter "max worker threads." (Other reasons for zombie processes exist, including something as simple as a poorly written frontend, but this is one of the main reasons.) You may need to coordinate with the DBA to alter this server setting.

Finding the Working SPIDs

You can tell if a SPID is actually performing work with this query:

```
SELECT spid, physical_io, cpu FROM master..sysprocesses
```

Run this query several times in succession. If the physical_io value increases, then the SPID is likely performing work. Physical_io is not a direct indicator of I/O activity incurred by the SPID, but it gives you a good idea of how much work the SPID is actually performing. (The accompanying CD-ROM contains a stored procedure called *sp_whoactive* which shows similar, but more detailed, information.)

The rogue user scenario. Pat is one of the scariest of all end user types: the kind that knows a little about the system but only enough to gum up the works. Pat's latest side project has been to use an ODBC-based spreadsheet to connect directly to the database, circumventing all of your regular transaction-processing controls. Somehow, she's managed to get in again, despite another password change.

Pat seems to be causing locking problems by starting a transaction and letting it run for a long time. Many blocks are caused by a single process holding locks for an extended period of time. Over a short time in a heavily used system, a single block causes a long chain of blocks. The best way to solve this problem is to clear the first transaction in the blocking chain, rather than take a few potshots at which process to kill.

We've included a stored procedure on the CD-ROM called *find_block_root.sp*. This Transact-SQL stored procedure will return one row per SPID at the head of a blocking chain. The program will display the query and locks held by the transaction.

Deadlocked transactions

Does this term remind you of a scene in your favorite action movie? Deadlocked transactions are among the nastiest type of database locking problems, mostly because there is not much we can do about them after they occur. Deadlocks, also known as *deadly embraces,* occur when one transaction acquires locks on Resource A and requests locks on Resource X at the same time that a second transaction that has locks on Resource X requests locks on Resource A. The two transactions are now stuck in a perpetual wait state. To illustrate a deadlock, assume that Joe has a shared lock on the sales table and requests an exclusive lock on the titles table. Simultaneously, Evelyn has a shared lock on the titles table and requests an exclusive lock on the sales table, on the same data pages as Joe.

Our sales clerks are caught in a deadlock. Joe's transaction cannot complete until Evelyn's transaction releases its locks and vice versa.

SQL Server automatically detects deadlocks and intervenes to resolve them. SQL Server resolves a deadlock by rolling back the first transaction that will break the deadlock for all pending transactions. (Older versions of SQL Server used to roll back the transaction with the least accumulated CPU time, allowing the "senior" transaction to complete.) Once any of the transactions in the deadlock are rolled back, the other transactions can acquire the locks they need to complete. Although there is little we can do to alter the way SQL Server handles deadlocks, SQL Server does issue an automatic notification (Error Number 1205) to the deadlock victim when he is rolled back:

```
Msg 1205, Level 13, State 2
Your server command (process id#%d) was deadlocked with another process and
has been chosen as deadlock victim.  Re-run your command.
```

After receiving a 1205 error, the deadlock victim's only recourse is to resend the transaction. There are a few features you can add to your applications to reduce the possibly of locking problems:

- Long-running transactions are the most common cause of deadlocks, and of locking problems in general. Keep transactions and their running time as brief as possible.
- Ensure that user interaction with a Transact-SQL program occurs either before or after execution of a transaction, never during a transaction.
- Use stored procedures to execute transactions, since stored procedures execute faster (and hold locks for a shorter time) than dynamic SQL statements.

- Include code in the transaction that will intercept 1205 messages and retry the transaction. Since the deadlock error interrupts any Transact-SQL processing, you can catch the 1205 error message only through the frontend application (that is, in the Visual Basic or PowerBuilder application).
- You can influence deadlock handling of a transaction with the command:

  ```
  SETDEADLOCKPRIORITY (LOW | NORMAL)
  ```

  When a session has the LOW setting, it will be the preferred deadlock victim. When a session has the NORMAL setting, default deadlock-handling occurs. Chapter 21, *Debugging Transact-SQL Programs,* has more information on the SET command.
- Optimizer hints can influence locking. For example, the HOLDLOCK hint can encourage long-running locks. On the other hand, the NOLOCK hint can improve locking concurrency but allows other problems such as dirty reads.
- Limit the number of records affected by a given transaction. For example, you could alter the frontend application to only retrieve data in blocks of 10 or 20 records at a time. Stored procedures and Transact-SQL batches could be similarly modified using the SET ROWCOUNT command to act only upon small batches of records.

When troubleshooting deadlocks, you can use trace flags 1204 and 1205 to find out more information about specific transactions. Trace flag 1204 provides high-level information about deadlocks, while trace flag 1205 provides more detailed information. Note that these trace flags return data only after a deadlock has occurred. They do not help reduce deadlocks; they only report on them. In order for these trace flags to work properly, they must be set when the server is starting. Refer to Chapter 21 for more detail on the syntax and usage of DBCC trace flags.

Optimistic Versus Pessimistic Concurrency Control

Now, a terminology lesson. The locking control methods we've discussed so far are also defined as *optimistic* and *pessimistic concurrency* controls. Think of pessimistic as the more restrictive forms of concurrency control, while optimistic concurrency controls are less restrictive.*

In general database theory, the most pessimistic database systems incur not only row-level locks but hold granularity all the way down to column-level locks. (That's obviously not SQL Server.) The pessimistic method assumes that many users will be competing for the same data. Thus, locks on the data should not be released until the user is absolutely done with the data. Pessimistic concurrency methods attempt to maximize data integrity at the cost of user concurrency. If you

* Hey, at least we're not talking about network interface cards (NIC) here. A less-restrictive NIC is known as a promiscuous NIC! How'd you like to have a promiscuous database?

issued a HOLDLOCK optimizer hint on every query, you'd be following a pessimistic concurrency method. Pessimistic locking schemes can introduce greater blocking problems but have greater data security and integrity.

Here's an example of a pessimistic fragment of a transaction:

```
BEGIN TRAN
SELECT COUNT(*) FROM authors (UPDLOCK HOLDLOCK)
```

This is an extremely pessimistic query that not only forces the more stringent update lock on the transaction but also holds those locks until a COMMIT or ROLLBACK is used.

Highly optimistic concurrency systems work on the assumption that few, if any, users will be competing for the same data. So, unlike a pessimistic system, a highly optimistic system only issues the lock at the precise moment of the update. Optimistic systems provide rapid user interaction and rarely incur blocks at the cost of data integrity.

Here's an example of a fragment of an optimistic transaction:

```
BEGIN TRAN
UPDATE titles
SET ytd_sales = ytd_sales + 25
FROM titles (PAGLOCK)
```

Normally, this UPDATE statement might lock the entire table. But by forcing different locking behavior with the PAGLOCK hint (explained in the next section), we can force the optimizer to choose a more optimistic locking strategy.

Although much of SQL Server's lock management is automated, you can use session-level settings and optimizer hints (available through the SET command and optimizer hints, respectively) to construct a more optimistic or pessimistic variation.

Tuning Locks

Most locking within SQL Server is handled automatically, but that does not mean you are powerless to affect the ways the server locks database resources. There are actually three avenues to affect locking: at the server level through lock escalation settings (beyond the scope of this book), at a session level through the SET command, and within the individual Transact-SQL statement through optimizer hints. The SET command and optimizer hints are discussed in detail in the next two sections.

Tuning locks through the SET command

The SET command can be grouped with a wide variety of keyphrases that produce all kinds of results. This section discusses only those variations of the SET command that affect locking. (Other permutations of the command are discussed in great detail in Chapter 21.) SET commands provide session-level control. Session-level control affects *everything* the user or system process does, as long as the user or process remains logged in. SET commands should usually be executed at the start of a user or system session. However, they can be used at any point during a session. Just keep in mind that SET parameters affect all transactions issued during the session.

The general syntax for the SET command is:

```
SET parameter_name parameter_value
```

For example, to set a session's transactions as the preferred deadlock victim, you'd use the command:

```
SET deadlockpriority low
```

The SET parameters that affect transaction or locking behavior are shown in Table 11-5.

Table 11-5. SET Commands That Affect Locking

SET Command	Vendor Support	Values	Description
CHAINED	Sybase	ON or OFF	Sets the current session to chained mode, marking a BEGIN TRANSACTION command before executing any implicit transactions of these commands: DELETE, FETCH, INSERT, OPEN, SELECT, and UPDATE.
CURSOR_ CLOSE_ON_ COMMIT	MS	ON or OFF	When set ON, the ANSI default behavior is enforced, telling SQL Server to close a cursor after committing or rolling back its transactions. COMMIT and ROLLBACK still work normally.
DEADLOCK-PRIORITY	MS	LOW or NORMAL	NORMAL does not affect processing. LOW tells SQL Server that any transaction initiated by this session should be the preferred deadlock victim.
IMPLICIT_ TRANSACTIONS	MS	ON or OFF	Causes SQL Server to open an implicit transaction for the following Transact-SQL commands: ALTER TABLE, CREATE, DELETE, DROP, FETCH, GRANT, INSERT, OPEN, REVOKE, SELECT, TRUNCATE, and UPDATE. SET does not affect any currently open transactions.

Table 11-5. SET Commands That Affect Locking (continued)

SET Command	Vendor Support	Values	Description
TRANSACTION_ ISOLATION_ LEVEL	MS, Sybase	READ COMMITTED or READ UNCOMMITTED or REPEATABLE READ or SERIALIZABLE (MS) 0 or 1 or 3 (Sybase)	This command can completely alter the way SQL Server locks records. Use this command with care! READ COMMITTED (on Microsoft) and 1 (on Sybase) is SQL Server's default lock handling, where "dirty reads" are prohibited and shared read locks are permitted. READ UNCOMMITTED (on Microsoft) and 0 (on Sybase) allow uncommitted changes to be read by other users; this is also known as a "dirty read." Under this setting, exclusive locks are ignored and shared locks aren't used. This is a very dangerous setting because other users and processes may act upon data that hasn't been committed to the database We recommend the use of the optimizer hint NOLOCK instead of this setting. REPEATABLE READ and SERIALIZABLE (on Microsoft) and 3 (on Sybase) are synonyms for the same functionality. REPEATABLE READ prohibits both dirty reads and nonrepeatable reads in SQL Server. We recommend the use of the optimizer hint HOLDLOCK instead of this setting.
XACT_ABORT	MS	ON or OFF	When set ON, SQL Server will abort all SQL statements in a transaction if any of the statements encounter an error. When set OFF, SQL Server will abort only the SQL statement that encountered the error, allowing all other statements in the transaction to complete normally.

In general, we do not recommend the use of SET commands to affect locking unless it's absolutely necessary. That means you should perform extensive testing before and after implementing any SET functionality. In many cases, SET has a much wider impact than meets the eye. It is often more effective to control specific locking behaviors with optimizer hints because they only affect the SQL statement where they are written.

Tuning locks through optimizer hints

Optimizer hints do a lot more than just affect locking on a specific transaction. Hints can also determine which indexes are used by a query, as well as the throughput method of a query. Optimizer hints provide direct control over the execution plan of a specific query; however, you should *never* implement hints without first researching the behavior and performance of the query. Most hints can be used only with SELECT statements (including a SELECT as a subquery in another type of statement), and a few can be used with the UPDATE statement. There are some distinct differences between the optimizer hints available on Microsoft and those available under Sybase.

For example, to force an update lock on a table while performing a simple SELECT statement executed on a Microsoft server, specify the following:

```
SELECT title_id,
    title,
    type,
    pub_id,
    price
FROM   titles (UPDLOCK)
WHERE  price > 20
```

As another example, this transaction executed on a Microsoft server forces an UPDATE statement to use only page locks, instead of allowing the transaction to escalate to a full table lock:

```
UPDATE  titles
SET     price = 15.99
FROM    titles (PAGLOCK)
WHERE   price IS NULL
```

Optimizer hints are not ANSI-compliant syntax and do not directly translate into languages used by other relational database systems.

In most cases, the optimization plan chosen by SQL Server's optimization engine is A-OK. Do not override SQL Server lightly! If application performance or locking is not up to par, the recommended procedure is:

1. Reevaluate database and table design.
2. Reevaluate indexing strategies.
3. Reevaluate query and transaction strategies.
4. Evaluate and test optimizer hints.

Table 11-6 details all the allowable optimizer hints.

Table 11-6. Optimizer Hints

Hint	Vendor	Usage	Description
FAST-FIRSTROW	MS	SELECT	Searches nonclustered indexes (and read-ahead features) for quickest data retrieval. The first rows may appear much faster than without the hint, but the query itself may take longer to complete.
INDEX	MS, Sybase	DELETE, SELECT, UPDATE	Overrides SQL Server's preferred index search in favor of the one specified by the hint. Syntax is INDEX = [index_name | index_ID]. You can use the shorthand INDEX = 0 to perform a table scan or INDEX = 1 to use the clustered index. Sybase syntax does not require the equals sign (=).
HOLDLOCK	MS, Sybase	SELECT	Holds a shared lock until the entire transaction is complete instead of releasing the lock as soon as the data is no longer needed. Can't be used with a SELECT statement that includes FOR BROWSE.
LRU or MRU	Sybase	DELETE, SELECT, UPDATE	The optimizer hints LRU and MRU (least recently used and most recently used, respectively) are mutually exclusive. They tell SQL Server the preferred buffer replacement strategy to use for the table. LRU forces the query optimizer to read the table into the cache on the MRU/LRU chain, while MRU purges the buffer from cache and renews it with the next buffer for the table.
NOLOCK	MS	SELECT	Disregards exclusive locks and refrains from issuing shared locks for the duration of the transaction. This hint allows transactions to read uncommitted and rolled back transactions, also known as "dirty reads," as if they were real data. This hint renders the application vulnerable to errors 605, 606, 624, and 625. They should be treated as 1205 errors. Refer to the "Deadlocked transactions" section, earlier in the chapter, for more information on the 1205 error.
NOHOLD-LOCK	Sybase	SELECT	Sybase's version of the NOLOCK hint.
PAGLOCK	MS	SELECT, UPDATE	Forces SQL Server to use shared page locks where a table lock might be used.

Table 11-6. Optimizer Hints (continued)

Hint	Vendor	Usage	Description
PARALLEL	Sybase	SELECT	Tells SQL Server to use a parallel partition or index scan (if the server is properly configured for parallel scans). You can use the syntax PARALLEL [level_of_parallelism], where level_of_parallelism is an integer value that specifies the number of worker processes that will scan the table or index in parallel. A value of 1 tells SQL Server to execute the query serially. You do not have to specify a level_of_parallelism.
PREFETCH	Sybase	DELETE, SELECT, UPDATE	The optimizer hint PREFETCH size tells SQL Server the I/O size, in kilobytes, of a table to bind in the cache. Valid values include 2, 4, 8, and 16. The procedure *sp_helpcache* shows the valid sizes for the cache an object is bound to or for the default cache.

SHARED	Sybase	SELECT	Tells SQL Server to use a shared lock instead of an update lock on the specified table or view. Other sessions seeking an update lock on the specified table or view will be permitted. Interestingly, you can use the SHARED optimizer hint only with the SELECT clause included as part of a cursor. For example:
			`DECLARE sample_shared CURSOR FOR`
			`SELECT  au_id, au_lname, au_fname`
			`FROM    authors SHARED`
			`WHERE   au_lname LIKE "GRE%"`

TABLOCK	MS	SELECT, UPDATE	For SELECT statements, forces a shared table lock during the transaction. For UPDATE statements, the hint forces an exclusive table lock for the duration of the transaction.
TABLOCKX	MS	SELECT, UPDATE	Forces an exclusive table lock for the duration of both SELECT and UPDATE transactions.
UPDLOCK	MS	SELECT	Causes a SELECT transaction to use update locks instead of shared locks during a transaction. This hint can be useful for situations in which you want to allow read transactions but not write transactions.

You have to be careful using multiple hints at one time, although you can get away with it. When combining multiple hints, remember these points:

- More restrictive hints preempt less restrictive ones. Thus, a TABLOCK would override a PAGLOCK hint if issued in a single transaction.
- Some hints—such as NOLOCK and HOLDLOCK—aren't allowed to be combined.

Hints override the functionality of any SET commands in effect.

Transactions and the Database

Of course, the net effect of a transaction within the database is to retrieve, add, delete, or modify data. But transactions do more than just affect a single table. Transactions actually affect the allocated space of tables, indexes, and views, the behavior and procession time of triggers, referential integrity, and the amount of free space in the database and the database transaction log. For example, as transactions are committed to the database, free space within the database is consumed. In fact, a database can even become so full that no new transactions are allowed to complete in that database. In this section, we'll analyze briefly how database objects are affected by transactions. We'll also discuss the DUMP and LOAD commands. Since these topics border on database administration issues, we'll go into only the higher-level details. However, it's important for you as an application developer to understand the strains and stresses a transaction-processing application places upon database objects.

What Is the Transaction Log?

We're not talking about some sort of pecan log here. The transaction log is a special system table, syslogs, that is used to record every logged transaction that occurs within a given database. (Some transactions, like SELECT . . . INTO and TRUNCATE, can be non-logged, as discussed in Chapter 3, *SQL Primer.*) The *transaction log,* or simply *log* for short, is used to ensure certain properties of a transaction (see "The ACID Test" sidebar early in this chapter). As logged operations occur within the database, they are written, audit trail style, into syslogs. By reviewing the data stored in the transaction log, the ability to roll back a transaction is guaranteed.

The log should usually be created on a separate *database device* from the database, especially for online transaction-processing applications. A database device is a preallocated file structure used to hold data and transaction logs. (You should read the SQL Server documentation if you'll be creating any user databases.) When a database is placed on a device, the amount of available space is predefined. In this sense, databases are kind of like a Tupperware bowl—you can cram only so much into them before you need either a larger bowl or a second bowl. Translating that analogy into SQL Server terms, you can do three things to add free space to a database:

1. Remove data
2. Expand the database device and the database
3. Add an additional database device to the database

As transactions are processed in a database, the syslogs table begins to fill up. In some cases, where data is added or updated, the database will expand. Other transactions, like DELETE statements, will erase data from the database. Unfortunately, it's difficult to predict how much space a transaction will consume. If a transaction adds an 80-byte record to a table, it might actually require 1.7K of space in the transaction log.

Every loggable transaction writes at least one record in syslogs in machine-readable format. (Don't try to read it yourself.) In fact, some transaction statements, like UPDATE, could write several records to the transaction log for a single transaction to take effect in the database. Similarly, a simple INSERT command not only writes the INSERT statement to the log, but also includes information about changes made to the tables' indexes. Interestingly, a single transaction issued at different times might consume different amounts of space in the log because it has used a different query plan. And don't forget that one transaction can actually affect many, many rows in a table or even multiple tables. That means that some transactions, especially very large transactions, can take up lots of space in the log. With some transactions, you'll even get this message:

```
Error : 1105, Severity: 17, State: 3

Can't allocate space for object 'Syslogs' in database 'pubs' because the
'logsegment' segment is full. If you ran out of space in Syslogs, dump the
transaction log. Otherwise, use ALTER DATABASE or sp_extendsegment to
increase the size of the segment.
```

Uh-oh! This error is a showstopper! You get an 1105 error when your transaction needs more space in the log than is available. If you initiate a transaction that causes an 1105 error, all transaction-processing work stops for all transactions that modify data in the database, not just your own. Certain transactions that do not modify data, like SELECT, can continue unabated. SQL Server halts all transactions until the transaction log is cleared (also known as "dumping" the log) or until it is augmented by adding more space to the log. In some cases, you're better off actually expanding the transaction log. Even so, the appearance of an 1105 error means that you'll have to restart your transaction once the cause of the error has been remedied.

Because this is such a horrible error to encounter on a production system, DBAs spend a lot of time carefully balancing the size of the transaction log against the size of its database. For instance, it's a common rule of thumb to create a transaction log that is no less than one-quarter to one-half the size of the database in a transaction-processing application. Decision support systems (DSSs) and data warehouse applications often have transaction logs that are much smaller. DBAs also implement database options "like truncate log on checkpoint" (usually on development systems) and special log-dumping tasks to control the accumulation of data in the transaction log. Please refer to the vendor's documentation for all the details on transaction log setup and administration.

Conversely, you also should spend a little time gauging the size and duration of your transactions against the size of the log. If you have applications that need to make an update on every record in a 20-megabyte table, but the transaction log is only 20 megabytes itself, you should probably break the transaction up into smaller pieces. Then, when each step of the transaction is successfully completed, you can dump the log (thus clearing it out) and continue on to the next step.

In addition to the size of a transaction, you also should evaluate the duration of a transaction. Even an itsy-bitsy transaction can fill up the log if it is left uncommitted for a long period of time. The duration of a transaction is significant because the transaction log cannot be truncated beyond the oldest open transaction. To illustrate, assume that the pubs database has a 30-megabyte transaction log and, after 45 minutes of processing, has accumulated 27 megabytes worth of data. Yikes! The log should be dumped immediately so that no one will encounter an 1105 error.

Unfortunately, a transaction was opened about 10 minutes earlier after the log had accumulated about 20 megabytes of data. Even if a DUMP TRAN command is issued now, *the log will be cleared only to the point of the oldest open transaction* (the one opened 10 minutes ago), leaving 20 megabytes of data in the log. Once that long-running transaction is closed, the log can be completely cleared. This is just one of many reasons why you should write short, succinct transactions. Figure 11-1 shows a graphic representation of the transaction log.

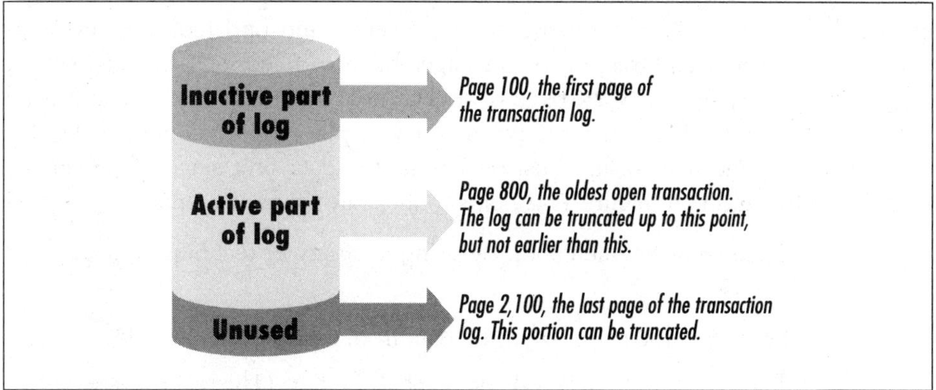

Figure 11-1. Open transactions and the transaction log

On Microsoft servers, you can use the command DBCC OPENTRAN (database_name) to retrieve information about the oldest open transaction. The DBCC command is discussed in detail in Chapter 21.

You can programmatically tell how much free space exists in the log (and the database for that matter) using the system stored procedure *sp_spaceused*. Unfortunately, *sp_spaceused* is not always accurate. System stored procedures, including *sp_spaceused*, are discussed in Chapter 17, *System and Extended Stored Procedures*.

Impact on Table and Indexes

In addition to consuming the free space of databases and their logs, transactions also have a profound impact on tables and indexes. Transactions affect tables with clustered indexes by causing *table fragmentation*. Transactions affect indexes by causing changes in *index statistics*. Table fragmentation and index statistics are within the domain of database administration, but we'll spend just a few moments on the topic since you might be administering your own database.

Tables without clustered indexes are said to have a *heap* structure. Heaped tables experience a less severe form of table fragmentation than tables built with a clustered index. Because new records are always inserted on the last data page of a heaped table, such a table doesn't experience noncontiguous data pages. However, heaped tables are fragmented by UPDATE and DELETE statements that erase data from data pages deep within the table.

Table fragmentation can occur on tables with clustered indexes that are the target of many transactions. As records are added, deleted, and updated, they are written and erased from data pages. As the pages become filled, SQL Server issues a page split that creates a new 2K page of data to hold new data. Unfortunately, the new data page created after the page split could be placed in a geographically distant location on the hard disk. Thus, over time, the data of a single table can be scattered hither and yon. Figure 11-2 helps to illustrate these concepts.

You can eliminate table fragmentation by using a variety of techniques; to name a few:

- Drop and re-create the table. Load the data from a backup table or via BCP.
- Drop and re-create the clustered index of the table. (This also re-creates all nonclustered indexes on the table.)
- Use the command DBCC DBREINDEX to rebuild the clustered and nonclustered indexes.
- LOAD the table from a dump.

Data Page 1
Data Page 2
Data Page 3
Data Page 4
Data Page 5

A full data page on a table

Row 5	01/01/99	345	'John Record'
Row 10	02/02/99	456	'George Record'
Row 15	03/03/99	567	'Paul Record'
Row 20	04/04/99	678	'Ringo Record'
Row 25	05/05/99	789	'Elton Record'
Row 30	06/06/99	890	'Robert Record'

Row 12	01/01/99	345	'Floyd Record'

Inserting a new record on a full page forces SQL Server to split the page, one of the most costly operations for the database.

SQL Server splits the data and/or index pages onto new allocations.

Row 5	01/01/99	345	'John Record'
Row 10	02/02/99	456	'George Record'
Row 12	01/01/99	345	'Floyd Record'

Row 15	03/03/99	567	'Paul Record'
Row 20	04/04/99	678	'Ringo Record'
Row 25	05/05/99	789	'Elton Record'
Row 30	06/06/99	890	'Robert Record'

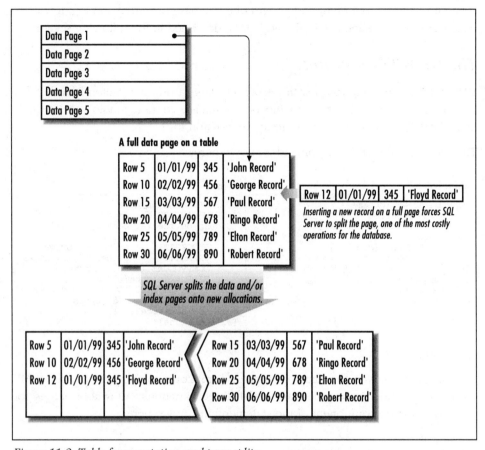

Figure 11-2. Table fragmentation and page splits

Index statistics are used by the query optimizer to determine which index(es) are used to execute a transaction. Statistics maintain information about the distribution of key values of an index. If the contents of a table are constantly being added to, erased, or changed (or the table has been cleared with a TRUNCATE TABLE command and then reloaded), the index statistics are no longer in sync with the real distribution of data in the table. The index statistics must be updated using the UPDATE STATISTICS command. You can find out the last time index statistics were updated for a given index using the STATS_DATE system function (on Microsoft only) or the DBCC SHOW_STATISTICS option.

A stored procedure called *update_stats* is included on the accompanying CD-ROM. This stored procedure can be run under an off-hours task to update all index statistics for all user databases.

When it comes to controlling the growth of a database or transaction log, few commands are as important as DUMP and LOAD, described in the following sections.

The DUMP Command

DUMP, having nothing to do with the world's largest dump at Staten Island, is the command that creates a backup file of a database, transaction log, or a single table. DUMP is also used to truncate the transaction log.

The syntax for the DUMP command is shown here:

Microsoft	Sybase
DUMP DATABASE {dbname | @dbname_parameter } | TABLE [[database.]owner.] table_name | TRAN[SACTION] {dbname | dbname_parameter } TO dump_device [, dump_device2 [..., dump_device3]] [WITH options]	DUMP DATABASE db_name | TRAN[SACTION]db_name TO dump_device [AT backup_server] [DENSITY = value, BLOCKSIZE = number_of_bytes, CAPACITY = number_of_kilobytes DUMPVOLUME = volume_name, FILE = file_name] [STRIPE ON device2 [AT backup_server] [BLOCKSIZE = number_bytes ...] ,device3...] [WITH options]

Microsoft DUMP

On a Microsoft server, the `dump_device` and `options` components of the DUMP command are held in common among all three variations. Allowable entries for the `dump_device` component of the statement are shown here:

```
dump_device =
{dump_device_name | @dump_device_name_parameter}
| {DISK | TAPE | FLOPPY | PIPE} =
{'temp_dump_device' | @temp_dump_device_parameter}
[VOLUME = {volid | @volid_var}]
```

You can simply list a dump device name (or a parameter with the value of a dump device name). A striped dump is created if you name more than one dump device. Alternatively, you can specify the type of dump device (DISK, TAPE, or FLOPPY) and the full pathname and filename (or parameter) for a temporary dump device. You can even specify a Windows NT Universal Naming Convention (UNC) path and filename or mapped drive letter using the DISK dump device type. Temporary dump devices are created when the DUMP command is executed, and do not have an entry in sysdevices at the time the command is executed. The PIPE dump device type allows you to dump to a specific named pipe. The PIPE option is included mostly for use by third-party vendors to build into their own applications. It's rarely used in normal Transact-SQL programs. The VOLUME specifier is a seldom-used option that allows you to assign a six-byte character string to the volume. The default volume for the first backup to a device is SQ0001.

Available options on a Microsoft server are as follows:

```
[[, ] {UNLOAD | NOUNLOAD}]
[[, ] {INIT | NOINIT}]
[[, ] {SKIP | NOSKIP}]
[[, ] {EXPIREDATE = {date | @date_parameter }
    |RETAINDAYS = {days | @days_parameter }}]
[[, ] STATS [= percentage]]
```

The UNLOAD/NOUNLOAD options are used only for dumps that go directly to tape. UNLOAD specifies that the tape will be rewound and unloaded when the dump is finished, while NOUNLOAD indicates that the tape will not be unloaded automatically after the dump. UNLOAD is the default. This option remains in effect for the duration of a user session.

The INIT/NOINIT options determine whether a dump device is overwritten (INIT) or appended to (NOINIT). NOINIT is the default. This option applies only to DISK and TAPE dumps. Options SKIP/NOSKIP are used only with TAPE dumps and indicate whether SQL Server should read the ANSI TAPE device header. NOSKIP is the default.

If you use the EXPIREDATE or RETAINDAYS parameter, you're telling SQL Server that the dump device cannot be overwritten until the specified date or number of days have passed, respectively. (Dumps can be appended to the dump device, though.) This option is available only with DISK and TAPE dumps and only in combination with INIT. (This value overrides the server's media retention configuration parameter.)

STATS is a nifty little option that, when you provide an integer value, returns the increments of the dump completed. Ten percent is the default, but five and twenty-five are commonly used. For example:

```
DUMP DATABASE pubs
TO   pubs_back
WITH noinit, stats = 12
```

Results:

```
Msg 3211, Level 10, State 4
12 percent dumped
Msg 3211, Level 10, State 4
24 percent dumped
Msg 3211, Level 10, State 4
36 percent dumped
Msg 3211, Level 10, State 2
48 percent dumped
Msg 3211, Level 10, State 2
60 percent dumped
Msg 3211, Level 10, State 2
72 percent dumped
Msg 3211, Level 10, State 2
84 percent dumped
Msg 3211, Level 10, State 2
```

```
96 percent dumped
Msg 3211, Level 10, State 1
100 percent dumped
Msg 4035, Level 10, State 1
Database 'pubs' (26467 pages) dumped to file <2> on device 'pubs_back'.
```

The DUMP DATABASE command allows you to make a backup copy of an entire database and transaction log. The database can then be reloaded using the LOAD command. The process is dynamic and can be run while users and processes are active on the system. There is no impact on the users, other than a possible slowdown in system responsiveness. SQL Server takes a snapshot of the database at a point in time. Only fully completed transactions are included in the dump. The user who executes the DUMP command must have the permissions needed to access the physical dump file. (Dump devices can be created using the system stored procedure *sp_addumpdevice*.)

The DUMP TRANSACTION command clears the inactive portion of the transaction log and makes a backup copy of a database's transaction log. It can be used only on databases that have separate database and log devices. This command has three special options usable only with DUMP TRAN: TRUNCATE_ONLY, NO_LOG, and NO_TRUNCATE:

TRUNCATE_ONLY
: Allows you to clear the transaction log without making a backup. You don't have to name a dump device when using this option.

NO_LOG
: Used when you've received the dreaded 1105 error and have no free space in the log. The NO_LOG option one-ups the TRUNCATE_ONLY option by stripping out the transaction log without making an entry in the log for the dump process. It's a good idea to issue a DUMP DATABASE command after dumping the log with either of these options.

NO_TRUNCATE
: A seldom-used option (you pray!) issued to recover a damaged database. NO_TRUNCATE allows a transaction log to be dumped even when the database is inaccessible by placing a special pointer in the master database. Then, if the master database and the log of the user database are undamaged, up-to-the-minute media recovery may be possible.

For example, to dump the transaction log of pubs on an hourly schedule (the dump device pubs_log_back has already been created using *sp_addumpdevice*), issue the following:

```
DUMP TRAN pubs TO pubs_log_back WITH NOINIT, STATS=5
```

In a pinch, when the pubs transaction log has filled to capacity, you'd issue the command:

```
DUMP TRAN pubs WITH NO_LOG
```

DUMP TRANSACTION can't be used on databases using the "truncate log on checkpoint" option. Also, any unlogged operation, such as BCP or SELECT . . . INTO, foils the operation. You'll have to issue a DUMP DATABASE command instead, as shown by the 4207 error message caused by issuing a DUMP TRAN command after an unlogged operation has occurred:

```
Error : 4207, Severity: 16, State: 2

DUMP TRANsaction is not allowed while the select into/bulk copy option is
enabled or if a non-logged operation has occurred: use DUMP DATABASE, or
disable the option with sp_dboption.
```

You can issue a DUMP TRANSACTION with TRUNCATE_ONLY if you receive a 4207 error.

The DUMP TABLE command allows you to make a backup copy of an individual table. This command is useful for situations in which backing up the whole database at one time is impractical. It does have its drawbacks; the most prominent is the fact that DUMP TABLE locks the database while dumping it. (It can also introduce data-integrity problems if the table being backed up has foreign keys to other tables.) To create a dump device for the employee table and dump it, issue the following commands:

```
SP_ADDUMPDEVICE 'disk','sales_back','c:\mssql\tranlogs\sales_back.dat'
GO

DUMP TABLE sales TO sales_back WITH STATS
GO
```

Sybase DUMP

Sybase, possibly due to its multiple hardware and operating systems perspective, has a variety of additional options, although the Sybase and Microsoft versions still hold many elements in common. For starters, Sybase allows you to:

```
DUMP TO dump_device AT backup_server.
```

(Refer to the syntax reference shown earlier.) This option allows you to dump a database across the network to up to 32 backup servers. For example:

```
DUMP DATABASE PUBS
TO pubs_back AT ZINFANDEL
```

When you specify the dump device, you also can utilize several options that aren't available or have different implementations under Microsoft. The device options are DENSITY, BLOCKSIZE, CAPACITY, DUMPVOLUME, and FILE:

DENSITY
: For use only on Unix machines and, thus, beyond the scope of this book.

BLOCKSIZE
: Entered in 2,048-byte increments, BLOCKSIZE overrides the default write density on tape devices.

CAPACITY
: In kilobytes, CAPACITY is the maximum amount of data allowed on a single tape value of the dump device. The minimum value is five data pages but should not be more than 70% of the size of the tape device.

DUMPVOLUME
: The same thing as Microsoft's VOLUME.

FILE
: Allows you to specify the name of the dump file, up to 17 characters in length. SQL Server will create a filename for you if you don't specify one.

The STRIPE ON command allows you to specify additional dump devices for quicker database dumps or to reduce the total number of volume changes to complete a dump. This option is really useful for huge databases. You can specify up to 31 more dump devices (for a total of 32 including the device specified in the TO clause). Once specified, the dump task will be split into equal portions with each portion dumped to a different device. Since the dumps are then run concurrently to the striped devices, the dump runs much faster.

There are additional WITH options that can be specified at the end of the DUMP command. They are:

```
DENSITY    = value,
BLOCKSIZE  = number_of_bytes,
CAPACITY   = number_of_kilobytes,
DUMPVOLUME = volume_name,
FILE = file_name
[[, ] {UNLOAD | NOUNLOAD}]
[[, ] {INIT | NOINIT}]
[[, ] {DISMOUNT | NODISMOUNT}]
[[, ] RETAINDAYS = days]
[[, ] NOTIFY = {CLIENT | OPERATOR_CONSOLE}]
```

The first five options were described with the device options earlier. The UNLOAD/NOUNLOAD options and the INIT/NOINIT options are the same as for Microsoft. The RETAINDAYS parameter is also the same as for Microsoft SQL Server, except that there is no EXPIREDATE alternative.

The DISMOUNT/NODISMOUNT options determine whether tapes in the dump device remain mounted. The default behavior is to dismount a tape device when the dump is completed. Specify the NODISMOUNT option to keep a tape mounted and online for later dumps or loads. You can override the default message destination (issued upon completion of the dump) by using the NOTIFY option. You can use the CLIENT parameter to route the message back to the client that initiated the DUMP, or you can use the OPERATOR_CONSOLE parameter to route the message back to the backup server console.

Also, unlike Microsoft, Sybase does not allow you to dump a table.

The LOAD Command

The LOAD command is, in many ways, analogous to the DUMP command. It shares many of the same options. The LOAD command can be used to load a database and its transaction log, only the log, or an individual table. It can also be used to retrieve an informative report about the contents of a dump device. The database should not be in use while a LOAD is being performed, especially since the data loaded overwrites any existing data in the target database, log, or table. This can be a real problem if you attempt to load while users are logged on (and a sure way to get attention for those of you readers who are "problem children"). It can also introduce data-integrity errors when loading a table that has foreign key relationships with other tables.

When you load a database, the database being loaded (the target) must be the same size as or larger than the database from where the dump was taken (the source). In addition, the target database must have the same size and order of data and log segments as the source. For example, assume that our pubs database started life as a 100-megabyte data segment and a 50-megabyte log segment. As the database grew, we added another 100 megabytes of data and 25 megabytes of log. Now we want to load a dump of the pubs database onto our development server. We cannot simply create a pubs database on the development server with a 200-megabyte data segment and 100-megabyte log segment; we must rebuild its data and log segments in the same way that they exist on the production server.

You can find out the sizes and segments of a database using the system stored procedure *sp_helpdb*. You can build a Transact-SQL script that will actually re-create a database in its exact segment size and order using the system stored procedure *sp_help_revdatabase*.

Loads should generally be performed only when the target and source data have originated on servers with the same version of SQL Server, hardware platform, default sort order, and default language. Otherwise, you should use BCP to move data. Microsoft SQL Server locks the target database for the duration of the load but otherwise requires no special handling. Sybase, on the other hand, requires that the target database be taken offline to perform a load. Once the database and transaction log loads are completed, the target database must be brought back online using the command:

```
ONLINE DATABASE db_name
```

The ONLINE DATABASE command also upgrades an older database and log to the most recent version of Sybase Adaptive Server.

The syntax for the LOAD command looks like this:

Microsoft	Sybase

`LOAD`
`    DATABASE {dbname |`
`        @dbname_variable}`
`| TABLE [[database.]owner.]`
`        table_name`
`| TRAN[SACTION] {dbname |`
`    @dbname_variable} | HEADERONLY`
`FROM dump_device [,dump_device2`
`    [.dump_device3]]`
`[WITH [UNLOAD | NOUNLOAD]`
`[[, ] SKIP | NOSKIP]`
`[[, ] STATS = number]`
`[[, ] FILE = file_number]`
`[[, ] STOPAT = {date_time |`
`    @date_time_var}]`
`[[, ] SOURCE = source_name]`
`[[, ] APPEND]]`
	`LOAD`
	`    DATABASE db_name`
	`| TRAN[SACTION]db_name`
	`FROM dump_device [AT backup_server]`
	`    [DENSITY   = value,`
	`     BLOCKSIZE  = number_of_bytes,`
	`     DUMPVOLUME = volume_name,`
	`     FILE = file_name]`
	`[STRIPE ON device2 [AT backup_server]`
	`    [BLOCKSIZE = number_bytes ...],`
	`     device3...]`
	`[WITH [DENSITY = density_value]`
	`[[, ] BLOCKSIZE = number_bytes]`
	`[[, ] DUMPVOLUME = volume_name]`
	`[[, ] FILE = file_name]`
	`[[, ] [DISMOUNT | NODISMOUNT]`
	`[[, ] [NOUNLOAD | UNLOAD]`
	`[[, ] LISTONLY [= full]]`
	`[[, ] HEADERONLY`
	`[[, ] NOTIFY = {CLIENT |`
	`        OPERATOR_CONSOLE}]]`

Many of the options in LOAD are identical to those in the DUMP command. For example, the entire dump_device clause has identical syntax and options to the Microsoft DUMP command. Additionally, the options UNLOAD/NOUNLOAD, SKIP/NOSKIP, and STATS are unchanged in LOAD.

Microsoft LOAD

Options unique to the Microsoft LOAD command include the following:

```
WITH
[[, ] FILE = file_number]
[[, ] STOPAT = {date_time | @date_time_var}]
[[, ] SOURCE = source_name]
[[, ] APPEND]
```

When multiple databases, logs, or tables are dumped to a single dump device, each is given a unique file number within the dump device. When you are loading from such a dump device, you can specify a FILE number to choose—anything other than the first item on the dump device. The default is the first file on the device. Use the Microsoft command LOAD HEADERONLY and examine the column sequence in the result set to find out the file number of each dump item. This is what the command returned on my test server's master database dump file:

```
LOAD HEADERONLY FROM masterdb_back
```

Results (edited for brevity):

```
Dumptype Database Striped Compressed Seq Volume... CreatDate  CreatTime...
-------- -------- ------- ---------- --- ------... ---------- ---------
1        master   0       0          1   SQL001... Jan  1, 98 06:25    ...
1        master   0       0          2   SQL001... Jan  9, 98 20:05    ...
1        master   0       0          3   SQL001... Jan 11, 98 23:20    ...

(3 row(s) affected)
```

The STOPAT option is very useful for recovering to a specific point in time. When *log* dumps have been performed in chronological order on a single dump device (using NOINIT to prevent overwriting), you can use the STOPAT option to tell SQL Server at what dump time to stop loading. Here's an example scenario. Assume that we perform a full database dump with INIT on the pubs database at 6:00 A.M. every day. Every hour after that, we dump the transaction log with NOINIT, thus appending to the end of the dump device. At 3:17 P.M., our server experiences a disk failure, necessitating a recovery from the dumps. We can recover right up to 3:00 P.M. (the time of our last dump) with a single command:

```
LOAD DATABASE pubs
FROM pubs_back
WITH stats, stopat = 'Jan 11, 1998 15:00'
-- use military time for clarity
GO
```

The APPEND and SOURCE options are used only with the LOAD TABLE command. The APPEND command tells SQL Server to add in any data that might already exist in the table, rather than overwrite it. The SOURCE command is used to identify the name of the source table when the source and target table have different names.

Sybase LOAD

As with Microsoft's version of the command, LOAD and DUMP are very similar for Sybase. The only command options unique to LOAD are LISTONLY and HEADERONLY. The HEADERONLY option is similar to Microsoft's LOAD HEADERONLY, described earlier. The option LISTONLY allows you to display information about all the dump devices stored on a single tape volume without actually loading any database or transaction log. The report produced by LISTONLY shows the database, device, date, and time of the dump, and the date and time the dump file can be overwritten. The option LISTONLY = FULL provides added information about the dump. In either case, the output reports are sorted by the ANSI tape label. LISTONLY overrides the HEADERONLY option.

Summary

This chapter has (we hope) shed some light on writing transactions in Transact-SQL and the locking implications of those transactions. Important topics to remember include:

- Writing implicit and explicit transactions
- Embedding error checking into a transaction
- Using named transactions to provide documentation features
- Adding savepoints to a transaction to enable partial rollbacks
- The dangers and concerns of nested transactions
- Observing locks and user sessions
- The types and scope of locks available in SQL Server
- Specific tips and techniques to troubleshoot blocked and deadlocked transactions
- The difference between optimistic and pessimistic concurrency controls
- Tuning locks with the SET command and optimizer hints
- The effect of transactions on the transaction log, tables, and indexes
- The use and syntax of the DUMP and LOAD statements

III

Functions and Extensions

Part III of this book discusses Transact-SQL functions and extensions to the language. Functions allow you to manipulate and transform data, obtain system information, perform data comparisons, and perform many other operations. This part of the book also discusses the query and reporting capabilities offered by various language extensions—the commands CASE, COMPUTE, CUBE, and ROLLUP.

Part III contains these chapters:

In this chapter:

12

Functions

Transact-SQL functions allow you to manipulate and transform data, obtain system information, perform data comparisons, and perform other operations. Transact-SQL provides standard ANSI SQL functions and also supports a number of powerful enhancements.

Functions may appear in a select list or in WHERE, GROUP BY, ORDER BY, HAVING, and COMPUTE clauses. Be careful when you use functions in a WHERE clause, because they may suppress the use of indexes. We'll discuss this in Chapter 20, *Transact-SQL Optimization and Tuning*. Functions may be nested up to 10 levels deep. This means that you can apply a function to another function that may contain a third function and so on, up to 10 levels. This limitation does not apply to Transact-SQL operations such as the concatenation of strings or arithmetic and Boolean operations.

Neither Sybase nor Microsoft currently supports user-defined functions. These functions would be a welcome enhancement of the language, and we hope that SQL Server vendors will listen to users and implement these functions in future versions.

In this chapter, we've grouped functions by use. Since some of them may be used for different purposes, they may appear in more than one section. Vendors' documentation and other sources of Transact-SQL usually classify *niladic* functions separately from other types. Niladic functions do not require any arguments and do not even need parentheses after the function name; examples include CURRENT_TIMESTAMP and USER. We have arranged these functions by use with other functions of a similar purpose.

Some functions perform automatic conversion of parameter datatypes, while others have restrictions on datatype use. In this chapter, we sometimes refer to all datatypes that store numeric data as NUMERIC, which includes TINYINT, SMALLINT, INT, REAL, FLOAT, DOUBLE, NUMERIC, DECIMAL, MONEY, and SMALLMONEY. We also refer to CHAR and VARCHAR data as STRING type, and to DATETIME and SMALLDATETIME as DATE type.

Table 12-1 contains a complete list of functions, showing the Microsoft and Sybase versions, and explaining briefly the differences between the two dialects.

Table 12-1. Implementation of Transact-SQL Functions by Microsoft and Sybase

Function	Microsoft/Sybase	Type
ABS	Both	Mathematical
ACOS	Both	Mathematical
ASCII	Both	String
ASIN	Both	Mathematical
ATAN	Both	Mathematical
ATN2	Both	Mathematical
AVG	Both	Aggregate
CEILING	Both	Mathematical
CHAR	Both	String
CHAR_LENGTH	Sybase only	String and text/image
CHARINDEX	Both	String
COALESCE	Microsoft 6.x, Sybase 11.5	System—NULL comparison
COL_LENGTH	Both	System—table column information
COL_NAME	Both	System—table column information
CONVERT	Both; but conversion rules are slightly different	Conversion
COS	Both	Mathematical
COT	Both	Mathematical
COUNT	Both	Aggregate
CURRENT_TIMESTAMP	Microsoft only	Date
CURRENT_USER	Microsoft only	System—session information
DATA_PGS	Sybase only	System—table size information
DATALENGTH	Both	System function; discussed in the "String Functions" section
DATEADD	Both	Date
DATEDIFF	Both	Date

Table 12-1. Implementation of Transact-SQL Functions by Microsoft and Sybase (continued)

Function	Microsoft/Sybase	Type
DATENAME	Both	Date
DATEPART	Both	Date
DB_ID	Both	System—database information
DB_NAME	Both	System—database information
DEGREES	Both	Mathematical
DIFFERENCE	Both	String
EXP	Both	Mathematical
FLOOR	Both	Mathematical
GETANSINULL	Microsoft only	System—database information
GETDATE	Both	Date
HEXTOINT	Sybase only	Conversion
HOST_ID	Both	System—session information
HOST_NAME	Both	System—session information
IDENT_INCR	Microsoft only	System—table column information
IDENT_SEED	Microsoft only	System—table column information
INDEX_COL	Both	System—table column information
INTTOHEX	Sybase only	Conversion
ISDATE	Microsoft only	System—type checking
ISNULL	Both	System—NULL comparison
ISNUMERIC	Microsoft only	System—type checking
LCT_ADMIN	Sybase only	System
LOG	Both	Mathematical
LOG10	Both	Mathematical
LOWER	Both	String
LTRIM	Both	String
MAX	Both	Aggregate
MIN	Both	Aggregate
NULLIF	Microsoft 6.x, Sybase 11.5	System—NULL comparison
OBJECT_ID	Both	System—object information
OBJECT_NAME	Both; Sybase function is more powerful	System—object information
PATINDEX	Both	String and text/image
PI	Both	Mathematical
POWER	Both	Mathematical
PROC_ROLE	Sybase only	System—session information

Table 12-1. Implementation of Transact-SQL Functions by Microsoft and Sybase (continued)

Function	Microsoft/Sybase	Type
RADIANS	Both	Mathematical
RAND	Both	Mathematical
REPLICATE	Both	String
RESERVED_PGS	Sybase only	System—table size information
REVERSE	Both	String
RIGHT	Both	String
ROUND	Both	Mathematical
ROWCNT	Sybase only	System—table size information
RTRIM	Both	String
SESSION_USER	Microsoft only	System—session information
SHOW_ROLE	Sybase only	System—session information
SIGN	Both	Mathematical
SIN	Both	Mathematical
SOUNDEX	Both	String
SPACE	Both	String
SQRT	Both	Mathematical
STATS_DATE	Microsoft only	System—object information
STR	Both	Conversion
STUFF	Both	String
SUBSTRING	Both	String
SUM	Both	Aggregate
SUSER_ID	Both	System—session information
SUSER_NAME	Both	System—session information
SYSTEM_USER	Microsoft only	System—session information
TAN	Both	Mathematical
TEXTPTR	Both	Text/image
TEXTVALID	Both	Text/image
TSEQUAL	Both	System
UPPER	Both	String
USED_PGS	Sybase only	System—table size information
USER	Both	System—session information
USER_ID	Both	System—session information
USER_NAME	Both	System—session information
VALID_NAME	Both	System

Aggregate Functions

Transact-SQL aggregate functions include the following:

AVG
: Computes average of a column

COUNT
: Counts rows

MAX
: Finds maximum value in a column

MIN
: Finds minimum value in a column

SUM
: Computes sum of column values

Aggregate functions compute a single value result, such as the sum or average value of a given column in a table. The number of values processed by an aggregate varies depending on the number of rows queried from the table. This behavior makes aggregate functions different from all other functions; others require a fixed number and type of parameters.

Here is the general syntax of an aggregate function:

```
aggregate_function :=
aggregate_function_name ( [ALL | DISTINCT] expression  | COUNT(*)
```

where:

```
aggregate_function_name := AVG | COUNT | MAX | MIN | SUM
```

The ALL operation is assumed by default. It is common practice to omit this keyword. When the DISTINCT operation is used, all rows with the same value are treated as if they were one row. The use of ALL and DISTINCT together is syntactically allowed, but makes no sense in MIN and MAX functions.

AVG and SUM

The AVG function computes the average of the values of a column or an expression. SUM, naturally, computes the sum. Both functions can be applied only to columns or expressions of numeric type and ignore null values. They can also be used to compute the average or sum of *distinct* values of a column or expression.

AVG(numeric_expression) and SUM(numeric_expression)
: Compute the average and sum of all values excluding NULL.

AVG(DISTINCT expression) and SUM(DISTINCT expression)

Compute the average and sum of all distinct values excluding NULL. Multiple rows with the same value are treated as one row with this value.

The following query computes average year-to-date sales for each type of books:

```
SELECT   type,
         average_ytd_sales = AVG( ytd_sales )
FROM     titles
GROUP BY type
```

Results:

```
type                average_ytd_sales
------------        -----------------
business            7697
mod_cook            12139
popular_comp        6437
psychology          1987
trad_cook           6522
UNDECIDED           (null)

(6 row(s) affected)
```

The next query produces total year-to-date sales for each type of book. Notice that in this example we did not give a name to the aggregate column, and it appears under a blank header in the result. An aggregate function, like any other expression applied to a column, suppresses the column header. Compare this to the previous query in which we explicitly assigned a header for the aggregate column:

```
SELECT   type,
         SUM( ytd_sales )
FROM     titles
GROUP BY type
```

Results:

```
type
------------        ---------------
business            30788
mod_cook            24278
popular_comp        12875
psychology          9939
trad_cook           19566
UNDECIDED           (null)

(6 row(s) affected)
```

COUNT

There are three variations of the COUNT function:

COUNT(*)
: Computes the number of rows, including those with null values.

COUNT(expression)
: Returns the number of rows with non-null values in a certain column or expression.

COUNT(DISTINCT expression)
: Calculates the number of distinct non-null values in a column or expression. Each group of rows with the same value of `expression` adds 1 to the result.

Do not believe those who tell you that COUNT(1) works faster than COUNT(*)—they provide the same performance! There is, however, a difference between COUNT(*) and COUNT(expression). If expression cannot return null values, always use COUNT(*) instead because it is faster.

The following query counts all rows in a table:

```
SELECT COUNT(*) FROM publishers
```

Results:

```
-----------
8

(1 row(s) affected)
```

The next query counts only those rows of the same table that have a non-null value of state:

```
SELECT COUNT( state ) FROM publishers
```

The result is lower than in the previous example because two publishers do not have a value in the state column:

```
-----------
6

(1 row(s) affected)
```

The next example counts the number of publishers in each state. If you want to use a reserved word for a column header, it has to appear in quotes after the column or expression the way 'count' does here.

```
SELECT    state, COUNT(1) 'count'
FROM      publishers
GROUP BY state
```

Results:

```
state count
----- -----------
(null)2
CA    1
DC    1
IL    1
MA    1
NY    1
TX    1

(7 row(s) affected)
```

The following query finds the number of different countries where publishers are located:

```
SELECT  COUNT( DISTINCT country ) 'Count of Countries'
FROM    publishers
```

Results:

```
Count of Countries
------------------
3

(1 row(s) affected)
```

MIN and MAX

The names of these functions speak for themselves. The functions:

```
MIN( expression )
MAX( expression )
```

find the minimum and maximum value in a set of rows. DISTINCT or ALL may be used with these functions, but they do not affect the result. Obviously, MIN and MAX will return the greatest and smallest number or date value, respectively, when applied to a numeric or date expression. But what happens with string data? The result is determined by the character set and sort order chosen at SQL Server installation. It defines the order of characters during any sorting, including finding the minimum or maximum value of a string expression.

The following query finds the worst and the best sales for any title on record:

```
SELECT  'MIN' = MIN( ytd_sales ),
        'MAX' = MAX( ytd_sales )
FROM    titles
```

Results:

```
MIN         MAX
----------- -----------
111         22246

(1 row(s) affected)
```

The last example is exactly what you should avoid in your code. Beware the performance implication of using more than one aggregate function in the same query. If you select either the MIN or the MAX function on an indexed column, SQL Server will use the index to quickly find the minimum or maximum value. But if you request both MIN and MAX in one query, it will result in a table scan that may take a very long time, depending on the table size. When you need both minimum and maximum values, run two separate SELECTS instead. This tip does not apply if you also select other aggregate functions that force a table scan anyway. When at least one of the aggregate functions requires that the whole table be scanned, then you may request MIN and MAX at the same time as well.

More Examples of Using Aggregate Functions

Let's find all possible aggregate functions on the prices of popular computing and business titles. There are only seven rows that will participate in our aggregation. The following query selects them all:

```
SELECT price FROM titles WHERE type IN ( 'popular_comp', 'business' )

price
--------------------------
19.99
11.95
2.99
19.99
22.95
20.00
(null)

(7 row(s) affected)
```

The next query returns all aggregates on the data set shown previously:

```
SELECT  AVG( price )                'AVG( price )',
        AVG( DISTINCT price )       'AVG( DISTINCT price )',
        SUM( price )                'SUM( price )',
        SUM( DISTINCT price )       'SUM( DISTINCT price )',
        MIN( price )                'MIN( price )',
        MAX( price )                'MAX( price )',
```

```
        COUNT( price )          'COUNT( price )',
        COUNT( DISTINCT price ) 'COUNT( DISTINCT price )',
        COUNT(*)                'COUNT(*)',
        COUNT(1)                'COUNT(1)'
FROM    titles
WHERE   type IN ( 'popular_comp', 'business' )
```

The results returned by this query are shown in Table 12-2:

Table 12-2. Examples of Using Aggregate Functions

Aggregate Function	Result	Comment
AVG(price)	16.31	Average of 2.99, 11.95, 19.99, 19.99, 20.00, and 22.95. NULL value in one row is ignored.
AVG(distinct price)	15.58	Average of 2.99, 11.95, 19.99, 20.00, and 22.95. NULL value in one row is ignored. Duplicate value of 19.99 in the table is considered only once.
SUM(price)	97.87	Sum of 2.99, 11.95, 19.99, 19.99, 20.00, and 22.95. NULL value in one row is ignored.
SUM(distinct price)	77.88	Sum of 2.99, 11.95, 19.99, 20.00, and 22.95. NULL value in one row is ignored. Duplicate value of 19.99 in the table is considered only once.
MIN(price)	2.99	Minimum value found in the column. NULL value is ignored.
MAX(price)	22.95	Maximum value found in the column. NULL value is ignored.
COUNT(price)	6	Count of rows where price has values other than NULL. Rows with NULL value are not counted.
COUNT(distinct price)	5	Count of distinct price values other than NULL. All rows with the same duplicate value are counted only once. Rows with NULL value are not counted.
COUNT(*)	7	Count of all rows that qualify for the WHERE clause conditions.
COUNT(1)	7	Count of all rows that qualify for the WHERE clause conditions. There is *no performance advantage* to using COUNT(1) instead of COUNT(*), and the result is the same.

Aggregate functions are often used in the HAVING clause of queries with GROUP BY.

The following query selects all categories (types) of books that have an average price for all books in the category higher than $15:

```
SELECT  type            'Category',
        AVG( price ) 'Average Price'
FROM    titles
GROUP BY type
HAVING  AVG( price ) > 15
ORDER BY 2
```

The next query selects all categories of books that have more than two books in the category and a price range between the most expensive and the least expensive book in the category of less than $10:

```
SELECT  type         'Category',
        COUNT(*)     'Number of Titles',
        MIN( price ) 'Least Expensive',
        MAX( price ) 'Most Expensive'
FROM    titles
GROUP BY type
HAVING  MAX( price ) - MIN( price ) < 10
    AND COUNT(*) > 2
```

The following example demonstrates different results returned by the same query applied to the same data set on servers with different sort orders (see Table 12-3):

```
CREATE TABLE #sort_order ( value VARCHAR(20) )
INSERT #sort_order VALUES ( 'abc' )
INSERT #sort_order VALUES ( 'XYZ' )
SELECT MIN( value ) from #sort_order
```

Table 12-3. Examples of Aggregate Functions on Servers with Different Sort Orders

SQL Server Sort Order	Result	Comment
Case-sensitive	XYZ	*X* has a lower ASCII code than *a*, so *X* is less than *a*.
Case-insensitive	abc	*XYZ* is compared with *ABC*, and *A* is less than *X*.

Mathematical Functions

Transact-SQL mathematical functions include the following:

ABS
: Absolute value

ACOS
: Angle (in radians) whose cosine is the specified argument

ASIN
: Angle (in radians) whose sine is the specified argument

ATAN
: Angle (in radians) whose tangent is the specified argument

ATN2
: Angle (in radians) whose tangent is argument1/argument1

CEILING
: Smallest integer greater than or equal to the argument

COS
: Cosine

COT
: Cotangent

DEGREES
: Converts radians to degrees

EXP
: Exponential value

FLOOR
: Largest integer less than or equal to the argument

LOG
: Natural logarithm

LOG10
: Base-10 logarithm

PI
: Pi constant

POWER
: Argument1 to the power of argument2

RADIANS
: Converts degrees to radians

RAND
: Pseudorandom FLOAT type value between 0 and 1

ROUND
: Rounds argument to the specified precision

SIGN
: -1 if the argument is negative, 0 if it is zero, and 1 if the argument is positive

SIN
: Sine

SQRT
: Square root

TAN
: Tangent

ABS and SIGN

The ABS and SIGN functions are specified as follows:

ABS(numeric_expression)
: Returns the absolute value of the argument. The result is of the same type as the argument.

SIGN(numeric_expression)

Returns 1 if the argument is positive, 0 if the argument is zero, or -1 if the argument is negative. The result is of the same type as the argument.

The following example finds the absolute values of numeric constants:

```
SELECT ABS( 123.45 ), ABS( -789 ), ABS( 3e-3 ), ABS( 0 )
```

Results:

```
--------- ----------- ------------------------ -----------
123.45    789         0.003                    0
Chapter 20
(1 row(s) affected)
```

The next example determines whether numeric constants are positive, negative, or zero:

```
SELECT SIGN( -50000000 ), SIGN( 98765.43e21 ), SIGN( 0 )
```

Results:

```
----------- ------------------------ -----------
-1          1.0                      0

(1 row(s) affected)
```

Use of ABS and SIGN is not limited to mathematical functions. See the "Characteristic Functions" section in Chapter 20 for more information.

Trigonometric Functions

Trigonometric functions in Transact-SQL are used primarily to implement mathematical and scientific applications. They include the following:

ACOS(float_expression)

Computes the angle (in radians) whose cosine is the specified argument

ASIN(float_expression)

Computes the angle (in radians) whose sine is the specified argument

ATAN(float_expression)

Computes angle (in radians) whose tangent is the specified argument

ATN2(float_expression1, float_expression2)

Computes the angle (in radians) whose tangent is between two specified arguments

COS(float_expression)

Computes the cosine of the specified angle (in radians)

COT(float_expression)

Computes the cotangent of the specified angle (in radians)

SIN(float_expression)
: Computes the sine of the specified angle (in radians)

TAN(float_expression)
: Computes the tangent of the specified angle (in radians)

The following example performs four different trigonometric functions:

```
SELECT SIN( 1.571 ), ASIN( 1 ), COS( 0 ), ATN2( 5, 5e2 )
```

Results:

```
------------------ ----------------- ------ ---------------------
0.999999979258613  1.5707963267949   1.0    0.00999966668666524

(1 row(s) affected)
```

DEGREES and RADIANS

The following functions convert angles from degrees to radians and vice versa:

DEGREES(numeric_expression)
: Converts argument in radians to degrees. Result type is the same as the argument.

RADIANS(numeric_expression)
: Converts argument in degrees to radians. Result type is the same as the argument.

For example:

```
SELECT  DEGREES( 3.141592 ), RADIANS( 60e0 ), RADIANS( 60 )
```

Results:

```
------------------------------- ---------------------- ---------
179.999962552063320000          1.0471975511966        1

(1 row(s) affected)
```

CEILING, FLOOR, and ROUND

The CEILING, FLOOR, and ROUND functions are used to round arguments as follows:

CEILING(numeric_expression)
: Finds the smallest integer greater than or equal to the specified argument. Returns result of the same type as the argument.

FLOOR(numeric_expression)
: Finds the largest integer less than or equal to the specified argument. Returns result of the same type as the argument.

ROUND(numeric_expression, precision)
: Rounds the argument `numeric_expression` so that it has `precision` significant digits.

The following query applies CEILING and FLOOR functions to book price:

```
SELECT  price,
        FLOOR( price )   AS 'floor',
        CEILING( price ) AS 'ceiling'
FROM    titles
WHERE   type = 'business'
```

Results:

```
price                floor                ceiling
-------------------- -------------------- --------------------
19.99                19.00                20.00
11.95                11.00                12.00
2.99                 2.00                 3.00
19.99                19.00                20.00

(4 row(s) affected)
```

The ROUND function requires some additional explanation. You could also say that this function rounds the number to the nearest $10^{precision}$. If the precision is positive, then the function rounds the argument expression to the nearest number with precision digits after the decimal point. When the precision is zero, the argument is rounded to the nearest integer value. Negative precision defines the number of significant digits to the left of the decimal point. After calculating the rounded result, the function converts it to the same type as the `numeric_expression`. This may result in additional rounding if the type does not support enough positions to the right of the decimal point. Table 12-4 shows examples of ROUND usage.

Table 12-4. Examples of Using ROUND Function

@prec	3	2	1	0	-1	-2	-3	-4
Rounding to nearest	0.001	0.01	0.1	1	10	100	1000	10000
ROUND (567.89, @prec)	567.89	567.89	567.90	568.00	570.00	600.00	1000.00	0.00

EXP and LOG

These functions compute exponentials and logarithms as follows:

EXP(float_expression)

Returns the exponential of the specified argument, which is equal to the *e* constant, or approximately 2.718282, to the power of `float_expression`

LOG(float_expression) and LOG10(float_expression)

Computes the natural and base-10 logarithms, respectively

The LOG function by itself is sufficient to calculate the logarithm of any base, but LOG10 is frequently used in applications, so it has been added for the programmers' convenience.

To calculate any base-N logarithm by using just the LOG function, use the following formula:

```
logn( x ) = LOG( x ) / LOG( n )
```

For example, LOG10(10000000) is equivalent to LOG(10000000) / LOG(10).

To compute a binary logarithm log2(x) use the following expression:

```
LOG( x ) / LOG( 2 )
```

For example:

```
SELECT  A = EXP( 10 ),
        B = LOG( EXP( 1.2345 ) ),
        C = LOG10( 1000000 ),
        D = LOG( 1024 ) / LOG( 2 )
```

Results:

```
A                    B             C             D
-------------------- ------------- ------------- -------------
22026.4657948067     1.2345        6.0           10.0

(1 row(s) affected)
```

POWER and SQRT

The POWER and SQRT functions have the following meanings:

POWER(numeric_expression, power)
: Returns the value of the `numeric_expression` argument to the power of `power`. The result is of the same type as the first argument.

SQRT(float_expression)
: Computes the square root of the specified argument. The result is a FLOAT datatype.

The POWER function may replace SQRT and, approximately, EXP using the following formulas, where x is any numeric expression:

```
SQRT[AZ23]( x ) = POWER( x, 0.5 )
EXP( x ) = POWER( 2.718282, x )
```

The difference between SQRT and POWER with the second argument of 0.5 is in the type of the result.

POWER returns the same type as the first argument, and may round it, while the SQRT result is a float, which is generally more precise. If you want POWER to return a floating-point result, you need to explicitly convert the first argument to a FLOAT type.

The POWER and SQRT functions may cause domain errors or arithmetic overflow errors. *Domain errors* occur when the result of a mathematical function is meaningless, such as SQRT(-1). *Arithmetic overflow* occurs when a function returns a result exceeding the maximum possible value for the result datatype, as in POWER(2, 31), which is "one greater" than the maximum allowed INT value.

Table 12-5 provides examples of POWER and SQRT.

Table 12-5. Examples of Using POWER and SQRT

Expression	Result
`SQRT( 4 )`	`2.0`
`POWER( 4, 0.5 )`	`2`
`SQRT( 5 )`	`2.23606797749979`
`POWER( 5, 0.5 )`	`2`
`POWER( convert( float, 5 ), 0.5 )`	`2.23606797749979`
`POWER( 2, 10 )`	`1024`
`POWER( 2e0, -1 )`	`0.5`
`POWER( 1.234, 5.678 )`	`3.300`
`POWER( 1.234e0, 5.678e0 )`	`3.29979892531597`
`POWER( -3, 3 )`	`-27`
`POWER( -1, 0.5 )`	`NULL, domain error occurred.`
`SQRT( -1 )`	`NULL, domain error occurred.`
`POWER( 2, 31 )`	`NULL, arithmetic overflow occurred.`
`POWER( 2e0, 31 )`	`2147483648.0`

RAND

The RAND() function returns a pseudorandom float value between 0 and 1. An optional integer seed may be specified as an argument if you need to generate the same sequence of random numbers. It is helpful in testing when the same sequence of random numbers is required over and over again.

You can use RAND to obtain random integers as well. For example, the following loop generates 10 pseudorandom integers between 0 and 99. The results may differ every time you execute this script.

```
DECLARE @i INT
SELECT  @i = 10
WHILE @i > 0
BEGIN
    SELECT  @i = @i - 1
    SELECT CONVERT( TINYINT, RAND() * 100 )
END
```

The script returns results in separate lines. We have put them in one line here to simplify presentation:

```
37, 53, 57, 60, 60, 16, 66, 45, 35, 5
```

PI

The PI() function returns a constant value of 3.141592653589793.

Why not use the hardcoded constant itself? Because if different programmers use different PI precision, then their applications may be incompatible and result in computation errors. The code is also more self-documenting when you use PI() than when you put the actual constant in your program.

String Functions

Transact-SQL string functions include the following:

ASCII
: Converts a character to a numeric ASCII code

CHAR
: Converts a numeric ASCII code to a character

CHAR_LENGTH
: Number of characters in a string

CHARINDEX
: Position of the first occurrence of a substring in a string

DATALENGTH
: Number of bytes in a character or binary string

DIFFERENCE
: Compares how two arguments sound and returns a number from 0 to 4; the higher result indicates the better phonetic match

LOWER
: Converts a string to lowercase

LTRIM
: Trims leading space characters

PATINDEX
: Position of the first occurrence of a pattern in a string

REPLICATE
: Repeats a string a number of times

REVERSE
: Reverses characters of a string

RIGHT
: Part of a string consisting of a given number of characters from its right

RTRIM
: Trims trailing space characters

SOUNDEX
: Returns a four-character code based on how the argument string sounds

SPACE
: Returns a string consisting of a given number of space characters

STUFF
: Replaces a part of one string with another string

SUBSTRING
: Extracts a part of a string

UPPER
: Converts a string to uppercase

String functions are extremely useful in business applications that manipulate character data. CONVERT and STR functions are also often used in expressions with string functions. Those functions are described later in this chapter.

+ (Concatenation)

Strictly speaking, concatenation is not a string function, but an operation. We have included it here because string expressions very often require concatenating results, so this operation is frequently used with string functions. The + operation has the following syntax:

```
char_or_binary_expression1 + char_or_binary_expression2
```

A concatenation (plus sign) function applied to two character or binary expressions concatenates their values. This may be semantically confusing, because the plus sign appearing between two numeric expressions adds their values. Therefore, the meaning of the function depends on argument definition, which may not be obvious from the context.

The result is a string whose length is equal to the total length of the arguments. However, if it exceeds the maximum length (255) of a character string supported by SQL Server, then the result is truncated without warning or error. Also, if the result is stored in a variable or column shorter than necessary, then extra characters on the right side are trimmed without warning or error.

A null value in any of the parameters is implicitly treated as a string of zero length. This is different from operations on other datatypes, where a null value in one of the parameters makes the whole result a null.

For example:

```
DECLARE @str1 CHAR(5), @str2 CHAR(5)
SELECT  @str1 = 'ABC', @str2 = NULL
SELECT  @str1 str1,
        @str2 str2,
        @str1 + @str2 + 'DEF' 'str1+str2+DEF'
```

Results:

```
str1  str2  str1+str2+DEF
----- ----- --------------
ABC   (null)ABCDEF
```

ASCII and CHAR

The ASCII and CHAR functions convert characters to ASCII codes and vice versa:

ASCII(char_expression)
: Returns the ASCII code of the first character of the argument.

CHAR(integer_expression)
: Returns a character given its ASCII code. Valid arguments are 0 through 255. A null value is returned for invalid arguments.

The following example selects ASCII codes:

```
SELECT  ASCII( 'A' )    'A',
        ASCII( 'a' )    'a',
        ASCII( 'abc' )  'abc',
        ASCII( '0' )    '0',
        ASCII( ' ' )    'space' ,
        ASCII( '
' )                     'Line Break'
```

Results:

```
A           a           abc         0           space       Line Break
----------- ----------- ----------- ----------- ----------- -----------
65          97          97          48          32          13

(1 row(s) affected)
```

The next example builds a string of characters from ASCII codes 32-127 and prints on three lines:

```
SET NOCOUNT ON
DECLARE @line1 VARCHAR(32),
        @line2 VARCHAR(32),
        @line3 VARCHAR(32),
        @code  TINYINT
SELECT @code = 32
WHILE @code < 64
```

```
BEGIN
    SELECT @line1 = @line1 + CHAR( @code ),      -- 32-63
           @line2 = @line2 + CHAR( @code + 32 ), -- 64-95
           @line3 = @line3 + CHAR( @code + 64 )  -- 96-127
    SELECT @code = @code + 1
END
PRINT @line1
PRINT @line2
PRINT @line3
```

Results:

```
 !"#$%&'()*+,-./0123456789:;<=>?
@ABCDEFGHIJKLMNOPQRSTUVWXYZ[\]^_
'abcdefghijklmnopqrstuvwxyz{|}~
```

CHARINDEX and PATINDEX

These functions are used to search strings for certain patterns, as follows:

CHARINDEX(substring, string)
: Finds the starting position of the first occurrence of the substring in the specified string. If no occurrence is found, then the result is zero. Both parameters may be string expressions.

PATINDEX(pattern, string)
: Finds the starting position of the first occurrence of the pattern in the specified string. If no occurrence is found, then the result is zero.

The string argument in PATINDEX may be a text or a character type. The pattern may (and usually does) include wildcard characters. It generally contains % (a percent character) in the first and the last position. The only cases in which a percent character is not included is when you test the string for a pattern occurrence at the very beginning of it or when you directly compare the string and the pattern.

Wildcard characters supported by PATINDEX are the same as those available with a LIKE comparison in a WHERE clause, as shown in Table 12-6.

Table 12-6. Wildcard Characters for PATINDEX

Wildcard Specification	Description
%	Any string of zero or more characters
_	Any single character
[ ]	Any single character within a given range (for example, [W-Z]) or a set of characters (for example, [01NYFT])
[^]	Any single character *not* within a given range (for example, [^W-Z]) or a set of characters (for example, [^01NYFT])

The following query returns titles that contain the words "computer" and "cooking" in any order:

```
SELECT  title
FROM    titles
WHERE   CHARINDEX( 'Computer', title ) > 0
    AND CHARINDEX( 'Cooking',  title ) > 0
```

Results:

```
title
----------------------------------------------------------------
Cooking with Computers: Surreptitious Balance Sheets
The Psychology of Computer Cooking

(2 row(s) affected)
```

The next query returns titles that have the word "cooking" followed by the word "computer" where the words may be separated by other text:

```
SELECT  title
FROM    titles
WHERE   PATINDEX( '%Cooking%Computer%', title ) > 0
```

The result consists of only one title compared to two in the previous example, because this query is more restrictive than the first one. It requires the words "Cooking" and "Computer" to appear in a certain order, as opposed to both words simply being present.

```
title
----------------------------------------------------------------
Cooking with Computers: Surreptitious Balance Sheets

(1 row(s) affected)
```

Table 12-7 provides additional PATINDEX examples.

Table 12-7. More Examples of Using PATINDEX

Function	Result	Comment
`CHARINDEX( 'de', 'abcdefg' )`	4	
`CHARINDEX( '%de%', 'abcdefg' )`	0	Percent is not treated as a wildcard character in CHARINDEX.
`PATINDEX( 'de', 'abcdefg' )`	0	
`PATINDEX( '%de%', 'abcdefg' )`	4	Compare this to CHARINDEX with the same arguments.
`PATINDEX( 'ab%', 'abcdefg' )`	1	Searching for a pattern at the beginning of a string. No percent sign in the first pattern position.

Table 12-7. More Examples of Using PATINDEX (continued)

Function	Result	Comment
`PATINDEX( '%fg', 'abcdefg' )`	6	Searching for a pattern at the end of a string. No percent sign in the last pattern position.
`PATINDEX( 'abcdefg', 'abcdefg' )`	1	Using PATINDEX to compare two strings.

DATALENGTH and CHAR_LENGTH

These functions determine the length of an argument as follows:

DATALENGTH(expression)
: Returns the length of **`expression`** in bytes. This function is most frequently used to determine the length of a VARCHAR column, variable, or expression, but the argument may be of any type supported by SQL Server.

CHAR_LENGTH(expression)
: Returns the number of characters in a string expression, excluding trailing blanks. It can be applied to string or TEXT data. This function is currently supported only by Sybase.

The result of DATALENGTH is the number of bytes needed to store the value internally, not the number of positions needed to print or display it. For example, when applied to an expression of type INT, DATALENGTH always returns 4, regardless of the value; for DATETIME it returns 8. It may be used with TEXT and IMAGE data as well.

For example:

```
SELECT  title,
        price,
        DATALENGTH( title ) 'Title Length',
        DATALENGTH( price ) 'Price Length'
FROM    titles
WHERE   type = 'popular_comp'
```

Results:

```
title                         price      Title Length Price Length
----------------------------- ---------- ------------ ------------
But Is It User Friendly?      22.95      24           8
Secrets of Silicon Valley     20.00      25           8
Net Etiquette                 (null)     13           (null)

(3 row(s) affected)
```

Table 12-8 provides additional examples of these functions.

Table 12-8. Examples of Using DATALENGTH and CHAR_LENGTH

Expression	Result
`DATALENGTH( 'ABC ' )`	5
`CHAR_LENGTH( 'ABC ' )`	3
`DATALENGTH( RTRIM( 'ABC ' ) )`	3
`DATALENGTH( 1234567890 )`	4
`DATALENGTH( 1e0 )`	8

DIFFERENCE and SOUNDEX

The DIFFERENCE and SOUNDEX functions attempt to compare how two strings sound when spoken. The algorithm is rather empirical, and sometimes the results are not what you would expect:

DIFFERENCE(string_expression1, string_expression2)
: Compares how two strings should sound and returns a "similarity level" of 0 (very different strings) through 4 (strings sound the same).

SOUNDEX(string_expression)
: Converts a character string into a code consisting of one character and three digits. In theory, strings that sound similar should result in the same code.

The algorithm for SOUNDEX is summarized in Table 12-9 and its code translation is in Table 12-10.

Table 12-9. SOUNDEX Algorithm

	Algorithm Step	Transformation of String "Difference and Soundex"
1	Truncate the argument expression at the first nonalphabetic character and ignore the remainder of the string. What this means is that only the beginning portion of the string up to the first nonletter matters for SOUNDEX. If the argument begins with a digit, space, or a special character, then the evaluated expression is a zero-length string that invariably results in code 0000.	Difference
2	Convert the string to uppercase.	DIFFERENCE
3	Strip all the letters A, E, H, I, O, U, W, and Y, except for the first position of the string. These are all the letters that have the result code digit of 0 from Table 12-10.	DFFRNC
4	Strip repeating characters with the same result code digit from Table 12-10 (when multiple letters with the same code appear in a row, keep only one).	DFRNC

Table 12-9. SOUNDEX Algorithm (continued)

	Algorithm Step	Transformation of String "Difference and Soundex"
5	Take the first four letters of what is left of the string. Ignore the remainder.	DFRN
6	Take the first letter of the string as the first character of the resultant code.	DFRN
7	Translate the second, third, and fourth letters of the string to code digits as shown in Table 12-10.	D165
8	If the result code is shorter than four characters, then pad it with trailing zeros up to four characters.	D165

Table 12-10. SOUNDEX Code Translation Table

Letter	A,E,H,I,O,U,W,Y	B,F,P,V	C,G,J,K,Q,S,X,Z	D,T	L	M,N	R
Result Code Digit	0	1	2	3	4	5	6

The examples in Table 12-11 demonstrate how the SOUNDEX algorithm may return the same code for very different-sounding strings.

Table 12-11. Examples of SOUNDEX Usage

Expression	Result	Comment
`SOUNDEX( "O'Reilly" )`	O000	Only the first character of the argument string is considered by SOUNDEX because there is a special character in the second position.
`SOUNDEX( "O'Brian" )`	O000	The value of SOUNDEX here is the same as in the previous example, because only the first character is considered.
`SOUNDEX( "at nine" )`	A300	Space character in the third position makes SOUNDEX ignore the word "nine."
`SOUNDEX( "at three" )`	A300	Space character in the third position makes SOUNDEX ignore the word "three," so the result is the same as in the previous example.
`SOUNDEX( " abcdef" )`	0000	Space in the first position makes SOUNDEX ignore the whole string.
`SOUNDEX( " VWXYZ" )`	0000	Space in the first position makes SOUNDEX ignore the whole string. This example demonstrates that the resulting SOUNDEX code is four zeros for any string that begins with a nonalphabetic character.
`SOUNDEX( "abcdef" )`	A123	
`SOUNDEX( "ACGJKQSXZR" )`	A260	Characters C, G, J, K, Q, S, X, and Z have the same code in the SOUNDEX translation table, so they all collapse into one digit—2—in the second position of the result.

Table 12-11. Examples of SOUNDEX Usage (continued)

Expression	Result	Comment
`SOUNDEX( "ACR" )`	A260	This string produces the same code as the previous one, because a single C results in digit 2 in the second position of the code (same as the previous string).
`SOUNDEX( "SQL" )`	S240	
`SOUNDEX( "Sequel" )`	S240	Vowels are ignored, so the code is the same as in the previous example.
`SOUNDEX( "Sport" )`	S163	
`SOUNDEX( "Spirit" )`	S163	Vowels are ignored, so the code is the same as in the previous example.

After looking at these examples, you probably wonder how best to describe what is it that SOUNDEX really does. Here is one sentence that summarizes the SOUNDEX algorithm: it converts a string argument into a code depending on the first letter and the following few consonants, considering similar-sounding ones the same and counting repeating ones as one.

The function has been criticized by users, and rightfully so. It is in many cases inaccurate and produces very different codes for phonetically similar strings. For example, you can search for an author name that you are not sure how to spell:

```
SELECT  au_fname, au_lname
FROM    authors
WHERE   SOUNDEX( au_lname ) = SOUNDEX( 'Grin' )
```

Results:

```
au_fname             au_lname
-------------------- ----------------------------------------
Marjorie             Green
Morningstar          Greene

(2 row(s) affected)
```

In this case SOUNDEX was helpful. But try searching for an author named Carsen. There are Karsen and Carson in the authors table. Strings have different SOUNDEX codes if they begin with a different first character. So the following query finds only one of them:

```
SELECT  au_fname, au_lname
FROM    authors
WHERE   SOUNDEX( au_lname ) = SOUNDEX( 'Carsen' )
```

Results:

```
au_fname             au_lname
-------------------- ----------------------------------------
Cheryl               Carson

(1 row(s) affected)
```

LOWER and UPPER

The following functions convert the case of strings:

LOWER(string_expression)
Converts all alphabetic characters of an argument into lowercase

UPPER(string_expression)
Converts all alphabetic characters of an argument into uppercase

Digits and special characters found in the string remain unchanged. These functions are especially useful on a case-sensitive server when you need to compare strings ignoring their case. For example:

```
SELECT  title
FROM    titles
WHERE   LOWER( title ) LIKE '% and %'
```

Results:

```
title
----------------------------------------------------------------------
Computer Phobic AND Non-Phobic Individuals: Behavior Variations
Onions, Leeks, and Garlic: Cooking Secrets of the Mediterranean

(2 row(s) affected)
```

The query finds all titles that contain the word "and" in uppercase, lowercase, or mixed case. On a case-insensitive server, though, all comparisons ignore the case, so the LOWER function would be unnecessary.

The LOWER and UPPER functions are also necessary in many situations in which you need to store a data element in a certain case or present retrieved information all capitalized or all lowercased. For example:

```
SELECT  LOWER( 'Alphabet' ), UPPER( 'warning' )
```

Results:

```
-------- -------
alphabet WARNING

(1 row(s) affected)
```

LTRIM and RTRIM

The following functions truncate space characters:

LTRIM(string_expression)
: Truncates leading and trailing space characters of an argument string

RTRIM(string_expression)
: Truncates trailing space characters of an argument string

These functions are frequently used in business applications to manipulate character data. For example, you may need to trim both leading and trailing blanks in some string directly entered by a user at runtime. The RTRIM function is often applied to CHAR data, because CHAR is padded with trailing space characters up to the declared length. You may want to strip these extra blanks before concatenating the string with another one.

The following example selects a book type trimmed of trailing spaces and enclosed in double quotes:

```
SELECT DISTINCT
        "Not trimmed" = '"' + type + '"',
        "Trimmed" = '"' + RTRIM( type ) + '"'
FROM   titles
```

Results:

```
Not trimmed    Trimmed
-------------- --------------
"business    " "business"
"mod_cook    " "mod_cook"
"popular_comp" "popular_comp"
"psychology  " "psychology"
"trad_cook   " "trad_cook"
"UNDECIDED   " "UNDECIDED"

(6 row(s) affected)
```

The following stored procedure searches for an author by last name. It trims spaces both on the left and right of an argument supplied by a user.

```
CREATE PROCEDURE search_author
    @last_name VARCHAR(40)
AS
SELECT  RTRIM( au_fname ) + ' ' + RTRIM( au_lname )
FROM    authors
WHERE   au_lname = LTRIM( RTRIM( @last_name ) )
GO
```

If the user specifies a name surrounded by blanks, the procedure still succeeds in finding the author:

```
EXEC search_author '  Carson '
```

Results:

```
------------------------------------------------------------
Cheryl Carson

(1 row(s) affected)
```

REPLICATE and SPACE

The REPLICATE and SPACE functions are used to produce strings of repeating character sequences.

REPLICATE(string_expression, integer_expression)
: Repeats the first argument the number of times specified by the second argument

SPACE(integer_expression)
: Repeats the space character the number of times specified by the argument

SPACE(n)
: Is equivalent to `REPLICATE( ' ', n )`

Table 12-12 provides examples of these functions.

Table 12-12. Examples of Using REPLICATE and SPACE

Expression	Result
`REPLICATE( 'Help', 4 )`	`'HelpHelpHelpHelp'`
`REPLICATE( '*', 20 )`	`'********************'`
`SPACE( 10 )`	`'          '`
`REPLICATE( ' ', 10 )`	`'          '`

REVERSE

The REVERSE() function returns the characters of the argument string in the reverse order. At first glance this function may seem exotic, because there is no equivalent in most other computer languages. But there are some expressions in which REVERSE comes in handy. For example, if you need to determine the position of the last space character in a string, you could use expressions from Table 12-13.

Table 12-13. Examples of Using REVERSE

Expression	Result	Comment
`CHARINDEX( ' ', REVERSE( 'This is a string' ) )`	7	This expression returns the position of the last space character in the argument string, counting from the right.
`DATALENGTH( 'This is a string' ) - CHARINDEX( ' ', REVERSE('This is a string' ) ) + 1`	10	This expression returns the position of the last space character in the argument string, counting from the beginning of the string.

SUBSTRING and RIGHT

The SUBSTRING and RIGHT functions extract a part of a character or binary string.

SUBSTRING (char_or_binary_expression, start, length)

Returns part of a `char_or_binary_expression` beginning with the `start` position.

RIGHT(char_expression, length)

Returns `length` rightmost characters of a `char_expression`. Zero or negative length returns null; `length` greater than the length of the `char_expression` returns the whole `char_expression`. Unlike the SUBSTRING function, RIGHT does not support the BINARY datatype.

If the first argument of the SUBSTRING function is of CHAR or VARCHAR datatype, then the result type is VARCHAR. For BINARY or VARBINARY arguments, the result is VARBINARY. The `length` is a mandatory parameter (unlike in substring function equivalents in some other computer languages) and specifies the number of bytes returned; `length` may exceed the number of available bytes in the argument string from the `start` position to the end. In such cases, the result string is shorter than length. If `start` is less than or equal to zero or is greater than the length of the first argument, or if `length` is zero, then the result is null. A negative length results in an error.

Very unfortunately, SUBSTRING does not work with TEXT type arguments, even if you need only a small part of a TEXT column that would fit in a CHAR type.

The accompanying CD-ROM contains the source code of stored procedure *sp_subtext*. This procedure extracts a substring up to 255 characters long from a TEXT column, given a start position and length. *sp_subtext* allows you to store the result in a local variable, unlike the READTEXT command.

The RIGHT function can always be replaced with an expression of SUBSTRING and DATALENGTH functions. It is just a more convenient and efficient way to perform extraction of a substring from the right.

Table 12-14 provides examples of these functions.

Table 12-14. Examples of Using SUBSTRING and RIGHT

Expression	Result
`SUBSTRING( 'abcdef', 2, 3 )`	bcd
`SUBSTRING( 'abcdef', 2, 0 )`	NULL
`SUBSTRING( 'abcdef', -12345, 1 )`	NULL
`RIGHT( 'abcdef', 4 )`	cdef
`SUBSTRING( 'abcdef', DATALENGTH( 'abcdef' ) - 3, 4 )`	cdef

STUFF

The STUFF function pastes (or "stuffs") one string into another. The function:

```
STUFF( char_expression1, start, length, char_expression2 )
```

replaces `length` characters of `char_expression1` beginning at `start` position with `char_expression2`. `start` values less than 1 or greater than the length of `char_expression1` produce a null result. Negative values of `length` also produce a null result.

Table 12-15 provides examples of using the STUFF function.

Table 12-15. Examples of Using STUFF

Expression	Result
`STUFF( 'turkey', 3, 2, 'stuffing' )`	tustuffingey
`STUFF( 'turkey', 4, 0, 'stuffing' )`	turstuffingkey
`STUFF( 'turkey', 4, 100, 'stuffing' )`	turstuffing
`STUFF( 'turkey', -1, 0, 'stuffing' )`	NULL
`STUFF( 'turkey', 7, 0, 'stuffing' )`	NULL

String Expressions

Transact-SQL provides very powerful string expressions and allows functions to be nested. For example, the following expression breaks a string consisting of city, state, and Zip Code into three separate elements. This is a practical task. Suppose that a user supplies address information as it is written on an envelope, but your database stores address elements separately. We have included comments to explain the complex expressions included here:

```
DECLARE @city_state_zip VARCHAR(80)
SELECT  @city_state_zip = 'Chicago, IL 60610'
```

```
SELECT  ------------------------------------------
        -- city is a part of the @city_state_zip
        -- from the first character to the position
        -- before the comma:
        SUBSTRING( @city_state_zip, 1,
            CHARINDEX( ',', @city_state_zip ) - 1          ) 'city',
        ------------------------------------------
        -- state is a part of the @city_state_zip
        -- from the position after the comma to the
        -- position of the last space, stripped of
        -- leading and trailing blank characters:
        RTRIM( LTRIM( SUBSTRING( @city_state_zip,
            CHARINDEX( ',', @city_state_zip ) + 1,
            DATALENGTH( @city_state_zip )
                - CHARINDEX( ' ', REVERSE( @city_state_zip ) )
                - CHARINDEX( ',', @city_state_zip ) + 1        ) ) ) 'state',
        ------------------------------------------
        -- zip is a part of the @city_state_zip
        -- from the position after the last space
        -- to the end:
        RIGHT( @city_state_zip,
            CHARINDEX( ' ', REVERSE( @city_state_zip ) ) - 1        ) 'zip'
```

Results:

```
(1 row(s) affected)

city                      state                 zip
------------------------- --------------------- --------------
Chicago                   IL                    60610

(1 row(s) affected)
```

In this example, we've used nested functions, and the code may look cryptic at first glance. For example, the expression:

```
CHARINDEX( ' ', REVERSE( @city_state_zip ) )
```

finds the position of the last space from the right in the variable. The REVERSE function puts the characters of the string backward, so Chicago, IL 60610 becomes 01606 LI ,ogacihC. Then CHARINDEX locates a space character in the inverted string. In this case, it is found in the sixth position. Therefore, the whole expression returns 6, which means that the space is the sixth character from the right in the original string.

You may be tempted to split this complex statement into several small SELECT statements that would use additional local variables to store intermediate results. In this example, that recoding would work fine because we parse a single local variable. However, coding that way may be too expensive if you need to process a set of rows. It is better to use one query, like the one shown in this section, than pay the severe performance penalty incurred by applying cursor processing.

Date Functions

Transact-SQL date functions include the following:

CURRENT_TIMESTAMP
: Current date and time

DATEADD
: Adds a number of dateparts (e.g., days) to a datetime value

DATEDIFF
: Difference between two datetime values expressed in certain dateparts

DATENAME
: Name of a datepart (e.g., month) of a datetime argument

DATEPART
: Value of a datepart (e.g., hour) of a datetime argument

GETDATE()
: Returns current date and time

The date functions manipulate DATETIME and SMALLDATETIME values. The CONVERT function may also be classified as a date function, because it can convert from and to the DATETIME type, among other things. That function is discussed in the "Type Conversion Functions" section later in this chapter. Several of the date functions refer to parts of dates, such as year, day, or minute. Table 12-16 shows Transact-SQL datepart names, abbreviations, and value ranges.

Table 12-16. Datepart Values

Datepart	Abbreviation	Range of Values
year	yy	1753–9999 for DATETIME or 1900–2079 for SMALLDATETIME
quarter	qq	1–4
month	mm	1–12
day of year[a]	dy	1–366
day	dd	1–31
week	wk	1–53
weekday	dw	1–7 (Sun.–Sat.)
hour	hh	0–23
minute	mi	0–59
second	ss	0–59
millisecond	ms	0–999

[a] Day of year can be used only by its abbreviation—dy.

CURRENT_TIMESTAMP and GETDATE

The CURRENT_TIMESTAMP and GETDATE() functions return the same value—the current date and time. You can say that they are synonyms in Transact-SQL. The result type is DATETIME.

CURRENT_TIMESTAMP
: Is a niladic function; it does not require any parameters and you do not even use parentheses with it.

GETDATE()
: Requires the parentheses, as shown, without arguments.

Microsoft has added CURRENT_TIMESTAMP to Transact-SQL for ANSI compliance in recent versions of SQL Server. Sybase does not support CURRENT_TIMESTAMP, so you need to use GETDATE() on Sybase systems.

It may be confusing, but CURRENT_TIMESTAMP is not related to TIMESTAMP columns. The function returns a DATETIME result, whereas TIMESTAMP columns contain binary values that do not convert to date and time.

GETDATE() is not supported by any SQL dialect other than Transact-SQL. Before CURRENT_TIMESTAMP was introduced by Microsoft, programmers had no choice but to use GETDATE(). Now it is probably wiser to use the standard ANSI SQL function CURRENT_TIMESTAMP instead, because it gives you compatibility with other ANSI-compliant SQL dialects. But use GETDATE() if your company still keeps SQL Server 4.x around or uses Sybase as well as Microsoft SQL Server.

DATEPART and DATENAME

The DATEPART and DATENAME functions return a part of a DATETIME value.

DATEPART(datepart, date_expression)
: Returns an integer representing the specified `datepart` of `date_expression`.

DATENAME(datepart, date_expression)
: Returns a character string representing the specified `datepart` of `date_expression`. For those dateparts that have no specific name (e.g., minute, day, year), the value is the datepart number in a character format. For days of the week and months, the function returns the actual name of the weekday or month.

A datepart may be specified by name or by the abbreviation provided in Table 12-16. We recommend using full names to avoid confusion, because abbreviations may sometimes be misleading. For example, "mi" means "minute," but could be misinterpreted as "millisecond," while "mm" means "month," but could be used mistakenly in place of "minute." A few extra keystrokes may save you from creating a bug and also will make your code self-documenting.

When you add milliseconds, remember that SQL Server supports time values with 3.33 milliseconds precision. Adding one millisecond to a datetime value does not change it, because it is rounded back to the same value. It may appear that the following code increments the @time variable 10 times until it reaches the New Year's mark and then executes the PRINT statement following the loop. However, the program loops endlessly, because adding one millisecond to a variable does not change its value:

```
SET NOCOUNT ON
DECLARE @time DATETIME
SELECT @time = '12/31/1999 11:59:59.990PM'
WHILE @time < '1/1/2000'
BEGIN
    SELECT @time = DATEADD( millisecond, 1, @time )
    PRINT 'Should old acquaintance be forgot'
END
PRINT 'And never brought to mind'
```

Results (an endless repetition of the same string):

```
Should old acquaintance be forgot
Should old acquaintance be forgot
Should old acquaintance be forgot
Should old acquaintance be forgot
Should old acquaintance be forgot
Should old acquaintance be forgot
Should old acquaintance be forgot
...
```

If you dare to execute this code, be ready to interrupt execution. From a query window, you can use the "Cancel Executing Query" button. In command-prompt ISQL, use Ctrl-C to stop the query.

Table 12-17 shows examples of these functions.

Table 12-17. Examples of Using DATEPART and DATENAME

Expression	Result	Result Type
`SELECT DATEPART( month, '2/14/1998' )`	2	INT
`SELECT DATENAME( month, '2/14/1998' )`	February	VARCHAR
`SELECT DATEPART( dy, '2/14/1998' )`	45	INT
`SELECT DATENAME( dy, '2/14/1998' )`	45	VARCHAR
`SELECT DATEPART( weekday, '2/14/1998' )`	7	INT
`SELECT DATENAME( weekday, '2/14/1998' )`	Saturday	VARCHAR
`SELECT DATENAME( year, '2/14/1998' )`	1998	VARCHAR

DATEADD and DATEDIFF

The DATEADD and DATEDIFF functions do the following:

DATEADD(datepart, number, date_expression)
Returns a datetime value computed by adding the specified `number` of `dateparts` to `date_expression`

DATEDIFF(datepart, date_expression1, date_expression2)
Returns the difference between two date expressions as the number of `dateparts`

The result of DATEDIFF is of type INT and cannot exceed the maximum range for INT values. Requesting the difference between two dates in small dateparts (such as milliseconds or seconds) causes arithmetic overflow when the range is exceeded.

The second parameter of DATEADD(`number`) must be of type INT or is converted to this type implicitly.

Table 12-18 shows examples of these functions.

Table 12-18. Examples of Using DATEADD and DATEDIFF

Expression	Result
`DATEADD( second, 2000000000, '1/1/2000' )`	`May 18 2063  3:33AM`
`DATEADD( second, -2000000000, '1/1/2000' )`	`Aug 15 1936  8:26PM`
`DATEADD( day, 1000000, '1/1/2000' )`	`Nov 28 4737 12:00AM`
`DATEADD( year, -1, '1/1/2000' )`	`Jan 1 1999 12:00AM`
`DATEDIFF( year, '12/31/1999', '1/1/2000' )`	`1`
`DATEDIFF( minute, '12/31/1999', '1/1/2000' )`	`1440`
`DATEDIFF( minute, '1/1/2000', '12/31/9999' )`	Message 535, Level 16, State 0 Difference of two datetime fields caused overflow at runtime.

The result of one of the example expressions:

```
DATEDIFF( year, '12/31/1999', '1/1/2000' )
```

requires additional explanation. The DATEDIFF function counts the number of datepart boundaries crossed between two dates, rather than rounding the interval to the nearest datepart. It may seem more correct to say that there are zero years between December 31, 1999, and January 1, 2000. However, there is one year-end boundary between the two, and the result of the function is 1.

The next example provides a solution you may find useful in different applications. It is often necessary to determine the elapsed time of a particular operation. Here is how you can do that:

```
DECLARE @start_time DATETIME
SELECT  @start_time = CURRENT_TIMESTAMP
<other statements>
SELECT  DATEDIFF( second, @start_time, CURRENT_TIMESTAMP )
            'Elapsed Time, sec'
```

This expression gives you the actual time between two events rather than the time that your process was utilizing CPU. You can obtain the latter with the help of the SET STATISTICS TIME ON command discussed in Chapter 21, *Debugging Transact-SQL Programs.*

Text and Image Functions

Transact-SQL text and image functions include the following:

TEXTPTR
: TEXT or IMAGE column pointer to be used with the READTEXT, WRITETEXT, or UPDATEXT commands

TEXTVALID
: Validates a pointer to a TEXT or IMAGE column and returns 1 if it is valid and 0 otherwise

The manipulation of TEXT and IMAGE data differs from the manipulation of other types, because this kind of data has several usage restrictions. These restrictions are outlined in Chapter 6, *Datatypes and Variables*. Transact-SQL provides several special functions to deal specifically with TEXT and IMAGE.

SET TEXTSIZE is a Transact-SQL statement (not a function) that limits the size of TEXT or IMAGE data returned by a SELECT statement.

Other functions that support TEXT and IMAGE data (as well as other datatypes) are PATINDEX, DATALENGTH, the Sybase-only function CHAR_LENGTH, discussed in the section on string functions; and CONVERT, discussed under "Type Conversion Functions."

The stored procedure *sp_subtext* found on the accompanying CD-ROM extracts a substring from a TEXT column and returns it in a variable.

TEXTPTR

The function:

```
TEXTPTR( text_or_image_column )
```

returns a binary string of type VARBINARY(16) containing an internal pointer to the `text_or_image_column`. This value may be used by the function TEXTVALID and the Transact-SQL commands READTEXT, UPDATETEXT, and WRITETEXT.

This example locates the pr_info TEXT value in the pub_info table for publisher 9901 and extracts a substring 16 characters long starting at the eighth position.

```
DECLARE @pointer varbinary(16)
SELECT  @pointer = TEXTPTR( pr_info )
FROM    pub_info
WHERE   pub_id = '9901'
READTEXT pub_info.pr_info @pointer 8 16
```

Results:

```
pr_info
-----------------------------------------------------------------
sample text data
```

TEXTVALID

The function:

```
TEXTVALID( 'table_name.text_or_image_column', text_pointer )
```

returns 1 if `text_pointer` is a valid pointer to the specified column of the specified table and returns 0 otherwise.

Type Conversion Functions

Transact-SQL type conversion functions include the following:

CONVERT
: Converts data from one datatype to another

STR
: Converts numeric data to character strings

HEXTOINT
: Converts platform-independent hexadecimal data to integer

INTTOHEX
: Converts integer data to platform-independent hexadecimal

Application programs often require that data be converted from one type to another. For example, you may need to concatenate a numeric value with a character string and a date. Transact-SQL does not allow concatenation of such different datatypes, but you can convert numeric and date values into strings and then concatenate them all together.

Transact-SQL provides several type conversion functions. The most versatile is the CONVERT function, which performs any datatype conversions supported by Transact-SQL. The STR function only converts from numeric types to character strings. Sybase has implemented two additional type conversion functions not supported by Microsoft: INTTOHEX and HEXTOINT; these convert integer data to platform-independent hexadecimal and vice versa.

The ROUND function may also be considered a type conversion function, because it changes the precision of numeric expressions. It is discussed in the earlier "Mathematical Functions" section.

CONVERT

The CONVERT function is a versatile Transact-SQL datatype conversion tool. Some other programming languages provide a separate function for every combination of type conversion. CONVERT does it all. The syntax of CONVERT is the following:

```
CONVERT( datatype[( length [, scale] )], expression [, style] )
```

where

`datatype[( length [, scale] )`
: Defines the type that you want to convert to.

`expression`
: Is the argument expression that you are converting.

`style`
: Is a parameter that specifies how to format datetime data. It is used only in DATETIME and SMALLDATETIME conversions to character strings.

For example:

```
SELECT  CONVERT( NUMERIC(5,2), '199.95' )          'CHAR to NUMERIC',
        CONVERT( CHAR(10), CURRENT_TIMESTAMP, 101 ) 'DATETIME to CHAR',
        CONVERT( BINARY(4), 1234567890 )            'INT to BINARY'
```

Results:

```
CHAR to NUMERIC DATETIME to CHAR INT to BINARY
--------------- ---------------- -------------
199.95          10/15/1997       0x499602d2
```

Converting DATETIME to CHAR

Transact-SQL allows you to use a wide variety of formats when converting datetime values to character. The format style is defined by the final argument of the CONVERT function (`style`).

Table 12-19 describes how different style values affect date and time formatting. Most formats allow you to represent the year with or without the century. We recommend that you always use four-digit year formats. With the threat of the looming year 2000 problem, it is better not to create even a potential for century-change bugs.

Table 12-19. CONVERT Date Format Styles

Name	Style	Format	Example
Default	0, 100	`Mon dd yyyy hh:mi[AM|PM]`	`Dec 31 1998 11:59PM`
USA	1	`mm/dd/yy`	`12/31/98`
	101	`mm/dd/yyyy`	`12/31/1998`
ANSI	2[a]	`yy.mm.dd`	`98.12.31`
	102	`yyyy.mm.dd`	`1998.12.31`
British/ French	3[a]	`dd/mm/yy`	`31/12/98`
	103[a]	`dd/mm/yyyy`	`31/12/1998`
German	4[a]	`dd.mm.yy`	`31.12.98`
	104[a]	`dd.mm.yyyy`	`31.12.1998`
Italian	5[a]	`dd-mm-yy`	`31-12-98`
	105[a]	`dd-mm-yyyy`	`31-12-1998`
	6	`dd Mon yy`	`31 Dec 98`
	106	`dd Mon yyyy`	`31 Dec 1998`
	7	`Mon dd, yy`	`Dec 31, 98`
	107	`Mon dd, yyyy`	`Dec 31, 1998`
	8, 108	`hh:mi:ss`	`23:59:59`
Default milliseconds	9, 109	`Mon dd yyyy hh:mi:ss:mmm[AM|PM]`	`Dec 31 1998 11:59:59:996PM`
USA	10	`mm-dd-yy`	`12-31-98`
	110	`mm-dd-yyyy`	`12-31-1998`
Japan	11a	`yy/mm/dd`	`98/12/31`
	111	`yyyy/mm/dd`	`1998/12/31`
ISO	12	`yymmdd`	`981231`
	112	`yyyymmdd`	`19981231`
Europe default milliseconds	13, 113[b]	`dd Mon yyyy hh:mi:ss:mmm`	`31 Dec 1998 23:59:59:996`
	14, 114[b]	`hh:mi:ss:mmm`	`23:59:59:996`

[a] These styles can be converted only one way—from datetime to a string. If you attempt backward conversion from a string formatted this way to datetime, CONVERT returns a NULL value and an arithmetic overflow message.

[b] Microsoft-only styles not supported by Sybase.

The following example finds the number of orders placed on every day of 1994:

```
SELECT  CONVERT( CHAR(10), ord_date, 101 ) 'Order Date',
        COUNT(*) 'Number of Orders'
FROM    sales
WHERE   DATEPART( year, ord_date ) = 1994
GROUP BY CONVERT( CHAR(10), ord_date, 101 )
```

Results:

```
Order Date Number of Orders
---------- ----------------
09/13/1994 2
09/14/1994 6
```

The next example selects the current date and time with the maximum possible precision:

```
SELECT CONVERT( CHAR(26), CURRENT_TIMESTAMP, 109 )
```

Results:

```
--------------------------
Oct 15 1997  6:23:05:070PM
```

You can also create your own formats by combining parts of other styles. For example, you may want to select date and time as mm/dd/yyyy hh:mi:ss:mmm in a 24-hour format. Transact-SQL does not convert datetime data to such a style. The next query solves the problem:

```
SELECT  CONVERT( CHAR(10), CURRENT_TIMESTAMP, 101 ) + ' ' +
        CONVERT( CHAR(12), CURRENT_TIMESTAMP, 114 )
```

Results:

```
-----------------------
10/15/1997 18:23:33:983
```

If your SQL Server has to talk to other systems, it may need to convert dates to ISO format with microseconds: yyyy-mm-dd-hh:mi:ss:mmmmmm. The next expression converts the current time into this format:

```
SELECT  SUBSTRING( CONVERT( CHAR(10), CURRENT_TIMESTAMP, 110 ), 7, 4 )
        + '-' +
        SUBSTRING( CONVERT( CHAR(10), CURRENT_TIMESTAMP, 110 ), 1, 6 )
                 + CONVERT( CHAR(12), CURRENT_TIMESTAMP, 114 ) + '000'
```

Results:

```
--------------------------
1997-10-15-18:24:31:006000
```

Converting CHAR to DATETIME

Strings in any of the supported formats may be converted to DATETIME implicitly. But in many cases, you still need to use the CONVERT function for explicit conversion.

As we mentioned before, some of the formats to which DATETIME data can be converted do not convert back to DATETIME from a string. Moreover, there are some additional string formats that may also be converted to DATETIME. SQL Server does not mind converting strings with incomplete information about date and time to the DATETIME type. It substitutes defaults for time elements that are not provided, as illustrated in Table 12-20.

Table 12-20. Default Date and Time Values in a String-to-DATETIME Conversion

DATETIME Element Not Specified	Default Value Substituted
Date (year, month, day)	January 1, 1900
Century omitted (2-digit year)	Years 50–99 convert to 1950–1999, years 00–49 convert to 2000–2049.
Hours, minutes, seconds, milliseconds	12:00 A.M.
A.M. or P.M. not specified	24-hour scale assumed
Minutes, seconds, milliseconds	0 minutes, 0 seconds, 0 milliseconds
Seconds, milliseconds	0 seconds, 0 milliseconds
Milliseconds	0 milliseconds
Any other omission of one or a combination of date and time elements	Error

For example, the following query selects a DATETIME value equal to 6:30 A.M. of the current day:

```
SELECT  CONVERT( DATETIME,
            CONVERT( CHAR(10), CURRENT_TIMESTAMP, 101 ) + ' 6:30AM')
```

Results:

```
---------------------------
Oct 15 1997  6:30AM
```

One important setting that affects how strings are interpreted when converted to DATETIME is the programmatically controlled DATEFORMAT, which specifies the order of day, month, and year numbers in a string. The following example demonstrates that, depending on the DATEFORMAT setting, the same expression may yield completely different results:

```
SET DATEFORMAT mdy
SELECT CONVERT( DATETIME, '01/02/03' )
SET DATEFORMAT ymd
SELECT CONVERT( DATETIME, '01/02/03' )
```

```
SET DATEFORMAT dmy
SELECT CONVERT( DATETIME, '01/02/03' )
```

Results:

```
---------------------------
Jan 2 2003 12:00AM

---------------------------
Feb 3 2001 12:00AM

---------------------------
Feb 1 2003 12:00AM
```

In order to avoid confusion and unpredictable results, we recommend that you use all four digits to specify a year and that you spell the month name rather than specify its number. Then, regardless of DATEFORMAT, the result is predictable. For example, instead of 01/02/03, use Jan 2 2003.

More examples are included in Table 12-21.

Table 12-21. Examples of CHAR to DATETIME Conversion

Value of Local Variable @string	Result of SELECT CONVERT(datetime, @string) on Server with DATEFORMAT Set to mdy
'12/31/98'	Dec 31 1998 12:00AM
'98.12.31'	NULL, arithmetic overflow occurred.
'1998.12.31'	Dec 31 1998 12:00AM
'31/12/1998'	NULL, arithmetic overflow occurred.
'31.12.1998'	NULL, arithmetic overflow occurred.
'31-12-1998'	NULL, arithmetic overflow occurred.
'December 31, 1998'	Dec 31 1998 12:00AM
'01:02:03'	Jan 1 1900 1:02AM
'01.02.03'	Jan 2 2003 12:00AM
'010203'	Feb 3 2001 12:00AM
'1998/12/31'	Dec 31 1998 12:00AM
'1999/12/31 23:59:59:999'	Jan 1 2000 12:00AM (milliseconds may get rounded)
' '	Jan 1 1900 12:00AM

We have intentionally made some of these examples counterintuitive to demonstrate how CONVERT handles differently formatted date and time strings.

Starting with SQL Server 6.5, Microsoft offers the ISDATE function, which validates whether a string could be converted to DATETIME. That function is discussed in the "System Functions" section later in this chapter. If you need to convert character data to DATETIME but are not sure if it is properly formatted, apply the ISDATE function first to check whether conversion is possible. This may help to avoid runtime errors.

Explicit and implicit conversions

SQL Server automatically converts between some datatypes when they are used in the same expression or comparison. You may still use the CONVERT function when you are unsure or in order to make your code more self-documenting.

Even when certain datatype conversions are supported, some values cannot be converted. For example, you cannot convert alphabetic characters to a numeric value, although a character string consisting of digits could be converted. In other cases, conversion may be allowed, but the result may be truncated, such as in a TEXT-to-CHAR conversion.

Conversion of numeric expressions may result in precision loss when the target type has a different number of decimal places, such as in the following example. The value is rounded when converted to NUMERIC(3,0) and truncated when converted to INT. To avoid confusion, you can use the ROUND function to perform rounding when you need it.

```
SELECT CONVERT( NUMERIC(3,0), 987.654 )

-----------
988

SELECT CONVERT( INT, 987.654 )

-----------
987
```

The rules that govern implicit and explicit conversion between datatypes are not always intuitive. Most numeric datatypes convert to each other implicitly. Currently supported conversions are shown in Table 12-22. In the table, I means conversion is implicit; E that it is explicit (use CONVERT); U that it is undefined; and X that it is not allowed. Where a slash (/) appears, the Microsoft behavior is on the left and the Sybase behavior is on the right.

Table 12-22. Transact-SQL Datatype Conversions

To:	TINYINT/ SMALLINT/INT	FLOAT/ REAL	NUMERIC/ DECIMAL	MONEY	SMALLMONEY	BIT	DATETIME/ SMALLDATETIME	CHAR/ VARCHAR	BINARY/ VARBINARY	TEXT	IMAGE
From:											
TINYINT/SMALLINT/ INT	I	I	I	I	I	I	X	E	I	X	X
FLOAT/REAL	I	I	I	I	I	I	X	E	X/I	X	X

Table 12-22. Transact-SQL Datatype Conversions (continued)

To:	TINYINT/ SMALLINT/INT	FLOAT/ REAL	NUMERIC/ DECIMAL	MONEY	SMALLMONEY	BIT	DATETIME/ SMALLDATETIME	CHAR/ VARCHAR	BINARY/ VARBINARY	TEXT	IMAGE
NUMERIC/DECIMAL	I	I	I	I	I	I	X	E	E/I	X	X
MONEY/ SMALLMONEY	I	I	I	I	I	I	X	E/I	I	X	X
BIT	I	I	I	I	I	I	X	E/I	I	X	X
DATETIME/ SMALLDATETIME	X	X	X	X	X	X	I	E	E/I	X	X
CHAR/VARCHAR	E	E	E	E	E	E	I	I	E/I	I	I
BINARY/VARBINARY/ TIMESTAMP	I	X/I	X/I	I	X/I	I	I	I	I	X	I
TEXT	X	X	X	X	X	X	X	E	X	U/X	X
IMAGE	X	X	X	X	X	X	X	X	E/I	X	U/X

It may be safer to use the CONVERT function than to rely on implicit conversion. It protects you from possible changes of these rules in future versions of SQL Server and also makes your code more self-documenting. Certain conversion rules differ in Microsoft's and Sybase's implementations. If you want to write portable code, use the least-common-denominator approach. For example, if one vendor supports implicit conversion and another only explicit, then use the CONVERT function.

The performance implications of using CONVERT are negligible. In many cases, SQL Server would have to implicitly perform the same or similar conversion anyway. But be careful not to apply CONVERT to index columns in a WHERE clause. Wrapping index columns in any expression or function disables the index.

Conversion rules may seem complicated, but they are the price of flexibility. Most other computer languages are not nearly as permissive as Transact-SQL and would never allow, for example, an automatic conversion of character to datetime or binary to money type.

Even if conversion between datatypes is supported, the target datatype should have sufficient length and precision to accept the new value. For example, you can generally convert an INT value into a TINYINT, but only if the INT value is within the allowed TINYINT range—between 0 and 255. Conversion between any integer, floating point, numeric, and money types fails if the value is outside of the target datatype range.

Precision may be lost and the resulting value may be either truncated to the nearest integer (when converted to integer types) or rounded to the nearest decimal digit determined by precision (when converting to floating-point or numeric types).

We have already discussed rules for missing datetime elements, such as missing time or missing date and what is substituted by default. Remember that milliseconds are rounded to the nearest smallest unit of time—every third millisecond. When DATETIME is converted to SMALLDATETIME, seconds and milliseconds are lost.

Character and binary strings are simply truncated to fit the target type length. Truncation does not result in any error or warning.

On Microsoft SQL Server, you may use the ISDATE and ISNUMERIC functions to check if a string could be converted to the DATETIME or NUMERIC type. These are discussed later in the "System Functions" section.

Sybase supports implicit conversions from any type other than TEXT to BINARY or VARBINARY. On Microsoft SQL Server, any type except for FLOAT, REAL, and TEXT can be converted to BINARY or VARBINARY when you need to look at the internal hexadecimal representation of the value. If the source value is longer than the target binary type, then only the rightmost bytes are converted. If the source is shorter than the target type, then it is padded with zeros on the left.

Converting any supported type to BIT promotes any nonzero value to 1.

STR

The STR function converts any numeric data to character strings. While CONVERT is very flexible and provides a variety of options, the STR function gives you better control over that particular type of conversion. It is easier to format the results of any numeric data conversion to character.

STR has the following syntax:

```
STR( numeric_expression [, length [, precision] ] )
```

where `length` defines the length of the resulting string in bytes, and `precision` defines the number of decimal positions. The default precision value is zero. Zero precision results in rounding to the nearest integer value. The default length is 10. If the specified or default length is insufficient to represent the result, then the whole string is filled with * characters to indicate overflow.

One more difference from CONVERT is that STR returns results right-justified, while CONVERT strings are left-justified. You may use this fact to format one way or another as needed.

It is possible to program any numeric-to-character conversion with the CONVERT function only, but STR allows you to write more compact code that is easier to read. Table 12-23 shows examples of STR use and how it could be replaced with CONVERT.

Table 12-23. STR and CONVERT Comparison Examples

Expression	Result
`STR( 123.456, 5, 1 )`	`123.5`
`CONVERT( CHAR(5), CONVERT( NUMERIC(5,1), 123.456 ))`	`123.5`
`STR( 123456 )`	~~bbbb~~123456
`CONVERT( CHAR(10), 123456 )`	123456~~bbbb~~
`RIGHT( SPACE(10) + RTRIM( CONVERT( CHAR(10), 123456 )), 10 )`	~~bbbb~~123456
`STR( 123456, 4 )`	`****`
`CONVERT( CHAR(4), 123456 )`	*~~bbb~~

INTTOHEX and HEXTOINT

Sybase provides two conversion functions (not currently supported by Microsoft) that deal with integer and platform-independent hexadecimal transformations.

HEXTOINT("hexadecimal_string")

Returns a platform-independent integer value of `hexadecimal_string`. The argument should be enclosed in quotes to distinguish it from platform-dependent binary data.

INTTOHEX(integer_expression)

Returns a platform-independent hexadecimal value of `integer_expression`. The result value is not prefixed with 0x as a binary type.

These functions are necessary to ensure that your application Transact-SQL code is portable from one type of hardware and operating system to another. Because Microsoft SQL Server runs on only one operating system (Windows NT), it does not need this function.

Table 12-24 shows examples of these functions.

Table 12-24. INTTOHEX and HEXTOINT Examples

Expression	Result
`HEXTOINT( "0x00010000" )`	`1024`
`INTTOHEX( 15 )`	`0000000F`

System Functions

Transact-SQL system functions include the following; for each, we show the values returned.

COALESCE
: First non-NULL argument from a list of arguments

COL_LENGTH
: Column length in bytes

COL_NAME
: Column name, given table ID, and column ID

CURRENT_USER
: Username in the current database of the current session

DATA_PGS
: Number of pages allocated for table data

DATALENGTH
: Argument length in bytes

DB_ID
: Database ID, given name

DB_NAME
: Database name, given ID

GETANSINULL
: Default nullability setting for new columns

HOST_ID
: Workstation ID of a given process

HOST_NAME
: Process hostname

IDENT_INCR
: Identity column increment value

IDENT_SEED
: Identity seed value

INDEX_COL
: Index column name, given table ID, index ID, and column sequential number in the index key

ISDATE
: Validates if a character string can be converted to DATETIME

ISNULL
: Returns the first argument if it is not NULL; otherwise, returns the second argument

ISNUMERIC
: Validates if a character string can be converted to NUMERIC

LCT_ADMIN
: Last-chance threshold control

NULLIF
: Returns NULL if two arguments are equal; otherwise, returns the first argument

OBJECT_ID
: Object ID, given name

OBJECT_NAME
: Object name, given ID

PROC_ROLE
: Verifies user roles

RESERVED_PGS
: Number of database pages reserved for a table

ROWCNT
: Estimated number of rows in a table

SESSION_USER
: Username in the current database

SHOW_ROLE
: All roles of a given user

STATS_DATE
: Date and time when index statistics were last updated

SUSER_ID
: System user ID of a given login name

SUSER_NAME
: Login name of given system user ID

SYSTEM_USER
: Login name for the current session

TSEQUAL
: Verifies whether TIMESTAMP value has changed

USED_PGS
: Number of database pages used for table data and indexes

USER
Username in the current database

USER_ID
User ID in the current database

USER_NAME
Username in the current database

VALID_NAME
Validates if a character string can be used as an identifier

System functions allow you to retrieve information from system tables and parameters. Some of them also provide a way to perform logical comparison of data.

ISNULL, NULLIF, and COALESCE: Null Comparisons

Several system functions are used in making comparisons to nulls:

`ISNULL( tested_expression, replacement_expression )`
Returns the value of the `tested_expression` if it is not null and the value of `replacement_expression` if `tested_expression` is null. Expressions must be of the same datatype or implicitly convertible to the same datatype. ISNULL does not support TEXT and IMAGE data.

`NULLIF( expression1, expression2 )`
Returns null if two expressions are equal; otherwise, returns `expression1`. Arguments may be of any Transact-SQL datatype except for TEXT and IMAGE. Microsoft has supported this function from Version 6.x, and Sybase added it in Version 11.5.

`COALESCE( expression1, expression2, … expressionN )`
Returns the first non-null expression from the given list. Arguments may be of any Transact-SQL datatype. Microsoft has supported this function from Version 6.x, and Sybase added it in Version 11.5.

In the following example of ISNULL, the query substitutes a dash for null values in an outer join:

```
SELECT  a.au_id,
        a.au_lname,
        title_id = ISNULL( t.title_id, '-' )
FROM    authors a,
        titleauthor t
WHERE   a.au_id *= t.au_id
    AND a.au_lname LIKE 'S%'
```

Results:

```
au_id       au_lname                                 title_id
----------- ---------------------------------------- --------
341-22-1782 Smith                                    -
274-80-9391 Straight                                 BU7832
724-08-9931 Stringer                                 -
```

The ISNULL function does not always work as you may expect on columns of an outer-joined table, as illustrated by the following example:

```
SELECT  a.au_id,
        a.au_lname,
        title_id = ISNULL( t.title_id, '-' )
FROM    authors a,
        titleauthor t
WHERE   a.au_id *= t.au_id
    AND a.au_lname LIKE 'S%'
    AND ISNULL( t.title_id, '-' ) = '-'
```

Results:

```
au_id       au_lname                                 title_id
----------- ---------------------------------------- --------
341-22-1782 Smith                                    -
274-80-9391 Straight                                 -
724-08-9931 Stringer                                 -
```

We've added one new condition to the WHERE clause, but the query still returns all three rows back; plus, it now loses the value of title_id even where it is available.

Believe it or not, vendors insist that the ISNULL behavior is by design. Indeed, SQL Server documentation warns you that you should get undefined results when you compare null to a column of an inner table participating in an outer join. (You could call it a "feature"!) By comparison, some other RDBMS vendors allow such comparison and return results not contradicting common sense.

The NULLIF function is equivalent to the following CASE expression, which we'll discuss in the next chapter:

```
CASE
    WHEN expression1 = expression2
    THEN NULL
    ELSE expression1
END
```

The COALESCE function is equivalent to the following CASE expression:

```
CASE
    WHEN expression1 IS NOT NULL THEN expression1
    WHEN expression2 IS NOT NULL THEN expression2
```

```
    ...
    WHEN expressionN IS NOT NULL THEN expressionN
    ELSE NULL
END
```

It may also be replaced with a series of nested ISNULL functions:

```
ISNULL( expression1,
ISNULL( expression2,
...
ISNULL( expression<N-1>, expressionN ) ... ) )
```

The following query selects the publisher name and state if it is located in the United States, or the specified country:

```
SELECT  pub_name,
        COALESCE( state, country ) 'location'
FROM    publishers
```

Results:

```
pub_name                                 location
---------------------------------------- --------------------------
New Moon Books                           MA
Binnet & Hardley                         DC
Algodata Infosystems                     CA
Five Lakes Publishing                    IL
Ramona Publishers                        TX
GGG&G                                    Germany
Scootney Books                           NY
Lucerne Publishing                       France

(8 row(s) affected)
```

The next query selects the number of titles available in each category. It substitutes null for UNDECIDED book type.

```
SELECT   NULLIF( type, 'UNDECIDED' ) 'category',
         COUNT(*) '# of titles'
FROM     titles
GROUP BY NULLIF( type, 'UNDECIDED' )
```

Results:

```
category     # of titles
------------ -----------
(null)       1
business     4
mod_cook     2
popular_comp 3
psychology   5
trad_cook    3

(6 row(s) affected)
```

ISDATE, ISNUMERIC, and VALID_NAME: Datatype Checking

Starting with SQL Server 6.5, Microsoft provides several very useful functions you can use to validate if a VARCHAR string could be converted to another type:

ISDATE(string_expression)
: Returns 1 if the `string_expression` could be converted to a DATETIME without an error and returns 0 otherwise.

ISNUMERIC(string_expression)
: Returns 1 if the `string_expression` could be converted to a NUMERIC type without an error and returns 0 otherwise.

VALID_NAME(character_expression)
: Returns 0 if `character_expression` is not a valid Transact-SQL identifier and a nonzero otherwise. A string may be deemed an invalid identifier if it contains illegal characters or if it is longer than 30 characters.

The following example selects all sales orders that have a numeric order number:

```
SELECT  stor_id, ord_num, title_id, qty
FROM    sales
WHERE   ISNUMERIC( ord_num ) = 1
```

Results:

```
stor_id ord_num              title_id qty
------- -------------------- -------- ------
6380    6871                 BU1032   5

(1 row(s) affected)
```

The following stored procedure finds all orders placed on a given date. It validates that the supplied date is properly formatted.

```
CREATE PROC get_orders
    @order_date VARCHAR(26)
AS

DECLARE @valid_date DATETIME

IF ISDATE( @order_date ) = 0
BEGIN
    SELECT 'Parameter', @order_date, 'is not a valid date format'
    RETURN
END
ELSE SELECT @valid_date = CONVERT( DATETIME, @order_date )

SELECT  stor_id, ord_num, title_id, qty
FROM    sales
WHERE   ord_date = @valid_date
GO
```

If we execute the procedure with an invalid date, it produces an error message and exits gracefully:

```
exec get_orders '02/30/1993'
```

Results:

```
--------- -------------------------- -------------------------
Parameter 02/30/1993                 is not a valid date format

(1 row(s) affected)
```

Now let's execute the same procedure with a valid date parameter:

```
exec get_orders '06/15/1992'
```

Results:

```
stor_id ord_num              title_id qty
------- -------------------- -------- ------
7067    P2121                TC3218   40
7067    P2121                TC4203   20
7067    P2121                TC7777   20

(3 row(s) affected)
```

DB-ID, DBNAME, and GETANSINULL: Retrieving Information About Databases

The following functions retrieve various types of information about databases:

DB_ID(['database_name'])
: Returns the ID of the given database. If no argument is given, then the ID of the current database is returned.

DB_NAME([database_id])
: Returns the name of the database identified by the given `database_id` or the name of the current database if no argument is specified.

GETANSINULL(['database_name'])
: Returns the status of the database option defining default nullability for columns of new tables. The value of the function is 1 if database option ANSI null default for the specified database is turned on and 0 otherwise. When this option is set, columns will allow null values unless their datatype explicitly restricts nulls. The current database is assumed if no argument is specified.

Here is an example of obtaining a single database ID:

```
SELECT DB_ID( 'pubs' )
```

Results:

```
------
4

(1 row(s) affected)
```

You can obtain the whole list of database IDs by executing the system stored procedure *sp_helpdb* or by querying the system table mastersys..databases:

```
SELECT dbid, name FROM master..sysdatabases
```

Results:

```
dbid   name
------ ------------------------------
1      master
3      model
5      msdb
4      pubs
2      tempdb

(5 row(s) affected)
```

The following example retrieves a single database name:

```
SELECT  DB_NAME( 4 )
```

Results:

```
------------------------------
pubs

(1 row(s) affected)
```

The same result may be selected with the following query:

```
SELECT  name
FROM    master..sysdatabases
WHERE   dbid = 4
```

OBJECT_ID, OBJECT_NAME, and STATS_DATE: Retrieving Information About Database Objects

OBJECT_ID('[owner_name.]object_name')

Returns the ID of the object from the system table sysobjects. The object ID is automatically assigned by SQL Server to every object and is guaranteed to be unique within its database. The function returns NULL if the specified object does not exist.

OBJECT_NAME(object_id [, database_id])

Returns the object name corresponding to the given `object_id` from the system table sysobjects. Microsoft's version of this function takes only one parameter, **object_id**, and works in the context of the current database. Sybase's implementation of OBJECT_NAME (starting with System 10) allows you to specify **database_id** as the second parameter, which makes it easy to obtain object names in other databases.

STATS_DATE(table_id, index_id)

Returns the date and time when index statistics were last updated. **table_id** is an object ID from system tables sysobjects and sysindexes. **index_id** is the value of the "indid" column from sysindexes for a specific table.

Here is an example of OBJECT_ID:

```
SELECT  titles      = OBJECT_ID( 'titles' ),
        byroyalty   = OBJECT_ID( 'byroyalty' ),
        titleview   = OBJECT_ID( 'dbo.titleview' ),
        sysobjects  = OBJECT_ID( 'sysobjects' ) ,
        my_proc     = OBJECT_ID( 'my_proc' )
```

Results:

```
titles      byroyalty   titleview   sysobjects  my_proc
----------- ----------- ----------- ----------- -----------
192003715   928006337   912006280   1           (null)

(1 row(s) affected)
```

This function may be used to check for object existence, as in the following example:

```
IF OBJECT_ID( 'my_proc' ) IS NOT NULL
BEGIN
    DROP PROC my_proc
    PRINT 'Dropped stored procedure my_proc'
END
```

The following example shows the use of the OBJECT_NAME function:

```
SELECT  OBJECT_NAME( 192003715 ), OBJECT_NAME( 2 )
```

Results:

```
------------------------------ ------------------------------
titles                         sysindexes

(1 row(s) affected)
```

Selecting OBJECT_NAME in the current database is equivalent to executing the following query:

```
SELECT  name
FROM    sysobjects
WHERE   id = <object_id>
```

In order to find the actual table and index name to which STATS_DATE refers, you may execute the following command:

```
SELECT  table_name = OBJECT_NAME( <table_id> ),
        index_name = name
FROM    sysindexes
WHERE   id    = <table_id>
    AND indid = <index_id>
```

DATA_PGS, RESERVED_PGS, ROWCNT, and USED_PGS: Retrieving Information About Table Sizes

Any database table size is characterized by several parameters:

- Number of rows
- Total space reserved for the table
- Space reserved for data
- Space reserved for indexes
- Space reserved, but not yet used, by data or indexes (derived from the previous three parameters)

SQL Server makes an effort to dynamically maintain this information in the system table sysindexes. However, due to implementation techniques, the information there is not always accurate. From the user's perspective, this is a bug. Vendors, however, insist that this design is due to performance considerations. They say that it would be too expensive in terms of SQL Server resources to maintain 100% accurate row and page counts in sysindexes.

Sybase provides several system functions to retrieve table size information from sysindexes. Microsoft maintains the same structure of sysindexes as in older versions, where table size parameters are directly available in sysindexes without special transformation. Both vendors support the system stored procedure *sp_spaceused*, which reports all parameters of a table size in kilobytes. However, the information returned by this procedure is also not guaranteed to be accurate, because it is also based on sysindexes. We discuss *sp_spaceused* in Chapter 17, *System and Extended Stored Procedures*.

The following functions retrieve information about table sizes:

DATA_PGS(object_id, {doampg | ioampg})
: Returns the number of pages reserved for table data (doampg) or index (ioampg). This function is supported only by Sybase. doampg and ioampg are the names of the columns in Sybase system table sysindexes.

RESERVED_PGS(object_id, {doampg | ioampg})
Returns the number of data or index pages reserved for the specified table. This function is supported only by Sybase.

ROWCNT(doampg)
Returns the number of rows in a table. This function is supported only by Sybase.

USED_PGS(object_id, doampg, ioampg)
Returns the number of pages used by the specified table and its clustered index. This function is supported only by Sybase.

Although the DATA_PGS function is not supported by Microsoft SQL Server, you can select the number of pages reserved for data and indexes from the system table sysindexes as follows:

```
SELECT  data_pages = SUM(
            CASE
                WHEN indid <   2 THEN dpages
                WHEN indid = 255 THEN used
                ELSE 0
            END ),
        index_pages = SUM(
            CASE
                WHEN indid NOT IN ( 0, 1, 255 ) THEN used
                ELSE 0
            END )
FROM    sysindexes
WHERE   id = <object_id>
```

In order to get results for table titles you can substitute `OBJECT_ID( 'titles' )` `for` `<object_id>` in the preceding and execute the query.

Results:

```
data_pages  index_pages
----------- -----------
3           2

(1 row(s) affected)
```

Remember that the size of a data page is 2 KB. Microsoft SQL Server 7.0 uses 8 KB pages. This query does not work on Sybase SQL Server except for 4.x versions, because the structure of system table sysindexes is now different from the one on Microsoft SQL Server.

You can issue the following query on Microsoft SQL Server to obtain the same result you'd get from the Sybase ROWCNT function:

```
SELECT  rows
FROM    sysindexes
WHERE   id = <object_id>
    AND indid < 2
```

Retrieving Information About Table Columns

The following functions retrieve information about table columns:

COL_LENGTH('table', 'column')
: Returns the length of the specified column of the specified table in bytes. The function reports the internal length of the column, not the actual length of any particular value. For variable-length character and binary columns, the result of COL_LENGTH is the declared maximum length. For TEXT and IMAGE columns, it is 16 bytes, because that is the length of the pointer to the TEXT or IMAGE data pages. The length of INT columns is 4 bytes; MONEY, 8 bytes, and so on.

COL_NAME(table_id, column_id)
: Returns the name of the column defined by the `column_id` in the table defined by the `table_id`.

DATALENGTH
: Returns the length in bytes of a given argument. We discussed this function under "String Functions," because it is most frequently used with string arguments.

IDENT_INCR('table_or_view')
: Returns the increment value set for the identity column of a specified table or view. The result is of a NUMERIC type. If `table_or_view` does not have an identity value or does not exist, then the result is NULL.

IDENT_SEED('table_or_view')
: Returns the seed value used at creation of the identity column of a specified table or view. The result is of a NUMERIC type. If `table_or_view` does not have an identity value or does not exist, then the result is NULL.

INDEX_COL('table_name', index_id, key_id)
: Returns the name of an index column of the specified table. `index_id` has a value of the ID column in the sysindexes table. `key_id` is the sequential number of the column in the index. If any parameter is invalid (nonexistent table, index, or key), then NULL is returned.

The following query is equivalent to issuing the COL_NAME function:

```
SELECT  name
FROM    syscolumns
WHERE   id = <table_id>
    AND colid = <column_id>
```

This example shows several of the functions:

```
SELECT  'table'  = OBJECT_NAME( id ),
        'column' = COL_NAME( id, colid ),
        'length' = COL_LENGTH( OBJECT_NAME( id ), COL_NAME( id, colid ) )
```

```
FROM    syscolumns
WHERE   id = OBJECT_ID( 'authors' )
```

Results:

```
table                          column                         length
------------------------------ ------------------------------ ------
authors                        au_id                          11
authors                        au_lname                       40
authors                        au_fname                       20
authors                        phone                          12
authors                        address                        40
authors                        city                           20
authors                        state                          2
authors                        zip                            5
authors                        contract                       1

(9 row(s) affected)
```

This example illustrates the use of IDENT_SEED:

```
SELECT IDENT_SEED( 'jobs' ) seed, IDENT_INCR( 'jobs' ) increment
```

Results:

```
seed                           increment
------------------------------ ------------------------------
1                              1

(1 row(s) affected)
```

Retrieving Information About User Session

The following functions retrieve information about the user session:

CURRENT_USER
: Returns the name of the user executing the command as defined in the current database. This is a niladic function and does not require any arguments.

HOST_ID()
: Returns the workstation identification.

HOST_NAME()
: Returns the name of the host process. By default, it is the name of the workstation or server running the process, but it can be explicitly set to any string at the time the connection is made. For example, if you use ISQL from a DOS prompt, you can control the hostname by using the /H switch.

PROC_ROLE("sa_role" | "sso_role" | "oper_role")
: Returns 1 if the current user has the specified role and returns 0 otherwise. This function is provided only by Sybase, because Microsoft SQL Server does not support roles.

SESSION_USER
: Is a niladic function. It requires no arguments and returns the name of the user in the current database. If the user's login does not have a user account in the current database, then the function returns 'guest'.

SHOW_ROLE()
: Returns all roles of the current user, or NULL if the user has no roles. This function is supported only by Sybase.

SUSER_ID(['login_name'])
: Returns the user's system login ID from table mastersys..logins.

SUSER_NAME([system_user_id])
: Returns the login name for the specified suid from table mastersys..logins.

SYSTEM_USER
: Is a niladic function. It requires no parameters and returns the login name as found in table mastersys..logins for the current user. It is equivalent to the function SUSER_NAME().

USER_ID(['user_name'])
: Returns the user ID in the current database—column uid from table sysusers.

USER_NAME([user_id])
: Returns the username in the current database as found in table sysusers for the given uid.

USER
: Is a niladic function. It requires no parameters and returns the user's name in the current database as found in the table sysusers. It is equivalent to the USER_NAME() function. If the current user does not have an account in the current database, then the result is 'guest'.

This example shows the use of many of these functions:

```
SELECT '
CURRENT_USER', CURRENT_USER, '
HOST_ID     ', HOST_ID(), '
HOST_NAME   ', HOST_NAME(), '
SESSION_USER', SESSION_USER, '
SUSER_ID    ', SUSER_ID(), '
SUSER_NAME  ', SUSER_NAME(), '
SYSTEM_USER ', SYSTEM_USER, '
USER_ID     ', USER_ID(), '
USER_NAME   ', USER_NAME(), '
USER        ', USER
```

Results:

```
-----------------------------...
CURRENT_USER dbo
HOST_ID      00000067
```

```
HOST_NAME    Test
SESSION_USER dbo
SUSER_ID     1
SUSER_NAME   sa
SYSTEM_USER  sa
USER_ID      1
USER_NAME    dbo
USER         dbo

(1 row(s) affected)
```

The workstation identification available through HOST_ID can also be obtained via the following query:

```
SELECT hostprocess FROM master..sysprocesses WHERE spid = @@spid
```

If you use ISQL with the HOST_NAME function, the following command:

```
isql /E /HTestProcess /Q"SELECT host_name()"
```

returns:

```
TestProcess
```

regardless of the workstation from which it was submitted.

In place of the SUSER_ID function, you could execute the following command to obtain the same information:

```
SELECT  suid
FROM    master..syslogins
WHERE   name = '<login_name>'
```

In place of SUSER_NAME, you could issue:

```
SELECT  name
FROM    master..syslogins
WHERE   suid = <system_user_id>
```

LCT_ADMIN and TSEQUAL: Other System Functions

These system functions don't fall into any of the other categories:

LCT_ADMIN({{ "lastchance" | "logfull" | "unsuspend"} , database_id} | "reserve", log_pages})

Controls the last-chance threshold of a transaction log. This function is supported only by Sybase and is used by database administrators.

TSEQUAL(timestamp1, timestamp2)

Compares two timestamp values. This function is very useful when your application selects a row without a holding a lock on it and later attempts to update the same row.

Consider the following scenario. User A selects a customer record for modification. It takes him five minutes to enter new address information. While he is doing that, User B selects the same customer record to change the credit rating. It takes her three minutes to enter the data. User B saves the row, then User A saves the same row, unknowingly overriding changes made by User B. To protect data from being lost due to concurrent access by multiple users, you could lock the table, but this would put some users on hold until locks are released.

Another method, called *optimistic concurrency,* allows any user to retrieve the record but also stores the timestamp value of the row at the time of SELECT. When a user saves the row, the previously saved timestamp should be compared to the current timestamp. If some other user has already modified the row, then the current timestamp is different. If the row has not changed, then the timestamp is the same.

The TSEQUAL function raises error 532, indicating that the timestamp has changed, and the UPDATE query fails. The error code should be analyzed by the application to determine further action. Usually the application should allow the user to retrieve the row again and reapply changes.

The following example creates a table with a TIMESTAMP column and executes two stored procedures—to retrieve title information and to update the on-hand quantity. The second procedure ensures that the row has not changed since retrieval. It uses the TSEQUAL function to compare the previously retrieved timestamp value to the current one.

```
SET NOCOUNT ON
CREATE TABLE ##new_titles (
    title_id    CHAR(6),
    on_hand_qty SMALLINT,
    ts          TIMESTAMP
)
INSERT  ##new_titles ( title_id, on_hand_qty )
VALUES               ( 'AA2000', 10000       )
GO

CREATE PROC ##get_title
    @title_id    CHAR(6),
    @on_hand_qty SMALLINT  OUTPUT,
    @ts          BINARY(8) OUTPUT
AS
SELECT  @on_hand_qty = on_hand_qty, @ts = ts
FROM    ##new_titles
WHERE   title_id = @title_id
GO

CREATE PROC ##update_title
    @title_id    CHAR(6),
    @on_hand_qty SMALLINT,
    @check_ts    BINARY(8)
```

```
AS
UPDATE  ##new_titles
SET     on_hand_qty = @on_hand_qty
WHERE   title_id    = @title_id
    AND tsequal( ts, @check_ts )
GO

DECLARE @title_id CHAR(6), @on_hand_qty SMALLINT, @ts BINARY(8)
-- retrieve one row and its current timestamp
EXEC ##get_title 'AA2000', @on_hand_qty OUTPUT, @ts OUTPUT
-- update the row if it has not changed since retrieval
EXEC ##update_title 'AA2000', 8000, @ts
-- one more attempt to update the row fails because it has been modified
-- by the first update since the timestamp was retrieved
EXEC ##update_title 'AA2000', 7500, @ts
GO
DROP TABLE ##new_titles
DROP PROC  ##get_title
DROP PROC  ##update_title
SET NOCOUNT OFF
GO
```

The first execution of ##update_title works fine. It changes the on-hand quantity and also the value of the timestamp column. The second attempt to update the same row fails with the following message:

```
Msg 532, Level 16, State 1
The timestamp (changed to 0x0000000100001f8e) shows that the row has been
updated by another user.
DB-Library Process Dead - Connection Broken
```

Suppose that two users take orders for new titles over the phone. User A receives an order for 2,000 items of title AA2000, and user B gets an order for 2,500 items of the same. They concurrently execute the ##get_title procedure to find out how many items are available. Both get an on-hand quantity of 10,000. User A wants to reduce the quantity by 2000 to reflect an order he has taken over the phone, so he executes procedure ##update_title to set the remaining quantity to 8,000. A minute later, User B tries to execute ##update_title to set the remaining on-hand quantity to 7500. But this is wrong, because the quantity has already changed. The procedure prevents User B from updating the row, because User A has already updated it.

Chapter 11, *Transactions and Locking*, discusses locking in detail.

Summary

This chapter discusses the Transact-SQL functions. Some of these functions are used in practically every application, while others are exotic or redundant. Knowing Transact-SQL functions is critical to success in SQL Server programming. Functions can be used in SELECT, WHERE, GROUP BY, ORDER BY, HAVING, and

COMPUTE clauses. They may be nested up to 10 levels deep. Note that Microsoft and Sybase implementations of Transact-SQL have diverged, and some functions are supported by only one vendor. Remember the following:

- Aggregate functions compute sum, average, minimum, and maximum values of a table column and count rows in a table. They are also used in HAVING and COMPUTE clauses of SELECT queries.
- Mathematical functions perform calculations; compute trigonometric, exponential, and logarithm values; produce absolute values; generate random numbers; and perform other functions.
- String functions are arguably the most frequently used functions. They concatenate strings (+), search strings for certain values (CHARINDEX and PATINDEX), extract parts of a string (SUBSTRING and RIGHT), convert to lower or uppercase (LOWER and UPPER), strip arguments of leading or trailing blanks (LTRIM and RTRIM), and provide other ways of transforming character data.
- Date functions find parts of a DATETIME value (DATEPART and DATENAME), add intervals to dates (DATEADD), calculate the difference between dates (DATEDIFF), and report current time (GETDATE and CURRENT_TIMESTAMP).
- Text and image functions manipulate TEXT and IMAGE data. These datatypes have a number of restrictions on use with other functions and require special handling.
- Type conversion functions transform data from one type to another. Transact-SQL has complicated rules for implicit and explicit type conversions. Use the CONVERT function to be sure of the result. CONVERT provides a variety of formatting styles when you convert DATETIME values to character strings.
- System functions retrieve values from system tables and internal SQL Server variables (e.g., USER_ID, HOST_NAME, COL_NAME, IDENT_SEED, OBJECT_ID, DB_NAME, etc.), compare values to NULL (ISNULL, NULLIF, and COALESCE), validate datatypes (ISDATE and ISNUMERIC), and perform other operations.

13

In this chapter:
- *CASE Expressions*
- *COMPUTE*
- *CUBE and ROLLUP*
- *Summary*

CASE Expressions and Transact-SQL Extensions

This chapter discusses several powerful Transact-SQL constructs: CASE, COMPUTE, CUBE, and ROLLUP. CASE expressions are relatively new to Transact-SQL but are ANSI standard and make some complicated programming tasks incredibly easy to implement. CASE often helps to improve query performance by an order of magnitude.

COMPUTE is a clause of a SELECT query. CUBE and ROLLUP are operators of a GROUP BY clause of a SELECT query, introduced by Microsoft in SQL Server 6.5. COMPUTE, CUBE, and ROLLUP all produce additional summary rows embedded in the result set. They are very helpful in report generation. CUBE and ROLLUP have been specifically added to Transact-SQL to improve support of multidimensional reporting and online analytical processing (OLAP) tools. COMPUTE, CUBE, and ROLLUP are Transact-SQL extensions of the SQL language; they are not ANSI standards.

CASE Expressions

CASE expressions are supported by Microsoft starting from SQL Server 6.0 and by Sybase from Version 11.5. This language construct is very efficient and makes many practical tasks easy. Essentially, CASE allows you to write expressions with conditional logic and use them anywhere expressions could be used. In this section, we'll discuss the syntax of CASE and provide some practical examples of its usage.

CASE Syntax

There are two forms of a CASE expression: simple and searched.

A simple CASE expression compares one value with a list of other values and returns a result associated with the first matching value. It has the following syntax:

```
CASE expression0
     WHEN expression1 THEN result_expression1
     [[WHEN expression2 THEN result_expression2] [...]]
     [ELSE result_expressionN]
END
```

This expression compares **expression0** with **expression1**, **expression2**, and so on, until it finds a match or reaches the end of the list. If it finds that an expression is equal to **expression0**, then it returns the corresponding **result_expression**. If no match is found at all, then it returns **result_expressionN**.

A searched CASE expression allows the analysis of several logical conditions and returns a result associated with the first one that is true. It has the following syntax:

```
CASE
    WHEN condition1 THEN expression1
    [[WHEN condition2 THEN expression2] [...]]
    [ELSE expressionN]
END
```

This expression evaluates **condition1**, **condition2**, and so on, until it finds one that is true or reaches the end of the list. If a true condition is found, then the result is the corresponding expression. If all conditions are false, then the result is **expressionN**. If the ELSE part of the CASE is not specified, and all conditions are false, then the result is NULL.

CASE stops searching the list as soon as it finds the first satisfying value (simple CASE) or condition (searched CASE). Therefore, it is important to organize WHEN elements in the right order, in case several elements may qualify.

Examples of CASE Usage

This section contains several examples showing the range of capabilities available with CASE expressions.

Example 1—Simple CASE expression

This example selects the list of authors except for those who live in California and indicates whether they have a contract. The report contract indicator is Yes or No rather than the bit values of 1 and 0 found in the contract column. The following query uses a simple CASE expression to produce the Yes/No contract indicator:

```
SELECT  au_fname,
        au_lname,
        CASE contract
            WHEN 1 THEN 'Yes'
            ELSE 'No'
```

```
        END 'contract'
FROM    authors
WHERE   state <> 'CA'
```

Results:

```
au_fname             au_lname                                 contract
-------------------- ---------------------------------------- --------
Meander              Smith                                    No
Morningstar          Greene                                   No
Reginald             Blotchet-Halls                           Yes
Innes                del Castillo                             Yes
Michel               DeFrance                                 Yes
Sylvia               Panteley                                 Yes
Anne                 Ringer                                   Yes
Albert               Ringer                                   Yes

(8 row(s) affected)
```

A traditional approach to this query implementation would be to use UNION. However, UNION requires two scans of the authors table, while CASE requires only one table scan.

```
SELECT  au_fname,
        au_lname,
        contract = 'Yes'
FROM    authors
WHERE   state <> 'CA'
    AND contract = 1
UNION ALL
SELECT  au_fname,
        au_lname,
        contract = 'No'
FROM    authors
WHERE   state <> 'CA'
    AND contract <> 1
```

The same result could be obtained in a single table scan without using CASE. The following query returns the same information. It is as efficient as the one with CASE but is not as easy to understand:

```
SELECT  au_fname,
        au_lname,
        SUBSTRING( 'No Yes', contract * 3 + 1, 3 ) 'contract'
FROM    authors
```

This query deserves some explanation. Remember that the contract column in the authors table is populated with values 1 and 0. When contract is equal to 1, then expression `contract * 3 + 1` is equal to 4 and `SUBSTRING('No Yes',4,3)` produces Yes. If contract is zero, then expression `contract * 3 + 1` yields 1 and `SUBSTRING('No Yes',1,3)` returns No. This technique was employed by Transact-SQL programmers seeking stellar query performance before CASE expressions were implemented. You can still use it today, but CASE is much easier to code and support. Although we discuss the *characteristic functions* approach in Chapter 20, *Transact-SQL Optimization and Tuning,* we recommend that you always use CASE expressions instead of characteristic functions.

Example 2—Searched CASE expression

This example reports how many titles have been sold in different year-to-date sales ranges. The following query uses a searched CASE expression in SELECT and also in the GROUP BY clause:

```
SELECT  CASE
            WHEN ytd_sales IS NULL  THEN 'Unknown'
            WHEN ytd_sales <=   200 THEN 'Not more than 200'
            WHEN ytd_sales <=  1000 THEN 'Between  201 and  1000'
            WHEN ytd_sales <=  5000 THEN 'Between 1001 and  5000'
            WHEN ytd_sales <= 10000 THEN 'Between 5001 and 10000'
            ELSE 'Over 10000'
        END 'YTD Sales',
        COUNT(*) 'Number of Titles'
FROM titles
GROUP BY
        CASE
            WHEN ytd_sales IS NULL  THEN 'Unknown'
            WHEN ytd_sales <=   200 THEN 'Not more than 200'
            WHEN ytd_sales <=  1000 THEN 'Between  201 and  1000'
            WHEN ytd_sales <=  5000 THEN 'Between 1001 and  5000'
            WHEN ytd_sales <= 10000 THEN 'Between 5001 and 10000'
            ELSE 'Over 10000'
        END
ORDER BY MIN( ytd_sales )
```

Results:

```
YTD Sales              Number of Titles
---------------------- ----------------
Unknown                2
Not more than 200      1
Between  201 and  1000 2
Between 1001 and  5000 9
Between 5001 and 10000 1
Over 10000             3

(6 row(s) affected)
```

Example 3—Simple CASE expression

This example discounts all computer-related titles by 25%. We define these as all titles of type popular_comp and all books with the word "computer" in the title. We discount all other titles by 10%. We exclude from the preceding discounts titles with year-to-date sales exceeding 10,000 and discount those by 5% only. Let's first select the data with current prices:

```
SELECT type, title = SUBSTRING( title, 1, 50 ), price FROM titles
```

Results:

```
type         title                                              price
------------ -------------------------------------------------- ------
business     The Busy Executive's Database Guide                19.99
business     Cooking with Computers: Surreptitious Balance Shee 11.95
business     You Can Combat Computer Stress!                    2.99
business     Straight Talk About Computers                      19.99
mod_cook     Silicon Valley Gastronomic Treats                  19.99
mod_cook     The Gourmet Microwave                              2.99
UNDECIDED    The Psychology of Computer Cooking                 (null)
popular_comp But Is It User Friendly?                           22.95
popular_comp Secrets of Silicon Valley                          20.00
popular_comp Net Etiquette                                      (null)
psychology   Computer Phobic AND Non-Phobic Individuals: Behavi 21.59
psychology   Is Anger the Enemy?                                10.95
psychology   Life Without Fear                                  7.00
psychology   Prolonged Data Deprivation: Four Case Studies      19.99
psychology   Emotional Security: A New Algorithm                7.99
trad_cook    Onions, Leeks, and Garlic: Cooking Secrets of the  20.95
trad_cook    Fifty Years in Buckingham Palace Kitchens          11.95
trad_cook    Sushi, Anyone?                                     14.99

(18 row(s) affected)
```

The following UPDATE query uses a searched CASE expression to perform price adjustment:

```
UPDATE  titles
SET     price = price *
            CASE
                WHEN ytd_sales > 10000
                    THEN 0.95   -- 5% discount
                WHEN type = 'popular_comp'
                    OR CHARINDEX( 'computer', LOWER( title ) ) > 0
                    THEN 0.75   -- 25% discount
                ELSE 0.9        -- 10% discount
            END
```

Once the update is done, we need to look at the new price list:

```
SELECT type, title = SUBSTRING( title, 1, 50 ), price FROM titles
```

Results:

```
type         title                                              price
------------ -------------------------------------------------- ------
business     The Busy Executive's Database Guide                17.99
business     Cooking with Computers: Surreptitious Balance Shee 8.96
business     You Can Combat Computer Stress!                    2.84
business     Straight Talk About Computers                      14.99
mod_cook     Silicon Valley Gastronomic Treats                  17.99
mod_cook     The Gourmet Microwave                              2.84
UNDECIDED    The Psychology of Computer Cooking                 (null)
popular_comp But Is It User Friendly?                           17.21
```

```
popular_comp Secrets of Silicon Valley                          15.00
popular_comp Net Etiquette                                      (null)
psychology   Computer Phobic AND Non-Phobic Individuals: Behavi 16.19
psychology   Is Anger the Enemy?                                9.86
psychology   Life Without Fear                                  6.30
psychology   Prolonged Data Deprivation: Four Case Studies      17.99
psychology   Emotional Security: A New Algorithm                7.19
trad_cook    Onions, Leeks, and Garlic: Cooking Secrets of the  18.86
trad_cook    Fifty Years in Buckingham Palace Kitchens          11.35
trad_cook    Sushi, Anyone?                                     13.49

(18 row(s) affected)
```

Without CASE, the same operation could be done with three separate UPDATEs as shown in the following code sample. However, it would require three table scans as opposed to one. A CASE expression makes the query much more efficient:

```
UPDATE  titles
SET     price = price * 0.95
WHERE   ytd_sales > 10000

UPDATE  titles
SET     price = price * 0.75
WHERE   ytd_sales <= 10000
    AND ( type = 'popular_comp'
    OR    CHARINDEX( 'computer', LOWER( title ) ) > 0
        )

UPDATE  titles
SET     price = price * 0.9
WHERE   ytd_sales <= 10000
    AND type != 'popular_comp'
    AND CHARINDEX( 'computer', LOWER( title ) ) = 0
```

Example 4—Cross-tab query

This example selects a cross-tab report of quarterly sales by year:

```
SELECT  DATEPART( year, ord_date ) 'Year',
        SUM(CASE DATEPART(quarter,ord_date) WHEN 1 THEN qty ELSE 0 END) Q1,
        SUM(CASE DATEPART(quarter,ord_date) WHEN 2 THEN qty ELSE 0 END) Q2,
        SUM(CASE DATEPART(quarter,ord_date) WHEN 3 THEN qty ELSE 0 END) Q3,
        SUM(CASE DATEPART(quarter,ord_date) WHEN 4 THEN qty ELSE 0 END) Q4
FROM    sales
GROUP BY DATEPART( year, ord_date )
```

Results:

```
Year        Q1          Q2          Q3          Q4
----------- ----------- ----------- ----------- -----------
1992        0           80          0           0
1993        60          165         0           25
1994        0           0           163         0

(3 row(s) affected)
```

This example provides a solution for a very popular business task of converting one-dimensional results (sales in this case) to a two-dimensional table. A similar query could show sales by month of a year, yearly sales by title, or use some other two dimensions. It is important that the number of values in one dimension (horizontal) should be fixed. In this example, there are four quarters in each year, so we know there will be a fixed number of columns in the result set. The number of values in the vertical dimension (years in this case) may be variable.

Example 5—CASE statement with subqueries

This example reports year-to-date sales of every title compared to the best, worst, and average of all titles.

```
SELECT  CASE
            WHEN ytd_sales IS NULL
                THEN 'Unknown'
            WHEN ytd_sales = ( SELECT MAX( ytd_sales ) FROM titles )
                THEN 'Bestseller'
            WHEN ytd_sales = ( SELECT MIN( ytd_sales ) FROM titles )
                THEN 'Worst'
            WHEN ytd_sales < ( SELECT AVG( ytd_sales ) FROM titles )
                THEN 'Below Average'
            ELSE 'At or Above Average'
        END 'Year-To-Date Sales',
        Title = SUBSTRING( title, 1, 50 )
FROM    titles
ORDER BY ISNULL( ytd_sales, -1 ) DESC
```

Results:

```
Year-To-Date Sales  Title
------------------- --------------------------------------------------
Bestseller          The Gourmet Microwave
At or Above Average You Can Combat Computer Stress!
At or Above Average Fifty Years in Buckingham Palace Kitchens
At or Above Average But Is It User Friendly?
Below Average       The Busy Executive's Database Guide
Below Average       Straight Talk About Computers
Below Average       Secrets of Silicon Valley
Below Average       Sushi, Anyone?
Below Average       Prolonged Data Deprivation: Four Case Studies
Below Average       Cooking with Computers: Surreptitious Balance Shee
Below Average       Emotional Security: A New Algorithm
Below Average       Is Anger the Enemy?
Below Average       Silicon Valley Gastronomic Treats
Below Average       Computer Phobic AND Non-Phobic Individuals: Behavi
Below Average       Onions, Leeks, and Garlic: Cooking Secrets of the
Worst               Life Without Fear
Unknown             The Psychology of Computer Cooking
Unknown             Net Etiquette

(18 row(s) affected)
```

The same result set could be obtained with six separate SELECT statements combined together through UNION or UNION ALL. But that approach would require additional table scans, and UNION would result in the creation of a temporary worktable. Overall, the code would be significantly less efficient. CASE allows us to considerably optimize query performance.

Example 5 demonstrates that you can use a subquery in a CASE statement. If performance of the query were an issue, we would declare three variables to hold maximum, minimum, and average ytd_sales values, then select these three values from the titles table in a single SELECT and use variables in place of subqueries.

COMPUTE

COMPUTE is a clause of a SELECT query. It produces summary rows in a result set for groups of rows and grand totals for the whole result set. COMPUTE appears in a query after ORDER BY and has the following syntax:

```
COMPUTE aggregate_function( column_or_expression )
[, aggregate_function( column_or_expression )...]
[BY column_or_expression [, column_or_expression ]...]
```

COMPUTE calculates aggregate functions on columns or expressions. An aggregate is produced for every group of rows defined by a combination of items in the BY list.

You usually need an ORDER BY clause if you want to use COMPUTE. The only exception is SELECT queries that use COMPUTE to obtain grand totals, where ORDER BY is optional. Items of the BY list should be the first items of the ORDER BY clause and should appear in exactly the same order. ORDER BY may have more items. You can use several COMPUTE clauses in the same SELECT statement when you need to calculate totals by smaller and larger groups and grand totals. The general syntax is the following:

```
ORDER BY item1 [, item2 ... [, itemN [, itemN1 [, itemN2 [, ...] ] ] ] ... ]
COMPUTE ... [ BY item1 [, item2 ... [, itemN  [, itemN1 ] ] ... ] ]
[ COMPUTE ... [ BY item1 [, item2 ... [, itemN ] ... ] ]
... ]
```

Aggregate functions can be applied only to items that appear in the BY list. If BY is omitted, then COMPUTE calculates grand totals for the whole result set.

The results of COMPUTE appear as separate rows in the output. Unfortunately, you have very little control over the formatting of these results, as you will see in a moment.

The following query selects all business and popular computing titles and their year-to-date sales. In addition, it computes average year-to-date sales for all selected rows:

```
SELECT  type, title_id, ytd_sales
FROM    titles
WHERE   type IN ( 'business', 'popular_comp' )
COMPUTE AVG( ytd_sales )
```

Results:

```
type         title_id ytd_sales
------------ -------- -----------
business     BU1032   4095
business     BU1111   3876
business     BU2075   18722
business     BU7832   4095
popular_comp PC1035   8780
popular_comp PC8888   4095
popular_comp PC9999   (null)

                      avg
                      ===========
                      7277

(8 row(s) affected)
```

The next example retrieves the same set of rows and computes total advance and average year-to-date sales for every type and also for the whole result set:

```
SELECT  type, title_id, advance, ytd_sales
FROM    titles
WHERE   type IN ( 'business', 'popular_comp' )
ORDER BY type
COMPUTE SUM( advance ), AVG( ytd_sales ) BY type
COMPUTE SUM( advance ), AVG( ytd_sales )
```

Results:

```
type         title_id advance                    ytd_sales
------------ -------- -------------------------- -----------
business     BU1032   5,000.00                   4095
business     BU1111   5,000.00                   3876
business     BU2075   10,125.00                  18722
business     BU7832   5,000.00                   4095

                      sum
                      ==========================
                      25,125.00
                                                 avg
                                                 ===========
                                                 7697
```

```
type         title_id advance                   ytd_sales
------------ -------- ------------------------- -----------
popular_comp PC1035   7,000.00                  8780
popular_comp PC8888   8,000.00                  4095
popular_comp PC9999   (null)                    (null)

                      sum
                      =========================
                      15,000.00
                                                avg
                                                ===========
                                                6437
                      sum
                      =========================
                      40,125.00
                                                avg
                                                ===========
                                                7277

(10 row(s) affected)
```

As these two examples demonstrate, computed aggregates always appear in the same columns to which they are applied and have a heading of the aggregate function name. What if you want your report to have some special text to the left of the aggregated value, such as "Total:"? Sorry, Transact-SQL cannot do that for you. It may also appear annoying that several aggregates for the same set of rows cannot appear in one line. In the previous example, SUM and AVG show up in a "staircase" style. Imagine what a report would look like if we computed a dozen aggregates. COMPUTE has its drawbacks, but for a quick-and-dirty result that still contains essential information, COMPUTE is a very useful tool.

It is important that COMPUTE aggregates be generated "on the fly," as SQL Server produces rows of the result set. This way, it does not have to make additional table scans in order to compute summary rows. This makes the query almost as fast as the same SELECT without COMPUTE.

The use and limitations of aggregate functions are discussed in more detail in Chapter 12, *Functions*. COMPUTE also imposes additional restrictions:

- The DISTINCT keyword cannot be used.
- Items of the COMPUTE clause should appear in the SELECT clause.
- ORDER BY is required if COMPUTE has a BY list.
- When COMPUTE is used with BY items, the COMPUTE clause should appear in the same order as the first items of the ORDER BY clause.
- COMPUTE cannot be used with SELECT INTO.

CUBE and ROLLUP

CUBE and ROLLUP are optional operators of a GROUP BY clause of a SELECT query. Microsoft has implemented them in SQL Server 6.5. Sybase does not support these operators. The general syntax of a GROUP BY is:

```
GROUP BY [ALL] expression1 [, expression2 [, ...] ] [WITH {CUBE | ROLLUP}]
```

Both CUBE and ROLLUP result in the generation of additional rows in the result set. These two switches have been added specifically to support OLAP and multidimensional reporting tools that usually require computation of summary values and present two-dimensional relational tables as multidimensional cubes.

We'll discuss the CUBE operator first, because ROLLUP produces just a "slice" of CUBE's results.

CUBE

A SELECT query using GROUP BY WITH CUBE returns all rows that it would return without the CUBE switch, *plus* super-aggregate rows for every possible combination of GROUP BY keys. The result set may be interpreted as a multidimensional *cube*, thus giving the name to the switch. This multidimensional geometry requires some abstract thinking. Nobody has ever seen a four-dimensional figure, let alone the fifth and higher dimensions. We can only imagine them. But we don't mean to imply that WITH CUBE is an operator used in theoretical math research. It has very practical applications in generating rows for multidimensional analysis tools, also known as OLAP.

Microsoft has added the CUBE operator specifically to support OLAP tools. Such systems typically present data as multidimensional cubes and have all possible aggregate values precomputed and ready to serve. Think of it as a fast-food restaurant that has all the regular menu items cooked before you even walk in. Many people prefer their meals cooked to order rather than microwaved. But here is the difference between burgers and data. As long as ingredients (raw data) do not change, you can cook summaries today and quickly fetch them a week later—it will be the same quality. You probably cannot do the same with your lunch.

A dimension of a data cube is an entity of values, such as years, states, book titles, or stores. Some applications require building and analyzing cubes with a dozen or more dimensions. Don't you like the terms used in multidimensional analysis, such as "slice and dice" or "drill down"?

WITH CUBE and WITH ROLLUP only support up to 10 dimensions. This should suffice for most practical purposes, even though online transaction processing (OLTP) gurus claim that 20 dimensions is a better limit.

For example, we can present the sales table as a three-dimensional cube. Dimensions are stores, titles, and year of the order date. The table in pubs is rather large for our example purposes, so we restricted the results to only those titles whose title_id begins with P. The following query selects all the data elements without super-aggregates:

```
SELECT   stor_id,
         title_id,
         DATEPART( year, ord_date ) 'year',
         SUM( qty ) 'qty'
FROM     sales
WHERE    title_id LIKE 'P%'
GROUP BY stor_id, title_id, DATEPART( year, ord_date )
```

Results:

```
stor_id title_id year        qty
------- -------- ----------- -----------
6380    PS2091   1994        3
7066    PC8888   1993        50
7066    PS2091   1994        75
7067    PS2091   1994        10
7131    PS1372   1993        20
7131    PS2091   1994        20
7131    PS2106   1993        25
7131    PS3333   1993        15
7131    PS7777   1993        25
8042    PC1035   1993        30

(10 row(s) affected)
```

You could also present these results as the 3-D cube shown in Figure 13-1.

Each cell of this cube contains a detail data element—a total number of books of a particular title sold in a particular store in a particular year. A cell is empty if none were sold. For example, a cell with coordinates stor_id = 7066, title_id = PC8888, and year = 1993 contains the value of 50.

Let's execute the same query with the CUBE option:

```
SELECT   stor_id,
         title_id,
         DATEPART( year, ord_date ) 'year',
         SUM( qty ) 'qty'
```

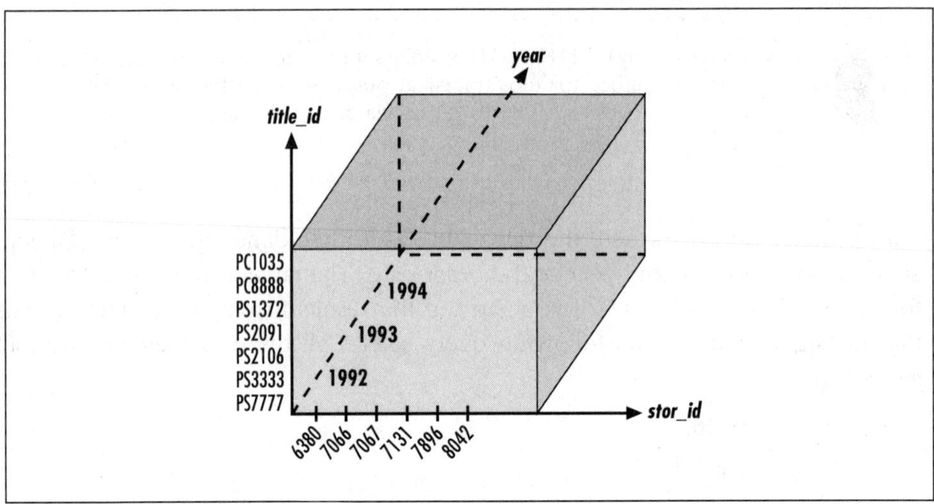

Figure 13-1. Graphical representation of SELECT WITH CUBE results

```
FROM     sales
WHERE    title_id LIKE 'P%'
GROUP BY stor_id, title_id, DATEPART( year, ord_date )
WITH CUBE
```

Now the result set contains 10 original rows plus 39 new rows:

```
stor_id title_id year        qty
------- -------- ----------- -----------
6380    PS2091   1994        3
6380    PS2091   (null)      3
6380    (null)   (null)      3
7066    PC8888   1993        50
7066    PC8888   (null)      50
7066    PS2091   1994        75
7066    PS2091   (null)      75
7066    (null)   (null)      125
7067    PS2091   1994        10
7067    PS2091   (null)      10
7067    (null)   (null)      10
7131    PS1372   1993        20
7131    PS1372   (null)      20
7131    PS2091   1994        20
7131    PS2091   (null)      20
7131    PS2106   1993        25
7131    PS2106   (null)      25
7131    PS3333   1993        15
7131    PS3333   (null)      15
7131    PS7777   1993        25
7131    PS7777   (null)      25
7131    (null)   (null)      105
8042    PC1035   1993        30
8042    PC1035   (null)      30
```

```
8042     (null)   (null)     30
(null)   (null)   (null)     273
(null)   PC1035   1993       30
(null)   PC1035   (null)     30
(null)   PC8888   1993       50
(null)   PC8888   (null)     50
(null)   PS1372   1993       20
(null)   PS1372   (null)     20
(null)   PS2091   1994       108
(null)   PS2091   (null)     108
(null)   PS2106   1993       25
(null)   PS2106   (null)     25
(null)   PS3333   1993       15
(null)   PS3333   (null)     15
(null)   PS7777   1993       25
(null)   PS7777   (null)     25
7066     (null)   1993       50
7131     (null)   1993       85
8042     (null)   1993       30
(null)   (null)   1993       165
6380     (null)   1994       3
7066     (null)   1994       75
7067     (null)   1994       10
7131     (null)   1994       20
(null)   (null)   1994       108

(49 row(s) affected)
```

The CUBE switch generates additional rows that contain NULL in one or more key columns. Each of these rows represents a super-aggregate for some key combination. In order to find total sales in a particular store for all titles and all years, you need to find a row in the result set with the desired stor_id and NULL in title_id and year columns. If you are interested in all sales of a particular title for a particular year, then you can search the cube for a row with this title_id and year and NULL in the stor_id column. The row with NULL in all three columns is the grand total of all sales.

The exact result (maybe in a different order) can be obtained through this cumbersome code:

```
-- 1. detail data
SELECT   stor_id,
         title_id,
         DATEPART( year, ord_date ) 'year',
         SUM( qty ) 'qty'
FROM     sales
WHERE    title_id LIKE 'P%'
GROUP BY stor_id, title_id, DATEPART( year, ord_date )
UNION ALL
-- 2. aggregate by store and title
SELECT   stor_id,
         title_id,
```

```
         NULL 'year',
         SUM( qty ) 'qty'
FROM     sales
WHERE    title_id LIKE 'P%'
GROUP BY stor_id, title_id
UNION ALL
-- 3. aggregate by store and year
SELECT   stor_id,
         NULL 'title_id',
         DATEPART( year, ord_date ) 'year',
         SUM( qty ) 'qty'
FROM     sales
WHERE    title_id LIKE 'P%'
GROUP BY stor_id, DATEPART( year, ord_date )
UNION ALL
-- 4. aggregate by title and year
SELECT   NULL 'stor_id',
         title_id,
         DATEPART( year, ord_date ) 'year',
         SUM( qty ) 'qty'
FROM     sales
WHERE    title_id LIKE 'P%'
GROUP BY title_id, DATEPART( year, ord_date )
UNION ALL
-- 5. aggregate by store
SELECT   stor_id,
         NULL 'title_id',
         NULL 'year',
         SUM( qty ) 'qty'
FROM     sales
WHERE    title_id LIKE 'P%'
GROUP BY stor_id
UNION ALL
-- 6. aggregate by title
SELECT   NULL 'stor_id',
         title_id,
         NULL 'year',
         SUM( qty ) 'qty'
FROM     sales
WHERE    title_id LIKE 'P%'
GROUP BY title_id
UNION ALL
-- 7. aggregate by year
SELECT   NULL 'stor_id',
         NULL 'title_id',
         DATEPART( year, ord_date ) 'year',
         SUM( qty ) 'qty'
FROM     sales
WHERE    title_id LIKE 'P%'
GROUP BY DATEPART( year, ord_date )
UNION ALL
-- 8. grand total
SELECT   NULL 'stor_id',
         NULL 'title_id',
```

```
         NULL 'year',
         SUM( qty ) 'qty'
FROM     sales
WHERE    title_id LIKE 'P%'
```

Not only is this script longer, it performs poorly. In our example, it took eight table scans and required 201 I/O operations compared to just one table scan and 24 I/O operations for the query with CUBE. The difference may be even more dramatic on large cubes with more than three dimensions.

By now, you may be wondering how you can use the CUBE operator in practical programming. If you have a multidimensional OLAP tool, it may take advantage of the switch by executing queries on your relational database and building data cubes. You do not have to code these queries; the software does it automatically. OLAP provides a user-friendly interface for you to access the cube data and retrieve details or aggregates from it.

Cube tables are very handy in implementing decision-support systems. You may build a system that produces reports with different summary data. Such systems usually allow you to enter different combinations of keys and request aggregates on an ad hoc basis. In order to speed up report generation, you may precompute all aggregates and keep them in a special cube table ready for retrieval. In our example, the cube table would have the following structure:

```
CREATE TABLE sales_cube (
    stor_id   CHAR(4)  NULL,
    title_id  CHAR(6)  NULL,
    ord_year  SMALLINT NULL,
    qty       SMALLINT NULL
)
```

A query using the CUBE operator populates the sales_cube table:

```
INSERT   sales_cube (
         stor_id, title_id,           ord_year,             qty )
SELECT   stor_id, title_id, DATEPART( year, ord_date ), SUM( qty )
FROM     sales
WHERE    title_id LIKE 'P%'
GROUP BY stor_id, title_id, DATEPART( year, ord_date )
WITH CUBE
```

We can set up a recurring task to refresh the table every night. After the table is populated, we can produce any report by selecting from the sales_cube table rather than from sales. For example, we can select the total quantity of sold books by year and title:

```
SELECT  ord_year, stor_id, qty
FROM    sales_cube
WHERE   title_id IS NULL
    AND ord_year IS NOT NULL
    AND stor_id  IS NOT NULL
```

Results:

```
ord_year stor_id qty
-------- ------- ------
1993     7066    50
1993     7131    85
1993     8042    30
1994     6380    3
1994     7066    75
1994     7067    10
1994     7131    20

(7 row(s) affected)
```

The next query selects total sales by title plus the grand total:

```
SELECT   ISNULL( title_id, 'Total:' ) 'title_id', qty
FROM     sales_cube
WHERE    ord_year IS NULL
    AND stor_id  IS NULL
ORDER BY ISNULL( title_id, 'zzzzzz' )
```

The ORDER BY clause of this query allows placing the grand total on the bottom of the result set:

```
title_id qty
-------- ------
PC1035   30
PC8888   50
PS1372   20
PS2091   108
PS2106   25
PS3333   15
PS7777   25
Total:   273

(8 row(s) affected)
```

Notice that queries on the sales_cube table do not require scanning and aggregating raw data. The performance benefits may be negligible on a tiny sample table. But any real decision-support database has millions of rows of data, and quick access to precalculated aggregates makes a huge difference.

ROLLUP

WITH ROLLUP is an option of the GROUP BY clause, which is very similar to WITH CUBE. In fact, it returns just a subset of the rows produced by CUBE. If you have gaps in your understanding of CUBE, please flip a few pages back and then come back here. CUBE and ROLLBACK are mutually exclusive. Only one option can be specified in any single query.

ROLLUP is useful in computing running sums and running averages. Unlike CUBE, which computes aggregates for any possible combination of keys of the GROUP BY, ROLLUP is sensitive to the order of items in the GROUP BY. For N items, it computes aggregates for any combination of the *first* N, N–1, N–2, . . . , 1, 0 items. This may be easier to demonstrate on a real query. Let's use the same example as in the previous section and replace CUBE with ROLLUP:

```
SELECT   stor_id,
         title_id,
         DATEPART( year, ord_date ) 'year',
         SUM( qty ) 'qty'
FROM     sales
WHERE    title_id LIKE 'P%'
GROUP BY stor_id, title_id, DATEPART( year, ord_date )
WITH ROLLUP
```

Remember that the same query with CUBE returned 49 rows. The ROLLUP option restricts it to only 26 rows:

```
stor_id title_id year        qty
------- -------- ----------- -----------
6380    PS2091   1994        3
6380    PS2091   (null)      3
6380    (null)   (null)      3
7066    PC8888   1993        50
7066    PC8888   (null)      50
7066    PS2091   1994        75
7066    PS2091   (null)      75
7066    (null)   (null)      125
7067    PS2091   1994        10
7067    PS2091   (null)      10
7067    (null)   (null)      10
7131    PS1372   1993        20
7131    PS1372   (null)      20
7131    PS2091   1994        20
7131    PS2091   (null)      20
7131    PS2106   1993        25
7131    PS2106   (null)      25
7131    PS3333   1993        15
7131    PS3333   (null)      15
7131    PS7777   1993        25
7131    PS7777   (null)      25
7131    (null)   (null)      105
8042    PC1035   1993        30
8042    PC1035   (null)      30
8042    (null)   (null)      30
(null)  (null)   (null)      273

(26 row(s) affected)
```

In this three-dimensional data set, the query with CUBE aggregates by any combination of keys in any combination of these items:

```
stor_id      title_id     year        SUM( qty )
stor_id      title_id     -           SUM( qty )
stor_id      -            year        SUM( qty )
-            title_id     year        SUM( qty )
stor_id      -            -           SUM( qty )
-            title_id     -           SUM( qty )
-            -            year        SUM( qty )
-            -            -           SUM( qty )
```

ROLLUP aggregates only half of them:

```
stor_id      title_id     year        SUM( qty )
stor_id      title_id     -           SUM( qty )
stor_id      -            -           SUM( qty )
-            -            -           SUM( qty )
```

A "conventional" script producing the same results as the query with ROLLUP follows. Compare it to a union of eight queries in the previous section; that is equivalent to CUBE.

```
-- 1. detail data
SELECT   stor_id,
         title_id,
         DATEPART( year, ord_date ) 'year',
         SUM( qty ) 'qty'
FROM     sales
WHERE    title_id LIKE 'P%'
GROUP BY stor_id, title_id, DATEPART( year, ord_date )
UNION ALL
-- 2. aggregate by store and title
SELECT   stor_id,
         title_id,
         NULL 'year',
         SUM( qty ) 'qty'
FROM     sales
WHERE    title_id LIKE 'P%'
GROUP BY stor_id, title_id
UNION ALL
-- 3. aggregate by store
SELECT   stor_id,
         NULL 'title_id',
         NULL 'year',
         SUM( qty ) 'qty'
FROM     sales
WHERE    title_id LIKE 'P%'
GROUP BY stor_id
UNION ALL
-- 4. grand total
```

```
SELECT    NULL 'stor_id',
          NULL 'title_id',
          NULL 'year',
          SUM( qty ) 'qty'
FROM      sales
WHERE     title_id LIKE 'P%'
```

The next example shows a case in which ROLLUP may be better than CUBE. It selects sales by year, quarter, and month. All three dimensions (year, quarter, and month) are of the same nature. We want totals by year/quarter/month, by year/quarter, and by year. Totals by month or quarter across all years are not important. ROLLUP produces only those super-aggregates we need:

```
SELECT    DATEPART( year,    ord_date ) 'year',
          DATEPART( quarter, ord_date ) 'quarter',
          DATEPART( month,   ord_date ) 'month',
          SUM( qty ) 'qty'
FROM      sales
GROUP BY DATEPART( year,    ord_date ),
          DATEPART( quarter, ord_date ),
          DATEPART( month,   ord_date )
WITH ROLLUP
```

The same query with CUBE would return extra rows that we do not need. The result set would be larger and would take more time to produce. Therefore, ROLLUP is more efficient than CUBE in cases like these. It returns the following results:

```
year        quarter     month       qty
----------- ----------- ----------- -----------
1992        2           6           80
1992        2           (null)      80
1992        (null)      (null)      80
1993        1           2           35
1993        1           3           25
1993        1           (null)      60
1993        2           5           165
1993        2           (null)      165
1993        4           10          15
1993        4           12          10
1993        4           (null)      25
1993        (null)      (null)      250
1994        3           9           163
1994        3           (null)      163
1994        (null)      (null)      163
(null)      (null)      (null)      493

(16 row(s) affected)
```

Summary

This chapter discussed several useful Transact-SQL constructs:

- CASE allows you to embed logical conditions in an expression wherever a function can be used. It is very helpful in many practical tasks. It has two forms: simple and searched. A simple CASE expression compares an expression to a list of other expressions or constants and returns the value associated with the first matching item. A searched CASE evaluates a list of logical expressions and returns the value associated with the first true condition. CASE is supported by Microsoft SQL Server 6.x and Sybase 11.5.
- The COMPUTE clause calculates aggregate functions on selected columns of a result set. It is usually accompanied by an ORDER BY clause. Rows generated by a COMPUTE appear in the result set with their own headers and have somewhat inflexible formatting.
- CUBE and ROLLUP are optional operators of a GROUP BY clause, supported by Microsoft SQL Server 6.5 and later. They generate additional rows with aggregated values. CUBE does it for every conceivable combination of key columns. It is very useful in building multidimensional data cubes for OLAP tools or custom-built decision-support applications. Results returned by CUBE contain all possible aggregates precomputed by every dimension and surface of the cube. ROLLUP also returns aggregated values, but only for a slice of all key combinations used by CUBE. It is useful in producing reports with running totals.

IV

Programming Transact-SQL Objects

While earlier parts of this book present the early courses of a meal, Part IV is the entrée. In these chapters, the details from earlier sections come together to explain how you can build the database objects that are the main workhorses of SQL Server: stored procedures, triggers, views, system stored procedures, and extended stored procedures.

Part IV contains these chapters:

- Chapter 14, *Stored Procedures and Modular Design*
- Chapter 15, *Triggers and Constraints*
- Chapter 16, *Views*
- Chapter 17, *System and Extended Stored Procedures*

14

Stored Procedures and Modular Design

Perhaps you've been slogging through this book, looking for a gem; you're nearing the edges of despair; and then, kaboom, you see neon lights, loud pompous music, a breathtaking view, and a culinary buffet all within a single section of the book. At least we hope this is how you'll feel after you've sampled the wares we plan on sharing with you in Part IV.

Stored procedures are to programmers what steroids are to many bodybuilders; you don't get anywhere without them. Once you acknowledge this, you need to learn how to abuse them as much as they abuse you. Pushing a stored procedure to the limit may not be the same as working with bleeding-edge technology, but it does often allow you to go home early and spend beeper-free nights engrossed in the latest Star Trek episode. In this chapter, we'll start to apply in greater detail all the building blocks we've introduced in the early parts of the book.

In this chapter, we look at stored procedures in detail, review their component parts, and see what role those components play in the construction of stored procedures. Once we've completed the dissection lesson, we'll review some of the many ways these procedures can be applied and issues that will need to be considered depending on how they are utilized. Finally, we'll conclude with a review of basic performance considerations that apply to stored procedures.

About Stored Procedures

A stored procedure is a precompiled set of Transact-SQL statements that can perform iterative conditional and set-based logic on the data in your database server. Stored procedures may have parameters passed to them and may also return result sets.

Besides providing you with the ability to batch Transact-SQL language statements, stored procedures also exhibit a number of special characteristics that enhance their usability. These are the following:

- A stored procedure is compiled when it is executed the first time. The query plan that is generated during this compile is then used for all future executions of this stored procedure or until you explicitly force the stored procedure to create a new query plan. When multiple users access the same stored procedure simultaneously, SQL Server generates a query plan for each user; these may differ based on the data being accessed in each instance.
- A user who does not have explicit access to the tables referred to in a stored procedure may still be given access to run the stored procedure and have data returned.
- A stored procedure that resides on a remote server can be executed from your local server if the required remote access permissions have been set up.
- A stored procedure can be executed from within a trigger.
- The Transact-SQL code of the stored procedure is contained in the syscomments table on the database in which the procedure was created.
- Parameters can be passed to a stored procedure.
- Results can be returned from a stored procedure.
- Stored procedures that are prefixed with *sp_* and are located in the master database can be executed from any database in a server.
- In Sybase, stored procedures prefixed with *sp_* that are stored in the sybsystemprocs database can also be executed from any database in a server.

Consider the following example:

```
CREATE PROCEDURE test_procedure_1
AS
        SELECT *
        FROM authors
GO
```

In this example, test_procedure_1 is the name of the procedure, and the SQL statements between the AS and the GO are the commands performed by this procedure. As we progress through this book, we'll develop a number of very sophisticated stored procedures that incorporate many of the concepts we're introducing.

Before we begin a complete dissection of a stored procedure, let's review how you find out what procedures you have in your database and also how you locate the text in the stored procedure. Many of you will probably be using tools or system stored procedures to do this. For those of you who want to find out this information directly, this is how it's done.

There are a couple of different routes you can choose when you want to locate your stored procedures. You can use the stored procedures created for you already by Microsoft or Sybase, or you can create your own and work directly with the system tables yourself. In this book, we'll show you the latter route since sufficient documentation exists on the former, and calling a stored procedure does not really teach you anything anyway.

To find the names of all the stored procedures in a particular database, you can run the following query:

```
SELECT name
FROM sysoobjects
WHERE type = 'P'
```

To find the actual code of the stored procedure, you can run the following SQL code:

```
SELECT   b.text
FROM     sysobjects a, syscomments b
WHERE    a.id = b.id
AND      a.type = 'P'
ORDER BY a.id, b.colid
```

To limit the comments text to a specific procedure, you would need to add the following line to the WHERE clause:

```
AND a.name = 'test_procedure_1'
```

On the accompanying CD-ROM, we've included some tools that reformat the text returned into chunks that can be directly run into the system again.

CREATE PROCEDURE

The CREATE PROCEDURE statement creates a stored procedure. The syntax for the Microsoft and Sybase versions differs slightly, as shown here.

Microsoft	Sybase

CREATE PROCEDURE
    [owner.]procedure_name[;number]
[[(]@parameter_name datatype [(length)
| (precision [,scale]_]
    [= default][OUTPUT]]
[,@parameter_name datatype [(length) |
(precision [,scale]_]
    [= default][OUTPUT],...]
[{FOR REPLICATION} | {WITH RECOMPILE}
    [{[WITH]|[,]} ENCRYPTION]]
AS SQL_statements
	CREATE PROCEDURE
	    [owner.]procedure_name[;number]
	[[(]@parameter_name datatype [(length)
	| (precision [,scale]_]
	    [= default][OUTPUT]]
	[,@parameter_name datatype [(length) |
	(precision [,scale]_]
	    [= default][OUTPUT],...]
	[{WITH RECOMPILE}]
	AS SQL_statements

WITH ENCRYPTION Option (Microsoft Only)

The WITH ENCRYPTION option allows you to encrypt the textual entry in syscomments of the stored procedure you are creating. Encryption prevents anyone from reviewing the contents of the stored procedure. Unfortunately for you, Microsoft does not include a decryption tool with SQL Server, which means that you cannot retrieve the unencrypted form of the procedure from syscomments. Furthermore, during an upgrade of the SQL Server, these procedures will not be upgraded, and you will have to reinstall them from your original source code. If you do elect to use encryption, make sure you have a backup copy of the stored procedure on disk somewhere.

The algorithm used for encryption in Microsoft's SQL Server is very simple and has been cracked using a couple of lines of Transact-SQL that require no knowledge of passwords or other secrets. Any user with read permission on syscomments can easily decrypt an encrypted object. For more details on the algorithm used, please refer to Tom Sager's article "Reverse Engineering a Database" in the magazine *SQL Server Update*, published by Xephon (November 1998 and December 1998).

Sybase's Adaptive Server Enterprise allows you to encrypt a procedure using the *sp_hidetext* system procedure; see Chapter 17, *System and Extended Stored Procedures*, for details.

FOR REPLICATION Option (Microsoft Only)

In general, replication can invoke a stored procedure when it passes data between servers. When you set up replication in Microsoft SQL Server, you can tell it to replicate data in a couple of different ways: "as is," without any changes between publisher and subscriber, is the most common method. However, you can optionally force all replicated records through a stored procedure by specifying the FOR REPLICATION option.

Stored procedures of this type are most commonly used to enable homegrown bidirectional replication (not normally supported in Microsoft SQL Server). For example, you could have a stored procedure that checks any incoming replicated data to ensure that it was created only on some other server. This would allow records created on server A to replicate out and to receive records from Server B. Server B would receive the record from Server A since it was not created on that server, but then replication would see it as a new transaction and pump it back out. Server A would get its own record back, but the logic in the stored procedure would filter it out.

WITH RECOMPILE Option

If this option is specified, SQL Server will not maintain a precompiled query plan for this procedure and will recompile this procedure every time it is executed. Setting this option effectively minimizes one of the major benefits of stored procedures, the fact that SQL Server doesn't recompile the procedure every time it executes. This option should be used only if the procedure accepts parameters and if *every* time this procedure is called the values are so radically different that the server would need to create a fresh query plan in order to prevent unnecessary table scans.

The benefit of the WITH RECOMPILE command is that when the data returned differs drastically from execution to execution or when users are allowed to use wildcard parameters that change the result set significantly, the procedure can create an appropriate query plan every time.

Examples of Simple Stored Procedures

In order to introduce stored procedures, this section presents several different procedures, each of which illustrates a simple technique. This book and its accompanying CD-ROM will also include many more sophisticated examples that show the real-world applications of these techniques.

Example 1—A procedure with no parameters

```
-- Drop this procedure if it already exists
PRINT "get_author_names"
GO
IF object_id('get_author_names') IS NOT NULL
BEGIN
    DROP PROCEDURE get_author_names
END
GO

CREATE PROCEDURE get_author_names
AS
-- Select a couple of columns from a table
   SELECT name = au_lname+" "+au_fname
```

```
    FROM   pubs.dbo.authors
    ORDER BY au_lname
GO
```

This example, if executed, would produce results similar to the following:

```
name
------------------------------
Bennet Abraham
Blotchet-Halls Reginald
Carson Cheryl
DeFrance Michel
del Castillo Innes
Dull Ann
Green Marjorie
Greene Morningstar
Gringlesby Burt
Hunter Sheryl
....
 (24 row(s) affected)
```

In this first example, we've created a simple procedure to select a couple of columns from a table. Probably the most important thing to learn from this example is the style of writing a procedure and good habits to get into. In this example, we first dropped the procedure if it already existed. We displayed a message with the procedure's name and then created the procedure. The code itself is indented, and we rigorously followed the style and conventions covered in Chapter 5, *Format and Style.* In the remaining examples, we'll leave out the leading code and header information to save space, but they are still implied.

Example 2—Procedure with an IF/ELSE structure

In this example we'll produce a year-to-date summary for sales reports. If the user passes a parameter in, then only a specific year is processed; otherwise, all years are processed. This example introduces both conditional processing and parameter passing.

```
CREATE PROCEDURE get_yearly_sales_summary @year INT = NULL
AS
    IF (@year <> NULL)
    BEGIN
        SELECT "ytd sales" =  (SUM(s.qty) * SUM(t.price)),
               "year" = @year
       FROM sales s,
            titles t
       WHERE t.title_id = s.title_id
       AND   DATEPART(YEAR,s.ord_date) = @year
       GROUP BY DATEPART(YEAR,s.ord_date)
    END
    ELSE
    BEGIN
        SELECT "ytd sales" =  (SUM(s.qty) * SUM(t.price)),
               "year" = DATEPART(YEAR,s.ord_date)
```

```
    FROM sales s,
         titles t
    WHERE t.title_id = s.title_id
    GROUP BY DATEPART(YEAR,s.ord_date)
 END
```

If you execute this procedure, you'll get results similar to the following (assuming that you left the parameter as NULL):

```
ytd sales                  year
-------------------------- -----------
3,831.20                   1992
38,610.00                  1993
14,630.88                  1994
```

Example 3—Procedure with a loop structure

In this example, we'll perform some conditional processing based on the date:

```
CREATE PROCEDURE display_job_info
AS
 DECLARE @job SMALLINT,
     @lineinfo VARCHAR(255)
 SELECT @job = 1

 WHILE @job <= 14 -- currently the max job id in pubs
 BEGIN

    SELECT @lineinfo = 'Job id: '+CONVERT(VARCHAR(3),@job)+' '+job_desc
    FROM   jobs
    WHERE  job_id = @job

    PRINT @lineinfo
    PRINT "Employees associated to this job"
    PRINT " "
    SELECT emp_id, fname
    FROM   employee
    WHERE  job_id = @job

    PRINT " "
    SELECT @job = @job + 1
 END
```

Results:

```
Job id: 1 New Hire - Job not specified
Employees associated to this job

emp_id    fname
--------- --------------------

Job id: 2 Chief Executive Officer
Employees associated to this job

emp_id    fname
--------- --------------------
PTC11962M Philip
```

```
...
Job id: 7 Marketing Manager
Employees associated to this job

emp_id    fname
--------- --------------------
L-B31947F Lesley
PDI47470M Palle
M-L67958F Maria
HAN90777M Helvetius

....
Job id: 14 Designer
Employees associated to this job

emp_id    fname
--------- --------------------
PSA89086M Pedro
KFJ64308F Karin
ENL44273F Elizabeth
```

Example 4—CASE expression

In the next example, we'll use a CASE expression to produce an evaluation of the year-to-date sales for a particular book:

```
CREATE PROCEDURE print_ytd_title_evaluation
AS
   SELECT performance_type =
   CASE
        WHEN ytd_sales < 1000 THEN 'Aweful'
        WHEN ytd_sales BETWEEN 1000 AND 5000 THEN 'Average'
        ELSE 'Brilliant'
   END,
   title,
   title_id,
   price
   FROM titles
```

Results:

```
performance_type  title                                title_id  price
-----------------------------------------------------------------------------
Average           The Busy Executive's Database Guide BU1032    19.99
Brilliant         You Can Combat Computer Stress!     BU2075    2.99
Average           Straight Talk About Computers       BU7832    19.99
Average           Silicon Valley Gastronomic Treats   MC2222    19.99
Brilliant         The Gourmet Microwave               MC3021    2.99
Brilliant         But Is It User Friendly?            PC1035    22.95
....

(19 row(s) affected)
```

Example 5—Temporary stored procedure

In the next example, we'll create a temporary stored procedure that calls a number of standard Transact-SQL functions and global variables:

```
CREATE PROCEDURE #temp_proc_test
AS
    SELECT "Current version" = @@version,
    "Current date " = GETDATE(),
    "Current database" = DB_NAME(),
    "Current user" = USER_NAME()
GO
```

Results:

```
Current version
Microsoft SQL Server  6.50 - 6.50.240 (Intel X86)    Dec 17 1996 15:50:46
Copyright (c) 1988-1996 Microsoft Corporation

Current date              Current database            Current user
Mar 8 1999  8:23PM        pubs                        dbo
```

Parameters

In general, parameters are used to pass values to a stored procedure. In Chapter 6, *Datatypes and Variables*, we discussed the declaration of variables in detail and how to create parameters for stored procedures. Here we'll expand upon the foundation laid in Chapter 6 and use parameters to enhance the functionality of our procedures.

No procedure can have more than 255 parameters passed to it. There can be two problems when passing a large number of parameters to a procedure: it can be extremely complicated to test a stored procedure that you do not know very well, and, for some, the need to pass many parameters may seem restrictive. A way to get around both of these problems is to use a definition table. In the definition table, you would record each parameter name, a description if desired, and a value. Then, in your stored procedure, you would call the definition procedure to set up these variables with the default values, which you can then use in your processing. If you use a definition table, you no longer have to remember the values that are passed to a procedure, and you have automatically created a test suite for your procedures.

This method will also require a minimal amount of disk access to retrieve the data contents from the underlying table and to populate the table to begin with. Although this method circumvents the need to pass parameters, it also means that every time you want to change the way the procedure works, you will need to modify the contents of the definition table. To decide whether this method makes sense for you, you'll want to evaluate the technique based on how your procedures are used in your organization and whether disk access would be a problem. This method has been included here since it is a handy technique to know about.

```
CREATE TABLE definition (theoption VARCHAR(32),
                         thevalue VARCHARS(128))
GO
INSERT definition VALUES ('CATEGORY','business')
INSERT definition VALUES ('YTDSALES','200')

-- Create a generic procedure to get a value from this definition file
CREATE PROCEDURE get_definition @defoption VARCHAR(32),
                                @defvalue VARCHAR(128) OUTPUT
AS
   SELECT @defvalue = thevalue
   FROM   Definition
   WHERE  theoption = @defoption
GO

CREATE PROCEDURE title_details_use_definition
AS
    DECLARE @SERVERTYPE VARCHAR(5),
            @CATEGORY VARCHAR(12),
            @YTDSALES MONEY,
            @CSALES VARCHAR(16)

EXEC get_definition @defvalue = @CATEGORY OUTPUT,
                    @defoption = 'CATEGORY'
EXEC get_definition @defvalue = @CSALES OUTPUT,
                    @defoption = 'YTDSALES'
SELECT @YTDSALES = CONVERT(MONEY,@CSALES)

SELECT t.title_id,
       t.title
FROM   titles t
WHERE  t.type = @CATEGORY
AND    t.ytd_sales >= @YTDSALES
```

There are two other ways in which this problem could have been solved. The first way would have been to hardcode all the values. The problem with this would be that you would either need to create a new procedure with different values every time the WHERE clause changes, or you would have to drop and re-create this procedure. The next example illustrates this method:

```
CREATE PROCEDURE hardcode_all_requirements
AS

SELECT t.title_id,
       t.title
FROM   titles t
```

```
WHERE  t.type = 'business'
AND    t.ytd_sales >= 200
```

Finally, you could have created two simple parameters for this procedure. With this particular example, this method would have been the most appropriate. There are not a large number of parameters; therefore, their values would probably change frequently and you would probably not need to create a sophisticated test suite to test it.

```
CREATE PROCEDURE parameterize_all_requirements @category VARCHAR(32),
                                               @ytdsales MONEY
AS
SELECT t.title_id,
       t.title
FROM   titles t
WHERE  t.type = @category
AND    t.ytd_sales >= @ytdsales
```

Regardless of which method you use, the results will be the same and will look similar to the following:

```
title_id  title
--------  ----------------------------------------------------------------
BU1032    The Busy Executive's Database Guide
BU1111    Cooking with Computers: Surreptitious Balance Sheets
BU2075    You Can Combat Computer Stress!
BU7832    Straight Talk About Computers
```

Table 14-1 provides a comparison of each solution.

Table 14-1. Comparison of Parameter Approaches

Method/Procedure Name	Advantages	Disadvantages
hardcode_all_parameters	Quick and easy.	You would have to rewrite the procedure if anything changed.
parameterize_all_requirements	All values are parameters, so a change would not necessarily require you to rewrite the procedure. The procedure is more versatile since it can be called under a number of different conditions without having to change the procedure itself.	You would now have to code somewhere in a calling program all the values for this procedure. Changes would require you to rewrite Transact-SQL code if this were a called procedure and its parameters were hardcoded. This procedure would have taken you slightly longer to implement.

Table 14-1. Comparison of Parameter Approaches (continued)

Method/Procedure Name	Advantages	Disadvantages
title_details_use_definition	Parameter changes are made to the definition table. If this procedure were called from another procedure, you might effectively save yourself maintenance time since you would probably not need to change the calling procedures call if the values change. Standard utilities would have been written to read this definition table and return the results to some program that uses it. It is easy to change the functioning of a procedure for non-Transact-SQL-literate users. It may help simplify test suite creation.	It's more time consuming to program. The program may be harder to understand. You now rely on a table being populated with values as opposed to code being parameterized. This solution is not applicable for all classes of problems. It is best used when there are a large number of parameters that rarely change or when you need to know precisely what parameters are passed to each procedure. You could create a trigger on the definition file to record all these changes into an audit table.

Each method has merits. Usually the deciding factor is who is going to use this procedure. If it's only you, then usually the parameter-driven or the hardcoded method will be appropriate. If, however, this procedure will need to be bulletproof and used on a large number of different platforms, in different SQL Server environments, and by a large number of individuals who may not even understand Transact-SQL, you would be better served by using a definition file or table to manage the procedure. Imagine for a moment that this were, in fact, a procedure to do an automated custom installation of a product.

Parameter Defaults

The problem with the previous example is that every time the procedure was called, values had to be entered for the two parameters that were created, @category and @ytdsales. In general, with a procedure like this one, the values passed to the procedure will be the same or will be modified very rarely. This type of procedure would benefit by allowing you to specify default values it will assume unless explicitly specified. In this example, only the declaration of the stored procedure has been amended to include defaults for the two parameters:

```
CREATE PROCEDURE parameterize_all_requirements
  @category VARCHAR(32) = 'business',
  @ytdsales MONEY = 200.00
AS
....
```

Since defaults have been specified for both of these variables, it is necessary to specify only the variable that changes. The following examples are all valid ways of calling this procedure now:

```
EXEC parameterize_all_requirements
EXEC parameterize_all_requirements @ytdsales = 100
EXEC parameterize_all_requirements @category = 'mod_cook'
EXEC parameterize_all_requirements @category = 'mod_cook', @ytdsales = 100
```

OUTPUT

The OUTPUT keyword for a parameter is used to indicate whether the value assigned to this variable during procedure execution should be returned to the calling process. This modifier can be very helpful since the return clause can only be used to return a single value, which in many cases may be insufficient for your purposes. Since a maximum of 255 parameters can be passed to a stored procedure, there can be at most 256 (including the return) values returned from a stored procedure in simple variables. Later on in this chapter, we'll look at ways to extend this limitation using result sets. The basic steps to using this feature are as follows:

- Create a stored procedure and include the OUTPUT keyword as part of the creation syntax.
- Execute the procedure including the OUTPUT keyword as part of the call.
- Use the variable's new value!

The following example illustrates this use of the OUTPUT keyword:

```
/* Step 1 - Create the procedure */
CREATE PROCEDURE Check_The_Output_Keyword @varint INT output,
                              @varchar VARCHAR(255) output,
                              @vardate DATETIME output
AS
   SELECT   @varint = db_id(),
            @varchar = @@version,
            @vardate = getdate()
GO
/* Step 2 - Call the procedure */
DECLARE     @lvarint INT,
            @lvarchar VARCHAR(255),
            @lvardate DATETIME

SELECT      @lvarint = 999,
            @lvarchar = 'Havent a clue',
            @lvardate = 'Feb 29 2004'

SELECT      @lvarint, @lvarchar, @lvardate

exec Check_The_Output_Keyword @varint = @lvarint output,
                @varchar =         @lvarchar output,
                @vardate =         @lvardate output
```

```
/* Step 3 - Display the new value */

SELECT @lvarint, @lvarchar, @lvardate
GO
```

Results:

When	@lvarint	@lvardate	@lvarchar
Before execution	999	Feb 29 2004 12:00AM	Haven't a clue
After execution	1	Nov 30 1997 12:52PM	Adaptive Server Enterprise/11.5/P/NT/OS 4.00/1/fbu/Wed Sep 10 03:56:32 PDT 1997

An interesting feature of the OUTPUT keyword on Sybase is that the stored procedure automatically displays the variables and their values after execution for all variables suffixed with the OUTPUT keyword.

RETURN

The RETURN keyword can be used to optionally specify a return value to the calling batch process. For a complete discussion of the RETURN keyword, refer to Chapter 7, *Conditional Processing*.

Types of Stored Procedures

Transact-SQL provides several distinct types of stored procedures:

- Permanent stored procedures
- Temporary stored procedures
- System stored procedures
- Extended stored procedures
- Remote procedure calls
- Auto execution procedures

In general, there are very few differences between the different types of stored procedures. However, certain types have special restrictions or additional features that you'll need to consider when deciding what type of procedure is most appropriate for your particular needs.

Permanent Stored Procedures

A *permanent stored procedure* can exist in any of your user databases. These stored procedures may act on data contained within the database where it resides or on data residing in other databases. Anyone can create procedures in a database, provided they have been given create procedure permission by the DBA. Owners of stored procedures can explicitly grant and revoke execution privileges to any stored procedure they have written.

Permanent stored procedures usually make up the majority of database objects in a SQL Server. These procedures generally contain application-related code. Typical categories of procedures that fall into this group are:

- Transaction processing routines—for example, a new order entry procedure.
- Batch processing routines—for instance, performing a day-end processing routine to move data to a historical database.
- Frequently run queries—for example, creating a daily sales status query to reflect current-day-calculated sales value or creating a transaction list report to reflect the day's transactions.
- Data-checking queries—perhaps creating an invoice-verification routine that totals all the line items to validate whether it still adds up to the calculated invoice total in case someone has erroneously run a delete!

The classifications we have introduced here shouldn't be considered definitive by any stretch of the imagination. The goal of a stored procedure is not to fit into a nice box but rather to serve some business purpose.

Persistent Temporary Stored Procedures

A *persistent temporary stored procedure* is any procedure found in the tempdb database. Every time the server is stopped and started again, tempdb is rebuilt from scratch, and all the objects users created in tempdb will be removed.

Global Temporary Stored Procedures (Microsoft Only)

A *global temporary stored procedure* is any stored procedure that is prefixed by ## during its creation process. These processes will exist as long as the session that creates them exists or as long as the last current process that is accessing the procedure exists, whichever is later. Procedures prefixed by ## can be called by any other process, provided they have the necessary access permissions. There are no special restrictions on these types of procedures.

Local Temporary Stored Procedures (Microsoft Only)

A *local temporary stored procedure* is any procedure that is prefixed by # when it is created. Only the creator of this procedure can use it. This procedure will be dropped as soon as the process that created it exits or the server is shut down, whichever is sooner. There are no special restrictions on these types of procedures.

System Stored Procedures

As part of the installation process, the master database on Microsoft SQL and sybsystemprocs on Sybase are populated with a large body of procedures designed to help you administer and track the database objects in your system. *System stored procedures* differ from regular stored procedures in only one respect: they can be executed in any database without having to explicitly specify the name of the database on which the procedure resides. Anyone who has DBO privilege in master or sybsystemprocs can create a system procedure. The rules relating to system stored procedures are covered in Chapter 17. An overview of the more commonly used system stored procedures is included in Appendix A, *System Tables.* Chapter 10, *Temporary Objects*, discusses temporary stored procedures in more detail.

Extended Stored Procedures

In the Microsoft SQL Server implementation, an *extended stored procedure* is part of the database kernel and exists outside of the system catalog tables. In Sybase ASE, however, an extended stored procedure is managed via the XP Server, which is an open server application that is bundled with the product. Both products allow you to write your own extended procedures and deliver them as part of your applications that reside on SQL Server. An extended stored procedure is written using C. Extended stored procedures are similar to standard stored procedures in that they are called using the EXECUTE command and may be passed parameters and return values and/or result sets. For example:

```
EXECUTE xp_cmdshell 'dir c:\'
```

Extended stored procedures cannot be dropped from SQL Server using the traditional DROP PROCEDURE command.

For a detailed discussion of Sybase- and Microsoft-specific extended stored procedures, see Chapter 17.

Remote Procedure Calls

The only difference between a *remote procedure call* and a permanent stored procedure is that with an RPC, the procedure resides on a different server. In order to execute a procedure that resides on a separate server, you need to do the following:

- Configure SQL Server to allow remote procedure calls; refer to your System Administration manual for details about this.

- Specify the server on which the procedure resides when the procedure is invoked. For example:

```
EXEC CHARDONNAY.master.dbo.sp_helpdb -- for MS SQL Server
EXEC CHARDONNAY.sybsystemprocs.dbo.sp_helpdb --  for Sybase SQL Server
```

- The NT Server must have RPC services installed and running.

In this example, the call is being made from a server other than Chardonnay, which has been configured to allow remote procedure calls with Chardonnay.

Auto Execution Procedures (Microsoft Only)

Microsoft SQL Server allows you to designate a procedure as an *auto execution procedure*, that is, one that executes every time SQL Server starts up. In order to do this, a procedure must conform to the following limitations:

- The procedure cannot accept parameters.
- The procedure must be owned by the SA.
- The procedure must be located in the master database.

In order to specify your procedure as auto execute, you can use the following three system procedures:

sp_makestartup
: This procedure requires the procedure name that needs to be set up as auto execute to be passed to it. This procedure checks that all the requirements stated previously have been met and then updates the category column in sysobjects with its current value | 16. (This is a bitwise operation to set the fifth position when it is not currently set. It applies only to auto execute procedures.)

sp_unmakestartup
: This procedure requires the procedure that needs to be removed from auto executing to be passed to it. Provided that this procedure is found, its category column in sysobjects is set to its current value &~16. (This is a bitwise operation to unset the fifth position if it is set. It applies only to auto execute procedures.)

sp_helpstartup
: This procedure lists all procedures that have been designated as auto execute procedures.

This feature is especially useful when you want to have the server execute a specific task every time the server is booted—for example, writing an audit trail log record, dumping a database, and performing specific processing requirements based on how your organization operates.

Advantages of Stored Procedures

Stored procedures have a number of advantages:

- They give you the ability to precompile an execution plan once that can be executed many times. The precompiled plan can be highly tuned and optimized compared to an ad hoc query or Transact-SQL script written to accomplish the same function.
- A stored procedure is a reusable object. A frequently used set of commands can be put in a procedure and executed from other procedures, batches, and applications.
- Using a stored procedure helps reduce network traffic. Instead of passing a large query with slightly different parameters over and over again from a client machine to the server, you pass a much-shortened EXEC <proc> @parms . . . command.
- Stored procedures allow you to isolate database (backend) logic and functions from the frontend and middle-tier applications. Each procedure is located in one place, the server, and can be easily modified when necessary. If you have a client application installed in multiple places with Transact-SQL code embedded there, then every change in this code requires recompiling and reinstalling the application on every client. Compare this to a stored procedure called from the same application. Changes to the procedure are made in only one place, the server, and the application remains unchanged. This helps to significantly reduce the amount of time required to change something.

Stored procedures are very popular because you can write the code once but execute it as often as needed. With a stored procedure, the logic you used to get to a result is at least recorded in syscomments and can easily be retrieved if you happen to misplace it in your circular filing system. Equally important, if you no longer need a stored procedure, it is a relatively trivial task to remove it from SQL Server.

Later on in this chapter, we'll look at good design techniques for stored procedures that enable you to write generalized procedures that solve a myriad of problems, as opposed to writing a stored procedure for every slightly different problem.

Stored Procedures Versus Other Objects

Using each of the Transact-SQL program constructs effectively is probably the most important thing you will learn to do as you master Transact-SQL. In order to help you, we've created a simple chart (Table 14-2) that summarizes suggested usage scenarios for each of the individual program constructs.

Table 14-2. Transact-SQL Object Usage

Object Type	Use When	Don't Use When
Stored procedure	Complicated processing logic. Iterative processing with little interaction with the user. Query will be run frequently.	Processing requires constant interaction with the user. Ad hoc query.
Views	Limit available data to user. Perform aggregate functionality in result set. Underlying base table volume is medium to low.	Large underlying base tables require frequent updates from the view.
Constraints	Simple integrity checks that do not require transaction rollback capabilities from within the constraint. Enforce referential integrity constraints where possible.	Logic is complex. Capability requires roll back of transaction within constraint.
Triggers	Logic is complex. Capability requires roll back of transaction within constraint. Require capability to roll back transaction from within the data modification operation. Create cascaded modification entries. Enforce referential integrity constraints, which cannot be done by constraints.	Simple logic that can as easily be performed using constraints, defaults, or rules.
Indexes	All the time.	Audit trail file with little or no query requirements.
Defaults	Simplify data capture and minimize standard data input.	Mandatory user data capture required.
Identity columns	Unique identifier required per table row.	Identifier needs to be strictly sequential with no sequence breaks. Need to change the identifier. Identifier needs to be unique.
Rules	Perform simple data range checks that may apply to multiple columns.	Rule is better handled by a constraint or trigger.
User types	Want to encourage data type consistency.	Few columns will be defined as this particular user type.

Executing Stored Procedures

In general, if a stored procedure is called as the first step in a batch, then the keyword EXECUTE does not need to be specified. In all other cases, the keyword EXECUTE needs to be specified as part of the call. For example:

```
sp_who
```

will execute since the batch consists only of the *sp_who* stored procedure. However, if the batch were to be extended to look like the following:

```
declare @v int
sp_who
```

Executing this batch would produce an error message similar to the following:

Microsoft	Sybase

`Msg 170, Level 15, State 1`
`Line2: Incorrect syntax near 'sp_who'.`
	`Server Message: Number 195, Severity 15`
	
	`'sp_who' is not a recognized parameter option`

To prevent this from happening, always prefix the keyword EXECUTE (described in the next section) to any stored procedure that needs to be executed.

EXECUTE and Dynamic SQL

The EXECUTE keyword is used to execute a stored procedure or a dynamically constructed SQL command (or commands) on a Microsoft installation. The EXECUTE command can be abbreviated to EXEC, as shown here:

```
EXECUTE sp_who
EXEC sp_who
```

One neat feature of SQL Server is the ability to execute a stored procedure where the name of the stored procedure is contained within a variable. For example, we might want to dynamically execute the system stored procedure *sp_who*. This is an important technique, because you might want to dynamically call one stored procedure over another using conditional statements like IF:

```
DECLARE @v VARCHAR(32)
SELECT  @v = 'sp_who'
EXEC    @v
```

Results:

```
spid   status     loginame    hostname  blk   dbname     cmd
------ ---------- ----------- --------- ----- ---------- ----------------
1      sleeping   sa                    0     master     MIRROR HANDLER
2      sleeping   sa                    0     master     LAZY WRITER
3      sleeping   sa                    0     master     CHECKPOINT SLEEP
```

```
4       sleeping    sa                          0     master     RA MANAGER
10      runnable    sa              NT_SQL      0     master     SELECT
```

In this version of the command, common to both Sybase and Microsoft platforms, the variable must *always* represent a stored procedure. That's because the EXEC command is expecting a stored procedure name. If we run the preceding example with a value other than a stored procedure, we'll get an error, as shown here:

```
DECLARE @v VARCHAR(32)
SELECT  @v = 'sauvignon'
EXEC    @v
```

Results:

```
Msg 2812, Level 16, State 4
Stored procedure 'sauvignon' not found.
```

In general, executing a remote procedure call (RPC) with EXEC is identical to executing a regular procedure. In a later section, we'll cover RPCs in greater detail.

EXEC()

Microsoft has extended the implementation of the EXEC command to allow you to execute dynamic SQL. Sybase also has its own flavor of this command through its *sp_remotesql* stored procedure. Essentially, both products work on the same fundamental concept in that they allow you to execute dynamic SQL at runtime as opposed to explicitly specifying your Transact-SQL prior to compilation. The most notable difference between this version of EXEC() and the stored-procedure-only version of EXEC is the addition of parentheses around the dynamically executed SQL string.

Here's a simple example:

```
EXEC( 'USE pubs' + ' ' +'SELECT au_id FROM authors WHERE au_lname = "Green"')
--OR
EXEC( 'USE pubs' + ' SELECT au_id FROM authors WHERE au_lname = "Green"')
--OR
EXEC('USE pubs SELECT au_id FROM authors WHERE au_lname = "Green"')
```

Results:

```
au_id
-----------
213-46-8915
au_id
-----------
213-46-8915
au_id
-----------
213-46-8915
```

As with the regular EXEC command, you can also encapsulate the value of the string to be executed within a variable. For example:

```
DECLARE @v VARCHAR(100)
SELECT @v = ('USE pubs' + ' ' +'SELECT au_id FROM authors WHERE au_lname =
"Green"')
EXEC (@v)
```

Results:

```
au_id
-----------
213-46-8915
```

There are a few rules that you need to follow when using the EXEC() function:

- Although it might appear otherwise, EXEC() is not limited to 255 characters as a VARCHAR variable would be. The string can be as long as necessary.
- Numeric data needs to be converted to a character string prior to execution.
- Functions cannot be used directly. You should pass a character expression composed of constants and variables to the EXEC() command.
- The dynamically executed code of EXEC() does not see local variables that might be declared in the main block of code. Local variables declared in the dynamic SQL are erased when the dynamic SQL has finished and do not pass outside.
- Much like local variables, temporary objects created outside of the EXEC() command are visible to the dynamic SQL, but those declared within the EXEC() command are dropped when the dynamic SQL completes and are not visible outside of the dynamic SQL process.
- EXEC() is not evaluated by SQL Server in any way prior to the execution of the batch in which the operations are called. This means that if you want to change a context, like a database where the command is executed, and then perform an operation within this new context, you need to perform both operations within EXEC() statements (as shown in the example).
- The USE command issued within an EXEC() command has no impact on the calling code; once the dynamic SQL is done, the database context switches back to where it was before.
- Similarly, SET commands issued by EXEC() impact only the dynamic code and not the main block of code. On the other hand, SET commands issued prior to the EXEC() statement are effective when EXEC() runs.

In and of itself, dynamic SQL execution is probably one of the most powerful features of SQL Server because you are no longer constrained by explicitly referring to an object prior to compilation. A simple use of this EXEC() feature is demonstrated here:

```
CREATE PROCEDURE Show_The_Data @Table varchar(30) = 'titles'
AS
```

```
        IF (SELECT object_id(@TblName)) = NULL
        BEGIN
            RAISERROR 25000 'Invalid Table selected'
            RETURN 1
        END

DECLARE @SQL_Statement varchar(255)

SELECT @SQL_Statement = 'SELECT * FROM '+@Table

EXEC(@SQL_Statement)
GO
```

As you can see, you've been able to create a generic procedure that applies to all tables in any database with very little effort.

Remote Procedure Calls (RPCs)

The computing environment in a modern enterprise typically comprises numerous database servers. They may contain unrelated databases or parts of the same model; some information may be redundant; and some may be partitioned across multiple servers. It is often necessary to access data scattered across many sources to produce the desired results. There are several ways to accomplish that. Your application running on a client machine may connect to several servers, pull necessary data elements from each one, and then merge them into one result set using its own powers. This approach has some disadvantages. It may place a heavy workload on a client and may require pulling a lot of data from each source to use only in behind-the-scenes processing.

SQL Server provides another mechanism for cross-server queries. It allows you to set up multiple servers as *remote* to one another and have them access one another's data when needed. A user connects to a single server and uses its objects. Whenever the process requires pulling data from another server, it can access it by database and object name prefixed with a remote server name. There is no need to make another connection and go through the authentication and logging-in process.

A remote SQL Server is defined as a server that users can access from their local server connection. They can execute stored procedures or address tables on a remote server. Connection to the remote server is managed by the local server to which the user is connected. The DBA has to configure and set up remote access and grant appropriate permissions for remote users.

Configuring a Remote Server

Each pair of remote servers is defined separately. Each one of the two remote servers needs to be configured to recognize its "partner." Information about remote servers is maintained in the system table master..sysservers. In order to add a new entry into this table, execute the system stored procedure *sp_addserver* in the master database:

```
sp_addserver server_name [, local]
```

The optional keyword LOCAL allows you to define the local server name (if it has not been set up yet) or to change it. It affects the value of the global variable @@servername. Typically, a local name is set at SQL Server installation. Given one parameter, *sp_addserver* adds the specified SQL Server to the list of remote servers. The value of column srvstatus of table sysservers indicates whether the entry describes the local server (srvstatus = 0) or a remote one (srvstatus = 1). Needless to say, there may be only one row for a local server and many for remote servers.

Figure 14-1 shows a typical RPC configuration.

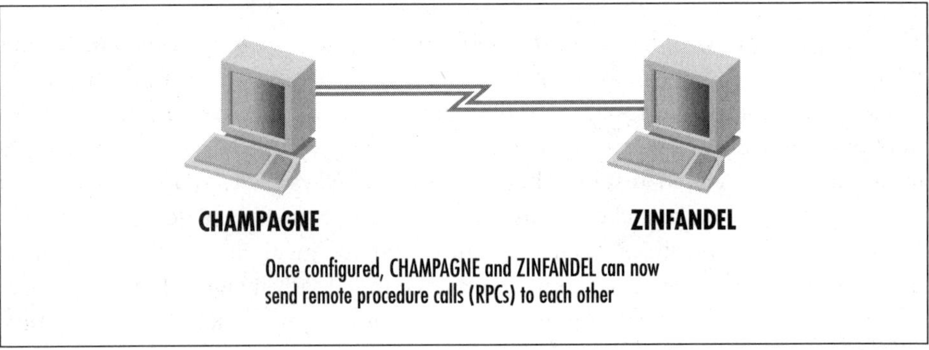
CHAMPAGNE
ZINFANDEL
Once configured, CHAMPAGNE and ZINFANDEL can now send remote procedure calls (RPCs) to each other

Figure 14-1. Remote procedure calls

For example, if you want SQL Servers CHAMPAGNE and ZINFANDEL to be remote to each other, execute the following command from CHAMPAGNE:

```
sp_addserver ZINFANDEL
```

which on successful completion returns a message:

```
Server added.
```

Then execute a similar command from ZINFANDEL:

```
sp_addserver CHAMPAGNE
```

At this point, SQL Server does not verify whether the remote server indeed exists. It simply modifies the contents of the system table. If a remote server does not exist or is not configured to allow remote access, your attempts to use remote objects will fail. You can review currently configured servers by executing another system stored procedure:

```
sp_helpserver
```

Results returned by the CHAMPAGNE server:

```
name                   network_name         status       id
---------------------- -------------------- ----------- ----
CHAMPAGNE              CHAMPAGNE                         0
ZINFANDEL              ZINFANDEL            rpc          1
```

In order to drop a remote server, use the following stored procedure:

```
sp_dropserver server_name
```

which returns a message:

```
Server dropped.
```

Setting configuration options

Before you can use a remote server, you may need to review configuration options. You may need to consult with the local DBA before altering these values. The configuration option "remote access" has to be set to 1, which is the default.

```
sp_configure 'remote access'
```

Additional advanced configuration options include "remote login timeout," and "remote query timeout." The remote login timeout parameter specifies the number of seconds SQL Server should wait before returning a remote login failure. The default value is 5. A zero value tells SQL Server to wait indefinitely. The remote query timeout parameter defines how many seconds SQL Server should wait for a remote query to return results. The default value of zero specifies an infinite wait.

You can limit the number of servers allowed to create a remote connection using the configuration option "remote sites."

If you change any of these configuration options, you have to restart SQL Server for the new settings to take effect.

Setting remote logins

The DBA must configure remote logins or establish a trusted mode for remote connections. Trusted mode means that a remote SQL Server will admit any user whose identity is validated by his or her local server. A discussion of remote logins and users is outside of the scope of this book.

Using Remote Objects

Accessing objects on a remote server requires prefixing them with a server name. For example, if you have a connection to local server CHAMPAGNE, you may select data from a table on remote server ZINFANDEL:

```
SELECT * FROM ZINFANDEL.pubs..discounts
```

Results look no different from those that could be returned by the local server:

```
discounttype                             stor_id lowqty highqty discount
---------------------------------------- ------- ------ ------- --------
Initial Customer                         (null)  (null) (null)  10.50
Volume Discount                          (null)  100    1000    6.70
Customer Discount                        8042    (null) (null)  5.00

(3 row(s) affected)
```

A Simple Remote Procedure Call

You can execute remote stored procedures in a similar way. For example:

```
EXECUTE ZINFANDEL.pubs.dbo.byroyalty 30
```

Results:

```
au_id
-----------
267-41-2394
472-27-2349

(2 row(s) affected)
```

Syntactically, you can reference remote objects as if they were local. Doing so, however, may have certain performance implications that we discuss later in this chapter. You should also consider what happens to transactions executed across multiple servers.

Adding Complexity to Remote Procedure Calls

Remote access allows you to unify data on many servers and, to some extent, treat this data as if it were on one big server. This is very useful when your database is partitioned across multiple servers or when you need to combine results from different offices of the same company. You may execute remote stored procedures to perform certain data manipulation and administration functions across many servers while logged in to just one.

Let's illustrate this concept with a more elaborate example. In our hypothetical company, we have four office locations, each with its own installation of SQL Server. Information is keyed and maintained locally in each office; however, management wants summary reports on a nightly basis.

As with many technical challenges, there is more than one correct way to solve this problem. Although we are concerned only with the last choice presented, some other valid choices include:

- Use SQL Server replication to bring all the data back to a central server; then run the management reports. (Not covered in this book.)

- Use the Bulk Copy Utility to export the data. FTP the data to a central server. Import the data with BCP. Then run the management reports.
- With Microsoft's implementation, use the SQL Transfer Manager to pull all the data together; then run the report. (Not covered in this book.)
- Use remote procedure calls (RPCs) to retrieve all the data from the other servers into a local report.

After some consideration, the SQL Server team decides that the first two choices (replication and BCP) would take too much development and maintenance time for the small amount of data needed back. The Transfer Manager option is ruled out, because the team supports both Sybase and Microsoft. The RPC option looks like a nice fit.

To pull back the data into a single report, we'll build a Transact-SQL program that executes the RPC reptq1 for each remote server found in the sysservers table. We'll use a cursor to loop through each entry in sysservers, including the local server.

```
-- A Transact-SQL program to execute an RPC call against all servers in
-- master..sysservers
SET NOCOUNT ON

-- Declare the variables and cursor
DECLARE @srvname      VARCHAR(30),
        @header_line  VARCHAR(50),
        @command_line VARCHAR(50)

DECLARE remote_servers_cursor CURSOR FOR
    SELECT srvname
    FROM   master..sysservers

-- Open the cursor and begin to retrieve data for each of the servers
OPEN remote_servers_cursor
FETCH NEXT FROM remote_servers_cursor INTO @srvname

WHILE (@@fetch_status <> -1)
BEGIN
    IF (@@fetch_status <> -2)
    BEGIN
        -- Build and print the report header for each remote server
        SELECT @header_line = ' ***** ' + RTRIM(@srvname) + ' ***** '
        PRINT ' '
        PRINT @header_line
        PRINT ' '

        -- Build and execute the RPC command line for each remote server
        SELECT @command_line = RTRIM(@srvname) + '.pubs..reptq2'
        EXEC   @command_line

    END

    FETCH NEXT FROM remote_servers_cursor INTO @srvname
END
```

```
-- Always close AND deallocate a cursor when you're done with it
CLOSE      remote_servers_cursor
DEALLOCATE remote_servers_cursor

GO
```

When we execute this RPC, the results look something like this (the result file has been edited for brevity):

```
 ***** BURGUNDY *****

type         pub_id title_id au_ord Name            ytd_sales
------------ ------ -------- ------ --------------- -----------
business     0736   BU2075   1      Green           18722

                                                    avg
                                                    ===========
                                                    18722

type         pub_id title_id au_ord Name            ytd_sales
------------ ------ -------- ------ --------------- -----------
psychology   0736   PS2091   2      Ringer          2045
psychology   0736   PS2091   1      Ringer          2045
```

...<results truncated>...

```
***** CHAMPAGNE *****

type         pub_id title_id au_ord Name            ytd_sales
------------ ------ -------- ------ --------------- -----------
business     0736   BU2075   1      Green           6658

                                                    avg
                                                    ===========
                                                    6658

type         pub_id title_id au_ord Name            ytd_sales
------------ ------ -------- ------ --------------- -----------
psychology   0736   PS2091   2      Ringer          2334
psychology   0736   PS2091   1      Ringer          2334
```

...<results truncated>...

Using this Transact-SQL script, you can easily retrieve the results of the reptq2 query for all servers found in master..sysservers. If you would rather compile the information from the remote servers and produce a report locally, you can use the INSERT . . . EXEC techniques described in Chapter 3, *SQL Primer*. INSERT . . . EXEC allows you to execute a local or remote stored procedure and insert the data directly into a table if you are using Microsoft SQL Server. Once the data is compiled into a single table, queries can produce a summarized report containing data from all servers.

Performance of Remote Objects

Building high-performance remote stored procedures is something of a black art. There are dangers and pitfalls to remote stored procedures that you never encounter when writing local stored procedures. For this reason, our recommendation is to use remote stored procedures primarily for data retrieval. Data modification via remote stored procedures can be a tricky business. Consider the following issues:

Locking and blocking
: Remote stored procedures must be fully capable of dealing with locks and blocking problems within their own code. Since they are executed on remote servers, there are few methods of intervention available to users and developers on the local server.

Remote transactions
: If the RPC executes a transaction on the remote server, you will have to add code to notify you on the local server. This involves some fancy footwork. The remote stored procedure could notify you of completion (either a transaction commit or rollback), using methods such as an email message (using *xp_sendmail*), another RPC back to the local server, or the raising of an error in the Windows NT event log.

Distributed transactions (Microsoft only)
: Some developers use *distributed transactions* to enable OLTP functionality across servers. A distributed transaction is a transaction initiated on a local server but completed on a remote server or servers. Such a transaction can be accomplished with remote stored procedures or by using the command BEGIN DISTRIBUTED TRANSACTION in combination with the Microsoft Distributed Transaction Coordinator (MS-DTC). (MS-DTC is beyond the scope of this book.) You can probably imagine the kinds of complications that can develop when trying to roll back a transaction that spans two or more servers. For example, if an RPC properly commits a transaction on Servers A and B, but not on Server C, how do you notify the other servers that they must roll back? It can be a huge programmatic mess.

Performance in general should be equivalent to the normal processing time of the stored procedure plus the added overhead of the network connection. Depending on the speed and reliability of your network link, remote stored procedures may execute quickly or slowly.

Stored Procedure Design

Ah, this is the part where your lids start to get very heavy and you suddenly have somewhere else you need to be. ***STOP. DO NOT TAKE ANOTHER STEP!*** This paragraph has been wired with an explosive charge and will blow up if you don't continue reading until the very end of this chapter! Maybe not, but at least we got you to read this paragraph.

A well-designed procedure may save you several weeks of unnecessary work and a whole lot of misery. The goal of this section is to introduce the fundamentals of design as they relate to stored procedures and to give you the tools necessary to create a well-designed stored procedure.

Naming Conventions

In Chapter 5, we covered format and style. System stored procedures are about the only stored procedures that have some limit on the names used. In order to create a system stored procedure that can be executed from any user database, the stored procedure name must start with *sp_* .

Modular Code and Block Structures

Modular code is a big term for a simple concept. Keep your code structured and logically grouped. In general, developing a behemoth procedure that does all things for all people will be both inefficient and likely beset by a large number of problems. Reducing a problem into a set of definite functions and then writing a series of stored procedures to deal with each of the subtasks simplifies the problem significantly. It also reduces the number of problems you will have to deal with later on. Another benefit of this approach is that you will be more likely to identify similar subtasks, which can be generalized further and can eliminate even more code from your programs. Remember: the less code you write, the less you will have to debug and, in many cases, the code will also be quicker. However, there are some exceptions, which we cover elsewhere in this book.

Wrappers

The procedures we have introduced in this chapter can be combined into a more complex routine, perhaps using a *wrapper*. A wrapper is a stored procedure or Transact-SQL script that calls subordinate stored procedures. You use a wrapper procedure to drive the ultimate execution of all subordinate stored procedures in the order in which they need to be run. The wrapper for the earlier example procedures looks similar to the following:

```
CREATE PROCEDURE my_wrapper_procedure
AS
        EXEC get_author_names
        EXEC get_yearly_sales_summary
        EXEC print_ytd_title_evaluation
```

Executing this procedure will produce a consolidation of all the results that were returned when each procedure was called individually.

To add another level of sophistication, you could create a wrapper that stores or transmits parameter values for use in the subordinate stored procedures. You could use parameters, variables, temporary tables, or permanent scratch tables to hold data that will be used in multiple subordinate procedures. Refer to the later section, "Passing a Temporary Table to a Nested Stored Procedure."

Nested Procedures

Procedures can be nested up to a maximum of 16 levels. The global variable @@nestlevel is updated every time a nesting is performed on both procedures and triggers. The wrapper concept introduced in the previous section is an excellent example of nesting since my_wrapper_procedure is the highest level procedure and it, in turn, calls a number of additional procedures like get_author_names. In this example, @@nestlevel would look similar to the following (assuming that it was actually checked during the call to each of these procedures):

Procedure	@@nestlevel
`my_wrapper_procedure`	1
`get_author_names`	2
`gey_yearly_sales_summary`	2
`print_ytd_title_evaluation`	2

Dependency

Dependency has two sides in the world of stored procedures. On one side, it involves understanding how a stored procedure will act when a dependent stored procedure is dropped or re-created. On the other side, it involves looking at how to code in the calling procedure to take into consideration the myriad of different results that can occur in these subordinate stored procedures.

When a dependent procedure is dropped and is then referenced by another procedure, SQL Server returns a server message. You will get a message similar to the following from the calling procedure:

```
Msg 2812, Level 16, State 4
Stored procedure 'xxxxxx' not found.
```

You can drop a subordinate procedure and re-create it with an entirely different purpose, and the calling procedure will correctly reference the new instance of this stored procedure. Depending on how you look at this, it can be both a good and a bad thing. It's good from the standpoint that you can independently change a stored procedure and not have to recompile all other procedures that reference it. It's bad in that SQL Server does not know that a procedure has changed and "warns" you that unpredictable results may occur. The following simple example shows both of these scenarios:

```
CREATE PROCEDURE part_b
AS
   SELECT *
     FROM authors
GO
CREATE PROCEDURE part_a
AS
   EXEC part_b
GO
EXEC part_a
GO
DROP PROCEDURE part_b
GO
EXEC part_a
GO
CREATE PROCEDURE part_b
AS
   SELECT *
     FROM titles
GO
EXEC part_a
GO
```

In the previous example, the user would have received different results from those expected because the called procedure was changed. The best defense against this type of problem is to implement a source code management system of some kind which can be used to track changes and, if necessary, restore the code to its original form. Being aware that problems like these can and do happen is the first step toward preventing them.

Transaction Rules

Transaction rules are like dependency checks; they are usually an afterthought. Transactions are discussed in greater detail in Chapter 11, *Transactions and Locking*. However, there are some important things you need to remember when you write a transaction within your stored procedures:

Volume
: If the procedure needs to modify a large volume of data, you need to decide whether data can be updated in smaller batches or whether it's an all-or-nothing problem. If it is the former, then you will be less concerned with the instantiation of a TRANSACTION block and more concerned with developing a procedure that allows you to process only a subset of data at a time. For example, use ROWCOUNT to update only a limited number of records at a time.

Function
: Does this procedure only select data, does it modify data, or does it call an extended stored procedure, like *xp_cmdshell*? When selecting data, you will

probably not implement any additional transaction checks. When modifying data, you may have to add explicit transactions to the code. When calling external stored procedures or custom-built functions, you lack significant ability to undo operations.

How critical it is for you to implement an explicit transaction will depend on the answer you come up with for the volume and function issues, since they will swing you in a particular direction. Just because you choose not to create an explicit transaction initially does not mean that you cannot change your mind at a later point.

Passing a Temporary Table to a Nested Stored Procedure

Perhaps one of the most useful techniques available with stored procedure design is creating a nested procedure and being able to pass into it either a temporary table or a permanent table that is only created in the calling procedure. Since the nested procedure needs to be created prior to the calling procedure, this may seem to be a problem. However, the solution itself is actually quite simple. Consider the following examples:

```
-- Create the table so that use_id procedure creation is a success
CREATE TABLE #id (id INT, iid INT)
GO

-- Create a procedure that uses this temporary table

CREATE PROCEDURE use_id
AS
   INSERT #id VALUES (1,1)
   INSERT #id VALUES (1,2)
   INSERT #id VALUES (1,3)
GO

-- Drop the table else the creator stored procedure will fail

DROP TABLE #id
GO

-- Create the calling stored proc which creates the table and calls use_id

CREATE PROCEDURE call_use_id
AS
   CREATE TABLE #id (id int, iid int)
   EXEC use_id
GO
```

In this script, the temporary table was created at the top so that all the inner procedures would be created successfully. Once they were created, the temporary table was dropped and the procedure that creates the temporary table was created. This approach has been used in many of the code examples you will find on the accompanying CD-ROM. The logic itself applies equally to permanent tables. You may have a permanent table that gets created in one procedure and is then populated in several nested procedures. Before those procedures can be created, the table must exist. The method described previously is how you would implement such a solution.

Conditional Data Retrieval

Often, it is necessary to return different data sets depending on the type of request being made. It is possible to code stored procedure logic to do this. Using the pubs database, we'll create a procedure to return different subsets of data for an author based on whether the report needs to be a summary or a detailed report:

```
CREATE PROCEDURE return_author_info
    @author_id char(11)='172-32-1176',
    @reptype char(1) = 'S'
AS
/* this procedure returns author information for a specific author */
/* S- Summary report, contains only financial information */
/* D- Detail report, contains financial and author information */

-- Error checking on rep type request
IF UPPER(@reptype) NOT IN ('S','D')
BEGIN
    PRINT "Invalid entry made, @reptype can only be (S)ummary or (D)etail"
    RETURN
END

IF (SELECT count(*)
     FROM  pubs..authors
     WHERE  au_id = @author_id) = 0
BEGIN
    PRINT "Invalid author_id specified, please try again"
    RETURN
END

-- Prepare the summary report

-- create structure for summary report
    CREATE TABLE #summary (au_id char(11) NULL,
        au_name VARCHAR(61) NULL,
        title_id CHAR(6),
        title VARCHAR(80),
        price MONEY,
        big CHAR(1),
        total_qty INT,
        total_revenue MONEY)

-- populate the summary structure
```

```
INSERT #summary
SELECT DISTINCT a.au_id,
    au_name = a.au_fname+' '+a.au_lname,
    t.title_id,
    t.title,
    t.price,
    '',
    SUM(s.qty),
    SUM(s.qty) * t.price
FROM   titles t,
       authors a,
       titleauthor ta,
       sales s
WHERE  ta.au_id = @author_id
   AND ta.au_id = a.au_id
   AND ta.title_id = t.title_id
   AND s.title_id = t.title_id
   AND s.title_id = ta.title_id
GROUP BY a.au_id,
         a.au_fname,
         a.au_lname,
         t.title_id,
         t.title,
         t.price

UPDATE #summary
   SET big_return = *
 WHERE total_return > 1000

    -- print the report contents

SELECT au_name,
       title,
       price,
        big,
       total_qty,
       total_revenue
FROM   #summary
ORDER BY title

    -- clean up
DROP TABLE #summary

-- Prepare the detail report
IF UPPER(@reptype) = 'D'
BEGIN
    -- create structure for detail report
    CREATE TABLE #detail (au_id VARCHAR (11),
       au_name VARCHAR(61),
       phone CHAR(12),
       address VARCHAR(40),
       city VARCHAR(20),
       state CHAR(2),
       zip CHAR(5))
```

```
    -- populate the detail structure
    INSERT #detail
    SELECT au_id,
        au_fname+' '+au_lname,
        phone,
        address,
        city,
        state,
        zip
    FROM   authors
    WHERE  au_id = @author_id

    -- print the report contents

    SELECT *
    FROM#detail

    -- clean up
    DROP TABLE #detail
END
GO
EXEC return_author_info '899-46-2035','S'
EXEC return_author_info '899-46-2035','D'
```

Results (drumroll please):

```
au_name       title                 price    big  total_qty total_revenue
------------- --------------------- -------- --- ---------- --------------
Anne Ringer   Is Anger the Enemy?   10.95    *    108        1,182.60
Anne Ringer   The Gourmet Microwave 2.99          40         119.60

(2 row(s) affected)

au_name       title                 price    big total_qty  total_revenue
------------- --------------------- -------- --- ---------- --------------
Anne Ringer   Is Anger the Enemy?   10.95    *    108        1,182.60
Anne Ringer   The Gourmet Microwave 2.99          40         119.60

(1 row(s) affected)

au_id       au_name     phone        address       city           state zip
----------- ----------- ------------ ------------- -------------- ----- -----
899-46-2035 Anne Ringer 801 826-0752 67 Seventh Av.Salt Lake City UT    84152
```

Data Formatting

Returning data in a way that is easy to read seems to be a simple goal. However, if you have ever spent several hours coding to line up report columns correctly, you know that this goal is often not that easy. SQL Server has limited data formatting capabilities since the size of the results column is determined by the underlying data type. If you want to change the default length of a column when displaying it, you have to use the CONVERT function.

For more complex data formatting, you will have to resort to writing logic in your stored procedures or using a report writing tool to reformat your data once SQL Server has selected it for you.

In the following example, we have reformatted results from a query prior to displaying it:

```
CREATE PROCEDURE create_store_labels
AS
    SET NOCOUNT ON
    DECLARE @stor_id CHAR(4),
    @stor_name VARCHAR(40),
    @stor_address VARCHAR(40),
    @city VARCHAR(20),
    @state CHAR(2),
    @zip CHAR(5),
    @jline VARCHAR(75)

DECLARE stor_select CURSOR
FOR SELECT stor_id,
    stor_name,
    stor_address,
    city,
    state,
    zip
FROM stores
ORDER BY zip

OPEN stor_select

FETCH stor_select
INTO @stor_id,
     @stor_name,
     @stor_address,
     @city,
     @state,
     @zip

/* Sybase: WHILE @@SQL_status = 0 */
WHILE @@fetch_status = 0
BEGIN

    PRINT @stor_id
    PRINT @stor_name
    PRINT @stor_address
    SELECT @jline = @city +','+@state+','+@zip
    PRINT @jline
    PRINT " "

FETCH stor_select
INTO @stor_id,
     @stor_name,
     @stor_address,
```

```
        @city,
        @state,
        @zip

END
CLOSE stor_select
DEALLOCATE  stor_select
/* Sybase: DEALLOCATE CURSOR stor_select */
GO
EXEC create_store_labels
-- partial results

8042
Bookbeat
679 Carson St.
Portland,OR,89076

7896
Fricative Bookshop
89 Madison St.
Fremont,CA,90019

7066
Barnum's
567 Pasadena Ave.
Tustin,CA,92789

7067
News & Brews
577 First St.
Los Gatos,CA,96745
```

In the next example, we'll use parameters and a generalized table to format the data returned based on the table requested:

```
CREATE PROCEDURE display_pubs_data
    @source VARCHAR(12) = 'store'
AS
CREATE TABLE #generalized_results (id VARCHAR(12),
    info VARCHAR(125))

   DECLARE @desc VARCHAR(40)
   SELECT @desc = "Report for "+UPPER(@source)+' table'

    PRINT @desc

   IF UPPER(@source) = 'STORE'
   BEGIN
       INSERT #generalized_results
       SELECT stor_id,
           stor_name+' '+stor_address+' '+city+' '+state+' '+zip
       FROM stores
   END
```

```
IF UPPER(@source) = 'AUTHOR'
   BEGIN
       INSERT #generalized_results
       SELECT convert(varchar(12),au_id),
           au_fname+' '+au_lname+' '+phone+' '+state+' '+zip
       FROM authors
    END

IF UPPER(@source) = 'EMPLOYEE'
   BEGIN
       INSERT #generalized_results
       SELECT e.emp_id,
           e.fname+'.'+e.minit+'.'+e.lname+' '+j.job_desc
       FROM  employee e, jobs j
       WHERE e.job_id = j.job_id
    END

IF UPPER(@source) = 'TITLE'
BEGIN
       INSERT #generalized_results
       SELECT convert(varchar(12),title_id),
           type+' : '+title+' '+convert(varchar(12),price)
       FROM titles
END

SELECT *
FROM #generalized_results
ORDER BY id
GO
```

Here's what happens when we execute the stored procedure with several different parameters:

```
exec display_pubs_data "STORE"

Report for STORE table
id   info
---- ------------------------------------------------------------------------
6380 Eric the Read Books 788 Catamaugus Ave. Seattle WA 98056
7066 Barnum's 567 Pasadena Ave. Tustin CA 92789
7067 News & Brews 577 First St. Los Gatos CA 96745
7131 Doc-U-Mat: Quality Laundry and Books 24-A Avogadro Way Remulade WA 98014

exec display_pubs_data "EMPLOYEE"

Report for EMPLOYEE table
id         info
---------- ----------------------------------------------------
A-C71970F  Aria. .Cruz Productions Manager
A-R89858F  Annette. .Roulet Managing Editor
AMD15433F  Ann.M.Devon Business Operations Manager
ARD36773F  Anabela.R.Domingues Public Relations Manager
CFH28514M  Carlos.F.Hernadez Publisher
CGS88322F  Carine.G.Schmitt Sales Representative

exec display_pubs_data "AUTHOR"
```

```
Report for AUTHOR table
id          info
----------- ----------------------------------------------------------
172-32-1176 Johnson White 408 496-7223 CA 94025
213-46-8915 Marjorie Green 415 986-7020 CA 94618
238-95-7766 Cheryl Carson 415 548-7723 CA 94705
267-41-2394 Michael O'Leary 408 286-2428 CA 95128
274-80-9391 Dean Straight 415 834-2919 CA 94609


exec display_pubs_data "TITLE"

Report for TITLE table
id     info
------ ----------------------------------------------------------
BU1032 business : The Busy Executive's Database Guide 19.99
BU1111 business : Cooking with Computers: Surreptitious Balance Sheets 11.95
BU2075 business : You Can Combat Computer Stress! 2.99
BU7832 business : Straight Talk About Computers 19.99
```

Data Security and Encryption

Data privacy is a serious issue. As data availability has increased, so has the need to implement more sophisticated security mechanisms. Imagine what would happen if everybody could see the human resources database in your company and could find out all the private details on your colleagues. SQL Server has a number of different techniques you can use to maintain data security. We'll briefly review these techniques in this section.

There are many ways to implement security on SQL Server. Each method has advantages, disadvantages, and a defined scope. Once you have a thorough understanding of the options available to you within SQL Server, you'll be able to choose the most appropriate method to use for a particular situation.

Rights and Privileges

SQL Servers are not unlike the rest of the world; someone always has to be in charge and have all the power. The SA account (for a Microsoft SQL Server) and the account with the sa_role (for a Sybase SQL Server) are these power junkies.

SQL Server allows you to create a number of different types of objects. In general, these objects are tables, views, triggers, indexes, defaults, rules, user types, and stored procedures.

In Sybase and Microsoft SQL Server, all database objects are owned by a particular user. The owner of the object may extend certain rights and privileges on these database objects to other users, to enable them to use and change data as necessary.

In order to be able to create database objects, a user has to be extended the necessary authority by the system administrator (SA) account on Microsoft SQL Server 6.5 or any user with the sa_role() in Sybase System 11.

The user who created an object is its owner, and that owner is given some rights and privileges as a result of ownership. For those of you who hold the SA account or have a user account that has been aliased as DBO, this would mean that the object is created with DBO as the owner. If you do not fall into this former category, then your object is created with your username in the particular database. This means that if other users want to reference an object you have created, they need to prefix the object name with your username.

Since Sybase and Microsoft treat security very differently, we'll discuss each approach separately. The Sybase implementation of security provides a number of extensions to establish a greater level of control in a database server.

The Transact-SQL commands GRANT and REVOKE are used to implement a form of discretionary control security. The following sections describe these commands and the objects they operate upon.

GRANT

GRANT is the command used to explicitly authorize a user or a group of users to use a particular object. By default, only the owner of an object or the database owner can use or see the data in an object. In order to confer this right or privilege to other users, you must issue the GRANT command as follows:

<table>
<tr><th>Microsoft</th><th>Sybase</th></tr>
<tr><td><pre>GRANT {ALL [privileges]|
    permission_list}
ON { table_name [(column_list)]
     | view_name[(column_list)]
     | stored_procedure_name
     | extended_stored_procedure_name}
TO {PUBLIC | name_list }

GRANT {ALL [privileges]
     | command_list}
TO {PUBLIC | name_list }</pre></td><td><pre>GRANT {ALL [privileges]|
    permission_list}
ON { table_name [(column_list)]
     | view_name[(column_list)]
     | stored_procedure_name
     | extended_stored_procedure_name}
TO {PUBLIC | name_list | role_name}
    [WITH GRANT OPTION]

GRANT {ALL [privileges]
     | command_list}
TO {PUBLIC | name_list | role_name}

GRANT {ROLE role_granted
    [, role_granted ...]}
TO grantee [, grantee ...]</pre></td></tr>
</table>

Here are some GRANT examples:

```
GRANT  UPDATE to mike
GRANT INSERT,UPDATE to purchasing
```

Both the GRANT and REVOKE commands operate on numerous levels, as described in the following sections.

Object level. On an object level, it is possible to restrict what objects an individual user can access. Objects that can be restricted include:

- Table
- Columns within a table
- View
- Stored procedure
- Extended stored procedure

Command level. Command-level restrictions allow you to explicitly allow or disallow an individual user from executing particular commands on the server. The following table lists which commands can be granted or revoked from an individual user:

Command	Microsoft	Sybase
CREATE DATABASE	X	X
CREATE DEFAULT	X	X
CREATE TABLE	X	X
CREATE PROCEDURE	X	X
CREATE RULE	X	X
CREATE VIEW	X	X
SET PROXY		X
SET SESSION AUTHORIZATION		X
DUMP DATABASE	X	
DUMP TRANSACTION	X	

Role level (Sybase only). Beginning with System 10, Sybase implemented roles into its database server technology. Microsoft has not implemented a similar technique up to and including v6.5. There are currently four different types of roles:

- System administrator (SA)
- System security officer (SSO)
- Operator
- User-defined role

Roles are important in Sybase; they allow you to assign responsibilities to individual users without explicitly stating each user. Administration is reduced since the role's nature and scope are defined once. Associating a user with a particular subset of responsibilities becomes a trivial task. This role affects the permissions you have, as well as the user ID of the owner assigned to the objects you create on the data server. This chapter covers roles in some detail, because the type of role you may have been assigned can affect your ability to create and manipulate database objects.

System administrator (SA) [sa_role()]. The system administrator role is given to those demigods of society intent on establishing rules and regulations that severely inhibit any reasonable persons intent on hacking in a database server. In SQL Server, the system administrator role need not be performed by a single person and can actually be distributed among a group of users.

The system administrator role covers the following types of tasks:

- Installating the database server
- Managing the physical disk resources used by the database server
- Granting or revoking permissions to the rest of the users of the database server
- Creating and removing logins in the database server
- Creating and removing users from the individual databases on a given database server
- Monitoring the server's functioning and preventing potential causes of failure
- Transferring data from one source to another
- Improving the performance of the database server by fine-tuning the databases that reside on it
- Creating and deleting individual databases
- Conferring ownership of databases to individual users
- Creating and deleting user groups
- Conferring all of the preceding on someone else by giving them the sa_role()

The system administrator is responsible for the day-to-day operations of the database server and for ensuring that it runs consistently.

System security officer (SSO) [sso_role()]. The system security officer is responsible for ensuring that the database server does not fall prey to subversive personalities intent on industrial espionage, among other things. The SSO in the Sybase world is responsible for the administration of all aspects of security. There is some overlap of responsibility between the SSO and the SA.

The tasks that the SSO would perform fall into the following categories:

- Creating and deleting all server login accounts
- Granting and revoking permission to use the set session authorization or the SET PROXY commands

- Granting, revoking, and administering a user-defined role
- Granting or revoking the operator or system security officer role
- Permitting the use of network-based security services
- Setting any security-related configuration parameters
- Changing any user's password and setting the password expiration interval
- Managing the audit system

Operator [oper_role()]. This role is reserved for the individual responsible for the backing up and restoring of a database. The tasks that are performed by this role are:

- Dumping a database
- Dumping a transaction
- Loading a database
- Loading a transaction

User-defined roles. Sybase SQL Server 11.5 includes the ability to define user roles. These roles work in a way that is similar to groups in the sense that they allow you to categorize your users in terms of the functions they perform. But they differ from groups in one important way; roles are server-wide, while groups are defined local to a particular database. Once a role has been created, the individual owners of objects still need to confer the necessary permissions to the role as is currently done with groups.

Roles have one further advantage over groups; they can be organized in a hierarchy. A role can inherit the characteristics of other roles in the server. For example, in a database server we may create a marketing_user role which gives access to the book titles. We also may create an editor_role which gives access to the marketing_user role and the authors tables. The editor_role can access both the marketing_user and the authors tables in this database because it has inherited the permissions of the marketing_user as well as its own.

Roles were implemented to enable database administrators to better track what is going on in a system. The biggest problem with the SA or DBO account is that it is nearly impossible to determine who did something on a server if she has been aliased as DBO. With roles, you never lose your identity (i.e., your login name), but you can still perform the tasks assigned to the role.

REVOKE

The REVOKE command is used to explicitly remove permissions to either objects or commands for a user or group of users. The REVOKE command options are similar to those offered by the GRANT command.

Microsoft	Sybase
`REVOKE {ALL [privileges]| permission_list} ON { table_name [(column_list)]	view_name[(column_list)]	stored_procedure_name	extended_stored_procedure_name} FROM {PUBLIC	name_list }`  `REVOKE {ALL [privileges]	command_list} FROM {PUBLIC	name_list }`	`REVOKE {ALL [privileges]| permission_list} ON { table_name [(column_list)]	view_name[(column_list)]	stored_procedure_name} FROM {PUBLIC	name_list	role_name} [CASCADE]`  `REVOKE {ALL [privileges]	command_list} FROM {PUBLIC	name_list	role_name}`  `REVOKE {ROLE role_granted [, role_granted ...]} FROM grantee [, grantee ...]`

Permissions list

Table 14-3 illustrates which permissions are supported for each type of object where the GRANT or REVOKE command has been executed. ALL can be used to explicitly grant every permission simultaneously.

Table 14-3. Permissions list

	SELECT	INSERT	UPDATE	DELETE	REFERENCES	EXECUTE
Table	X	X	X	X	X	
Stored procedure						X
View	X	X	X	X		
Column	X		X		X	

Encryption

Both vendors provide the capability to encrypt the database code of an object, although each has implemented it differently. Microsoft includes the ENCRYPTION specifier as part of its CREATE syntax, while Sybase uses a system stored procedure, *sp_hidetext,* for its implementation. You may want to consider using encryption when you need to protect your intellectual property rights. Consider the following scenario: you develop an application for a client, you install the application and provide support, but your contract says that you don't give the client your source code. Otherwise, your clients may be at liberty to take your product, maintain it themselves, and cut off your ongoing service agreement. Your product's installation does not even have to be performed from source code scripts. For example, you develop a database and a bunch of stored procedures in-house. You create all procedures encrypted, dump your database, and send the dump to the client. They just load it on their server. They cannot get to your source code, but they can still use the application.

In another case, you may wish to create a procedure that stores the SA password in it and does some administration function, as in the following code for Microsoft:

```
CREATE PROCEDURE become_sa_for_a_moment
WITH ENCRYPTION
AS
     DECLARE @cmd varchar(255)
          SELECT @cmd = 'c:\SQL11\bin\iSQL -Usa -Pblooper -SCHARDONNAY -ic:\
                  SQL1\scripts\hereitis.SQL'
          EXEC xp_cmdshell @cmd,NOOUTPUT
GO
```

In order to implement encryption in Sybase, you'd need to do the following:

```
CREATE PROCEDURE become_sa_for_a_moment
AS
     DECLARE @cmd varchar(255)
     SELECT @cmd = 'c:\SQL11\bin\iSQL -Usa -Pblooper -SCHARDONNAY -ic:\SQL1\
scripts\hereitis.SQL'
     EXEC xp_cmdshell @cmd,NOOUTPUT
GO
sp_hidetext "become_sa_for_a_moment"
GO
```

In this example, the password for SA has been written into the procedure. You probably wouldn't want just anyone to be able to read the code for this procedure and find out the SA password. By using the WITH ENCRYPTION option, no one will be able to read the code for this procedure in syscomments and gain access to this sensitive information.

If you were to select the code for this procedure from syscomments, then you would see something similar to the following:

```
/* syscomments */
id  number colid texttype language text
-----------------------------------------------------------------------------
1264007534  1  1 6  0  L såvùO_Oéf:3j"ØË%ê! ._ '_ ø,Ét';/f<ó-F\__'·k'È¥<vé*Á mÈ_
>_$®;y}R ,ï«  §ûH/_jp cçÍâÎ_B!æÌ<ÒZœõeV cPÙhàà_‰ºí…ö{§VÊ"P_JÓª§t… Õ¡çL«™Z¬  Ç§ëCŒi?_-
  ‡®¯_ÅƒË>-˜…¤^_ r-\ÄÓnÌôu_^  üWì_å_ _öE9ÄÆÂ FdŒs‡

(1 row(s) affected)
```

If you had to re-create this procedure for some reason, you would have to use your original source code file, since there is currently no mechanism to decrypt encrypted code within SQL Server. We think this is a feature of the product!

No matter how tempted you may be, do not remove these lines from syscomments, since you will not be able to upgrade these procedures when you install a newer version of SQL Server. Removing entries from any system table is a bad idea, because the vendor's technical support staff will not offer you any assistance if you have a problem afterward.

Note that, as noted earlier in the chapter, Microsoft's V6.5 implementation of ENCRYPTION has significant limitations.

The Importance of Ownership

Object ownership is unfortunately one of those concepts that needs to be covered not because it is exciting, but because it may affect the way you code. In addition, it can potentially save you hours of misery trying to debug code that actually works.

When you write Transact-SQL code, you have the option of specifying the owner name before any database object, since it is possible to create multiple versions of the same object but with different owners. The database server assumes that if you don't specify the owner name explicitly in your code, it must first see if you have an object of that name owned by yourself. If you do, the server will pick up your instance of the object. If you don't, the server will check to see if there is an instance owned by the DBO. If there is, the server picks up that instance. If the server cannot find an instance owned by the DBO, it assumes that the object is missing and sends you an error code. For example:

```
SELECT  pub_id,
    pub_name
FROM    dbo.publishers

/* may be the same as */

SELECT  pub_id,
    pub_name
FROM    publishers
```

It is important to be aware of the issues of ownership when you write Transact-SQL code, since it may affect the way you write your code. For example, this code:

```
IF EXISTS (SELECT name
           FROM sysobjects
           WHERE name = 'publishers')
   DROP TABLE publishers
```

may return an error if there is a table called publishers but it is not owned by you. In this example, it would be better to write the code as follows:

```
IF EXISTS (SELECT name
           FROM sysobjects
           WHERE name = 'publishers'
```

```
        AND uid = USER_ID() )
    DROP TABLE publishers
```

Think Modular

There is always more than one way to write a query. In this book, we look at a number of ways since each technique we present here represents one of our tried-and-trusted ways of getting SQL Server to do what we want it to do with the minimum amount of CPU and disk utilization. In general, the KISS (keep it simple, stupid) principle is as applicable in stored procedure design as it is in every other aspect of computing. The simpler a stored procedure is, the more likely it is to perform in optimal fashion.

We have found that by applying modular design techniques to stored procedure design, we create a versatile bunch of stored procedures that we can use in a wide variety of circumstances. Furthermore, development is speeded up, since creating multiple stored procedures (where each performs an atomic function) is quicker and simpler than creating one behemoth procedure that does everything. More than likely, the behemoth would end up doing nothing since it wouldn't work, or it would consume so many resources in attempting to run that it may just as well not work.

Performance Issues

Now that we have covered some of the basic design concepts, it's time to review some of the major performance issues you may have to deal with when using stored procedures. We've dedicated an entire chapter to this topic—Chapter 20, *Transact-SQL Optimization and Tuning*—so please consider this section an appetizer and not the main course.

Compilation

One of the reasons executing a stored procedure is quicker than executing simple SQL is that the system precompiles the code in a stored procedure and builds a query plan for it. It then uses this query plan in all subsequent executions of this stored procedure. Another reason stored procedures are so much more efficient in general is because there is a reduction in network traffic. The query plan itself is not created until the first time the stored procedure is executed. This is because SQL Server does not know at compile time what values may be passed to the stored procedure. SQL Server can evaluate this only after the procedure is run for the first time. The query plan itself is stored in sysprocedures. Please don't rush to check this system table out because the data is stored in a binary form and is basically unreadable.

To help SQL Server choose an optimal query plan, you should make sure, the first time any procedure is run, that the parameters passed to the procedure are as realistic as possible. The result is that the query plan SQL Server selects will hold for the majority of cases this procedure will process. Each time SQL Server reboots, the query plans are discarded and new ones are created. SQL Server may not necessarily choose the same plan when it reboots.

Recompile

There are several methods that can be used to recompile a stored procedure. Each method achieves the same objective.

- The stored procedure can be created with the WITH RECOMPILE option as part of its declaration. Doing this will cause the server to recompile the stored procedure every time it is run and create a fresh query plan for it.
- The stored procedure can be executed with the WITH RECOMPILE option in the EXEC command.
- By performing an UPDATE STATISTICS on any table that is called by a stored procedure, SQL Server will flag all affected stored procedures and create a new query plan the next time they are executed.
- Dropping a procedure and re-creating it will also cause a stored procedure to be recompiled again when it is next executed. Every time you drop and re-create a stored procedure, it is assigned a different unique ID.
- The server can be stopped and restarted. This will cause all previously existing query plans to be lost; SQL Server will then re-create new query plans the next time a procedure is called after startup. This may seem like a radical solution. However, when your data has changed significantly, as is often the case in a data warehouse, this may be the simplest solution.
- Finally, the *sp_recompile* stored procedure can be called for a specific procedure, which will create a fresh query plan the next time the stored procedure is executed. The syntax for *sp_recompile* is covered in Chapter 17.

You should usually recompile a stored procedure when one or more of the following occurs:

- The indexes on the data the procedure uses have changed.
- The volume of data the procedure processes has changed.

Whenever SQL Server recompiles a stored procedure, it extends the existing query plan. SQL Server does not simply remove all record of it and create a new one. This means that if you continually recompile a stored procedure, over time its query plan will grow extremely large, consume unnecessary resources, and no longer be fast. To prevent this from happening, you need to drop the procedure and re-create it. There is also a size limitation on stored procedure text. In Sybase, this limitation is 16 MB. On Microsoft, as of V6.5, the limitation is currently 64 KB. The procedure cache configuration option must be large enough to hold the compiled version of your stored procedure.

Indexing

Many times, you'll need to create a temporary table or a permanent scratch table in the course of a stored procedure's processing. This introduces some complex challenges because earlier versions of SQL Server require a referenced object to exist in order for a stored procedure to properly execute. (One way to get around this problem is to use "wrapper" stored procedures, as we explained earlier.) This is especially troubling when the temporary table also needs an index or two.

There are a couple of different ways to create indexes in a stored procedure so that the stored procedure actually takes advantage of them. Unfortunately, you have to do some creative programming. When SQL Server creates the query plan, an index does not exist, since it exists only after the first time the stored procedure is run. Two different methods are described here that do the same thing.

```
-- Create table so we can create the inner stored procedure
CREATE TABLE #nauthors (au_id VARCHAR(11),
    au_lname VARCHAR(40),
    au_fname VARCHAR(20),
    phone CHAR(12),
    address VARCHAR(40),
    city VARCHAR(20),
    state CHAR(2),
    zip CHAR(5),
    contract BIT)
GO

-- Create a procedure that can utilize an index
CREATE PROCEDURE use_the_index
AS
SELECT au_id
FROM   #nauthors
GO

-- Drop this table so we can create the outer stored procedure
```

```
DROP TABLE #nauthors
GO

-- Create a procedure to populate a table with data
-- and also create an index on it
CREATE PROCEDURE high_level_nest
AS

CREATE TABLE #nauthors (au_id VARCHAR(11),
    au_lname VARCHAR(40),
    au_fname VARCHAR(20),
    phone CHAR(12),
    address VARCHAR(40),
    city VARCHAR(20),
    state CHAR(2),
    zip CHAR(5),
    contract BIT)

INSERT #nauthors
SELECT *
FROM   pubs..authors

CREATE INDEX ind1 ON #nauthors (id)

EXEC use_the_index
GO
```

Another method you can use is to refer to the index by number explicitly in your SELECT statement. You cannot use the name of the index, since it does not exist at that point and will result in a compilation error. Only Sybase SQL Server Version 11.0 allows us to use this method. Neither Sybase Adaptive Server 11.5 nor Microsoft SQL Server 6.5 allows us to use this approach. Microsoft does not even allow us to process the query. Sybase allows the query to be run but returns a warning that the specified optimizer hint does not exist and that the server will choose a more appropriate index. You may wish to try the following example on your server version to see if you can use this method since it's so much simpler to code than the other approach:

```
CREATE PROCEDURE refer_to_the_index
AS
SELECT *
INTO   #nauthors
FROM   pubs..authors

CREATE INDEX ind1 ON #nauthors (au_id)
SELECT au_id
FROM   #nauthors (1)
GO
```

On Microsoft SQL Server 6.5, you'll get this response:

```
Msg 307, Level 16, State 1
Index id 1 on table '#nauthors'(specified in the FROM clause) does not exist.
```

Summary

This chapter has looked at stored procedures in detail and introduced all the major topics that relate to stored procedures:

- The purpose of stored procedures
- How to create stored procedures via CREATE PROCEDURE
- Types of stored procedures
- Advantages of stored procedures
- When to use stored procedures rather than other Transact-SQL objects
- How to execute stored procedures and use dynamic SQL
- How to use remote procedure calls (RPCs), a variant of stored procedures
- General design considerations for building stored procedures
- Conditional data retrieval and the use of stored procedures where specific subsets of data are required
- The use of data formatting when returning data sets
- Data security and encryption in SQL Server

In this chapter:
- *Triggers*
- *Interaction of Triggers and Constraints*
- *Summary*

15

Triggers and Constraints

A trigger or constraint can be created to execute every time an insert, update, or delete operation occurs on a particular table. Triggers and constraints are created in order to enforce some form of integrity requirement that has been determined, usually in the analysis or design phase of the project. Refer to Chapter 2, *Database Analysis and Design*, for a more detailed explanation of project phases.

In this chapter, we'll review how triggers and constraints are created, what they can do for you, and how they are used in applications.

Triggers

A trigger is similar to a stored procedure, except that it is attached to a particular table. A trigger is executed every time a data-modification operation, such as an insert, update, or delete, occurs. Triggers are used to enforce integrity rules. The nature of these rules is determined by the particular application for which they are created. In some cases, triggers may be used to check that an entry you've created has a reciprocal entry elsewhere. They may be used to delete or create related records when appropriate. Trigger code can, with few exceptions, include most valid Transact-SQL commands and functions that we've discussed elsewhere in this book.

Traditionally, triggers have been used to enforce integrity rules in a database and ensure that when a data-modification operation occurs (i.e., insert, update, or delete) any necessary prerequisites to the action have been met.

From Version 6.00 of Microsoft and System 10 of Sybase, constraints can now be used to perform some of the same tasks as triggers. Even though constraints are embedded in the actual table definition, at this point they lack the functionality to be as flexible as triggers. In reality, constraints and triggers should be combined.

When the check being performed is straightforward, it is usually practical to implement it using a constraint. When the check is more convoluted and cannot be coded as a constraint, it can instead be coded as a trigger.

Although triggers are executed automatically, they are only executed once higher-level integrity checks have been performed. In general, the hierarchy for data-modification operations is as shown in Figure 15-1.

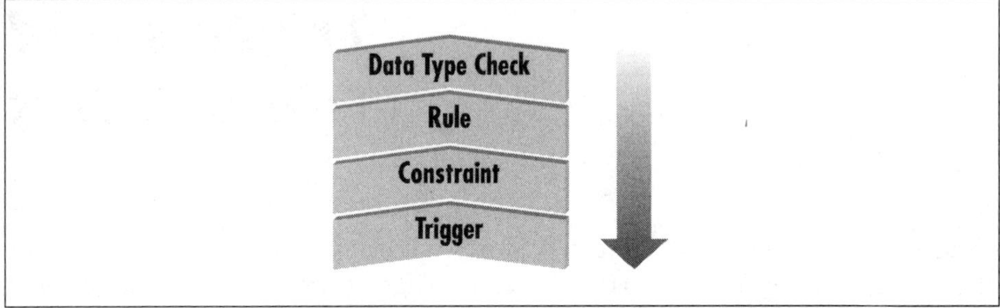

Figure 15-1. Integrity check hierarchy

Triggers allow you to do an explicit rollback of the transaction if a check fails or to initiate additional transactions such as cascading deletes and updates. A trigger can also reference other objects in a server or even cause an action to be executed on a remote server using remote procedure calls (RPCs).

Creating Triggers

Before a trigger can be used, it must be created. The syntax to create a trigger is as follows:

Microsoft

```
CREATE TRIGGER
    [owner.]trigger_name
ON [owner.]table_name
FOR {INSERT, UPDATE}
    [WITH ENCRYPTION]
AS
    {IF UPDATE(column_name)
        [{AND |OR}UPDATE
    (column_name)]...]
        SQL_statements
    {IF UPDATE (column_name)
        [{AND |OR} UPDATE
    (column_name)]...
        SQL_statements]...
```

Sybase

```
CREATE TRIGGER
    [owner.]trigger_name
ON [owner.]table_name
FOR {INSERT, UPDATE}

AS
    {IF UPDATE (column_name)
        [{AND |OR}UPDATE
    (column_name)]...]
        SQL_statements
    {IF UPDATE (column_name)
        [{AND |OR} UPDATE
    (column_name)]...
        SQL_statements]...
```

To create a trigger, you must specify the table to which the trigger relates, as well as the data-modification operation(s) for which it is to be performed. The following example creates a simple trigger on the authors table to display a message every time a record gets created or modified:

```
CREATE TRIGGER Print_Authors_Msg_UI
ON authors
FOR INSERT,UPDATE
AS
IF (SELECT @@rowcount ) > 0
     PRINT "Entry made in the authors table"
```

Removing Triggers

There are two ways to drop a trigger. The first is to explicitly issue a DROP TRIGGER statement as follows:

```
DROP TRIGGER [owner.][Trigger Name]
```

For example:

```
DROP TRIGGER Print_Authors_Msg_UI
```

Alternatively, if a new trigger is created on a table for the same operation as the old trigger, then the existing trigger is automatically dropped even if the procedure does not have the same name!

Trigger Ownership

Since a trigger is associated with a particular table, only the owner of the table can create a trigger for it. A user who has access to a table with a trigger defined for it does not need special permission to execute the procedure. The INSERT, UPDATE, and DELETE operations—not an explicit call—are what cause a trigger to execute.

The INSERTED and DELETED Pseudotables

The power of a trigger lies in the ability to check the data that has just been added to or deleted from a table. In order to do this, two special tables called the *inserted pseudotable* and the *deleted pseudotable* temporarily exist during the execution of the trigger. The inserted and deleted table structures are exactly the same as the underlying table to which they refer. During an insert operation, only the inserted pseudotable exists. During a delete operation, only the deleted pseudotable exists. During an update operation, both tables exist because the inserted table stores the afterimage of the operation. The deleted table stores the before image of the operation.

In the following example, a trigger will be created on the titleauthor table to check that a valid entry exists in both the authors and the titles table:

```
CREATE TRIGGER Author_Titles_Check_UI
ON titleauthor
FOR insert,update
```

```
AS
/* This trigger checks to see whether a valid entry exists in the titles */
/* table as well as an entry in the authors table for a given titleauthor */
/* record */

DECLARE @rcount int

/* If there are no records exit */

SELECT @rcount = @@rowcount
IF @rcount = 0
    RETURN

/* Titles check */

IF (SELECT count(*)
    FROM titles a,
         inserted b
    WHERE a.title_id = b.title_id) <> @rcount
BEGIN
    RAISERROR 50001"Cannot create entry for non-existent title"
    ROLLBACK TRANSACTION
    RETURN
END

/* Authors check */

IF (SELECT count(*)
          FROM authors a,
               inserted b
       WHERE a.author_id = b.author_id) <> @rcount
BEGIN
    RAISERROR 50001 "Cannot create entry for non-existent author"
    ROLLBACK TRANSACTION
    RETURN
END
```

In this example, the inserted table had the same structure as the titleauthor table, as shown in Figure 15-2.

Figure 15-2. titleauthor table layout

The trigger was used to perform a FOREIGN KEY check in both the authors and the titles structure prior to the commit of the transaction. In this example, if a single entry had been incorrect, the entire transaction would have been rolled back, and a message would have been displayed to the user.

The deleted table works in a similar fashion. One of the most common uses of triggers is to cascade the impact of an event (for example, delete any child entries that exist for that particular example). The next example contains a simple illustration of this technique. This trigger will be created on the authors table to delete any entries in the titleauthor table once an author is deleted:

```
CREATE TRIGGER TitleAuthorRemove_D
ON authors
FOR DELETE
AS
DELETE titleauthor
FROM deleted a,
     titleauthor b
WHERE a.author_id = b.author_id
```

IF UPDATE()

One additional feature unique to a trigger is the IF UPDATE() function. This function can be specified in an update trigger. It allows you to check whether a particular field was updated and executes a particular test only if the field was modified. This is very useful when there are a large number of FOREIGN KEY checks that need to be performed or columns that cannot be modified under any circumstances. In the next example, we create an update trigger on the authors table to illustrate the use of IF UPDATE():

```
CREATE TRIGGER AuthorChecks_U
ON authors
FOR UPDATE
AS

DECLARE @rcount int
SELECT @rcount = @@rowcount

IF UPDATE(au_id)
BEGIN
    RAISERROR 50001 "Cannot change the author id. Must delete and re-create"
    ROLLBACK TRANSACTION
    RETURN
END

IF UPDATE(contract)
BEGIN
    IF (SELECT contract
        FROM inserted
        WHERE contract IN (0,1)) <> @rcount
    RAISERROR 50001"Can only change the contract indicator to 0 or 1"
     ROLLBACK TRANSACTION
     RETURN
END
```

```
IF UPDATE(au_lname)
BEGIN
    IF (SELECT a.au_lname
          FROM deleted a,
   inserted b
  WHERE a.au_lname = 'SMITH'
    AND b.au_lname = 'SMITHERS'
    AND a.au_id = b.au_id ) > 0
  BEGIN
       UPDATE authors
       SET a.au_lname = b.au_lname
       FROM authors a,
            deleted b
       WHERE a.au_id = b.au_id
 END
END
```

In this example, the trigger checks to see that the au_id column is never updated, that the contract column contains only a 0 or a 1, and that the au_lname field was not changed from SMITH to SMITHERS. A violation in either the checks for au_id or the conract column would cause the trigger to be rolled back. A violation in au_lname wouldn't cause the trigger to be rolled back, but the trigger would update all the last names to their original values.

The first two rules could also be maintained using constraints. The update on au_lname is an example of a business rule that has been incorporated into a business object. This type of rule can only be implemented via a trigger today.

Trigger Transactions

We've briefly introduced the transaction concept. When a data-modification operation occurs, there are three specific phases of transaction processing that the data passes through:

Before image
: The table contains the original data prior to the operation. The transaction begins here.

During image
: The inserted and deleted pseudotables contain a copy of all data added to or removed from the table. The underlying table also holds the modified data as well as other rows not affected by the transaction. The transaction would be in progress, and the trigger would perform all necessary checks.

After image
: The table contains all changed data. The inserted and deleted tables are discarded. The transaction would have completed. In the case of the trigger performing a rollback transaction, the data in the table would revert to the before-image stage.

Types of Rollbacks

There are two primary ROLLBACK commands that can be issued within a trigger:

ROLLBACK TRIGGER
: This will roll back the entire trigger, excluding any RPCs that may have executed. This command optionally calls RAISERROR. The trigger will also roll back any cascaded operations it has caused. The ROLLBACK TRIGGER will cause SQL Server to abort the command that caused the trigger to fire in the first place. SQL Server will also abort the execution of the trigger at this point.

ROLLBACK TRANSACTION
: This will roll back the entire transaction, excluding any RPCs that may have been executed. The trigger is not aborted. In general, if you issue a ROLLBACK TRANSACTION, you will probably want to exit the trigger at that point. To ensure that this happens, add a RETURN after the ROLLBACK TRANSACTION; this is similar to the way we've implemented our error checks in the previous examples.

In a trigger, the operation of these commands does not actually differ unless explicit savepoints have been defined in the trigger itself. For more information about savepoints, see the discussion of transactions in Chapter 11, *Transactions and Locking*. In the examples given, we've used rollback transactions to maintain consistency across versions and products. The alternate form is used in the next example:

```
CREATE TRIGGER PublisherChecks_UI
ON titles
FOR insert,update
AS
DECLARE @rcount int
SELECT @rcount = @@rowcount
IF @rcount = 0
        RETURN

IF (SELECT count(*)
          FROM publishers a,
                inserted b
        WHERE a.pub_id = b.pub_id) <> @rcount
BEGIN
        ROLLBACK TRIGGER WITH RAISERROR 50001
        "Cannot create entry for non existent publisher"
       RETURN
END
```

Nested and Cascaded Triggers

There are subtle differences between nested and cascaded triggers.

A Trigger in Slow Motion

Lights, Camera, Action . . .

The Scene:

Deep inside the SQL Server kernel an overzealous commander SQL Server is acting out control fantasies on unsuspecting users.

The Event:

An unsuspecting user issues a query that causes a trigger to be fired.

The Action:

Captain SQL Server creates a savepoint before any action is taken on the data. This is done so Captain SQL Server can roll back the entire transaction, excluding RPCs should it be necessary.

Captain SQL Server builds the deleted and the inserted tables with the before images and the after images, respectively.

Captain SQL Server then updates the underlying table with the changes.

Captain SQL Server then runs the trigger to check to see that the data changes were valid.

If the data changes were valid, Captain SQL Server will commit the changes; otherwise, the transaction will be rolled back.

The user may get a message saying that a certain number of rows were modified or a rude message informing the user that he messed up.

Captain SQL Server removes the inserted and deleted tables and continues operations as normal.

Cut.

Nested triggers

A nested trigger is actually a set of two or more triggers that fire on related tables but that may have differing goals. For example, when you issue an update to the sales table, you may also cause an insert operation on a sales_history record (you may want to create a copy of each sales entry in the sales_history file). Likewise, issuing a delete on the sales table may also result in a delete on this sales history record, this time to remove the sales_history record. For example:

```
CREATE TABLE  sales_history  (
title_id tid,
total_orders int)

CREATE TRIGGER Sales_I
ON sales
FOR INSERT
AS
```

```
-- Assume that a record for each title already exists in the sales_history
table -- for this example

UPDATE sales_history
SET       a.total_orders = a.total_orders +b.qty
FROM      inserted b,
     sales_history a
WHERE a.title_id = b.title_id

GO
```

In this example, an insert to the sales table will cause an update to the sales_history table.

Cascaded triggers

Cascading triggers, on the other hand, merely perpetuate the same operation to subordinate tables. For example, if you delete a title from the titles table, you also want to delete all related records from the titleauthor table. Thus, the same sort of delete operation was cascaded to the subordinate table, as shown here:

```
CREATE TRIGGER Title_Delete_D
ON publishers
FOR delete
AS
DECLARE @rcount int
SELECT @rcount = @@rowcount
IF @rcount = 0
    RETURN

DELETE titles
  FROM titles a,
       deleted b
 WHERE b.pub_id = a.pub_id
```

In this trigger example, every time a publisher is deleted, all titles that exist in the titles table for that particular publisher are deleted as well. However, if you look at the titles table, the title_id is also found in several other tables, including titleauthor, sales, and roysched. If the title were removed without removing the entries in these other tables, then there would be incomplete data sitting in the system. A trigger similar to the following may be created on the titles table to handle such a delete operation:

```
CREATE TRIGGER AncilliaryTableDelete_D
ON titles
FOR delete
AS
DECLARE @rcount int
SELECT @rcount = @@rowcount
IF @rcount = 0
    RETURN
```

```
DELETE sales
  FROM sales a,
       deleted b
 WHERE b.title_id = a.title_id

DELETE roysched
  FROM roysched a,
       deleted b
 WHERE b.title_id = a.title_id

DELETE titleauthor
  FROM titleauthor a,
       deleted b
 WHERE b.title_id = a.title_id
```

It is currently possible to cascade a trigger to a maximum of 16 levels. To perform nested trigger operations, SQL Server needs to be configured properly. The configuration option "allow nested triggers" must be set to 1. This configuration option is set using the *sp_configure* system stored procedure.

Firing Triggers

Any INSERT, DELETE, or UPDATE will cause a trigger to fire, provided that a trigger has been created for that type of operation.

Since the SELECT keyword does not modify data, no trigger will execute when any SELECT statement is executed. On Sybase SQL Server, the system table sysobjects contains columns called instrig, updtrig, deltrig, and seltrig. The first three columns store object IDs for INSERT, UPDATE, and DELETE triggers. There is anecdotal evidence that Sybase had planned to implement SELECT triggers as well, hence the column seltrig. This idea was never implemented, but the column has remained for posterity.

A trigger will always execute once for every set of rows processed by an INSERT operation, no matter how many rows were inserted by the command.

One critical thing to remember is that if the trigger fails, then all records are rolled back and no partial updates are allowed.

Performance Considerations

Triggers are a great mechanism for ensuring data integrity. However, since they always execute whenever the specified operation is performed, it's critical to ensure that triggers perform only necessary checks. Here are some guidelines:

- Use unique indexes rather than triggers to maintain data consistency.

- Remember that cascading deletes initiate transactions on many related tables, which can make processing appear slower to a user, especially if that user is only aware that the parent record is being deleted. For that reason, cascading triggers may be dangerous if someone carelessly deletes a parent row without considering that many other rows will be gone as well. (It is sometimes safer to use constraints to restrain the deletion of parent rows until all child records are gone.)
- Always consider the number of records that will be updated when you create triggers, especially on UPDATE triggers. A carte blanche UPDATE on a table may cause your trigger logic to be executed on large volumes of records, which may cause your log to fill up since a trigger runs within a transaction.
- A trigger is not executed when BCP (the Bulk Copy Program), described in Appendix C, *The BCP Utility*, is used to load data into tables.

Triggers and Replication

Replication can be quite a thorny issue if you make heavy use of triggers. The big problem with triggers and replication on a Microsoft SQL Server database is SQL Server's use of deferred UPDATE statements. That means that INSERT and DELETE transactions aren't affected by the cohabitation of replication and triggers on a particular database. An INSERT or DELETE is the same on both the publishing and the subscribing server.

However, SQL server's use of deferred *UPDATE* statements also means that UPDATE statements may experience problems. In effect, SQL Server's deferred UPDATE model translates an UPDATE command into a separate INSERT statement of a record containing its new values, followed by a DELETE statement of the record containing its old values.

Thus, a server publishing replicated data may fire an UPDATE trigger with its own special logic for a given transaction. But when that publishing server sends the data on to the next subscribing server, it receives an INSERT and DELETE transaction—possibly with very different, even conflicting, trigger logic.

The general idea is to be very careful when using triggers and replication in tandem. Furthermore, you should thoroughly test all transaction scenarios against replicated tables that possess triggers to ensure that your business logic is properly maintained.

Interaction of Triggers and Constraints

Contraints are discussed in some detail in Chapter 3. Here, we discuss constraints in relation to triggers.

A constraint allows you to apply simple referential integrity checks to a table. Constraints are called before triggers. An important point to remember about constraints is that while only a single trigger of a given type (INSERT, UPDATE, or DELETE) may exist on a table at any given time, *many* constraints may exist on a single table. A constraint is similar to a trigger in that it is associated with a particular table, and it enforces data-integrity rules. From an operational standpoint, constraints differ from triggers in three significant ways:

- Only the INSERT, UPDATE, or DELETE command that initiated constraints is rolled back in the event of failure.
- Constraints may be included in the CREATE TABLE statement of the owning table.
- Constraints are less extensive in functionality than triggers, but they are easier to create and maintain.

There are four primary types of constraints that are currently supported by SQL Server:

PRIMARY/UNIQUE
: Enforces uniqueness of a particular table column

DEFAULT
: Specifies a default value for a column in case an INSERT operation does not provide one

FOREIGN KEY
: Validates that every value in a column exists in a column of another table

CHECK
: Checks that every value stored in a column is in some specified list

Each type of constraint performs a specific type of action. Microsoft SQL Server and Sybase SQL Server support both table- and column-level constraints, as we discussed in Chapter 3.

Sometimes triggers and constraints do not get along well. For example, in Microsoft SQL Server 6.x, FOREIGN KEY constraints are checked first, very often disabling triggers on the same table. Table 15-1 may help you select between constraints and triggers.

Table 15-1. Trigger and Constraint Selection Matrix

Type/Event	Constraint	Trigger
FOREIGN KEY	Easy to implement. Doesn't support complex rules. Restricts dropping of a referenced table. All tables must be resident within the same database.	Implementation is more complicated than constraints. Can support any complex rules. Doesn't restrict dropping of a referenced table. Can handle cross-database foreign keys.
DEFAULT	Easy to implement. Doesn't support complex rules.	Implementation is more complicated than constraints. Can support any complex rules.
CHECK	Easy to implement. Doesn't support complex rules.	Implementation is more complicated than constraints. Can support any complex rules.
PRIMARY KEY, UNIQUE KEY	Easy to implement. An alternative is to use a CREATE UNIQUE INDEX statement.	Implementation is more complicated than constraints.
Complex business rules (such as "The total amount of cash withdrawals from the account on any day should not exceed $500")	Doesn't support complex rules.	Specifically designed for this type of logic.
Error log	SQL Server can be configured to write constraint violation messages to the error log, but this method is not flexible.	Can be programmed to write specific events to the error log.
Error handling	Supports only standard constraint violation error messages.	Can be programmed to report any user-defined error message and perform additional complex error-handling functions.
Effect of trigger or constraint during a BCP process	BCP is a nonlogged operation. The constraint does not execute.	BCP is a nonlogged operation. The trigger does not execute.

Summary

This chapter looked at triggers, which are used to maintain data integrity within your tables; we described both the syntax used to create triggers and the different methods used to remove a trigger. In addition, we discussed:

- The different types of triggers that can be created
- The use of the insert and deleted pseudotables
- Transaction specifics and cascade logic
- The differences between constraints and triggers, and suggestions on where each should be used

In this chapter:
- *About Views*
- *Managing Views*
- *Querying Views*
- *View Dependencies, Permissions, and Data Manipulations*
- *Limitations of Views*
- *View Overhead*
- *Summary*

16

Views

Around 3:00 P.M. every afternoon, I start wishing for a cube with a view. There are two reasons for this. First, I'm often in some dreadful meeting at about that time. And second, like most of us in corporate America, I seldom see a window during the course of the day. At least the SQL Server relational database provides us with views, however, and although they're not the kind I'm often hoping for, they are very useful structures indeed.

About Views

The best way to understand a *view* is to think of it as a virtual table. A view's contents are *not* based on a stored set of data values in a table of the database; rather, the contents are defined by a query. This query is defined by using a standard SELECT statement against tables on the same server. The contents of the view are the result set of the executed query. The view is presented to you as if it were any other table with rows and columns. Once the view is defined, you can perform most SQL data-manipulation statements against the view. Certain restrictions do apply to inserting, updating, and deleting data. We'll cover these restrictions later in this chapter.

The table(s) used in the view are known as *base tables*. Data manipulation using a view reflects data in the base tables. Any updates applied to the base tables will be reflected in the view in real time. Data that is updated through a view is updated in the base table in a real-time fashion as well. Here's an example of a simple view:

```
CREATE VIEW author_royalties
AS
SELECT A.au_fname "First_Name",
       A.au_lname "Last_Name",
       SUM(T2.royalty * T2.ytd_sales/100) "Paid_Royalties"
FROM authors     A
```

```
JOIN titleauthor T1 ON A.au_id  = T1.au_id
JOIN titles      T2 ON T1.title_id = T2.title_id
GROUP BY A.au_lname, A.au_fname
GO
```

To extract data from the view, specify:

```
SELECT * FROM author_royalties
```

Results:

```
First_Name           Last_Name                                Paid_Royalties
-------------------- ---------------------------------------- --------------
Abraham              Bennet                                   409
Reginald             Blotchet-Halls                           2113
Cheryl               Carson                                   1404
Michel               DeFrance                                 5339
Innes                del Castillo                             243
Ann                  Dull                                     409
Marjorie             Green                                    4902
Burt                 Gringlesby                               409
Sheryl               Hunter                                   409
Livia                Karsen                                   37
Charlene             Locksley                                 333
Stearns              MacFeather                               424
Michael              O'Leary                                  796
Sylvia               Panteley                                 37
Albert               Ringer                                   256
Anne                 Ringer                                   5584
Dean                 Straight                                 409
Johnson              White                                    407
Akiko                Yokomoto                                 409
```

In certain circumstances, you can not only issue a SELECT statement against a view, you can also perform INSERT, UPDATE, and DELETE statements on the view. We'll provide more detail on that sort of activity later in the chapter.

Managing Views

Before a view can be used, it must be created. We'll cover the syntax options for creating a view in this section. Basically, the syntax to create a view is very simple; we need to apply only a few lines of code around a standard SELECT statement.

View Syntax

The syntax to create a view is as follows:

Microsoft	Sybase

`CREATE VIEW [owner.]view_name`
`[(column_name [, column_name]...)]`
`[ WITH ENCRYPTION]`
`AS select_statement`
`[WITH CHECK OPTION]`
	`CREATE VIEW [owner.]view_name`
	`[(column_name [, column_name]...)]`
	`AS select_statement`
	`[WITH CHECK OPTION]`

Each view must be given a unique **view_name** within the user's account that conform to SQL Server's rules for object identification.

An interesting "feature" of Microsoft SQL Server is the ability to create local temporary views using the pound symbol (#). #view_name can be used to create what SQL Server treats as a temporary view, but SQL Server does not allow you to access the view.

The **column_names** in views are usually optional, since SQL Server will default to the name of the columns in the SELECT statement as the names of the columns of the view. There's one exception to this behavior. Column names are required if the view contains a column that is derived from a formula, arithmetic expression, or function, or in situations in which two or more columns in the SELECT statement have the same name. **column_name** can be either a column list at the beginning of the create view or embedded aliases in the SELECT statement syntax. The limits and rules of table column names apply to column names used in a view.

Our general recommendation is to avoid the **column_name** syntax in favor of using column aliases in the SELECT statement. In our opinion, this approach improves readability, especially in very large views.

In the following example, by omitting the **column_name** list, the view column names are given the same names as the **column_name** list used in the SELECT statement.

```
CREATE VIEW v_pub_info
AS
SELECT  pub_id, pub_name, city
FROM    publishers
```

To see the columns created by the preceding code, invoke the *sp_help* system stored procedure from ISQL:

```
sp_help v_pub_info
```

Results:

```
Name          Owner            Type                     when_created
------------  ---------------  -----------------------  ---------------------
v_PubInfo     dbo              view                     Jan 3 1998  1:24PM

Data_located_on_segment
-----------------------
not applicable
```

```
Column_name Type     Length Prec Scale Nullable TrimTrailing   FixedLen
                                                Blanks         NullInSource
----------- -------- ------ ---- ----- -------- -------------- --------------
pub_id      char     4      no   yes   no
pub_name    varchar  40     yes  yes   no
city        varchar  20     yes  yes   no

Identity                       Seed                    Increment
----------------------------   ---------------------   ------------------------
No identity column defined.    (null)                  (null)

No constraints have been defined for this object.

No foreign keys reference this table.
```

By adding the column name label as a literal in double quotes into the SELECT statement, we can modify the view's `column_name`. This works well with a long select list where you have computed columns or where you need to use two columns with the same name from different joined tables. We used this technique earlier in a view that created the computed column for total advances.

Here's another example:

```
CREATE VIEW v_pub_info2
AS
SELECT  pub_id "Publisher_Id",
        pub_name     "Publisher_Name",
        city         "Publisher_City"
FROM    publishers
```

This will create the view with the following column names:

```
Column_name
-------------------------------
Publisher_Id
Publisher_Name
Publisher_City
```

A less common, though equally valid, approach to use when creating a view is to explicitly define the column names. The results from the preceding CREATE VIEW can also be achieved with the following syntax:

```
CREATE VIEW v_pub_info2  (Publisher_Id,Publisher_Name,Publisher_City)
AS
SELECT  pub_id, pub_name, city
FROM    publishers
```

The list of columns in this view is the same as in the previous example.

WITH ENCRYPTION (Microsoft only)

When you create a view, the syscomments system table contains the text of the view syntax used in the CREATE VIEW statement. The contents of syscomments are usually plain old text and can be viewed using the *sp_helptext* system stored procedure (or even just a SELECT on syscomments). Using this clause will cause the text of the view syntax to be encrypted in the syscomment tables.

For example:

```
sp_helptext v_pub_info2
```

Results:

```
text
---------------------------------------------------------------------------
CREATE VIEW v_pub_info2 (Publisher_Id,Publisher_Name,Publisher_City)
AS
SELECT  pub_id, pub_name, city
FROM    publishers
```

As you can see, this is a good way to review the query behind any view. However, if the nature of the database requires that the view syntax be concealed from the users or other developers, then the view could be created using the following syntax:

```
CREATE VIEW v_pub_info2 (Publisher_Id,Publisher_Name,Publisher_City)
WITH ENCRYPTION
AS
SELECT  pub_id, pub_name, city
FROM    publishers
```

If you attempt to use the *sp_helptext* system stored procedure, the following will occur:

```
sp_helptext v_pub_info2
```

Results:

```
The object's comments have been encrypted.
```

Using the WITH ENCRYPTION clause will keep the view code from being re-created during a database upgrade. You will have to maintain the view text in a separate file to be applied after the upgrade.

AS select_statement

This is the section of the statement that defines the view. Just about any kind of SELECT you can imagine is acceptable, with the following restrictions:

- ORDER BY, COMPUTE, or COMPUTE BY clauses cannot be used.
- The INTO keyword is not allowed.
- Temporary tables cannot be referenced.

- You must have SELECT permission on all objects referenced in the view. Other appropriate DML permissions (INSERT, UPDATE, or DELETE) must exist to perform that operation with a view.

WITH CHECK OPTION

This option forces any updates done via the view to adhere to the SELECT statement's WHERE clause criteria. Normally, views allow data entry against their base tables. When you enable the WITH CHECK OPTION, the view disables data entry or updates to a record if the change makes the record inaccessible to the view.

Here's an example where we've created a view showing the authors living in Tennessee (TN).

```
CREATE VIEW v_TN_authors
AS
SELECT au_id,
       au_lname,
       au_fname,
       phone,
       address,
       city,
       state,
       zip,
       contract
FROM   authors
WHERE  state = 'TN'
WITH CHECK OPTION
```

This statement will create a view named v_TN_authors with the columns au_id, au_lname, au_fname, phone, addresses, city, state, zip, and contract for all authors whose state equals TN. The WITH CHECK OPTION disables the modification of the state field to any value other than TN, since this would eliminate the row from the view. Here's an example:

```
UPDATE v_TN_authors
SET    state = 'KY'
```

This is how SQL Server would respond:

```
Msg 550, Level 16, State 2
The attempted insert or update failed because the target view either
specifies WITH CHECK OPTION or spans a view which specifies WITH CHECK OPTION
and one or more rows resulting from the operation did not qualify under the
CHECK OPTION constraint.
```

Getting Information About a View

As we've shown, SQL Server has two very helpful system stored procedures that can be used to get information concerning a view:

sp_help `<database object name>`
: Displays the column names for the view

sp_helptext `<database object name>`
: Displays the values stored in syscomments for a specific database object

Chapter 17, *System and Extended Stored Procedures*, provides details on all of the system stored procedures.

Renaming Views

If you create a view and later need to modify the name for any reason, the system stored procedure *sp_rename* can be used to rename the view in the database. Refer to Chapter 17 for more information about this system stored procedure. There are a few pitfalls associated with using *sp_rename*, so read up on the topic before using it, and be careful.

Dropping Views

To remove a view from the database, use the following syntax.

```
DROP VIEW [owner.]view_name,
          [owner.]view_name...]
```

As you can see, there's really nothing fancy about dropping a view. The syntax is identical for Microsoft and Sybase.

Now that you've seen how to build and manipulate views, what are some of the ways views are used?

Querying Views

Views are most commonly used only for data retrieval. Typical application-development uses for views include the following:

Hiding data complexity
: Sometimes your end users are exposed to the actual data structures within a database. You can shield them from exceedingly complex join conditions (or other complexities in the data) by providing them access to views instead of base tables.

Customizing data
: You can deploy computed or derived fields for use in a database through views. Doing so provides you with the advantage of displaying a single set of computed values to multiple applications. That way, business logic is embedded in the views and not in the frontend application.

Enforcing business rules
: By limiting the amount or type of data made available to an application, certain types of business rules can be enforced.

Data exports
: Performing BCP (the Bulk Copy Program) can rapidly export (and import) data, but it has virtually no ability to format exported data. Instead, the data can be formatted into a view. Then, the data can be BCPed out in the desired format.

Enforcing security
: Views can be used to implement horizontal security and vertical security. *Horizontal security* is the process of restricting the actual rows a user sees, based on the WHERE clause of the view. *Vertical security* is the process of restricting the columns available to the users, based on the SELECT clause of the view.

We'll discuss each of these concepts in greater detail in the following sections.

Hiding Data Complexity

SQL statements can often become rather complex. We need a means to simplify the users' perception of the data and their manipulation of it. Views achieve this by allowing the user to work with a single set of rows and columns. However, behind the scenes, the view may consist of several base tables with complex join criteria. Complex calculations may daunt an end user, but placing them in a view can easily conceal these. Views can be used to simplify data access to the user.

For example, if every time we list authors' names with the stores in which their books are available, the following SELECT statement would need to be coded to join all the tables. See Figure 16-1 for an entity-relationship diagram.

```
SELECT  a1.au_lname,
        a1.au_fname,
        s1.stor_name
FROM    authors a1,
        titleauthor ta,
        sales sa,
        stores S1
WHERE   a1.au_id    = ta.au_id
    AND ta.title_id = sa.title_id
    AND sa.stor_id  = s1.stor_id
```

The same statement can be coded into a view by the following syntax:

```
CREATE VIEW v_storeauthors
AS
SELECT  a1.au_lname,
        a1.au_fname,
```

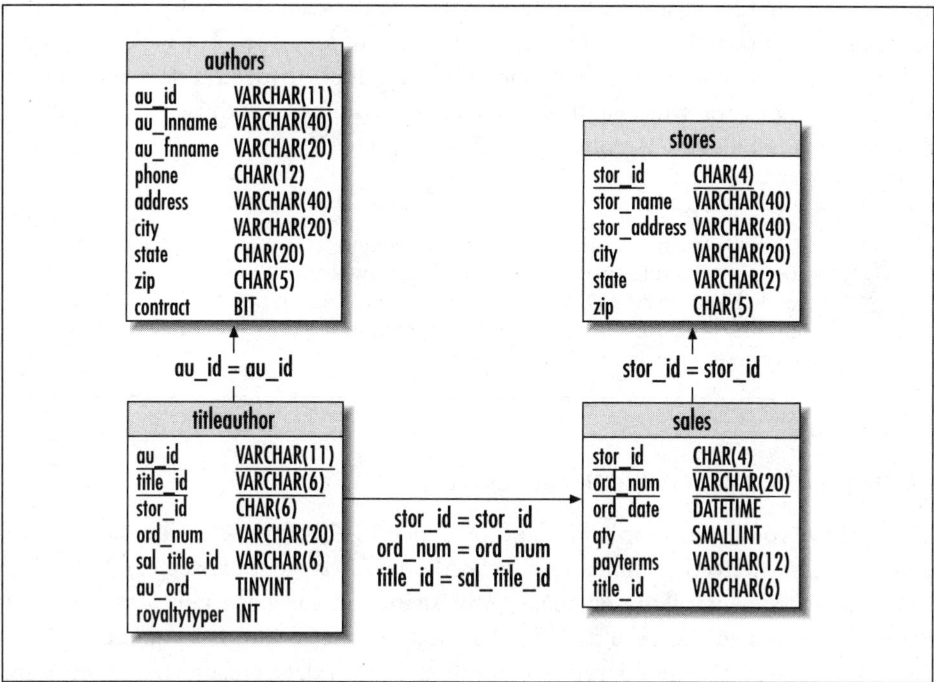

Figure 16-1. Hiding data complexity in a view

```
        s1.stor_name
FROM    authors a1,
        titleauthor ta,
        sales sa,
        stores S1
WHERE   a1.au_id     = ta.au_id
    AND ta.title_id = sa.title_id
    AND sa.stor_id  = s1.stor_id
```

The same type of complexity can be simplified with denormalization; however, that introduces additional data storage overhead and data modification anomalies that could add to the complexity of the data entry applications.

Once the previous view is coded, the users of the database can now do the following SELECT to retrieve information that relates authors to the stores where their books have been sold.

```
SELECT au_lname,
       au_fname,
       stor_name
FROM   v_storeauthors
```

This view is simpler to access for the end user of the database if she is allowed to access the database directly. The user of v_storeauthors does not have to understand that the titleauthor and sales tables are required to determine which stores are selling books for which authors. If you add columns for those tables used in the view, many other users could reuse this one view.

This view only addresses code complexity. The query, as written before, will still execute the same query with the four-table join as coded in the CREATE VIEW statement. The load on the database will be the same for the view as for the initial query. We'll discuss view overhead later in this chapter.

Using Views to Customize Data

Views allow you to develop computed or derived fields for use in the database. If you add these derived columns to a view, the users of the database can use these values as extensions of the database. Any change in the base tables of the view will be reflected in the result set of the view the next time it is queried. Using views in this way also standardizes computations and data presentation formatting across any application that queries the view.

Suppose, for example, that the pubs database supported several mailing label and form letter applications—each one created by the administrative assistant for a department of the firm. Recently, the firm has established a business policy that all applications follow the same style for address labels. To accomplish this, the following view (containing a computed column) could be used:

```
CREATE VIEW v_authorsmailing (au_id, name)
AS
SELECT au_id,
       RTRIM(au_lname) + ', ' + RTRIM(au_fname)
FROM authors
```

Now all users will have the same author name formatting. By doing the following SELECT against this view, you'll retrieve the formatted author's name instead of the unformatted author's name:

```
SELECT name
FROM v_authorsmailing
```

Results:

```
name
------------------------------------------------------------
White, Johnson
Green, Marjorie
Carson, Cheryl
O'Leary, Michael
```

```
Straight, Dean
Smith, Meander
Bennet, Abraham
Dull, Ann
Gringlesby, Burt
Locksley, Charlene
Greene, Morningstar
Blotchet-Halls, Reginald
Yokomoto, Akiko
del Castillo, Innes
DeFrance, Michel
Stringer, Dirk
MacFeather, Stearns
Karsen, Livia
Panteley, Sylvia
Hunter, Sheryl
McBadden, Heather
Ringer, Anne
Ringer, Albert

(23 row(s) affected)
```

If there were ever a need to change the format of the presentation of the author's name, then a single change to the view v_authorsmailing would be reflected in all applications using the view. This makes code maintenance very simple and reduces the need to modify the base table. This is all done with virtual data and eliminates the need to store the additional data for a formatted name on the database.

You can follow this same principle in adding computed columns to a view. Columns like total advances per author can be computed in a view. Then each application using the view could take advantage of a single column from a view, rather than having to develop its own total advances calculation. The following view computes total advances per author:

```
CREATE VIEW v_author_advances
AS
SELECT  a1.au_id,
        au_lname,
        au_fname,
        sum(advance) "total_advance"
FROM    authors a1,
        titleauthor ta,
        titles t1
WHERE   a1.au_id    = ta.au_id
    AND ta.title_id = t1.title_id
GROUP BY a1.au_id,
        au_lname,
        au_fname
```

Now, any time you need to determine total advances for an individual, you can code the following SELECT:

```
SELECT au_lname,
       au_fname,
```

```
       total_advance
FROM   v_author_advances
WHERE  au_id = '213-46-8915'
```

Results:

```
au_lname                         au_fname             total_advance
-------------------------------- -------------------- --------------------
Green                            Marjorie             15,125.00

(1 row(s) affected)
```

Note that views like this one may have performance implications. In this example, SQL Server creates a worktable every time you need to query from the view. On a large table, such a query may take a long time. When you create views with slow underlying SELECT statements, expect the retrieval of a result set from a view to take the same time as the query on which it is based.

Using Views to Implement Business Rules

Normally we associate the implementation of business rules with stored procedures; however, certain scenarios can use views to control business processes. This method basically uses views to focus on specific data from a table or group of tables. By limiting the data available to the user, certain business rules can be implemented.

For example, if a certain number of processes are valid only for employees who are new hires, you can code the following view:

```
CREATE VIEW v_new_hires
AS
SELECT emp_id,
       fname,
       minit,
       lname,
       job_id,
       job_lvl,
       pub_id,
       hire_date
FROM   employee
WHERE  job_id = 1  -- Job Code 1 denotes a new hire
```

Now, to validate any action that is valid only for a new hire, all that's required is to select against the v_new_hires view. This view would make new-hire validation consistent across many different applications. So if the job_id value used to indicate a new hire changed from 1 to 99, then a single change to the view could update this business rule in all the different applications using the v_new_hires view. This is much less tedious than having to locate all the sections of application code that reference the new hire business rule to make the same change.

The following code is an example of how the v_new_hires could be implemented:

```
DECLARE @input_emp_id empid

SELECT  @input_emp_id = 'PMA42628M'

IF EXISTS (SELECT * FROM v_new_hires WHERE emp_id = @input_emp_id)
    PRINT "NEW HIRE"
ELSE
    PRINT "EXISTING EMPLOYEE"
```

This code segment declares an input variable for employee ID using the user-defined datatype of empid. Then a value is assigned to the input_employee_id variable. Finally, the IF . . . ELSE block determines whether the employee is a new hire and prints a message indicating whether the employee is a new hire or an existing employee.

Data Exporting

Many times you have to interface data from your system into another. Views are ideal for this use in two key scenarios:

- When you need to export data: export tools such as SQL Server's BCP (Bulk Copy Program) are limited in the ways in which data can be formatted and filtered.
- When interfacing with other systems: you want to limit the impact of changes from one system to the next.

In these cases, views will isolate your system's internal table structure from the other systems to which it interfaces.

Utility programs such as BCP are limited in the queries that are supported. In some situations in which the data must undergo some heavy manipulations for it to be usable in another system, it is much easier to develop a BCP task to export data based on a view rather than attempting to format and filter the data within BCP. For example, to export the author's name as one field, the view query would be coded to handle the formatting of the first_name and last_name fields as one. Or if the items being exported deal with multiple table joins or other complex WHERE clause criteria, these conditions can be coded in the view. Then the data could be extracted with a single BCP task.

By utilizing views when exporting to another system, you are limiting the exposure to other systems should the internal table structure of your system change. If interfaces to other systems are based on the base tables, then any data denormalization done to optimize your system would also require changes to the interface code and testing of the other systems. However, if you used a view to hide your database design from the other system, a change to your data design would require changes only to the view query, not to the actual interface code touching your system. In this case, views are acting much like an API (Application Program Interface).

Here's an example that is rather simple but illustrates the point. In this hypothetical scenario, our company contracts out all payroll services. As a result, we have to send out an ASCII file that contains any newly hired employees. Also, we're required to provide hire dates for each employee in a nonstandard format. We can meet all of these needs by using BCP against a specially crafted view:

```
CREATE VIEW employee_extract
AS
SELECT emp_id,
       job_lvl,
       CONVERT(CHAR(8),hire_date,10) "hire_date"
FROM   employee
WHERE  job_id = 1
```

Views for Simple Security

Views control access to the data by two primary means: limiting either the number of rows or the columns available to the user. By combining a "security" view with properly administered permissions on the base tables, end users are effectively restricted from any data within a database. On the other hand, using security views, end users can also have access to any data they need. To this end, data access is accomplished by creating views to handle the specific data needs of the user and granting the user access only to the specific views.

Once you have granted a user specific permissions to a view, you can delete the same privilege to the underlying base table.

By limiting the number of rows, we control the data itself. Views are among the best methods of implementing data security within the database. Ownership of the data cannot be subdivided within a single table. However, a view can be constructed on top of a table that provides the end user with only the rows and columns he is authorized to see. This is known as a *value dependent subset*.

For example, you may need to create a view that controls the employee records a user can see. Many times, managers can update information about only those employees who report directly to them. As an example, the following view allows a user to access information about only those employees whose job level is less than 100:

```
CREATE VIEW v_employee_staff
AS
SELECT emp_id,
```

```
        fname,
        minit,
        lname,
        job_id,
        job_lvl,
        pub_id,
        hire_date
FROM    employee
WHERE   job_lvl < 100
```

Once the view is created, the user must have grants to the v_employee_staff view. Permissions to the employee table can then be limited. This would be useful where a certain group of employees can access data about only those employees who are below their job level.

Vertical security

There are other means of controlling columns that could be considered sensitive information. One scenario uses *vertical security* to control what the end user sees. Vertical security means that data security is ensured by allowing the end user to see only a specific subset of columns. Basically, vertical security is ensured through the column_list of the SELECT statement. So, the developer may wish to limit certain columns of a table from being published on the Internet, such as the author's address or phone number. A view like the one shown here reveals only those columns that the developer feels are safe to show:

```
CREATE VIEW v_internet_data
AS
SELECT au_lname, au_fname
FROM   authors
```

By leaving the author's phone number and address out of the view, there is no way for the user to access the data columns. (Of course, the developer might still slip up and write the frontend application using the base tables.)

Horizontal security

Another way views provide data security is by limiting the records that are available to the user. This is known as *horizontal security*. Horizontal security is ensured through the WHERE clause of the SELECT statement. For example, if the user can see only the average royalty, the following view could be created:

```
CREATE VIEW v_avg_royalty (type, avg_royalty)
AS
SELECT type, AVG(royalty)
FROM   titles
GROUP BY type
```

Using the v_avg_royalty view would allow a user to analyze the average royalty by type of book without having access to the actual royalty amounts for any given author.

Dynamic Views for Advanced Security

The previous section detailed ways in which you can build views that provide useful, but rather rudimentary, forms of security. The biggest drawback to the methods shown is that the logic of the security must be hardcoded into the view. Thus, in the v_employee_staff view, a user can see all of the employees classified as "staff-level" because their job_lvl is less than 100.

```
CREATE VIEW v_employee_staff
AS
SELECT emp_id,
       fname,
       minit,
       lname,
       job_id,
       job_lvl,
       pub_id,
       hire_date
FROM   employee
WHERE  job_lvl < 100
```

The weaknesses of this approach are many:

- What if the user querying the view has a job_lvl far less than 100? Do you want that user to see records about employees of a higher grade?
- What if a user, such as the human resources director (or her secretary), is officially a "staff-level" user? This specific job requires greater access than a staff-level user. Or what if your organization has many levels of access to the data—what then?
- What if you want managers to see all job_lvls in their division but none of the employees in other divisions?

These questions, and others, can be answered by applying a more advanced security model against views. Typically, this approach is accomplished by creating *dynamic views*. Dynamic views are views that get a portion of their information from system tables, system functions, or even customized lookup tables. By linking the query of the view to these external data sources, the view is able to retrieve data based on the specific needs of the end user issuing the query.

One example of this approach is to use the system table sysusers. Although a detailed discussion of creating users is beyond the scope of this book, a little background will help you get the idea. Users are created through the SQL Server GUI or by using the system stored procedure *sp_adduser*. Once a user is created, information about that user is stored in the system table sysusers. Because sysusers is a table just like any other, it can be queried in a view.

For example, our company may have decided to create several different user types: manager, staff, and superuser. You can create a view that will show different rows to different users, depending on their user types. Suppose that you have a group of users named manager. You want to give all manager users a full view of the employee table and limit other users to viewing employees with job_lvl < 100. The following view accomplishes this goal:

```
CREATE VIEW v_employees
AS
SELECT emp_id, fname, minit, lname, job_id, job_lvl, pub_id, hire_date
FROM   employee
WHERE  job_lvl < 100
    OR ( SELECT  name
         FROM    sysusers
         WHERE   uid = user_id()      -- the ID of the user currently logged on
         ) = 'managers'
```

Depending on the needs of your application, you could construct a more robust security table that stores information about your users. The table might store things like the user ID, department, and flag columns that indicate if a user can access certain data resources. You could then build queries that dynamically combine information from the security table and the other base tables.

An even more robust method of building dynamic views is based on use of the CASE statement, described in Chapter 13, *CASE Expressions and Transact-SQL Extensions*. You can use the power and versatility of the CASE statement to derive a new value for each column of the view. The advantage of using CASE within a view is the total flexibility in data retrieval. The disadvantage of using CASE within a view is the large amount of code required to achieve the desired results. However, this is very often an acceptable compromise.

Here's an example of a dynamic view built using CASE statements. In this hypothetical case, we have constructed an intranet application. We don't want anyone outside of the organization to have access to this data. We can control exactly what the end user sees using a SELECT statement that combines the functionality of CASE and the system function HOST_NAME(). The system function allows us to determine whether the workstation connecting to SQL Server uses our organizational default of pubs_% or a some other, unacceptable value:

```
CREATE TABLE v_authors
AS
SELECT
    CASE
        WHEN HOST_NAME() LIKE 'PUBS_%' THEN au_fname
        ELSE 'access denied'
    END "au_fname",
    CASE
        WHEN HOST_NAME() LIKE 'PUBS_%' THEN au_lname
        ELSE null
    END "au_lname",
    CASE
        WHEN contract=1 AND HOST_NAME() LIKE 'PUBS_%' THEN 'Yes'
        WHEN contract=0 AND HOST_NAME() LIKE 'PUBS_%' THEN 'No'
```

```
        ELSE null
    END "contract"
FROM    authors
```

If any of our internal workstations query this view using any variation of SELECT * FROM v_authors, they receive this information:

```
au_fname             au_lname                                 contract
-------------------- ---------------------------------------- --------
Johnson              White                                    Yes
...<deleted for brevity>
Albert               Ringer                                   Yes

(23 row(s) affected)
```

But if a workstation is outside of our organization (that is, it has an unacceptable workstation name), they see these results:

```
au_fname             au_lname                                 contract
-------------------- ---------------------------------------- --------
access denied        (null)                                   (null)
...<deleted for brevity>
access denied        (null)                                   (null)

(23 row(s) affected)
```

As you can see, views built using CASE and other external sources of data, such as system functions, provide some amazing capabilities.

View Dependencies, Permissions, and Data Manipulations

The topic of dependencies, codependencies, permissions, and manipulations sometimes makes good "psychobabble" small talk at parties. But most party-goers would give you blank stares if you brought up the topic of view dependencies and permissions.

As we've said, views are virtual tables based on other database objects. Views can be based on table objects, other views, or a combination. Obviously, views are *dependent* on these other preexisting objects. SQL Server must be able to keep up with not only the permissions of end users to the underlying database objects but also the permissions of the views themselves. Views are made up of other objects. So retrieving a usable result set is dependent on the permissions granted to its underlying objects.

The enforcement of the view permissions occurs at runtime. Thus, if permissions are not defined properly, you will not know until an end user attempts to execute the application.

Since views are dependent on the underlying database objects that are used in the view's SELECT statement, bad things can happen to the view when the underlying objects are dropped or changed. For example, views that select from database objects that have been dropped return this message (note that the object_name shown here is a generic (and not a specific) object in the pubs database):

```
Msg 208, Level 16, State 1
Invalid object name 'object_name'.

Msg 4413, Level 16, State 1
View resolution could not succeed because the previously mentioned objects,
upon which the view directly or indirectly relies, do not currently exist.
These objects need to be recreated for the view to be usable.
```

Similar problems occur if the tables (or views) beneath a view are radically altered (especially if columns referenced in a view are dropped). The view will stop working with error #207, as shown here:

```
Msg 207, Level 16, State 2
Invalid column name 'column_name'.
```

Even if a column is simply renamed, you'll encounter this error. Interestingly, changing the datatype of an underlying column will not affect the dependent view, as long as the column name and order of the columns do not change in the underlying database object.

It's important to think of a view as a preparsed SELECT statement. If the SELECT statement, as written in the view, will work—OK. But if changes occur in the underlying database object that invalidate the SELECT statement, then the view is dead in the water.

Permissions

Views are often used as security devices because end users may have permissions to use a view without having any permissions to its underlying objects. Thus, an end user can have SELECT, INSERT, UPDATE, and DELETE permissions on a view. The end user can execute all of these DML statements against the view (and consequently the database objects it is built upon) without having these same permissions on the underlying table. (There are some limitations to inserting or updating data through a view, which are discussed later.)

For example, given the following simple view:

```
CREATE VIEW v_titles1
AS
SELECT *
FROM  titles
```

The view v_titles1 is dependent on the table titles. As long as the owner of the v_titles1 view and the titles table are the same user, there won't be permission problems. However, permission problems can arise when the views are built upon database objects with different owners, especially when the owners haven't granted subsequent permissions to users of the view.

SQL Server will allow you to *create* a view dependent on another object in which you do not have permissions. Unfortunately, SQL Server doesn't allow you to *use* such a view.

For example, assume that the title and sales tables are owned by different users. The user creating the v_titles2 table shown later is the owner of the titles table but doesn't even have SELECT permissions on the sales table. This restriction keeps a user from accessing the sales information without the permissions of the owner of the sales table. The user would actually be allowed to create the view shown next but would be unable to retrieve any data from it. So, given the following modification to v_titles1:

```
CREATE VIEW v_titles2
AS
SELECT title,
       SUM(qty) as "Qty"
FROM  titles t1,
       sales s1
WHERE  t1.title_id = s1.title_id
GROUP BY title
```

A query of:

```
SELECT * FROM v_titles2
```

yields a result of:

```
Msg 229, Level 14, State 1
SELECT permission denied on object v_titles2, database pubs, owner dbo
```

Yet if we make one small change and grant SELECT permissions on the view v_titles2, the end user will get this result for the very same query:

```
title                                                         Qty
------------------------------------------------------------  ------
But Is It User Friendly?                                      30
Computer Phobic AND Non-Phobic Individuals: Behavior Variations  20
Cooking with Computers: Surreptitious Balance Sheets          25
Emotional Security: A New Algorithm                           25
Fifty Years in Buckingham Palace Kitchens                     20
Is Anger the Enemy?                                           108
Life Without Fear                                             25
```

```
Onions, Leeks, and Garlic: Cooking Secrets of the Mediterranean  40
Prolonged Data Deprivation: Four Case Studies                    15
Secrets of Silicon Valley                                        50
Silicon Valley Gastronomic Treats                                10
Straight Talk About Computers                                    15
Sushi, Anyone?                                                   20
The Busy Executive's Database Guide                              15
The Gourmet Microwave                                            40
You Can Combat Computer Stress!                                  35
```

This little demonstration proves that when you need added security for your application or database, you can avoid granting end users direct access to base tables and instead control their access to data through views.

Data Manipulations Through Views

Views not only allow you to perform SELECT statements, but they also let you perform INSERT, UPDATE, and DELETE statements against a view. Of course, the user attempting the data manipulation must have the right explicitly granted to perform the DML command on the view.

We strongly recommend that you do not allow DML operations other than SELECT on a view built upon two or more base tables.

Data manipulation through a view works best, without a doubt, when the view is built upon a single base table. Most attempts at data manipulation through views that access two or more tables are asking for trouble. In any case, even if the view has more than one base table, a DML statement executed against the view may only impact the columns of a single table. If you attempt an invalid DML operation against a view, SQL Server will generally return an error message that is derived from the base table, not the view itself. For example, the INSERT operation shown here:

```
INSERT INTO titleauthor
   (au_id)
VALUES('262-32-1339')
```

will result in the following response from SQL Server:

```
Msg 233, Level 16, State 2
The column title_id in table titleauthor may not be null.
```

However, if you alter the INSERT operation like this:

```
INSERT INTO titleauthor
   (au_id, au_fname, au_lname)
VALUES(''262-32-1339','Vlad','The Impaler')
```

you'll now get a new error:

```
Msg 207, Level 16, State 1
Invalid column name 'au_fname'.
```

This error occurs because there is no column au_fname in the titleauthor view. Other restrictions on the behavior of DML statements are covered in the next section.

Limitations of Views

While views provide a number of benefits to the user and developer of SQL Server applications, they have a number of restrictions that must be followed:

- Views can contain only a single SQL statement.
- Views can be created only in the current database.
- Views cannot have rules, defaults, or triggers associated with them.
- Views cannot be based on temporary tables.
- Views created with the SELECT * statement will not automatically add the new columns to the view if the base table is changed. The view must be dropped and re-created. (This is the default behavior of SQL Server. Stored procedures have the same constraint.)
- You can't INSERT or UPDATE a view built on multiple tables when the DML statement affects more than one base table. If you still want to update a view that utilizes two tables joined together, only one of the tables can be updated at one time.
- You cannot INSERT into a view with a computed column. An UPDATE statement can change any column that is not computed.
- You can't INSERT into a view unless all NOT NULL columns in the base tables have values supplied within the INSERT statement or have a default constraint. Otherwise, the view has no way to supply the base tables with values for the NOT NULL columns.
- READTEXT or WRITETEXT commands cannot be applied to a view that contains TEXT or IMAGE columns.
- Views do not return the expected result set defined with an outer join and are then queried using a qualification on the column from the inner table. This will always return all rows from the inner table; however, rows that do not meet the qualification are returned with null values in the column of rows that don't meet the qualification. This means that you should avoid creating views with an outer join SELECT, because they may cause problems when somebody else uses them.

- Views cannot be created inside an explicit transaction—that is, between a BEGIN TRAN and a COMMIT TRAN block of Transact-SQL.

View Overhead

As with all database objects, views require some level of database overhead. Of course, the obvious overhead is the storing of the view information, including the actual SELECT statement source in the system tables in the database. So, utilizing a view in an application will require a little more disk space. However, given any sizable database application, this overhead will be negligible. Furthermore, disk space is so cheap these days that view overhead is seldom an issue.

Views do not normally take longer to return a result set than do normal queries. However, we've seen situations in which sloppy developers have built views on top of views on top of views on top of views, ad nauseam. This kind of construct can cause *very* slow data retrieval and manipulation. (Very complex nested views can actually crash the server!) Always construct your views against base tables and not against other views.

Perhaps the most important "overhead" of a view can be seen by looking at the most common alternative to a view—building a specialized permanent table to store the data that would be presented by the view. When you compare these two alternatives, you must weigh the cost of generating the SELECT statements required by the view at runtime against the costs of creating and managing a permanent table.

There are some other factors to consider with database performance and the use of views. When comparing the initial execution of a view to other simple SQL statements, you'll note that views frequently require slightly less CPU time than a standard SELECT statement to obtain the same results. However, once the SELECT statement has been used once, SQL Server caches it into memory. Queries in cache are usually quicker on the second execution than the same view. In this circumstance, the first execution of a view takes up a little overhead, but on subsequent executions, the SELECT statement seems to be a little faster.

Neither case we've discussed would be a strong argument to use or not use a view due to extra overhead. The differences are noticeable only when either using a very large database or tracing CPU time using performance-monitoring tools. The best recommendation is to analyze views versus queries only when there are questionable runtime performance issues.

Summary

Views are a very useful database object and, if used properly, can make the life of application developers and database users much easier. This chapter discussed ways to utilize views to hide data complexity, customize data columns, standardize data column formatting across multiple applications, implement business rules, and simplify data exporting. We also looked at:

- View dependencies
- Limitations of views
- Working with views through Transact-SQL commands
- View overhead

Most client/server applications using SQL Server will utilize views for all the items mentioned here to get the job done and to make the developer's code more straightforward with fewer SQL complexities.

17
System and Extended Stored Procedures

In earlier chapters, we've covered the general techniques and syntax required to create stored procedures. In this chapter, we focus on system stored procedures (SSPs) and extended stored procedures (ESPs).

System Stored Procedures

System stored procedures are those procedures that reside in the master database or (on Sybase) in the sybsystemprocs database and whose names start with a reserved prefix *sp_*. The SQL Server installation process creates a number of vendor-supplied system stored procedures. You can also develop your own system procedures or obtain additional system procedures from other sources and install them on your server. We have included a set of our own "add-on" system stored procedures on the CD-ROM that accompanies this book.

What makes system procedures "special" to SQL Server? All you have to do is to prefix your procedure name with *sp_* and create it in the master database (or sybsystemprocs on Sybase). Then your procedure may be executed from any other database. If the name of a system procedure is not prefixed with a database name, then it works in the context of the current database. This means that if the procedure references any objects, it looks for them in the current database at the time of execution rather than in the database in which the procedure resides. By comparison, a regular stored procedure looks for objects specified by name only in the database in which it was created.

The key difference between system and regular procedures is how they treat objects that are not prefixed with a database name in their code. A regular procedure will always access the same object in the same database. For example, if it refers to table my_table, then it expects to find that table in the database where the procedure is created. A system stored procedure looks for some objects in the current database where it is executed from. For example, if your system stored procedure refers to a stored procedure my_procedure, then it will look for this procedure in the databases where you execute it, and not its home database (master for Microsoft, sybsystemprocs for Sybase). The same applies to system tables that are found in ever database (e.g., sysindexes or sysobjects), but not to user tables. If your system stored procedure refers to table my_table, then it expects to find iti n the database of residence (master or sybsystemprocs), and not in the current database.

Which database is the "current database" for these purposes? This question is very important for system stored procedures. If you are in the pubs database and execute *sp_help*, then it returns the list of objects in your current database—pubs. But what if you prefix the name of the system procedure with a different database name, such as tempdb..sp_help? The "current database" for *sp_help* execution becomes tempdb, even though you may be in pubs when you execute it. Therefore, it will return the list of objects in tempdb.

A regular stored procedure always runs in the context of the database where it was created. If your current database is master and you want to execute the stored procedure byroyalty, then you have to prefix it with the name of its home database—pubs..byroyalty.

Not all stored procedures supplied by a vendor are considered system stored procedures. For example, Microsoft SQL Server also has several stored procedures in the msdb database that are created at server installation time and that support SQL Executive task scheduling. They are not considered system stored procedures, because they do not reside in the master database and their names do not begin with *sp_*. Creating a procedure in a user database with a prefix of *sp_* does not make it a system procedure. But if you create it in master (or sybsystemprocs on Sybase), it will become a system procedure. Also, if you create a procedure in the master database but give it a name not starting with *sp_*, then SQL Server treats it as a regular stored procedure that just happens to reside in master.

You may also find references to catalog stored procedures in SQL Server documentation or other sources. These are system procedures that work with the system catalog tables. The term *catalog procedure* does not define a special class of SQL Server objects and may often be used interchangably with the term *system stored procedure.*

Common System Stored Procedures

In the following sections, we've compiled a summary of the more commonly used system stored procedures—what they do and what their syntax looks like on Microsoft and Sybase SQL Server. For some of the more obscure options, you will need to refer to your system documentation.

sp_addmessage

Syntax:

Microsoft	Sybase
`sp_addmessage message_num, severity, message_text [,language [,REPLACE]]`	`sp_addmessage message_num, message_text [,language [,REPLACE]]`

This procedure is used to add a user-defined message to the system. This message can then be referenced by subsequent PRINT, RAISERROR, and *sp_bindmsg* requests. User-defined messages must begin at 50001 in Microsoft and 20000 in Sybase. By specifying REPLACE to be true, you may optionally choose to replace an existing copy of the message. In Microsoft, the severity level must be between 1 and 25. However, only the system administrator can add messages with a severity level greater than 18. The message text cannot exceed 255 characters.

Successfully executing this procedure will return a message similar to the following:

```
New message added.
```

sp_addtype

Syntax:

```
sp_addtype typename,phystype [,nulltype]
```

This procedure adds user-defined datatypes to your system. In general, a name needs to be specified for the type, and you must specify its physical underlying datatype and whether this field allows nulls.

Successfully executing this procedure will return a message similar to the following:

```
New type added.
```

sp_bindefault

Syntax:

```
sp_bindefault defname,objname [,FUTUREONLY]
```

This procedure is used when a user-defined default needs to be bound to a column or user-defined datatype.

To call this procedure, you will need to know the name of the default and the object to which it is to be bound. FUTUREONLY can be used if you are binding to a user-defined datatype and want only new columns created after this bind to be affected by this default. If this option is not specified, all existing columns with this user datatype will have the default bound to them.

Successfully executing this procedure will return a message similar to the following:

```
Default bound to datatype.
```

sp_bindrule

Syntax:

```
sp_bindrule [defname,objname [,FUTUREONLY]]
```

This procedure is used when a user-defined rule needs to be bound to a column or user-defined datatype.

To call this procedure, you will need to know the name of the rule and the object to which it is to be bound. FUTUREONLY can be used if you are binding to a user-defined datatype and want only new columns created after this bind to be affected by this rule. If this option is not specified, all existing columns with this user datatype will have the rule bound to them.

Successfully executing this procedure will return a message similar to the following:

```
Rule bound to datatype.
```

sp_configure

Syntax:

Microsoft	Sybase

`sp_configure [ configuration_option [ , new_value ] ]`	`sp_configure [ configuration_option [ , new_value ] | group_name | non_unique_parameter_fragment]`
	
	`sp_configure "configuration file",0,{"WRITE" | "READ" | "VERIFY" | "RESTORE" } "file name"`

This procedure allows you to review and control SQL Server configuration options. It sets very critical parameters that may seriously affect the well-being of your SQL Server. Therefore, permission to execute this procedure belongs to the SA. When executed without parameters, *sp_configure* reports current settings for configurable options.

Sybase stores all configuration options in an external file as well as in the system tables. In order to support this usage, Sybase includes a second usage of the *sp_configure* command. The file is usually the name of the server suffixed by a revision number. An example of this would be *CHARDONNAY.001*. The file can be located in the directory where your SQL Server is installed—for example, *c:\sql11*.

Results of *sp_configure* on Microsoft SQL Server follow (actual numbers on your server may vary).

Highlighted lines in the report are advanced options in Microsoft's terminology. They may be hidden from the sp_configure report if you set the "show advanced options" parameter to 0.

name	minimum	maximum	config_value	run_value
affinity mask	**0**	**2147483647**	**0**	**0**
allow updates	0	1	0	0
backup buffer size	1	10	1	1
backup threads	0	32	5	5
cursor threshold	**-1**	**2147483647**	**-1**	**-1**
database size	2	10000	2	2
default language	0	9999	0	0
default sortorder id	**0**	**255**	**52**	**52**
fill factor	0	100	0	0
free buffers	**20**	**524288**	**409**	**409**
hash buckets	**4999**	**265003**	**7993**	**7993**
language in cache	3	100	3	3
LE threshold maximum	2	500000	200	200
LE threshold minimum	**2**	**500000**	**20**	**20**
LE threshold percent	1	100	0	0
locks	5000	2147483647	25000	25000
logwrite sleep (ms)	-1	500	0	0
max async IO	1	255	8	8
max lazywrite IO	**1**	**255**	**8**	**8**
max text repl size	0	2147483647	65536	65536
max worker threads	10	1024	255	255
media retention	0	365	0	0
memory	2800	1048576	163840	163840
nested triggers	0	1	0	0
network packet size	512	32767	4096	4096
open databases	5	32767	20	20
open objects	100	2147483647	5000	5000
priority boost	**0**	**1**	**0**	**0**
procedure cache	1	99	10	10
RA cache hit limit	**1**	**255**	**4**	**4**
RA cache miss limit	**1**	**255**	**3**	**3**
RA delay	**0**	**500**	**15**	**15**
RA pre-fetches	**1**	**1000**	**3**	**3**
RA slots per thread	**1**	**255**	**5**	**5**
RA worker threads	0	255	3	3
recovery flags	0	1	0	0
recovery interval	1	32767	5	5
remote access	0	1	1	1
remote conn timeout	-1	32767	10	10
remote login timeout	**0**	**2147483647**	**5**	**5**

```
remote proc trans       0     1           0      0
remote query timeout    0     2147483647  0      0
remote sites            0     256         10     10
resource timeout        5     2147483647  10     10
set working set size    0     1           0      0
show advanced options   0     1           1      1
SMP concurrency         -1    64          0      1
sort pages              64    511         64     64
spin counter            1     2147483647  10000  0
tempdb in ram (MB)      0     2044        0      0
time slice              50    1000        100    100
user connections        5     15          250    250
user options            0     4095        0      0
```

Older versions of Sybase formatted *sp_configure* results the same way, but recent versions present them differently. Sybase and Microsoft have many proprietary configuration options.

Configuration options are controlled by the SA of your SQL Server and affect different aspects of tuning and adjustment to certain hardware and application requirements. Some of the notable parameters are:

Memory
: The amount of RAM allocated to SQL Server out of the total amount of memory available on the machine. The unit of measurement is a 2-KB page. In the preceding example, 320MB of memory is allocated to SQL Server (163840/512).

Locks
: The maximum number of rows that may be contained in the system table master..syslocks. Sometimes SQL Server may run out of this resource, in which case it terminates transactions that require more locks. A higher setting requires more memory allocated to managing locks that could otherwise be given to data cache.

Procedure cache
: Sets the percentage of total memory allocated to SQL Server for use by stored procedure plans. A higher setting reduces the size of the data cache. It improves the performance of stored procedures if there are many of them in your system but reduces the performance of all queries that could benefit from extra data cache.

User connections
: Limit the number of concurrent processes running on SQL Server. This number is dictated by your SQL Server license.

LE parameters
: Control locks escalation.

RA parameters
: Control read-ahead management.

In order to check a single setting, execute *sp_configure* with one parameter, the option name. For example:

```
sp_configure 'memory'
```

The results are formatted the same way as for all parameters but consist of only the information relating to that option.

To modify a configuration parameter, you need SA authority. Some settings take effect as soon as you execute the command RECONFIGURE WITH OVERRIDE. Others become effective only when you shut down and restart SQL Server. For example, the following command allows direct updates on system tables (something that vendors recommend you never attempt on your own):

```
sp_configure 'allow updates', 1
GO
RECONFIGURE WITH OVERRIDE
GO
```

sp_dboption

Syntax:

```
sp_dboption [ database_name, option_name, { TRUE | FALSE } ]
```

This stored procedure is used by the DBA to control database options. Some of these options may influence your stored procedures and Transact-SQL batch programs as follows:

select into or bulkcopy
: Allows nonlogged operations, such as SELECT INTO and the BCP utility with the IN option, to be performed in the database. (With Microsoft SQL Server, BCP, described in Appendix C, will still work even when the option is turned off, but it will run in a slow logged mode. Sybase's ASE will return an error message and prevent the BCP option from occurring.) This option expedites certain transactions, but it should not be used in databases in which a loss of data is very expensive or when transaction logs must be preserved by periodic backups.

trunc. log on chkpt.
: Usually goes hand in hand with SELECT INTO. If you allow nonlogged operations in the database, then you don't care about the transaction log. In those cases, it usually makes sense to tell SQL Server to truncate the transaction log in this database on every checkpoint event, which occurs every few minutes. Recent versions of Sybase have less use for this option, because the DBA can set up the transaction log thresholds to automatically dump it when percentages are exceeded. For example, a 75% threshold causes the log to dump when it's 75% full.

read only
: Prevents any data modification in the database.

DBO use only
: Restricts database use to its owner.

single user
: Does not allow more than one user to access the database at the same time.

sp_depends

Syntax:

```
sp_depends object_name
```

The purpose of this stored procedure is to report relations between database objects. It is supposed to return the list of all objects that `object_name` references and the list of objects that reference `object_name`. The only problem is that it doesn't always work as expected.

This is an ill-implemented system procedure. It is buggy by design, and we advise that you stay away from it.

Let us explain what is fundamentally wrong with this procedure. References between objects are recorded in the system table sysdepends, which is located in every user database. Every time you create a stored procedure, trigger, or view that refers to other tables, views, or stored procedures, entries are added to sysdepends to describe these new links. The idea is to maintain a schema of relations between database objects. Unfortunately, this does not work as expected. First of all, links to objects in other databases are not recorded. Second, if you drop an object that other objects depend upon, its links are destroyed. If you then re-create the same object again, these references (or dependencies) are not restored. They are added only for objects on which a newly created one depends.

In a typical user database, you periodically have to drop and re-create some objects. For example, you may need to make changes in a stored procedure called by several other procedures and triggers or to modify a view that some stored procedures select from. After a while the sysdepends table in such a database contains only a partial schema of object relations. The system stored procedure *sp_depends* reports object dependencies based on this incomplete system table. You cannot rely on these results and are better off not using it at all.

The results of *sp_depends* may be reliable only if all objects in the database have been created in the strict order of dependency and if objects referred by other ones have never been dropped and re-created. This may be achieved only in a very tightly controlled production environment in which the DBA is aware of the sysdepends problem and takes special care to drop and re-create all dependent objects at the same time he drops or re-creates the objects to which they refer. For example, you can rely on *sp_depends* in an unaltered pubs database supplied by the vendor.

sp_help

Syntax:

```
sp_help [ object_name | user_defined_datatype ]
```

This stored procedure either returns a complete list of objects in the current database (when executed with no parameters) or provides information about one particular object or user-defined datatype. Object information is formatted depending on the object type, as demonstrated by the following examples.

This example obtains the list of all database objects; this is somewhat similar to executing *DIR* from DOS or *ls* from Unix:

```
sp_help
```

Results in the pubs database on Microsoft SQL Server:

```
Name                           Owner           Object_type
------------------------------ --------------- -----------------
titleview                      dbo             view
authors                        dbo             user table
discounts                      dbo             user table
employee                       dbo             user table
jobs                           dbo             user table
pub_info                       dbo             user table
publishers                     dbo             user table
roysched                       dbo             user table
sales                          dbo             user table
stores                         dbo             user table
titleauthor                    dbo             user table
titles                         dbo             user table
employee_insupd                dbo             trigger
sysalternates                  dbo             system table
sysarticles                    dbo             system table
syscolumns                     dbo             system table
syscomments                    dbo             system table
sysconstraints                 dbo             system table
sysdepends                     dbo             system table
sysindexes                     dbo             system table
syskeys                        dbo             system table
syslogs                        dbo             system table
sysobjects                     dbo             system table
sysprocedures                  dbo             system table
sysprotects                    dbo             system table
syspublications                dbo             system table
```

```
sysreferences                dbo           system table
syssegments                  dbo           system table
syssubscriptions             dbo           system table
systypes                     dbo           system table
sysusers                     dbo           system table
byroyalty                    dbo           stored procedure
reptq1                       dbo           stored procedure
reptq2                       dbo           stored procedure
reptq3                       dbo           stored procedure
DF__authors__phone__03D09CBB  dbo          default
DF__employee__hire_d__3473D416 dbo         default
DF__employee__job_id__2FAF1EF9 dbo         default
DF__employee__job_lv__3197676B dbo         default
DF__employee__pub_id__328B8BA4 dbo         default
DF__jobs__job_desc__25319086  dbo          default
DF__publisher__count__09897611 dbo         default
DF__titles__pubdate__0F424F67  dbo         default
DF__titles__type__0D5A06F5     dbo         default

User_type Storage_type Length Prec Scale Nullable Default_name Rule_name
--------- ------------ ------ ---- ----- -------- ------------ ---------
empid      char         9                no       none         none
id         varchar      11               no       none         none
tid        varchar      6                no       none         none
```

Getting help on a table produces a comprehensive report that contains information on table columns and their attributes, indexes, keys, and constraints:

```
sp_help authors
```

Results (slightly formatted for presentation):

```
Name     Owner  Type         When_created
-------- ------ ------------ --------------------
authors  dbo    user table   Apr 3 1996  3:45AM

Data_located_on_segment
------------------------------
default

Column_name Type     Length Prec Scale Nullable TrimTrailing  FixedLen
                                                Blanks        NullInSource
----------- -------- ------ ---- ----- -------- ------------- -------------
au_id       id       11     no   yes   no
au_lname    varchar  40     no   yes   no
au_fname    varchar  20     no   yes   no
phone       char     12     no   yes   no
address     varchar  40     yes  yes   no
city        varchar  20     yes  yes   no
state       char     2      yes  yes   yes
zip         char     5      yes  yes   yes
contract    bit      1      no   (n/a) (n/a)

Identity                    Seed   Increment
--------------------------- ------ -------------
No identity column defined. (null) (null)
```

```
index_name    index_description                    index_keys
------------- ------------------------------------ ------------------
UPKCL_auidind clustered, unique, primary key       au_id
              located on default
aunmind       nonclustered located on default      au_lname, au_fname

constraint_type        constraint_name              status_enabled
    status_for_replication
    constraint_keys
---------------------- ---------------------------- --------------
    ----------------------
    ------------------------------------------------------------
CHECK on column au_id  CK__authors__au_id__02DC7882  Enabled
    Is_For_Replication
    ((au_id like '[0-9][0-9][0-9]-[0-9][0-9]-[0-9][0-9][0-9][0-9]'))
CHECK on column zip    CK__authors__zip__04C4C0F4    Enabled
    Is_For_Replication
    ((zip like '[0-9][0-9][0-9][0-9][0-9]'))
DEFAULT on column phone DF__authors__phone__03D09CBB  (n/a)
    (n/a)
    ('UNKNOWN')
PRIMARY KEY (clustered) UPKCL_auidind                 (n/a)
    (n/a)
     au_id

Table is referenced by
----------------------------------------------------
pubs.dbo.titleauthor: FK__titleauth__au_id__1312E04B
```

Help on views is very similar to that on tables, with the exception that views have no keys, indexes, or constraints. The following help on stored procedures includes information about all parameters:

```
sp_help byroyalty
```

Results:

```
Name          Owner   Type              When_created
------------- ------- ----------------- -------------------
byroyalty     dbo     stored procedure  Apr 3 1996  3:45AM

Data_located_on_segment
-----------------------
not applicable

Parameter_name   Type   Length Prec Scale Param_order
---------------- ------ ------ ---- ----- -----------
@percentage      int    4      10   0     1
```

There is not much that *sp_help* can tell you about other objects, except for object name, owner, type, and creation date.

In Microsoft SQL Enterprise Manager or ISQL/W, you can quickly obtain *sp_help* results on any object if you highlight the object name in a query window and press Alt-F1.

sp_helpconstraint

Syntax:

```
sp_helpconstraint tablename
```

This procedure returns information about any constraints that have been defined in this database. For example, executing *sp_helpconstraint* for authors in pubs returns results similar to the following:

```
Object Name
---------------------------------------------------------------------------
authors

constraint_type              constraint_name              status_enabled
    status_for_replication
    constraint_keys
--------------------------  ---------------------------  ----------------
    ----------------------
    -----------------------------------------------------------------------
CHECK  on  column au_id     CK__authors__au_id__02DC7882Enabled
    Is_For_Replication
    ((au_idlike'[0-9][0-9][0-9]-[0-9][0-9]-[0-9][0-9][0-9][0-9]'))
CHECK  on  column zip       CK__authors__zip__04C4C0F4  Enabled
    Is_For_Replication
    ((ziplike'[0-9][0-9][0-9][0-9][0-9]'))
DEFAULT on  columnphone     DF__authors__phone__03D09CBB(n/a)
    (n/a)
    ('UNKNOWN')
PRIMARY KEY (clustered)   UPKCL_auidind                 (n/a)
    (n/a)
    au_id

Table is referenced by
---------------------------------------------------------------------------
----------------------------------------------
pubs.dbo.titleauthor: FK__titleauth__au_id__1312E04B
```

This tells you what constraints exist for the authors table: two CHECK constraints, one DEFAULT constraint, and one PRIMARY KEY constraint, as well as any FOREIGN KEY constraints associated with this table, titleauthor.

sp_helpdb

Syntax:

```
sp_helpdb [ database_name ]
```

This stored procedure provides information about all databases (when executed without a parameter) or a particular database. In order to get help on all databases, execute the following from any database:

```
sp_helpdb
```

Results (obtained on one of our servers):

```
name      db_size       owner    dbid   created     status
--------- ------------- -------- ------ ----------- -----------------------
master    50.00 MB      sa       1      Apr  3 1996 trunc. log on chkpt.
model     1.00 MB       sa       3      Apr  3 1996 no options set
msdb      8.00 MB       sa       5      May  7 1997 trunc. log on chkpt.
pubs      3.00 MB       sa       4      Apr  3 1996 trunc. log on chkpt.
tempdb    1002.00 MB    sa       2      Jan 28 1998 select into/bulkcopy
TEST      5000.00 MB    sa       6      May  8 1997 select into/bulkcopy,
                                                    trunc. log on chkpt.
```

The "status" column in the result set contains a description of all database options in effect. It is derived from a bitmap column "status" of the system table, master..sysdatabases. The result set is sorted by database name.

In order to obtain help on a particular database, execute the stored procedure with a database name as a parameter, as in the following:

```
sp_helpdb pubs
```

Results:

```
name      db_size       owner    dbid   created     status
--------- ------------- -------- ------ ----------- ----------------------
pubs      3.00 MB       sa       4      Apr  3 1996 trunc. log on chkpt.

device_fragments               size          usage
------------------------------ ------------- ------------------------------
master                         1.00 MB       data and log
master                         2.00 MB       data and log

device                         segment
------------------------------ ------------------------------
master                         default
master                         logsegment
master                         system
```

This result consists of one line in the same format as in the previous case (for all databases), followed by a description of database segment sizes and fragment allocation and the list of database segments.

sp_helpdevice

Syntax:

```
sp_helpdevice [ logical_device_name ]
```

This procedure provides information about all database devices or a particular one. In order to get the list of all devices, execute:

```
sp_helpdevice
```

Results:

```
device_name   physical_name
description
status cntrltype device_number low        high
------------- ----------------------------
-------------------------------------------
------ --------- ------------ ----------- -----------
diskdump      nul
disk, dump device
16     2         0            0           20000
pubs_dump     F:\MSSQL\BACKUP\pubs_dump.DAT
disk, dump device
16     2         0            0           0
diskettedumpa a:sqltable.dat
diskette, 1.2 MB, dump device
16     3         0            0           19
diskettedumpb b:sqltable.dat
diskette, 1.2 MB, dump device
16     4         0            0           19
MSDBData      D:\MSSQL\DATA\MSDB.DAT
special, physical disk, 6 MB
2      0         127          2130706432  2130709503
MSDBLog       D:\MSSQL\DATA\MSDBLOG.DAT
special, physical disk, 2 MB
2      0         126          2113929216  2113930239
tempdb2       D:\MSSQL\DATA\tempdb2.DAT
special, physical disk, 1000 MB
2      0         2            33554432    34066431
test1         E:\MSSQL\DATA\test1.DAT
special, physical disk, 2000 MB
2      0         1            16777216    17801215
test2         E:\MSSQL\DATA\test2.DAT
special, physical disk, 2000 MB
2      0         3            17801216    18825215
test3         E:\MSSQL\DATA\test3.DAT
special, physical disk, 1000 MB
2      0         4            18825216    19337215
master        D:\MSSQL\DATA\MASTER.DAT
special, default disk, physical disk, 60 MB
3      0         0            0           30719
```

The most important information returned by *sp_helpdevice* is the mapping of logical device names to physical NT filenames associated with logical devices. This mapping is derived from system table sysdevices.

If you specify a device name as a parameter, the result set consists of only one row for the given device, in the same format as the preceding.

sp_helpgroup

Syntax:

```
sp_helpgroup [group_name]
```

This procedure details any information about groups that have been defined in this database. This procedure returns the name of the group as well as the group ID associated with this group.

Executing this procedure may return results similar to the following:

```
Group_name          Group_id
-----------------------------------------
public              0
another_group       16384
```

User-defined groups begin at 16384 on Microsoft SQL Server and 16390 on Sybase SQL Server.

sp_helpindex

Syntax:

```
sp_helpindex table_name
```

This stored procedure reports on all of the indexes of a table. The format is the same as index information generated by *sp_help* executed on a table. This is not surprising, because *sp_help* executes *sp_helpindex* when it generates help on a table. When you only care about indexes, executing *sp_helpindex* is quicker than *sp_help*.

sp_helpjoins (Sybase Only)

Syntax:

```
sp_helpjoins lefttable, righttable
```

This stored procedure details all the likely join candidates for two tables or views. The procedure follows three levels of probability to determine the join candidates and returns those entries that return a match at the highest level:

Highest probability
: Any foreign keys or common keys; requires an entry in syskeys for this to work

Medium probability
: Similar user type

All else fails probability
: Same physical datatype

sp_helpkey

Syntax:

```
sp_helpkey [table_name]
```

This procedure is called to display information on the PRIMARY, FOREIGN, and COMMON keys associated with this table or view. Alternatively, this procedure will return key information about all keys defined in the system. In order for this procedure to return meaningful information, you must have executed the *sp_primarykey, sp_foreignkey,* or *sp_commonkey* system procedures previously on the objects in this database.

sp_helprotect

Syntax:

```
sp_helprotect name [,username]
```

This procedure allows you to review any permission settings that have been defined in a database for a database object (table, view, stored procedure) or user.

sp_helpsql (Microsoft), sp_syntax (Sybase)

Syntax:

```
sp_helpsql ['topic']
sp_syntax [,'module',[language]]
```

This is the online help system available within SQL Server. Topics are broken down into the following catagories in Microsoft SQL Server:

Datatypes
The datatypes SQL Server supports

Expressions
Any valid expressions you can enter

Wildcard characters
Any wildcard characters you can use

Text functions
All text functions the system supports

Mathematical functions
Any mathematical functions you may care to use

Functions
Any other functions not covered under the other topics

In addition to these categories, help is also available on all the Transact-SQL commands and system stored procedures.

Sybase also supports the notion of categories, broken down as follows:

- OpenVMS
- Transact-SQL
- Unix utility
- System procedure

To be able to use the Sybase procedure *sp_syntax*, you will need to install the sybsyntax database as well as this procedure. The sybsyntax database is installed as part of a typical Sybase ASE installation procedure.

sp_helptext

Syntax:

```
sp_helptext object_name
```

This stored procedure retrieves the Transact-SQL source code of the specified object—a stored procedure, trigger, view, rule, or default. Information is derived from the "text" column in system table syscomments, found in every database. The procedure doesn't allow table names to be specified as parameters, because CREATE TABLE statements are not kept in syscomments. On Microsoft SQL Server, you cannot obtain the source of those objects created using the WITH ENCRYPTION option. The procedure still works for them but returns unintelligible encrypted text.

sp_helptext has one bug by design. The source code of an object reconstructed by the procedure has extraneous line breaks at some places. It looks as if someone just went through your code clicking in random places and then hitting the Enter key. As a result, you can't use the output of *sp_helptext* to re-create the object unless you painfully search for all unauthorized line breaks and paste broken lines together. This problem arises from the way information is stored in system table syscomments. The "text" column is of type VARCHAR(255). SQL Server treats source code of any new object as a stream of bytes, where line breaks are represented by two special characters—ASCII codes 13 and 10 (a.k.a. Line Feed and Carriage Return). Sometimes only one of these characters may be used, depending on the editor you use to write your source code.

SQL Server tries to pack as much information per row of syscomments as possible. It sticks several lines of source code into one row of syscomments. If the last line doesn't fit, SQL Server breaks it and begins the next row of syscomments with the remainder of the last line. As a result, syscomments column text contains something like that shown in Figure 17-1.

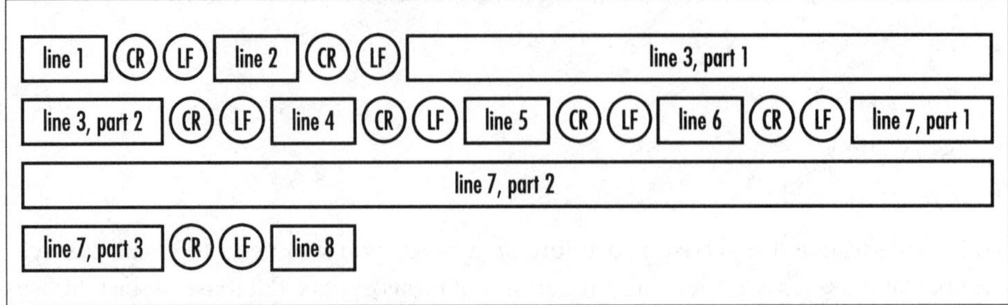

Figure 17-1. Storage of Transact-SQL source code in syscomments

This example represents a Transact-SQL object consisting of eight lines of the source code. SQL Server packs them in lines up to 255 characters and, in this case, they all fit into four rows of the syscomments table. Note that line 7 has wrapped more than once—apparently it is a long line, longer than 255 characters. We have used LF and CR tags to indicate line feed and carriage return characters.

Now back to the *sp_helptext* stored procedure. The algorithm of the procedure is simple—it selects the text column from syscomments for a given object. It doesn't care that extra line breaks appear in the code where one row of syscomments ends and the next one starts. In our example, three additional line breaks will appear in the object code: one in line 3 and two in line 7. All CR LF characters will also be displayed as line breaks. It may be easier to demonstrate this using an example, as follows:

```
sp_helptext reptq2
```

Results:

```
text
--------------------------------------------------------------------------


CREATE PROCEDURE reptq2 AS
select type, pub_id, titles.title_id, au_ord,
   Name - substring (au_lname, 1,15), ytd_sales
from titles, authors, titleauthor
where titles.title_id = titleauthor.title_id AND authors.au_id =
 titleauthor.au_id
   AND pub
_id is NOT NULL
order by pub_id, type
COMPUTE avg(ytd_sales) BY pub_id, type
COMPUTE avg(ytd_sales) BY pub_id
```

Note the two **boldfaced** lines. This was, in fact, one line in the original source code, but it got broken when reconstructed from syscomments. In this case, the break occurs in the middle of a column name. If you copy this result to a query window and try to execute it in order to re-create the object, it will fail because pub and _id are invalid column names.

Is it possible to write a Transact-SQL stored procedure that would retrieve the source code without breaking lines? We offer you our stored procedure, *sp_helpcode,* included on the CD-ROM accompanying this book. That procedure also takes the object name as a parameter and reconstructs the source code, pasting broken lines together. Due to the Transact-SQL limitation of the maximum length of CHAR and VARCHAR data as 255 characters, we couldn't make our stored procedure perfect. In case the original object includes lines longer than 255 characters, they will be broken into pieces. But *sp_helpcode* breaks lines intelligently—at a blank character closest to position 255. It also appends a comment line at the end of the result set when artificial line breaks have been added.

Most frontend tools today include a function that retrieves the source code of an object from syscomments. They don't insert extraneous line breaks; we encourage you to use them.

sp_helpuser

Syntax:

```
sp_helpuser [name_in_database]
```

This procedure details information about users, groups, and aliases in the current database. This procedure is useful for identifying what groups a user belongs to and whether the user's login name is different from his username.

sp_hidetext (Sybase Only)

Syntax:

```
sp_hidetext [objname [, tabname [, username]]]
```

This procedure is used to encrypt an object in a database. If the procedure is called with no parameters, *all* objects within the database will be encrypted. You can also encrypt a table or a view using this procedure. You can also specify the user for whom you want an object encrypted. For example:

```
sp_hidetext @tabname ='authors'
```

will hide the code for the table authors.

sp_lock

Syntax:

```
sp_lock [ spid1 [ , spid2 ] ]
```

This stored procedure reports locks placed by all processes (when executed with no parameters), one specified process, or two specified processes. Information is retrieved from the system table master..syslocks. It changes dynamically as processes submit new transactions and queries in progress move to new pages in tables. *sp_lock* is extremely valuable in on-the-fly analysis of query performance.

For example, you can obtain a complete list of locks currently being held by all processes as follows:

```
sp_lock
```

Results:

```
spid   locktype          table_id    page        dbname
------ ----------------- ----------- ----------- ---------------
12     Sh_intent         16003088    0           pubs
12     Sh_intent         192003715   0           pubs
12     Sh_page           192003715   402         pubs
12     Sh_intent         288004057   0           pubs
12     Sh_page           288004057   424         pubs
15     Sh_intent         704005539   0           master
15     Ex_extent         0           376         tempdb

(1 row(s) affected)
```

These results show that there are currently two processes on our SQL Server that hold locks. Spid 15 is our own process from when we executed the *sp_lock* procedure. It places some locks of its own while *sp_lock* is in progress. We can disregard it for the purposes of our performance monitoring.

Let's analyze locks issues by spid 12. The first step is translating values in the table_id column to real table names. Column dbname provides the name of the database where each lock is held. The table_id is the object ID found in the sysobjects table in each respective database. We can obtain table names by executing the following query:

```
SELECT  id, name
FROM    pubs..sysobjects
WHERE   id IN ( 16003088, 192003715, 288004057 )
```

Note that we have pasted distinct object ids from *sp_lock* results in the IN list.

Results:

```
id          name
----------- ------------------------------
16003088    authors
192003715   titles
288004057   titleauthor

(3 row(s) affected)
```

This information, coupled with *sp_lock* output, tells us that the query executed by spid 12 holds shared locks on three tables. This indicates a SELECT query. *sp_lock* output also shows that all three tables have a lock on page 0. This indicates a table-level lock and may be an indication of an inefficient query.

Real production servers may have hundreds of concurrent users executing numerous queries and holding thousands of locks. It's impractical to analyze *sp_lock* output that consists of many pages of information. You can narrow the focus by using one or two SPIDs as parameters. The result set will contain the same information filtered for specified SPIDs.

As our example demonstrates, the process of translating object IDs to table names is somewhat cumbersome and requires an additional manual step. On Sybase SQL Server, it is possible to get table names directly from syslocks with the following query:

```
SELECT  l.spid,
        locktype = v.name,
        table_name = OBJECT_NAME( l.id, l.dbid ),
        l.page,
        dbname = DB_NAME( l.dbid )
FROM    master..syslocks l, master..spt_values v
WHERE   l.type = v.number
    AND v.type = 'L'
--  uncomment the following line and substitute spid unless you want all
--  AND l.spid = <spid>
ORDER BY 1, 5, 3, 2, 4
```

This query uses the Sybase-only version of the built-in function OBJECT_NAME, which allows you to specify the database ID as the second parameter.

On Microsoft SQL Server, there is no straightforward way to get table names. We have included our own procedure, *sp_locktab,* on the CD-ROM, and it reports table names instead of object IDs. Table names come at a price of slower performance of our procedure compared to standard *sp_lock* when syslocks contains many rows. The source code of the procedure is compact enough, so we included it here as an example:

```
CREATE PROC sp_locktab
-- Produce sp_lock report with table names instead of object ids
-- For Microsoft SQL Server 6.5
-- Date:    02/04/1998
    @spid1 SMALLINT = NULL,
    @spid2 SMALLINT = NULL
AS
DECLARE @dbid CHAR(3), @dbname VARCHAR(30), @db_count INT
CREATE TABLE #locks (
    id          INT          NOT NULL,
    dbid        SMALLINT     NOT NULL,
    page        INT          NOT NULL,
    type        SMALLINT     NOT NULL,
    spid        SMALLINT     NOT NULL,
    table_name VARCHAR(30)  NULL
)
CREATE TABLE #db ( dbid SMALLINT )

INSERT  #locks ( id, dbid, page, type, spid )
```

```
SELECT   *
FROM     master..syslocks
WHERE    ( @spid1 IS NULL AND @spid2 IS NULL )
    OR   spid IN ( @spid1, @spid2 )

INSERT #db SELECT DISTINCT dbid FROM #locks

SELECT @db_count = @@rowcount

WHILE @db_count > 0
BEGIN
    SET ROWCOUNT 1
    SELECT  @db_count = @db_count - 1,
            @dbid     = STR( dbid, 3 ),
            @dbname   = DB_NAME( dbid )
    FROM    #db
    DELETE  #db -- only one row is deleted here
    SET ROWCOUNT 0
    EXEC ( '
        UPDATE  #locks
        SET     table_name = o.name
        FROM    #locks l, ' + @dbname + '..sysobjects o
        WHERE   l.dbid = ' + @dbid + '
            AND l.id   = o.id
    ' )
END

SELECT  spid,
        locktype = name,
        table_name,
        page,
         dbname = DB_NAME( dbid )
FROM    #locks l, master..spt_values v
WHERE   l.type = v.number
    AND v.type = 'L'
ORDER BY 1, 5, 3, 2, 4

DROP TABLE #locks
DROP TABLE #db
GO
```

sp_monitor

Syntax:

```
sp_monitor
```

This procedure is used to display a series of statistics about the server. Only users who have sa_role() may run this procedure. Executing this procedure will return results similar to the following

```
last_run                  current_run                 seconds
--------                  -----------                 -----------
Mar  1 1998 10:17PM       Mar  1 1998 10:18PM         58
```

```
cpu_busy                 io_busy                  idle
--------                 -------                  ----
12(0)-0%                 33(0)-0%                 23788(58)-100%

packets_received         packets_sent             packet_errors
----------------         ------------             -------------
130(3)                   1055(15)                 1(0)

total_read         total_write        total_errors       connections
----------         -----------        ------------       -----------
2312(5)            630(4)             0(0)               0(0)
```

Each statistic follows a similar form:

```
current_value(previous_value)-time_since_ran%
```

The results are broken down into different components:

- The time that has passed since this procedure was run previously
- The ratio of CPU to I/O to system idle rates
- The number of network packets that have been sent and received by client connections, as well as any packet errors
- The total number of reads, writes, errors, and connections that have occurred since the last execution of this procedure

The results measured from *sp_monitor* are held in system global variables. The first time *sp_monitor* is run after the server is started, the results in parentheses will be meaningless. You should use *sp_monitor* as a monitoring tool since it can help focus your performance and tuning efforts.

sp_password

Syntax:

```
sp_password old_password, new_password [, login_id]
```

This stored procedure changes your password. Naturally, if you don't remember the old password, you can't set a new one. The only exception is made for the SA, who can specify NULL instead of `old_password`. This allows administrators to reset the passwords of forgetful users. You may prefer to use the GUI interface to SQL Server to change your password. Nevertheless, you should remember the syntax of *sp_password* in cases in which the command-line ISQL turns out to be the only way you can access SQL Server.

sp_primarykey

Syntax:

```
sp_primarykey tablename, column1 [, column2, column3, . . . column8]
```

This procedure is used to define a primary key on a view or table. Each time this procedure is called, an entry is made in the system table syskeys.

sp_recompile

Syntax:

```
sp_recompile table_name
```

This system stored procedure forces every stored procedure and trigger that references the specified table in the current database to be recompiled the next time they run. Query plans for procedures and triggers are compiled when they are first used after SQL Server restarts. If you then add or update your data or create new indexes, previously compiled plans may no longer be optimal. SQL Server doesn't automatically notice that and continues using the same plan. One of the methods to tell it that new plans are needed for all procedures, triggers, and views associated with a particular table is to execute *sp_recompile.*

Stored procedures created or executed using the WITH RECOMPILE option are recompiled every time they run. They do not benefit from your executing *sp_recompile*, but there is no harm either. You also don't have to run *sp_recompile* if you are planning to restart SQL Server soon, because it will then recompile every object upon restart anyway.

We recommend that you execute *sp_recompile* for tables on which you create new indexes or modify a lot of data. The procedure takes very little time to execute, because it doesn't perform the actual compilation of new plans. It simply marks every related object for recompilation once it is used again.

In certain cases, Microsoft SQL Server 6.5 automatically creates a new query plan if you add a new index to the table, without requiring you to do an *sp_recompile.* This is contrary to the documentation. Using a similar test, we also checked Sybase, which did not automatically recompile the procedure.

sp_remotesql (Sybase Only)

Syntax:

```
sp_remotesql server, query [,query2, . . . ,query254]
```

This procedure can be used to send a query to a remote server or the local server, execute the query, and return the results to this client. The server must exist in sysservers and should have been added using the *sp_addserver* function. In order to use this procedure, you will need to have installed Component Integration Services (included on the ASE installation CD-ROM).

sp_rename

Syntax:

```
sp_rename old_name, new_name
```

This stored procedure renames an object or a user-defined datatype. This procedure may seem innocent enough—just a name change in system table sysobjects or systypes—but it may be a very dangerous stored procedure in certain situations. The problem is that *sp_rename* does not take care of references made by other objects to the renamed one.

Suppose that we rename table titleauthor to titleauthor_history, and then create a new table titleauthor. What happens to stored procedures that access titleauthor? Will they go to the new object under this name or still to the old one, even though it has been renamed? If you are new to this problem, then it's almost guaranteed that you won't even guess right. We don't mean to imply that you can't figure it out. It's just that SQL Server does the least natural and intuitive thing in this case. Right after you execute *sp_rename,* all stored procedures, triggers, and views will continue working with the old object, ignoring the name change. This is due to the fact that the object ID has not changed. It was recorded with every reference to the table in other objects, and those objects continue to think that it is still the same table. However, if you drop and re-create any of the stored procedures that reference the renamed object, a new link will be established. This time, SQL Server will look for an object currently named titleauthor. Since we have created a new table under this name, it will be used by newly created (or re-created) objects. Imagine that some procedures keep using the old physical table titleauthor_history, and some (that you happened to re-create) use titleauthor. What an awful mess!

In some systems, you may have dozens or hundreds of stored procedures that refer to the renamed object. If you want them to access the *old* one, you have to modify the source code of every related procedure, trigger, and view and then re-create them. If you want them to access a new object under the same name (titleauthor in our example), you should simply drop and re-create every procedure, trigger, and view that refers to this object. It may take a very long time. Besides, how do you find all objects with references to the renamed one? If you're thinking about using the system procedure *sp_depends*, think again. Read our warnings about this procedure first!

The safest approach, if you need to rename an object, is to create a new one under the desired name and then drop the old one. If this is a table, you also need to copy all the data before you drop the old object, which could be a very resource-intensive process. So you have to evaluate your alternatives depending on the size of the table. If you drop an old object, what happens to all related objects? Interestingly, nothing bad, if you create a new object under the same name. Every stored procedure, trigger, and view will realize that the physical object has changed and will find the new one by name. This switch is completely transparent to the user. If you simply drop an object and do not substitute a new one, related objects will not function as common sense suggests.

sp_renamedb

Syntax:

```
sp_renamedb old_database_name, new_database_name
```

This procedure is used to change the name of a user database to a new name. In order to rename a database, you must first put it into single-user mode.

In Sybase SQL Server, a database cannot be renamed if it is referenced by any other table in another database. The check is based on the current entries in the system table sysreferences.

sp_serveroption

Syntax:

```
sp_serveroption [server_name, option_name, {TRUE |FALSE}]
```

This procedure is used to set server options. The option sets differ between Microsoft and Sybase SQL Server. Microsoft SQL Server options include:

dist
: Distribution server

dpub
: Combination publisher/subscriber server

pub
: Publication server

rpc
: Remote server

sub
: Subscription server

Sybase SQL Server options are specifically for remote servers. Options include:

net password encryption
: Indicates whether client-side password encryption is required when connecting to this remote server.

readonly

Defines this remote server as a read-only server. Component Integration Services needs to be used to take advantage of this option.

rpc security model A

Specifies the way RPC calls are to be handled. This model does not perform mutual authentication, message confidentiality, or message integrity.

timeouts

This option allows you to enable or disable the normal timeout code that is listened to by the local server. If this option is unset, the connection will not be automatically dropped after one minute if there is no logical connection established.

sp_spaceused

Syntax:

Microsoft	Sybase
`sp_spaceused [ table_name ] [[,] @updateusage = { TRUE | FALSE }`	`sp_spaceused [ table_name ]`

This stored procedure reports space usage for the whole database (when executed with no parameters) or for a particular table. The output format is different depending on whether a table name is specified, as the following examples demonstrate.

In order to obtain space usage for the current database, execute the following:

```
sp_spaceused
```

Results (on our pubs database):

```
database_name                  database_size      unallocated space
------------------------------ ------------------ ------------------
pubs                           3.00 MB            1.77 MB

reserved           data               index_size         unused
------------------ ------------------ ------------------ ------------------
1262 KB            188 KB             114 KB             960 KB
```

Note that the column headed "unused" may be very confusing. It does not show the amount of free space left in the whole database. In this case, it is the total amount of space reserved for tables but not filled with data. The database also has unallocated space that is not reserved for any table and may be taken by the first object that claims more room to grow. Most of the unused space may be reclaimed on a particular table if you re-create its clustered index.

The following is an example of a space usage report on a particular table:

```
sp_spaceused authors
```

Results (on our pubs database):

```
name            rows          reserved    data    index_size unused
--------------- ------------ ----------- ------- ----------- ---------
authors         23            64 KB       2 KB    8 KB        54 KB
```

The procedure reports not only space usage but also the number of rows in the table. This is a much quicker way of getting the row count than running the SELECT COUNT(*) query, right? Wrong! We strongly advise you not to rely on *sp_spaceused* to give you accurate results about the number of rows or space usage by table or for the whole database. The problem is that it derives results from the system table sysindexes. By design, SQL Server does not guarantee that the contents of this table are always accurate. It makes a considerable effort to keep track of space used and the number of rows. However, very often the numbers get out of hand. This happens when SQL Server experiences a heavy workload and some transactions terminate abnormally and roll back. SQL Server also gets confused when you drop an index. You can say that SQL Server is sometimes too busy to keep track of what's going on.

The data in sysindexes may be corrected by several methods. The oldest method is to execute the DBCC CHECKDB command. As a side effect, it fixes the sysindexes information when it encounters any discrepancy. But the price of this fix may be enormous, as DBCC CHECKDB may take hours or even days on large tables.

Microsoft has also introduced a new DBCC option in recent versions—DBCC UPDATEUSAGE. It fixes the sysindexes information faster than DBCC CHECKDB. You may force DBCC UPDATEUSAGE to be executed right before *sp_spaceused* retrieves its results. This is possible through a Microsoft-only syntax:

```
sp_spaceused authors, @updateusage = TRUE -- for table authors only
```

or:

```
sp_spaceused @updateusage = TRUE            -- for the whole current database
```

Beware that this may take some time, depending on the size of the table or database.

sp_spaceall

You may sometimes need to get space usage on every table in a database. Executing *sp_spaceused* on all tables may not be very convenient. Also, you may want results formatted as a table, rather than as numerous separate single-table reports. We offer you (on the accompanying CD-ROM) our system stored procedure *sp_spaceall* for Microsoft SQL Server 6.x. It reports space usage by every table in the current database, as well as a percentage of each table in the total. The percentage may be calculated on the number of rows, space reserved, space used for data, or indexes. Results may be ordered by any column.

Syntax:

```
sp_spaceall [ table_type ] [ , percent_and_order_by ]
```

where table_type may be one of the following:

s
: System tables only

u
: User tables only (default)

us
: All tables

The `percent_and_order_by` argument specifies the name of the result set column that should be used to calculate the percentage compared to the database total and also to order the result: name, reserved, rows, data, index_size, or unused. For example, in order to obtain space usage for all user tables in database pubs, ordered by name, execute the following:

```
sp_spaceall u, name
```

The percent column in this case is calculated for reserved numbers, because it would be meaningless on the name column.

Results:

```
name                       rows reserved data index_size unused reserved %
-------------------------- ---- -------- ---- ---------- ------ ----------
authors                    23   64       2    8          54     5.071
discounts                  3    16       2    0          14     1.268
employee                   43   64       4    8          52     5.071
jobs                       14   32       2    4          26     2.536
pub_info                   8    80       36   4          40     6.339
publishers                 8    32       2    4          26     2.536
roysched                   86   48       4    4          40     3.803
sales                      21   64       2    8          54     5.071
stores                     6    32       2    4          26     2.536
titleauthor                25   96       2    12         82     7.607
titles                     18   64       4    8          52     5.071
------------------------ ---- -------- ---- ---------- ------ ----------
Total: data and log = 3 MB 1102 1262     188  114        960    100.0
```

sp_unbindefault

Syntax:

```
sp_unbindefault objname [,FUTUREONLY]
```

This procedure allows you to unbind a previously bound default from a user-defined datatype or column. You may optionally choose to unbind only a default from future instances of a particular datatype and not affect any defaults that have already been bound to existing user-defined datatype columns.

sp_unbindrule

Syntax:

```
sp_unbindrule objname [;FUTUREONLY]
```

This procedure allows you to unbind a previously bound rule from a user-defined datatype or column. You may optionally choose to unbind only a rule from future instances of a particular datatype and not affect any rules that have already been bound to existing user-defined datatype columns.

sp_who

Syntax:

```
sp_who [ login_name | spid ]
```

This is probably the most popular system stored procedure. It is important to know who else is logged in to SQL Server and who is doing what. The *sp_who* procedure reports all system processes connected to SQL Server, including internal system processes (when executed without parameters). You may also filter the results by a specific login name or by a system process ID (SPID). Results are retrieved mainly from the system table master..sysprocesses.

Results (on Microsoft):

```
spid  status    loginame  hostname     blk  dbname  cmd
----- --------- --------- ------------ ---- ------- ---------------
1     sleeping  sa                     0    master  MIRROR HANDLER
2     sleeping  sa                     0    master  LAZY WRITER
3     sleeping  sa                     0    master  CHECKPOINT SLEEP
4     sleeping  sa                     0    master  RA MANAGER
10    sleeping  WOLFGANG  WMOZART      0    pubs    AWAITING COMMAND
11    runnable  JOHANN    JBACH        0    master  SELECT
12    sleeping  PYOTR     PTCHAIKOVSKY 0    master  AWAITING COMMAND
13    runnable  ANTONIO   AVIVALDI     0    pubs    INSERT
14    sleeping  GIUSEPPE  GVERDI       0    tempdb  AWAITING COMMAND

(1 row(s) affected)
```

Results (on SYbase):

```
fid spid status     loginame origname hostname  blk dbname cmd
--- ---- ---------- -------- -------- --------- --- ------ ---------------
0   2    sleeping   NULL     NULL               0   master NETWORK HANDLER
0   3    sleeping   NULL     NULL               0   master DEADLOCK TUNE
0   4    sleeping   NULL     NULL               0   master MIRROR HANDLER
0   5    sleeping   NULL     NULL               0   master HOUSEKEEPER
0   6    sleeping   NULL     NULL               0   master SHUTDOWN HANDLER
0   7    sleeping   NULL     NULL               0   master CHECKPOINT SLEEP
0   8    running    sa       sa       JBACH     0   master SELECT
0   9    background NULL     NULL               0   t1     REP AGENT
```

The most notable columns of the result set are:

spid
: A unique ID assigned to every process running on SQL Server

loginame
: User login name

blk
: The SPID of the process blocking this process (zero indicates no blocks)

dbname
: The name of the current database used by the process

cmd
: The command currently executed by the process, or AWAITING COMMAND if idle

Do not trust the "status" column; that may be very misleading. It is supposed to tell you whether a process is running, but it is derived from a very volatile and unreliable column status of system table sysprocesses. The status of "sleeping" very often doesn't mean that the process is idle.

Chapter 11, *Transactions and Locking*, shows an example of *sp_who* usage.

We offer you a better (in our opinion) way of measuring the activity of system processes. On the accompanying CD-ROM, you will find the stored procedure *sp_whoactive,* which takes two snapshots of the sysprocesses table with several seconds' delay. Processes that have moving activity indicators are reported as "active." The most important activity indicators are the physical and logical I/O incurred by every process. Our procedure also counts the number of rows in the syslocks table held by every process. Changes in this number indicate activity. This method allows you to quickly spot the most active processes that consume more resources. With the help of *sp_whoactive,* it may be much easier to tell whether a process is really busy or just "frozen" and not moving at all.

Another helpful stored procedure on the CD-ROM is *sp_inputbuffer.* It works on Microsoft SQL Server only and returns DBCC INPUTBUFFER results for every system process. This may be more informative than the "cmd" column of *sp_who.*

Creating Your Own System Procedures

If you are not happy with the standard set of system stored procedures, you can create your own. This is a common practice. Transact-SQL programmers often create system stored procedures that are in some respects better than those provided by vendors.

You may also find third-party stored procedures, such as those we've included on the accompanying CD-ROM, as well as those published in other SQL Server books or in many locations on the Web. As with any shareware or freeware, these programs require careful screening and evaluation to establish that they are reliable and safe to use in your environment. We encourage you to use our stored procedures. We have tested them on many different servers and, to the best of our knowledge, they are safe to use.

SQL Server allows you to drop and re-create standard system procedures. However, we strongly advise against such practice. The next SQL Server upgrade could reinstall a vendor's version and cause havoc in your applications relying on customized enhancements. Moreover, off-the-shelf applications that you purchase may rely on standard versions of system stored procedures and break on your own.

Extended Stored Procedures

Extended stored procedures provide a way to extend SQL Server functionality beyond Transact-SQL. An extended stored procedure is a separate program compiled as a dynamic link library (DLL) and registered on SQL Server in a special way. You can execute this program as if it were a standard stored procedure. Implementation is transparent to a user who runs the procedure with a regular EXEC command, passes parameters, and receives certain results back.

SQL Server comes with a set of vendor-supplied extended stored procedures. They also provide some additional extended procedures that you may find useful but that are not officially supported.

Typically, an extended stored procedure is written to access resources outside of SQL Server databases, such as operating system files. Such procedures may also offer better performance on heavy computing tasks that do not access data as much as they crunch numbers. Writing such a function in C++ may be more efficient than coding it in Transact-SQL.

Extended stored procedures allow you to build a library of useful functions that you could distribute as an add-on product to SQL Server in the form of a DLL file. For example, you could use extended stored procedures to manipulate objects other than data stored in relational tables such as multimedia files. You could implement a database of graphics files and use extended stored procedures to search images by color, shape, or pattern. The possibilities are virtually limitless. Extended stored procedures can do anything a computer is capable of doing.

The following sections describe the Microsoft and Sybase implementations of extended stored procedures and then summarize the syntax and usage of the most popular procedures.

Microsoft Implementation

You can develop extended stored procedures for Microsoft SQL Server using the Open Data Services (ODS) API. You can write your C functions with the ODS API and compile a DLL. Therefore, extended procedures become a dynamic part of SQL Server. They are executed by the same NT service that runs SQL Server, rather than as separate services. This means that extended procedures share the same address space and security with the Windows NT MSSQLServer service. The Microsoft implementation uses NT's structured exception handling (SEH) to keep traps in extended stored procedures from crashing the server. A problem with this usage is that it is possible to corrupt SQL Server's memory via a rogue pointer. This can ultimately crash the server.

The Microsoft model simplifies administration and improves the performance of extended procedures. However, poorly written extended procedures may cause access violations and corrupt memory used by SQL Server. Therefore, the system administrator should carefully review and test every custom-made extended stored procedure before registering it on SQL Server.

Sybase Implementation

On Sybase, extended stored procedures are implemented as a separate Open Server application—XP Server. This application is a separate process that does not share memory with SQL Server. Sybase's approach offers more protection than Microsoft's extended procedure implementation on SQL Server; however, Microsoft's method offers better performance.

XP Server is installed as part of the Adaptive Server installation. It communicates with SQL Server via remote procedure calls (RPCs). Sybase Adaptive Server automatically starts XP Server when the first extended procedure is called. The service shuts down when Adaptive Server shuts down.

Registering Extended Procedures

You may compile all or several of your extended procedures into one or more DLL files and install them on your SQL Server. Every extended stored procedure must be registered on SQL Server with *sp_addextendedproc*. The syntax is:

```
sp_addextendedproc procedure_name, DLL_name
```

You can obtain information about the DLL file of a registered extended procedure, or all of them, by executing *sp_helpextendedproc*. In order to unregister an extended procedure, execute *sp_dropextendedproc*.

xp names, unlike *sp_* ones, are case-sensitive regardless of the server code page and sort order. On a case-insensitive server, you could use either *SP_WHO* or *sp_who,* but only *xp_sendmail,* not *XP_SENDMAIL.*

xp_cmdshell

Syntax:

```
xp_cmdshell command_string [, no_output]
```

This stored procedure is an extremely powerful tool. It performs commands as if they were submitted from the operating system command prompt. Therefore, you have the ability to run any programs or command files outside of SQL Server and manipulate files from within Transact-SQL code.

Before we discuss this process in more detail, be aware that there are some real security issues with *xp_cmdshell* in the Microsoft implementation. By default, Microsoft SQL Server executes the command shell process with the permissions of the NT user account configured to start SQL Server. Depending on your point of view, this can be a serious security risk. The DBA may configure a separate NT account to execute *xp_cmdshell* commands submitted by non-SA users. Sybase has been a bit more cautious with its implementation of *xp_cmdshell* and uses a combination of roles and a context mode for this command to limit which users can execute this procedure.

In the call to *xp_cmdshell,* command_string may be a literal string or a local variable. The optional parameter NO_OUTPUT suppresses the output. For example, you can check the contents of the root directory on the C: drive on your SQL Server as follows:

```
EXEC master..xp_cmdshell 'dir c:\'
```

Results (on our notebook computer):

```
output
--------------------------------------------------------------------------
Volume in drive C has no label.
 Volume Serial Number is 2357-B517
(null)
 Directory of C:\
(null)
05/07/97  01:13p        <DIR>          Program Files
```

```
05/07/97  12:29p        <DIR>          WINNT
05/07/97  01:25p        <DIR>          TEMP
10/30/97  11:13p                   512 BOOTSECT.DOS
11/05/97  10:38p        <DIR>          DRIVERS
05/07/97  08:03p        <DIR>          MSSQL
10/23/97  10:40p        <DIR>          DOS
05/31/94  06:22a                54,645 COMMAND.DOS
05/31/94  06:22a                 9,349 WINA20.386
05/09/97  04:06a        <DIR>          BITWARE
08/19/96  07:50p                 6,907 PMXFM.EXE
02/15/98  11:49a            53,477,376 pagefile.sys
10/30/97  11:43p                    65 CONFIG.SYS
08/24/96  11:11a                93,812 COMMAND.COM
10/30/97  11:02p                   489 NETLOG.TXT
05/30/97  09:39a        <DIR>          Utils
11/21/97  08:48a                   111 autoexec.bat
              17 File(s)    53,643,266 bytes
                           897,613,824 bytes free

(24 row(s) affected)
```

If you couple *xp_cmdshell* with SQL Server 6.5's capability to insert the results of any stored procedure into a table, you can manipulate the results. For example, if you want the output in the previous example to include only file and directory names, you can execute the following script:

```
CREATE TABLE #result ( line VARCHAR(255) NULL )
INSERT  #result ( line ) EXEC master..xp_cmdshell 'dir c:\'
SELECT  line
FROM    #result
WHERE   line like
           '[0-9][0-9]/[0-9][0-9]/[0-9][0-9]  [0-9][0-9]:[0-9][0-9][ap]%'
DROP TABLE #result
```

Results:

```
(24 row(s) affected)

line
------------------------------------------------------------------------------
05/07/97  01:13p        <DIR>          Program Files
05/07/97  12:29p        <DIR>          WINNT
05/07/97  01:25p        <DIR>          TEMP
10/30/97  11:13p                   512 BOOTSECT.DOS
11/05/97  10:38p        <DIR>          DRIVERS
05/07/97  08:03p        <DIR>          MSSQL
10/23/97  10:40p        <DIR>          DOS
05/31/94  06:22a                54,645 COMMAND.DOS
05/31/94  06:22a                 9,349 WINA20.386
05/09/97  04:06a        <DIR>          BITWARE
08/19/96  07:50p                 6,907 PMXFM.EXE
02/15/98  11:49a            53,477,376 pagefile.sys
10/30/97  11:43p                    65 CONFIG.SYS
08/24/96  11:11a                93,812 COMMAND.COM
```

```
10/30/97  11:02p              489 NETLOG.TXT
05/30/97  09:39a     <DIR>        Utils
11/21/97  08:48a              111 autoexec.bat

(17 row(s) affected)
```

Email Processing

Several extended stored procedures in both Sybase and Microsoft SQL Server allow you to handle email received by SQL Server and send email messages from SQL Server. The setup and administration of mail accounts to use with SQL Server is beyond the scope of this book.

The following extended stored procedures process mail messages:

xp_sendmail
: Sends a mail message

xp_readmail
: Reads a mail message

xp_deletemail
: Deletes a mail message

xp_findnextmsg
: Is used to obtain an internal ID of the next message in the inbox

xp_processmail
: Is a procedure that calls *xp_findnextmsg*, *xp_readmail*, and *xp_deletemail* in succession to process the next incoming message in the queue

Syntax:

```
xp_sendmail
@recipient = recipient [; recipient2; [...; recipientN]]
        [, @message = message]
        [, @query = query]
        [, @attachments = attachments]
        [, @copy_recipients = recipient [; recipient2; [...; recipientN]]]
        [, @blind_copy_recipients = recipient [; recipient2; [...;
            recipientN]]]
        [, @subject = subject]
        [, @type = type]
        [, @attach_results = {'true' | 'false'}]
        [, @no_output = {'true' | 'false'}]
        [, @no_header = {'true' | 'false'}]
        [, @width = width]
        [, @separator = separator]
        [, @echo_error = {'true' | 'false'}]
        [, @set_user = user]
        [, @dbuse = dbname]

xp_readmail
[ @msg_id = msg_id]
```

```
[, @type = type [OUTPUT]]
        [, @peek = {'true' | 'false'}]
        [, @suppress_attach = {'true' | 'false'}]
        [, @originator = @sender OUTPUT]
        [, @subject = @subject_line OUTPUT]
        [, @message = @body_of_message OUTPUT]
        [, @recipients = @recipient_list OUTPUT]
        [, @cc_list = @cc_list OUTPUT]
        [, @bcc_list = @bcc_list OUTPUT]
        [, @date_received = @date OUTPUT]
        [, @unread = {'true' | 'false'}]
        [, @attachments = @temp_file_paths OUTPUT])
        [, @skip_bytes = @bytes_to skip OUTPUT]
        [, @msg_length = @length_in_bytes OUTPUT]

xp_deletemail [@msg_id = ] msg_id

xp_findnextmsg
[ @msg_id = msg_id [OUTPUT]]
        [, @type = type]
        [, @unread_only = {'true' | 'false'}]

sp_processmail [@subject = subject] [[,] @filetype = filetype] [[,]
    @separator = separator] [[,] @set_user = user] [[,] @dbuse = dbname]
```

Microsoft SQL Server supports MAPI-compliant mail systems (MAPI stands for Mail Application Programming Interface). The @type parameter of mail-handling stored procedures must comply with this specification—IP[M | C].Vendorname.subclass. Sybase 11.5 supports only the CMC:IPM type of the MAPI specification.

Using these extended procedures, you can program your SQL Server to automatically receive and process email messages and send its own mail. For example, your SQL Server can send users reports automatically every night; this way, they'll have them in their email boxes in the morning. It can send messages triggered by certain business rules defined on your database, such as a low on-hand quantity of a product your company sells or an overdue payment on a customer account. Your DBA may program the server to report the status of recurring tasks and database space free on a daily basis. The number of applications is virtually unlimited.

Note that *xp_sendmail* has several options on how to send information. You can include everything in the message text, attach a file with any data, or attach the results of a query. Queries cannot access your local temporary tables, so be sure to refer to permanent tables or global temporary ones.

In order to read and delete incoming messages, you need to know the message ID assigned by SQL Server. The stored procedure *xp_findnextmsg* returns an ID for one message in the inbox. You need to supply this ID to the *xp_readmail* or *xp_deletemail* procedure to indicate which particular message you want to open or discard.

Query by Email

SQL Server may be taught to act on certain email messages, such as requests for reports or commands to execute a stored procedure. Provided that you take care of the security and ensure that you do not open doors for anyone to control your SQL Server, this may be a very powerful mechanism for remote interaction with SQL Server. One strong advantage is that you could have a virtually unlimited number of occasional users without paying for extra licenses.

In this model, users simply send email to SQL Server with their queries; SQL Server reads them, executes them, and replies by email with result sets attached. This approach may be great for an Internet application on which online response is not required. You publish an email address for your SQL Server on the Web, users send it email with requests for information or some other data, and SQL Server responds automatically. It's a perfect world of low-cost marketing or an information-sales channel, isn't it? We only hope that none of our readers will use this procedure to build applications that send *spam* (unsolicited email advertising) to hundreds or thousands of people.

In order to implement this "Query by Email" application, you need to schedule a task on SQL Server to run every minute and check for incoming messages. The check is done by *xp_findnextmsg*. If it finds new messages, then it processes them one at a time. Processing of a single message begins with reading the message by *xp_readmail* and storing the body of the message in a local variable. You are limited to 255 bytes here, unless you want to allow file attachments to incoming emails and implement more sophisticated attachment parsing and processing. Assuming that the incoming request is executable Transact-SQL code, you execute it and save the results in a global temporary table. Microsoft's capability to store the results of a dynamic query or a stored procedure in a table is very useful here. For example, if you create a global temporary table ##result and an incoming request is stored in variable @request, you can execute it as follows:

```
INSERT ##result EXEC ( @request )
```

The information may be sent back to the incoming message originator by *xp_sendmail* with the ##result table contents as an attachment. Once an incoming email is processed, you should delete it by *xp_deletemail.*

A more restricted (and hacker-proof) model would only allow senders to supply parameters to a predefined set of stored procedures. For example, they could send your SQL Server product names. Your mail-processing job could pass these names received in incoming messages to a stored procedure that derives product information, current price, availability, and shipment options from your database. Another stored procedure could report order processing status by order number. Results may be sent back to the sender. Limiting options of incoming requests prevents an unauthorized person from executing any Transact-SQL command on your server.

The *xp_processmail* procedure is useful in email query processing. Using this procedure, you can take one incoming message that is expected to contain a single Transact-SQL query, execute this query, mail the results back to the message sender, and delete the incoming message. Parameters in the procedure are:

@subject = subject
: When specified, the procedure will process only incoming messages that contain this subject in their subject line. If this parameter is not specified, then the procedure will attempt to process any messages.

@filetype = filetype
: Specifies file name extension that should be used for the result set file attached to the reply message. ".TXT" is used by default.

@separator = separator
: Specifies column delimiter for the resultset . The default is "TAB," which indicates that the tab character should be used to separate columns.

@set_user = user
: Specifies the user whose permissions should be used to execute the query. "guest" is the default.

@dbuse = dbname
: Specifies the database where the query should be executed. "master" is the default.

Here are some examples:

```
EXEC xp_sendmail 'Tchaikovsky_Peter', 'Transaction log in msdb is full.'
EXEC xp_readmail @msg_id     = @message_id,
                 @originator = @originator OUTPUT,
                 @message    = @query OUTPUT
EXEC xp_deletemail @message_id
EXEC xp_findnextmsg @msg_id = message_id OUTPUT
```

xp_logevent

Syntax:

```
xp_logevent error_number, message [, severity]
```

This procedure allows you to write messages directly to the Windows NT event log. Parameters are:

error_number
: Is user-defined and must be greater than or equal to 50,000

message
: Is the message to be written into the event log, up to 255 characters

severity
: May be one of the following three values: informational, warning, or error

xp_msver (Microsoft Only)

Syntax:

```
xp_msver [ option_name ]
```

This extended stored procedure reports system parameters. You can use it to quickly check the total memory, number, and type of processors, NT version, SQL Server version, and service pack. For a list of options, see the list in the Name column in the following output.

Results (returned by our notebook PC):

```
Index  Name                 Internal_Value Character_Value
------ -------------------- -------------- -----------------------------------
1      ProductName          (null)         Microsoft SQL Server
2      ProductVersion       393266         6.50.201
3      Language             1033           English (United States)
4      Platform             (null)         NT INTEL X86
5      Comments             (null)         NT INTEL X86
6      CompanyName          (null)         Microsoft Corporation
7      FileDescription      (null)         SQL Server Windows NT
8      FileVersion          (null)         1996.04.02
9      InternalName         (null)         SQLSERVR
10     LegalCopyright       (null)         Copyright © Microsoft Corp. 1996
11     LegalTrademarks      (null)         Microsoft® is a registered
                                           trademark of Microsoft
                                           Corporation. Windows(TM) is a
                                           trademark of Microsoft Corporation
12     OriginalFilename     (null)         SQLSERVR.EXE
13     PrivateBuild         (null)         (null)
14     SpecialBuild         131073         (null)
15     WindowsVersion       90505220       4.0 (1381)
16     ProcessorCount       1              1
17     ProcessorActiveMask  1              00000001
18     ProcessorType        586            PROCESSOR_INTEL_PENTIUM
19     PhysicalMemory       39             39 (41082880)
20     Product ID           (null)         50700-419 0020595

(20 row(s) affected)
```

Summary

This chapter covered system stored procedures and extended stored procedures in some detail. Beside describing the rules regarding their creation and initiation, it discussed:

- The function and use of the most commonly used system procedures
- The nuances of the Sybase and Microsoft inplementiations of the extended stored procedures and some basic uses of these procedures

Performance Tuning and Optimization

Part V provides the tools you'll use to polish and fine-tune your Transact-SQL programs. We'll explain how to design Transact-SQL programs that are effective and bug-free and how to maintain code using methods that will reduce your workload when maintenance is an issue. We'll provide oodles of tips, tricks, and techniques for eking out extra performance from a Transact-SQL program. We'll also give you the information you need to test, diagnose, and debug your Transact-SQL program.

Part V contains these chapters:

In this chapter:

- *Coding for Reuse*
- *The Black Box Program*
- *Categorization Schemas*
- *RETURN*
- *RAISERROR*
- *Temporary Data Storage*
- *Using Parameters Effectively*
- *Help*
- *Summary*

18

Transact-SQL Code Design

Design is one of those topics that every author likes to write a chapter about. We are no different. We have methods that work for us, and this is the place where we get to stand on our soapbox and espouse the virtues of these methods. In all seriousness, design is critical since this is where the foundation is laid for the work that is eventually produced in the form of a database or Transact-SQL code. If the design is lacking, you can be sure that the code will necessarily follow. In this chapter, we'll cover some of the design techniques we particularly like to use, and we'll also try to explain why these techniques make sense to us. If you are interested in learning more on this topic, there is a large body of literature devoted to it. But be warned; much of this literature is full of hot air!

In the first section of this chapter, we'll describe some basic techniques that can be used during the design process. Later on, we'll cover the methods you can use within stored procedures to implement these techniques.

Coding for Reuse

Very few of us can afford to buy a shirt, wear it once, and then throw it away. Yet every day we write code, use it once, and then throw it away. If you had to count the number of hours you've spent on this type of code, you would probably be horrified by the amount of time involved. Can we avoid this type of situation? In general, yes. Code is rarely written to be executed once, contrary to the assurances our user community may give us that a query needs to be run just this once. Coding for reuse is mostly about writing code that takes into consideration the fact that things change. Let's look at a simple example to illustrate this point.

A user asks us to write a report to display all the titles for the author Marjorie Green and the price for each title.

The fields to be included in this report are au_fname, au_lname, title, type, and price. The user would like this to be a stored procedure so he can execute it every month to see how many titles this author has. You are asked to write this procedure at 4:50 P.M. on a Friday evening. Here is what you do:

```
CREATE PROCEDURE get_marjorie_green_titles
AS
-- Procedure to get all the books for Marjorie Green
SELECT a.au_fname,
         a.au_lname,
         t.title,
         t.type,
         t.price
    FROM authors a,
         titles t,
         titleauthor at
    WHERE a.au_id = at.au_id
        AND      t.title_id = at.title_id
        AND      a.au_fname = 'Marjorie'
        AND      a.au_lname = 'Green'
```

You run the report for the user and get results similar to the following:

```
au_fname  au_lname   title                                type       price
--------- ---------- ------------------------------------ ---------- -------
Marjorie  Green      The Busy Executive's Database Guide  business   19.99
Marjorie  Green      You Can Combat Computer Stress!      business   2.99

(2 row(s) affected)
```

You deliver your report at 4:59 P.M., and disappear for the weekend. Next week comes and the user wants another report exactly like the one for Marjorie Green, except this time she needs it for Dean Straight. You now have two choices; you can either create a new copy of the Marjorie Green procedure, and substitute Dean for Marjorie and Straight for Green, or you can create one procedure for both authors and just call it something different. Assuming that you choose the latter option—since it is the more practical solution and would result in a procedure that can be reused—the procedure will now look similar to the following:

```
CREATE PROCEDURE get_any_author_titles
@au_fname varchar(20),
@au_lname varchar(40)
AS
-- Procedure to get all the books for any author
    SELECT a.au_fname,
         a.au_lname,
         t.title,
         t.type,
```

```
        t.price
    FROM authors a,
        titles t,
        titleauthor at
    WHERE a.au_id = at.au_id
        AND       t.title_id = at.title_id
        AND       a.au_fname LIKE @au_fname

        AND       a.au_lname LIKE @au_lname
```

Now, you can put in Dean Straight or Marjorie Green or any other author, for that matter, and you can get all titles for a given author. In this situation, by writing reusable code, you have achieved savings in three areas:

Future time
: Time that would have been spent creating individual reports.

User time
: The user can now create a report for every author without requiring your help.

Database storage space
: Every stored procedure you create consumes space on the server.

By anticipating that the user may want to run this report for other authors and by coding accordingly (for example, pass in parameters for the author's name, which took all of 30 seconds to code), you can save yourself from having to re-create the solution again. Reality might have even been worse, since more than a couple of days might have passed, and you might not even be able to remember what you called the procedure in the first place. In this case, you'd have to spend half an hour hunting it down, only to find that it was a two-minute procedure to begin with!

In the rest of this chapter, we'll focus on other techniques that can be used to write reusable code and areas in which they can be utilized effectively.

The Black Box Program

Black boxes are things that are designed to produce a desired result without requiring you to understand how they do it. Imagine how much more complicated life would be if we had to understand how the dishwasher or washing machine worked in order to be able to wash dishes or clothes. For many of us, dishwashers and washing machines are black boxes. All we need to know is what objects need to go into them and how to start the machine; then we simply wait for those clean dishes and clothes to come out at the end.

Programs can be designed on the same principle. For many of you, the system stored procedures are probably black boxes. You may not know how the *sp_helpdevice* procedure works, but you do know that if you call it, it gives a list of the devices in a server. As your level of understanding of both Transact-SQL and the system tables grow, you will probably start to penetrate those black boxes in order to tweak them so they reflect more appropriate information for your own environment.

Before you start to do this, there are a number of rules you need to follow in order to create a black box program. As the name implies, a black box must be reliable and return consistent results with the minimum of fuss.

There are a wide variety of uses for black box routines in both application design and database administration. Black box programs can be written to be very flexible; the *sp_help* procedure is a good example of that. Black box programs can also be written to focus on something specific like *sp_helpdevice*.

The ICU of Black Box Design

Independent
: A black box routine should be written to depend on database objects that are permanent.

Consistent
: A black box routine should always return results in a consistent manner.

User friendly
: A black box routine should be easy to use and require minimal understanding on the part of the user to execute.

In general, there are three phases to writing a black box: selecting a candidate program or code segment to convert into a more robust piece of code, modifying the code to conform with this more generalized model of programming, and testing the code. The following sections describe each of these phases.

Selecting the Candidates

There are no hard-and-fast rules to follow that determine what procedures are black box candidates; a candidate procedure in one system is not necessarily a candidate in another. However, answering yes to one or more of the following questions would probably indicate that this procedure should be generalized if possible:

- Does this code segment get called in more than one place? An example is the calculation of mortgage payments in a bank financing system.

- Does this code segment always have similar inputs or can they be parameterized? For example, the future value, present value, interest rate, and number of payment are all standard parameters to the formula.
- Does this code segment always produce similar results? In our example, the result is the monthly mortgage payment.
- Does this code segment include complicated logic?

A financial calculation is a good example of a piece of code that will be called from many different places in a given system. You would not want to code this same formula 50 times in the application. You should define it once and call it 50 times. Then if the formula ever changed, you would have to change it only once! In this example, we decide to create a mortgage payments calculator routine called calculate_mortgage_payments.

Once you have selected some candidate code segments, the next phase is to modify their code to make them more robust.

Coding the Candidates

The difficult part is over; you've already figured out for what pieces of code you want to create more generic counterparts. The amount of work you will have to perform here is dependent on two things:

- How much code is there in your system that needs to be changed to use this generalized code segment?
- How complicated is the code you are trying to generalize?

There are two phases to the code change. First, the code that is to be generalized needs to be coded and tested to see that it will function the way it is expected to. Second, the programs that originally called this code will need to be changed to refer to this new generalized procedure.

In general, any code segments that currently include the piece of code that is being generalized will need to be modified to include a call to the generalized procedure, along with any applicable parameters. Using our earlier example of the mortgage payments calculation, suppose this formula was used in many different client programs, such as Power Builder. You could have done one of two things:

- Change the Power Builder frontend to call the calculate_mortgage_payments routine and pass in the appropriate values at runtime.
- Revise the original code that contained the original mortgage payments calculator routine to call the new calculate_mortgage_payments routine. We don't suggest you do this; it adds unnecessary overhead and is less elegant. You should consider doing something like this only if it is not known where this

procedure was called to begin with (if this is the case, then you are in trouble before you even start).

Testing the Candidates

Once you have written the "generalized" version of the procedure (e.g., calculate_mortgage_payments), you will need to test it and check to see that it works consistently and produces the same results as the original procedure, which had the calculation hardcoded into it. Assuming that the new code does work correctly, then all the other programs that called it will need to be tested.

Categorization Schemas

Another technique we use to help in code design is categorization schemas.

Categorizing Transact-SQL code for categorization's sake is not really a good idea. Developing a categorization schema to structure your design process is. What do we mean by this? A categorization schema can be viewed as a skeleton that can be applied to a database to facilitate the creation of a functional database. By using a categorization schema, you will be less inclined to write one procedure to do everything, since it would be difficult to categorize the program according to its function (besides the fact that the procedure would probably consume way too many resources). Before we apply a categorization schema to our pubs database, we first need to introduce it.

Informational Programs

Informational programs are those programs that only return a subset of data. These types of programs do not change the underlying data in the database. These programs can be broken down further as follows:

Complete select
: All the data for a particular table(s) is returned.

Key select
: Data for a particular record determined by its primary key is returned.

Specific select
: This is almost the same as key select; the only difference is that there is no primary key in this type of table. For example, a transaction log may require all constituent components in order to select a record from a table.

Operational Programs

These programs may modify the data directly in a table or tables, or may modify some value that is passed to the program to begin with:

Create

These types of programs create data in some form or other. The data created may be as simple as inserting data into a table, or it may generate some value, for example, a number returned to the calling program.

Remove

These types of programs remove data from some dataset. Typically, these programs will require some key value to be entered in order to determine the scope of deletion.

Change

These types of programs change data from one form to another. These programs may need a key (like the remove programs) in order to determine the scope of the change. They may not necessarily change a record in a table (like the create category); they may also change a value (such as converting a sentence to uppercase).

Now that we've introduced this categorization schema, let's apply it to the pubs database.

Imagine that we have decided to create a new and improved pubs database that has more functionality than the existing database. In order to do this, we build a matrix to overlay the pubs tables to the schema already introduced, as shown in Table 18-1.

Table 18-1. Categorization Schema Matrix for pubs Database

Table	Create	Remove	Change	Complete Select	Key Select
authors	X	X	X	X	X
publishers	X	X	X	X	X
titles	X	X	X	X	X
titlesauthor	X		X	X	X
stores	X	X	X	X	X
sales	X	X	X	X	X
roysched	X	X	X	X	X
discounts	X	X	X	X	X
jobs	X	X	X	X	X
pubs_info	X	X	X	X	X
employee	X	X	X	X	X

Now that we've established the basic functionality we want to create for this program, we can build a list of procedures that would need to be written. These are listed in Table 18-2.

Table 18-2. Matrix of Procedures Required for pubs Database

Procedure Name	Description
ins_authors	Create a new authors record
del_authors	Delete an authors record
mod_authors	Modify an authors record
get_all_authors	Get all the authors records
get_one_author	Get a specific authors record
ins_publishers	Create a new publishers record
del_publishers	Delete a publishers record
mod_publishers	Modify a publishers record
get_all_publishers	Get all the publishers records
get_one_publishers	Get a specific publishers record
ins_titles	Create a new titles record
del_titles	Delete a titles record
mod_titles	Modify a titles record
get_all_titles	Get all the titles records
get_one_titles	Get a specific titles record
ins_stores	Create a new stores record
del_stores	Delete a stores record
mod_stores	Modify a stores record
get_all_stores	Get all the stores records
get_one_stores	Get a specific stores record
ins_sales	Create a new sales record
del_sales	Delete a sales record
mod_sales	Modify a sales record
get_all_sales	Get all the sales records
get_one_sales	Get a specific sales record
ins_roysched	Create a new roysched record
del_roysched	Delete a roysched record
mod_roysched	Modify a roysched record
get_all_roysched	Get all the roysched records
get_one_roysched	Get a specific roysched record
ins_discounts	Create a new discounts record
del_discounts	Delete a discounts record
mod_discounts	Modify a discounts record
get_all_discounts	Get all the discounts records
get_one_discounts	Get a specific discounts record
ins_jobs	Create a new jobs record

Table 18-2. Matrix of Procedures Required for pubs Database (continued)

Procedure Name	Description
del_jobs	Delete a jobs record
mod_jobs	Modify a jobs record
get_all_jobs	Get all the jobs records
get_one_jobs	Get a specific jobs record
ins_pubs_info	Create a new pubs_info record
del_pubs_info	Delete a pubs_info record
mod_pubs_info	Modify a pubs_info record
get_all_pubs_info	Get all the pubs_info records
get_one_pubs_info	Get a specific pubs_info record
ins_employee	Create a new employee record
del_employee	Delete an employee record
mod_employee	Modify an employee record
get_all_employee	Get all the employee records
get_one_employee	Get a specific employee record
ins_titlesauthor	Create a new titlesauthor record
del_titlesauthor	Delete a titlesauthor record
get_all_titlesauthor	Get all the titlesauthor records
get_one_titlesauthor	Get a specific titlesauthor record

In the time it took to extrapolate out the original matrix, we've created a comprehensive list of the basic procedures that need to exist for the database. We can also use this information to determine the time it will take to build these procedures. By using a simple categorization schema, we have managed to structure our thinking to the point where we actually have an ordered work plan as well.

If you think about it, probably every database you have ever worked with requires the basic functions we've listed in Table 18-2. If you look on the CD-ROM provided with this book you will find a file called *spgen.sql*, which includes code for a stored procedure called *sp_genprocs*. This procedure has been written to generate Transact-SQL code in the form of stored procedures for all of the preceding functions. The code is currently designed to generate either a SELECT of all the data or a SELECT based on key values.

Now that you've generated code to support these basic functions, you can spend your time writing the procedures that cover any complicated business logic that may apply to your database.

The rest of this chapter covers the methods you can use to write the type of code just described.

RETURN

The RETURN keyword is used to indicate whether the procedure succeeded or failed. SQL Server has a predefined list of values to which it will set RETURN if the procedure fails. By default, RETURN is set to 0 if the procedure succeeds. You can set RETURN to any numeric value greater than 0 if you choose. In Chapter 7, *Conditional Processing*, we cover the restrictions associated with this keyword in more detail.

RAISERROR

The RAISERROR keyword is used to display a message whenever a particular condition arises. Usually the message indicates that an error of some kind has occurred and that processing has been aborted. The messages themselves can be stored in the sysusermessages table within any database and can be called by number. The power of the RAISERROR keyword is that the system logs a message to the log file whenever an error occurs. Depending on your application, these messages can be used to track certain key events in your application. Consider the following code fragment:

```
-- Prevent this routine from running in Year 2000 because it is
--      currently WRONG
IF datepart(year,getdate()) = 2000
BEGIN
        RAISERROR 50000 "This date calculation routine assumes there are
        28 days in February for 2000"
        RETURN
END
```

Here, we wanted to track whether this procedure gets called during the year 2000, since it contains an error that has not been fixed for one reason or another. It is critical that every time it is called, it gets brought to someone's attention. By using the RAISERROR keyword, an entry will be made in the error log file, which usually gets read by someone (we hope). In Chapter 9, *Error Handling*, we cover the nuances of the RAISERROR keyword in greater detail.

Temporary Data Storage

Temporary tables are one of the most powerful features of Transact-SQL. They exist for only a limited period of time, while the procedure that is using them is being run. In this chapter, we focus on how they can be used within programs to enhance functionality. In Chapter 10, *Temporary Objects*, we cover all the details relating to their use. In general, temporary tables are used in the generalized scenarios described in the following sections.

Static Temporary Data Store

Sometimes you need to store a subset of data items that you use throughout a procedure. Assuming that the table is very small, it doesn't make sense to create a permanent table to hold only a couple of values that have a limited purpose. If all the data in a table is less than 2K, it will always be read in anyway! Consider the following stored procedure:

```
CREATE PROCEDURE get_specific_authors
AS
        CREATE TABLE #the_authors (au_lname varchar(40))
        INSERT #the_authors VALUES ('Green')
        INSERT #the_authors VALUES ('Straight')

SELECT a.au_fname,
             a.au_lname,
             t.title,
             t.type,
             t.price
        FROM    authors a,
             titles t,
             titleauthor at,
             #the_authors ta
        WHERE a.au_id = at.au_id
            AND      t.title_id = at.title_id
            AND      a.au_lname = ta.au_lname
```

Here we have created a temporary table to store a list of authors for whom we want to run the query. In order to change the values in #the_authors, the procedure will have to be edited and re-created. For a more extensive example of this type of temporary stored procedure, refer to the stored procedure *sp_genprocs* included on the CD-ROM.

Intermediate Results

Often, it is necessary to perform complex manipulations on some data set. For either performance reasons or due to the way the data is stored, the final data set may need to be built across multiple queries. The way this is done is by using temporary tables while the data set is being prepared. The following example illustrates this point:

```
CREATE PROCEDURE get_complex_author_info
AS
-- Prepare the basic structure for all the authors
SELECT a.au_fname,
         a.au_lname,
         ytd_sales = CONVERT(MONEY,0),
         ytd_advances = CONVERT(MONEY,0),
         ytd_royalties = CONVERT(MONEY,0)
     INTO #ytd_author_info
```

```
FROM   authors a

-- Update only Straight and Green to these fixed values

UPDATE #ytd_author_info
SET ytd_sales = 10.00,
    ytd_advances = 1.00,
    ytd_royalties = 3.00
FROM #ytd_author_info
WHERE au_lname = 'Green'

UPDATE #ytd_author_info
SET ytd_sales = 1220.00,
    ytd_advances = 144.00,
    ytd_royalties = 35.00
FROM #ytd_author_info
WHERE au_lname = 'Straight'

-- Do something else if required
SELECT *
FROM #ytd_author_info
ORDER BY au_lname, au_fname

DROP TABLE #ytd_author_info
```

Results:

```
au_fname      au_lname          ytd_sales    ytd_advances  ytd_royalties
------------  ----------------  -----------  ------------  -----------
Abraham       Bennet            0.00         0.00          0.00
Reginald      Blotchet-Halls    0.00         0.00          0.00
Cheryl        Carson            0.00         0.00          0.00
Michel        DeFrance          0.00         0.00          0.00
Innes         del Castillo      0.00         0.00          0.00
Ann           Dull              0.00         0.00          0.00
Marjorie      Green             10.00        1.00          3.00
Morningstar   Greene            0.00         0.00          0.00
Burt          Gringlesby        0.00         0.00          0.00
Sheryl        Hunter            0.00         0.00          0.00
Livia         Karsen            0.00         0.00          0.00
Charlene      Locksley          0.00         0.00          0.00
Stearns       MacFeather        0.00         0.00          0.00
Heather       McBadden          0.00         0.00          0.00
Michael       O'Leary           0.00         0.00          0.00
Sylvia        Panteley          0.00         0.00          0.00
Albert        Ringer            0.00         0.00          0.00
Anne          Ringer            0.00         0.00          0.00
Meander       Smith             0.00         0.00          0.00
Dean          Straight          1,220.00     144.00        35.00
Dirk          Stringer          0.00         0.00          0.00
Johnson       White             0.00         0.00          0.00
Akiko         Yokomoto          0.00         0.00          0.00
```

In this example, we used #ytd_author_info to record intermediate results that we were building as we progressed through the procedure get_complex_author_info.

The table existed for only a short period of time and went away once it had served its purpose. We did not need to check for its existence since we created it during the SELECT INTO section of the procedure.

Passing Complex Data to Other Procedures

Sometimes we need to pass more than simple values to a called procedure. When this is required, one way of doing it is through the use of temporary tables. Consider the following enhancement to the get_complex_author_info procedure:

```
CREATE TABLE #ytd_author_info (au_lname varchar(40),
                     au_fname varchar(20),
                     ytd_sales money,
                     ytd_advances money,
                     ytd_royalties money)

GO

CREATE PROCEDURE calculate_ytd_info @au_lname varchar(40) = ''
AS

IF @au_lname = 'Green'
BEGIN
        UPDATE #ytd_author_info
        SET ytd_sales = 10.00,
            ytd_advances = 1.00,
            ytd_royalties = 3.00
        FROM #ytd_author_info
        WHERE au_lname = 'Green'
    END

IF @au_lname = 'Straight'
BEGIN
        UPDATE #ytd_author_info
        SET ytd_sales = 1220.00,
            ytd_advances = 144.00,
            ytd_royalties = 35.00
        FROM #ytd_author_info
        WHERE au_lname = 'Straight'
    END

GO

DROP TABLE #ytd_author_info
GO

CREATE PROCEDURE get_complex_author_info
AS
    -- Prepare the basic structure for all the authors
SELECT  a.au_fname,
        a.au_lname,
```

```
    ytd_sales = CONVERT(MONEY,0),
    ytd_advances = CONVERT(MONEY,0),
    ytd_royalties = CONVERT(MONEY,0)
INTO #ytd_author_info
FROM   authors a

-- Update only Straight and Green to these fixed values

exec calculate_ytd_info @au_lname = 'Green'
exec calculate_ytd_info @au_lname = 'Straight'

-- Do something else if required
SELECT *
FROM #ytd_author_info
ORDER BY au_lname, au_fname

DROP TABLE #ytd_author_info
```

If this procedure were to be executed, it would yield the same result set as the previous version did.

In this example, we've created a second procedure, calculate_ytd_info, which is now sent the data that has been compiled to this point so that this procedure can further update the final data set. It would have been more difficult to code this example if we had used simple parameter values passed to the procedure.

There are many more elaborate ways in which we can utilize temporary data storage in Transact-SQL code, as we'll see in subsequent sections.

Using Parameters Effectively

Use parameters for those procedures that require only the simplest data to be passed to or return from them. In general, you can pass only 255 variables to any procedure, and you can optionally specify each one of these variables as type OUTPUT. This means you can return the result they assume after any data manipulation to the calling procedure. Each parameter can take a default or can be made mandatory, requiring the user to specify a value every time the procedure is called. Certain datatypes cannot be passed as parameters, which limits their scope.

Parameters are possibly the most frequently used technique for writing generalized code, considering that you can use them to specify all the data that changes on every execution. Consider the mortgage payment calculator routine discussed earlier. It would not have been possible to create such a routine if it were not for parameters. Or, maybe more accurately, it would have been far more complicated!

In Chapter 14, *Stored Procedures and Modular Design*, we cover many details relating to parameters.

Help

Help is often ignored in procedures. The presumption is that because a procedure is usually small, you don't need help. Buzzzzzzzzzz, wrong! Tell that to the authors of 20-plus page procedures. There are several ways you can implement help in your procedures; we'll discuss two possible methods here. For both methods, we'll assume that the procedure includes a parameter called @displ_help, which, when set to Y, indicates that help for this procedure should be displayed.

Hardcoded Help

The most simplistic way to implement a help system is to add PRINT statements to your procedure. This is done to display some help text whenever the @displ_help variable is set to Y, as the following code fragment illustrates:

```
IF UPPER(@displ_help) = 'Y'
BEGIN
    PRINT "This procedure does a whole bunch of interesting things"
    PRINT "In order to call it correctly you need to pass in the  "
    PRINT "following useless information which it doesn't actually"
    PRINT "do anything with but it looks good."
END
```

Results:

```
This procedure does a whole bunch of interesting things
In order to call it correctly you need to pass in the
following useless information which it doesn't actually
do anything with but it looks good.
```

An alternative to this approach would be to create a generalized help system, described in the next section.

A Generalized Help System

In order to create a generalized help system, you will need to add an extra table to your database and create a routine that retrieves help for a particular procedure based on some value passed. The benefit of such an approach is that it is a way to compile documentation for your system and store it on the database; you can utilize this documentation in a myriad of different places. A simple help system based on this approach follows.

```
-- Create a table to hold the help information

CREATE TABLE help_data (proc_name varchar(32), id int, lineinfo varchar(255))
GO

-- Populate this table with the help information we want to display
```

```
INSERT help_data VALUES ("bull_procedure",1, "This procedure does a whole
bunch of interesting things")
INSERT help_data VALUES ("bull_procedure",2, "In order to call it correctly
you need to pass in the  ")
INSERT help_data VALUES ("bull_procedure",3, "following useless information
which it doesn't actually")
INSERT help_data VALUES ("bull_procedure",4, "do anything with but it looks
good.")
GO

-- Create a routine to display the help for any procedure

CREATE PROCEDURE display_help @proc_name varchar(32)
AS
    SELECT lineinfo
    FROM help_data
    WHERE  proc_name = @proc_name
    ORDER BY id
GO

-- Apply this to the original code fragment

IF UPPER(@displ_help) = 'Y'
EXEC display_help "bull_procedure"
```

Results:

```
lineinfo
------------------------------------------------------------------------------
------------------------------------------------------------------------------
------------------------------------------------------------------------------
------------------------
This procedure does a whole bunch of interesting things
In order to call it correctly you need to pass in the
following useless information which it doesn't actually
do anything with but it looks good.
```

The amount of coding required to provide help for a single procedure may seem somewhat elaborate—but only if, in fact, there is only one procedure that needs help. However, if all of your procedures need help, coding in the help system involves nothing more than adding a call to each procedure. Assuming that you are using *sp_genprocs*, described earlier, it is actually very simple to add this call to each of the generated routines. Inserting the help lines into your data file would then be the only task required to get the help system to work.

The help system described here could be extended to be context-sensitive by adding a context parameter to the display_help procedure and by adding a context to the table containing the data itself. However, we will leave that one up to you.

Depending on your requirements, you may also consider using the sysusermessages table if you only have very simple help messages and do not require multiple lines of help.

Summary

This chapter has provided an overview of design considerations as they relate to Transact-SQL. We've introduced the following topics that will help you write more robust and reusable code:

- Coding for reuse
- The black box program and how it is coded
- How to categorize your procedures in order to help in the design and implementation stages
- The use of the RETURN keyword to vary the way you work
- The use of the RAISERROR keyword to return messages to the user and the log file
- The use of temporary tables to store intermediate result sets
- Using parameters effectively
- Implementing help in your programs

19

Code Maintenance in SQL Server

Code maintenance is as much a function of system administration as it is a function of development. The system administration component deals with the backup and recoverability of the code, as well as the consistency of the code across a distributed environment. The development component is related to functionality and operability. As a developer (particularly if you're working on an application that will be deployed on many servers), it behooves you to have a fully developed methodology for the management of code across your servers. To help you develop a well-thought-out methodology that can help you plan the management of your code, we'll look at the following major components of the methodology::

SQL Server system tables
: Basic tools you use to develop the methodology

Source code management
: What it is and how you go about implementing it

Code maintenance
: Issues you need to consider once the programs have been changed

Related topics
: Indirect factors that will affect your methodology

Using SQL Server System Tables

The system tables hold all the information about everything in the server. This information, or *metadata*, is extremely valuable. SQL Server could not run without it. This metadata can be used to find out all sorts of interesting things about your database. You can use the information to reverse-engineer DDL statements used to create database objects, as well as commands used to create devices and databases, add logins and users, grant permissions, and manipulate other objects stored in your system tables. (Note that ad hoc query code is not stored in your system tables.) In Appendix A, we cover the system tables in detail and describe their functionality and what information is located in which table. In this chapter, we'll look at ways you can use these tables to find information about what is on your server, to reverse-engineer code, and to generate new code.

What is the distinction between reverse engineering and creating new code? In the former case, we use SQL Server's metadata to create a carbon copy of what is already there. In the latter, we use information from the system tables, namely the table definitions, to create a new procedure. For example, we could create a default INSERT statement for a table based on its structure in sysobjects and syscolumns. We'll discuss these approaches in more detail in the following sections.

Reverse-Engineering Existing Code

Included on the CD-ROM accompanying this book is a whole slew of utilities specifically designed to help you reverse-engineer the code in your server (assuming you are not lucky enough to have a third-party software utility to do it for you). If you have Microsoft SQL Enterprise Manager or Sybase Central, you will probably be using this tool to reverse-engineer most of your code already. The one advantage of our scripts is that they are purely Transact-SQL based. This means that you can just pop them onto a disk and upload them into a server. Moreover, our Transact-SQL scripts can be set up as a task on the server. So you can regularly reverse-engineer your Transact-SQL code to a backup directory (you cannot do that with the GUI tools). They consume very little space and can be used as templates for your own work if you choose.

If you wrote Transact-SQL code to do something to your server, you can probably write a query to determine what you wrote originally, as long as it was not an ad hoc query. This is great when you lose your original code or when you are experimenting with different ways of doing something on your SQL Server.

Engineering New Code

Ultimately, you use your SQL Server to store data. You may build a wide variety of objects around this data, but their purpose is to affect how this data is created or removed. You can use your system catalog tables to write utilities that generate new code based on the objects in your database. For example, you may want to create a procedure that generates a generic insert procedure for each structure in your database, taking into consideration those procedures that have identity columns. An example of such a procedure is *sp_genprocs*, which is described in Chapter 18, *Transact-SQL Code Design*.

There are many more things you can do. You could compare the contents of two databases' system tables to determine what the differences are from a structural standpoint and then generate code to move data from one structure to another. Another common use of the system tables is to generate DUMP and DBCC scripts using sysdatabases and sysdevices to determine the scope and destination of the dump. Your imagination is about the only limit to what you can do when it comes to engineering new code.

Once you get to know the system tables described in Appendix A, you can leverage the data contained in those tables to ease writing new code. Here's a hypothetical situation: management has decided that the pubs database needs a user ID strictly for report queries. You've decided to call the user ID pubs_readonly. Granting all the appropriate rights might take you quite a while if you had to use the GUI to add SELECT privileges to pubs_readonly for every table. Instead, you could write a quick script based on the sysobjects table to extract the GRANT statements needed to perform the operation:

```
SET NOCOUNT ON
GO

SELECT  'GRANT SELECT ON ' + LOWER(name) + ' TO pubs_readonly'

FROM     sysobjects
WHERE    type = 'U'
ORDER BY name
GO
```

The results are a nice little Transact-SQL script that you can cut and paste back into ISQL:

```
--------------------------------------------------------------
GRANT SELECT ON authors TO pubs_readonly
GRANT SELECT ON discounts TO pubs_readonly
GRANT SELECT ON employee TO pubs_readonly
GRANT SELECT ON jobs TO pubs_readonly
GRANT SELECT ON pub_info TO pubs_readonly
GRANT SELECT ON publishers TO pubs_readonly
GRANT SELECT ON roysched TO pubs_readonly
GRANT SELECT ON sales TO pubs_readonly
GRANT SELECT ON stores TO pubs_readonly
GRANT SELECT ON temp_authors TO pubs_readonly
GRANT SELECT ON temp_output_container TO pubs_readonly
GRANT SELECT ON titleauthor TO pubs_readonly
GRANT SELECT ON titles TO pubs_readonly
```

Similarly, you could write a small Transact-SQL query against the sysservers table on Microsoft SQL Server to extract a ready-made batch of RPCs:

```
SELECT   'EXEC ' + UPPER(srvname) + '.master.dbo.sp_who
' + 'GO
```

```
    ' -- These extra lines are needed so that the GO appears properly in the
      -- script.
FROM     master..sysservers
ORDER BY srvname
```

As before, the results come out looking like a nicely ordered Transact-SQL script:

```
EXEC BURGUNDY.master.dbo.sp_who
GO
EXEC CHARDONNAY.master.dbo.sp_who
GO
EXEC MERLOT.master.dbo.sp_who
GO
EXEC SAUVIGNON.master.dbo.sp_who
GO
EXEC SHIRAZ.master.dbo.sp_who
GO
EXEC ZINFANDEL.master.dbo.sp_who
GO
```

Many of the system stored procedures that ship with the database either act upon data stored in the system tables or are driven directly by data stored in the system tables.

Interdependence of Server-Side Objects

Whenever you create server-side code objects (that primarily means objects like stored procedures, views, and triggers, but also includes check constraints, rules, and defaults), you must reference other database objects. For example, a view must be constructed from one or more base tables specified in the view SELECT statement. Even in this simple example, the database objects are deeply intertwined. The view cannot exist without its base tables. Similar restrictions exist when creating other types of server-side code.

The important point to remember is that any changes to an underlying object might have a negative impact on any objects built on top of it. For example, suppose that you want to add a new column to the authors table. That's no big deal, right? But what if you have some stored procedures or views based on the authors table that issue the command SELECT * FROM authors? Then you have a problem, because the dependent database objects no longer select all of the columns contained in the table (although it may not fail outright).

The SQL Server query engine compiles server-side code when you issue the CREATE statement. If the code is successfully parsed and compiled, certain sets of data about the object are stored in the database:

- The source code of the database object is stored in sysobjects.
- The tree structure of the database object is stored in the sysprocedures system table. The tree structure of a server-side coded object is a hierarchical, binary

representation of the original source code, listing local and external object references. The tree structure is initialized or "sequenced" when the server-side object is created.

- The query plan of the object is also stored in a system table. The query plan is constructed as the server-side object is executed and brought into memory. All references to other database objects are translated into their object identifier, and the code is fully compiled. Once in memory, the query plan need not be reparsed or "sequenced" since that was completed when the object was created. The query plan then stays in memory (unless it gets bumped out because it has been inactive for a long time and another active process needs the cache space) so that it can be processed by other processes without spending any plan-compilation overhead.

This information is maintained for stored procedures but not for every type of server-side objects. Triggers, views, rules, defaults, and check constraints are compiled only when they are executed. Thus, their plan information is generally stored directly in the procedure cache rather than in the sysprocedures table.

When a server-side object is compiled, all of the database objects on which it depends must exist in a valid state. When a server-side object is compiled, all references to other database objects are resolved. Errors may occur when the server-side object is executed if any changes have taken place on its underlying database objects. To be blunt, the validity of a stored procedure, trigger, or view is dependent on the validity of all database objects on which it depends.

Source Code Management

Many of us work on large projects where there are lots of developers, each of whom is responsible for a different section of the overall system. In such projects, source code management is critical. In database applications, source code management also encompasses DDL (Data Definition Language) and DDM (Data Manipulation Language) code. Source code management is critical for several reasons:

Recoverability
: The ability to re-create what has been done due to a disaster

Integrity
: The confidence that there is only one active version of a program lying around

Ease of modification
: The knowledge of where the source code is located

It is remarkably easy to write a simple SELECT to retrieve some data from your database. Because Transact-SQL makes it so easy to quickly write a procedure to solve some immediate problem and then pop it into the database, it tends to be as quickly forgotten, and the source code to the procedure ends up being lost forever. Those of you who work with a DBA may know that you may need to jump through several hoops to get code stored in your database.

In general, the hierarchy of misery ranges from "Yeah, sure. Here is the SA password" to "Have you filled in, in triplicate, a request form, attached the necessary code, and had it signed by several managers?" Those of you living in the former realm are probably more at risk for losing code than those in the latter group. For those in the latter group, there is probably a copy of your code somewhere (if only so the DBA can hang you with it later if performance issues arise).

There are a number of standard steps you will need to follow to implement code management within your organization. You may need to go through several iterations of these steps depending on how large your organization is and how much uncontrolled code you have lying around.

Tool Selection

First you need to decide whether your organization should consider purchasing a source code management tool. You will need to consider the following factors when making this decision. If you answer yes to one or more of these questions, you should probably seriously consider purchasing a source code management tool, since it will simplify the administrative burden of maintaining code.

- Is there more than one developer writing code?
- Is there more than one active version of this code or application?
- Does this application sit on several different platforms?
- Does the code change frequently?
- Is this code backed up on a regular basis?

If your organization is a good candidate for source code management, go shopping. There are many excellent code management software utilities on the market today. Select the one that fits best into your organization's technological infrastructure and your budget.

Directory Structure

Early in the process, you should decide on a directory structure to implement. This is critical, since it's imperative that you group similar code in a logical fashion so it's easy to maintain multiple source trees. This book showcases two different vendor product offerings for SQL Server, and you have no doubt seen many subtle differences between the products. How would you like to write code to support both of these products? It's not fun—we know. Table 19-1 lists some suggestions on ways to logically group your code. You may decide to use combinations of these grouping schemas within your own organization.

Table 19-1. Alternates for Code Directory Structures

Group	Purpose	Positive	Negative
Function	Group your code based solely on the function or application to which it belongs—for example: SalesOrderProcessing PurchaseOrder-Processing GeneralLedger	Extremely practical method when there are numerous distinct applications or functions within an application. Usually an excellent high-level schema for your applications, to which you can add on some of the other grouping schemas at lower levels.	Often need to create a hierarchy; otherwise, you may not be able to manage the code easily.
Server	Use the server name as the basis for your directory structure—for example: CHARDONNAY SHIRAZ MERLOT	Easy to manage when the number of servers is small. Useful when an application is distributed across multiple servers.	When you have several hundred servers in your organization, this grouping may no longer be meaningful or effective. When you have multiple copies of an application distributed across multiple servers, this structure may lead to unnecessary duplication of code.
Database	Use your database names as a means to identify logically grouped code—for example: pubs financials euromonetaryunit	Great scheme when you have multiple databases in an application, which are duplicated across multiple servers, since you can eliminate duplicate code using this approach.	May be meaningless on its own. Different applications may have similarly named databases, causing confusion for some developers.

Table 19-1. Alternates for Code Directory Structures (continued)

Group	Purpose	Positive	Negative
DDL	Either use a group to hold similar Transact-SQL code together or expand on this further to define each type of object—for example: DDL Triggers Tables Constraints Indexes Rules Defaults Procedures Batch	All similar type of code is grouped under the same structure, which may speed up the installation process. Allows you to install a specific subset of code quickly.	May be extremely problematic when there are large numbers of dependencies in the application. To compensate, you would need to define some form of dependency list, which would have to be considered every time code is reinstalled.
Operating platform	You would define either hardware or operating systems here—for example: Solaris SUN NT Alpha	This may be necessary if you support applications that reside on multiple platforms and have different programming variations associated with the operating system or hardware.	You may end up duplicating a lot of source code using this approach, depending on how much code needs to be customized for the host platform.
Software version	Define the version of a database management tool or similar software product that distinguishes features—for example: MSSQLV421 SYBASE11 SYBASE115 MSSQL65 MSSQL70 SYBASE119	Different versions of software often support differing levels of functionality. This may be the only way you can manage different product features, since it will impact the code you write.	You may end up duplicating a lot of source code using this approach, depending on how much code needs to be customized per software version.

In general, you will use combinations of these approaches, as the following examples demonstrate:

HumanResources\Employees\DDL
: HumanResources is an application, Employees is a database, and *DDL* is the directory that points to where all the primary database object code is stored.

HumanResources\CHARDONNAY\Configuration
: CHARDONNAY is the server, and *Configuration* is a directory that holds all the configuration information for that particular server.

HumanResources\NT\SybaseSQL115
: NT represents an operating platform, and SybaseSQL115 is the version of Sybase being run on that platform, with all the applicable code underneath.

Source Files

You must decide how you are going to store your code in your new directory structure. In general, you will do either one of the following:

- Place related code into the same file and potentially have multiple database objects in the same file.
- Place a single object in a single file.

Believe it or not, figuring out which is the best approach is actually quite tough. When you have a lot of dependencies in your code, you may be inclined to put dependent code all within the same file. This is fine, but you have to consider how you would handle multiple programmers wanting to modify different objects in the same file. Using the latter method would resolve that issue, but you'd then need to worry about putting everything into the database in the correct order. Constraint implementation in SQL Server has actually made this issue loom larger than before. If you go for the one-object-per-file scenario, you will need to maintain a list somewhere which stores the dependencies relating to objects. You may actually want to consider maintaining a database somewhere with this information. Later in this chapter (and in Appendix A), we'll discuss how you could use the metadata that is already in your system catalog tables to help you maintain separate source files.

Locating the Source of Transact-SQL Code

One of the most difficult steps in managing your source code involves finding out where (and from whom) the code originated. You might say that this is where the fun really begins (note the strong sarcasm!). We've been dealing with infrastructure issues up to this point. Now you will need to actually find out how well managed your code really is.

The first thing to do here is to hunt down any programmers (other than yourself) who have been involved with the application you are trying to put under source management. Anything they didn't properly document in the original programs should be documented now. The objective here is to find the code that was originally written and is currently in production and then to place it into the source file structures you have created by now. Usually, you will find that several key components of your code are missing. You are also likely to find several key programmers who refuse to give you any assistance. If, in fact, this proves to be the case, you may need to generate a clean set of source code based on what already exists within SQL Server. Here are some steps to follow when generating source code:

1. Do a simple query on your database to identify how many of each type of objects are in your database:

```
SELECT type,
       count(*)
FROM   sysobjects
GROUP BY type
```

2. Once you have gotten a feel for the numbers, figure out when was the last time the code changed on these objects, using Transact-SQL similar to the following. This code will give you the creation date of each object in your database, grouped by type, and a cute little checklist:

```
SELECT name,
    type,
    crdate,
    code_found = "[  ]",
    src_manage = "[  ]",
    dependencies = "[  ]"
FROM   sysobjects
ORDER BY type,crdate desc
```

3. Store these results in a file; then make a note as each piece of source code is located and placed under the source code management system.
4. You will have to do one of two things when you actually begin checking off each object. Either create your code from scratch again by reverse-engineering the objects from the database or just move the most recent copy of your source code to its new home on your source code server.
5. If you prefer to resort to reverse-engineering the code, the good news is that the CD-ROM accompanying this book has a number of Transact-SQL utilities designed to do just that. Table 19-2 briefly describes each utility and its purpose.

Table 19-2. Transact-SQL Reverse-Engineering Utilities

Filename	Purpose
rtable.sql	Reverse-engineer a table
ratable.sql	Reverse-engineer all tables in a database
rindex.sql	Reverse-engineer indexes for a particular table in a database
raindex.sql	Reverse-engineer all indexes for a database
gserver.sql	Reverse-engineer the contents of the master database into code form
rdefault.sql	Reverse-engineer binding of defaults
rrule.sql	Reverse-engineer binding of rules

Users of Microsoft SQL Enterprise Manager and Sybase Central may choose to use their built-in reverse-engineering utilities instead. However, the GUI tools require user intervention, while these stored procedures can be executed from the ISQL command-line utility or as Windows NT (or SQL Server) tasks.

There are a couple of gotchas you'll need to consider when using these utilities:

- The procedures don't take object dependencies into consideration. There are two major types of dependencies: temporary tables and permanent database objects. The temporary tables are created in order to reverse-engineer the database objects in the first place. The permanent database objects (that is, tables, procedures, rules, views, and defaults) are the second dependency that needs to be created in order to be able to create these procedures. The first type is more problematic to deal with than the second, since the code necessary to create temporary tables already exists in the database system catalog tables. In order to find the structure of these temporary tables, you will need to scan your syscomments or source code files for the miscreant CREATE TABLE # statement. Once you locate the code, you can then copy and paste the code to the top of your generated file.
- If you do need to use procedures like the ones just mentioned to re-create your source code (this may occur if you are using an earlier version of Microsoft or Sybase SQL Server), then you need to remember to create the objects in your database using a very specific order. Since this approach is *not* the preferred approach and using the respective vendors' utilities is, we will only briefly cover the order here:

  a. Create all groups in the database.

  b. Create all users in the database.

  c. Create all user data types.

  d. Create all defaults.

  e. Create all rules.

  f. Create all tables.

  g. Bind your defaults to your tables.

  h. Bind your rules to your tables.

  i. Create all constraints.

  j. Create all triggers.

  k. Create all procedures.

l. Grant all necessary permissions.

m. Populate the tables with their data.

n. Create all indexes.

If you follow this order, then the number of errors you get for missing objects will be kept to a minimum. You can solve the errors using either an imprecise method or a precise method. The imprecise method involves repeatedly trying to create the object until it passes. Very often, the reason the code failed was because there was an object it was dependent on that was missing. Those entries that cannot be created using that method probably require you to add some extra code, like a temporary table, to the file first; otherwise, it will never work.

Those of you who would like to minimize wading through the error messages can use the stored procedure *sp_grep* included with the CD-ROM to identify object dependencies.

After you have explicitly defined and properly ordered all object dependencies, store the list in a safe place to ensure that future database installations follow the same order. After all, there's no sense in going through this pain and suffering again. When you are loading procedures, keep in mind that SQL Server will allow you to create a stored procedure with missing dependent procedures. It just returns a warning.

Ongoing Maintenance

Now that you have your code organized and know where everything is, it is probably time to change it. Before you start that process, you may want to take a few minutes to decide:

- If no formal source code tool is being used, how are you going to track who is working with a piece of code, and are you going to prevent changes being overwritten by someone else?
- How are you going to manage object dependencies and the files that record ordering information?

Once you address these issues, you can turn to the art of code maintenance. Code maintenance deals with how to actually make sure changes make their way to the right place and how to minimize the amount of code you write to begin with.

Code Maintenance

Throughout this book, we have covered many techniques that can help speed up code development either by following good coding practices or by following good design approaches. However, no matter how well you design or write a program, it will change. Proper code maintenance eases this process, especially in an application that will have a long life span or many developers supporting it. Code maintenance has five major steps:

1. Check the program out of your source code manager.
2. Perform the code changes.
3. Test the code changes.
4. Check the program back into your source code manager.
5. Implement the code changes.

This chapter focuses on step 5. Steps 1 and 4 are more a function of either your source code management tool or the manual source code management process you have implemented. Step 2 is really what the rest of this book is dedicated to, and step 3 is covered in Chapter 21, *Debugging Transact-SQL Programs.*

Testing Code

Everybody knows about testing. We have all had experience with this at one stage of life or another. Program testing is where you find out how bad your coding really is. It's also an opportunity to find out how you can avoid running certain suspect components of your code. In general, there are four phases to testing, compilation, unit, system, and integration, which are summarized in Table 19-3:

Table 19-3. Phases of Testing

Phase	Description	Production Ready?
Compilation	The program is "run" into the server. You are trying to check that your syntax is correct and that you correctly reference all your database objects. This step completes when the object parses and compiles properly.	Contrary to popular belief, just because a program compiles doesn't mean it can be put into production.
Unit	The program is called and you determine whether it returns the correct results. This step completes once you have proved that this program works on its own.	You may be slightly more ready than you were before, but what about all those things you changed and removed? What else is going to fall over because of what you did?

Table 19-3. Phases of Testing (continued)

Phase	Description	Production Ready?
System	You put the program into a test environment with all its fellow object and dependent procedures. You perform full regression testing on your application using all your existing test suites. This step completes once you have proven that the application as a whole has not been adversely affected by the change.	Close—at least you now know that everything within the application works.
Integration	If you have applications that share data or do things like RPCs, you will probably need to perform some type of integration testing as well, since dependent systems may call the very object that has changed. This step completes once all dependent systems have been tested and are functioning correctly. These dependent systems may also need to change as a result of the change you implemented.	Now you are ready. All systems that may depend on your application in some way have also been checked out, and all of the systems are working harmoniously.

When done properly, testing can be very time-consuming. However, the benefits outweigh the cost of time, since properly tested systems rarely have problems. Usually, when they do, they are easy to fix since the whole development process has been managed more precisely from the beginning, and there has been a lot more communication among everyone involved.

Once all the testing has been completed and all bugs that were found during testing have been ironed out, it is time to put the program into production.

Version Control Across Multiple Servers

If you've ever had to work in a multiserver environment, you probably know how tough it is to keep the servers in sync. In fact, if you have to support a single application on lots of geographically dispersed servers, you're probably contending with this very issue.

One technique used to track and verify that your stored procedures and other server-side code objects are at the correct version involves the use of *program headers*. Remote procedure calls and text-searching techniques are discussed in a later section.

Here's a little example of how to do that. Imagine that we have three office locations: New York, Los Angeles, and Chicago. Each office has its own respective server: SAUVIGNON, ZINFANDEL, and BORDEAUX. It's the DBA's job to ensure that the changes have been properly distributed to all production servers.

The easiest way to do that involves these steps:

1. Insist that server-side objects contain a program header that contains a standardized object name and version number. The program header is a comment block close to the top of the object. Chapter 5, *Format and Style,* has a good example of this under "Header Comments."
2. Use a remote procedure call to the stored procedure search_tsql_text (as shown in the following section, "Searching Through Source Code"), *sp_grep* (on the accompanying CD-ROM), or a stored procedure of your own making to determine if the specific program header exists on the remote server. For example:

   ```
   sauvignon.pubs..search_tsql_text 'batch_summary_rpt ver 1.1.7'
   ```

3. Your RPC call should return the name of a single database object—something like the following:

   ```
   Searching for string " batch_summary_rpt ver 1.1.7 "

   Objects Containing Search Str
   ------------------------------
   batch_summary_rpt
   ```

If the RPC retrieves the name of a specific database object, you know that you have the correct version of the database object on that server. If your search doesn't retrieve any data, you know that the server queried by the RPC does not have the necessary object. You can then create the needed object on the remote server.

We've included a command-prompt utility called *dbCompare* on the accompanying CD-ROM. *dbCompare* reads and compares database schemas between two databases on Microsoft SQL Server. It reports any inconsistencies, such as different table structures, indexes, missing objects, different source code, sp parameters, and so on. It's very helpful when you have to ensure that your application objects are the same across multiple servers.

Searching Through Source Code

Let's kick back and hypothesize for a moment (no, not about being filthy rich!). Assume that several years have passed, and the pubs database has grown significantly, both in the amount of data it stores and in the number of server-side objects used in applications. In fact, there are now so many stored procedures in the database that it's kind of tough to tell who's doing what. Now let's assume that we have to make a major change to a stored procedure called review_titles, one that might require us to touch every stored procedure that is dependent on it. How can we quickly find out what other objects depend on review_titles?

You might be tempted to use *sp_depends*, but it's a sad fact that *sp_depends* won't tell us much about the dependencies of nested stored procedures. Fortunately, you can simply perform a query on the syscomments table. (The stored procedure *sp_grep* that is found on the CD-ROM is more reliable and effective, but it's too big to print here. We recommend *sp_grep* before search_tsql_text.) Here's an example stored procedure that searches the syscomments table for a particular string. If it finds any records matching the search string, it returns the name:

```
CREATE PROC search_tsql_text @search_string VARCHAR(50)
AS

SET NOCOUNT ON

DECLARE @output_line VARCHAR(100)

SELECT  @output_line = 'Searching for string "' + UPPER(@search_string) + '"'

PRINT   @output_line
PRINT   ' '

SELECT name AS "Objects Containing Search Str"
FROM   sysobjects
WHERE  id IN
    (SELECT DISTINCT id
     FROM   syscomments
     WHERE  text like '%' + @search_string +'%')
ORDER BY name

GO
```

You could easily modify this stored procedure to show additional information, such as the type of database object. Here's what it looks like when executed:

```
search_tsql_text 'review_titles'
```

Results (these are the names of objects associated with a much larger pubs database):

```
Searching for string " review_titles "

Objects Containing Search Str
------------------------------
batch_summary_rpt
biweekly_titles_rpt
```

```
closed_titles_charge_build
title_change_veri_rpt
tr_del_from_usage
```

If you'd rather not create a stored procedure to search for a string in the system table, then you can simply cut and paste the SELECT statement. Then, you can later replace the parameter with the text of the search string.

Related Topics

There are a number of benefits to leveraging code stored within the database server; many of these concepts were pioneered by Sybase, which is generally credited with the development of stored procedures:

Execute permissions
: You can provide a SQL Server login with only execute permissions on a stored procedure. Then the user can access data and functionality within a database without ever actually having to read and write permissions in that database. In this way, stored procedures can be used to provide security much as views can be, as discussed in Chapter 14.

Remote procedure calls (RPCs)
: Remote procedure calls enable you to pull data from a remote server and use it on the local server. The brave of heart can even use RPCs to construct distributed applications.

Transactional security
: Relational databases offer table, column, and referential integrity by default. However, Transact-SQL code allows you the flexibility to ensure that transactions, even those spanning multiple tables and many steps, are always performed properly.

Load balancing
: Running code on the server lets you build client-based applications that are leaner and meaner. On a properly configured server, server-side code can mean a big improvement in the performance of a client/server application.

Whenever you create a stored procedure, trigger, or view, you are in fact storing the Transact-SQL code of that object in the SQL Server database—in the syscomments table of the local database, to be exact. Not only does the table provide all of the text of Transact-SQL objects, it also provides you with a means of re-creating and backing up the original scripts used to create the object. In this sense, the database server is a *repository* for server-side code. By addressing other system tables, such as sysobjects, in queries, you can quickly generate application code that might take a long time to code by hand.

The accompanying CD-ROM contains a stored procedure called *sp_helpcode* that reconstructs object source code without line breaks (unlike *sp_helptext*). This stored procedure is useful for database objects like stored procedures, triggers, views, and any other database object whose metadata is stored in the system table syscomments.

Summary

This chapter described the management and maintenance of Transact-SQL code, both within the database server and external to the server in source files. In this chapter we've examined:

- The importance of SQL Server system tables in managing and reviewing source code, and how to use system tables to generate new Transact-SQL code
- The relationship that exists within server-side objects, and methods to troubleshoot object dependencies
- Source code management techniques
- Code maintenance and ways to reverse-engineer existing source code and implement code changes across multiple servers
- Some related aspects of managing your data on your database

20

Transact-SQL Optimization and Tuning

Performance optimization and tuning are very hot database development and support topics. Very often, more resources are spent on optimization than on the original development process. In our experience (confirmed by many industry experts), 80% of performance gains on SQL Server come from making improvements in Transact-SQL code, not from devising crafty configuration adjustments or tweaking the operating system.

This chapter concentrates on Transact-SQL code optimization. Your first optimization task is to decide which component of your system takes priority in optimization efforts. Your goal may be to achieve faster response time, add more concurrent users, improve the overall number of transactions per day, or achieve a combination of objectives. Remember: *improvements in one area often require compromises in others.*

It is impossible to talk about Transact-SQL optimization without mentioning physical database design. This chapter also briefly discusses how to design your database depending on your application type.

SQL Server has a built-in query optimizer that makes important decisions about your query execution. It chooses the order in which tables are joined, which index to use on each table, and whether to employ special tricks such as creating worktables and breaking queries into steps. In most cases, it optimizes queries just fine. The Transact-SQL command SET SHOWPLAN ON allows you to view the query plan chosen by the optimizer. If you don't like it and want to enforce your own plan, then you can use special Transact-SQL commands and so-called optimizer hints to override the optimizer's decisions. Other commands allow you to display performance statistics, analyze index efficiency, and evaluate the cost of all query execution plans.

Creating and using proper indexes is crucial to Transact-SQL performance. A good index may improve query performance by a factor of a thousand. In this chapter we discuss different index options and when to use them. We have also assembled numerous miscellaneous optimization tricks, including a discussion of the *characteristic functions* technique.

This book does not cover SQL Server configuration tuning or operating system optimization. Please refer to your vendor's documentation and to other books on SQL Server databse administration and Windows NT administration.

About Optimization

There are several ways to measure performance and, consequently, there are several parameters to optimize in a Transact-SQL program. The performance of a database application may be evaluated by one or more of the following criteria:

- Average response time of a transaction
- Maximum response time of a transaction
- Percentage of transactions whose response time does not exceed a certain time limit
- Throughput—the number of transactions per unit of time
- Concurrency—the number of users served simultaneously within a specified response time

The industry-standard TPC benchmarks (issued by the Transaction Performance Council) measure the performance of a system by the number of transactions per second and the average price per transaction. Different TPC benchmarks are designed for different types of applications. TPC-C represents a transaction mix typical for an online transaction processing (OLTP) system, while TPC-D is representative of a data warehouse activity. Without diminishing the importance of TPC benchmarks, we recommend that you perform your own testing for *your* applications on *your* hardware in *your* environment. TPC results are achieved on specific hardware and network configurations that may have little in common with yours—not to mention that every application and database schema is different and may require specific optimization techniques.

A user's perception of application performance may be the most important factor of its evaluation. Very often, it has little to do with your point of view and may be based on prior experience with legacy systems, comparison with other similar applications, and factors unrelated to the database part of the application. For example, an inefficient network may kill your efforts to optimize Transact-SQL code, a poorly designed GUI may require that a user makes dozens of clicks to receive desired results, and an untrained user may submit an ad hoc query that brings the whole server to a halt. In this chapter, we focus on Transact-SQL performance optimization and tuning and related areas of database design. But you should keep in mind all of the many components that may influence overall application performance:

- Server hardware
- Server operating system
- Network hardware and topology
- Network operating system
- Application architecture
- Middleware tier
- Client computer hardware
- Frontend applications
- Database design
- Backend (Transact-SQL) programs

From the user's perspective, all these factors contribute to an application's response time. When a user clicks on a button in his GUI interface and it takes three minutes to display the results, he doesn't care what takes so long. He just wants the system to be faster. Your first task is to find and isolate bottlenecks. If the poor performance is caused by SQL Server, then you have some work to do.

It is important to realize that in many cases there is no clear-cut tuning solution. Optimization is usually a series of trade-offs. For example, you may sacrifice overall throughput to improve concurrency, or you may optimize average response time at the expense of throughput. In some cases, you might achieve stellar performance of a decision-support query but pay the price by slowing down online transactions. Most importantly, you often have to choose between better performance and lower price. More expensive systems naturally have more power to perform better. As with any other optimization task, tuning Transact-SQL programs requires that you develop criteria to measure the success of your tuning efforts. It depends on your particular application goals and requirements. Talk to your users to determine what is most important to them. Choose which parameters should not exceed certain limits and which ones are critical to overall performance. You may even need to assign weights to different criteria reflecting their relative importance.

Sometimes a user's perception of poor response time may be alleviated with an approach that has nothing to do with programming. One of us once developed a decision-support application that constantly caused user complaints. It could take up to five minutes to bring back results of certain queries because of the large amount of data that had to be processed. There was no more room for SQL code optimization, and the client didn't want to pay for faster server hardware. But the angry users turned into happy campers when we modified the GUI application to randomly display prestored graphic images while waiting for a query to come back. We allowed users to bring their own favorite pictures and scanned them into a stack of images. The concept was the same as in some modern screensavers, although very novel at the time this application was developed. Users were happy watching pictures of landscapes, animals, and Clint Eastwood (the department manager brought this one himself). Of course, you might argue that times have changed and today they would demand 3-D graphics, animation, sound, and real-time stock quotes.

Any optimization effort requires an investment of time. Your day will not stretch beyond 24 hours, no matter how little sleep you allow yourself. Before you spend your precious time on Transact-SQL code optimization, find out whether it is the backend program that causes poor performance. It may turn out that your colleague network administrator or your colleague GUI developer has to improve his part of the performance equation.

If you narrow down the problems to SQL Server, investigate which stored procedure or table is causing the trouble. In many cases, you will find that only one place in your code requires extra work. Do not spend time optimizing pieces that are not causing complaints. Isolating and prioritizing bottlenecks is probably more important than rewriting inefficient queries.

An often-overlooked approach to optimization involves evaluating the workload on the database system and trying to balance it more evenly throughout the day, week, and month. Monitor system usage for several weeks to determine the busiest hours of the day and the busiest days of the week and month. Shift all maintenance jobs and long-running reports to off-peak hours and days. It usually requires no code changes but yields incredible performance gains. Empowered with your research results, managers may even consider shifting the working hours of the staff. Spreading work evenly helps to alleviate users' competition for limited server resources during peak hours.

Efficient Physical Database Design

This section looks at the database models, datatypes, and partitioning approaches that yield the best results.

Optimizing the Database Model

Different physical database models may be used to store the same data. Some are optimized for decision-support systems (DSSs), while others are better tuned for OLTP applications. When you design your physical database, you have to choose what is more important: SELECT query performance or the performance of transactions that modify data, like INSERT, UPDATE, and DELETE. You also have to take into consideration storage requirements. It may be possible to improve the performance of certain types of queries by allocating more space to store redundant information.

A normalized schema typically achieves high transactions-per-second marks and good response time for online transactions. It uses database space efficiently, because data redundancy is minimized or nonexistent. However, decision-support queries and reports are usually slow and more difficult to program on normalized schemas.

A denormalized design, on the other hand, excels in DSS applications and fails in OLTP systems. It is optimal for data retrieval and less efficient for modifications. It also requires extra database space to maintain redundant data and to store additional indexes.

The *star schema* is a special database design that is optimized for data warehouses. A typical star schema consists of a fairly large fact table that is composed of foreign keys to smaller dimension tables. Examples of dimensions are geographical location (country, state, or city), time (year, quarter, month, or day), product, salesperson, customer, and so on. This model is optimized for data analysis that requires aggregating certain data dimensions. Queries on a star schema typically join the fact table with a number of dimension tables. The downside is that current versions of SQL Server may not be fully optimized to take advantage of this model. You have to exercise special care when you join many tables in one query.

One frequently made design mistake involves running online transactions and decision-support queries in the same database. They just cannot coexist peacefully. A single long-running report may put on hold all short online transactions on the same table. One possible solution to this problem is to periodically make a copy of the OLTP database to a special reporting database and run all reports there. The data is delayed in the reporting database by several hours or even days, but DSS tasks usually do not require an up-to-the-minute level of detail. The price is the extra database space needed for the reporting database.

Efficient Datatypes

Database design includes choosing proper datatypes for table columns and deciding which ones allow null values. These choices are normally driven by business requirements, but you often have flexibility in which datatype to choose. For example, Transact-SQL has many types to store "numbers:" BIT (0 or 1 values only), TINYINT, SMALLINT, INT, SMALLMONEY, MONEY, REAL, DOUBLE, NUMERIC, and even CHAR and VARCHAR.

The rule of thumb is to use a datatype that allows storing the same or a larger range of values in fewer bytes. Narrow columns make narrow tables, and narrow tables allow you to store more rows on a single data page. Narrow columns also mean more efficient narrow indexes. They translate into fewer physical disk I/O operations when you work with the table. This can lead to better performance.

Consider carefully which columns should allow null values. Each column with the NULL option adds an overhead of several bytes to every row in which it has some value. Expressions with such columns are somewhat slower compared to columns that do not allow nulls. On the other hand, nullable columns may save a lot of space if only a small percentage of rows have non-null values. This results in a leaner table that can be scanned more quickly. In any case, do not declare a column with the NULL option "just in case." Some extra analysis may help you improve performance.

When you alter tables to add new columns, you have no choice but to allow NULL for them. If analysis shows that columns with the NOT NULL option would make transactions faster, consider re-creating the table and making them NOT NULL. You may need to reload table data at this point, but it's a one-time price for an optimized table. Increased performance will pay you back over time with hefty interest.

The variable-length datatypes VARCHAR and VARBINARY are similar to nullable types in their advantages and disadvantages. They add an extra few bytes per row to the length and slow down transactions. But if the average actual length is much shorter than the maximum declared one, these types may save space and offer better performance than fixed-length types.

If your table contains a series of flags with Yes/No or False/True type of information, the best datatype for such columns is BIT. This type is especially effective when you have several columns of type BIT in a table. Up to eight such columns may be packed into just one byte of storage. Keep in mind that you can use the BIT type only for new tables and not to alter existing ones. This is because BIT does not allow the NULL option, which is required for columns added with the ALTER TABLE command.

Database Partitioning

"Divide and conquer" is a two-millennium-old motto, but it still applies to many aspects of our life. Dividing tables and databases into smaller, more manageable chunks is one of the most popular optimization techniques. This technique is called *partitioning*.

Horizontal partitioning

Horizontal partitioning is the process of splitting a table into pieces with the same structure but fewer rows in each. Examples of split criteria are historical data versus current data, by year, or by sales region. The main advantage of horizontal partitioning is that queries that work with only one portion of the data do not affect transactions on other portions.

For example, suppose that the sales table in pubs has grown very large as a result of increased sales. Users constantly complain about degrading performance when they attempt to work with sales data. You analyze their transactions and determine that there is a conflict between transactions submitted by the marketing research group and the sales department. Marketing analysts need to run decision-support queries on past sales data while salespeople process new orders and add rows into the table. Long-running queries often block new data inserts, causing frustration among the operators taking orders and the customers on the other end of the line. You also find out that the marketing analysis is based only on data from past years, and only one year at a time. In order to prevent a war between marketing and sales and, most importantly, to keep the sales growing, you decide to split the table into several annual ones: sales1995, sales1996, sales1997, . . . , sales_current. Now all new orders are entered into sales_current, while decision-support queries are restricted to other tables. Of course, extra work is required to separate annual sales data and store it in several tables.

In a few days, you notice that people from the two departments can eat lunch at the same table again. Their problems may be over, but you have just created a support challenge for yourself. All applications and maintenance jobs have to take into consideration the partitioned design. When a new year begins, you have to add a new table and move the past year's data into a new historical "container."

In this example, optimized transaction performance is achieved at the expense of more complicated programming and administrative support.

Vertical partitioning

Vertical partitioning is the process of splitting tables into parts, with fewer columns in each but the same number of rows as in the original. Instead of one wide table, you create two or more narrow ones that are related one-to-one by their primary key. All vertically partitioned tables combined take more space than the original table because the primary key has to be replicated across all of them.

The advantage of this approach is in isolating frequently accessed columns from rarely used ones. A narrow table with the most popular columns becomes more efficient than the original one, because it takes less space and requires fewer I/O operations to scan. In cases in which you need columns from more than one part of the partitioned table, you have to join them. Such transactions are more expensive than they would be on the original table. But if you do your analysis correctly, they will be rare. When you improve the performance of 95% of your transactions at the expense of slightly slowing down the remaining 5%, you increase the overall throughput and the average response time.

For example, suppose that your analysis of table titles usage shows frequent access to the columns title_id, type, pub_id, and price. The remaining columns are used only when the row is originally inserted and also in night batch reports that do not have strict performance requirements. You can partition the table into two tables, as shown in Table 20-1.

Table 20-1. Vertical Partitioning of the Titles Table

Before Partitioning	After Partitioning

<pre>CREATE TABLE titles (
    title_id CHAR(6)   NOT NULL,
    title   VARCHAR(80) NOT NULL,
    type   CHAR(12)   NOT NULL,
    pub_id   CHAR(4)   NULL,
    price   MONEY   NULL,
    advance   MONEY   NULL,
    royalty   INT   NULL,
    ytd_sales INT   NULL,
    notes   VARCHAR(200)   NULL,
    pubdate   DATETIME   NOT NULL
)</pre>
	<pre>CREATE TABLE titles_main (
	    title_id CHAR(6) NOT NULL,
	    type CHAR(12) NOT NULL,
	    pub_id CHAR(4) NULL,
	    price MONEY NULL
	)
	
	CREATE TABLE titles_info (
	    title_id CHAR(6) NOT NULL,
	    title VARCHAR(80) NOT NULL,
	    advance MONEY NULL,
	    royalty INT NULL,
	    ytd_sales INT NULL,
	    notes VARCHAR(200) NULL,
	    pubdate DATETIME NOT NULL
	)</pre>

The titles_main table still contains a row for every title. But now it requires up to 10 times less storage space than the original titles table, depending on the number of rows, null values, and VARCHAR values length. The titles_info table is not used by critical transactions. In this example, vertical partitioning improves performance where it most matters, at the expense of slowing down night batches that nobody complains about.

As in the case of horizontal partitioning, you have to do some extra work to maintain partitioned tables. It may be a good idea to create views that join parts of a partitioned table, so that someone who wants to look at the original structure could still do it. In our example, you could create a view:

```
CREATE VIEW titles
AS
SELECT  a.title_id,
        b.title,
        a.type,
        a.pub_id,
        a.price,
        b.advance,
        b.royalty,
        b.ytd_sales,
        b.notes,
        b.pubdate
FROM    titles_main a, titles_info b
WHERE   a.title_id = b.title_id
```

This view simplifies the maintenance of old stored procedures and triggers. If they used to refer to the table before partitioning, they will access the same data via the view of the same name.

Indexing Strategies

Creating proper indexes is the most critical aspect of Transact-SQL performance optimization. Very often, a new index can reduce the response time of a query from several hours to several seconds. When this happens, you have your moment of programmer's glory. Everybody notices dramatic improvements, and it takes no extra hardware resources. Managers and users love it! But there is another side to this coin. Poorly chosen indexes result in horrible response time and immense aggravation of the same managers and users.

The SQL Server optimizer can analyze and choose indexes for you, but it can only choose from existing ones. It is difficult to overstate how important good indexes are to query performance. Spend extra time analyzing and creating the best indexes for any query that you expect to show good performance.

More Versus Fewer Indexes

Before we compare different index types and options, we need to realize that creating more indexes is not always better. Every new index on a table may improve *some* of the SELECT, INSERT, UPDATE, and DELETE queries but may slow down *every other* INSERT, UPDATE, and DELETE transaction on the same table. This is because SQL Server has to update every index to include or delete keys of affected rows or change pointers to pages where updated rows reside if they change location. The slowdown is usually within one or several percentage points of the transaction response time, but these taxes add up if you create many indexes.

In some companies, creation of indexes is a DBA's prerogative. But programmers are the ones who write SQL code that uses them. Very often, they have a better idea of what index they need for a particular transaction, while a DBA has a general view of the database and SQL Server as a whole. Cooperation between both groups is the key to success.

Decision-support applications and data warehouses typically require more indexes per table in order to satisfy all possible queries. They also are tolerant of slower modification queries, because those are limited to data loads and usually run during nonpeak hours as batch jobs. At the other extreme are OLTP applications that are very sensitive to decreases in performance of INSERT, UPDATE, and DELETE transactions.

Indexes require special maintenance in databases with volatile data. If you insert, delete, and update all or a large percentage of records in a table, the DBA must schedule an UPDATE STATISTICS job to keep indexes useful. You may even experience dramatic drops in query response times. All of a sudden, the same stored procedure that took a second yesterday takes 10 minutes today. Users are unable to perform their work. If you see these symptoms, find out which table is constantly locked (run system stored procedure *sp_lock*) and then ask the DBA to update the statistics on that table. Very often, doing so "miraculously" puts your performance back on track.

In general, new indexes improve the overall performance of an application. For example, consider an application in which the addition of a new index could significantly improve a rarely executed report query at the expense of marginally slowing down frequently executed update transactions.

Figure 20-1 illustrates the flow of transactions in three scenarios. Each thin line represents a single online transaction (normally quick). A bold line represents a long-running report query. All transactions are lined up along the time axis. They start at different moments and take the amount of time expressed by the length of the line.

- Scenario A shows the normal flow of update transactions. Each one takes about the same time, and they don't block one another because they update different parts of a big table.
- Scenario B illustrates the impact of the report execution (shown as a solid bold line) on update transactions. There is no index to optimize the report in

this scenario. It quickly locks the whole table. Every update that starts while the report query is in progress is delayed. The average response time rises dramatically. The response time bar on the right side of the picture has two parts—actual execution time, which is the same as in scenario A, and average delay due to blocks caused by the report query (shown as a black bar).

- Scenario C demonstrates the transaction flow after an index is added. The index improves the performance of the report query so that it is several times better. It prolongs the actual execution time of every update transaction by several percentage points. However, the average delay caused by the report goes down. Therefore, the average response time of the update transactions also improves. In this scenario, everybody wins. This is a clear-cut case when you must add the index. Unfortunately, not every situation is so obvious. You need to consider all the consequences of a new index with respect to a particular application and usage patterns. Sometimes you have to choose and make some transactions faster at the expense of other ones.

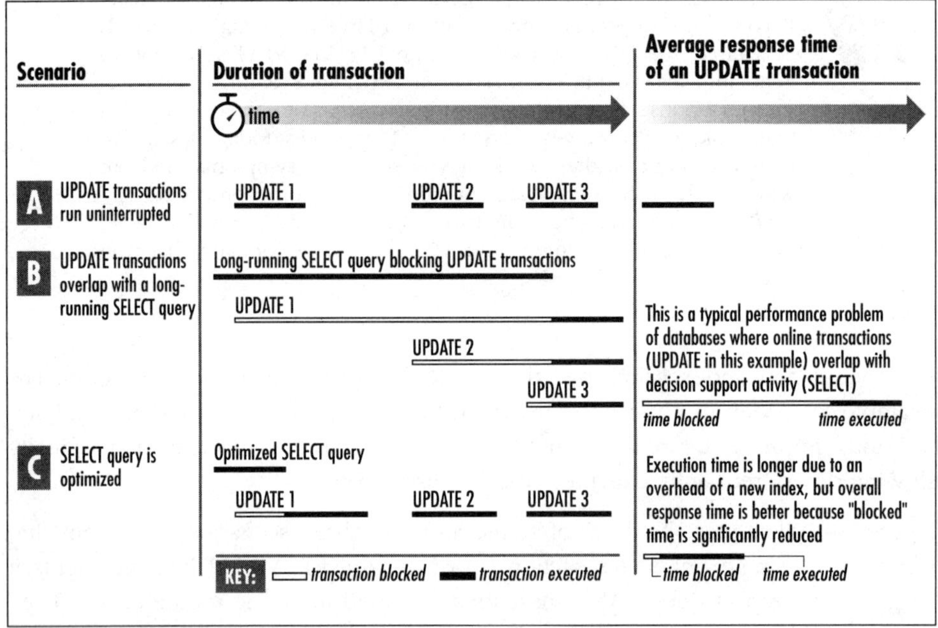

Figure 20-1. Influence of an index on transaction performance

Clustered Versus Nonclustered Indexes

The SQL Server optimizer dearly loves clustered indexes. They are more efficient for many types of queries than nonclustered ones. The trouble is that you can't have more than one clustered index per table. For example, if you have two important queries on the same table using different keys in the ORDER BY clause, you have to choose which one is more critical. You can create a clustered index to optimize one report and a nonclustered index for another. It's possible that the non-clustered index will not be very efficient for the second report and won't even be chosen by the optimizer. In such conflict situations, you have to consider carefully which query is more important to optimize first.

It is important to have a clustered index on every table. Such indexes help manage database space more efficiently. Tables without a clustered index have a tendency to expand over time and use more space for the same number of rows. Current versions of SQL Server have automatic garbage collection on the page and extent level. A database page allocated to a table may be reused by the same table when all rows from it are deleted. An extent may be reused by any object once all eight pages of it become empty. But as long as a single row remains on a page of a table without a clustered index, it will not be reused to insert new data. The only exception is the very last page of the table. All new rows are added to the bottom of the table. Compare this situation to tables with a clustered index, where new rows may be inserted in the middle of a table and added to partially used pages.

Avoid creating a clustered index on a monotonicallly increasing key. It forces all the new rows to go to the end of the table. Examples of such a key are columns with the IDENTITY property, columns used to store the current date and time, and TIMESTAMP columns. Such a clustered index forces all users inserting data to compete for the last page of the table. This may cause last-page locking contention—also known as a "hotspot." The most disappointing part, though, is the fact that such indexes are usually less efficient than nonclustered ones. If you have an IDENTITY column, you are not likely to search for all rows given a range of keys but will probably often select a specific row by its IDENTITY key. It is also rare that you would sort by this column since it has no business meaning. A nonclustered index on such a column is typically better, because it's almost as efficient as a clustered one in terms of access and allows you to create a clustered index for some other purpose.

Clustered indexes are good for queries that use:

- GROUP BY clauses that use all or the first few columns of the clustered index key.
- ORDER BY clauses that use all or the first few columns of the clustered index key.
- WHERE clause conditions comparing the clause to the first or the first few columns of the clustered index key and retrieving many rows.
- Long keys (either based on long columns or composite keys comprised of many columns), because a clustered index on a long key takes no extra space for the leaf level. A nonclustered index on a long key may be quite large, because it takes a lot of space to store keys of the leaf level of the index.

The first three types benefit from the fact that requested rows are located together on consecutive rows of the table. SQL Server has to find only the first qualifying row and then keep on scanning until all rows are done. Several rows found on a single page reduce the number of I/O operations needed to access all the data. Additionally, Microsoft SQL Server has a performance booster—the read-ahead feature that automatically detects sequential reads from the same table and prefetches data pages before the query asks for them. With a nonclustered index, it usually turns out that requested rows are scattered around different pages, and it may take a separate I/O operation to get every row. Therefore, a query using a clustered index is much more likely to take advantage of read-ahead.

Nonclustered indexes are good for accessing one or a few rows. When you retrieve one row, you cannot take advantage of multiple rows located on the same page. They also are efficient for queries that can find all columns necessary to produce results in an index. In such cases, SQL Server doesn't even look at data pages. It uses indexes to process the whole transaction. Most indexes have keys narrower than the underlying table. They take less space than the tables to which they belong. Therefore, it takes fewer I/O operations to scan the index than the table, and the whole transaction has a better response time.

Clustered indexes usually have one less B-tree level on top of the leaf data pages than nonclustered ones. In such cases, it takes one extra I/O to access a row via a nonclustered index compared to a clustered one. But the benefit may be negligible when index pages are found in cache, and this extra I/O is an inexpensive logical one (in data cache).

Short Versus Long Index Keys

Indexes with short keys are generally more efficient than those with long keys, because more keys fit on a single page and the whole index takes less space. Consequently, the index is faster to scan and more likely to fully fit into the data cache. Of course, columns comprising an index key should be chosen based on application requirements and the underlying data model. Very often, you have a choice of adding an extra column to the key that doesn't make a big difference in index selectivity. It may be more efficient to make the index leaner and meaner rather than use long composite keys, even though they may be more *selective*. A longer key means that fewer keys fit on a single database page, and the index may require more levels in the B-tree. As a result, it takes more I/O operations to get the same data through this index, and transactions slow down.

Covering Indexes

Sometimes it pays to create an index with a long composite key that includes all columns needed to process a certain critical query. A nonclustered index that includes (or *covers*) all columns used in a query is called a *covering index*. When SQL Server can use a nonclustered index to resolve the query, it will prefer to scan the index rather than the table, which typically takes fewer data pages. Provided that an index key is not too long, SQL Server can place more keys than actual table rows on a single page. The whole index takes fewer pages than table data. If your query uses only columns included in the index, then SQL Server may scan this index to produce the desired output.

For example, suppose that your application allows a wildcard search on the employee last name:

```
SELECT lname FROM employee WHERE lname LIKE '%ttlieb%'
```

This query does a table scan on the employee table. But if we create the following covering index, the query becomes more efficient:

```
CREATE INDEX employee_lname ON employee ( lname )
```

In this case, the table is small and the data occupies only two pages. But the index employee_lname is even more compact; it takes only one page. Therefore, with the help of the covering index, the same query requires only one physical I/O operation instead of two.

In this case, if the query uses several columns, the covering index has to include them all, as in the following example:

```
SELECT  fname, lname
FROM    employee
WHERE   lname LIKE '%ttlieb%'
    AND job_lvl < 200
```

A covering index for this query has to include three columns:

```
CREATE INDEX employee_name_lvl ON employee ( lname, fname, job_lvl )
```

It is important not to overdo your indexes. If a covering index benefits only a single query but takes a toll on every INSERT, UPDATE, or DELETE transaction on the same table, then it may not be a good idea to create the covering index. Making covering index keys too wide reduces their benefits, because an index on a wide key takes more space and may not be much more effective than scanning the data pages of the table.

Helping SQL Server Choose Indexes

The mere existence of indexes is not enough for SQL Server to use them. You have to specify conditions in the WHERE clause that take advantage of these indexes. If you have only partial conditions for a composite key, specify WHERE clause conditions for the leftmost columns of the key.

For example, suppose you have a table with an index on columns a, b, c and d. Depending on your WHERE clause conditions, SQL Server may use all or fewer columns of the index, or not use the index at all, as shown in Table 20-2.

Table 20-2. Usage of Composite Key Columns

WHERE Clause Conditions	Key Columns That May Be Used
`WHERE a = @a AND b = @b AND c = @c AND d = @d`	a, b, c, d
`WHERE a = @a AND b = @b AND c = @c`	a, b, c
`WHERE a = @a AND b = @b AND d = @d`	a, b
`WHERE a = @a AND c = @c AND d = @d`	a
`WHERE b = @b AND c = @c AND d = @d`	Index cannot be used (unless all columns needed for the query may be found in the index, in which case SQL Server may do an index scan instead of a table scan)

Index Selectivity

Index selectivity measures the duplication of index key values in the table. You may say that an index with unique keys has perfect selectivity. The opposite is an index in which all key values are the same. That one has the worst possible selectivity and is obviously useless. The selectivity of an index is a measure of how many different index keys are found in the table related to the total number of table rows.

The following formula estimates the selectivity of a particular index:

Index Selectivity =
Number of Distinct Keys in the Index / Number of Table Rows

The closer this mark is to 1, the better for the optimizer. The existence of duplicate keys lowers selectivity and reduces the effectiveness of the index. As a rule of thumb, nonclustered indexes with selectivity less than 0.1 are not efficient, and the optimizer refuses to use them for queries. It may take more I/O operations to complete a transaction using a nonselective index than to do a table scan. Exceptions may be made in special cases in which all columns needed for the query are found in the index and access to data pages is not needed.

Microsoft SQL Server also measures *index density,* which is inversely related to selectivity. In other words, the higher the selectivity of an index, the lower its density. Use the DBCC SHOW_STATISTICS command discussed later in this chapter to obtain index density information.

The density of an index with a composite key may be measured for all columns of the key, as well as for the first one, two, or more columns. The density of partial keys is important in cases in which only the first few columns of the key appear in a WHERE clause (see Table 20-2) and SQL Server has to decide whether to use the index.

Nonselective indexes aren't always bad. They may be efficient when they cover all columns of a query. For example, suppose that we add a column called gender of type CHAR(1) to the employee table and store values of M and F in it. You could then write a query to calculate the number of male and female employees:

```
SELECT  gender, COUNT(*) FROM employee GROUP BY gender
```

Without an index on the gender column, the optimizer has to scan the whole table to find the answer. If you create an index on this column, it may improve the query performance:

```
CREATE INDEX employee_gender ON employee ( gender )
```

Even though the index is very nonselective and is not good for any other task, your specific query is optimized by scanning the index, which takes much less space than the whole table.

The benefits of following this approach should be carefully weighed against the increased transaction cost required to maintain the index, as well as the database space it takes.

SQL Server Query Optimizer

The *query optimizer* is your invisible partner in Transact-SQL programming. It analyzes every query you submit to SQL Server and chooses the best execution plan for it. It is quite intelligent, very fast, never complains about night work, nor asks for a raise. It may sometimes make a mistake, just as your human colleagues do, and may come up with an inefficient execution plan. There are ways to give it direct orders, and it follows them precisely, regardless of what it thinks of your decision. If it were human and had some sense of humor, it would be a perfect partner to work with.

Partnership means that you have to do your share of work. The optimizer is not flawless. It may overlook the best solutions, and it is not smart enough to remember past mistakes. It cannot go beyond existing indexes, and it does not recognize obsolete index statistics. The good news is that you can help it.

Every Transact-SQL query requires SQL Server to create and execute a little (or not so little) program. There may be numerous ways to execute the same query. The query optimizer has to choose the best join order, which indexes to use for search arguments and join conditions, and whether to create worktables. All these choices result in the creation of a *query execution plan*—an internal program that SQL Server executes to process your query.

SQL Server processes every query in several steps. It parses the query, compiles the best (in its educated opinion) execution plan, and places the chosen plan in the procedure cache. Then it executes the query. Once the query is complete, SQL Server removes the plan from the cache.

Stored procedures, views, and triggers are handled differently. The first time somebody invokes an object after SQL Server is restarted, a plan is created for this object and placed in the procedure cache. The plan for a stored procedure depends on the actual values of parameters passed to the stored procedure at the first execution. The plan doesn't disappear from the cache after execution is complete. It may be used again and again by subsequent calls. Procedures created with the WITH RECOMPILE option are an exception, because their plans are recompiled and reoptimized at every execution.

When a user executes a stored procedure, SQL Server checks the procedure cache and, if there is a plan and it's not used by another user, that plan is reused. But if two users attempt to use the same object, SQL Server compiles another instance of the plan. This is because procedures are not reentrant and each user needs a separate copy of the plan. The second plan may be different from the first one, because parameters passed to the procedure may be different and table statistics may have changed since the first plan was compiled. If more than two users execute the same object concurrently, then multiple instances of the plan are created. All plans are dropped from the procedure cache when SQL Server shuts down.

The system table sysprocedures contains a parsed tree of each stored procedure, trigger, and view. It has references to databases and other objects resolved, but it's not compiled and optimized. The SQL Server procedure cache contains completely compiled and optimized procedure plans. At this point, all join orders are defined, indexes are chosen, and decisions are made on the use of worktables and execution methods.

Join Order

Queries that involve joining two or more tables may be performed in several ways. The more tables you join, the more possible join orders SQL Server may come up with. The number of possible join order permutations is the factorial of the number of tables involved:

```
Number_of_possible_join_orders = Number_of_joined_tables !
```

Table 20-3 shows the number of possible join orders for different numbers of joined tables.

Let's use sequential numbers to indicate different tables and denote a join by combining those numbers. Then we can list all possible join orders for a two-table join

Table 20-3. Number of Join Orders

Number of Joined Tables	Number of Possible Join Orders
1	1
2	2
3	6
4	24
5	120
6	720
7	5,040
8	40,320
9	362,880
10	3,628,800
11	39,916,800
12	479,001,600
13	6,227,020,800
14	87,178,291,200
15	1,307,674,368,000
16	20,922,789,888,000

as 12 and 21. There are six orders for three tables: 123, 132, 213, 231, 312, and 321. There are 24 ways to join four tables:

```
1234    2134    3124    4123
1243    2143    3142    4132
1324    2314    3214    4213
1342    2341    3241    4231
1423    2413    3412    4312
1432    2431    3421    4321
```

Now that you've got the idea, try writing down all possible orders for a 16-table join as an exercise.

OK, if you are still reading, then you know that we're kidding. Those who have started working on the exercise should not enter the ranks of SQL Server programmers. This task will keep them busy for the rest of their lives anyway. Of course, the optimizer could do the work much faster than a human, but the number is still much too high to properly consider. Even if the optimizer could evaluate a million different join orders per second, it would still take 242 days to find the best plan for a 16-way join.

Evaluating every plan involves considering different indexes on each table and the possibility of creating worktables to improve the performance. This means that the number of conceivable query execution plans is even greater than the number of join orders. Past versions of Microsoft and Sybase SQL Server did not handle joins of more than four tables well. Programmers had to break large queries into several steps using temporary tables or use optimizer hints, which we will discuss later in this chapter. Sybase 11.x can optimize six-table joins quite well and in some cases more than that. Microsoft no longer suggests that you limit queries to any specific number of tables, provided that you do not exceed 16 tables. It appears to be able to find good plans for multitable joins. We assume that the optimizer uses an expert algorithm to focus on best plan branches only and thus avoids evaluating every possible join order.

A similar approach is used in computer chess-playing programs. They do not consider every possible move and concentrate only on the most promising directions. This allows such programs to go deeper in the analysis of particular branches.

Query Cost Analysis

How does the optimizer choose the best execution plan? It uses a cost analysis that assigns a cost to every plan. The cost is computed based on the number of physical I/O and logical I/O operations that the optimizer predicts for a certain plan execution. Microsoft says that physical I/O has a weight of 14 cost units and logical I/O a weight of 2 cost units. Sybase prices physical I/O higher at 18 units and logical I/O the same as Microsoft. These numbers may give a fair valuation for an average server, but your particular server hardware and storage system may show different performance. If you use very fast disks and a slow CPU machine, then the ratio between the price of physical versus logical I/O could be, for example, 5. But if your storage system is not sufficiently optimized, your disks are not well partitioned, and the RAID disk array is not properly configured, then you could observe that disk access is 10 or 15 times more expensive than memory access.

Our personal experience indicates that many servers deviate from the vendor numbers. A typical ratio is 10 or higher. We suspect that this deviation could be attributed to the fact that there are many ways to incorrectly configure a storage system, while RAM, in most cases, does not require special configuration. Many administrators fail to optimize their disks for SQL Server and do not take full advantage of the optimizer's potential. It's also possible that SQL Server vendors choose the ratio of physical versus logical I/O price based on some specific hardware configuration that doesn't match yours.

RAID technology is a must in today's disk optimization techniques. It also helps to have multiple disk controllers in your storage system. It is a good idea to place your operating system on a disk or RAID array that is separate from your databases. OLTP applications typically benefit from separating data and transaction log segments. The next step is separating data and indexes. In some cases, you may even decide to place two frequently joined tables on two separate physical devices to achieve better performance for queries that involve both tables. Different RAID levels are optimal for different types of applications. However, a higher level of storage optimization requires extra research and administration work. Besides, the number of physical devices on a server is limited. A RAID disk array will serve most noncritical applications just fine.

Other factors that may shift weights in the cost evaluation are the following:

- Caching of data pages; this may turn some physical I/O into logical I/O.
- Placing tempdb in RAM in Microsoft SQL Server.
- Assigning RAM to hold named data caches in Sybase.
- The *read-ahead* ability of Microsoft SQL Server; this prefetches data into the cache before SQL Server hits the necessary pages. Read-ahead performs I/O in larger blocks and is, therefore, faster than normal physical I/O operations.

The query optimizer may miss some of these factors and not take them into consideration when it estimates the cost of each plan. As a result, it may undervalue certain plans and feel unreasonably good about other ones. Fortunately, SQL Server gives programmers a great deal of flexibility in forcing a particular plan. (We will go into more detail on this issue later in this chapter.)

Index Selection

As we've mentioned, using the right indexes is the most important aspect of optimization. The query optimizer selects the best indexes to do the following:

- Evaluate filter conditions on each table
- Satisfy join conditions
- Find column values without going to the actual data pages

Filter conditions are also known as *search arguments* (SARGs). A SARG compares table columns to a constant, a variable, or an expression containing constants and variables. Based on the SARG criteria, the optimizer may find an index that significantly narrows down the number of table rows qualifying for the result set.

For example, the system table sysobjects has a unique clustered index on the ID column. The following query has a SARG on the ID column and can use the clustered index to satisfy the selection. We have "wrapped" it into SET SHOWPLAN commands, explained a bit later, to obtain the execution plan:

```
SET SHOWPLAN ON
GO
SET NOEXEC ON
GO
SELECT  *
FROM    sysobjects
WHERE   id = 8
GO
SET NOEXEC OFF
GO
SET SHOWPLAN OFF
GO
```

Both Microsoft SQL Server and Sybase chose to use the clustered index in this case. SHOWPLAN output differs because Sybase provides more information, even though it describes the same plan.

<table>
<tr><th>Microsoft</th><th>Sybase</th></tr>
<tr><td><pre>STEP 1
The type of query is SELECT
FROM TABLE
sysobjects
Nested iteration
Using Clustered Index</pre></td><td><pre>QUERY PLAN FOR STATEMENT 1 (at line 1).

    STEP 1
        The type of query is SELECT.

        FROM TABLE
            sysobjects
        Nested iteration.
        Using Clustered Index.
        Index : sysobjects
        Ascending scan.
        Positioning by key.
        Keys are:
            id
        Using I/O Size 2 Kbytes.
        With LRU Buffer Replacement
        Strategy.</pre></td></tr>
</table>

In order to join two tables with reasonable performance, you need an index on joined columns of at least one of these tables. One table may be scanned, or searched by SARG, while the second one is joined through an index.

For example, review the plan of the following query:

```
SET SHOWPLAN ON
GO
SET NOEXEC ON
GO
SELECT  o.name 'table', i.indid, i.name 'index'
FROM    sysobjects o, sysindexes i
WHERE   o.id = i.id
```

```
    AND i.indid > 0
GO
SET NOEXEC OFF
GO
SET SHOWPLAN OFF
GO
```

The query plan is the same for both vendors, even though the output is different:

Microsoft	Sybase

STEP 1
The type of query is SELECT
FROM TABLE
sysindexes i
Nested iteration
Table Scan
FROM TABLE
sysobjects o
Nested iteration
Using Clustered Index
	QUERY PLAN FOR STATEMENT 1 (at line 1).
	
	    STEP 1
	        The type of query is SELECT.
	
	        FROM TABLE
	            sysindexes
	            i
	        Nested iteration.
	        Table Scan.
	        Ascending scan.
	        Positioning at start of table.
	        Using I/O Size 2 Kbytes.
	        With LRU Buffer Replacement
	        Strategy.
	
	        FROM TABLE
	            sysobjects
	            o
	        Nested iteration.
	        Using Clustered Index.
	        Index : sysobjects
	        Ascending scan.
	        Positioning by key.
	        Keys are:
	            id
	        Using I/O Size 2 Kbytes.
	        With LRU Buffer Replacement
	        Strategy.

Here, the optimizer had some choice. It could scan the sysobjects table and then join every row of sysobjects to sysindexes. The optimizer chose to scan sysindexes instead and then join to sysobjects. The price of this second plan is indeed lower. To verify that fact, we used the optimizer hints discussed later in this chapter to explicitly force the first and then the second join order and compared the price in terms of page I/O operations. For now, we'll spare you the details of this testing. Our results showed 165 I/O operations for the first plan (sysobjects-sysindexes) versus 92 I/O operations for the second plan (sysindexes-sysobjects).

SHOWPLAN Output

One of the things we like about the query optimizer is that it provides feedback in the form of a query execution plan. In the previous section, we showed you some basic SHOWPLAN output to analyze our queries. Now we are going to explain

SHOWPLAN in more detail and describe messages you may encounter in query plans. Understanding this output brings your optimization efforts to a new level. You no longer treat the optimizer as a "black box" that touches your queries with a magic wand.

The following command instructs SQL Server to show the execution plan for every query that follows in the same connection (or process) or turns this option off:

```
SET SHOWPLAN { ON | OFF }
```

Very often, you only want to see the query plan without actually executing it. Another SET command disables the execution of Transact-SQL code but validates for syntax and semantics errors and also allows the SHOWPLAN setting to work.

```
SET NOEXEC { ON | OFF }
```

Once you have issued SET NOEXEC OFF, the only command that may be executed is SET NOEXEC ON. Disabling the execution of queries is a very good idea when you are just testing the plan. Most new queries have a chance of producing an inefficient plan and not returning results for ages. Combining the SET SHOWPLAN ON and SET NOEXEC ON commands, you can review the plan and verify that it is reasonable before actually executing the query.

These settings do not take effect immediately, but they start working from the next step. In other words, you have to issue a GO command before the SHOWPLAN or NOEXEC setting is changed.

Here is some typical Transact-SQL code used to obtain an execution plan for a query without actually running it:

```
SET SHOWPLAN ON
GO
SET NOEXEC ON
GO
<query>
GO
SET NOEXEC OFF
GO
SET SHOWPLAN OFF
GO
```

We'll discuss SHOWPLAN's output in several examples. To avoid an annoying redundancy, we won't repeat the SET commands shown previously. But note that every example in this section provides a query that should be substituted for the <query> tag in this script and assumes the same SET SHOWPLAN and SET NOEXEC "wrapping."

The order of these steps is very important. For example, you have to turn the SHOWPLAN on before setting NOEXEC on. If you did it in the reverse order, then SET NOEXEC ON would force SQL Server to ignore the SET SHOWPLAN command.

SHOWPLAN output differs for Microsoft SQL Server 6.5 and Sybase 11.5, but essentially it is very similar. Sybase's plans in the current version are more informative. They provide information about index names, key columns, and other details not available from Microsoft.

The following simple query selects all rows from the table authors. It has no choice but to scan the whole table, because we don't provide any WHERE clause:

```
SELECT * FROM authors
```

The SHOWPLAN results confirm that this is a table scan:

<table>
<tr><th>Microsoft</th><th>Sybase</th></tr>
<tr><td><pre>STEP 1
The type of query is SELECT
FROM TABLE
authors
Nested iteration
Table Scan</pre></td><td><pre>QUERY PLAN FOR STATEMENT 1 (at line 1).

    STEP 1
        The type of query is SELECT.

        FROM TABLE
            authors
        Nested iteration.
        Table Scan.
        Ascending scan.
        Positioning at start of table.
        Using I/O Size 2 Kbytes.
        With LRU Buffer Replacement
        Strategy.</pre></td></tr>
</table>

Some of the SHOWPLAN tags explain what SQL Server is going to do with the query in plain English, while others may appear puzzling. Table 20-4 provides a brief explanation of every message supported by both Sybase and Microsoft. Sybase has introduced many new SHOWPLAN messages in its recent versions. You will find Sybase-only messages in Table 20-5.

Table 20-4. SHOWPLAN Messages Used by Microsoft and Sybase

SHOWPLAN Message	Explanation
STEP n	In many cases, SQL Server executes a query in several steps. For example, this happens if you use GROUP BY, ORDER BY, DISTINCT, or subqueries.
The type of query is query_type	Explains the type of query—for example, SELECT, INSERT, TABCREATE (for CREATE TABLE command), etc.
The type of query is SELECT (into a worktable)	Indicates that SQL Server has to create a worktable. This happens if the query has a GROUP BY clause or a DISTINCT clause, or under other conditions explained in more detail in Chapter 10, *Temporary Objects*.

Table 20-4. SHOWPLAN Messages Used by Microsoft and Sybase (continued)

SHOWPLAN Message	Explanation
The update mode is { direct | deferred }	Microsoft SQL Server has two methods of performing changes to the data (UPDATE, INSERT, DELETE, and SELECT INTO commands)—*direct update* (or update in place) and *deferred update*. A deferred update deletes updated rows from the table and then reinserts them with modified values. Direct updates are more efficient because they modify table rows on the same database page, but you can't force them. Sybase uses these and two additional update mode methods described in Table 20-5.
GROUP BY	Appears in plans of queries with a GROUP BY clause.
Scalar Aggregate	Appears in plans of queries that contain aggregate functions (e.g., SUM, MAX, or COUNT), but do not contain a GROUP BY clause. Every aggregate function in such queries returns just one number. Compare this with the next message.
Vector Aggregate	Appears in plans of queries that contain aggregate functions (e.g., SUM, MAX, or COUNT), and a GROUP BY clause. Every aggregate function in such queries returns a "vector" of numbers—one per group.
FROM TABLE table_ name	Reports the name and alias (if used) of the table from which the data is retrieved. For joins and subqueries, this message appears separately for every table in the same order in which the optimizer decided to join them. This order may differ from the one in which tables are listed in the FROM clause of the query.
TO TABLE	Reports the table in which the data is inserted, updated, or deleted.
Worktable n	Appears when the optimizer decides to create a worktable in order to process the query. Conditions of worktable creation are discussed in more detail in Chapter 10. This may signal a performance problem.
Worktable created for SELECT INTO	This actually refers to the new table created by a SELECT INTO query. It is not a worktable, but a permanent or temporary table.
Worktable created for DISTINCT	Appears in queries that use the DISTINCT keyword, except for those cases in which the optimizer can use an existing index to retrieve all DISTINCT values. Avoid adding DISTINCT to your queries unless you are certain that it's necessary. If you apply it to a large result set that is already distinct, it causes an unnecessary creation of a huge worktable. This dramatically slows down the query and may overflow the tempdb database.

Table 20-4. SHOWPLAN Messages Used by Microsoft and Sybase (continued)

SHOWPLAN Message	Explanation
Worktable created for ORDER BY	Queries with ORDER BY require creation of a worktable, except for those cases in which the table has an index on the key used for ordering. If the index is not clustered, the optimizer may still end up rejecting it and creating a worktable, depending on the number of rows that may be affected. Try to create clustered indexes on columns that are frequently used in ORDER BY clauses. Unfortunately, you can have only one such index per table, so if you have different ordering criteria in your queries, choose the most frequently used or the most critical key on which to build a clustered index.
Worktable created for REFORMATTING	*This is a sign of trouble!* The optimizer uses the reformatting strategy as a last resort when you join large tables without meaningful indexes. Instead of scanning both tables, SQL Server creates a worktable and populates it with qualifying rows from the smallest table (it only picks columns used in the query). It then creates a clustered index on this worktable—the best for the join criteria. Finally, it joins the larger table with the worktable using the clustered index that it has created. Extra time spent building the worktable is typically less than the time required to scan the table multiple times.
This step involves sorting	Appears in queries with DISTINCT and ORDER BY that cannot use an index. Sorting is done on worktables.
Using GETSORTED Table Scan	Indicates that SQL Server sorts rows in a worktable.
Nested iteration	Indicates that SQL Server joins this table with the previous one. The algorithm of a join is a loop, in which the optimizer passes through one table and, for every qualifying row, makes an indexed lookup or a scan of the second table.
EXISTS TABLE: nested iteration	Indicates usage of a table for an existence test. This may be an EXISTS, IN, ANY, =, <, >, <=, >=, or <> condition.
Table Scan	*Watch out for this one!* It indicates that there is no good index to search the table. In some cases, you intend to scan the whole table to get the result. However, when you use WHERE clause conditions to filter out certain rows or to join tables, you may expect some index to be used. The optimizer decides whether any of the existing indexes will satisfy the search. Review each instance of a table scan carefully to determine if an index exists but for some reason is rejected or if a new one could be created. This is especially important in joins of large tables. A table scan on both joined tables is a sure performance killer.
Using Clustered Index	This one speaks for itself. Clustered indexes are usually the most efficient for a query.
Index: index name	Reports a nonclustered index used for a table search. The fact that some index is used does not guarantee that it is the most efficient one for this specific query. Review index names and keys to determine whether this is indeed the one you expected the optimizer to choose.

Table 20-4. SHOWPLAN Messages Used by Microsoft and Sybase (continued)

SHOWPLAN Message	Explanation
Using Dynamic Index	Indicates that SQL Server uses an index that it has built itself on a worktable. Appears in queries with OR conditions or IN lists in the WHERE clause. SQL Server often has to build a worktable to satisfy such queries. It searches the table for every OR condition or IN list element and adds row IDs to the worktable. A row ID is a pointer to a data page and row number on the page. SQL Server treats this worktable as a dynamic index that may be used to access the data. Generally, OR and IN are not very efficient constructs.
{ Ascending | Descending } scan	Reports the scan direction of a table or index.
{ AND | AND NOT | OR | OR NOT } EXISTS nested iteration	Indicates a nested iteration to satisfy an existence or nonexistence test. Review these messages carefully, because existence and nonexistence tests may be inefficient when they are not supported by proper indexes. The plan for the nested iteration search follows this message.
SUBQUERY: nested iteration	Indicates a nested iteration subquery that involves an aggregate. SHOWPLAN output includes a subquery plan right after this message.
WITH CHECK OPTION	Indicates modification of a view that was created WITH CHECK OPTION. It requires existence tests and may be the bottleneck when there is no proper index.

Table 20-5. SHOWPLAN Messages Used Only by Sybase

SHOWPLAN Message	Explanation
The update mode is { deferred_varcol | deferred_index }	The deferred_varcol method is used to update variable-length columns. The deferred_index method is used for index modification.
Evaluate Grouped aggregate_type AGGREGATE	Appears for queries that contain an aggregate and a GROUP BY or COMPUTE BY clause. The aggregate_type indicates the type of an aggregate function.
Evaluate Grouped ASSIGNMENT OPERATOR	Appears for queries with a COMPUTE BY clause. It indicates that SQL Server populates a worktable in one step and then computes aggregates for the COMPUTE BY in the second step.
Evaluate Ungrouped aggregate_type AGGREGATE	Appears for queries that contain aggregate functions but no GROUP BY clause and also for queries that use COMPUTE.
Evaluate Ungrouped ASSIGNMENT OPERATOR	Appears for queries with a COMPUTE clause used to compute a scalar aggregate.
Auxiliary scan descriptors required: n	Indicates that the query requires referential integrity checking.
Keys are: column_list	Lists the columns that are used in the index. Sometimes only the first few columns of a composite index are used, thus reducing the efficiency of the index.

Table 20-5. SHOWPLAN Messages Used Only by Sybase (continued)

SHOWPLAN Message	Explanation
Positioning at start of table	Indicates a table scan from the first row of the table.
Positioning by Row Identifier (RID)	Appears for queries with OR conditions that cause the creation of a dynamic index.
Positioning by key	Indicates that SQL Server uses an index to find the qualifying row.
Positioning at index { start | end }	Indicates a scan of a nonmatching nonclustered index. This strategy is used when all columns required for the query are found in a nonclustered index that is more efficient to scan than the table itself. It is better than a table scan but may still take a very long time if the index itself is also large. Find out what caused this message and whether optimization is possible.
Scanning only the last page of the table	This message indicates usage of a scalar MAX function (without a GROUP BY clause). SQL Server flips to the last page to find the answer. You could say that it is as impatient as many book readers.
Scanning only to the first qualifying row	This message indicates the usage of a scalar MIN function (without a GROUP BY clause). SQL Server stops scanning the table upon finding the answer.
Index contains all needed columns. Base table will not be read.	Indicates that a nonclustered index contains all columns needed to process the query and that it is more efficient than using the data pages of the table itself.
Using n Matching Index Scans	Appears for a query using OR conditions or an IN list.
Log Scan	Indicates that a trigger invoked as a result of an INSERT, UPDATE, or DELETE query requires building an inserted and/or deleted table.
Using I/O size n Kilobytes	Possible sizes are 2, 4, 8, and 16. The optimizer chooses large I/O sizes for some types of queries, provided that the table, index, or database used in the query has a data cache with large I/O sized pools.
With { LRU | MRU } Buffer Replacement Strategy	Indicates the cache usage strategy chosen for the query. LRU strategy means that data pages read into cache replace the *least recently used* buffer. It is used for queries modifying data on pages, pages used more than once by the same query, index pages, and in some other cases. The MRU strategy uses the *most recently used* buffer and is typically used for data pages that are needed only once. It is also called "fetch and discard."
Total estimated I/O cost for statement n (at line m): c	This message is printed when the SA enables resource limits. The cost of the query reflects the number of physical and logical I/O operations estimated for the query. It has no unit of measure and should be used to compare the price to other queries or other plans of the same query. The estimated cost may differ from the actual cost.

Table 20-5. SHOWPLAN Messages Used Only by Sybase (continued)

SHOWPLAN Message	Explanation
Query Plan for Statement n (at line n)	This is the header of a plan for each query.

Optimizer Hints

The optimizer may be your friend, but sometimes you may want to hit it with something heavy for insisting on making the wrong decisions. If it chooses a particular join order or an index for a certain query, it will consistently make the same choice given the same data to process. Even if the query turns out to be a disaster and never returns, the optimizer learns nothing from its mistake. Such cases are not very frequent (thank God!). But if you experience a situation in which the optimizer makes a poor choice, you have to build the query plan yourself.

Transact-SQL includes special syntax constructs that allow you to force one or another plan. Microsoft calls them *optimizer hints*. Sybase has similar capabilities but doesn't have any special name for them. Throughout this chapter, we will use the term "optimizer hints" to describe any "plan enforcement" commands.

All optimizer hints may be classified depending on what aspect of the plan they control:

- Join-order hints
- Index-selection hints
- Locking-type hints

Join Order Optimizer Hints

Both Sybase and Microsoft have a special command that tells SQL Server to join tables in the same order in which they appear in the FROM clause of a query. This command is:

```
SET FORCEPLAN ON
```

It takes effect only within the current SQL Server connection and is effective immediately upon execution. It impacts all queries that follow in the same step and after, until you turn the option off by executing another command:

```
SET FORCEPLAN OFF
```

When you force a particular join order, SQL Server obligingly does what it's told. However, it may still choose or reject indexes on each particular table. If you want to control index selection as well, you have to use more optimizer hints.

Here is an example. The following query joins three tables and could have six possible join orders. If you analyze the WHERE clause conditions, you'll notice that two of them don't make any sense: titles-authors-titleauthor and authors-titles-titleauthor, because the tables authors and titles are not linked by any conditions. But if you decide to force one of these inefficient join orders, you can do that. Compare the plans in Table 20-6. They were produced by Microsoft SQL Server, but Sybase's output is very similar. We added extra rows to the authors and titles tables before executing the query to make the plan more realistic.

Table 20-6. Impact of SET FORCEPLAN ON on a Query Plan

Query Without FORCEPLAN	Query With FORCEPLAN

`SELECT  t.title, a.au_lname`
`FROM    titles t,`
`        authors a,`
`        titleauthor ta`
`WHERE   ta.au_id = a.au_id`
`    AND ta.title_id =`
`        t.title_id`
	`SET FORCEPLAN ON`
	`GO`
	`SELECT  t.title, a.au_lname`
	`FROM    titles t,`
	`        authors a,`
	`        titleauthor ta`
	`WHERE   ta.au_id = a.au_id`
	`    AND ta.title_id =`
	`        t.title_id`
	`GO`
	`SET FORCEPLAN OFF`
	`GO`

`STEP 1`
`The type of query is SELECT`
`FROM TABLE`
`titleauthor ta`
`Nested iteration`
`Table Scan`
`FROM TABLE`
`titles t`
`Nested iteration`
`Using Clustered Index`
`FROM TABLE`
`authors a`
`Nested iteration`
`Using Clustered Index`
	`STEP 1`
	`The type of query is SELECT`
	`FROM TABLE`
	`titles t`
	`Nested iteration`
	`Table Scan`
	`FROM TABLE`
	`authors a`
	`Nested iteration`
	`Table Scan`
	`FROM TABLE`
	`titleauthor ta`
	`Nested iteration`
	`Table Scan`

In this example, forcing a plan is a poor choice. The original plan chosen by the optimizer used clustered indexes on two tables. The plan that we forced had to scan every table. This would be disastrous on big tables. The moral of the story is: don't force a plan unless you are certain that it improves your query performance.

The SET FORCEPLAN command may be useful in situations in which you can't guarantee that statistics on indexes are always up to date, particularly if you join many tables in one query. The optimizer may get confused by too many choices and outdated index statistics and create a plan that takes an infinity to execute.

Index-Selection Optimizer Hints

The syntax for forcing a particular index on a table differs slightly between Microsoft and Sybase. You can explicitly specify an index by name for any table in the FROM clause as shown here:

Microsoft	Sybase
`table_name ( INDEX = { index_name | indid } )`	`table_name ( INDEX { index_name | indid } )`

Note that Sybase syntax has no equals sign in front of the index_name or indid.

There is also an old syntax for index enforcement that is still supported by both vendors. It was the only way on SQL Server 4.x versions to explicitly specify an index. This syntax requires knowing the value of the "indid" column from the sysindexes table for a particular index of a particular table:

```
table_name ( indid )
```

In order to obtain the indid for the table_name table, you can query sysindexes like this:

```
SELECT  name, indid
FROM    sysindexes
WHERE   id = OBJECT_ID( 'table_name' )
```

The query returns the name and indid of every index of the specified table. Tables that have no clustered index result set will also contain a row with indid = 0 and the table name in the name column. Clustered indexes always have indid = 1. Non-clustered indexes have indid automatically assigned by SQL Server in the order of creation, starting with 2. Tables that contain TEXT or IMAGE columns will also report sysindexes rows with indid = 255. This indid cannot be used in an optimizer hint.

For example, execute the following query in the pubs database to search for indexes on the titleauthor table:

```
SELECT  name, indid
FROM    sysindexes
WHERE   id = OBJECT_ID( 'titleauthor' )
```

Results:

```
name                           indid
------------------------------ ------
UPKCL_taind                    1
auidind                        2
titleidind                     3

(3 row(s) affected)
```

You can use a hint of (1) to force a clustered index on any table, provided that there is one. A hint of (0) forces a table scan to ignore any indexes. Table 20-7 contains some examples.

One more optimizer hint that influences index selection is FASTFIRSTROW, which is supported only by Microsoft. It makes sense on queries with an ORDER BY

Table 20-7. Examples of Index-Selection Optimizer Hints

Query	Description
`SELECT * FROM titleauthor WHERE au_id = '267-41-2394'`	You let the optimizer decide which index to choose and whether to use one at all.
`SELECT * FROM titleauthor ( 1 ) WHERE au_id = '267-41-2394'`	Explicitly forces the clustered index (provided that there is one).
`SELECT * FROM titleauthor ( 0 ) WHERE au_id = '267-41-2394'`	Forces a table scan by suppressing any indexes.
`SELECT * FROM titleauthor ( index = UPKCL_taind ) -- on Sybase delete "=" sign above WHERE au_id = '267-41-2394'`	Forces the clustered index on the titleauthor table by index name.
`SELECT * FROM titleauthor ( index = titleidind ) -- on Sybase delete "=" sign above WHERE au_id = '267-41-2394'`	Forces index titleidind on the titleauthor table by index name. This index is extremely inefficient here. We use it only to illustrate that the optimizer obligingly follows your instructions, no matter how wrong they may be.
`SELECT * FROM titleauthor ( 3 ) WHERE au_id = '267-41-2394'`	Forces index titleidind on the titleauthor table by indid value. This method was the only one available on old versions of SQL Server, but we recommend you avoid it now, because indid values may change if your DBA drops and recreates table indexes. This may destroy all carefully tuned plans referring to specific index IDs.

clause, when the table has a nonclustered index matching your ordering criteria. Without this hint, the SQL Server optimizer shoots for the best possible response time of the whole transaction. It often decides not to use a nonclustered index if scanning the table and sorting it in a worktable returns the whole result faster. But it may still take a long time, and a user may be waiting impatiently. Instead, you may choose to receive the *first row* more quickly and take extra time to get all the other rows, rather than getting the whole result set in the minimum amount of time. The hint forces use of a nonclustered index for a query with ORDER BY, provided that there is a matching one.

For example, your application may populate the first screen with a few rows to give the user some food for thought while the query continues. The last row arrives later than it would without the hint, but from the user's perspective, the performance is better when the first screen is populated quickly.

Locking Optimizer Hints

Shared locks placed by a SELECT command are released as soon as the query finishes, even if it is executed within a transaction (BEGIN/COMMIT TRAN). But both

Sybase and Microsoft support a special hint that allows extending locks until the end of the transaction. If you specify HOLDLOCK after a table name in the WHERE clause, SQL Server will keep the lock until the transaction either commits or rolls back.

For example:

```
SET NOCOUNT ON

DECLARE @ytd_sales INT

BEGIN TRAN

SELECT  @ytd_sales = MAX( ytd_sales )
FROM    titles HOLDLOCK

SELECT  'Best year-to-date sales:', @ytd_sales

UPDATE  titles
SET     notes = notes + ' Bestseller'
WHERE   ytd_sales = @ytd_sales

COMMIT TRAN
```

Normally, locks on the titles table would be released right after the first SELECT query, but the HOLDLOCK hint extends them until the transaction commits.

Microsoft SQL Server provides a number of additional optimizer hints that allow you to control the type of locks: NOLOCK, UPDLOCK, TABLOCK, PAGLOCK, and TABLOCKX. Sybase has its own exclusive hint—NOHOLDLOCK.

Why would you need to change a lock type? In most cases, you are better off with the locking strategy chosen by the optimizer. However, there may be situations in which you want to override the default behavior.

For instance, escalation of page-level locks to a table level occurs only after a configurable threshold is exceeded. This setting is the same for all databases and all tables on your SQL Server. Suppose that you have a special query and you know in advance that it will exceed the threshold number of locked pages and escalate to a table-level lock anyway. Instead of allowing SQL Server to start by allocating page-level locks and manage the increasing number of them waiting for the threshold to be exceeded, you can simply tell it to use a table-level lock right away.

It may be necessary to control lock type in order to fight deadlocks. By requesting an exclusive lock on a table, you reduce the chance that you will deadlock with another transaction on this table. But be careful using this technique. You may end up reducing deadlocks but instead dramatically increase live locks, which means poor response time for users.

Another useful technique is to set the whole database dedicated to DSS or data warehouse applications to the read-only mode. SQL Server does not manage locks in such databases, because all locks would be shared and there would be no lock conflicts. You may turn the read-only mode off when you run data load jobs. The single-user database mode also suppresses lock management, because a single user cannot have lock conflicts. Therefore, you may completely avoid lock management in a DSS database by using the read-only mode for production time and the single-user mode for data load time.

Use direct locking control with discretion (as with any other optimizer hints). When you override normal SQL Server behavior, you take the responsibility for query performance. In most cases, you are better off leaving the grunt work to the machine. But if you are still excited about the opportunities to mandate lock types, see Table 20-8 for a description of these hints.

Table 20-8. Locking Optimizer Hints

Locking Optimizer Hint	Description
NOLOCK	Places no locks on the table and ignores any existing locks placed by other processes. Accessing a table in such a manner is also known as a "dirty read." Your process may select pages modified by an uncommitted transaction. Other processes may violate consistency of your results and cause error 605, 606, 624, or 625. Your application may retry the same query upon receiving any of these messages. This optimizer hint may be very efficient when you need to select data from a table that may be updated by other processes at the same time. Suppose that you are retrieving only columns that are never updated. Normally, your query would place a shared lock on the table and prevent other processes from updating it until you are done. But when you specify NOLOCK, you allow other processes to continue uninterrupted. This may dramatically improve concurrency, especially if you know that processes do not modify the data that you are retrieving. One practical task is to generate reports on large tables in OLTP systems. If your process requires a table scan on a table updated by short transactions in other processes, try NOLOCK to avoid lengthy locks.
HOLDLOCK	This hint extends shared locks placed on a table by a SELECT query until the end of a transaction. It makes sense in SELECT queries executed within a BEGIN TRANSACTION—COMMIT TRANSACTION block. Normally, shared locks are released as soon as the SELECT query finishes. Use HOLDLOCK when you want to make sure nobody else will update the data you have selected until your transaction is complete.

Table 20-8. Locking Optimizer Hints (continued)

Locking Optimizer Hint	Description
UPDLOCK	This hint allows you to place *update* locks instead of *shared* ones. Locks are held through the end of the transaction as they would be for an UPDATE query. Use UPDLOCK to protect data you are selecting from being updated by other processes until your transaction completes.
TABLOCK	Places a shared lock, rather than page locks, on the whole table. The lock is held until the end of the command. Use HOLDLOCK in addition to TABLOCK if you want to extend it through the end of a transaction. This hint reduces lock management to the minimum, because it is much less expensive for SQL Server to hold a lock on the whole table than to remember each and every locked page. Use it when you know that the table is likely to be locked completely anyway and you want to spare SQL Server the effort of locking pages until it reaches the lock escalation threshold. It is especially important if your lock escalation threshold is set very high.
PAGLOCK	Forces page-level rather than table-level shared locks. This hint allows you to ignore the configured lock escalation threshold and keep acquiring page-level locks. One practical task that may benefit from this hint is to generate a historical report on a table to which online users add new data. Suppose that the table has no clustered index, so new records are added to the last page. Your query may select 95% of rows but not today's records. Normally, it would lock the whole table and suspend online transactions until it's done. With PAGLOCK, you lock pages with historical data but not new records on the last page. Be careful when using this hint, because it may cause your SQL Server to run out of locks (a configurable resource).
TABLOCKX	Places an exclusive lock on the whole table. The lock is held through the end of the transaction. This hint gives you full control of the table. You avoid the risk of somebody else starting a transaction on the same object. Lock management is minimal, because SQL Server keeps only one record to lock the whole table, versus multiple records to lock individual pages. You should be aware, though, that you eliminate any concurrency on the table for as long as your transaction continues.

Query Analysis

This section describes how you can analyze your queries and determine how to make them run more efficiently.

Isolating Bottlenecks in Transact-SQL Code

When you determine that the performance problems of your applications are related to SQL Server code, you still need to narrow the problem down further. Before you rush to tune stored procedures, determine priorities by isolating the tables and procedures that cause the most trouble.

A typical real-life situation is a call that you get in the middle of a busy day from a user complaining about poor response time. She may even tell you that everybody's application is "frozen" or that "nothing moves on the screen," and when people reboot and restart the application, they get the same hourglass icon. Chapter 21, *Debugging Transact-SQL Programs,* describes procedures you can use to narrow down performance problems to a single process or even a table or stored procedure. Isolate bottlenecks to set priorities in your tuning efforts. Once you know which stored procedure causes the most trouble, you can start by optimizing it first. Chances are that you will improve the overall performance substantially and that further tuning will not even be necessary.

We know from personal experience how difficult it may be for a programmer to curb perfectionism. The desire to constantly improve and optimize a program that already works may be hard to suppress. There is probably no program that could not be made even better. Print a banner "If it ain't broke, don't fix it," and put it on the wall behind your monitor. Every time you feel the urge to optimize a stored procedure, ask yourself if it's worth it.

Narrowing Down Performance Problems

We'll describe the process of investigating performance problems in Chapter 21. Here is a brief summary of the steps:

- If users complain about constant poor response time or sudden sporadic slowdowns, try to monitor lengthy blocks with the system stored procedure *sp_who.* Analyze the "blk" column of the result set, which indicates the SPID of the blocking process. Find the blocking processes that are not blocked themselves; they are probably running slow-performing queries.
- Enclosed on the CD-ROM is a stored procedure, *sp_whoactive,* which you may install on your SQL Server. It makes two snapshots of SQL Server activity and determines which processes consume I/O resources and hold locks. It quickly narrows down your search for troublemakers to one or a few expensive processes.
- Once you isolate potential troublemakers (we mean system processes, of course), find out what tables they are using by executing *sp_lock.* Translate database names and object IDs reported by *sp_lock* into table names.
- Find the type of query for each problem process in the *sp_who* output. On Microsoft SQL Server, execute DBCC INPUTBUFFER for each suspected SPID to obtain the actual commands it executes.

Collecting Evidence

Before you accuse a particular query of poor performance and try to correct it, you need to collect the evidence—information about the plan, tables used in the query, their indexes, related objects, and usage patterns.

Here is the checklist of items and answers you need to obtain in order to analyze a query:

- Transact-SQL code of the query.
- Table structures for every table involved in the query.
- Indexes and constraints on the table.
- Table sizes in data pages, index pages, and the number of rows.
- Index selectivity or density (may be obtained by the DBCC SHOW_STATISTICS command explained later in this chapter).
- All items listed previously for constraints that may be validated as a result of an INSERT, UPDATE, or DELETE query.
- Source code of triggers that may be fired as a result of an INSERT, UPDATE, or DELETE query.
- All items listed previously for every table affected by these triggers.
- Query plan generated with the help of the SET SHOWPLAN ON command.
- How often the query is executed.
- Whether it is executed by a human user or by an automatic job scheduler.
- The performance requirements to this query and which ones it fails to meet.
- Whether the performance is consistent or sporadic. Is there any noticeable pattern in performance degradation over time or during different periods of the month, week, or day? If multiple users execute the query, do they all experience the same performance problem or is it isolated to a subset of users?
- If there were a sudden drop in performance, what changed in any related objects or in the system in general shortly before the drop? Watch out for dropped indexes, significant amounts of data inserted into tables, increased workload, or changes in the operating system, SQL Server configuration, hardware, network, client software, application, or source code of related objects. This usually gives you the list of "primary suspects"—things that could be responsible for performance problem.
- Do other processes block the query while it is running? Use the system stored procedure *sp_who* to check if it is a victim of other inefficient processes.

Analyzing Evidence

The amount of information collected about a single query may sometimes be enormous. If nothing jumps out at you as an obvious reason for poor performance, then start with the most likely causes.

Analyze the query plan and check whether it uses proper indexes. If indexes aren't used as you expected, ask the DBA whether an UPDATE STATISTICS has been done on these indexes lately. This is especially important if a lot of data has been inserted or modified in related tables.

Check whether the query is a victim of another inefficient process or transaction: see if it is blocked for extended periods of time by other processes. If so, then concentrate your efforts on optimization (or sometimes termination) of the guilty processes. If your query is blocked and you need to know the command executed by the blocking process, you can use the command DBCC INPUTBUFFER (spid) on Microsoft SQL Server. It reports the last 255 characters sent to the server by the process whose SPID you specify. Unfortunately, permission to execute this useful command belongs to the SA only.

Impact of Triggers and Constraints on Performance

Triggers and constraints on tables involved in your INSERT, UPDATE, or DELETE query may turn out to be hidden performance killers. The problem is that you don't see them when you look at the query code. You have to remember to review the code of triggers that may fire and constraints that may need to be checked by the query. It is possible that the query itself uses the right indexes but fires a trigger that performs some additional work that takes forever. What if an index on a table affected by the trigger has been dropped or never existed? It may turn out that your query deleting a single row causes a delete trigger to scan some other huge table.

Analyze all triggers that may be fired by your transaction. If they automatically make changes in other tables, then analyze triggers on those tables as well. Sometimes this may go several levels deep. Make sure that every trigger is optimized—that tables used by trigger queries have good indexes to expedite this transaction. It takes only one inefficient trigger to kill the performance.

In addition to triggers, constraints require efficient indexes on tables linked to the one you modify.

Analyzing Query-Performance Statistics

SQL Server provides the ability to benchmark your transactions by sampling I/O activity and elapsed execution time. Certain DBCC commands may be used to obtain a very detailed explanation of any index statistics and the estimated cost of every possible execution plan.

SET STATISTICS IO

The SET STATISTICS IO ON command forces SQL Server to report actual I/O activity on executed transactions. It cannot be paired with the SET NOEXEC ON option, because it only makes sense for those commands that execute. Once the option is turned on, every query produces additional output that contains I/O statistics. The output looks different on Microsoft SQL Server and Sybase. In order to turn the option off, execute SET STATISTICS IO OFF.

For example, the following script obtains I/O statistics for a simple query counting rows of the syscomments table in the pubs database:

```
SET STATISTICS IO ON
GO
SELECT COUNT(*) FROM syscomments
GO
SET STATISTICS IO OFF
GO
```

Results:

Microsoft	Sybase

`-----------`
`        127`
`Table: syscomments  scan count 1,`
`logical reads: 16,  physical reads: 1,`
`read ahead reads: 0`
	`Total writes for this command: 0`
	`-----------`
	`        127`
	`Table: syscomments  scan count 1,`
	`logical reads: (regular=16 apf=0`
	`total=16), physical reads: (regular=1`
	`apf=0 total=1),  apf IOs used=0`

In addition, we executed a system stored procedure to obtain table size statistics for our analysis:

```
sp_spaceused syscomments
```

The output is practically the same on Microsoft SQL Server and Sybase:

```
name          rows   reserved data       index_size   unused
------------- ------ ------------------ ------------ --------
syscomments   127    192 KB   120 KB    8 KB         64 KB
```

What can we tell by looking at this information?

- The query didn't have to scan the whole table. The number of data pages in the table is 60, but it took only 16 I/O operations to obtain the result. It indicates that the query has found an index that could be used to compute the result, and scanning the index took less I/O than it would take to scan all data pages.

- Index pages were mostly found in the data cache. This is because we executed the query shortly after other queries on syscomments, and the table and its index were already cached. Your mileage may vary.
- Microsoft has reported no read-ahead activity. In this case, data and index pages were already cached. For a table scan on a large table, read-ahead would probably kick in and cache necessary pages before your query requested them. Read-ahead turns on automatically when SQL Server determines that your transaction is reading database pages sequentially and believes that it can predict which pages you'll need next. A separate SQL Server connection virtually runs ahead of your process and caches data pages for it. The configuration and tuning of read-ahead parameters is beyond the scope of this book.

In this example, the query was executed as efficiently as it could be. No further tuning is required.

SET STATISTICS TIME

The elapsed time of a transaction is a volatile measurement, since it depends on the activity of other users on the server. However, it provides more of a real measurement than the number of data pages (which doesn't mean anything to your users). Users are concerned about the seconds and minutes they spend waiting for a query to come back, not about data caches and read-ahead efficiency. The SET STATISTICS TIME ON command reports the actual elapsed time and CPU utilization for every query that follows. Executing SET STATISTICS TIME OFF suppresses the option.

```
SET STATISTICS TIME ON
GO
SELECT COUNT(*) FROM titleauthors
GO
SET STATISTICS TIME OFF
GO
```

Results:

```
SQL Server Execution Times:
   cpu time = 0 ms.  elapsed time = 8672 ms.
SQL Server Parse and Compile Time:
   cpu time = 10 ms.

-----------
25

(1 row(s) affected)


SQL Server Execution Times:
   cpu time = 0 ms.  elapsed time = 10 ms.
```

```
SQL Server Parse and Compile Time:
   cpu time = 0 ms.
```

The first message reports a somewhat confusing elapsed time value of 8,672 milliseconds. This number is not related to our script and indicates the amount of time that has passed since the previous command execution. You may disregard this first message. It took SQL Server only 10 milliseconds to parse and compile the query. It took 0 milliseconds to execute it (shown after the result of the query). What this really means is that the duration of the query was too short to measure. The last message that reports a parse and compile time of 0 ms refers to the SET STATISTICS TIME OFF command (that's what it took to compile it). You may disregard this message. We have highlighted the most important messages in the output.

The elapsed and CPU time are shown in milliseconds. The numbers may vary on your computer (but don't try to compare your machine's performance to our notebook PCs, because this is not a representative benchmark). Moreover, every time you execute this script, you may get slightly different statistics, depending on what else your SQL Server was processing at the same time.

If you need to measure the elapsed duration of a set of queries or a stored procedure, it may be more practical to implement it programmatically, as we'll show in a minute. The reason is that the STATISICS TIME command reports the duration of every single query, and you have to add things up manually when you run multiple commands. Imagine the size of the output and the amount of manual work in cases in which you time a script that executes a set of queries thousands of times in a loop! Instead, consider the following script to capture time before and after the transaction and report the total duration in seconds (you may use milliseconds if you prefer):

```
DECLARE @start_time DATETIME
SELECT  @start_time = GETDATE()
< any query or a script that you want to time, without a GO >
SELECT  'Elapsed Time, sec' = DATEDIFF( second, @start_time, GETDATE() )
GO
```

If your script consists of several steps separated by GO, you can't use a local variable to save the start time. A variable is destroyed at the end of the step, defined by the GO command, where it was created. But you can preserve the start time in a temporary table like this:

```
CREATE TABLE #save_time ( start_time DATETIME NOT NULL )
INSERT #save_time VALUES ( GETDATE() )
GO
< any script that you want to time (may include GO) >
GO
SELECT  'Elapsed Time, sec' = DATEDIFF( second, start_time, GETDATE() )
FROM    #save_time
DROP TABLE #save_time
GO
```

DBCC

DBCC stands for *Database Consistency Check;* the DBCC command provides many useful options. The most famous (or infamous) use allows DBAs to check the consistency of a database and look for database corruption. The DBCC commands (DBCC CHECKDB, DBCC NEWALLOC, DBCC CHECKCATALOG, and others) are briefly discussed in Chapter 21. They may take an enormous amount of time on large databases and may lock tables, therefore creating performance problems. If your analysis of *sp_who* results shows that a process is blocked by another process executing DBCC, then you need to talk to your DBA. Normally, commands that check database consistency should not be executed while users are accessing the system. But DBCC has many additional options, and some of them may be useful in your Transact-SQL programming work.

DBCC SHOW_STATISTICS (Microsoft only)

This command is very useful in analyzing index effectiveness. It shows statistics on a specified index of a particular table. The syntax is:

```
DBCC SHOW_STATISTICS ( table_name, index_name )
```

The output contains information about index density, which defines how many rows potentially have the same key. For composite keys, the output contains information about partial keys consisting of the first few columns of the index, as well as information for the whole key. You can say that index density is the opposite of selectivity. Selective indexes have low density. Indexes with high density are not very selective and are unlikely to be used by the optimizer in query plans. For example:

```
USE master
GO
DBCC SHOW_STATISTICS ( syscomments, syscomments )
GO
```

Results:

```
Updated              Rows        Steps       Density
-------------------- ----------- ----------- ------------------------
Jan 21 1998  9:05PM  4471        320         0.000738525

(1 row(s) affected)

All density              Columns
------------------------ ------------------------------
0.00852328               id
0.00852328               id, number
0.000223664              id, number, colid
0.000223664              id, number, colid, texttype

(4 row(s) affected)

Steps
```

```
-----------
    9051068
   12527078
      . . .
 2096010498
 2128010612
 2144010669

(320 row(s) affected)

DBCC execution completed. If DBCC printed error messages, see your System
Administrator.
```

If we multiply the number shown in the "All density" column by the total number of rows, we can determine how many rows have the same full or partial key. In this example, a key consisting of values for the "id", "number", and "colid" columns provides perfect selectivity: 0.000223664 * 4471 = 1.000001744. Selectivity of 1 means that the any key defined by these columns is associated with only one row in the table. If a query specifies only an "id" column value, then such a partial key points to 38 rows on average (0.00852328 * 4471 = 38.10758488). This is still quite a selective key. The optimizer will use this index for queries that specify a partial key in the WHERE clause, like the following:

```
SELECT text FROM syscomments WHERE id = 2144010669
```

DBCC SHOWCONTIG (Microsoft only)

This command helps you decide when to re-create a clustered index. It provides information about table fragmentation. This is similar to the hard disk fragmentation that occurs on any computer after weeks of creating and modifying files. Disks need defragmentation every so often in order to stay efficient. Database tables are very much the same in this respect. After the data undergoes modifications, some database pages may be allocated in different places in the database. The most efficient allocation is when all pages occupy a contiguous area in the database. The more pieces it is broken into, the less efficient the table becomes, because SQL Server has to work harder to scan all the pages. To defragment a table, drop and re-create a clustered index on it.

The syntax of this DBCC command is:

```
DBCC SHOWCONTIG ( table_id [, indid ] )
```

For example:

```
DBCC SHOWCONTIG ( 6, 1 )
```

Results:

```
DBCC SHOWCONTIG scanning 'syscomments' table...
[SHOW_CONTIG - SCAN ANALYSIS]
--------------------------------------------------------------------------
Table: 'syscomments' (6)  Indid: 1  dbid:1
```

```
TABLE level scan performed.
- Pages Scanned................................: 936
- Extent Switches..............................: 335
- Avg. Pages per Extent........................: 7.9
- Scan Density [Best Count:Actual Count].......: 34.82% [117:336]
- Avg. Bytes free per page.....................: 757.3
- Avg. Page density (full).....................: 62.40%
- Overflow Pages...............................: 0
- Disconnected Overflow Pages..................: 0
DBCC execution completed. If DBCC printed error messages, see your System
Administrator.
```

Statistics returned by the DBCC command are explained in Table 20-9.

Table 20-9. Statistics Returned by DBCC

Statistics	Description
Pages Scanned	Number of database pages used by the table (when you specify indid of 1 or 0) or a nonclustered index (when you specify indid > 1).
Extent Switches	All pages of a table or index are linked into a chain. Access to the table or index is more efficient when all pages of each extent are linked together into a segment of this chain. The DBCC command scans the chain of pages and counts the number of times it has to switch between extents. If the number of extent switches exceeds the number of pages divided by eight, then there is room for optimization.
Avg. Pages per Extent	Space for each table is reserved in extents of eight pages. Some pages are unused because the table has never grown to use them or because rows have been deleted from a page. The closer this number is to eight, the better. A lower number indicates that there are many unused pages that decrease performance of table access.
Scan Density [Best Count: Actual Count]	Scan Density shows how contiguous the table is. The closer the number is to 100%, the better. Lower numbers indicate fragmentation. Best Count shows the ideal number of extent switches that could be achieved on this table. Actual Count shows the actual number of extent switches.
Avg. Bytes free per page	The average number of free bytes per page used by the table or index. The lower the number, the better. High numbers indicate inefficient space usage. The highest possible number of free space is 2,014—the size of a database page minus overhead. This, or a close number, will be displayed for empty tables. For tables with large rows, this number may be relatively high even after optimization. For example, if row size is 1,005 bytes, then only one row will fit per page. DBCC will also report the average free space as 1,005 bytes, but don't expect another row to fit into the same page. In order to fit a row of 1,005 bytes, you'd also need additional room for row system overhead.
Avg. Page density (full)	Shows how full an average page is. Numbers close to 100% are better. This number is tied to the previous one and depends on the row size as well as on the clustered index fillfactor. Transactions performed on table rows change this number because they delete, insert, or move rows around by updating keys.
Overflow Pages	Reserved for system use.

Table 20-9. Statistics Returned by DBCC (continued)

Statistics	Description
Disconnected Overflow Pages	Reserved for system use.

If your statistics are far from perfect, you can ask your DBA to rebuild a clustered index on the table in order to freshen it up. If you don't have a clustered index, then create a dummy one and drop it. This operation may be very time-consuming on large tables and requires free space in the database equal to 1.25 times the total size of data pages used by the table. Unfortunately, it may not be feasible on large tables in critical production systems. You may often have to live with fragmented tables or use programmatic methods of compressing them.

DBCC TRACEON

For those of you who enjoy reading computer memory dumps at the dinner table, we'll show some additional commands that you might use to peek at the optimizer's worksheets.

The DBCC TRACEON (trace_flag) command is one of several methods used to activate SQL Server trace flags. Some of them are particularly interesting for query analysis; these are shown in Table 20-10. Any trace flag may be disabled by the DBCC TRACEOFF (trace_flag) command.

Table 20-10. Trace Flags for Query Analysis

Trace Flag	Description
302	Reports statistics on page usage, actual selectivity, estimated physical and logical I/O usage.
310	Reports join order. You may as well use the SHOWPLAN output for this purpose.
3604	Sends output generated by the trace process to the client. Set this flag in conjunction with other flags in order to see the output of activated traces. By default, trace information goes into the SQL Server ERRORLOG file.

For example:

```
DBCC TRACEON( 3604 )
DBCC TRACEON( 302 )
DBCC TRACEON( 310 )
GO
SELECT  a.au_lname, ta.royaltyper
FROM    authors a, titleauthor ta
WHERE   a.au_id    = ta.au_id
GO
DBCC TRACEOFF( 3604 )
DBCC TRACEOFF( 302 )
DBCC TRACEOFF( 310 )
GO
```

The job of interpreting results is not for the faint of heart. Using trace flags may sometimes be your last resort when you can't understand the optimizer's reasoning. Reading this output may also help you learn the internals of the SQL Server optimizer. We leave it to your discretion how often you want to use it. Results produced by our sample script on Microsoft SQL Server follow:

```
*******************************
Leaving q_init_sclause() for table 'authors' (varno 0).
The table has 69 rows and 5 pages.
Cheapest index is index 0, costing 5 pages per scan.

*******************************
Leaving q_init_sclause() for table 'titleauthor' (varno 1).
The table has 25 rows and 1 pages.
Cheapest index is index 0, costing 1 pages per scan.

*******************************
Entering q_score_join() for table 'authors' (varno 0).
The table has 69 rows and 5 pages.
Scoring the join clause:
AND (!:0x1afb63c)  (andstat:0x2)
  EQ (L:0x1afb628)  (rsltype:0x2f rsllen:255 rslprec:11 rslscale:0
  opstat:0x0)
    VAR (L:0x1afb58a)  (varname:au_id varno:0 colid:1
    coltype(0x27):VARCHAR colen:11 coloff:-1 colprec:11 colscale:0
    vartypeid:101 varnext:1afb34e varusecnt:1 varlevel:0 varsubq:0)
    VAR (R:0x1afb5de)  (varname:au_id varno:1 colid:1
    coltype(0x27):VARCHAR colen:11 coloff:-1 colprec:11 colscale:0
    vartypeid:101 varnext:1afb3d8 varusecnt:1 varlevel:0 varsubq:0)

Unique clustered index found--return rows 1 pages 2
Cheapest index is index 1, costing 2 pages and generating 1 rows per
scan.
Join selectivity is 69.
*******************************

*******************************
Entering q_score_join() for table 'titleauthor' (varno 1).
The table has 25 rows and 1 pages.
Scoring the join clause:
AND (!:0x1afb63c)  (andstat:0x2)
  EQ (L:0x1afb628)  (rsltype:0x2f rsllen:255 rslprec:11 rslscale:0
  opstat:0x0)
    VAR (L:0x1afb5de)  (varname:au_id varno:1 colid:1
    coltype(0x27):VARCHAR colen:11 coloff:-1 colprec:11 colscale:0
    vartypeid:101 varnext:1afb3d8 varusecnt:1 varlevel:0 varsubq:0)
    VAR (R:0x1afb58a)  (varname:au_id right:1afb5de varno:0 colid:1
    coltype(0x27):VARCHAR colen:11 coloff:-1 colprec:11 colscale:0
    vartypeid:101 varnext:1afb34e varusecnt:1 varstat:0x884
    varlevel:0 varsubq:0)

Scoring clause for index 1
Relop bits are: 0x80,0x4
Estimate: indid 1, selectivity 6.250000e-002, rows 1 pages 2
```

```
Scoring clause for index 2
Relop bits are: 0x80,0x4
Estimate: indid 2, selectivity 6.250000e-002, rows 1 pages 3
Cheapest index is index 0, costing 1 pages and generating 25 rows per
scan.
Cost join selectivity is 1.
Best join selectivity is 16.
*******************************

QUERY IS CONNECTED

J_OPTIMIZE: Remaining vars=[0,1]

permutation: 0 - 1

NEW PLAN (total cost = 232):
JPLAN (0x34ff594) varno=0 indexid=0 totcost=80 pathtype=sclause
class=join optype=? method=NESTED ITERATION outerrows=1 rows=69
joinsel=1 lp=5 pp=5 cpages=5 ctotpages=5 corder=1 cstat=0x20
matcost=10181 matpages=2 crows=69 cjoinsel=1

JPLAN (0x34ff5f0) varno=1 indexid=0 totcost=152 pathtype=sclause
class=join optype=? method=NESTED ITERATION outerrows=69 rows=25
joinsel=16 lp=69 pp=1 cpages=1 ctotpages=1 corder=1 cstat=0x20
crows=25 cjoinsel=1 joinmap=[0]

permutation: 1 - 0
WORK PLAN (total cost = 336):

NEW PLAN (total cost = 186):
JPLAN (0x34ff594) varno=1 indexid=0 totcost=16 pathtype=sclause
class=join optype=? method=NESTED ITERATION outerrows=1 rows=25
joinsel=1 lp=1 pp=1 cpages=1 ctotpages=1 corder=1 cstat=0x20
matcost=10079 matpages=1 crows=25 cjoinsel=1

JPLAN (0x34ff5f0) varno=0 indexid=1 totcost=170 pathtype=join
class=join optype=? method=NESTED ITERATION outerrows=25 rows=25
joinsel=16 lp=50 pp=5 cpages=2 ctotpages=5 corder=1 cstat=0x4 crows=1
cjoinsel=69 joinmap=[1] jnvar=1 refindid=0 refcost=0 refpages=0
reftotpages=0 ordercol[0]=1 ordercol[1]=1

WORK PLAN (total cost = 202):

CHOSE PLAN:
JPLAN (0x34fe9f4) varno=1 indexid=0 totcost=16 pathtype=sclause
class=join optype=? method=NESTED ITERATION outerrows=1 rows=25
joinsel=1 lp=1 pp=1 cpages=1 ctotpages=1 corder=1 cstat=0x20
matcost=10079 matpages=1 crows=25 cjoinsel=1

CHOSE PLAN:
JPLAN (0x34fea50) varno=0 indexid=1 totcost=170 pathtype=join
class=join optype=? method=NESTED ITERATION outerrows=25 rows=25
joinsel=16 lp=50 pp=5 cpages=2 ctotpages=5 corder=1 cstat=0x4 crows=1
cjoinsel=69 joinmap=[1] jnvar=1 refindid=0 refcost=0 refpages=0
reftotpages=0 ordercol[0]=1 ordercol[1]=1
```

```
TOTAL # PERMUTATIONS: 2
TOTAL # PLANS CONSIDERED: 4

FINAL PLAN (total cost = 186):
JPLAN (0x34fe9f4) varno=1 indexid=0 totcost=16 pathtype=sclause
class=join optype=SUBSTITUTE method=NESTED ITERATION outerrows=1
rows=25 joinsel=1 lp=1 pp=1 cpages=1 ctotpages=1 corder=1 cstat=0x20
matcost=10079 matpages=1 crows=25 cjoinsel=1

JPLAN (0x34fea50) varno=0 indexid=1 totcost=170 pathtype=join
class=join optype=SUBSTITUTE method=NESTED ITERATION outerrows=25
rows=25 joinsel=16 lp=50 pp=5 cpages=2 ctotpages=5 corder=1 cstat=0x4
crows=1 cjoinsel=69 joinmap=[1] jnvar=1 refindid=0 refcost=0
refpages=0 reftotpages=0 ordercol[0]=1 ordercol[1]=1
```

DBCC SQLPERF (Microsoft only)

DBCC SQLPERF can be used to obtain general SQL Server performance statistics. The same parameters can also be tracked in real time using the SQL Server Performance Monitor. The syntax of the command follows:

```
DBCC SQLPERF ( {IOSTATS | LRUSTATS | NETSTATS | RASTATS
    [, CLEAR]} | {THREADS} | {LOGSPACE} )
```

SQLPERF options are explained in Table 20-11.

Table 20-11. DBCC SQLPERF Options

DBCC SQLPERF Option	Description
IOSTATS	Reports I/O usage since the server was started or since these statistics were cleared.
LRUSTATS	Reports cache usage since the server was started or since these statistics were cleared.
NETSTATS	Reports network usage.
RASTATS	Reports read-ahead usage.
CLEAR	This option is used in conjunction with one of the four discussed previously. Clears the specified statistics and generates no output.
THREADS	Maps the Windows NT system thread ID to a SQL Server SPID. The output contains the login name, physical and logical (reported as CPU) I/O activity, and memory usage statistics.
LOGSPACE	Reports the percentage of transaction log space used. This option can be used only if the transaction log is located on its own database segment.

The amount of information you can obtain with these commands may seem too much to digest. Well, we think it *is* too much. For most practical purposes, you don't need to monitor all performance statistics. But you may be interested in a particular parameter that you suspect is causing performance problems. In such cases, DBCC SQLPERF may come in handy.

Optimization Tips and Techniques

The tips and techniques described in this section are applicable in a narrow class of programming tasks. Knowing them expands your resources in performance optimization. We have chosen to use Microsoft SHOWPLAN output in all examples in this section, because this output is more compact and still shows all the critical information. Sybase's query plans are essentially the same for our sample queries, although they include some additional messages.

Subqueries Optimization

As a good rule of thumb, try to replace all subqueries with joins. The optimizer may sometimes automatically *flatten out* subqueries and replace them with regular or outer joins. But it doesn't always do a good job at that. Explicit joins give the optimizer more options to choose the order of tables and find the best possible plan. When you optimize a particular query, investigate whether getting rid of subqueries makes a difference.

The following queries select the names of all user tables in the pubs database and the clustered index name for each table, if one exists. If there is no clustered index, then the table name still appears in the list with a dash in the clustered index column. Both queries return the same result set, but the first one uses a subquery, while the second employs an outer join. Compare the query plans produced by Microsoft SQL Server:

Subquery Solution

```
SELECT  name 'table',
        ISNULL(
            ( SELECT  name
              FROM    sysindexes i
              WHERE   i.id = o.id
                  AND i.indid = 1
            ), '-'
        ) 'clustered index'
FROM    sysobjects o
WHERE   type = 'U'
```

```
STEP 1
The type of query is SELECT
FROM TABLE
sysobjects o
Nested iteration
Table Scan
FROM TABLE
Worktable 1
SUBQUERY : nested iteration
GROUP BY
Vector Aggregate
  FROM TABLE
  Sysindexes i
  Nested iteration
  Using Clustered Index
  TO TABLE
  Worktable 1
```

Outer Join Solution

```
SELECT  o.name 'table',
        ISNULL( i.name, '-'
        ) 'clustered index'
FROM    sysobjects o, sysindexes i
WHERE   i.id =* o.id
    AND i.indid = 1
    AND o.type = 'U'
```

```
STEP 1
The type of query is SELECT
FROM TABLE
sysobjects o
Nested iteration
Table Scan
LEFT OUTER JOIN : nested iteration
  FROM TABLE
  sysindexes i
  Nested iteration
  Using Clustered Index
```

Results are the same in both cases:

```
table                          clustered index
------------------------------ ------------------------------
authors                        UPKCL_auidind
publishers                     UPKCL_pubind
titles                         UPKCL_titleidind
titleauthor                    UPKCL_taind
stores                         UPK_storeid
sales                          UPKCL_sales
roysched                       -
discounts                      -
jobs                           PK__jobs__job_id__243D6C4D
pub_info                       UPKCL_pubinfo
employee                       employee_ind

(11 row(s) affected)
```

A solution using an outer join is more efficient. It does not require creating a worktable for subquery processing.

UNION Versus UNION ALL

Whenever possible, use UNION ALL instead of UNION. The difference is that UNION has a side effect of eliminating all duplicate rows and sorting results, which UNION ALL doesn't do. Selecting a distinct result requires building a temporary worktable, storing all rows in it, and sorting before producing the output. In some cases, that's exactly what you need to do, and then UNION is your friend. But if you don't expect any duplicate rows in the result set, use UNION ALL. It simply selects from one table or a join and then selects from another, attaching results to the bottom of the first result set. UNION ALL requires no worktable and no sorting (unless other unrelated conditions cause that). In most cases, it's much more efficient. One more potential problem with UNION is the danger of overflowing the tempdb database with a huge worktable. It may happen if you expect a large result set from a UNION query.

The following queries select the names of all user tables in the pubs database and the names of temporary tables found in the tempdb database. The only difference between the two solutions is the use of UNION versus UNION ALL. But the addition of the ALL keyword makes a huge difference in the query plan. The first solution requires a worktable and sorting the results before they are returned to the client. The second query is much more efficient, especially for large tables. In this example, both queries return the same result set, although in a different order. In our testing, we had two temporary tables at the time of execution. Your results may vary.

UNION Solution

```
SELECT  'pubs  ' AS 'database',
        Name     AS 'table'
FROM    pubs..sysobjects
WHERE   type = 'U'
UNION
SELECT  'tempdb' AS 'database',
        Name     AS 'table'
FROM    tempdb..sysobjects
WHERE   type = 'U'

STEP 1
The type of query is INSERT
The update mode is direct
FROM TABLE
Pubs..sysobjects
Nested iteration
Table Scan
TO TABLE
Worktable 1
STEP 2
The type of query is INSERT
The update mode is direct
FROM TABLE
Tempdb..sysobjects
Nested iteration
Index : ncsysobjects
TO TABLE
Worktable 1
STEP 3
The type of query is SELECT
This step involves sorting
FROM TABLE
Worktable 1
Using GETSORTED Table Scan
```

UNION ALL Solution

```
SELECT  'pubs  ' AS 'database',
        Name     AS 'table'
FROM    pubs..sysobjects
WHERE   type = 'U'
UNION ALL
SELECT  'tempdb' AS 'database',
        name     AS 'table'
FROM    tempdb..sysobjects
WHERE   type = 'U'

STEP 1
The type of query is SELECT
FROM TABLE
pubs..sysobjects
Nested iteration
Table Scan
STEP 2
The type of query is SELECT
FROM TABLE
tempdb..sysobjects
Nested iteration
Index : ncsysobjects
```

Results:

```
database table
-------- ------------------------
pubs     authors
pubs     discounts
pubs     employee
pubs     jobs
pubs     pub_info
pubs     publishers
pubs     roysched
pubs     sales
pubs     stores
pubs     titleauthor
pubs     titles
tempdb   #test01_______0000000001
tempdb   #test02_______0000000001

(13 row(s) affected)
```

```
database table
-------- ------------------------
pubs     authors
pubs     publishers
pubs     titles
pubs     titleauthor
pubs     stores
pubs     sales
pubs     roysched
pubs     discounts
pubs     jobs
pubs     pub_info
pubs     employee
tempdb   #test01________0000000001
tempdb   #test02________0000000001

(13 row(s) affected)
```

Extraneous WHERE Clause Conditions

You will help the optimizer if you provide it with all possible WHERE clause conditions. We all learned at school that if A=B and B=C, then A=C. We don't know which school the optimizer went to, because it is unable to figure that out. Consider the query:

```
SELECT  *
FROM    a, b, c
WHERE   a.key = b.key
    AND b.key = c.key
```

It's a three-table join and should have six possible join orders: abc, acb, bac, bca, cab, cba. However, the WHERE clause limits the optimizer's options to abc and cba, because it does not provide conditions to join tables a and c directly. This does reduce the amount of work for the optimizer, since there are fewer join orders to consider. However, we recommend including extra conditions that are obvious to you, but not to the optimizer:

```
SELECT  *
FROM    a, b, c
WHERE   a.key = b.key
    AND b.key = c.key
    AND a.key = c.key
```

It does not change the result returned by the query but allows the optimizer to consider all six join orders. Maybe one of the four extra plans, which would otherwise not even be evaluated, is the most efficient.

Compare the following queries and their plans produced by Microsoft SQL Server. The second query offers the optimizer an extra condition and allows it to pick a different join order.

Minimal WHERE Clause Conditions	Additional WHERE Clause Conditions
SELECT st.stor_id, st.state, sa.ord_num, sa.qty, d.discount FROM stores st, sales sa, discounts d WHERE st.stor_id = sa.stor_id AND sa.stor_id = d.stor_id	SELECT st.stor_id, st.state, sa.ord_num, sa.qty, d.discount FROM stores st, sales sa, discounts d WHERE st.stor_id = sa.stor_id AND sa.stor_id = d.stor_id **AND st.stor_id = d.stor_id**
STEP 1 The type of query is SELECT FROM TABLE discounts d Nested iteration Table Scan FROM TABLE **sales sa** Nested iteration Using Clustered Index FROM TABLE **stores st** Nested iteration Using Clustered Index	STEP 1 The type of query is SELECT FROM TABLE discounts d Nested iteration Table Scan FROM TABLE **stores st** Nested iteration Using Clustered Index FROM TABLE **sales sa** Nested iteration Using Clustered Index

The join order has changed with the addition of one seemingly unnecessary condition. In this example, performance may be about the same in both cases, but in other situations, extra conditions make a big improvement. Let the optimizer decide which plan is best.

Results are the same in both cases:

```
stor_id state ord_num              qty    discount
------- ----- -------------------- ------ --------
8042    OR    423LL922             15     5.00
8042    OR    423LL930             10     5.00
8042    OR    P723                 25     5.00
8042    OR    QA879.1              30     5.00

(4 row(s) affected)
```

We inserted more rows into the pubs tables used in these queries to execute this test. If you try the same on standard tiny pubs tables, you will probably see no index use in query plans.

Functions and Expressions That Suppress Indexes

When you apply built-in functions or expressions to indexed columns, the optimizer cannot use indexes. Try to rewrite these conditions in such a way that index keys are not involved in any expression.

The problem in the following example is very similar to the additional WHERE clause conditions problem. Again, you know that if A=B then A-B=0, but SQL Server doesn't. You have to help it and remove any expressions around numeric columns that form an index. The following queries select a row from the table jobs by a unique key that has a unique clustered index. If you apply an expression to the column, the index is suppressed. But once you change the condition job_id - 2 = 0 to job_id = 2, the optimizer uses the clustered index.

Query With Suppressed Index	Optimized Query Using Index
SELECT * FROM jobs **WHERE job_id - 2 = 0**	SELECT * FROM jobs **WHERE job_id = 2**
STEP 1 The type of query is SELECT FROM TABLE jobs Nested iteration **Table Scan**	STEP 1 The type of query is SELECT FROM TABLE jobs Nested iteration **Using Clustered Index**

The following table contains more examples of queries that suppress an index on columns of different types and shows how you can rewrite them for optimal performance.

Query With Suppressed Index	Optimized Query Using Index
DECLARE @job_id VARCHAR(5) SELECT @job_id = '2' SELECT * FROM jobs **WHERE CONVERT(VARCHAR(5), job_id) = @job_id**	DECLARE @job_id VARCHAR(5) SELECT @job_id = '2' SELECT * FROM jobs **WHERE job_id = CONVERT(SMALLINT, @job_id)**
SELECT * FROM authors **WHERE au_fname + ' ' + au_lname = 'Johnson White'**	SELECT * FROM authors **WHERE au_fname = 'Johnson' AND au_lname = 'White'**
SELECT * FROM authors **WHERE SUBSTRING(au_lname, 1, 2) = 'Wh'**	SELECT * FROM authors **WHERE au_lname LIKE 'Wh%'**
CREATE INDEX employee_hire_date ON employee (hire_date) GO -- Get all employees hired -- in the 1st quarter of 1990: SELECT * FROM employee **WHERE DATEPART(year, hire_date) = 1990 AND DATEPART(quarter, hire_date) = 1**	CREATE INDEX employee_hire_date ON employee (hire_date) GO -- Get all employees hired -- in the 1st quarter of 1990: SELECT * FROM employee **WHERE hire_date >= '1/1/1990' AND hire_date < '4/1/1990'**
-- Suppose that hire_date may -- contain time other than 12AM -- Who was hired on 2/21/1990? SELECT * FROM employee **WHERE CONVERT(CHAR(10), hire_date, 101) = '2/21/1990'**	-- Suppose that hire_date may -- contain time other than 12AM -- Who was hired on 2/21/1990? SELECT * FROM employee **WHERE hire_date >= '2/21/1990' AND hire_date < '2/22/1990'**

SELECT INTO Versus INSERT . . . SELECT

Avoid using SELECT INTO unless it takes a few seconds or unless you are the only user in the database in which SELECT INTO creates a new table. It locks system tables in the database in which you create a new table for as long as it takes to execute. It may block all other users trying to create objects in the same database. It is especially critical on temporary tables, because users of all databases share the same tempdb. Your SELECT INTO that takes a long time blocks the users of all databases from creating temporary objects.

The benefit of SELECT INTO is that it is not logged. It allows you to populate a bigger table in one shot compared to using CREATE TABLE followed by an INSERT . . . SELECT statement. However, contrary to popular belief, SELECT INTO is not a better performer than a logged INSERT. Most of the time it is even slower.

One area in which SELECT INTO is a time saver is in creating empty tables with the same structure as an existing table. For example:

```
SELECT * INTO #authors FROM authors WHERE 1=0
```

This statement makes a quick copy of the authors table structure to a temporary table. Condition WHERE 1=0 is always false, which guarantees that no records are entered into the #authors table. The query has an almost instant response time, so it does not block other users. It saves you time, because you don't have to enter a CREATE TABLE statement with numerous column descriptions. But it does not improve the performance of the code.

Direct Versus Deferred UPDATE

SQL Server uses two main update methods for INSERT, UPDATE, DELETE, and SELECT INTO operations: *direct* update and *deferred* update. Sybase has also introduced deferred_varcol and deferred_index methods in recent versions.

A direct update changes data in place and is more efficient than a deferred update. Sybase further classifies direct updates as updates *in place*, *cheap direct* updates, and *expensive direct* updates.

A deferred update is the most expensive method of modifying a table. SQL Server executes a deferred update in several steps. First it deletes the updated rows, and then it reinserts them. Both operations are logged.

There is no special Transact-SQL syntax to force a direct or a deferred update, but there are rules that govern which method is chosen. Knowing these rules may let you optimize your UPDATE statements by helping SQL Server choose the direct update method.

Beware that rules change from one version to another and are now different between Microsoft and Sybase.

An update in place (or direct update) on Microsoft SQL Server is possible when all of the following conditions are met:

- The table does not contain a trigger for UPDATE.
- The table is not used for replication.
- Only one table is used in the UPDATE statement.
- Columns comprising the clustered index are not updated.
- Updated columns are fixed-length. If some are variable-length, then the total length of the updated row should be precisely the same as before the UPDATE.
- The updated row differs from the old row by no more than 50% of all bytes in all columns.

- If several columns are updated, they should be in contiguous blocks with no more than two gaps between contiguous blocks. Noncontiguous blocks within eight bytes are considered contiguous for this test. Remember that the physical order of columns in the table may be different from the order in which you listed them in the CREATE TABLE statement; SQL Server shifts all variable-length and nullable columns to the end of the row.
- When a single row is updated, there should be a unique index covering the WHERE clause conditions used in the UPDATE statement. SQL Server must know in advance that you are updating only one row.

Update in place (or direct update) that affects multiple rows is possible under these conditions:

- Only fixed-length non-nullable columns are updated.
- Columns comprising the clustered index are not updated.
- If a nonclustered index is used to perform the UPDATE, then the updated column may not be a part of this index key.

We don't encourage you to count bytes figuring out how many contiguous blocks of columns you are updating or whether changing one more byte would exceed the 50% limit for direct updates. But if you follow several guidelines, you may improve your application performance without spending too much time on fine-tuning:

- Use fixed-length nonnullable columns, as long as doing so doesn't result in wasted space and doesn't violate your business rules.
- Place columns that are updated at the same time close to one another in the table structure. This increases your chances of satisfying the rule for contiguous blocks of columns.
- Try to create a unique index to cover WHERE clause conditions used for single-row updates.

UPDATE . . . FROM and DELETE . . . FROM

Transact-SQL offers an extension to ANSI-SQL syntax for UPDATE and DELETE commands that may be very efficient in many cases. It allows you to specify a FROM clause and join several tables in an UPDATE or DELETE command.

In order to update the titleauthor table, the following ANSI SQL solution executes two subqueries. The UPDATE . . . FROM command in the right column replaces it with a join.

ANSI SQL (Supported by Transact-SQL)	Transact-SQL

<pre>UPDATE titleauthor
SET   royaltyper = 90
WHERE   au_id = (
 	
  SELECT au_id
  FROM   authors
  WHERE   au_lname = 'Ringer'
      AND au_fname = 'Albert')
 	
    AND title_id = (
 	
  SELECT title_id
  FROM   titles
  WHERE   title =
              'Life Without Fear')</pre>
	<pre>UPDATE titleauthor
	SET royaltyper = 90
	FROM authors a, titles t
	WHERE titleauthor.au_id =
	                  a.au_id
	    AND a.au_lname = 'Ringer'
	    AND a.au_fname = 'Albert'
	    AND titleauthor.title_id =
	                  t.title_id
	    AND t.title =
	            'Life Without Fear'</pre>

<pre>STEP 1
The type of query is SELECT
Scalar Aggregate
FROM TABLE
authors
Nested iteration
Index : aunmind
STEP 2
The type of query is SELECT
Scalar Aggregate
FROM TABLE
titles
Nested iteration
Index : titleind
STEP 3
The type of query is UPDATE
The update mode is direct
FROM TABLE
titleauthor
Nested iteration
Using Clustered Index
TO TABLE
Titleauthor</pre>
	<pre>STEP 1
	The type of query is UPDATE
	The update mode is deferred
	FROM TABLE
	authors a
	Nested iteration
	Index : aunmind
	FROM TABLE
	titleauthor
	Nested iteration
	Table Scan
	FROM TABLE
	titles t
	Nested iteration
	Using Clustered Index
	TO TABLE
	titleauthor</pre>

In the next example, we update a row in the titles table that has a specific order recorded in the sales table. Note that the ANSI SQL solution has to execute essentially the same subquery twice, because the column title_id is needed for the WHERE clause, and the column qty is used in the SET clause.

ANSI SQL (Supported by Transact-SQL)	Transact-SQL

<pre>UPDATE titles
SET   ytd_sales = ytd_sales + (
    SELECT qty
    FROM   sales s
    WHERE   s.stor_id = '9999'
        AND s.ord_num = '999999')
WHERE   title_id = (
    SELECT title_id
    FROM   sales s
    WHERE   s.stor_id = '9999'
        AND s.ord_num = '999999')</pre>
	<pre>UPDATE titles
	SET ytd_sales = ytd_sales +
	                    s.qty
	FROM sales s
	WHERE titles.title_id =
	              s.title_id
	    AND s.stor_id = '9999'
	    AND s.ord_num = '999999'</pre>

ANSI SQL (Supported by Transact-SQL)	Transact-SQL
STEP 1 The type of query is SELECT Scalar Aggregate FROM TABLE sales s Nested iteration Using Clustered Index STEP 2 The type of query is SELECT Scalar Aggregate FROM TABLE sales s Nested iteration Using Clustered Index STEP 3 The type of query is UPDATE The update mode is direct FROM TABLE titles Nested iteration Using Clustered Index TO TABLE titles	STEP 1 The type of query is UPDATE The update mode is deferred FROM TABLE sales s Nested iteration Using Clustered Index FROM TABLE titles Nested iteration Using Clustered Index TO TABLE titles

The following queries demonstrate that you can apply the same technique to DELETE commands.

ANSI SQL (Supported by Transact-SQL)	Transact-SQL

DELETE sales
WHERE   EXISTS (
    SELECT 1
    FROM   titles t
    WHERE   sales.title_id =
                t.title_id
    AND   t.title =
              'Life Without Fear')
	DELETE sales
	FROM titles t
	WHERE sales.title_id =
	            t.title_id
	    AND t.title =
	            'Life Without Fear'

SET NOCOUNT ON

You have already noticed that successful queries return a system message specifying the number of rows they affect. In many cases, you don't need this information. The SET NOCOUNT ON command allows you to suppress the message for all subsequent transactions in your session, until you issue the SET NOCOUNT OFF command. We know that this is a double-negative, but Transact-SQL is not always elegant.

This option has more than a cosmetic effect on the output generated by your script. It reduces the amount of information passed from the server to the client. Therefore, it helps to lower network traffic and improves the overall response time of your transactions. The time to pass a single message may be negligible, but think about a script that executes some queries in a loop and sends kilobytes of useless information to a user.

Consider adding SET NOCOUNT ON at the beginning of every stored procedure and script that doesn't require row counts in the output.

SET ROWCOUNT

SET ROWCOUNT limits the number of rows affected by all subsequent queries. This command is very efficient in numerous programming tasks. The syntax on Microsoft and Sybase has diverged since Microsoft SQL Server 6.5 added a very useful option of using variables with SET ROWCOUNT, as shown here:

Microsoft	Sybase
`SET ROWCOUNT { numeric_constant |` `    @variable }`	`SET ROWCOUNT numeric_constant`

SET ROWCOUNT sets the maximum number of rows that may be affected by a SELECT, INSERT, UPDATE, or DELETE query. The setting is immediately effective upon execution of the command and impacts only the current session. In order to remove this limit, execute SET ROWCOUNT 0.

Some practical tasks are much more efficient to program with SET ROWCOUNT than with standard SQL commands. Let us demonstrate it with several examples.

One of the most popular queries in almost any database is a request for the top n items from a list. In the case of the pubs database, we could search for the top five best-selling titles. Compare the two solutions: with SET ROWCOUNT and without.

Pure ANSI SQL	Transact-SQL Using SET ROWCOUNT

`SELECT  title, ytd_sales`
`FROM    titles a`
`WHERE   ( SELECT  COUNT(*)`
`          FROM    titles b`
`          WHERE   b.ytd_sales >`
`                  a.ytd_sales`
`        ) < 5`
`ORDER BY ytd_sales`
	`SET ROWCOUNT 5`
	
	`SELECT   title, ytd_sales`
	`FROM     titles`
	`ORDER BY ytd_sales`
	
	`SET ROWCOUNT 0`

The pure ANSI SQL solution executes a correlated subquery that may be inefficient, especially in the case in which there is no index on ytd_sales to support it. The second solution uses SET ROWCOUNT to stop the SELECT query after it has found the first five rows. In this case, we also have an ORDER BY clause that forces sorting of the whole table before results may be retrieved. On a large table, we would create an index on ytd_sales to avoid sorting. The query would then use the index to find the first five rows and stop. Compare this to the first solution, which would scan the whole table and execute a correlated subquery for every row. The difference in performance is negligible on a small table. But on a large table, it may amount to hours of processing time for the first solution versus seconds for the second one.

Parameters Versus Variables

Values assigned to local variables inside a script or stored procedure may be very important for the optimizer. Depending on the value of a variable at execution time, it may choose a different query plan. But it doesn't know the value of a local variable in advance and has to make some assumptions about this value during the parse and compilation phase. If these assumptions prove wrong, you end up with an inefficient query.

The optimizer assumes a 25% hit accuracy for variables and parameters.

If local variables are important in your script, consider creating a stored procedure and passing their values to the procedure as parameters. Since the optimizer knows the parameters before it compiles a stored procedure, it makes the right choice based on runtime values. The following example demonstrates the technique:

Local Variables Solution	Parameters Solution

`DECLARE @title_id VARCHAR(11)`
`SELECT  @title_id = '%'`
`SELECT  *`
`FROM    titleauthor`
`WHERE   title_id LIKE @title_id`
	`CREATE PROC get_titleauthor`
	`    @title_id VARCHAR(11)`
	`AS`
	`SELECT  *`
	`FROM    titleauthor`
	`WHERE   title_id LIKE @title_id`
	`GO`
	
	`DECLARE @title_id VARCHAR(11)`
	`SELECT  @title_id = '%'`
	`EXECUTE get_titleauthor @title_id`
	`        WITH RECOMPILE`

`STEP 1`
`The type of query is SELECT`
`FROM TABLE`
`Titleauthor`
`Nested iteration`
`Index : titleidind`
	`STEP 1`
	`The type of query is SELECT`
	`FROM TABLE`
	`titleauthor`
	`Nested iteration`
	`Table Scan`

In this case, a table scan is more efficient than an index scan, because the value of @title_id is %, which causes retrieval of all rows. Reading every row of the table is inevitable, and using the table scan takes fewer I/O operations than using the non-clustered index titleind. In the first query, the optimizer makes an assumption that you are assigning a value to @title_id that limits the search to several rows. It does not analyze the actual value used in the code. In this example, the assumption is wrong, and we end up with an inefficient plan. Once we convert the query into a stored procedure and pass it a parameter, as shown in the right column of the table, the optimizer realizes that a table scan is the best technique and uses it.

We have specified WITH RECOMPILE in the optimized script. This option guarantees that the optimizer will be able to make the decision about whether to use the index based on the value of @title_id passed at each execution.

Assumptions About Temporary Table Size

A similar problem to the one described in the previous section exists with temporary tables created at runtime. The optimizer is unable to estimate the size of a temporary table unless it exists prior to compile time. The optimizer always assumes that a temporary table has only 100 rows and uses 10 data pages. Obviously, this may be wrong in many cases. The optimizer also refuses to recognize indexes that you dynamically build on temporary tables.

In order to allow the optimizer to take the actual table size into account, you can use a technique similar to the one described in the previous section. Split your code into a separate stored procedure. The optimizer will know the size of the temporary table and whether any good indexes exist before the procedure is executed and will choose the best plan based on the accurate information. For example:

Table Created in the Same Script

```
CREATE TABLE #pub (
    pub_name VARCHAR(40) NOT NULL,
    title    VARCHAR(80) NULL,
    employee VARCHAR(51) NULL
)
GO

INSERT   #pub
SELECT   p.pub_name,
         t.title,
         e.fname + ' ' + e.lname
FROM     publishers p,
         titles     t,
         employee   e
WHERE    p.pub_id *= t.pub_id
    AND p.pub_id *= e.pub_id

CREATE CLUSTERED INDEX pubind
ON #pub ( pub_name )
WITH ALLOW_DUP_ROW

SELECT   *
FROM     #pub
WHERE    pub_name =
             'New Moon Books'
GO
DROP TABLE #pub
GO
```

Table Passed to a Stored Procedure

```
CREATE TABLE #pub (
    pub_name VARCHAR(40) NOT NULL,
    title    VARCHAR(80) NULL,
    employee VARCHAR(51) NULL
)
GO
CREATE PROC get_pub
AS
SELECT   *
FROM     #pub
WHERE    pub_name =
             'New Moon Books'
GO
INSERT   #pub
SELECT   p.pub_name,
         t.title,
         e.fname + ' ' + e.lname
FROM     publishers p,
         titles     t,
         employee   e
WHERE    p.pub_id *= t.pub_id
    AND p.pub_id *= e.pub_id

CREATE CLUSTERED INDEX pubind
ON #pub ( pub_name )
WITH ALLOW_DUP_ROW

EXEC get_pub WITH RECOMPILE
GO
DROP TABLE #pub
GO
DROP PROC get_pub
GO
```

<table>
<tr><th>Table Created in the Same Script</th><th>Table Passed to a Stored Procedure</th></tr>
<tr><td><pre>
-- plan of the highlighted SELECT:
STEP 1
The type of query is SELECT
FROM TABLE
#pub
Nested iteration
Table Scan
</pre></td><td><pre>
-- plan of the highlighted SELECT:
STEP 1
The type of query is SELECT
FROM TABLE
#pub
Nested iteration
Using Clustered Index
</pre></td></tr>
</table>

Loop Optimization

This section describes techniques you can use to optimize loop processing in your programs.

Move invariant operations outside of the loop

If you are familiar with other programming languages, then you are probably aware of loop-optimization techniques. You should try to put all operations outside the loop if they don't change inside. This reduces the amount of unnecessary repetitive work. The SQL Server optimizer doesn't automatically recognize such inefficiencies and clean the code for you (compilers of some other languages do). You have to write efficient loops yourself, as in the following example.

These scripts print a table of square roots for all numbers from 1 to 100:

<table>
<tr><th>Inefficient Loop Operations</th><th>Optimized Script</th></tr>
<tr><td><pre>
SET NOCOUNT ON
DECLARE @message VARCHAR(25),
        @counter SMALLINT
SELECT @counter = 0
WHILE @counter < 100
BEGIN
    SELECT @counter = @counter + 1
    SELECT @message =
            REPLICATE('-', 25)
    PRINT @message
    SELECT @message =
       str(@counter, 10) +
       str(SQRT(CONVERT(FLOAT,
            @counter)), 10, 4)
    PRINT @message
END
</pre></td><td><pre>
SET NOCOUNT ON
DECLARE @separator VARCHAR(25),
        @message   VARCHAR(25),
        @counter   SMALLINT
SELECT @counter = 0,
        @separator =
            REPLICATE('-', 25)
WHILE @counter < 100
BEGIN
    SELECT @counter = @counter + 1
    PRINT @separator
    SELECT @message =
       Str(@counter, 10) +
       Str(SQRT(CONVERT(FLOAT,
            @counter)), 10, 4)
    PRINT @message
END
</pre></td></tr>
</table>

The second script executes the function REPLICATE('-', 25) only once, compared to 100 times in the first script. Results produced by both scripts are identical:

```
-------------------------
         1    1.0000
-------------------------
         2    1.4142
-------------------------
         3    1.7321
-------------------------
```

```
            4    2.0000
                   . . .
-------------------------
           99    9.9499
-------------------------
          100   10.0000
```

Replace loops with queries

It may often be possible to replace loops with SQL queries. A single query is almost always more efficient than multiple iterations. For instance, we could rewrite the loop shown in the previous example as follows:

```
SELECT  REPLICATE( '-', 25 ) + '
' + str( ( a.id - 1 ) * 10 + b.id, 10 )
  + str( SQRT( CONVERT( FLOAT, ( a.id - 1 ) * 10 + b.id ) ), 10, 4 )
FROM    sysobjects a, sysobjects b
WHERE   a.id <= 10
    AND b.id <= 10
```

This script uses the fact that there are rows in the system table sysobjects with id column values of 1 through 10. If we join this table to itself and apply filters on column id values to take 10 rows from one instance of sysobjects and 10 rows from the second instance, then we get 100 rows (10 times 10). In order to produce numbers 1 through 100, we use expression (a.id-1)*10+b.id. The code may look tricky, but it returns the same results much faster than a loop.

Characteristic Functions

Characteristic functions are a special technique of coding Transact-SQL expressions that reduces the number of passes on tables. The technique was discussed in a series of articles and, later, in the book *Optimizing Transact-SQL: Advanced Programming Techniques** by D. Rozenstein, A. Abramovich, and E. Birger. We must mention that some of the Transact-SQL expressions that use the same technique appeared in messages posted on Usenet newsgroups by other people in 1991 through 1993. Nevertheless, Mr. Rozenstein and his coauthors deserve full credit for developing a set of rules, creating generic solutions for several common business tasks, and deriving many practical applications, as well as popularizing the approach.†

A typical characteristic function embeds IF . . . ELSE logic into an expression. Some computer languages provide a built-in function called "immediate IF" which serves the same task. For example, Oracle has a somewhat similar function called DECODE. FoxPro, Clipper, and dBase offer the IIF function. Transact-SQL didn't have such a function until the introduction of CASE.

* SQL Forum Press, ISBN 0-9649812-0-3

† They also hold the trademark on the term "characteristic functions."

CASE expressions, described in Chapter 13, *CASE Expressions and Transact-SQL Extensions*, have effectively eliminated the need for characteristic functions. But the approach has been used by many programmers to achieve superb query performance, and chances are that you will encounter these functions in some older code. Characteristic functions are still a reasonable performance-optimization technique if you have Microsoft SQL Server prior to Version 6.0 or any Sybase version prior to 11.5.

If your version of SQL Server supports CASE expressions, forget about characteristic functions and use CASE. With older versions of Transact-SQL, carefully consider if the performance gains of applying characteristic functions in each case justify the nightmare of explaining this code to someone.

Let's start with a simple example that shows what characteristic functions can do and why they are more efficient than CASE expressions. Suppose that we need to produce a report that contains every book title and a column called bestseller that contains 1 if year-to-date sales are 10,000 or more and 0 otherwise. We have implemented this task using "traditional" SQL and with a characteristic function:

Traditional SQL	Characteristic Function Solution

`SELECT title, bestseller = 1`
`FROM titles`
`WHERE ytd_sales >= 10000`
`UNION ALL`
`SELECT title, bestseller = 0`
`FROM titles`
`WHERE ytd_sales < 10000`
	`SELECT title,`
	`bestseller = sign( sign(`
	`ytd_sales - 10000 ) + 1 )`
	`FROM titles`

The expression used to calculate the bestseller column is an example of a characteristic function:

```
sign( sign( ytd_sales - 10000 ) + 1 )
```

This statement deserves a more detailed explanation. The following table explains it step-by-step:

ytd_sales	ytd_sales - 10000	sign(ytd_sales - 10000)	sign(ytd_sales - 10000) + 1	sign(sign(ytd_sales - 10000) + 1)
> 10000	> 0	1	2	1
= 10000	0	0	1	1
< 10000	< 0	-1	0	0

Therefore, the whole expression returns either 1 or 0, depending on whether ytd_sales have reached the point of 10,000.

Performance of our second query is substantially better than the "traditional SQL" one. In this case, we had to use UNION ALL to combine two parts of the report. The traditional query had to scan the titles table twice. Now, imagine if this table contained millions of rows. The whole table wouldn't fit into the data cache, and both table scans would have to read the whole table from disk. Performance of the characteristic function solution would be twice as good.

Note that SQL Server takes very little time to compute expressions like the preceding one. All computations occur in the server's memory and require no disk access. Performance of the query is primarily determined by the number of physical and logical disk reads.

The big downside of characteristic functions is that they are difficult to code and support. It is absolutely critical to include comments in your code explaining the purpose of every characteristic expression. The preceding example is one of the simplest things you can do with characteristic functions. More complicated expressions may be virtually impossible to decrypt by anyone but the original programmer.

Table 20-12 shows characteristic expressions for all Boolean functions on one or two numeric operands.

Table 20-12. Characteristic Functions on Numeric Operands

Boolean Expression	Characteristic Function Returning 1 IF the Boolean Expression IS TRUE and 0 IF FALSE	Equivalent Alternative Characteristic Function
a = b	1 - ABS(SIGN(a - b))	1 - SIGN(ABS(a - b))
a != b	ABS(SIGN(a - b))	SIGN(ABS(a - b))
a < b	1 - SIGN(SIGN(a - b) + 1)	1 - SIGN(1 - SIGN(b - a))
a <= b	SIGN(1 - SIGN(a - b))	SIGN(SIGN(b - a) + 1)
a > b	1 - SIGN(1 - SIGN(a - b))	1 - SIGN(SIGN(b - a) + 1)
a >= b	SIGN(SIGN(a - b) + 1)	SIGN(1 - SIGN(b - a))
a IS NULL	ISNULL(a * 0, 1)	--
a IS NOT NULL	1 - ISNULL(a * 0, 1)	--

Encoding of conditions on CHAR and VARCHAR types is different. Particular characteristic functions may depend on the length of operands. For example, to compare two strings, a and b, of the same length with no trailing spaces, you can use the CHARINDEX function. CHARINDEX(a, b) returns 1 if strings are the same, and 0 otherwise. Null values and the presence of trailing spaces require additional coding efforts. For example, to compare strings that may be of different lengths and ignore trailing spaces, you would have to use the following expression:

```
CHARINDEX( '~' + RTRIM( a ) + '~', '~' + RTRIM( b ) + '~' )
```

We have used the tilde character (~) to delimit strings in case their length is different and string a occurs partially in string b (e.g., a='DEF' and b='ABCDEF'). The addition of delimiters guarantees that strings are compared precisely. Use of the delimiter assumes that the delimiter character itself is not used in any of the two compared strings and that the length of neither string exceeds 253 characters.

DATETIME and SMALLDATETIME values may be compared with the DATEDIFF function as shown in Table 20-13.

Table 20-13. Characteristic Functions on DATETIME Operands

Boolean Expression	Characteristic Function
a = b, where a and b are not further than 24 days apart	`ABS( SIGN( DATEDIFF( millisecond, a, b ) ) )`
a = b, for any values a and b, comparing only the date portion	`ABS( SIGN( DATEDIFF( day, a, b ) ) )`
a = b, for any values of a and b	`CHARINDEX( CONVERT( CHAR(26), a, 109 ), CONVERT( CHAR(26), b, 109 ) )`
a != b	1 - `CharacteristicFunction`(a=b) *one of the three expressions above, depending on the values of a and b*

Characteristic functions also exist for >, >=, <, and <= comparison of DATETIME values, but they are rather complicated. As we mentioned, with the introduction of CASE expressions, these characteristic functions have a purely theoretical interest.

Operations on Boolean conditions may be encoded using the following formulas on corresponding characteristic functions:

Logical Expression	Characteristic Function Expression
NOT Condition1	1 - `CharacteristicFunction`1
Condition1 AND Condition2	`CharacteristicFunction`1 * `CharacteristicFunction`2
Condition1 OR Condition2	SIGN(`CharacteristicFunction`1 + `CharacteristicFunction`2)
Any one of two conditions (Condition1 and Condition2) is TRUE and another is FALSE	1 - ABS(SIGN (`CharacteristicFunction`1 + `CharacteristicFunction`2 - 1))
Both conditions (Condition1 and Condition2) are TRUE or both are FALSE	ABS(SIGN(`CharacteristicFunction`1 + `CharacteristicFunction`2 - 1))

Empowered with all these expressions, we can code virtually any logical condition in a Transact-SQL query.

The whole characteristic functions approach consists of two parts. One is the idea of embedding conditional logic in queries in order to minimize the number of passes through tables, eliminate subqueries, or reduce the number of tables in joins. This technique is extremely valuable, and we strongly encourage you to take advantage of it whenever possible. You should, however, use CASE expressions to program any logical conditions and not any of the preceding tricky functions.

The second part of the technique involves encoding conditional expressions with built-in functions such as SIGN, ABS, and CHARINDEX. This technique was a smart workaround that bypassed a Transact-SQL deficiency on older SQL Server versions. However, with the introduction of CASE expressions in Microsoft SQL Server 6.0 and Sybase Adaptive Server 11.5, the technique became obsolete. CASE provides performance at least as good as characteristic functions and is incredibly easier to code and support. If you have to resort to characteristic functions because you are using an old version of SQL Server, try to limit their use to cases in which performance gains are significant.

For additional information on CASE, refer to Chapter 13, where we programmed a table-pivoting query that demonstrated how to use CASE to program conditional logic.

Summary

This chapter discussed various Transact-SQL optimization and tuning techniques and approaches. SQL Server performance is a composite of many factors. Transact-SQL programming is only one of them, but a very important one. These are the main topics:

- The most important optimization criteria are response time, throughput, and concurrency. A number of factors contribute to SQL Server performance level: hardware, operating system, network, frontend and middleware applications, and, finally, database design and Transact-SQL code.
- Efficient database design is crucial to your programming efforts. It may be very difficult, if not impossible, to write efficient queries in a poorly designed database. The database model should be chosen based on applications using the database. OLTP applications benefit from high normalization and little redundancy. DSS applications, on the other hand, may require that you denormalize your schema for performance. It may be necessary to perform database or table partitioning in order to resolve performance bottlenecks. Efficient datatypes optimize data storage and reduce I/O activity required to access the same data.
- Indexes are a key factor in query optimization. Additional indexes slow down update transactions but benefit certain queries. The optimization of indexes is

often a trade-off in which you choose which queries to optimize and which ones to slow down as a result.

- SQL Server uses a cost-based query optimizer that evaluates different possible query-execution plans and chooses the one that promises to be the least expensive in terms of physical and logical I/O resources. It decides on the join order, which indexes to use on each table, and when to create worktables or convert queries to other forms.
- The SET SHOWPLAN command allows you to review the query plan generated by the optimizer. It is very helpful in query analysis. In our discussion we review the messages that you may encounter in a query plan and explain how to interpret them.
- SQL Server provides a number of ways to override the optimizer when you want to force your own query plan. You can control join order, index selection, and lock strategy with optimizer hints. These are special language elements that instruct SQL Server on how to build a particular query plan.
- We discussed query analysis and how to isolate Transact-SQL bottlenecks. A number of Transact-SQL commands may be used to obtain query performance statistics.
- We covered a number of optimization techniques, tricks, and tips, and we used numerous examples to demonstrate efficient language elements and programming approaches.

21

In this chapter:
- *Testing Versus Debugging*
- *Successful Debugging*
- *Specific Debugging Techniques*
- *The SET Command*
- *Debugging Utilities*
- *Summary*

Debugging Transact-SQL Programs

This chapter describes how to debug Transact-SQL programs. Don't confuse debugging with *testing*. In fact, there is an entire genre of computer books devoted to the subject of software testing and quality assurance. We won't be covering much of that here. Instead, this chapter focuses on the procedures and means of investigating and fixing errors in programming. This chapter will also suggest some specific tools that are available to debug a Transact-SQL program.

Testing Versus Debugging

Writing a Transact-SQL program usually follows a simple chronology. A program must be defined, written, and tested. Testing should reveal if there are any bugs in the program. If there are, the program must be debugged and retested until it is free of bugs.

Testing and debugging should usually be kept as distinct as possible. In fact, the author of a program is probably the last person you want to test that program. For some reason, the author unconsciously makes allowances for the weaknesses of a program, enabling it to pass tests that a different tester would catch. Of course, you don't have any choice on a one-person assignment, but in a team environment, the tester and author should be different individuals.

Testing has three objectives or steps:

1. Ensure that the Transact-SQL program works as it should. For example, a report program should produce the correct results, a data entry screen should return a result set in a timely manner, and a monthly closedown process should tabulate the summary records correctly. This step should usually be done by the author of the program. The program should then be handed off to a tester for Steps 2 and 3.

2. Verify that the Transact-SQL program does not fail when subjected to unusual, but foreseeable, circumstances. So-called "break testing" should check for things like the following: the program doesn't keel over when an unusually large or small number is passed as a parameter, the process becomes deadlocked, or an alphanumeric value is passed to a numeric parameter.
3. Confirm that the program plays well with other programs. It is essential that your Transact-SQL program doesn't perform operations that conflict with other Transact-SQL programs, including stored procedures, triggers, and batch routines.

If you have the resources, it's advisable to have the program author perform only the usual "unit tests" to ensure that the program meets its stated requirements. If a test plan does not exist, the programmer should write one for the program to meet each of the three main objectives of testing. The program and test plan should then go to a tester, who subjects the program to a rigorous set of drills. Each step of the test plan could reveal a bug. The tester should document the results of each step in the test plan, including both successes and failures. The failures are finally compiled into a bug report that is returned to the original programmer. The programmer must now root out the cause of each documented bug and repair it without breaking anything else. After the programmer has made the necessary changes, the program should go through the testing cycle *again* to make sure that the bug fixes haven't introduced any new problems. (Sadly, that happens a lot.)

Debugging is often one of the most difficult parts of writing a program. That's because debugging requires healthy doses of both good programming skills and a good business understanding of the requirements of the program. Debugging gets even harder when the debugger is not the original programmer. For this reason, many of the recommendations we make throughout this book are designed to ease the arduous task of debugging. For example, programs that don't have any documentation or that inconsistently use whitespace are much harder to debug than programs that are uniformly implemented.

Successful Debugging

Debugging is one of those nebulous areas of human endeavor that is more art than science. This section does not hope to present every tip or technique for successful debugging. Instead, we'll discuss several of the most salient techniques to employ when repairing a program in a rational and methodical approach. The good news about these tips and strategies is that they can be applied to any programming language, not just Transact-SQL. Specific techniques for analyzing and fixing Transact-SQL problems are discussed later in this chapter.

The best way to approach debugging is to use a logical, methodical routine. Perform the same steps with every debugging task, even in those situations in which you have a good idea what the problem is before you begin. The application of a rational and logical debugging plan will yield good results, no matter what programming language you use. The following sections can help you define a debugging template.

Collect Information About the Problem

Although collecting information about errors in a Transact-SQL program seems like the first logical thing to do, it's certainly not the first thing many programmers do. Instead, they squander untold amounts of time by immediately jumping back into their program, reviewing their code, line by line, before they have all the facts. When you're gathering information about an error or failure, here are a few things to do:

- *Record the error number and message, if available.* Believe it or not, there are some developers who, when encountering a problem, do not record this information. Recording the error number and message is useful both for general errors returned by SQL Server and for specific application errors coded by the developer. With error number and description in hand, you can then turn to other resources, such as the SQL Server Books On-Line or Sybooks, hardcopy documentation, or the vendor support web site to find out more information about the specific error.
- *Reproduce the error.* Getting a problem to occur predictably is a significant step in determining the cause of the problem. This can also provide you with useful information about those situations that do *not* cause the problem to occur. For example, if you cannot reproduce the error on your workstation, but you can on another tester's workstation, the problem could be directly related to the software installed only on that person's machine.
- *Narrow the test case.* Sometimes problems occur in applications with many unknowns: stored procedures with lots of parameters, client applications with multiple server connections, or database administration tasks with many routines, to name just a few examples. When debugging any code with multiple components, you'll get better results by narrowing down the test case into smaller functional segments. For example, we were recently developing a data migration routine. The program would fail without loading any records. If we had stopped testing at this point, we would have had to analyze all of the code that initiated the bulk data load. Instead, we reduced the size and variety of the test data and were able to determine that the data load failed only after it encountered a record whose dates were in an unusual format. We were able to narrow the test case down to a specific problem that could be easily corrected.

- *Document situations in which the program does not fail.* A program's successes can sometimes be as revealing as its failures. A Transact-SQL program that fails only intermittently can be difficult to debug, unless you have detailed information about the environment in which the program succeeded. These details can help you narrow down the troublesome section of code and/or the conditions that cause a failure. For example, if a batch routine seems to work well every time it is run off-schedule, you should examine the batch environment for its regularly scheduled runs. Perhaps another application is scheduled to run at the same time and is generating blocks that are interfering with your program.

Even if you think you know the cause of a bug, you should be sure to record some minimal information. The more you know when you tackle the problem, the easier it'll be to solve the problem.

Don't forget to record a little information about the bug fix in the program itself! This will help future programmers maintain the Transact-SQL program and avoid the same mistake themselves.

Analyze Before Repeating

One of the most important aspects of programming to understand is the set of business rules behind the application. Often, if you cannot properly summarize the purpose of a program, you will not be able to properly code it. Similarly, if you cannot properly summarize the effect of a bug, you will not be able to fix it. That's why you spend time collecting information about the problem. With adequate information and analysis, you'll be able to summarize the problem as "Inactive clients are not reactivated when they initiate new sales," "Inventory is not decremented on an advanced sale initiated on the web site," or whatever.

Once you've sorted through the pages of printer output trying to get an understanding of the bug, you might be inclined to say, "Hmmm, looks like a simple fix. I'll make these few changes, recompile, and retry." Although this is an extremely common practice, it's not the best way to debug—for a couple of reasons. First, you don't *really* know what's causing the error. When you fully understand an error, you usually know exactly what changes are needed to fix it. If you're unsure about the error, then you're just taking a potshot by examining the impact of a change. Second, even if the change repairs the error, you can be certain only that the change has stopped the bug from occurring under the same (or similar) circumstances. Since you don't truly know the root of the bug, you cannot be certain that all occurrences of the bug are fixed.

Conversely, by gaining a complete understanding of the bug through analysis, you can take the steps needed to fix the bug under all conditions. You can aid this process by performing a mental walk-through of the code based on the change, without actually executing the program. (Who ever said programmers lack imagination?) Sample several scenarios of the program to test the hypothetical fix. After you're satisfied that the change addresses every aspect of the problem, then perform a full test of the solution. You're no longer making changes and reiterating a test; now you are verifying a fix.

Assumptions = Ouch!

When you have to troubleshoot an application, successful and effective analysis is aided by verifying every assumption of your program. And, in general, your program will be rife with assumptions. When you prepare to implement a fix, make sure your assumptions are valid.

For instance, one of the most frequent assumptions in testing a program is that the inputs are valid. This can also be one of the most dangerous assumptions to make. These problems are most maddening because there might not be anything at all wrong with your program. Only the data driving the program is faulty.

If the bugs in a program defy explanation, it's time to verify the assumptions. Make a list of all the assumptions you make in the program—including the data driving the program—and test them. The bug fix may not even require a change to the program!

Back Up, Back Up, Back Up

Everybody faithfully backs up their personal workspace, right? Yeah, sure.

Only two months before starting this book, I lost weeks of data when my laptop hard drive crashed. You can imagine the ribbing I got from my coworkers. Here I was, responsible for the backup of nearly 100 SQL Server installations across the country (which were quite reliable, thank you very much) and my very own laptop goes boom. After eating a large slice of humble pie, I quickly set about automating a backup for my local workstation.

Laugh all you want, but this one gets everybody eventually. And if you're not prepared, it'll get you sooner. Take the following steps to facilitate backups:

- Archive the original Transact-SQL program version.
- Give new versions of the Transact-SQL program script a new name. (Remember, this is the script filename, not the name of the stored procedure.)

- Frequently save changes. If possible, keep one or more backup copies in another geographic location. (Keep a copy at home and one at work or possibly at another office site.) If your firm has the resources, use a version control system like PVCS or SourceSafe to provide even stronger source code control.

The idea is to have the original version of the program and each subsequent revision as a snapshot in time. Since most operating systems, and Windows NT specifically, support long filenames, there is no reason not to keep multiple versions of a Transact-SQL program on hand. That way, you won't have to waste time reversing any changes to a program. You can simply shift back to a preceding version of the program and continue from there.

With so many utilities available in current operating systems, it's almost inexcusable not to at least perform automated backups of your data directories. The wide availability of versioning and change management software can also reinforce protective measures for important applications and files.

Only One Change at a Time

I don't know how many programmers I've seen who encounter a bug within their program and, while debugging the program, decide to make a few "housekeeping" updates. They change a few variable datatypes, add a few lines of output, and alter an error message or two. Before they know it, they have no way to verify that the bug has been fixed; in addition, their changes may have introduced new bugs! In those cases in which they got lucky and apparently fixed the bug, they don't know which of the changes actually did the trick.

Now the whole debugging process is gummed up. The changes will have to be reversed until the programmer can get a clearer understanding of what's happening. (By this time, the spouse is calling to see if it's gonna be a Domino's night.) Unless you're making very simple changes, the extra time spent on multiple tests is worth the heightened productivity.

Fix the first problem you encounter. That's the motto of many Transact-SQL programmers. Because a Transact-SQL program is processed serially in order of the first command to the last, fixing a single error early in the program may clear up many error messages appearing later in the compile sequence. A common example of this concept is a datatype mismatch early in the program when variables are declared. Every time the variable is referenced from there on out will generate a compile error. Fixing the datatype mismatch at the very top of the program clears all subsequent error messages.

Hand in hand with making only one change at a time are the concepts of *unit tests* and *system tests*. Under unit testing, you test only a single unit of code at a time. (The unit could be an entire program or a module within a program.) Once all of the units are verified as working properly, the entire application can be tested as a whole in a system test. Individual program tests aren't needed during the system test because they were individually validated. Time can be devoted to the application that calls each program unit.

Seek Help

There's a Southern saying—"If it was a snake, it'd have bit me"—meaning that the thing you were looking for is right in front of you. This saying certainly holds true when you've been debugging for hours (or even days). The main thing you need at a time like this is a fresh pair of eyes. Those eyes could be your own, or they could be somebody else's. (Don't go imagining a scene from some kind of slasher movie!)

It's very common for programmers to get comfortable with a program that's taken up a lot of their time. It has now become an old friend (or enemy). At that point, they don't even read it any more. Consequently, they don't even see the bugs staring them in the face. Somehow, the programmer manages to internalize certain assumptions about the program that might not be true. The first thing to do in that case is (your boss is gonna love this) take a break. When you're buried layers deep in a program, it's difficult to maintain an objective and fresh perspective. When you lose your perspective, easily detected bugs slip by completely unnoticed. Here's an example of a common war story among programmers, "I beat my head against a wall for a whole day over this program! And then, in the shower the next day, BAM! It comes to me!" So, be sure to take a break. It'll help keep your mind clear.

In some cases, programmers go to the extent of working on several Transact-SQL programs at one time. When coding gets a little stale, they'll put that particular program aside for a day or two to work on a fresh program. When they're ready to return to the original program, they then read and scrutinize it as if it were somebody else's program. This gives them a fresh perspective and helps them to see other errors that might have slipped by. In fact, we know of someone who goes to the extent of pretending that they're another person before they start to review their own program, including changing their voice, accent, and mannerisms. (This might signal the onset of multiple personality disorder!) But, heck, it helps them debug the program. So more power to them!

If a trip to the water cooler doesn't provide any relief, you can always turn to another person for assistance. Often, the simple act of explaining the program and the bug will help you to find the solution yourself. When you explain the problem to another developer, you must reiterate the function and behavior of the program. Perhaps you lost track of a parameter and have a name mismatch; the logic to an IF statement may be flawed; or an important query may have a faulty WHERE clause. On the other hand, you might be able to get that one bit of information you need to find or fix a bug. Even if your coworker cannot help with the problem, you've still given him an implied compliment by showing you respect his opinion. It also shows that you're not embarrassed by mistakes. Asking for help actually does improve and encourage teamwork.

If you don't have ready access to other talented programmers, you still have avenues for seeking help. Both vendors (Microsoft and Sybase) have numerous online support venues. Table 21-1 discusses several available ways to get help.

Table 21-1. Support Sources

Way to Get Support	Description
comp.databases.mssql	An Internet newsgroup dedicated to Microsoft SQL Server.
comp.databases.sybase	An Internet newsgroup dedicated to Sybase Adaptive Server.
CompuServe MSSQL Forum	CompuServe's forum dedicated to several distinct discussions about Microsoft SQL Server.
http://www.microsoft.com/sql	Microsoft's web site devoted to SQL Server.
http//support.microsoft.com	Microsoft's method of access to its searchable online Knowledge Base.
http://www.sybase.com	Sybase provides a variety of electronic support services through their web site, including technical information libraries, online product manuals, FAQs, and infobases.
http://www.swynk.com	An independent web site with useful information about a number of Microsoft products, including SQL Server.
http://www.tiac.net/users/sqltech/	An independent web site full of handy tips for Sybase, including links, sample programs, and other information.

Get It Right the First Time

Obviously, the most effective way to debug an application is to write one with few bugs in it in the first place. This is tougher than it sounds since we're all under the gun to get the code out fast. It takes time and energy to be careful and methodical. On the other hand, the payoffs for high-quality code on the first go-around more than compensate. Writing a usable program from the get-go can improve your reputation as a guru, make a positive impression on the boss at review time, help keep those slipping schedules on track, and provide a free hour here or there to delete all that spam you're receiving. Here are three strategies that can help you write better code from the start:

- Before beginning, understand the business purpose for the program. How can you write a good piece of code if you don't understand its objective? Once you know what the program is intended to do, visualize the overall structure of the program. You should have a plan for matching the intended function of the program with the program specifications before writing even a single line of code. Programs designed this way are much less likely to introduce gross errors of logic.
- Just as you should use modeling tools to create a top-down schema of your database (as discussed in Chapter 2, *Database Analysis and Design*), you should also impose top-down design techniques on your Transact-SQL programs. With complex programs, it is easy to get lost in all the minutiae of coding the specifications. Instead, start with a pseudo-code or plain-English outline of the program. At each step of the program, dig down into the details needed to implement that single component of the program. This will isolate the complexities of the program steps and engender a modularized program.
- When you start coding, break the program into small, tightly integrated modules. These modules can be tested and implemented separately. Some general-purpose modules, such as an error-handling block, can be reused in different programs. (Now, we're not talking object-oriented here.) Don't write a single, meandering program that's hard to read, comprehend, and maintain.

Combine these tips with other strategies laid out elsewhere in this book to write Transact-SQL programs that are of higher quality, readability, and maintainability. When you combine all of this wisdom, the strategies can reduce the occurrence and severity of bugs in your program.

Specific Debugging Techniques

Transact-SQL in itself is admittedly weak in debugging features. Unlike some other programming languages that include integrated development environments, Transact-SQL lacks features such as program stepping, breakpoints, or observable variable values. To get around these weaknesses, we have to use a little creative programming (most people call those "kludges").

In this section, we'll discuss specific coding techniques used to debug and troubleshoot a Transact-SQL program. Among the points we'll discuss are performing initial programming in batch mode, the DBCC and SET commands, DBCC trace flags, and utilities available to assist with debugging. In the case of the DBCC and SET commands, these commands offer many capabilities outside of the realm of debugging. We'll also explain these other non-debugging features of the DBCC and SET commands, although in less detail.

It seems obvious that you should do your development in a separate development database or server, but some developers still develop within their production environment. On the surface, the most obvious problem is the possible modification or corruption of production data. But there can also be very negative impact incurred if a developer alters existing stored procedures, tables, views, or other database objects. Avoid the dangers and pitfalls altogether by creating a separate development database with a manageable subset of data taken from the production database.

If you can afford it, get a completely separate development server. Developers can coexist with end users on a production server if they have their own database. However, developers frequently request server reboots to install new software, service packs, or whatever. (Not that a programmer would *ever* develop code that might actually cause a problem that requires shutting down and restarting the server!)

Performing Initial Programming as a Batch

Whenever you are coding a Transact-SQL object, whether it be a stored procedure, view, or trigger, it's usually best to code the application in a Transact-SQL batch (or batches) first. For example, when writing a new view to summarize author advances by title ID, it's better to code the SELECT statement first in batch mode. Once you've honed the SELECT statement down to the exact result set you want, you can then reissue the statement couched in the CREATE VIEW command.

For example, here's our first shot at the SELECT statement that retrieves author advances by title ID:

```
SELECT "SSN"           = a.au_id,
    "Author"           = a.au_fname + a.au_lname
    "Title ID"         = t.title_id,
    "Total Advance"    = SUM(t.advance)
FROM authors    a,
    titleauthor ta,
    titles      t
WHERE   a.au_id      = ta.au_id
    AND ta.title_id = t.title_id
GROUP BY a.au_id, a.au_lname, a.au_fname, t.title_id
GO
```

Results:

```
SSN            Author                    Title ID  Total Advance
------------   -----------------------   --------  ------------------------
172-32-1176    JohnsonWhite              PS3333    2,000.00
213-46-8915    MarjorieGreen             BU1032    5,000.00
213-46-8915    MarjorieGreen             BU2075    10,125.00
<...some lines omitted for brevity...>
899-46-2035    AnneRinger                PS2091    2,275.00
998-72-3567    AlbertRinger              PS2091    2,275.00
998-72-3567    AlbertRinger              PS2106    6,000.00

(25 row(s) affected)
```

Well, that's the data we want but not the format. The author column is all messed up. If we had coded the view without first trying it in a Transact-SQL batch, we would not have received an error. However, we wouldn't have gotten the data in the format we wanted either. If we had coded this as a view to begin with, we'd have to drop the view before continuing. Let's take another crack at it, this time improving the appearance of the author column:

```
SELECT "SSN"           = a.au_id,
    "Author"           = SUBSTRING(RTRIM(a.au_fname) + ' '+
                         RTRIM(a.au_lname),1,25),
    "Title ID"         = t.title_id,
    "Total Advance"    = SUM(t.advance)
FROM authors     a,
    titleauthor ta,
    titles      t
WHERE   a.au_id      = ta.au_id
    AND ta.title_id = t.title_id
GROUP BY a.au_id, a.au_lname, a.au_fname, t.title_id
GO
```

The results should look better, since we've spent some time formatting the author column:

```
SSN         Author                    Title ID Total Advance
----------- ------------------------- -------- -------------------------
172-32-1176 Johnson White             PS3333   2,000.00
213-46-8915 Marjorie Green            BU1032   5,000.00
213-46-8915 Marjorie Green            BU2075   10,125.00
<...some lines omitted for brevity...>
899-46-2035 Anne Ringer               PS2091   2,275.00
998-72-3567 Albert Ringer             PS2091   2,275.00
998-72-3567 Albert Ringer             PS2106   6,000.00

(25 row(s) affected)
```

The principal idea to remember when writing a specialized Transact-SQL program, such as a stored procedure, trigger, or view, is that these are preparsed and (if it's a stored procedure) precompiled sets of Transact-SQL code. By testing the code in a standard Transact-SQL batch environment, you can confirm the proper functioning and behavior of the application without the need to DROP the object if there is a problem.

Adding Debugging Messages to a Transact-SQL Program

Assume for a moment that we need to write a stored procedure on Microsoft SQL Server that will run the command DBCC UPDATEUSAGE on every user database, plus master and msdb. The stored procedure, when completed, will be added to our schedule as a nightly maintenance program. Here's an example of what the finished product might look like on a Microsoft server using a cursor:

```
CREATE PROCEDURE update_sysindex
AS
/*
   01/16/98 - J.S. Bach - Updates the values of sysindexes on a nightly basis
                          for Microsoft server.
*/
SET NOCOUNT ON

-- declare the variables used in the program
DECLARE @dbname     VARCHAR(30),
    @cmd_line       VARCHAR(100)

-- declare the cursor that finds each user database, except for model and
-- tempdb
DECLARE dbname_cursor CURSOR FOR
    SELECT name
    FROM   sysdatabases
    WHERE  name NOT IN ('model', 'tempdb')

OPEN dbname_cursor
FETCH NEXT FROM dbname_cursor INTO @dbname

-- perform the DBCC UPDATEUSAGE command on each user database
WHILE (@@fetch_status <> -1)
BEGIN
    IF (@@fetch_status <> -2)
    BEGIN
        SELECT @cmd_line =
            'DBCC UPDATEUSAGE (' + RTRIM(@dbname) + ')
             WITH COUNT_ROWS, NO_INFOMSGS'
        EXEC  (@cmd_line)
    END
    FETCH NEXT FROM dbname_cursor INTO @dbname
END

-- gracefully close and terminate the cursor
CLOSE dbname_cursor
DEALLOCATE dbname_cursor
GO
```

However, it takes a seasoned veteran to be able to write a program like this without any testing or debugging. One of the most common approaches to take is to insert PRINT commands that tell you the current value of variables and the status of the control-of-flow structures, such as loops. Here's an earlier version of the program loaded with debugging messages to tell the programmer what is happening inside the program:

```
CREATE PROCEDURE update_sysindex1
AS
/*
   01/16/98 - J.S. Bach - Updates the values of sysindexes on a nightly
                          basis.
*/

SET NOCOUNT ON

DECLARE @dbname    VARCHAR(30),
     @cmd_line     VARCHAR(100),
     @output_line VARCHAR(75)

DECLARE dbname_cursor CURSOR FOR
     SELECT name
     FROM   sysdatabases
     WHERE  name NOT IN ('MODEL', 'TEMPDB')

OPEN dbname_cursor
FETCH NEXT FROM dbname_cursor INTO @dbname

-- messages are commonly built by concatenating dynamic and hard-coded
-- information, and then printed as shown here
SELECT @output_line = 'Starting cursor with ' + UPPER(@dbname) + ' database.'
PRINT  @output_line
PRINT ' '

WHILE (@@fetch_status <> -1)
BEGIN
     IF (@@fetch_status <> -2)
     BEGIN
          -- tell which database is being processed
          SELECT @output_line = "Updating "  + RTRIM(@dbname)
          PRINT  @output_line

          -- drop the NO_INFOMSGS option on the DBCC command to get a full
          -- report of its activities
          SELECT @cmd_line =
               'DBCC UPDATEUSAGE (' + RTRIM(@dbname) + ') WITH COUNT_ROWS'
               --, NO_INFOMSGS' is retained for the final product

          -- print the exact command being executed
          PRINT 'Command executed:'
          PRINT  @cmd_line
          EXEC  (@cmd_line)
```

```
        PRINT ' '
    END
    FETCH NEXT FROM dbname_cursor INTO @dbname
END

PRINT 'Closing and terminating cursor'

CLOSE dbname_cursor
DEALLOCATE dbname_cursor
GO
```

Results (edited for brevity):

```
Starting cursor with DISTRIBUTION database.

Updating distribution
Command executed:
DBCC UPDATEUSAGE (distribution) WITH COUNT_ROWS
DBCC UPDATEUSAGE: Sysindexes row for Table 'MSsubscriber_jobs' (IndexId=2)
updated:
    USED Pages: Changed from (4261) to (40) pages
    RSVD Pages: Changed from (4270) to (47) pages
DBCC execution completed. If DBCC printed error messages, see your System
Administrator.

Updating master
Command executed:
DBCC UPDATEUSAGE (master) WITH COUNT_ROWS
DBCC UPDATEUSAGE: Sysindexes row for Table 'helpsql' (IndexId=2) updated:
    USED Pages: Changed from (2) to (51) pages
    RSVD Pages: Changed from (8) to (56) pages
DBCC execution completed. If DBCC printed error messages, see your System
Administrator.

Updating msdb
Command executed:
DBCC UPDATEUSAGE (msdb) WITH COUNT_ROWS
DBCC UPDATEUSAGE: Sysindexes row for Table 'syshistory' (IndexId=1) updated:
    RSVD Pages: Changed from (75) to (96) pages
DBCC execution completed. If DBCC printed error messages, see your System
Administrator.

Updating pubs
Command executed:
DBCC UPDATEUSAGE (pubs) WITH COUNT_ROWS
DBCC UPDATEUSAGE: Sysindexes row for Table 'pub_info' (IndexId=255) updated:
    USED Pages: Changed from (17) to (74) pages
    RSVD Pages: Changed from (24) to (80) pages
DBCC execution completed. If DBCC printed error messages, see your System
Administrator.

Closing and terminating cursor
```

This fully enunciated result set lets you know everything that happened within the stored procedure. But what if you want to know what's happening in a Transact-SQL program as it is about to happen, rather than after it's all done? Because a stored procedure is processed as a single unit, no output from the PRINT commands appears until the procedure completes all commands. For long-running stored procedures, that means you might wait for minutes, or even hours, before receiving a single result set. Even though many of your PRINT statements have already successfully executed, the result set for a stored procedure will not be returned until all commands within the stored procedure have finished. That's another good reason to test the program as a Transact-SQL batch before compiling the code as a view, trigger, or stored procedure.

In some cases, you may want the output of a PRINT command to appear *before* a time-consuming piece of code executes. There are a couple of ways to tackle this problem:

1. Rewrite the stored procedure as a Transact-SQL script, writing each piece of code as a separate batch (with its own GO statement). In this scenario, PRINT statements will return their output as soon as the GO is processed. However, this approach has the downside that not all Transact-SQL programs can be broken into multiple batches. Some programs might use a single set of local variables throughout or might contain very large BEGIN . . . END blocks.
2. Write the stored procedure in such a way that the output is actually recorded in a table (using an INSERT statement), rather than printed on the screen. You can query the message table to determine what steps the stored procedure has completed.

DBCC Command Summary

DBCC is SQL Server's Database Consistency Checker and catch-all utility. Many of the variations of DBCC are used to verify the integrity of a SQL Server database, much like a *chkdsk* command in MS-DOS or the *fsck* command on Unix. However, it seems that often, if the development teams couldn't find a good place to put a useful new command, they'd stick it into DBCC. DBCC does lots of different things: checking the logical and physical consistency of a database, monitoring memory usage and server performance, pinning a table into the active data cache, and forcing the re-creation of a table's indexes. In most cases, DBCC isn't corrective. It usually only alerts you to problems so that you can manually fix the problems of the database or server. You should remember that many, if not most, of the DBCC commands are not actually used for debugging. However, DBCC is a useful command, and since it does assist with debugging, we decided to cover it here in its entirety.

Table 21-2 shows all the variations of DBCC currently supported by the vendors and their general usage category. We'll discuss the DBCC commands that show up in the debugging category in greater detail later.

Table 21-2. DBCC Commands and Usage Categories

DBCC Command	Category
CHECKALLOC	Database consistency check
CHECKCATALOG	Database consistency check
CHECKDB	Database consistency check
CHECKIDENT	Database consistency check
CHECKSTORAGE	Database consistency check
CHECKTABLE	Database consistency check
FIX_AL	Database consistency check
FIX_TEXT	Database consistency check
INDEXALLOC	Database consistency check
NEWALLOC	Database consistency check
TABLEALLOC	Database consistency check
TEXTALL	Database consistency check
TEXTALLOC	Database consistency check
UPDATEUSAGE	Database consistency check
dll_name (FREE)	Database and server configuration
DBREPAIR	Database and server configuration
SHRINKDB	Database and server configuration
INPUTBUFFER	Debugging
LOG	Debugging
OPENTRAN	Debugging
OUTPUTBUFFER	Debugging
PAGE	Debugging
TRACEOFF	Debugging
TRACEON	Debugging
TRACESTATUS	Debugging
DBREINDEX	Performance tuning and monitoring
GAMINIT	Performance tuning and monitoring
MEMUSAGE	Performance tuning and monitoring
PAGE	Performance tuning and monitoring
PERFMON	Performance tuning and monitoring
PINTABLE	Performance tuning and monitoring
PROCCACHE	Performance tuning and monitoring

Table 21-2. DBCC Commands and Usage Categories (continued)

DBCC Command	Category
REINDEX	Performance tuning and monitoring
ROWLOCK	Performance tuning and monitoring
SHOWCONTIG	Performance tuning and monitoring
SHOW_STATISTICS	Performance tuning and monitoring
SQLPERF	Performance tuning and monitoring
TUNE	Performance tuning and monitoring
UNPINTABLE	Performance tuning and monitoring
USEROPTIONS	Performance tuning and monitoring

A more detailed breakdown of each command appears in Table 21-3. All the DBCC commands shown in Table 21-2 and Table 21-3 are prefixed with the string DBCC when used in Transact-SQL. Thus, to find the oldest open transaction within the current database, you'd use the Transact-SQL command:

```
DBCC OPENTRAN(pubs)
GO
```

When a database name or database ID is needed to run the specific DBCC command, the current database is assumed if no value is supplied. Similarly, if the DBCC command acts against a specific table ID or index ID and no value is supplied, the command acts upon all tables in the current (or specified) database or all indexes of the specified table, respectively. For those DBCC commands that return a lot of information, you can use the optional clause WITH NO_INFOMSGS to reduce the amount of information returned by the command. For example, compare the output of this batch both with and without informational messages:

```
PRINT '*** DBCC with informational messages'
GO

DBCC CHECKCATALOG(pubs)
GO

PRINT ' '
PRINT '*** DBCC without informational messages'
GO

DBCC CHECKCATALOG(pubs) WITH NO_INFOMSGS
GO
```

The results are quite different:

```
*** DBCC with informational messages
Checking pubs
```

```
The following segments have been defined for database 4 (database name pubs).
virtual start addr      size      segments
--------------------    ------    --------------------------
                2052    512
                                       0
                                       1
               10756    1024
                                       0
                                       1
           234881024    512
                                       2
DBCC execution completed. If DBCC printed error messages, see your System
Administrator.

*** DBCC without informational messages
DBCC execution completed. If DBCC printed error messages, see your System
Administrator.
```

Most programmers use the WITH_NOINFOMSGS for programs that do not require human intervention to operate.

The CD-ROM accompanying this book contains three stored procedures that automate certain DBCC checks. *sp_dbback* integrates common DBCC commands with your nightly database dump. That way you can be certain that you never dump a corrupt database. *sp_dbback* does not dump an inconsistent database, instead raising an error message in the Windows NT event log. The stored procedure *update_stats* provides an automated means of updating the index statistics for all user databases. The stored procedure *sp_reinit_ndx* rebuilds all indexes and reestablishes fillfactors on user tables in a given database.

Operations performed by DBCC, especially database integrity checks, can be very long running and resource intensive. (The DBCC commands most likely to cause this sort of performance hit are NEWALLOC, CHECKDB, CHECKCATALOG, and, in some cases, TEXTALL). Moreover, SQL Server databases require frequent DBCC checks to remain healthy. To lighten the impact on end users and important batch processes, DBAs typically schedule DBCC checks to occur in the off-hours when no one is using the system. On extremely large databases, the database consistency check commands should be run with the NOINDEX option to speed performance and then run normally on a less-frequent schedule.

Table 21-3 shows a detailed breakdown and explanation of each DBCC option. We'll give extra attention to the commands that fall in the debugging category.

Table 21-3. DBCC Command Options

DBCC Option	Permissions	Vendor Support	Description

Microsoft—
`CHECKALLOC [(database_name [NOINDEX])]`
 	
Sybase—
`CHECKALLOC [(database_name [, FIX | NOFIX])]`
	SA or DBO	MS, Sybase	Retained only for backward compatibility. Use the NEWALLOC command instead. The Sybase version of this command allows you to fix allocation errors found by the DBCC command. The database must be in single-user mode first. The default is NOFIX.

`CHECKCATALOG [(database_name)]`	SA or DBO	MS, Sybase	Checks for consistency between the system tables of a given database and reports on the segments defined. For example, every stored procedure recorded in sysobjects would be cross-checked in syscomments, and CHECKCATALOG would ensure that every type in syscolumns has a matching entry in systypes.

Microsoft—
`CHECKDB [(database_name [NOINDEX])]`
 	
Sybase—
`CHECKDB [(database_name [,SKIP_NOINDEX])]`
	SA or DBO	MS, Sybase	Runs the CHECKTABLE option against every table in the specified database or the current database if no database is declared.
			
			Sybase allows the DBCC check to skip all nonclustered indexes on the table when you include the keyword SKIP_NOINDEX.

`CHECKIDENT [(table_name)]`		MS	Verifies that the internal identity value for a table is valid compared to the maximum identity value in the column. If the values are out of sync, the internal identity value is reset to equal the maximum value in the identity column. This can avert error number 2627 on identity columns that also serve as primary or unique keys.
`CHECKTABLE (table_name [, NOINDEX | index_id])`	SA, DBO, or table owner	MS, Sybase	This option checks the linkage between data and index pages, index pointer consistency, index sorting, page offsets, and data consistency for a specific table. When run on syslogs (the transaction log), CHECKTABLE reports on free and used space in the log. The command can be executed against a single, specific index by specifying the table name and index ID.

Table 21-3. DBCC Command Options (continued)

DBCC Option	Permissions	Vendor Support	Description
			The NOINDEX option is used in conjunction with CHECKCATALOG, CHECKDB, CHECKTABLE, and NEWALLOC. It can also be used to check only the consistency of the clustered index of a table, or, if none exists, the data with the NOINDEX keyword. This can really speed up a DBCC check, especially on large tables. NOINDEX is effective only on user-defined tables and has no effect when DBCC is run against system tables.
`DREINDEX ([ 'database.owner.table_name' [, index_name [, fillfactor [, {SORTED_DATA | SORTED_DATA_REORG}]]]])`	SA, DBO, or table owner	MS	Rebuilds one or more indexes for a table and establishes original or new index fillfactors. This command provides the flexibility of not having to know the structure of the table or dependent objects. You can simply provide the table name to rebuild all indexes on a given table or specify a specific index. By providing a new fillfactor value from 1 to 100, you can specify how full (as a percentage) each index page should be when it is re-created. A fillfactor value of 0 uses the original fillfactor of the index. The optional SORTED_DATA and SORTED_DATA_REORG keywords tell SQL Server that it does not need to sort the data when re-creating a clustered index because the data is already sorted. (They will still verify the sort and will terminate the process if they find values out of order.) SORTED_DATA does not copy data or rebuild nonclustered indexes and is consequently faster. SORTED_DATA_REORG, on the other hand, always rebuilds the physical data and index pages according to the fill factor specified. If you specify one of the optional parameters (like index_name, fillfactor, or SORTED_DATA), all preceding parameters must be specified.

Table 21-3. DBCC Command Options (continued)

DBCC Option	Permissions	Vendor Support	Description
`DBREPAIR (database_name, DROPDB [, NOINIT])`	SA	MS, Sybase	This command was used largely to drop a damaged database. It has been superseded by the DROP DATABASE command and the *sp_dbremove* system stored procedure. The command can be used only on a database that has no users in it (including the person issuing the DBCC DBREPAIR command). The NOINIT keyword (Microsoft only) ensures that the allocation pages of the dropped database are not modified.
`dll_name (FREE)`	SA	MS	Frees, or unloads, a specific dynamic link library (DLL) from SQL Server's memory. Normally, once the DLLs of an extended stored procedure are executed, they are held in memory until SQL Server is recycled. The command DBCC dll_name (FREE) allows you to unload any such DLL without having to stop and restart SQL Server.
`FIX_AL`	SA	MS	A variation of the NEWALLOC option that corrects error 2540. The database must be in single-user mode for this command to work.
`FIX_TEXT (table_name | table_id)`	SA, table owner	Sybase	If the character set has been changed, FIX_TEXT upgrades text values to the new multibyte character set. This command should be run if Sybase Adaptive Server's character set is ever changed on an existing table with TEXT fields.
`INDEXALLOC ({table_name | table_id}, index_id [, {FULL | OPTIMIZED | FAST | NULL} [, FIX | NOFIX]])`	SA, table owner	Sybase	An abbreviated version of CHECKALLOC that verifies a single index on a specified table to ensure that all pages are correctly allocated and used. The check runs in OPTIMIZED mode by default. FULL mode reports all allocation errors. OPTIMIZED reports on Object Allocation Map (OAM) allocation errors but not unreferenced allocation errors. FAST does produce an exception report of 2521-level errors but doesn't produce an allocation report. If you specify a check mode, you may also specify whether you want the DBCC check to fix or bypass detected allocation errors with the FIX and NOFIX keywords.

Table 21-3. DBCC Command Options (continued)

DBCC Option	Permissions	Vendor Support	Description
`INPUTBUFFER (spid)`	SA	MS	Retrieves the first 255 bytes of the current input buffer for a specific SPID. The input buffer is the command sent from the client to the server. In other words, it shows what users and system processes are currently executing. Some processes don't contain an input stream, causing the command to return an error. Use the system stored procedure *sp_who* to find a specific user's SPID.
`GAMINIT (dbid)`	SA	MS	Proactively populates the Global Allocation Map (GAM) rather than allowing the GAM to be populated as needed. This DBCC command is seldom needed, except in certain Very Large Database (VLDB) environments. This function is typically used to control spurious periods of inactivity during heavy database access during random disk accesses. The command must be executed when SQL Server starts, before any other database activity takes place. It can take several minutes to prepopulate the GAM. The larger the database, the longer DBCC GAMINIT will take.
`LOG`	SA	MS	When issued after the DBCC TRACEON(3604) command, displays information on each record in the log file of a database. Some transaction types are easy to decipher, like ENDXACT or BEGINXACT. Here are some other transaction types that are less obvious: • IINSERT and IDELETE are the DML commands acting upon an index. • DNOOP and INOOP are deferred deletes or inserts, respectively. • INSIND is an indirect insert. • CHGSYSINDSTAT is a change to a statistics page in sysindexes. • CHGSYSINDPG is a change to a data page in sysindexes.

Table 21-3. DBCC Command Options (continued)

DBCC Option	Permissions	Vendor Support	Description
`MEMUSAGE`	SA	MS	This variation of DBCC provides a report showing how the server's memory was allocated at startup, how much memory is consumed by the 20 largest objects in the buffer cache, and how much memory is consumed by the 12 largest objects in the procedure cache. Multiple objects in the procedure cache are summed in the report. MEMUSAGE also differentiates between precompiled *trees* and compiled *plans* of objects in the procedure cache.
`NEWALLOC [(database_name [NOINDEX])]`	SA or DBO	MS	NEWALLOC is an update of the CHECKALLOC command that doesn't stop processing when an error is encountered. NEWALLOC checks data and index pages against their extent structures for all tables in a given database. The command also reports the number of extents used by objects for an allocation unit (that is, 512K, 32 extents, or eight 2K pages), the number of pages marked as used by the objects, and the number of pages actually used by objects. NEWALLOC is an important preventive maintenance command. It should be used at regular intervals when the database is experiencing minimal usage.
`OPENTRAN ({database_name} | {database_id}) [WITH TABLERESULTS]`	SA or DBO	MS	Reports information about the oldest active transaction (and the oldest distributed and nondistributed replication transactions), if any exist within the database. Otherwise, no results are returned. WITH TABLERESULTS formats the result set for readability and easy insertion into a table for comparisons. OPENTRAN is very useful for discovering if open transactions exist in the transaction log, since only the inactive portion of a log can be dumped with the DUMP TRAN statement. OPENTRAN allows you to identify the SPID of any transactions preventing a complete log dump, enabling you to terminate the offending process.

Table 21-3. DBCC Command Options (continued)

DBCC Option	Permissions	Vendor Support	Description
`OUTPUTBUFFER (spid)`	SA	MS	Retrieves the current output buffer of the specific SPID in hexadecimal and ASCII format. The output buffer is the result set sent from the server to the client. An error is invoked when this command is used on processes that don't have output streams.
`PAGE ({dbid|dbname}, pagenum [,print_option] [,cache_option] [,logical_option])`		MS, Sybase	Prints out the contents of a specific page in a given SQL Server database based on the dbid or database name and the exact page number provided. Print options are 0, 1, or 2: 0 The default; prints only page header information. 1 Prints header, row, and offset informa tion. 2 The same as 1, except in block format. Cache options are 0 and 1: 0 Retrieves page numbers from disk rather than cache. 1 The default; retrieves the page number from disk only if it's not in cache. The logical options differentiate between a virtual page number (0) and a logical page number (1), which is also the default.
`PERFMON`	SA	MS	Retrieves the performance statistics generated by the DBCC commands SQLPERF IOSTATS, SQLPERF LRUSTATS, and SQLPERF NETSTATS—in that order.
`PINTABLE (database_id, table_id)`	SA	MS	All pages of a table specified by this command will remain in the data cache until the DBCC UNPINTABLE command is used. That's not to say that the table is automatically read into cache. Instead, as data, index, or text pages are read into the cache, they are not flushed out later. This command should be used with caution. It doesn't provide a performance boost in every case. In fact, very large tables can consume the entire data cache, necessitating a server restart. A table remains "pinned" even after restart.

Table 21-3. DBCC Command Options (continued)

DBCC Option	Permissions	Vendor Support	Description
`PROCCACHE`	SA	MS	Returns a report showing the current status of the server's procedure cache. Information reported includes the number of possible procedures in the cache, the number of buffer slots that have a procedure, the number of buffer slots that have an executing procedure, the total size of the cache, the size of procedure cache consumed by procedures, and the size of procedure cache consumed by executing procedures.
`REINDEX (table_name | table_id)`	SA, table-owner	Sybase	Runs a fast version of CHECKTABLE that scans indexes on a user table. If any errors are discovered, a message is printed and the index is dropped and re-created. If everything is OK (or there are no indexes on the table), a message is returned. No reindexing is done if the table itself is corrupt.
`ROWLOCK (dbid, tableid, set)`	SA or DBO	MS	Engages insert row-level locking (IRL) on a Microsoft SQL Server (Version 6.5). Values for set include 1 to engage IRL and 0 to disengage IRL for a given table. Note that the ID for the database and table must be provided, not the name.
`SHOW_STATISTICS (table_name, index_name)`	SA, DBO, or table owner	MS	Displays the statistical information about the distribution page of an index for a given table. This is very useful for determining if the index is performing efficiently. The lower the density shown, the more selective the index. DBCC SHOW_STATISTICS is discussed more fully in Chapter 20, *Transact-SQL Optimization and Tuning*.
`SHOWCONTIG (table_id [index_id])`	SA or DBO	MS	Tells if a table is fragmented or not by traversing the page chain of a specified index or the data leaf level (if only a table ID is provided). This is very useful for determining if the index is performing efficiently. DBCC SHOWCONTIG is discussed more fully in Chapter 20.

Table 21-3. DBCC Command Options (continued)

DBCC Option	Permissions	Vendor Support	Description
`SHRINKDB (database_name [, new_size [, 'MASTEROVERRIDE']])`	SA or DBO	MS	When used with only a database name, this command returns a report showing the smallest possible size of the database. Objects that prevent the database from being further reduced in size are also listed. To shrink the combined data and log portions of a database, list a new size in 2K pages. The database must be in single-user mode to shrink it. Usually, the log will be reduced, although there's no reliable way to predict that. After shrinking the database, use the ALTER DATABASE statement to readjust the size of the data or log portion. It's a good idea to dump both master and the database you're working with (although not to the same dump device), both before and after shrinking it. The command is fully logged and recoverable (except on master). We generally recommend dropping and re-creating the database in the desired size instead of using DBCC SHRINKDB. No database can be reduced below the size of the model database or by an amount not measurable in allocation units (512K). The server must be restarted in single-user mode to shrink either master or tempdb. The MASTEROVERRIDE keyword must be used when shrinking master.
`SQLPERF ({IOSTATS | LRUSTATS | NETSTATS | RASTATS | WAITSTATS [CLEAR]} |{THREADS} | {LOGSPACE})`	Any user	MS	Returns performance statistics in four categories since the server was last started or the statistics were last cleared. IOSTATS provides I/O statistics. LRUSTATS (least recently used) cache provides information about the server cache. NETSTATS returns information about network use. RASTATS shows read-ahead statistics. CLEAR clears all statistics without showing them. WAITSTATS shows information about the time SQL Server spent waiting on a resource, reported per lock type and per transaction.

Table 21-3. DBCC Command Options (continued)

DBCC Option	Permissions	Vendor Support	Description
			THREADS enables you to map a Windows NT system thread ID to a SQL Server SPID. In reality, this is less useful than it sounds, since a single SPID may be served by many different Windows NT threads under thread pooling. Results also include the login name, I/Os, CPU utilization, and memory usage for the SPIDs. LOGSPACE returns the log size, log space used by percentage, and status of each database on the server that has a separate log device. Databases without a separate log device appear in the report but always show a log size of 0, with 0 space used. A status of 1 indicates that log and data are on the same device, while a status of 0 means that log and data are on separate devices. DBCC SQLPERF is discussed more fully in Chapter 20.
`TABLEALLOC ({table_name | table_id},index_id [, {FULL | OPTIMIZED | FAST | NULL} [, FIX | NOFIX]])`	SA, table-owner	Sybase	An abbreviated version of CHECKALLOC that verifies a specified table to ensure that all pages are correctly allocated and used. The check runs in OPTIMIZED mode by default. FULL mode reports all allocation errors. OPTIMIZED reports on Object Allocation Map (OAM) allocation errors but not unreferenced allocation errors. FAST produces an exception report of 2521-level errors but doesn't produce an allocation report. If you specify a check mode, you may also specify whether you want the DBCC check to fix or bypass detected allocation errors with the FIX and NOFIX keywords.
`TEXTALL [({database_name | database_id}[, 'FULL' | FAST])]`	SA or DBO	MS	Automatically executes a TEXTALLOC command against all tables that contain a text or image column.
`TEXTALLOC [({table_name | table_id}[, 'FULL' | FAST])]`	SA or DBO	MS	Verifies the allocation and linkages of a single table containing text or image columns. A FULL check (the default if no value is supplied) runs against all allocation pages in the database, while a FAST check only verifies the linkage of the text chains and that the pages in the chain are allocated.

Table 21-3. DBCC Command Options (continued)

DBCC Option	Permissions	Vendor Support	Description
`TRACEOFF (trace#)`	SA	MS, Sybase	Engages a specific trace flag. See "Using DBCC Trace Flags" later in this chapter for more details.
`TRACEON (trace#)`	SA	MS, Sybase	Disengages a specific trace flag. See "Using DBCC Trace Flags" later in this chapter for more details.
`TRACESTATUS (trace_flag# [trace_flag#...])`	SA	MS	Returns the status of on (1) or off (0) for a specific trace flag or flags. You can substitute a -1 for the trace flag number to retrieve the status of all active trace flags.
`TUNE ( ASCINSERTS, {0 | 1 } , table_name | CLEANUP, {0 | 1 } | CPUAFFINITY, START_CPU [, ON| OFF] | DEVIOCHAR VDEVNO, "batch_size" | DONEINPROC { 0 | 1 } | MAXWRITEDES, WRITES_PER_BATCH )`	SA	Sybase	Enables and disables special performance switches.
`UNPINTABLE (database_id, table_id)`	SA	MS	Marks a pinned table (done with the DBCC PINTABLE command) as "unpinned", although the table will remain in cache as long as it used normally. The table will be removed from the cache only when it is aged and flushed to disk.
`UPDATEUSAGE ({0 | database_name} [,table_name [,index_id]]) [WITH COUNT_ROWS]`	SA or DBO	MS	Reports on and corrects inaccuracies in the sysindexes table. The columns rows, used, reserved, and dpages are adjusted for clustered indexes, although size data is not retained for nonclustered indexes. Specifying a zero instead of the database name will update the current database. The command returns a result only if inaccuracies are present in the sysindexes table; otherwise, no result is returned. The command is fully logged unless it is executed against syslogs. The WITH COUNT_ROWS clause updates the rows column of sysindexes with the current count of rows in the table. The command tells you what rows and columns it updated, but only when it actually makes a change.

Table 21-3. DBCC Command Options (continued)

DBCC Option	Permis-sions	Vendor Support	Description
			This command takes a long time to run, especially on large tables or databases. It also acquires a shared table lock on the table being processed. We recommend that you use this command only when you detect incorrect values and only during off-hours. Be sure to put the database in single-user mode if syslogs is to be processed.
`USEROPTIONS`	Any user	MS	Retrieves all SET options active in the current session. For more information about SET, see "The SET Command" later in this chapter.
`[WITH NO_INFOMSGS]`	--	MS	This key phrase can be attached to the end of a DBCC command to prevent the printing of informational messages. Only error messages will be printed. This helps real problems stand out, particularly with DBCC commands that produce a lot of output, like DBCC NEWALLOC.

Many of the commands mentioned in this table are covered in detail elsewhere in the book. For example, the command DBCC OPENTRAN, although a debugging command, is discussed in Chapter 11, *Transactions and Locking*, in the context of transactions. The performance-tuning and monitoring commands are discussed in Chapter 20, along with other performance-tuning concepts. Database consistency checks, however, are discussed only in this chapter (and in the sample stored procedures on the CD-ROM accompanying this book) since they are primarily reserved for database administration tasks.

Using DBCC Debugging Commands

The majority of DBCC debugging functionality is embodied in the trace flag. However, DBCC INPUTBUFFER and DBCC OUTPUTBUFFER can be of great help in debugging those errors that are most difficult to find. These are commands that are near and dear to the snoops of the Transact-SQL world. In effect, these commands allow you to eavesdrop on a client connection or process. DBCC INPUTBUFFER allows you to see the first 255 bytes sent from the client to the server—things like DML statements and whatnot. Conversely, DBCC OUTPUTBUFFER enables you to see the first 255 bytes sent by the server to the client—usually result sets or error messages.

Let's hypothesize. You've just received a complaint that two users of the pubs database are experiencing slow performance. (Never can please those users, can you?) Since you and many other users are working normally, it must have something to do with the activities of the users. A few minutes of research show that connectivity from their workstations to the server is fine. Perhaps the problem resides within the application. Let's find out what they were doing in the app by using the *sp_who* system stored procedure. Here are the results:

```
spid   status     loginame     hostname     blk   dbname     cmd
------ ---------- ------------ ------------ ----- ---------- ----------------
1      sleeping   sa                        0     master     MIRROR HANDLER
2      sleeping   sa                        0     master     LAZY WRITER
3      sleeping   sa                        0     master     CHECKPOINT SLEEP
4      sleeping   sa                        0     master     RA MANAGER
10     sleeping   sso          WKSTN9501    0     master     AWAITING COMMAND
11     sleeping   sa           CHAMPAGNE    0     master     AWAITING COMMAND
12     sleeping   sa           CHAMPAGNE    0     master     AWAITING COMMAND
13     runnable   sso          WKSTN9501    0     master     EXECUTE
14     sleeping   Terry        WKSTN9589    0     pubs       AWAITING COMMAND
15     runnable   Dwayne       WKSTN9508    0     pubs       SELECT
16     sleeping   Evelyn       WKSTN9534    17    pubs       SELECT
17     sleeping   Dean         WKSTN9577    0     pubs       UPDATE
18     runnable   Anthony      WKSTN9590    0     pubs       SELECT
19     sleeping   sa           CHAMPAGNE    0     distributi AWAITING COMMAND
```

Ahah! We have an obvious problem with spid 17. It appears that user Dean (spid 17) is blocking Evelyn (spid 16). Let's find out what he's executing that is causing the block using DBCC INPUTBUFFER:

```
DBCC INPUTBUFFER(17)
GO
```

Results:

```
Input Buffer
--------------------------------------------------------------------------
BEGIN TRAN
    UPDATE titles
    SET    ytd_sales = ytd_sales + (SELECT SUM(qty)
                                    FROM   sales s
                                    WHERE  s.title_id = t.title_id)
    FROM   titles t
```

No wonder blocking is occurring! This is a terrible transaction. It will wait indefinitely for Dean to manually enter a COMMIT TRAN or ROLLBACK TRAN statement. Not only that, the UPDATE statement itself issues an exclusive table lock, effectively blocking anyone wishing to access the titles table. Now that we know what's going on, we can cancel the transaction for now and insist that Dean rewrite the transaction to be a little more polite to other users of the application.

Making use of the output buffer stream is a little more cumbersome. In fact, it takes quite a trained eye to make use of the output buffer. The command DBCC OUTPUTBUFFER allows you to view data sent from the server to the client in both hex and ASCII formats, but it's somewhat more difficult to make out. Here's what the output buffer for spid 17 looks like:

```
Output Buffer
---------------------------------------------------------------------------------
00172f78:  04 01 00 1a 00 00 00 00 fd 05 00 d4 00 00 00 00  ................
00172f88:  00 fd 14 00 c5 00 12 00 00 00 00 fd 10 00 c1 00  ................
00172f98:  01 00 00 00 45 16 00 00 01 00 23 00 43 68 61 6e  ....E.....#.Chan
00172fa8:  67 65 64 20 64 61 74 61 62 61 73 65 20 63 6f 6e  ged database con
00172fb8:  74 65 78 74 20 74 6f 20 27 70 75 62 73 27 2e 09  text to 'pubs'..
00172fc8:  55 53 4e 41 54 4e 54 31 31 00 01 00 fd 00 00 e2  CHAMPAGNE......
00172fd8:  00 00 00 00 00 4c 4c 41 54 49 4f 4e 5f 53 45 51  .....LLATION_SEQ
00172fe8:  3f 63 68 61 72 73 65 74 3d 69 73 6f 5f 31 20 73  ?charset=iso_1 s
00172ff8:  6f 72 74 5f 6f 72 64 65 72 3d 6e 6f 63 61 73 65  ort_order=nocase
00173008:  20 63 68 61 72 73 65 74 5f 6e 75 6d 3d 31 20 73   charset_num=1 s
00173018:  6f 72 74 5f 6f 72 64 65 72 5f 6e 75 6d 3d 35 32  ort_order_num=52
00173028:  ff 51 00 c1 00 01 00 00 00 ff 41 00 ca 00 01 00  .Q........A.....
00173038:  00 00 79 00 00 00 00 fe 08 00 e0 00 01 00 00 00  ..y.............
00173048:  32 03 30 30 30 fd 00 00 00 00 00 00 00 00 00 00  2.000...........
00173058:  00 00 00 00 00 00 00 00 00 00 00 00 00 00 00 00  ................
00173068:  00 00 00 00 00 00 00 00 00 00 00 00 00 00 00 00  ................
00173078:  00 00 00 00 00 00 00 00 00 00 00 00 00 00 00 00  ................
00173088:  00 00 00 00 00 00 00 00 00 00 00 00 00 00 00 00  ................
00173098:  00 00 00 00 00 00 00 00 00 00 00 00 00 00 00 00  ................
001730a8:  00 00 00 00 00 00 00 00 00 00 00 00 00 00 00 00  ................
001730b8:  00 00 00 00 00 00 00 00 00 00 00 00 00 00 00 00  ................
001730c8:  00 00 00 00 00 00 00 00 00 00 00 00 00 00 00 00  ................
001730d8:  00 00 00 00 00 00 00 00 00 00 00 00 00 00 00 00  ................
001730e8:  00 00 00 00 00 00 00 00 00 00 00 00 00 00 00 00  ................
001730f8:  00 00 00 00 00 00 00 00 00 00 00 00 00 00 00 00  ................
00173108:  00 00 00 00 00 00 00 00 00 00 00 00 00 00 00 00  ................
00173118:  00 00 00 00 00 00 00 00 00 00 00 00 00 00 00 00  ................
00173128:  00 00 00 00 00 00 00 00 00 00 00 00 00 00 00 00  ................
00173138:  00 00 00 00 00 00 00 00 00 00 00 00 00 00 00 00  ................
00173148:  00 00 00 00 00 00 00 00 00 00 00 00 00 00 00 00  ................
00173158:  00 00 00 00 00 00 00 00 00 00 00 00 00 00 00 00  ................
00173168:  00 00 00 00 00 00 00 00 00 00 00 00 00 00 00 00  ................
00173178:   .

(1 row(s) affected)

DBCC execution completed. If DBCC printed error messages, see your System
Administrator.
```

Not what you'd call the most informative of reports, is it? The result set returned by DBCC OUTPUTBUFFER usually contains information like:

- Result set data sent to the client connection
- Current server context
- Current database context
- Operating system files involved in the output stream

- Stored procedures used by the SPID
- Environmental settings for the session
- Tables and columns used in the result set

Both the DBCC INPUTBUFFER and the DBCC OUTPUTBUFFER commands rely on the content of the tabular data stream to produce results. Certain system processes, and user processes on certain rare occasions, do not produce an input or output buffer. In those cases, both DBCC commands return this result set:

```
The specified SPID does not process input/output data streams.
DBCC execution completed. If DBCC printed error messages, see your System
Administrator.
```

DBCC Sybase-style

Sybase has taken a divergent approach to DBCC when compared with Microsoft. Sybase has created a special database for maintaining DBCC check data, especially information generated by DBCC CHECKSTORAGE. This database is called, mercifully, *dbccdb*. This database has its own administrative requirements and idiosynchrasies.

Sybase has provided a number of stored procedures to maintain and report on data stored in dbccdb. Here's a sampling:

sp_dbcc_configreport
: Reports the configuration settings of a specified database

sp_dbcc_deleteall
: Deletes all old results from dbccdb for a specified database

sp_dbcc_deletehistory
: Truncates old results from DBCC CHECKSTORAGE commands for a specified database

sp_dbcc_evaluatedb
: Reevaluates configurations and recommends new settings for the specified database based on the latest DBCC CHECKSTORAGE command

sp_dbcc_faultreport
: Reports faults found in a specified database or by a specified date

sp_dbcc_statisticsreport
: Reports statistics information held in the dbcc_counter table generated by CHECKSTORAGE on or before a specified date

sp_dbcc_summaryreport
: Reports on all CHECKSTORAGE operations for a specified database or by a specified date

sp_dbcc_updateconfig
: Updates the configuration parameters for the specified database

Using DBCC Trace Flags

DBCC trace flags are a lot like a coffee table with many newsmagazines on it. You can get lots of great information from them, but you have no idea when a specific issue will go missing because a friend or family member has absconded with one. DBCC trace flags are similar in some ways because they can greatly aid in debugging problems but are not part of the supported feature set of SQL Server. That means that the vendors can add or remove specific trace flags with impunity. Speaking of the vendors: don't expect them to answer questions or provide support regarding trace flags. They will generally balk at offering support for questions about trace flags.

Don't build any long-term functionality based on DBCC trace flags. Continued usability or future compatibility are by no means assured! Treat them as an as-is feature.

There's a whole slew of documented and undocumented trace flags. You should be very careful about experimenting with trace flags. Use them only when they are needed to diagnose a specific problem. In fact, the vendors prefer that you use trace flags only when you're directed to by a primary support provider (i.e., Microsoft or Sybase).

DBCC trace flags are specialized settings that affect or initiate specific server behavior. They can be engaged by a number of different methods, but we're concerned only with activation through the DBCC command. That's because the DBCC command gives you the flexibility to set and reset a trace flag during the course of your session. Since trace flags remain in effect until terminated, it's important to remember to turn them off as soon as you're done with the debugging session. To enable a trace flag, use this syntax:

```
DBCC TRACEON (trace_flag_number)
GO
```

So, if you wanted to turn on trace flag 3604, you'd enter the command:

```
DBCC TRACEON (3604)
GO
```

To disable a trace flag, you'd use this syntax:

```
DBCC TRACEOFF (trace_flag_number)
GO
```

Similarly, to turn off the 3604 trace flag that was previously engaged:

```
DBCC TRACEOFF (3604)
GO
```

Trace flags can also be enabled at SQL Server startup by adding a –T trace_flag_number switch to the command line (or in the *SETUP.EXE* parameters option). For example,

```
sqlservr -dc:\mssql\data\master.dat -ec:\mssql\log\
errorlog -T1204 -T1205
```

The –T switch is case-sensitive (it must be capitalized). To add multiple trace flags, leave a space between additional flags (as shown in the example). Trace flags started this way remain in effect until the server is restarted without the trace flags. This approach is usually less flexible and desirable than using the DBCC TRACEON and DBCC TRACEOFF commands.

Did you forget which, if any, trace flags you're using? Use the DBCC TRACESTATUS command to find out if any trace flags are in effect during your current session:

```
DBCC TRACESTATUS (-1)
GO
```

You can also use DBCC to check for specific trace flags by entering the number of the specific trace flag within the parentheses. If you want to check for more than one trace flag, simply place a comma between each trace flag number within the parentheses. For example:

```
DBCC TRACESTATUS (-1,3502,3604)
GO
```

Note that trace flags are *very* specific to versions of the database. Table 21-4 assumes that you are using Microsoft SQL Server Version 6.5 (service pack 4) or Sybase Adaptive Server 11.5 (initial release). Each of the trace flags currently supported by Microsoft is detailed in Table 21-4.

The SET Command

Table 21-4. DBCC Trace Flags

Trace Flag	Description
–1	Enables a trace flag for all client connections instead of the current client connection. Always used in combination with other trace flags. Trace flag –1 impacts only currently opened processes. The trace flag must be reissued to trace any sessions started after it was first initialized.
106	An informational trace flag that disables line number information on syntax errors.
107	Causes all numbers with a decimal point to be treated like a FLOAT datatype instead of a DEC.

Table 21-4. DBCC Trace Flags (continued)

Trace Flag	Description
110	Turns off ANSI SELECT characteristics.
204	A backward compatibility switch that enables non-ANSI standard behavior. For example, old versions of SQL Server ignored trailing blanks in LIKE pattern searches and allowed queries that contained aggregate functions to have items in the GROUP BY clause that were not in the select list.
206	Tells SQL Server to use the SETUSER statement in backward compatibility mode.
237	Turns off the requirements to create a foreign key on tables not owned by the creator. When engaged, trace flag 237 disables ANSI-standard behavior by requiring only SELECT permission and disabling the requirement for referenced values to exist in the foreign key table.
242	Tells SQL Server to use correlated subqueries in non-ANSI-standard backward compatibility mode.
243	Tells SQL Server to use the nullability behavior of SQL Server Version 4.2. For example, under Version 4.2, a whole Transact-SQL batch will fail when a nullability error is encountered (like inserting a null value into a NOT NULL column) at compile time. But when runtime nullability errors were encountered, Version 4.2 allowed a row to be skipped and batch processing to continue.
244	Tells SQL Server to stop checking for and allow *interim constraint violations*. An interim constraint violation is a fancy name for the worktables used to enable self-referencing DELETE statements, multirow UPDATE statements, and INSERT . . . SELECT statements.
246	Derived or null columns must be explicitly named in a SELECT . . . INTO or CREATE VIEW statement, and when they aren't so named, they raise an error. Trace flag 246 disables this type of error reporting.
302	Prints information about query optimization for all queries issued during the current connection. The report includes the selectivity of the index (if available), the estimated physical and logical I/O of the indexes, and whether the statistics page is used. Trace flag 302 is most useful in conjunction with trace flag 310.
310	Provides details about the join order used in queries issued during the current session. Superseded in value by the command SET SHOWPLAN ON.
320	Disables join-order heuristics used in ANSI joins. You can watch join-order heuristics by using trace flag 310. Microsoft SQL Server uses join-order heuristics to reduce the number of permutations when choosing the best join order.
323	Reports on the use of UPDATE statements using update-in-place.
325	Shows the cost of using nonclustered indexes or sorts to perform an ORDER BY clause.
326	Reports the estimated and actual costs of sorts used in a query.
330	Provides greater information about joins when using SET SHOWPLAN ON.
342	Disables the costing of pseudo-merge joins, thus significantly reducing time spent on the parse and compile phase for certain types of large, multitable joins. You can also use the command SET FORCEPLAN ON to disable the costing of pseudo-merge joins because the query is forced to use the order specified in the FROM clause.

Table 21-4. DBCC Trace Flags (continued)

Trace Flag	Description
349	Fixes a performance bug in views in which the view is defined with a subquery in its SELECT. But a direct query for the exact same SELECT statement yields much faster performance. Trace flag 349 fixes this behavior.
506	Trace flag 506 enforces ANSI-style comparisons between variables and parameters containing null (and always producing a result of null). Trace flag 506 is superseded by the command SET ANSI_NULLS ON.
652	Disables read-ahead functionality for the server.
653	Disables read-ahead functionality for the current connections. When used in combination with the –1 trace flag, it disables read-ahead functionality for all currently active processes.
1081	Extends the life span of index pages in cache by delaying the entrance of data pages into cache. This can improve performance on databases where retaining the index pages in cache is more important than reducing data page I/O.
1140	Eliminates the extent-chain scan when attempting to allocate a page to an existing table.
1200	Reports the lock promotion, type of lock requested, and SPID for queries in a given session.
1204	Shows deadlocking information, including the types of locks encountered and the current command affected.
1205	Shows detailed information about the current command in process at the time of deadlock.
1211	Provides additional lock management functionality, such as enabling retry on allocation lock collision.
1609	By default, the *sp_sqlexec* extended stored procedure sends commands directly to the Open Data Services language event handler. This trace flag enables the unpacking and checking of RPC information sent by *sp_sqlexec*. Microsoft servers now have the more flexible EXECUTE command.
1704	Shows when a temporary table is created or dropped.
2701	Normally, @@error has a value of 0 for messages with a severity level of 10 or less when issued by RAISERROR. This trace flag sets the value of @@error to 50,000 for messages with a severity level of 10 or less.
3002	Forces backups into Microsoft SQL Server 6.0 compatibility mode, meaning that the database must be in DBO-only mode when performing a dump.
3502	Enters a message in the SQL Server error log at the start and end of each checkpoint.
3503	Tells if the checkpoint noted at the end of automatic recovery was skipped for a given read-only database.
3505	In Microsoft SQL Server, DUMP statements directed to tape automatically use hardware compression if it is available. Trace flag 3505 disables this behavior.
3604	Sends all trace output to the client workstation's standard output device (usually the screen).

Table 21-4. DBCC Trace Flags (continued)

Trace Flag	Description
3605	Sends all trace output to the SQL Server error log. When run from the command line, the output is duplicated on the screen where the *SQLSERVR.EXE* command was run.
3607	At startup, skips the automatic recovery process for all databases.
3608	At startup, skips the automatic recovery process for all databases except master. This trace flag is useful when the master database must be recovered.
3609	At startup, skips the creation of the tempdb database. This trace flag is useful when the device(s) that make up tempdb or model database are having problems.
3640	For all client sessions, prohibits the sending of DONE_IN_PROC messages that are sent by each completed statement of a stored procedure. Similar to the command SET NOCOUNT ON, except that it applies to all clients at once.
4022	At startup, skips the execution of all startup stored procedures.
4030	Shows the byte and ASCII data stream from the client to the server (the server input stream). Functionally similar to the command DBCC INPUTBUFFER.
4031	Shows the byte and ASCII data stream from the server to the client (the server output stream). Functionally similar to the command DBCC OUTPUTBUFFER.
4032	Same as trace flag 4031, but shows only the ASCII data stream. Trace flag 4032 is used instead of trace flag 4031 when rapid output response is needed.
5302	Alters default behavior of SELECT . . . INTO (and other processes) that lock system tables for the duration of the transaction. This trace flag disables the locking of system tables with SELECT . . . INTO during an implicit transaction.
7501	Forces the use of Microsoft SQL Server 6.0 behavior for dynamic cursors. With Microsoft SQL Server 6.5, dynamic cursors are automatically engaged with forward-only cursors providing faster processing and alleviating the need for unique indexes.
7502	Disables cached cursor plans for extended stored procedures.
8202	On a Microsoft SQL Server publishing database, the log reader sometimes replicates UPDATE statements as UPDATE commands and at other times as DELETE/INSERT pairs. This trace flag causes all UPDATE commands to replicate as DELETE/INSERT pairs.
8501	Writes detailed information about MS-Distributed Transaction Coordinator context and state changes to the log.

Like the DBCC command, the SET command has many permutations and variations. However, the SET command is focused on controlling query-related behavior for the duration of a process (like a stored procedure or trigger) or for the duration of an end user's work session. That means that a SET command, once activated, remains in effect until it is specifically revoked. In triggers and stored procedures, the SET command remains in effect until processing has completed, at which point it rolls back.

Be careful when using SET in a Transact-SQL batch. It takes effect only at the end of the batch. So if you want a SET command to be in effect during the entirety of a given Transact-SQL program, place it in a batch at the start of the program.

The various SET commands affect different aspects of a user's session. Thus, certain SET commands are usually used in certain situations. For example, you would probably use a different set of commands (no pun intended) when doing performance tuning from the set you'd use for debugging a stored procedure. As a result, some variations of the SET command get a great deal of coverage in other chapters and receive commensurately less in this chapter. For example, those SET commands that deal with transactions and locking are discussed in Chapter 11, while those that affect performance tuning are discussed in Chapter 20. Table 21-5 gives an overview of each SET command.

Table 21-5. The SET Command

SET Command	Vendor Support	Description
SET ANSI_DEFAULTS {ON | OFF}	MS	Sets all of the ANSI-compliance settings on or off, including ANSI_NULLS, ANSI_NULL_DFLT_ON, ANSI_PADDING, ANSI_WARNINGS, ARITHABORT, CURSOR_CLOSE_ON_COMMIT, IMPLICIT_TRANSACTIONS, and QUOTED_IDENTIFIER.
SET ANSI_NULL_DFLT_OFF | ANSI_NULL_DFLT_ON	MS	These are mutually exclusive options. When set to ANSI_NULL_DFLT_OFF, the session will define new columns without ANSI null compatibility (new columns without explicit nullability will be defined as NOT NULL), overriding the default database nullability set by the *sp_dboption* system stored procedure. Ensures ANSI null compatibility when set to ANSI_NULL_DFLT_ON.
SET ANSI_NULLS {ON | OFF}	MS	Sets ANSI-standard behavior in comparison operations EQUAL (=) and NOT EQUAL (<>), so that any operation containing a null evaluates to null. Use of this command requires the use of the IS NULL and IS NOT NULL operators to compare null values. Null is not acceptable as an argument while enabled.
SET ANSI_PADDING {ON | OFF}	MS	This setting causes variable-length datatypes (VARCHAR and VARBINARY) to be padded with spaces to their full length, while fixed-length columns (CHAR, INT, SMALLINT, and TINYINT datatypes) that allow nulls are padded in the event of a null value.

Table 21-5. The SET Command (continued)

<table>
<tr><th>SET Command</th><th>Vendor Support</th><th>Description</th></tr>
<tr><td>SET ANSI_PERMISSIONS {ON | OFF}</td><td>Sybase</td><td>By default, this setting is OFF. This command indicates whether SQL-92 standards will be applied to UPDATE and DELETE statements.</td></tr>
<tr><td>SET ANSI_WARNINGS {ON | OFF}</td><td>MS</td><td>Generates error messages whenever
• An overflow or divide-by-zero error occurs
• Nulls appear in aggregate functions like AVG, COUNT, MAX, MIN, or SUM
• An INSERT or UPDATE attempts to load a value exceeding the maximum length of a character or binary column (the DML statement is also aborted)</td></tr>
<tr><td>SET ANSINULL {ON | OFF}</td><td>Sybase</td><td>Same as Microsoft's SET ANSI_NULLS.</td></tr>
<tr><td>SET ARITHABORT {ON | OFF}</td><td>MS, Sybase</td><td>Causes any query experiencing an overflow or divide-by-zero error to terminate. Any results processed by the query prior to the error will be returned. Otherwise, the query will return null and a warning message.
Sybase allows the added keywords ARITH_OVERFLOW and NUMERIC_TRUNCATION using the syntax SET ARITHABORT [ARITH_OVERFLOW | NUMERIC_TRUNCATION] {ON | OFF}. The two settings are *not* mutually exclusive. Both can be in effect at one time.
ARITH_OVERFLOW impacts arithmetic errors caused by overflow or divide-by-zero errors. NUMERIC_TRUNCATION impacts arithmetic operations caused by the loss of scale from conversion to an exact numeric datatype.</td></tr>
<tr><td>SET ARITHIGNORE {ON | OFF}</td><td>MS, Sybase</td><td>Causes any query experiencing an overflow or divide-by-zero error to return NULL. Any results processed by the query prior to the error will be returned. Otherwise, the query will return null and a warning message.
Sybase allows the added keyword ARITH_OVERFLOW. It is optional and has no impact on the statement.</td></tr>
<tr><td>SET CHAINED {ON | OFF}</td><td>Sybase</td><td>Same as Microsoft's SET IMPLICIT_TRANSACTIONS.</td></tr>
<tr><td>SET CHAR_CONVERT {OFF | ON [WITH {ERROR | NO_ERROR}]
|
charset [WITH {ERROR | NO_ERROR}]}</td><td>Sybase</td><td>Enables or disables character conversion between the client and server, if they are using different character sets. The charset value may be the character set's name or ID. If set OFF, no conversion occurs. The WITH ERROR option notifies the client application if a conversion error occurs, while the WITH NO_ERROR option does not send a notification of errors to the client.</td></tr>
</table>

Table 21-5. The SET Command (continued)

SET Command	Vendor Support	Description
SET CIS_RPC_HANDLING {ON | OFF}	Sybase	Sets the default for outbound RPC calls to be handled by Component Integration Services (CIS) when set ON.
SET CLOSE ON END TRAN {ON | OFF}	Sybase	Same as Microsoft's SET CURSOR_CLOSE_ON_COMMIT.
SET CURSOR_CLOSE_ON_COMMIT {ON | OFF}	MS	This has nothing to do with the average single guy's fear of commitment. This setting specifies that cursors close when a transaction is committed or rolled back. This behavior conforms to ANSI standards.
SET CURSOR_ROWS number	Sybase	Sets the number of rows for each cursor fetch request from a client. Doesn't affect a FETCH . . . INTO operation.
SET DATEFIRST number	MS, Sybase	Normally, the value 7 (Sunday) is the first day of the week in the United States. This command sets another day of the week between 1 (Monday) and 7 (Sunday) as the first day. Useful for date functions and calculations.
SET DATEFORMAT date_format	MS, Sybase	Normally, DATETIME and SMALLDATETIME values are entered in the order of month-day-year in the United States. This command allows the date_formats of dateparts to be rearranged as mdy, myd, dmy, dym, ydm, or ymd.
SET DEADLOCKPRIORITY [LOW | NORMAL]	MS	Described in detail in Chapter 11, this setting can set a session as the preferred victim in any deadlock situations (LOW). A setting of NORMAL causes the session to be handled normally for deadlock resolution.
SET DISABLE_DEF_CNST_CHK {ON | OFF}	MS	Tells SQL Server to check for violation of constraints during data modifications, also known as *interim deferred violations*. Since these violations can sometimes resolve themselves before the transaction concludes, this setting disables the reporting of such temporary violations. This option also reduces the number of worktables generated by some queries and, in such cases, can improve performance.
SET FIPS_FLAGGER {level | OFF}	MS, Sybase	Enables ANSI SQL-92 FIPS 127-2[a] compliance at three different levels. An error message is generated whenever an operation conflicts with the specified ANSI settings. Values for level may be ENTRY, INTERMEDIATE, and FULL. When set OFF, no messages are generated when an operation conflicts with a specific ANSI FIPS setting.

Table 21-5. The SET Command (continued)

SET Command	Vendor Support	Description
SET FLUSHMESSAGE {ON | OFF}	Sybase	This is what most men's brains do when their significant other asks them to relay an important message to a mutual friend or coworker. In SQL Server, however, this setting tells Adaptive Server when it can return messages to the user. When set ON, messages are returned immediately as they are generated, rather than allowing them to be stored in the message buffer.
SET FMTONLY {ON | OFF}	MS	Queries will not return rows to a client when this setting is invoked. Only metadata (headers) are returned to the client.
SET FORCEPLAN {ON | OFF}	MS	This setting forces the SQL Server optimizer to process joins in the exact order as the tables appear in the FROM clause.
SET IDENTITY_INSERT {[[database].owner.]tablename} {ON | OFF}	MS, Sybase	Allows a session to directly update or insert identity values into one (and only one) table. Only one table can have this behavior enabled at any given time. If the identity value inserted or updated is greater than the current identity value, the new inserted value will be used as the current value.
SET IMPLICIT_TRANSACTIONS {ON | OFF}	MS	Issues an implicit transaction whenever certain SQL and Transact-SQL commands are issued. Refer to Chapter 11 for more details.
SET LANGUAGE language_name	MS, Sybase	Enables system messages in the language named, as long as the language set is installed on the server. The default is us_english. Refer to the section "Server Character Set" in Chapter 4, *Transact-SQL Fundamentals*, for more information.
SET NOCOUNT {ON | OFF}	MS, Sybase	Disables the message executed at the end of each statement, telling how many rows were affected while processing the statement. Processing of stored procedures can be greatly speeded up by eliminating the DONE_IN_PROC messages, thus reducing network traffic.
SET NOEXEC {ON | OFF}	MS, Sybase	Allows compilation of queries but prevents execution. Usually used in conjunction with SHOWPLAN to debug or tune a query. This setting prevents the execution of any subsequent statements, including other SET statements, until this feature is disengaged.

Table 21-5. The SET Command (continued)

SET Command	Vendor Support	Description
SET NUMERIC_ ROUNDABORT {ON | OFF}	MS	Setting this option ON tells SQL Server to terminate any transaction that causes a loss of precision in an arithmetic operation. Common causes include addition or subtraction when the number is too large or small to represent or round errors in multiplication or division operations. When set OFF, data is rounded off, and processing continues normally.
SET OFFSETS {keyword_list}	MS, Sybase	Used only in DB-Library applications, this setting returns the position of the keyword_list in relation to the beginning of the query. Valid keyword values include COMPUTE, EXECUTE, FROM, ORDER, PARAM, PROCEDURE, SELECT, STATEMENT, and TABLE.
SET PARALLEL_ DEGREE number	Sybase	Sets the upper limit for the number of working threads used to execute a parallel query. The value is stored in the Sybase global variable @@parallel_ degree. The number cannot exceed the maximum number of worker threads allowed per query as set in the "max parallel degree" configuration parameter.
SET PARSEONLY {ON | OFF}	MS, Sybase	This statement is useful for checking large and involved Transact-SQL programs because it checks the syntax (and returns error messages if any syntax errors exist) without generating a sequence tree, compiling, or executing the query. Not for use in stored procedures or triggers.
SET PREFETCH {ON | OFF}	Sybase	Allows or disallows large I/Os to the data cache.
SET PROCESS_LIMIT_ ACTION {ABORT | QUIET | WARNING}	Sybase	When set to ABORT, PROCESS_LIMIT_ACTION tells Adaptive Server to abort a parallel query when an insufficient number of worker threads are available to process the query. When set to QUIET, adjusts the plan downward to meet the maximum allowed worker threads. When set to WARNING, a warning message is issued when the plan is adjusted.
SET PROCID	MS, Sybase	Used only in DB-Library applications, this setting returns the internal identification number of a stored procedure before it returns a result set created by the stored procedure.
SET PROXY login_ name	Sybase	On Sybase, this setting allows you to assume the full persona of another user, including login ID, permissions, and suid of a specified login_name.

Table 21-5. The SET Command (continued)

SET Command	Vendor Support	Description
SET QUOTED_IDENTIFIER {ON | OFF}	MS, Sybase	Tells SQL Server not to check any identifier within double quote marks for keyword violations. Refer to the "Quoted Identifiers" section in Chapter 4 for more information.
SET REMOTE_PROC_TRANSACTIONS {ON | OFF}	MS	Tells Microsoft SQL Server to start a DTC transaction whenever a remote stored procedure is executed.
SET ROLE {"sa_role" | "sso_role" | "oper_role" | role_name [WITH PASSWD "password"]} {ON | OFF}	Sybase	Sets a specified role ON or OFF during the current session. By default, all roles granted to a user are turned on when they log in. This function can toggle those settings interactively during their session. The WITH PASSWD option requires that the correct password be provided.
SET ROWCOUNT {number | @int_variable}	MS, Sybase	This powerful, and possibly disruptive, command tells SQL Server to halt execution once the specified number of rows are returned (for a query) or acted upon (for a transaction). The value may be a literal number or a variable. All Transact-SQL statements within the user's session stop processing once they have affected the specified number of rows. This behavior even impacts triggers and cursors. A rowcount of 0 returns all rows.
SET SCAN_PARALLEL_DEGREE number	Sybase	Allows a numeric setting up to the value of the "max scan parallel degree" configuration parameter to be put into effect for the current session. This value is the maximum degree of parallelism for hash-based scans.
SET SELF_RECURSION {ON | OFF}	Sybase	Determines whether a Sybase trigger can initiate a transaction that will cause the trigger to fire again. This option is set off by default.
SET SESSION AUTHORIZATION login_name	Sybase	The same as SET PROXY, though this command is SQL standard.
SET SHOWPLAN {ON | OFF}	MS, Sybase	Provides a great deal of information about the processing plan for each query, including index and table usages.
SET SORT_RESOURCES {ON | OFF}	Sybase	When ON, this setting generates and prints a description of the sorting plan for a CREATE INDEX statement.

Table 21-5. The SET Command (continued)

SET Command	Vendor Support	Description
SET STATISTICS {IO | TIME} {| SUBQUERYCACHE} {ON | OFF}	MS, Sybase	IO provides a great deal of information about I/O generated for each table in each query, including number of scans, logical reads from pages in cache, and physical reads from pages on disk. TIME provides the parse, compile, and execution time, in milliseconds, for each command. SUBQUERYCACHE, allowable on Sybase only, shows the number of cache hits, misses, and number of rows stored in the subquery cache for each subquery.
SET STRING_RTRUNCATION {ON | OFF}	Sybase	By default, INSERT or UPDATE statements that attempt to insert oversized CHAR or VARCHAR values are truncated without raising a SQLSTATE exception. When set ON, an exception is raised whenever such a string is truncated.
SET TABLE COUNT NUMBER	Sybase	By default, Sybase Adaptive Server will consider up to four tables while optimizing a single join. This SET command allows you to set the value anywhere from 1 to 8.
SET TEXTSIZE number	MS, Sybase	Crops TEXT datatype data in a result set to the specified size, in bytes, impacting the global variable @@textsize. The default size is 4K.
SET TRANSACTION ISOLATION LEVEL	MS, Sybase	This setting controls the default locking behavior for all transactions issued during the current connection. Refer to Chapter 11 for more details.
SET TRANSACTIONAL_ RPC {ON | OFF}	Sybase	When ON, RPC transactions are handled by the Component Integration Service (CIS). When OFF, RPC transactions are handled by the Adaptive Server site handler.
SET XACT_ABORT {ON | OFF}	MS	Discussed fully in Chapter 20, this setting controls how the currently executing transaction terminates. When set ON, the entire transaction will be rolled back when any single error appears. When set OFF, only the statement that raised the error will terminate; all other statements in the transaction will continue normally.

[a] Federal Information Processing Standard 127-2

If you get the urge, you can use the system stored procedure *sp_configure* user options instead of the SET command on a Microsoft server. Refer to Chapter 17, *System and Extended Stored Procedures*, for details on this system stored procedure. You can query the @@options global variable to determine what user options have been set.

Debugging Utilities

There are a number of add-on utilities available to help debug the most difficult Transact-SQL program or application. They are mentioned here to let you know where to look in case you need more assistance debugging a particularly difficult problem.

There are several reasons we don't cover the utilities in detail. None of the tools are integrated components of the programming environment. Most of the tools are used to debug some portion of the application but not Transact-SQL code itself. And in several cases, you actually have to load the debugging utility from another product or download it from a web site. Plus, not all of the debugging tools are verified for use against both Microsoft and Sybase database platforms. Please refer to the system documentation for full instructions on using these debugging tools. Tools available include:

Makepipe and Readpipe
: Shipped with both Microsoft and Sybase databases, these two command-line utilities are designed to help test network named pipes.

PRINTDMP
: When a Microsoft SQL Server process generates an access violation, it often produces a specific stack trace named with a *.DMP* extension. This file can only be read using the PRINTDMP utility stored in *\MSSQL\BINN*.

ODBCPing
: This 32-bit application, stored in the *\MSSQL\BINN* directory of Microsoft SQL Server installations, is used to test connectivity between two servers, especially for processes like replication.

ODBCSpy
: Shipped on Microsoft's ODBC Software Developer's Kit (SDK), the ODBCSpy utility can be used to trace all ODBC calls made to a specific ODBC data source from a client perspective. Tracing is quite informative and includes full descriptions of error messages returned by SQL Server. A minimal trace utility called ODBC Driver Manager is included in the ODBC Administrator of the ODBC SDK.

SQL Trace
: Microsoft's graphical utility that monitors and records SQL Server 6.5 database activity in real time or focuses on specific users, applications, and processes from the server perspective. SQL Trace ships with Microsoft SQL Server Version 6.5 and later.

Transact-SQL Debugger
: One of the true ironies of Microsoft product packaging is that its first Transact-SQL debugger does not ship with Microsoft SQL Server. You can only get it

from the Microsoft Visual C++ or Microsoft Visual Studio products (in fact, they're slightly different versions). This utility requires installation of both server and client components to function properly. But when properly set up, it can provide a wide variety of useful debugging features, including step-through, break processing, viewable variables and parameters, and so on.

Windows NT Performance Monitor
: Available with both Microsoft and Sybase installations, this utility allows you to monitor a wide variety of counters and objects specific to SQL Server, its internal processes, and its user connections. As indicated by its name, it is mostly used by DBAs to measure system performance, but it can also be useful for determining if a specific Transact-SQL program or process is consuming too many resources, locking out other users, and so on.

Summary

This chapter discussed both general and specific debugging techniques for Transact-SQL programs, including:

- An overview of debugging and the basic characteristics of the debugging process. Many of the techniques presented here are generic to debugging regardless of the language being used.
- A series of debugging tools specific to SQL Server and ways in which they can be utilized to speed up the debugging process.
- The use of the SET command, an invaluable tool for debugging and other purposes.

VI

Appendixes

Part VI of this book contains several summary appendixes:

- Appendix A, *System Tables*
- Appendix B, *What's New for Transact-SQL in Microsoft SQL Server 7.0*
- Appendix C, *The BCP Utility*

System Tables

The system catalog tables are the heart of SQL Server. No database object can exist in SQL Server without an entry of some form being made in the system catalog tables. It is very important to learn as much as you can about the system tables, since that knowledge can influence the way you work. On the CD-ROM accompanying this book, you will find a large number of procedures designed to ease the administrative functions of SQL Server. Many of these stored procedures manipulate or read data from these system tables.

Perhaps one of the most interesting things that can be gleaned from the system tables is how similar Microsoft and Sybase's SQL Servers actually are. In recent years, each of these products has made incredible strides in terms of its individual evolution. In spite of their variations, however, they still follow a similar paradigm of thinking, which is played out in their system catalog tables. For those of us who have to work with both architectures, the system catalog tables are still close enough to require learning only once.

In this appendix, we will briefly explain the system tables. Once you become familiar with the tables and commands, you will be able to start writing your own stored procedures to get information from the system catalog tables.

We don't cover every column in detail. Rather, we have focused on the main columns that we frequently use when working with SQL Server. The remaining columns we've left for you to explore on your own. These columns are well covered in the system documentation that accompanies your particular version of SQL Server.

The best tips anyone can give you on maximizing your utilization of the system catalog tables are these:

- Review the coding of the system stored procedures.

- Learn the system table entity-relationship diagram.
- Understand what type of data is stored in each of the system catalog tables.

The table descriptions given here are valid for Microsoft SQL Server through Version 6.5 and Sybase Adaptive Server architecture through Version 11.5

System Tables in the master Database

The tables and most of the options described in the following sections are applicable to both Microsoft and Sybase SQL Server. In a few cases, we'll note differences between the implementations.

spt_values

This table contains all the constants for SQL Server and their descriptions. It is essentially a lookup table for SQL Server. The lookups are broken into groups like Configuration Options or Index Types. Within the groups are the permissible values each group may have. For example, for Index Types, the permissible values are Nonclustered, Clustered, and so on. Each of these values would have a number value associated with it, in this case, 0 and 16. These values would then be used by SQL Server every time it was trying to refer to a clustered or nonclustered index, as opposed to using the names. Many of the system stored procedures refer to this table to get descriptive text for these values, which may be found on the numerous system tables. The most important columns are:

name
: Option name

number
: A value associated with the option; 1 indicates that this is a type description

type
: Option type name

low
: Either the value for the option or the start value for those options that have a range of values associated with them

high
: The end value for fields that contain value ranges

syscharsets

This table contains all the character sets and the sort orders that have been defined for the SQL Server. The most important columns are:

id

Character set or sort order ID. If this is a sort order, then this field will be the combination of the sort order ID and the character set that this sort order is based on (csid).

type

Entry type. For character sets, the values are between 1,000 and 1,999. For sort orders, the values are between 2,000 and 2,999.

csid

0 if this is a character set and the ID of the character set if this is a sort order.

name

Unique name of the character set or sort order.

description

Entry description.

definition

Definition of the character set or sort order.

sysconfigures

This table contains all the permissible configurable parameters within SQL Server, as well as their default values. The values contained here do not change when you modify a configuration parameter. Instead, the syscurconfigs table is updated with the actual value that is used at runtime. The most important columns are:

config

This is a unique identifier for each configurable option in the server.

value

This is the value for this configuration option.

comment

This field contains the name of the configuration option. Sybase has also added a name column, which contains similar values to this field, although not exactly the same.

status

This field contains 1 if this is a dynamically configurable option and 0 if the option will take effect only on a reboot. In Microsoft, a value of 2 indicates that this field will be displayed only if the "show advanced options" configuration option is set.

syscurconfigs

This table is dynamic. It is rebuilt in both Microsoft and Sybase every time you query it. This table contains the current configuration values of the server. The most important columns are:

config
: Identifier of the configuration option.

value
: Currently effective value of the configuration option.

comment
: On Microsoft SQL Server, this field contains configuration option names. On Sybase, this field details the amount of memory that this particular option consumes. A # in this field indicates that this parameter is sharing memory with other resources. The value after the # mark indicates the parameter with which it is sharing memory.

status
: Indicates whether this field is dynamic or static—that is, whether this option will take effect immediately or after the server is rebooted.

sysdatabases

This table stores information about the databases that have been defined on this server. This is one of the most important tables in the master database, since no database can exist on the server without being defined here. The most important columns are:

name
: Database name.

status
: A bitmap of database current status and database options. The database options are values set using the *sp_dboption* stored procedure. The current status of the database is set by SQL Server during startup, once recovery of a database is complete or once the database has been brought online after a database dump.

crdate
: The date the database was created.

dumptrdate
: The last time the database was dumped.

sysdevices

This table stores information about the database devices that have been created on this SQL Server. In order to be able to create a database on a device, the device first has to be defined and recorded in this table. The most important columns are:

low
: The first virtual page number associated with the device

high
: The last virtual page number associated with the device

status
: A bitmap of options and settings for the device

name
: Device logical name

physname
: Device physical name

mirrorname
: Associated mirror device name

cntrltype
: Device type

syslanguages

This table contains an entry for each language other than us_english that has been defined for this particular SQL Server. The most important columns are:

langid
: Unique language identifier.

dateformat
: Date formatting order that applies to this language, for example, mdy.

datefirst
: The first day of the week in this language. Valid options are 1 through 7, where 1 = Monday and 7 = Sunday.

upgrade
: The last SQL Server upgrade version for this language.

name
: Official language name.

alias
: An alternate name of the language.

months

A comma-separated list of full month names, ordered from January to December. Each month name may not exceed 20 characters.

shortmonths

A comma-separated list of abbreviated month names, from January to December. Each month name may not exceed nine characters.

names

A comma-separated list of day names from Monday to Sunday.

Sybase and Microsoft invert their usage of name and alias. This means that if Francais is the name in Microsoft, Sybase puts this name in the alias column.

syslocks

This table contains information about the currently active locks in the system. It is dynamic and changes frequently as resources are used. The most important columns are:

id

Object ID that has a lock on it.

dbid

Database ID where the object resides.

page

If the lock is held on a page, this is the page ID. If the lock is on an extent, this column contains the page ID of the first page of the extent. For table-level locks, the value is zero.

type

Lock type (see Table A-1).

spid

ID of the system process that issued the lock.

Table A-1. Lock Type Values in Microsoft and Sybase SQL Server

Microsoft	Sybase
1 – Exclusive table lock	1 – Exclusive table lock
2 – Shared table lock	2 – Shared table lock
3 – Exclusive intent lock	3 – Exclusive intent lock

Table A-1. Lock Type Values in Microsoft and Sybase SQL Server (continued)

Microsoft	Sybase
4 – Shared intent lock	4 – Shared intent lock
5 – Exclusive page lock	5 – Exclusive page lock
6 – Shared page lock	6 – Shared page lock
7 – Update page lock	7 – Update page lock
8 – Exclusive extent lock	8 – Exclusive extent lock
9 – Update extent lock	9 – Update extent lock
11 – Next extent lock	11 – Next extent lock
12 – Previous extent lock	12 – Previous extent lock
257 – – Blocked exclusive table lock	256 – Lock is blocking another process
258 – Blocking shared table lock	512 – Demand lock
259 – Blocking exclusive intent lock	
260 – Blocking shared intent lock	
261 – Blocking exclusive page lock	
262 – Blocking shared page lock	
263 – Blocking update page lock	
264 – Blocking exclusive extent lock	
265 – Blocking update extent lock	

syslogins

This table holds information about all the users who can log onto this SQL Server. A user account cannot be created in any database unless a login has been created for this user first. The most important columns are:

totcpu
: Total number of CPU cycles consumed by this user since the last time the values were cleared

totio
: Total number of I/O cycles consumed by this user since the last time the values were cleared

dbname
: The name of the default database for this user

name
: User login name

password
: Encrypted user password

In SQL Server Versions 4.x and before, the password column was not encrypted. Therefore, a devious SA could learn anybody's password and then log in as another user, potentially causing damage traceable back to this unsuspecting person. In recent versions, both vendors have encrypted the column as they strengthened SQL Server security.

sysmessages

This table stores the message text for all system- and user- defined warning and error messages in SQL Server. It is referenced when the RAISERROR command is called. The most important columns are:

error
: Unique error number

langid
: Language associated with the message

severity
: Severity of the error message

description
: Description of the error message

sysprocesses

This table stores information about active processes in this server. Once a process exits the server, its entry is removed. This table is not a physical database table, but rather a dynamic view built by SQL Server. You cannot directly update or modify rows in it, even if you allow updates on system tables, and entries come and go in it as users come and go on the system. When a user consumes resources or performs some action on the server, this table is updated accordingly. The most important columns are:

spid
: System process ID for the connection.

status-connection status:

runnable
: The process is actually doing something useful or at least consuming resources. The number of runnable processes at any single instance is determined by the number of SQL Server CPUs configured to belong to your server. Sybase also refers to each CPU available to the server as an "engine."

sleeping

The process is catching up on some much-needed rest, since the server has decided to help out some other poor process. However, you probably don't need to worry about this, since the process may be sleeping for only a very brief period of time. The report is based on the state of the server at the millisecond this request was run.

lock sleep

The process cannot continue until some other process (whose SPID will be in the blocked column) completes its operation, because both processes are competing for the same object.

hostname

The name of the host who spawned this process. Typically, this will be the client machine name or application name. You may be able to define the hostname of your process when you establish a connection. For example, command-prompt ISQL uses the switch –H*hostname* to make the specified hostname string the hostname of your process.

program_name

The name of the program that is being used to connect to SQL Server.

cmd

The type of action this process is performing. It will typically be a Transact-SQL command that the process is executing, such as SELECT, INSERT, UPDATE, DELETE, CREATE INDEX, and so on. Inactive processes will have the value of AWAITING COMMAND in this column.

cpu

The amount of logical I/O this process has consumed since it first began. This is one of the most useful columns to watch, since it indicates whether this query has been a resource hog. Logical I/O is nine times less expensive than physical I/O. The goal should be to have your logical I/O exceed your physical I/O. The query will also likely be quicker if it is run from memory and is not being satisfied by going to the disk to retrieve the results.

physical_io

The number of physical I/O reads this command has consumed since it began. This counter differs from cpu in that it starts from zero every time a new command is issued for this process. This column is the most important one to watch as you try to identify any potential resource hogs in your user community.

memusage

The amount of memory allocated to this process.

dbid

ID of the database in which this process is working.

suid

Login for the user and owner of this process.

blocked

Whenever this field has a number in it, the status field will contain LOCK SLEEP. Locking is covered in more detail in Chapter 11, *Transactions and Locking*.

sysremotelogins

This table stores information about users who can execute remote procedure calls on this server. In order to be able to call an RPC on this server, these remote users' servers will have to have been previously defined in sysservers. The most important columns are:

remoteusername

Username on the remote server

remoteserverid

ID of the remote server based upon the entry in sysservers

suid

User login ID on this server

status

A bitmap of options defined for this user

sysservers

This table stores information about remote servers known to the local server. This information is used to determine whether remote procedure calls can be executed on another server. Sybase uses this table to define the backup server as well. The most important columns are:

srvname

The name of the remote server

srvstatus

A bitmap of options defined for the server

srvnetname

Server name in the operating system

sysusages

This table stores the relationship between the databases defined in the server and the devices where the databases are located. There can be many entries for a database in this table, since every database can have many physical device fragments attached to this database. The most important columns are:

dbid
: ID of the database that owns the segment

segmap
: Segment type (data, log, data and log)

lstart
: Logical address of the segment within the database

size
: Segment size

vstart
: Virtual address of the segment within the device

Sybase-Specific System Tables in the master Database

Sybase has added a number of system tables, described in the following sections.

sysengines

This table contains an entry for each SQL Server CPU or engine that is online. This table stores usage activity and is extensively used by the system stored procedure *sp_monitor* to monitor the engine utilization.

syslisteners

This table holds information on the network protocols that can be used to connect to the server. It is dynamic and is built every time a user queries it.

sysloginroles

This table contains an entry for each login that has been assigned a system role in SQL Server—that is, DBO, SSO or oper, sybase_ts, and navigator—and replication will have an entry for each role that is associated with the login records in this table.

syslogshold

This table holds information about the oldest active transaction in the server and the replication server transaction point that may apply to this database. It is dynamic and is built whenever a user queries it.

sysmonitors

This table stores information about each monitor counter being stored on the SQL Server.

sysresourcelimits

This table contains any resource limits defined for a particular login or application. Every time this login or application executes a query, command, or stored procedure, the system verifies that it does not consume more than its allocated share of resources.

syssecmechs

This table contains information about security mechanisms and services that are supported on this server. It is dynamic and is built every time a user queries it.

syssrvroles

This table describes each user-defined role and all system roles.

systestlog

This table is used on the B1-level secure server implementation.

systimeranges

This table contains time ranges for resource limitations. SQL Server allows you to create named time ranges that can be applied to resource limitations. These time ranges specify when the resource limitations apply. This allows you to specify periods when a resource limitation can be activated, for example, Monday to Friday, 9:00 A.M. to 12:00 A.M.

System Tables in All Databases

The following sections describe the system tables that are present in all databases on SQL Server (including the master database).

sysalternates

This table contains a row for each database user who has an alias. An alias allows extending to a user all permissions granted to another user of a database. It has two columns:

suid
: System user ID (as found in master..syslogins).

altsuid
: System user ID of a user to whom another user (identified by suid) is aliased.

sysarticles (Microsoft Only)

This system table supports replication. It has a row for each article posted by the publishing server.

syscolumns

This table contains one row for each column of every table or view and each parameter of every stored procedure. The most important columns are:

id
: Object ID of the table, view, or stored procedure (as found in sysobjects)

colid
: Column ID, sequential 1-based number of a column within its object

status
: A bitmap describing whether the column allows NULL values, if it has an IDENTITY property, or if it is an OUTPUT parameter of a stored procedure

type
: Physical storage type (as found in systypes)

length
: Maximum length in bytes

usertype
: User datatype (as found in systypes)

cdefault
: Object ID of the default (if any) associated with the column

domain
: Object ID of the rule or check constraint associated with the column

name
: Column name, unique within its object

prec
: Precision (for numeric datatypes)

scale
: Scale (for numeric datatypes)

syscomments

This table contains Transact-SQL source code for stored procedures, views, triggers, rules, defaults, check constraints, and default constraints of the database. You won't find CREATE TABLE and CREATE INDEX statements in syscomments. They may be reconstructed from other system tables. The table may also be used to store user-defined comments about objects, but this feature is rarely used.

The whole CREATE statement is treated as a stream of bytes that may include line feed and carriage return characters. SQL Server breaks the whole source code of the object into pieces of up to 255 bytes and stores them in syscomments, taking as many rows as needed.

Sybase stores up to 255 bytes in every syscomments row, while Microsoft SQL Server alternates between 255 and 249 bytes. Every other line is not longer than 249 characters. This should not concern you, unless you are writing your own system stored procedures that access syscomments.

This table has a composite primary key consisting of four columns:

id
: Related to ID of the object in sysobjects.

number
: For grouped stored procedures; indicates grouping number.

colid
: Sequential syscomments row number for the object; 1-based.

texttype
: Indicates whether the row is a part of the source code or a user-supplied comment. On Microsoft SQL Server, it also may indicate encryption.

text
: Used to store the object's source code or user-defined comments in a VARCHAR(255) field. We don't particularly like the name of this column, because it is the same as the name of a Transact-SQL datatype. Just remember that the type of the text column is not the TEXT datatype.

sysconstraints

This table associates constraints with tables and columns. The most important columns are:

constid
: ID of the constraint

id
: ID of the table on which this constraint is defined

colid
: Column ID (as in syscolumns) if this is a column-level constraint, or 0 if it is a table-level constraint

status
: A bitmap that defines constraint type

sysdepends

This table is supposed to contain references between objects. For example, if a stored procedure references three tables and calls one other procedure, then sysdepends should contain an entry for every pair of related objects—four rows in this example. However, there is a serious flaw in how SQL Server manages data in this table. Everything works perfectly when you create all objects in the hierarchical order of dependency—tables first, then views on tables, then views on previously defined views, then stored procedures that do not call other procedures, then procedures that call previously defined procedures. However, if you drop and re-create an object that is used by other objects, SQL Server forgets all the links associated with it. All objects continue to function, but the dependencies are gone from sysdepends. We strongly advise you never to rely on sysdepends information or on the related system stored procedure, *sp_depends,* that uses this table. Just pretend this table does not exist.

Note one more limitation: dependencies can be stored only for objects within the current database.

sysindexes

This table contains a row for every index of every table and a row for the data pages level of tables that have no clustered index. The primary key is defined on two columns:

id
: Links to an object (table) in sysobjects.

indid

The value of the index ID tells the type of index:

0

For the data page level of a table without a clustered index.

1

For the clustered index on the table (if it exists).

2–254

For nonclustered indexes (the next available number is automatically assigned at new index creation).

255

For the chain of data pages containing TEXT or IMAGE data (if the table has columns of these types). indid column values may be very important, because you can use them in Transact-SQL code to force specific indexes. See Chapter 20, *Transact-SQL Optimization and Tuning*, for more details.

Other important columns are:

name

The name of the table if indid = 0; the index name if indid is between 1 and 254; and the table name prefixed with a *"t"* if indid = 255. Index names have to be unique for each table, but the same name may be used for indexes of different tables.

status

A bitmap that contains index options.

minlen and maxlen

The minimum and maximum possible length of a row based on column definitions.

keycnt

Number of columns comprising a composite index key.

keys1 and keys2

Bitmaps referencing columns of a table from which the index key is made. Information stored in these columns is used by the INDEX_COL function.

Several columns contain information about the number of rows and the space used by the table. On Microsoft SQL Server and old versions of Sybase, these columns are:

rows

For rows with indid of 0 or 1, contains an estimated count of rows in the table. SQL Server tries to keep it accurate but does not guarantee that it is. It is set correctly if you execute a time-consuming DBCC CHECKDB, DBCC CHECKTABLE, or Microsoft-specific DBCC UPDATEUSAGE.

reserved, dpages, and used
: Combined for all sysindexes rows of a table; may be used to estimate space usage by the table.

On recent Sybase versions, these columns have been replaced with two new ones:

doampg and ioampg
: These columns contain page numbers for internal table allocation maps. They are used by the Sybase-only built-in functions DATA_PGS, RESERVED_PGS, and USED_PGS.

syskeys

This table contains information about table keys. The most important columns are:

id
: Object ID of the table as found in sysobjects

depid
: Object ID of the dependent table referenced by the key

type
: A bitmap describing the key type

syslogs

This table contains database transaction log records. It is one of the most critical tables in every database and is used almost constantly by SQL Server. However, there is very little useful information you can derive from this table if you try to select from it. If you expect that it contains all the data modified by your transactions and logged in the transaction log, you will be disappointed. The syslogs table is only the tip of an iceberg. Actual transaction log information is stored separately on database pages that you cannot access with a SELECT query. You cannot directly update, insert, or delete data in syslogs. It has two columns:

xactid
: Transaction ID (not practically useful to review).

op
: Operation code. This number may be used for very high-level analysis of database activity. Each operation, such as UPDATE, INSERT, or DELETE, has a special operational code. So, when you select op from syslogs, you see how many operations of each type have been executed since the last time the transaction log was dumped and in which order they were executed.

sysobjects

This table contains a list of all database objects: system and user tables, stored procedures, triggers, views, defaults, rules, and constraints. Indexes and keys are not considered database objects and are described in the sysindexes and syskeys tables, respectively. The most important columns are:

name
: Object name

id
: Object ID, unique within its database

uid
: User ID of the object owner (as found in *sysusers*)

type
: Object type (see Table A-2)

crdate
: Object creation date and time

deltrig
: Object ID of the DELETE trigger if it exists, or 0

instrig
: Object ID of the INSERT trigger if it exists, or 0

updtrig
: Object ID of the UPDATE trigger if it exists, or 0

Table A-2. Object Types for Microsoft and Sybase SQL Server

type	Microsoft	Sybase
C	CHECK constraint	
D	DEFAULT constraint	Default
F	FOREIGN KEY constraint	
K	PRIMARY KEY or UNIQUE constraint	
L	Log	Log
P	Stored procedure	Stored procedure
R	Rule	Rule
RF	Stored procedure for replication	
RI		Referential integrity constraint
S	System table	System table
TR	Trigger	Trigger
U	User table	User table
V	View	View

Table A-2. Object Types for Microsoft and Sybase SQL Server (continued)

type	Microsoft	Sybase
X	Extended stored procedure	
XP		Extended stored procedure

sysprocedures

This table contains information about the execution plans of stored procedures, triggers, views, defaults, rules, and check constraints. There is little practical reason to query this table directly.

sysprotects

This table contains information about granted and revoked permissions on database objects. The most important columns are:

id
: Object ID that has a permission granted or revoked (as found in sysobjects).

uid
: ID of user or group that has a permission granted or revoked (as found in sysusers).

action
: Permission description code. You may translate it to a meaningful description with the help of the following query:

```
SELECT  name
FROM    master..spt_values
WHERE   type = 'T'
AND     number = <action>
```

protecttype
: Permission type code. Execute the following query to obtain permission description:

```
SELECT  name
FROM    master..spt_values
WHERE   type = 'T'
AND     number = <protecttype>
```

columns
: Bitmap indicating columns to which permission applies.

The stored procedure *sp_helprotect* reports information contained in sysprotects.

syspublications (Microsoft Only)

This table contains information about publications posted by the publishing server.

sysreferences

This table contains information about foreign key constraints. The most important columns are:

constid
: Foreign key constraint ID

fkeyid (Microsoft) or tableid (Sybase)
: Object ID of the referencing table (as found in sysobjects)

rkeyid (Microsoft) or reftabid (Sybase)
: Object ID of the referenced table (as found in sysobjects)

keycnt
: Number of columns comprising the foreign key

fkey1 ... fkey16 (Microsoft) or fokey1 ... fokey16 (Sybase)
: Column ids of the referencing table (as found in colid of the syscolumns table)

rkey1 ... rkey16 (Microsoft) or refkey1 ... refkey16 (Sybase)
: Column ids of the referenced table

This system table is a vivid example of a poor database design. Its structure does not allow for expansion of a foreign key beyond 16 columns. Vendors will have to make serious structural changes if they want to allow longer keys in future SQL Server versions.

---

syssegments

This table contains information about database segments. Segment management is beyond the scope of this book.

syssubscriptions (Microsoft Only)

This table contains information about published articles and their links to servers' subscribers.

systypes

This table contains information about system and user-defined datatypes. Rows describing system datatypes are added at database creation and cannot be removed or altered. User-defined datatypes are added by the system stored procedure *sp_addtype*. They are defined based on system datatypes. The most important columns are:

uid
User ID of the datatype creator (as found in sysusers)

usertype
User type ID

variable
Indicator of variable-length types

allownulls
Indicator of nullable types

type
Physical datatype

length
Physical length in bytes

tdefault
Object ID of the default (if any) associated with the datatype

domain
Object ID of the check constraint (if any) associated with the datatype

name
Datatype name

prec
Precision (for numeric types)

scale
Scale (for numeric types)

sysusers

This table contains information about database users and user groups. Each user is associated with a login contained in master..syslogins. A user cannot be a member of more than one user group. All users are also considered members of public, regardless of their group. All users have permissions granted to public in addition to permissions granted to their user group and to them directly. Every database normally contains system-defined users:

DBO
Associated with SA login

guest
A special account for guest users

public
Refers to all users

Users may be added to a database with the system stored procedure *sp_adduser* and deleted with *sp_dropuser*. Groups are added with *sp_addgroup* and deleted with *sp_dropgroup*. Information from sysusers may be retrieved with the procedures *sp_helpgroup* and *sp_helpuser*.

The most important columns are:

suid
: System user ID (as found in master..syslogins) for users; a negative number for user groups

uid
: User ID, unique within this database

gid
: User ID of the user group (it links back to the sysusers table, which contains groups as well as users)

name
: The name of the user or user group, unique in this database

Summary

This appendix summarized system tables and discussed some of the key fields that record valuable system information. The discussion is divided into three major sections:

- Master database system tables—those system tables that can only be found in the master database and control the functioning of the overall SQL Server products.
- Sybase-specific system tables in the master database—Sybase has added a number of tables into its system diagram.
- System tables in all databases—each user database, including the master database, also contains a number of tables that hold database-specific information.

B

What's New for Transact-SQL in Microsoft SQL Server 7.0

The fact that the software industry is constantly updating software releases is both a boon and a bane to authors. On the one hand, an author might have the opportunity to develop additional editions of her book (if the market is willing) every time the software is upgraded. On the other hand, the material can become out of date as quickly as the software it's based upon. At the time we're writing this book, Microsoft SQL Server is nearing a major release milestone—Version 7.0. This appendix summarizes the changes in this version.

General SQL Server Changes

The majority of changes to the Microsoft SQL Server are at the database engine level. Here are the highlights of general changes to Microsoft SQL Server in Version 7.0:

- An entirely new lock manager that enables row-level locking and a lightweight locking mechanism known as a "latch." (Get it, "locks" and "latches"? These database designers go in for metaphors.)
- A redesigned query-processing engine that is much faster and enables higher degrees of CPU scalability.
- A revamped file management system that removes the need for preallocated database and transaction log devices.
- An innovative resource manager that allows for the dynamic allocation of memory, file space, locks, open objects, and other database settings that previously had to be hand-tuned.

There are many, many more improvements and enhancements to Microsoft SQL Server. The primary strategy behind the redesign of Microsoft SQL Server is the need to establish a core DBMS product that will be competitive in the marketplace for the next 5 to 10 years. Of course, upgrades and supplements will be provided, but the core DBMS is established in Version 7.0. Similarly, Sybase upgraded many of the core DBMS components of Adaptive Server in the Version 11.5.

Despite all of the changes in Microsoft SQL Server and Sybase Adaptive Server in the latest releases, Transact-SQL has seen little change. The following sections detail those areas of Transact-SQL that have experienced a change, as well as those areas of the new product that have a direct impact on Transact-SQL, such as new optimizer hints that support row-level locking.

Transact-SQL Changes

The majority of enhancements in Transact-SQL are found in these areas:

- Expanded storage sizes
- Datatype changes and Unicode
- SQL manager
- DDL
- Cursors
- Changes in SELECT
- Distributed queries
- Compatibility
- Miscellaneous enhancements

Expanded Storage Sizes

There have been numerous improvements in the Microsoft SQL Server file storage engine. As a result, many database objects are now sized quite differently from older versions of SQL Server. Table B-1 summarizes the differences.

Table B-1. Expanded Storage Sizes

Item	Size in Version 6.x	Size in Version 7.0
Maximum tables per query	16	256
Maximum foreign keys per table	13	253
Maximum columns per table	255	1,024
Maximum row size	1,962	8,060

Table B-1. Expanded Storage Sizes (continued)

Item	Size in Version 6.x	Size in Version 7.0
Maximum items in an ORDER BY or GROUP BY clause	16	Unlimited
Maximum total bytes in an ORDER BY or GROUP BY clause	900	8,060
Maximum parameters per stored procedure	255	1,024
Maximum identifier length of an object name (identifiers)	30	128

Datatype Changes and Unicode

This section summarizes the major datatype changes affecting Transact-SQL.

Datatype sizes

As a result of changes in the SQL Server storage engine, CHAR and BINARY datatypes—and their variable-length siblings VARCHAR and VARBINARY—now support a maximum size of 8,000 bytes, which allows you to store 8,000 ASCII characters or 4,000 Unicode characters. Ee-wow! That's a big improvement over 255. In the same "bigger is better" vein of thought, TEXT and IMAGE datatypes now hold up to two gigabytes of data and can be accessed with the SUBSTRING function. BIT datatypes are now nullable. And considerable speed improvements are available for TEXT, IMAGE, DECIMAL, and NUMERIC datatypes. You can now create a table of the following example definition:

```
CREATE TABLE pub_info
(
    pub_id  CHAR(4) NOT NULL REFERENCES publishers(pub_id)
                         CONSTRAINT upkcl_pubinfo PRIMARY KEY CLUSTERED,
    logo    IMAGE   NULL,
    pr_info VARCHAR(2000)   -- was TEXT datatype in Version 6.5
)
```

Now you can create tables with extremely large fields as a normal CHAR or VARCHAR datatype and avoid all the difficulties of accessing TEXT or IMAGE data.

CURSOR datatype

The new CURSOR datatype is quite an odd little bird. You should use the CURSOR datatype only when you have to create a cursor variable or as a cursor OUTPUT parameter. The CURSOR datatype cannot be used in a CREATE TABLE statement. Only a few operations are allowed with this datatype. You can use it in the SET variable statement or in the new CURSOR_STATUS function; you can use it as an output parameter from a stored procedure and as the source of an OPEN, FETCH, or CLOSE command in a CURSOR statement. For example:

```
-- Use the CURSOR datatype
DECLARE @variable_a CURSOR
```

```
DECLARE @variable_b CURSOR

-- Declare the cursor
DECLARE tnames_cursor CURSOR LOCAL FOR SELECT name
    FROM sysobjects WHERE type = 'U'

-- Set the values
SET @variable_a = tnames_cursor
SET @variable_b = @variable_b

-- Opens and fetch from tnames_cursor
OPEN  @variable_a
FETCH @variable_b       -- get the first row, but from a different variable
FETCH tnames_cursor     -- get the second row, but from the actual cursor
                        --   itself

-- Close the explicit cursor, but can still access the variables
DEALLOCATE tnames_cursor
```

You can now use the CURSOR datatype as shorthand for the cursor itself.

UNIQUEIDENTIFIER datatype

The UNIQUEIDENTIFIER datatype contains a globally unique identification number stored as a 16-byte binary string, also known as a GUID. This datatype should be used for scenarios in which uniqueness must be maintained in data that is merged from many tables into a single table. The process for generating a GUID is derived from a variety of different components, as shown here:

```
<time_low>-<time_mid>-<time_hi_and_version>-<clock_seq_hi_and_reserved>-
<clock_seq_low>-<node>
```

The dashes are not stored in the column but are added to the display value of the field for better readability. The UNIQUEIDENTIFIER datatype requires special handling. The *only* operations that are allowed against it are equal (=) and not equal (<>), IS NULL and IS NOT NULL. With the exception of IDENTITY, column constraints and properties are OK with the UNIQUEIDENTIFIER datatype.

GUID is preferred over IDENTITY when data must have a single column to uniquely identify a row across multiple tables and/or servers. Only one GUID column is allowed per table.

UNICODE datatypes

Microsoft SQL Server 7.0 now includes native Unicode formats, implemented as new datatypes within SQL Server. Even some of Microsoft SQL Server's internal metadata is now stored as Unicode. The implementation of Unicode now is up to par with the UCS-2 character set. For the uninformed, Unicode is an international standard code system that stores each character in two bytes. Because of its two-byte storage, Unicode allows for 65,000+ possible different characters, compared to 256 different characters that may be stored in one byte. Thus, different codes may be assigned to letters of different national alphabets, because there are fewer than 65,000 different letters in all world languages (including hieroglyphics). Unicode datatypes thereby provide the benefit of storing a string in Chinese, English, or Russian (but not all of them at the same time in one data element). As long as your application is using ODBC 3.6 or higher or OLEDB, you can take advantage of Unicode characters in the application.

With Unicode, Microsoft has introduced several new datatypes NCHAR, NVARCHAR, and NTEXT. The NCHAR and NVARCHAR datatypes are Unicode implementations of CHAR and VARCHAR. As with CHAR and VARCHAR, the new maximum size of these fields is 8,000 bytes; 8,000 bytes amounts to storing 4,000 Unicode characters, since each one takes two bytes of storage. These datatypes always behave as if SET ANSI_PADDING=ON were set prior to using the datatype.

A lot of the metadata in Microsoft SQL Server 7.0 uses Unicode. For example, the new SYSNAME user datatype is NVARCHAR(128). Both system catalogs and system stored procedures use them. It's a good idea to reacquaint yourself with any system stored procedure or system table that you *think* you know well. Believe us when we tell you "They've changed!"

To enter data into the Unicode columns NCHAR, NVARCHAR, and NTEXT, you must precede the literal string with a capital "N." For example, to insert the value Francais spécialités, the INSERT command should contain the value "N Francais spécialités." If you forget the N prefix, bad things will happen. Generally, the data, not Unicode, will be stored in the installed page code. Thus, the client might not see the intended results if you leave the N prefix off.

The NTEXT field is a Unicode version of the TEXT dataype and allows you to store up to two gigabytes of characters. Character data is implicitly converted to and from the NCHAR and NVARCHAR datatypes. No special CONVERT clause is necessary.

The functions LIKE and SUBSTRING are usable with Unicode datatypes. Concatenation also works with Unicode datatypes, although you have to be careful using NULL concatenation. Currently, NULL concatenation on CHAR and VARCHAR columns behaves as follows: 'string' + NULL = 'string'. Using Unicode datatypes, that command would result in a NULL value. To achieve the same results, you would have to use the ISNULL function:

```
'string' + ISNULL(nchar_expression, ' ')  = 'string'
```

SQL Manager

Changes to the SQL Manager focus on building more robust caching mechanisms. Caching is an extremely valuable performance booster. Thus, adding new methods for caching SQL plans can dramatically improve the performance of Transact-SQL operations.

A unified cache

In Microsoft SQL Server 7.0, the SQL Manager now utilizes a *unified cache*. Gone are the days of separate data and procedure caches. Now, a single cache exists that buffers both frequently used data and frequently used Transact-SQL objects like stored procedures, views, and triggers. This enhancement now decreases the amount of DBA tuning needed to properly balance the memory needs of data and procedural objects. Any excess memory that might have been consumed by an improperly sized data or procedure cache is now free to be used by either. Also, the memory setting of Microsoft SQL Server 7.0 is auto-tuning by default.

Shared query plans

Another change found in the SQL Manager is in the use of *shared query plans*. Formerly, Microsoft SQL Server maintained a separate compiled query plan with each invocation of a stored procedure or Transact-SQL command. So, in Microsoft SQL Server 6.5, two users could invoke the same query and get entirely different query plans. Now, in Microsoft SQL Server 7.0, the SQL Manager maintains one compiled plan in read-only format for all users. As users invoke the stored procedure or Transact-SQL command, the object is reused according to the specific parameters passed to it. Shared query plans aren't used in every situation, though. For example, shared query plans are not used with implicitly resolved code. An implicitly resolved query is one in which the object's owner is left for SQL Server to extrapolate, as shown here:

```
SELECT *
FROM   pubs..authors
```

This query is implicitly resolved because SQL Server has to check internally to see who owns the author table. On the other hand, the following query is explicitly resolved:

```
SELECT *
FROM   pubs.jsbach.authors
```

There is also no sharing of query plans if the execution environment differs. For example, the following two queries will have entirely different query plans:

Joe executes:

```
SET ANSI_WARNINGS ON
SELECT * FROM titles
```

Evelyn executes:

```
SET ANSI_WARNINGS OFF
SELECT * FROM titles
```

So, Joe and Evelyn cannot leverage a shared query plan because their environments differ too much. If, however, they had the same execution environment, then SQL Server would utilize a shared query plan (and data cache) for the two queries.

New caching mechanisms

Microsoft SQL Server now has four new caching mechanisms to further speed Transact-SQL processing: ad hoc, auto-parameter, marked parameters, and prepare/execute. Each new method is designed to speed a certain type of Transact-SQL operation. Each mechanism has advantages and disadvantages. Table B-2 summarizes the uses of the new caching mechanisms.

Table B-2. New Caching Mechanisms in Microsoft SQL Server 7.0

Caching Mechanism	Used For
Ad hoc	User-issued queries and random reports
Auto-parameter	Highly repetitive operations with few changes between executions of the operation
Marked parameter	Applications that execute a block of Transact-SQL code many times and by multiple instance
Prepare/execute	Applications in which Transact-SQL programs or stored procedure calls frequently move between the client and the server

As a developer, you have to explicitly tell SQL Server when you want it to use marked parameter and prepare/execute caching mechanisms. You should use *some* form of caching if a Transact-SQL statement or batch is used by multiple applications or called by frequently used stored procedures. Ad hoc query caching is useful for user interaction and report generation. Auto-parameter caching is also useful for the DBA performing repeated DML operations, but is of less use to a developer. Developers should focus more on marked parameter caching and prepare/execute caching. If a Transact-SQL statement or batch is reused by the current or other instances, you might prefer to use prepare/execute caching with parameters. If the Transact-SQL statement or batch might be shared among multiple instances, marked parameter caching might be a better choice. It's probably a good idea to use ad hoc query caching for user interaction and report generation.

Ad hoc caching. Ad hoc caching affects all Transact-SQL statements executed in an ad hoc environment. Thus, queries executed by end users using ISQL/W, SQL Enterprise Manager, report writers, and other processes external to the DBMS may be cached. Then the cache will be reused any time that same query is invoked after it has been cached. Ad hoc caching affects the code of users and processes that execute Transact-SQL commands that exactly match each other and are under 8,000 characters in size. For example, any one of the following queries would be cached when first executed. Subsequent invocations of the same query would come directly from the cache without recompiling:

```
SELECT * FROM sales WHERE qty = 1.0
SELECT * FROM sales WHERE qty = 1.0
SELECT * FROM sales WHERE qty = 2.0
SELECT * FROM sales WHERE qty = 5
SELECT * FROM sales WHERE qty = 15
SELECT * FROM sales WHERE qty < 1.5
SELECT * FROM sales WHERE qty < 1 OR stor_id <= 7896
```

Auto-parameter caching. Auto-parameter caching is a mechanism Microsoft SQL Server uses to speed simple DML statements like INSERT, UPDATE, DELETE, and SELECT. With this technique, Microsoft SQL Server attempts to guess which constants in the DML statement might serve as parameters based on certain predefined templates. After parsing is finished, Microsoft SQL Server then looks for plans that match. If a match is found, the compiled query plan is pulled from the cache. If no match is found, then a new plan is compiled.

The templates used for each DML statement when auto-parameter caching is used are shown here:

```
INSERT <table> VALUES({<constant>|NULL|DEFAULT},...)

DELETE <table>
WHERE <key-expression>

UPDATE <table> SET <colname> = <constant>
WHERE <key-expression>

SELECT {* | <column>,..,<column>} FROM <table>
WHERE <key-expression>
```

As mentioned earlier, auto-parameter caching is for use with relatively simple DML statements. Therefore, the `key-expression` may contain only column names, constants, the AND operator, and the = operator. The following are examples of two queries that would use the same auto-parameter caching plan:

```
SELECT * FROM sales WHERE qty = 1.0
SELECT * FROM sales WHERE qty = 2.0
```

In this case, the auto-parameter cache plan uses the parameter float @p in the template, as in SELECT * FROM sales WHERE qty = @p. Here's another pair of queries that will use the same query plan. This time, the parameter INT @p will be used in the query template:

```
SELECT * FROM sales WHERE qty = 5
SELECT * FROM sales WHERE qty = 15
```

Auto-parameter caching will not be used in this last pair of queries:

```
SELECT * FROM sales WHERE qty < 1.5
SELECT * FROM sales WHERE qty < 1 OR stor_id <= 7896
```

Marked parameter caching. Marked parameter caching is a new technique available to Open Database Connectivity (ODBC) and Transact-SQL applications. This technique requires the application developer to make explicit calls in the ODBC and Transact-SQL code. Marked parameter caching provides a procedure-like processing model to externally stored client programs.

When using ODBC, the command *SQLExecDirect* is used (as of beta 3). When using Open Linking and Embedding Database (OLEDB), the proper command to use is *ICommand::Execute* (as of beta 3). Syntax and usage for these programming environments are beyond the scope of this book. You can use marked parameter caching with Transact-SQL though. You can enable marked parameter caching in a Transact-SQL application using the system stored procedure *sp_executesql*. The general syntax for *sp_executesql* is shown here:

```
sp_executesql(@batch_text   NVARCHAR(4000),
              @batch_params NVARCHAR(4000),
              param1,.. paramN)
```

So, to execute the cached SQL statements shown earlier in this section as marked parameter queries, you would issue these commands:

```
sp_executesql('SELECT * FROM sales WHERE qty = @p','FLOAT @p',1.0)
sp_executesql('SELECT * FROM sales WHERE qty = @p','INT @p',5)
sp_executesql('SELECT * FROM sales WHERE qty < @p','FLOAT @p',1.5)
sp_executesql('SELECT * FROM sales WHERE qty < @p1 OR stor_id <= @p2','INT
              @p1, INT@p2',1,7896)
```

Prepare/execute caching. Prepare/execute caching is used mostly with ODBC, OLEDB, and Active-X Data Object (ADO), although it does have a Transact-SQL implementation. Prepare/execute caching allows you to cache frequently used ODBC or OLEDB operations, including cursors. The operation is shared across users and doesn't force the application to send text to the server at each user execution. In some situations, prepare/execute caching also reduces tempdb utilization.

The prepare/execute caching mechanism uses three system stored procedures within a Transact-SQL application: *sp_prepare*, *sp_execute*, and *sp_unprepare*. The syntax of all three is shown here:

```
sp_prepare(@handle        INT OUTPUT,
           @batch_text    NVARCHAR(4000),
           @batch_params  NVARCHAR(4000))

sp_execute(@handle        INT, param_value1,...)

sp_unprepare(@handle      INT)
```

Here's an example of a Transact-SQL batch that places a query in cache, executes the query, then removes it from cache:

```
-- Declare the handler parameter
DECLARE @handle INT

-- Load the SELECT statement into cache
sp_prepare @handle OUTPUT, 'SELECT * FROM sales WHERE qty = @p','@p FLOAT'

-- These two commands execute the query based on the cached plan
sp_execute @handle, 1.0
sp_execute @handle, 5

-- The query is removed from cache
sp_unprepare @handle
```

DDL Enhancements

There are a number of quite exciting DDL enhancements in Microsoft SQL Server 7.0. Here's the short list of changes:

- Deferred name resolution
- Computed columns
- Incremental DDL: ALTER TABLE ADD COLUMN, ALTER TABLE DROP COLUMN, ALTER TABLE ALTER COLUMN, ALTER VIEW/PROCEDURE/TRIGGER
- Multiple and recursive triggers

Deferred name resolution

In previous versions of SQL Server, if name resolution failed at compile time, then the entire DDL statement often failed. For example, the following Transact-SQL batch will fail on a SQL Server 6.5 installation:

```
-- the sales_preview table doesn't exist yet
CREATE PROCEDURE preview1 @p INT
AS
SELECT * FROM sales_preview WHERE qty >= @p
GO

CREATE TABLE sales_preview (qty INT)
GO

EXEC preview1
GO
```

In SQL Server Version 7.0, if name resolution fails at compile time, the DDL statement is allowed. Later, name resolution is resolved at runtime. So, the preceding Transact-SQL batch will succeed on a SQL Server 7.0 installation.

Computed columns

In Version 6.5 of SQL Server, computed columns were the domain of views and queries. Now, computed columns may be built directly into a table. As with computed columns in a view, a computed column in a table is a virtual column. The syntax of a table with a computed column follows this format:

```
CREATE TABLE name (
    <column_name> AS <expression>
)
```

Computed columns resemble views in their behavior. They are read only, cannot be indexed, and cannot be bound to a constraint. The values are evaluated as they are queried, not as the data is stored in the table. The expression that builds the computed column value may have columns, constants, or functions. Subqueries, though, are not allowed. For example:

```
CREATE TABLE dear_diary (
    date_of_entry DATETIME,
    comments      VARCHAR(4000),
    weather_type  VARCHAR(15),
    celsius       REAL,
    farenheit  AS (32 + 9*Celsius/5)
)
```

That's a very cool new feature! Don't forget: you cannot insert data into a computed column.

Incremental DDL

If you have been working with Microsoft SQL Server for very long, you may be aware of how difficult it has been to make significant alterations to an existing database object. Most difficult of all was removing a column from a table. Now, in Microsoft SQL Server 7.0, things have changed for the better. Here are some new DDL statements that are making our lives a little easier:

ALTER TABLE . . . ADD COLUMN
: Now allows the addition of both nullable and non-nullable columns. A default value is required for non-nullable columns. When the command is executed, the new column will be populated with the default value.

ALTER TABLE . . . DROP COLUMN
: Yippee! You can now drop an existing column from a table without having to jump through the same flaming hoops that Microsoft SQL Server 6.5 required. All indexes and constraints that depend on the column must already be dropped for the command to work. You still have to watch out for the existence of dropped columns in any Transact-SQL objects in the database or external Transact-SQL program. A block of Transact-SQL code that refers to a

dropped column will still fail as in Version 6.5. It's just much easier to drop columns from a table in Version 7.0.

ALTER VIEW/PROCEDURE/TRIGGER
: This command allows you to substitute new Transact-SQL code for an existing object. The existing object retains permissions and dependencies when it is altered. Of course, changes to the Transact-SQL code are not checked in any calling objects, so you must be sure that your altered object still produces the output expected by any programs that might call it; if you don't, you'll encounter errors at runtime. The ALTER VIEW statement now allows global variables within the definition of the view.

ALTER TABLE . . . ALTER COLUMN
: You can now use this command to change the datatype of an existing column to a datatype compatible with data stored in the column. This implies that there is conversion of actual alphabetic characters to integers, for example. The original column cannot have the TIMESTAMP, TEXT, or IMAGE datatypes. The columns have some other restrictions. They may not be computed columns, nor may they be used in an index.

ALTER TABLE . . . DISABLE
: This command allows you to temporarily enable and disable triggers and constraints. This is a wonderful option for the DBA or developer who is attempting to load a table with data but doesn't want to subject the load process to trigger or constraint overhead.

Added together, these new DDL commands allow you to incrementally change an existing object without having to drop and re-create it. You still have the added challenge of maintaining the current definition of your Transact-SQL programs, but at least your coding work is eased.

Multiple and recursive triggers

There are some big changes in the way triggers are handled in Microsoft SQL Server Version 7.0. Microsoft SQL Server now allows the creation of multiple triggers on a table for INSERT, UPDATE, and DELETE statements. By adding conditional logic to multiple triggers, you can effectively construct a scenario in which only one trigger fires for each application that accesses a given table. Other uses might include invoking multiple actions based on the operations occurring on one table.

The NOT FOR REPLICATION clause has been added to the CREATE TRIGGER and ALTER TRIGGER statements to tell the trigger not to execute when a replication login fires it.

When you issue a CREATE TRIGGER statement against a table that already has a trigger of the same type, the existing trigger will be overwritten. If the names are different, a new trigger will be created and added to the table.

The order of execution for multiple triggers on a single table is not defined and should be considered simultaneous.

Earlier versions of SQL Server did not support recursive triggers. Now, if a trigger modifies the table in which it resides, that same trigger can be fired as a result of its own operation. (This functionality is enabled by setting the RECURSIVE TRIGGERS option using *sp_dboption.*)

The RECURSIVE TRIGGERS option (when enabled) may cause problems in existing triggers coded without recursion in mind. Use it with care.

For example, assume that the sales table in pubs has two update triggers, tr_upd1 and tr_upd2. An end user updates the sales table. Triggers tr_upd1 and tr_upd2 both fire simultaneously. The pseudotables inserted and deleted contain only those rows corresponding to the UPDATE statement issued by the end user that fired the triggers. Based on the Transact-SQL code, the trigger tr_upd1 issues a second UPDATE statement, recursively firing tr_upd1 and tr_upd2. Again, the Transact-SQL code of the two triggers executes and (if you've coded the darned thing properly) finishes its operation.

Cursors

The ubiquitous, but very nonrelational, cursor has become more potent in SQL Server 7.0. For example, locking for cursors has been greatly improved. These improvements in cursor locking mean reduced concurrency and blocking issues. Locking improvements include separate locking for any transactions invoked by the cursor. Cursors that span transactions can behave differently for each transaction. And cursors are now allowed to perform updates with the READ UNCOMMITTED isolation level.

Here are some other changes to cursors you will probably encounter:

- Scoped cursors
- Cursor information
- DECLARE CURSOR

Scoped cursors

Now, cursors may be *local* or *global* in scope, just like variables. Local cursors are accessible only during the current session and are deallocated at the end of the process or procedure. Global cursors remain allocated until explicitly deallocated and can be referenced in any stored procedure or batch executed by the connection. The cursor is only implicitly deallocated when the current session disconnects. The syntax for creating a scoped cursor follows this format:

```
DECLARE cursor_name CURSOR [GLOBAL | LOCAL] AS SELECT...
```

Unless otherwise specified, cursors default to global scope based on the DEFAULT TO LOCAL CURSOR database option. You may change this setting using the *sp_dboption* system stored procedure. Local cursors are available within the current batch or stored procedure of the current session, while global cursors are open throughout the currently active session. Once a global cursor is declared and opened, its data may be fetched at any time within the currently open session. For example:

```
CREATE PROCEDURE proc_fragment
AS
BEGIN
    ...
    -- first, the global cursor
    DECLARE neato_global_cursor GLOBAL ...
    OPEN    neato_global_cursor

    -- now, the local cursor
    DECLARE neato_local_cursor LOCAL ...
    OPEN neato_local_cursor
END

EXECUTE proc_fragment

-- the next command will work because the global cursor is still allocated
FETCH my_global_cursor

-- the next command will fail because the local cursor is now deallocated
FETCH my_local_cursor...
```

Cursor information

Some changes in the way we retrieve information about cursors are to be found in Microsoft SQL Server 7.0. First, the cursor_status function now exists to tell if a cursor variable points to a cursor and to tell if the cursor is closed, open, or deallocated. The following system stored procedures now provide this information:

sp_describe_cursor
: Returns information about the cursor, including concurrency, model, row count, number of columns, and its last operation

sp_describe_cursor_columns
: Provides information about the columns in a cursor's result set

sp_describe_cursor_tables
: Provides information about the base tables of a cursor

sp_cursor_list
: Returns information about multiple cursors (all global cursors, all local cursors, or both)

DECLARE CURSOR

The DECLARE CURSOR command has been reinforced to include functions that could previously be specified only directly through ODBC or OLEDB. The new syntax for DECLARE CURSOR is shown here:

```
DECLARE cursor name CURSOR
    [ GLOBAL | LOCAL ]
    [ SCROLL | FORWARD_ONLY ]
    [ STATIC | KEYSET | DYNAMIC ]
    [ READ_ONLY | SCROLL_LOCKS | OPTIMISTIC ]
FOR <select statement>
    [ FOR UPDATE [ OF column list ] ]
```

The other syntax, described earlier in this book, meets ANSI SQL-92 standards and is still available. In this new verbiage, extensions were added to allow you to define cursors similar to those specific to ODBC, ADO, and DB-Library APIs. The two forms are mutually exclusive. So if you use the SCROLL or INSENSITIVE keywords before the CURSOR keyword, you can't use any keywords between the CURSOR and FOR keywords and vice versa. Other keywords are detailed in Table B-3.

Table B-3. Additional DECLARE CURSOR Keywords

Keyword	Description
FORWARD ONLY	Indicates that the cursor can scroll only from the first to the last row. FETCH NEXT is the only fetch option allowed. This setting is the default, unless STATIC, KEYSET, or DYNAMIC is specified, although these settings are supported with FORWARD_ONLY. It is mutually exclusive of SCROLL. When issued alone, the cursor acts as a DYNAMIC cursor.
STATIC	Indicates that the cursor will make a temporary working copy of the data used by the cursor. These temporary worktables are housed in tempdb, where all modifications take place. This cursor disallows the modification of actual data.
KEYSET	Builds a special temporary worktable in tempdb called the *keyset* that freezes the membership and order of rows used by the cursor when the cursor is opened. (The keyset keeps track of each row's unique identifier.) As you scroll through a keyset cursor, changes made to the nonkey values of the base tables are visible. Inserts are not visible. Rows deleted (or updated in a deferred update) from the keyset cursor will raise an @@fetch_status value of -2.
DYNAMIC	Tells that the cursor should immediately reflect all changes to the data as the cursor is scrolled. Absolute and relative fetch options are not allowed with dynamic cursors. The data values, order of rows, and membership of rows in the cursor can change on each fetch.

Table B-3. Additional DECLARE CURSOR Keywords (continued)

Keyword	Description
SCROLL_LOCKS	Indicates that rows read by the cursor are locked to ensure the success of positional DELETE and UPDATE. The row is locked as it is read into the cursor, then released as a new record is scrolled.
OPTIMISTIC	Mandates that optimistic locking should be used. Thus, updates and deletes made through the cursor will not succeed if the row has been altered since it was read in by the cursor. The cursor doesn't lock the row as it is read. Instead, the record is verified as unaltered by a timestamp (if available) or a checksum value (if no timestamp is available). If the timestamp or checksum reveals that the row was modified after the cursor read the record, the positional update or delete will fail.

Changes in SELECT

Some changes in queries are not visible in the Transact-SQL code. For example, SQL Server now supports the parallel execution of an individual query. That means that a query that has a lot of processing to do may actually be split into smaller units and executed on multiple processors simultaneously. The query optimizer will usually parallelize queries that have to examine huge numbers of records to produce a relatively small result set. Large queries that have joins, aggregations, and UNIONs are likely candidates for parallel execution.

Other changes in the Transact-SQL syntax are more obvious. This section discusses a few such changes in the SELECT statement, including SELECT TOP, WHERE CONTAINS, and WHERE FREETEXT. There are also several new optimizer hints available with the SELECT statement.

SELECT TOP

Have you ever been working on a Transact-SQL query and thought to yourself "All I really want are the first 10 rows of this result set!" In Version 6.5 and earlier, you would have to combine your DML statement with the command SET ROWCOUNT x (where x was the number of rows you wanted to affect) to limit the scope of the DML statement. You can now request similar behavior for queries using the SELECT TOP command. SELECT TOP is a variation of the SELECT statement that is preferred over SET ROWCOUNT and can be used in the subqueries of other DML statements such as UPDATE and DELETE.

SET ROWCOUNT cannot be used in a view, but SELECT TOP can. You now have some exciting new capabilities in a SQL Server view.

The syntax is essentially the same as a regular SELECT statement, except that TOP is mutually exclusive of the ALL and DISTINCT options. Here's the syntax:

```
SELECT {ALL | DISTINCT | TOP n [PERCENT] [WITH TIES]} ...
```

The TOP n keyword tells SQL Server to return only the first n rows of the query result set. If you use an ORDER BY clause, you'll get the first n rows sorted by the ORDER BY clause. Otherwise, you'll get the first n rows from the table heap. The PERCENT keyword tells SQL Server that you want to retrieve the first n percent of rows in the table (values are rounded to the next higher integer if the percentage yields a fraction of rows) in the result set. The WITH TIES option may be used only with TOP and an ORDER BY clause. The WITH TIES option then causes the result set to be sorted according to how the ORDER BY clause is written. Thus, you can sort the TOP n records retrieved, rather than all the records of the result set with only the TOP n records retrieved.

Here's an example of using SELECT TOP:

```
SELECT TOP 10 au_lname,
              au_fname
FROM          authors
ORDER BY      au_id DESC
```

You can enable the same behavior in UPDATE, DELETE, or INSERT . . . SELECT statements by using a subquery.

WHERE CONTAINS and WHERE FREETEXT

Another significant enhancement is available with SELECT in Version 7.0. Currently, searches through TEXT columns can be quite time-consuming. Now, you have the option of using the WHERE CONTAINS and WHERE FREETEXT keywords to perform full-text indexing during a SELECT against TEXT and NTEXT columns. Full-text indexing is not enabled by default in SQL Server 7.0 and is based on technology developed for Microsoft Index Server (a web search tool).

The WHERE CONTAINS clause is approximately equivalent for searches on TEXT columns to a WHERE LIKE clause on character columns. The WHERE FREETEXT clause offers functionality on a TEXT column that is more similar to a WHERE = clause for character columns. In either case, the function must be in the format:

```
function(column_name, 'search_text_string')
```

Here are some examples:

```
SELECT auth_name,
       title
FROM   books
WHERE  CONTAINS(summary,'Transact-SQL AND programming')

SELECT company,price
```

```
FROM   books
WHERE  CONTAINS(description,'bunny rabbits NEAR() hunting')

SELECT help_text
FROM   on_line_help
WHERE  FREETEXT(help_text,'Debugging Transact-SQL?')
```

New optimizer hints and the OPTION clause

There are quite a few new optimizer hints added in with those available under Version 6.5. Microsoft has divided these new hints into several categories: table hints, join hints, and query hints. *Table hints* are basically the syntax used in Version 6.5, where the hint is placed with the FROM clause. There are some new table hints that affect the isolation level or how a table is read. *Join hints* are to be placed with the JOIN clause and affect the way a join between two tables is processed. Finally, Microsoft has introduced a whole slew of new *query hints* that affect the general strategy SQL Server employs when building the query plan.

In some cases, these new categories have somewhat different syntax from Version 6.5. Each variation in syntax is explained with its hint category. In addition, Microsoft has introduced a new clause, OPTION, to handle hints in a more structured fashion.

Table hints. In addition to the old hints you might have used in Version 6.5, Microsoft has added quite a few new ones. The majority of the new table hints are used to affect the isolation level utilized by the query engine or to offer a method of exploiting row-level locking features found in Version 7.0. The following list describes the new table hints available in Version 7.0:

READCOMMITTED
: This hint tells SQL Server to use the same locking semantics as a transaction running at READ COMMITTED isolation level. Chapter 11, *Transactions and Locking*, has more information about isolation levels.

READPAST
: This hint tells SQL Server to read right past locked rows and skip them. This hint is a synonym for setting @@lock_timeout to 0. The READPAST hint works only for transactions at the READ COMMITTED isolation level and is effective only for reading past row-level locks. It has no effect on page or table locks.

READUNCOMMITTED
: This hint is the same as the NOLOCK hint in Version 6.5.

REPEATABLEREAD
: SQL Server scans with the same locking semantics as a transaction running at REPEATABLE READ isolation level. Chapter 11 has more information about isolation levels.

ROWLOCK

This hint forces SQL Server to use shared row locks where shared pages or table locks would normally be used.

SERIALIZABLE

This hint is the same as HOLDLOCK hint in Version 6.5.

As mentioned earlier, table hints may be written as a part of the FROM clause (same syntax as in Version 6.5). The OPTION clause may be used only for query hints, not for table or join hints.

Join hints. Microsoft has added some nifty new join hints that enable you to exploit the join execution algorithm used by SQL Server's query processing engine. You may include one hint per ANSI join. When you use a join hint, the query engine forces the join order for all tables based on the positioning of the ON keyword(s). If you're using a full outer join without an ON clause, you can add parentheses to indicate your desired order. You may choose between LOOP, HASH, or MERGE join strategies when using the optimizer hint. Each hint is mutually exclusive of the other. For example, the following SELECT statement is forced to join two tables using a merge strategy and two others using a hashing strategy:

```
SELECT a.au_fname, a.au_lname, t.title_id
FROM authors a
INNER (MERGE) JOIN titleauthor ta ON a.au_id     = ta.au_id
INNER (HASH)  JOIN titles t       ON t.title_id = ta.title_id
```

Query hints with OPTION. Query hints are used to apply a given hint throughout the entire query. The hint strategy is applied to all operations of the query. The use of these hints requires that you include an OPTION clause at the end of the SELECT statement. The option clause should be used with the outermost SELECT statement (if nested) or with the last SELECT statement (if used with a UNION). Sometimes the use of hints will force SQL Server to generate an invalid plan. If this ever happens, SQL Server will fall back on a recompiled plan without using the specific query hints. A SQL Server Profiler event will also be generated. (If SET SHOWPLAN_TEXT or SHOWPLAN_ALL is active, a warning message will also appear in its output.)

Query hints take precedence over table or join hints.

There are a number of new query hints. Many of them duplicate the function of a table or join optimizer hint. However, the query hints apply to all operations within the query. Here's a more complete listing of query hints available in Version 7.0. Query hints shown on the same bullet and separated by a pipe mark (|) are mutually exclusive of one another:

HASH GROUP or ORDER GROUP
: The hint tells SQL Server to handle GROUP BY or COMPUTE aggregations using either hashing or ordering strategies.

MERGE UNION, HASH UNION, or CONCAT UNION
: This query hint affects the processing of UNION statements by forcing the optimizer to use the merging, hashing, or concatenation strategy. If more than one hint is specified, SQL Server chooses the least expensive strategy specified.

FAST n
: This hint tells the SQL Server optimizer to build the query plan for fast retrieval of the first n rows (where n is a nonnegative integer). Once n number of records have been returned, the query continues execution and returns a full result set.

FORCE ORDER
: By using FORCE ORDER, the default optimizer behavior is overridden. Joins are performed in the exact order of the query.

ROBUST PLAN
: The ROBUST PLAN hint offers an unusual tweak. It is possible to create a table that exceeds SQL Server's ability to process it, because a row might contain many variable-length columns. In these situations, an error does not occur until the actual data stored in such a row exceeds the maximum allowable row size. So rows stored in an oversized record can usually be processed without error, as long as they're equal to or smaller than the maximum potential size. Keeping these factors in mind, the ROBUST PLAN query hint tells the query optimizer to attempt a plan optimized for the maximum potential row size. This may cost you somewhat in performance, but you gain in that SQL Server raises an error immediately rather than deferring the error until query execution time.

Here's an example of the query hints using the OPTION clause; we'll force the GROUP BY operation to be processed using an ordering algorithm, and we'll also force the optimizer to join in the order shown in the query:

```
SELECT a.au_fname,
       a.au_lname,
       SUBSTRING(t.title, 1, 15) AS "Title"
FROM   authors a
    INNER JOIN titleauthor ta ON a.au_id = ta.au_id
    INNER JOIN titles t       ON t.title_id = ta.title_id
```

```
GROUP BY a.au_lname,
         a.au_fname,
         t.title
ORDER BY au_lname ASC,
         au_fname ASC
OPTION (ORDER GROUP, FORCE ORDER)
```

To apply a query hint to a UNION query is a little more tricky, since the hint has to deal with two separate queries. The easy thing to remember is that query hints go at the *end* of the query, as shown here:

```
SELECT *
FROM   titles t1
UNION
SELECT *
FROM   title_archives t2
OPTION (MERGE UNION)
```

Distributed Queries

SQL Server 7.0 now supports distributed Transact-SQL queries against a wide variety of data sources from a single DML statement. The preparatory work to allow distributed queries is about the same as that needed to allow RPCs. Refer to Chapter 14, *Stored Procedures and Modular Design*, for more information about setting up for remote procedure calls. However, instead of using the system stored procedure *sp_addserver*, you use the system stored procedure *sp_addlinkedserver*. The syntax is simple:

```
sp_addlinkedserver 'server_name'.
```

SQL Server's capabilities far surpass simple DML statements against other SQL Server databases. In fact, SQL Server is now capable of querying heterogeneous data sources such as other relational database systems (e.g., Oracle, Sybase, Informix, or Microsoft Access). Distributed queries may even be executed against nonrelational data sources like FoxPro or even Microsoft Excel. This process is actually not too complex to implement but goes beyond the scope of a book on Transact-SQL. Please refer to the vendor documentation for more information on heterogeneous queries.

Once you've done all the groundwork to allow distributed queries by linking the target servers, you can actually issue a DML statement across multiple servers using a four-part object name in the form:

```
server_name.[database_name.[owner_name].]object_name
```

For example:

```
SELECT * FROM MERLOT.pubs.dbo.authors
```

This command will execute across the LAN/WAN environment and retrieve a result set from the MERLOT server, assuming that it was properly linked with the *sp_addlinkedserver* system stored procedure. This same system stored procedure is used to link other ODBC-compliant databases such as Oracle, Informix, DB2, or Sybase. It can also be used to link non-ODBC data sources like Microsoft Excel or Visual FoxPro.

You can use distributed queries and the four-part object names for SELECT, INSERT, UPDATE, and DELETE. You can even use it to construct local views, since the four-part object names are a component of a valid SELECT statement. The DML statements can take place on either the local or remote server without restriction, if both servers are running Microsoft SQL Server and MS-DTC. (Some restrictions apply to other data providers.) DDL statements are not supported with distributed execution.

Compatibility

Compatibility between Microsoft SQL Server 7.0 and previous releases is a key point of concern to those with applications deployed in earlier versions of the product. The good news is that the vast majority of applications written for Version 6.0 or 6.5 will run without any modification. This functionality is ensured on a database-by-database basis through the system stored procedure *sp_dbcmptlevel*. Even when you have set the database compatibility level to Version 6.5, most functions unique to Version 7.0 (about 99%) are still available to the database. The idea is to use *sp_dbcmptlevel* to upgrade an application's database to a 7.0 server running under Version 6.5 compatibility mode. Then, at your convenience, you can upgrade the application and database coding to fully utilize Version 7.0 features.

When running in Version 7.0 mode, there are a few new keywords to avoid: TOP, ROWGUIDCOL, PENROWSET, CONTAINS, and RESTORE. Also, the GROUP BY clause implies the sort order of a query as if an ORDER BY clause were present. Trace flag 204 is no longer available. (That's the trace flag that provided Version 4. 2 GROUP BY behavior.)

Information Schema Views

The system tables have been changed in Microsoft SQL Server 7.0. Microsoft has provided views to all of the Version 6.5-style system tables, such as sysdatabases or sysdevices. However, the system tables have been further augmented by ANSI-standard system catalog views called *information schema views*.

The information schema views are internal, system table-independent views of SQL Server metadata. They're most useful because they remain unchanged even if the system tables are altered. Furthermore, information schema views are ANSI SQL standard according to the definition of INFORMATION_SCHEMA.

INFORMATION_SCHEMA is defined for all databases and contains metadata for all data objects stored in that database. According to the ANSI standard, a three-part naming convention is used. Microsoft uses the three-part naming standard but with slighltly different terminology. Microsoft refers to the ANSI-standard catalog as a database, schema as *owner*, and object as (drumroll please) *object*. User-defined datatypes are called domains by Microsoft.

Here's a listing of all views found in INFORMATION_SCHEMA:

```
information_schema.check_constraints
information_schema.column_domain.usage
information_schema.column_privileges
information_schema.columns
information_schema.constraint_column_usage
information_schema.constraint_table_usage
information_schema.domain_constraints
information_schema.domains
information_schema.key_column_usage
information_schema.referential_constraints
information_schema.schemata
information_schema.table_constraints
information_schema.table_privileges
information_schema.tables
information_schema.view_column_usage
information_schema.views
information_schema.view_table_usage
```

New Functions

There are a great many new functions added in Version 7.0. Table B-4 summarizes these new functions. A few functions that relate to file structures used exclusively in SQL Server 7.0 (such as FILE_ID) are not included in the list. For the purposes of this table, an expression (as shown in the Syntax column) may be a constant, a column name, another function, a subquery, and any combination of arithmetic, bitwise, or string operators.

Table B-4. New Functions

Function	Type	Syntax	Description

CAST	String	`CAST(expression AS data_type)`	A new ANSI-standard method for converting expressions between system datatypes. A synonym for CONVERT used for datatype conversion. For example:
			`SELECT CONVERT(char(20), ytd_sales)`
			`FROM titles`
			Is the same as:
			`SELECT CAST(ytd_sales AS char(20))`
			`FROM titles`

COLUMN-PROPERTY	Property	`COLUMNPROPERTY (id, column, 'property')`	Returns a wide variety of information about a column or procedure parameter. Integer values for each property may be 1 (true), 0 (false), or null if the property is not applicable. Column properties are: AllowsNull IsIdentity IsIdNotForRepl IsOutParam IsRowGUIDCol Precision Scale UseAnsiTrim
CONTAIN-STABLE	Full-text search	`CONTAINSTABLE (table, {column | *}, '<contains_search_condition>')`	Allows end users to execute full-text queries, with result sets returned by rank (or their accuracy based on the full-text search). This function is referenced in the FROM clause of a SELECT statement as if it were a regular table name.
CURSOR_STATUS	System	`CURSOR_STATUS ({ {'local', cursor_name} | {'global', cursor_name} | {'variable', cursor_variable} })`	This is a fancy scalar function that allows the caller of a stored procedure to tell if the procedure has returned a cursor and result set for a given parameter. You may check on local or global cursors or use a variable, as defined with the CURSOR datatype. The result set of this function is a SMALLINT, with values ranging from -3 to 1. The values have different meanings depending on whether you are checking the status of a named cursor or are using a variable. The general meanings of the values are: -3 Cursor does not exist -2 Not applicable -1 Cursor is closed 0 Result set is empty 1 Result set is not empty (has zero or more rows)

Table B-4. New Functions (continued)

Function	Type	Syntax	Description
DATABASE-PROPERTY	Prop-erty	`DATABASEPROPERTY ('database', 'property')`	Returns a wide variety of information about a database. Integer values for each property may be 1 (true), 0 (false), or null if the property is not applicable. Database properties, which are mostly self-explanatory, include: IsAccessible IsBulkCopy IsBypass IsCorrupt IsDboOnly IsInLoad IsNoCheckPoint IsOffline IsReadOnly IsSingleUser IsSuspect IsTruncLog
DAY	Date	`DAY(date)`	Returns an integer value for the day-date part of the specified date; as such, it is equivalent to DATEPART(dd, date)
FREETEXT-TABLE	Full-text search	`FREETEXTABLE (table, {column | *}, 'freetext_string')`	Allows end users to execute full-text queries, with result sets returned according to their rank (or their accuracy based on the full-text search). Results are based upon values that match the meaning, but not the exact wording, of the text specified by the freetext_string. This function is referenced in the FROM clause of a SELECT statement as if it were a regular table name.
FULLTEXT-CATALOG-PROPERTY	Full-text search	`FULLTEXTCATALOG-PROPERTY (catalog_name, property)`	Returns information about the full-text catalog status and usage. Since the full-text search capabilities of SQL Server 7.0 are beyond the scope of this book, please refer to the system documentation for more information.
FULLTEXT-SERVICE-PROPERTY	Full-text search	`FULLTEXTSERVICE-PROPERTY (property)`	Returns information about the full-text service-level properties. Since the full-text search capabilities of SQL Server 7.0 are beyond the scope of this book, please refer to the system documentation for more information
GETCHECK SUM	System	`GETCHECKSUM ('column')`	Returns a 32-bit cyclic redundancy check (CRC) on a specified row or rows in a table.

Table B-4. New Functions (continued)

Function	Type	Syntax	Description
INDEX-PROPERTY	Prop-erty	`INDEXPROPERTY (table_id, 'index', 'property')`	Returns a wide variety of information about an index. Integer values for each property may be 1 (true), 0 (false), or null if the property is not applicable. Index properties, which are mostly self-explanatory, include: IndexFillFactor IsAllowDupKey IsAllowDupRow IsClustered IsDefaultFillFactor IsIgnoreDupRow IsPadIndex IsUnique

IS_MEMBER	System	`IS_MEMBER ({'group' | 'role' })`	Returns a Boolean value that indicates whether the current user is a member of the specified Windows NT group or SQL Server role. If IS_MEMBER returns a null value, then either the group or role is invalid. For example:
			`IF IS_MEMBER ('db_owner') = 1`
			`PRINT 'Congrats!  You're the owner."`

IS_SRVROLE-MEMBER	System	`IS_SRVROLEMEMBER ('role' [,'login'])`	Returns a Boolean value that indicates whether the current user login is a member of the specified server role. When a null value is returned, the role or login ID is invalid.
LEFT	String	`LEFT (expression, starting_position)`	Returns the remaining characters on the lefthand side of the specified expression starting at the specified position. The starting position must be a positive whole number.
LEN	String	`LEN (expression)`	Similar to DATALENGTH on Microsoft or CHARLEN on Sybase, this function returns a specified number of characters (rather than bytes) of a given expression. LEN doesn't count trailing spaces.
MONTH	Date	`MONTH(date)`	This function is basically equivalent to the function DATEPART (mm, date).

NEWID	System	`NEWID()`	Returns a 16-byte binary string used to generate globally unique identifiers, such as those used in the UNIQUEIDENTIFIER datatype. For example, here's a CREATE TABLE statement that takes advantage of this function:
			`CREATE TABLE sample (`
			`sample id UNIQUEIDENTFIER NOT NULL`
			`DEFAULT NEWID(),`
			`description VARCHAR(500) NULL)`

Table B-4. New Functions (continued)

Function	Type	Syntax	Description
OBJECT-PROPERTY	Prop-erty	`OBJECTPROPERTY (id,'property')`	As with other property functions, this function returns all sorts of information about database objects. Because this function is a catchall for all database objects, it can potentially return an avalanche of data. Refer to the vendor documentation for more detail.
PARSE-NAME	System	`PARSENAME ('object_name', { 1 | 2 | 3 | 4 } )`	For a specified object name, returns: 1 Object name 2 Object owner 3 Database owner 4 Server name If there's an error, PARSENAME returns null.
PERMIS-SIONS	System	`PERMISSIONS ([object_id [, 'column']] )`	This function returns permission information for a given database object. This is useful for determining if the current user can perform a certain operation. The result set of the function is a large and somewhat complex bitmap, where each value indicates a different level of permission. Refer to the vendor documentation for more details.
QUOTE-NAME	String	`QUOTENAME ('character_string' [, 'quote_character'])`	Returns a Unicode string with double quote marks needed to make the input string a valid Microsoft SQL Server quoted identifier. The quote character defaults to [ ] but may also be a single or double quote.
REPLACE	String	`REPLACE ('expression1', 'expression2', 'expression3')`	Replaces all values of expression2 with the values of expression3 found in expression1. (Whew!) For example, the following statement replaces all occurrences of the string DUCK that are found in the string "It is now DUCK season!" with the string WABBIT: `SELECT REPLACE('It is now DUCK season!','DUCK','WABBITT')`
STDEV	Mathe-matical	`STDEV (expression)`	Returns the statistical standard deviation of all non-null values for a given expression. Usable only with numeric columns.
STDEVP	Mathe-matical	`STDEVP (expression)`	Returns the statistical standard deviation of the population of all non-null values for a given expression. Usable only with numeric columns.
SUSER_ID	System	`SUSER_SID (['login'])`	Returns a security identification number (SID), as an integer, for the user's login name.

Table B-4. New Functions (continued)

Function	Type	Syntax	Description
SUSER_SNAME	System	`SUSER_SNAME ([server_user_sid])`	Returns the login identification name from a user's security identification number (SID), as an integer, for the user's login name.
SYSTEM_USER	System	`SYSTEM_USER`	Returns the SQL Server login identification name, if the user is logged into the SQL Server (e.g., SA). Otherwise, it returns the Windows NT login identification name, such as DOMAIN\super_user.

TRIGGER_NESTLEVEL	System	`TRIGGER_NESTLEVEL ([object_id])`	Returns the number of triggers executed for the DML statement that fired the trigger and can determine the current level of nesting. For example:
			`IF ((SELECT TRIGGER_NESTLEVEL`
			`OBJECT_ID('sales') ) ) > 3 )`
			`RAISERROR('Trigger sales nested`
			`more than 3 levels.',16,-1)`

TYPEPROPERTY	Property	`TYPEPROPERTY (type, property)`	Returns information about a given system or user datatype. Properties include: Precision Scale AllowsNull UseAnsiTrim
VAR	Mathematical	`VAR(expression)`	Returns the statistical variance of all non-null values for a given expression. Usable only with numeric columns.
VARP	Mathematical	`VARP(expression)`	Returns the statistical variance of the population of all non-null values for a given expression. Usable only with numeric columns.
+ and -	Date	N/A	Provides addition and subtraction for date fields.

Upgrades to the SET Command

The SET command now enjoys several additions. You can now use the SET command to assign the value of variables. You are no longer forced to use the `SELECT @variable_name = value` syntax. For example, to assign the value of today's date and time to a variable, you could use this command:

```
SET @todays_date = GETDATE()
```

Of course, the variable must be created using the DECLARE command before the SET command can be used.

There are several new and/or improved SET commands:

- ANSI_NULLS (slightly altered behavior)
- CONCAT_NULL_YIELDS_NULL

- LOCK_TIMEOUT
- QUERY_GOVERNOR_COST_LIMIT
- SHOWPLAN_ALL
- SHOWPLAN_TEXT

Behavior has been changed for SET_ANSI_NULLS. It now takes effect only in the next batch subsequent to its activation. It does not take effect when invoked within a stored procedure, instead producing a warning message.

The command SET CONCAT_NULL_YIELDS_NULL ON will produce a null value for a concatenation operation if any operand within the concatenation is NULL.

You can also override the new server configuration parameter "query_governor_ cost limit" using the command SET QUERY_GOVERNOR_COST_LIMIT.

The SET command now supports a neato-keen feature called LOCK_TIMEOUT. SET LOCK_TIMEOUT allows you to control the maximum amount of time you allow a process to be locked by other processes or users. You can use this feature to program an application to allow a user to resume an activity if he is locked out or blocked for a certain period of time.

The command SET SHOWPLAN is not entirely new, but is certainly improved. It now includes SHOWPLAN_ALL and SHOWPLAN_TEXT. The SHOWPLAN_ALL command displays a great deal of query plan information about a query, including the parent identification number of the node being displayed, while SHOWPLAN_TEXT, a subset of SHOWPLAN_ALL, features a more readable and user-friendly reporting format. Here's an example of the report produced by SET SHOWPLAN_TEXT, which is represented in two parts. The first part shows the text of the Transact-SQL command, while the second shows a hierarchical tree detailing each step taken in the execution plan of the command:

```
SET SHOWPLAN_TEXT ON
GO

SELECT *
FROM   authors
WHERE  address like '10 Miss%'
GO
```

The result set looks like this:

```
StmtText
-----------------------------------------------------------
SELECT *
FROM   authors
WHERE  address like '10 Miss%'

(1 row(s) affected)
```

```
StmtText
-----------------------------------------------
  |--Filter(Like(authors.address, '10 Miss%'))
       |--Clustered Index Scan(pubs..authors)

(2 row(s) affected)
```

Other New Transact-SQL Statements

Here is a brief list of important new Transact-SQL commands, or old commands that have important new features. More information about each of these commands is available in the SQL Server 7.0 system documentation.

NOT FOR REPLICATION clause
: Added to both ALTER TRIGGER and CREATE TRIGGER. This feature tells a trigger not to execute when a replication login modifies the table involved in the trigger operation.

BACKUP statement
: Added to allow full or partial database backup operations, and to log backups. It is essentially the same as the DUMP command.

BULK INSERT command
: This BCP-like command performs non-logged copies, moving a database table to or from an external data file in a user-specified format.

COMMIT/ROLLBACK command
: May now include the optional keyword WORK. COMMIT WORK is virtually identical to COMMIT TRAN, except that you cannot identify a user query with it. There's also a new ROLLBACK WORK statement, too.

CREATE STATISTICS command
: Creates a statistics histogram on a table and associated statistics groups for the specified column or set of columns of the table. This is an advanced command and should not be used by novices. Only the table owner can execute CREATE STATISTICS.

Three new DBCC commands
: DBCC CHECKFILEGROUP performs allocation and integrity checks on all tables in the specified filegroup. DBCC SHRINKDATABASE can shrink the actual file size of a given database. DBCC SHRINKFILE reduces the size of a specific data file within a database.

DENY statement
: In the security arena, this new statement enhances security by creating an explicit entry in the security system that denies a permission from a security account in the current database. This differs from Version 6.5, which only allowed you to revoke (or essentially not grant) a certain set of privileges.

DENY also prevents the security account from inheriting permission through a group or role membership.

RESTORE command

The older LOAD statement has been supplanted by the RESTORE command (although LOAD still exists). The RESTORE statement allows full or partial database backups or log backups to be restored. An added bonus is that both LOAD DATABASE and RESTORE DATABASE will automatically create the master database if it doesn't already exist. For user databases, you do not need to create the database before restoring it. SQL Server 7.0 will now create the destination database as part of the restore operation.

REVOKE statement

REVOKE has been changed to only remove or deny access. Formerly, in Version 6.5, it could also be used to create a negative entry in the sysprotects system table.

New System Tables

The times, they are a-changin'. The system tables used in SQL Server Version 7.0 reflect the growing design of the system. These new system tables augment the metadata stored in a Version 6.5 SQL Server. Here is a brief description of each new system table found in Version 7.0 that is not found in Version 6.5:

System Table	Description
backupfile	Stores one row per data or log file that was backed up
backupmediafamily	Maintains metadata about each medium involved in the backup family backup set
backupmediaset	Tells about the backup media set
backupset	Describes the backup set
MSagent_parameters	Stores parameters associated with agent profiles
MSagent_profiles	Stores one row for each defined replication agent profile
MSarticles	Stores one row for each article being replicated by a publisher
MSdistpublishers	Stores one row for each remote publisher supported by the local distributor
MSdistributiondbs	Stores one row for each distribution database defined on the local distributor
MSdistribution_agents	Stores one row for each distribution agent running at the local distributor
MSdistribution_history	Stores history rows for the distribution agents associated with the local distributor

System Table	Description
MSdistributor	Holds all distributor properties
MSlogreader_agents	Stores one row for each log reader agent running at the local distributor
MSlogreader_history	Contains the history rows of the log reader agents associated with the local distributor
MSmerge_agents	Stores one row for each merge agent running at the subscriber
MSmerge_contents	Contains one row for each row modified in the current database since it was published
MSmerge_delete_conflicts	Stores information dealing with delete conflicts
MSmerge_genhistory	Stores data about each generation known to a subscriber within the retention period
MSmerge_history	Stores history rows for previous updates to subscriber
MSmerge_replinfo	Stores one row for each replica made from the local server
MSmerge_subscriptions	Stores one row every time the subscriber is serviced by the merge agent
MSmerge_tombstone (sounds scary!)	Stores information on deleted rows and allows those deletes to propagate to other subscribers
MSpublication_access	Stores a row for each login that has access to the specific publication or publisher
MSpublications	Stores one row for each publication replicated by a publisher
MSpublisher_databases	Stores one row for each publisher/publisher database pair serviced by the local distributor
MSreplication_objects	Contains one row for each object that is associated with replication in a subscriber database
MSreplication_subscriptions	Stores information about each distribution agent servicing the local subscriber database
MSrepl_commands	Stores rows of replicated commands
MSrepl_errors	Contains rows with extra replication agent failure information
MSrepl_originators	Stores one row for each modifiable subscriber where the transaction originated
MSrepl_transactions	Stores one row for each replicated transaction
MSrepl_version	Stores one row with the current version of replication installed

System Table	Description
MSsnapshot_agents	Stores one row for each snapshot agent associated with the local distributor
MSsnapshot_history	Stores history rows for the snapshot agents associated with the local distributor
MSsubscriber_info	Stores one row for each publisher/subscriber pair that is receiving push subscriptions from the local distributor
MSsubscriber_schedule	Holds default merge and transactional synchronization schedules for each publisher/subscriber pair
MSsubscriptions	Stores one row for each subscription serviced by the local distributor
MSsubscription_properties	Stores rows for the parameter information for pull distribution agents
restorefile	Stores one row per restored file
restorefilegroup	Stores one row per restored filegroup
restorehistory	Holds one row per restore operation
sysallocations	Stores one row for each allocation unit
sysaltfiles	Stores one row for each file in a database
sysarticleupdates	Stores information on the articles that are updated
syscacheobjects	Contains information on how the database cache is being used
syscategories	Stores the categories used to organize jobs, alerts, and operators
sysdownloadlist	Contains the queue of download instructions for all target servers
sysfiles	Contains metadata about each database file
sysfilegroups	Maintains metadata about each database filegroup
sysfulltextcatalogs	Shows information about full-text catalogs
sysjobhistory	Stores information about the execution of scheduled jobs
sysjobschedules	Stores schedule information for jobs that will be executed
sysjobs	Stores information for each scheduled job that will be executed
sysjobservers	Stores the association or relationship of a particular job with one or more target servers
sysjobsteps	Stores information for each step in a job that will be executed

System Table	Description
syslockinfo	Stores information on all granted, converting, and waiting lock requests
sysmembers	Stores a row for each member of a database role
sysmergearticles	Stores one row for each merge article defined in the local database
sysmergepublications	Stores one row for each merge publication defined in the database
sysmergeschemachange	Stores information about schema changes
sysmergesubscriptions	Stores one row for each known subscriber and is a local table at each publisher
sysmergesubsetfilters	Stores information about how to rejoin partitioned articles
sysperfinfo	Stores the SQL Server version of counters used by Windows NT Performance Monitor
syspermissions	Stores all information about permissions, both granted and denied
sysoledbusers	Stores one row for each user and password mapping for a specified linked server
sysreplicationalerts	Tells which conditions cause replication alerts to fire
systargetservergroupmembers	Tells about the target servers currently enlisted in a multiserver group
systargetservergroups	Tells about the target server groups currently enlisted in an entire multiserver environment
systargetservers	Tells about the target servers currently enlisted in a multiserver operation domain
systaskids	Stores a mapping of tasks created in earlier versions of SQL Server to the current version

Changes to Columns in System Tables

Many system tables were hanging around in Version 6.5. They're still with us in Version 7.0, but have undergone a few changes. This section only shows those tables that were described in Appendix A and only indicates where columns were dropped. Many system tables had changes in the datatypes or added new columns, but that shouldn't affect any existing Transact-SQL application. Don't write queries directly on the system tables. Instead, starting with Version 7.0, you can write to the ANSI-standard schema views which will not change as the system tables do.

sysdatabases

These columns have been dropped:

logptr
dumptrdate

sysdevices

These columns have been dropped:

mirrorname
stripeset

sysindexes

These columns have been dropped:

distribution
segment
rowpage
keys1
keys2

sysobjects

The "schema" column has been dropped.

sysprocesses

The "gid" column has been dropped. The table also includes a new column, "open_tran", that tells how many transactions a process has.

The following system tables (discussed in Appendix A) have sustained only changes to column datatypes. Everything else about the tables (with the possible exception of a new column or two) is the same:

sysarticles
syscharsets
syscolumns
syscomments
sysconfigures
sysconstraints
syscurconfigs
syslanguages
syslogins
sysremotelogins
sysservers
systypes

New Configuration and Database Options

A number of new server configuration options have been included with Version 7. 0 of Microsoft SQL Server. Since both server-wide and database-wide configuration options are beyond the scope of this book, we'll simply list them for you. If you think you need to know more about these, please refer to the system documentation.

The following are the new server configuration parameters in SQL Server 7.0:

cost threshold for parallelism
extended memory size
index create memory
lightweight pooling
max degree of parallelism
max server memory
min query memory per query
min server memory
query governor cost limit
query wait(s)
remote proc trans
scan for startup procs
time slice
Unicode comparison style
Unicode locale id

The following are the new database configuration parameters in SQL Server 7.0:

autoclose
autoshrink
ANSI nulls
ANSI warnings
concat null yields null
cursor close on commit
merge publish
quoted identifier
recursive triggers
torn page detection

Summary

For ease of reference, this appendix summarized the new Transact-SQL features in Microsoft's SQL Server 7.0.

C

The BCP Utility

The Bulk Copy Program (BCP) is designed to facilitate the import and export of data from your tables to ASCII files. As its name implies, it batches the loading and extraction process. You would be well served to take some time to look at this utility, since BCP is one of the most extensively used and versatile utilities packaged with SQL Server. You can use it to assist in many varied tasks you'll need to perform, like data backup, data manipulation, and data creation.

BCP does not fire rules and triggers.

BCP is a command-line program and supports two states—in and out, used as follows:

in
: To load data into a table

out
: To export data from a table; the data in the table is not removed

BCP Command

Table C-1 shows the BCP command format for Microsoft and Sybase.

Microsoft allows you to use either hyphens (-) or slashes (/) when specifying command-line switches.

Table C-1. BCP Command Summary

Microsoft	Sybase
bcp [[database_name.]owner.]table_name	bcp [[database_name.]owner.]table_name
{in | out} datafile	[:partition_id]
[-a packet size]	{in | out} datafile
[-b batchsize]	[-a display_charset]
[-c]	[-A size]
[-e errfile]	[-b batchsize]
[-E]	[-c]
[-f formatfile]	[-e errfile]
[-F firstrow]	[-E]
[-i path_and_name]	[-f formatfile]
[-L lastrow]	[-F firstrow]
[-m maxerrors]	[-g id_start_value]
[-n]	[-I interfaces_file]
[-o path_and_name]	[-J client_charset]
[-P password]	[-L lastrow]
[-r row_terminator]	[-m maxerrors]
[-S server]	[-n]
[-t field_terminator]	[-P password]
[-U username]	[-q datafile_charset]
[-v]	[-r row_terminator]
	[-R remote_server_principal]
	[-S server]
	[-t field_terminator]
	[-T text_or_image_size]
	[-U username]
	[-v]
	[-X]
	[-z language]

For historical reasons, different versions of BCP use different header information in the BCP format file, described later in the "BCP Format Files" section. The version numbers correspond to the version of Open Client used to write the BCP program (i.e., the BCP version number). If you want to use BCP format files for different versions of SQL Server, you will need to create a different format file for each version of SQL Server. In order to find out which version of BCP you are using, use the -v option with BCP.

BCP supports an interactive mode as well. When you select this mode (i.e., you do not specify a transfer protocol), the program interactively prompts you to specify the storage type of each field in the table as well as any length and terminator details. Once all the fields in the data set being imported or exported are specified, you can specify a filename for this format file.

Using the interactive mode can help you to create a skeleton template file that can be amended as additional information about the data becomes known.

BCP Options and Command Switches

The BCP switches are case-sensitive. Table C-2 summarizes their use under Microsoft and Sybase.

Table C-2. BCP Switches Summary

Switch	Purpose	Microsoft	Sybase
a *display_charset*	Problems can arise if BCP is being run from a terminal with a different character set from the one on the machine on which the actual BCP operation is being performed. Use this option with the -J option to specify the character set translation file.		X
a *packet_size*	Specifies the number of bytes per network packet that is sent to and from SQL Server, ranging in value from 512 to 65,535. The default for this field is 4,096. Changing this field may enhance or degrade performance.	X	
A *size*	Specifies the number of bytes per network packet that is sent to and from SQL Server. You may vary this value. This field may range from default network packet size to maximum network packet size. The value selected must be a multiple of 512. Changing this field may enhance or degrade performance.		X
b *batchsize*	Specifies the number of records in a batch to be copied into the server. SQL Server defaults the batch to 1. If you are loading a large volume of records, you should consider using larger batches. For example, 1,000 might be useful, since the batch size directly affects the transaction size and can have an adverse effect on performance or the log.	X	X
c	The bulk copy operation is performed using the CHARACTER datatype for all fields. Tabs (\t) are used to delimit fields and new lines (\n) are used to delimit rows.	X	X
e *errfile*	Specifies the path and filename of the error file for errors occurring during a bulk copy.	X	X

Table C-2. BCP Switches Summary (continued)

Switch	Purpose	Micro-soft	Sybase
E	If the identity values are in the table to be imported, then this switch must be specified. Otherwise, SQL Server will try to assign a unique row ID to each row being copied.	X	X
f *format-file*	Specifies the path and filename of the format file to be used for this BCP operation. The format file allows you to customize the layout of the data that is being either loaded or extracted from the database.	X	X
F *firstrow*	Specifies the first row from which to start the BCP process.	X	X
g *id_start_value*	Specifies the starting identity value to be used when copying the data in.		X
i *path_and_name*	Specifies the path and name of a file that directs input for a BCP operation. Commonly used to build a BCP script file.	X	
I *interfaces_file*	Specifies a nondefault interfaces file to use for this BCP process. This comes from the Sybase world, where an interface file is used to hold the connection information for each server. Under NT, the *SQL.INI* file performs this function.		X
J *client_charset*	Specifies a character set to use on the client where it differs from the SQL Server character set. Using this switch with no arguments disables character set conversion and should be used when both the server and the client use the same character set.		X
L *lastrow*	Specifies the last row for this BCP process. This is useful if you want to load only the first 1,000 records (or some other arbitrary number).	X	X
m *maxerrors*	Specifies the maximum number of errors that are allowed prior to the BCP process being aborted. The default value is 10.	X	X
n	The bulk copy operation is performed using the native mode or character mode for each field. If this table is being copied out to reload on another server, you should use the (c) option instead	X	X
o *path_and_name*	Specifies the path and name of a file where output generated by BCP is directed. Commonly used to capture error messages during the BCP operation.	X	
P *password*	Specifies the password to use for the login.	X	X
q *datafile_charset*	Allows the BCP process to be run on file systems in which the character set is different from the client's character set.		X

Table C-2. BCP Switches Summary (continued)

Switch	Purpose	Micro-soft	Sybase
r *row_terminator*	Specifies an optional row terminator.	X	X
R *remote_server_principal*	Specifies the principal name for the sever that has been defined according to the security mechanism. This field is required only when the server's principal name differs from the server's network name.		X
S *server*	Specifies the name of the server to which to connect. This is where the data will be loaded into or exported out of.	X	X
t *field_terminator*	Specifies an optional field terminator.	X	X
T *text_or_image_size*	Specifies the maximum length of data the SQL Server will use. The default is 32K. This applies to TEXT and IMAGE fields.		X
U *user-name*	Specifies the SQL Server login name to use for the bulk copy operation.	X	X
v	Returns the version information for the program, as well as a list of all switches.	X	X
X	Enables the client-side password encryption for this session.		X
z *lan-guage*	Specifies the official name of the language that the BCP program should use when it is displaying all prompts and error messages.		X

Data Export with BCP (Out)

In most cases, only a small subset of options is actually used when issuing the BCP command. A sample of a typical BCP command is shown here:

```
bcp pubs..authors out authors.txt -Usa -P -SMERLOT -c
```

In this example, the authors table is bulk copied out using character type mode. As you may have noticed, you don't need to specify switches in any particular order. BCP displays messages similar to the following to detail its progress:

```
Starting copy.....
402 rows copied.
Clock time(ms.): total = 1 Avg = 0 (402000.00 rows per sec.)
```

This means that 402 records were copied and it took one millisecond to copy all the rows. The last line contains the statistics for this BCP process. If the table has more than 1,000 rows in it, BCP will send incremental status messages that say "1,000 rows copied" for each 1,000 rows sent to or from the server.

Data Import with BCP (In)

Here is an example of issuing a typical BCP command for input, using common options:

```
bcp pubs..authors in authors.txt -Usa -P -SMERLOT -c
```

In this example, the authors table is copied in using character type mode. BCP displays messages similar to the following to detail its progress:

```
Starting copy.....
402 rows copied.
Clock time(ms.): total = 1000 Avg = 2 (402.00 rows per sec.)
```

This means that 402 records were copied and it took one second to copy all the rows. The last line contains the statistics for this BCP process, displayed at the end. If the table has more than 1,000 rows in it, BCP will send incremental status messages that say "1,000 rows copied" for each 1,000 rows sent from the server.

As you can see from this example, the time taken to perform the BCP in is significantly higher than the time taken to BCP data out. Depending on the options that have been set in this database, you may have to use the slow BCP mode (see "BCP Performance Considerations" later in this appendix).

BCP Field Type Versus Database Field Type

The BCP format file allows you to specify a different datatype from the data set being imported or exported. This is very useful when you are importing or exporting numerics and DATETIME datatypes. You can tell BCP to treat these columns as a SQLCHAR or character field when you export or import them, even if they are actually numerics. You would want to do this because SQL Server treats noncharacter datatypes very differently and often stores them in an encoded form, which limits your ability to manipulate the raw data if you export it as its original datatype. A similar problem occurs when you are importing noncharacter type data that was not created using SQL Server to begin with.

In order to decide which datatype you want to use to export or import data, you should first establish where the data is coming from, where the data is going, and whether the data structures are dissimilar. If either the source or destination is not a SQL Server or if the data structures are dissimilar, then you will probably find that you need to use the character data type (SQLCHAR) in your format file.

BCP Performance Considerations

BCP works in two modes: *fast* or *slow*. To use the fast mode, all indexes need to be dropped on the table that is being copied into, and the database option for bulkcopy needs to be set on this database. The specific database option syntax differs slightly between products, so please refer to your system manuals for the specific syntax on your server. When you use the fast mode, SQL Server logs only the page allocations and not the actual data inserts into the transaction log. This can be very useful if you have only a small transaction log or if time is critical. However, you will need to weigh this approach against the time it will take you to create your indexes after the BCP process has finished. If you decide to use the slow (or normal) mode, remember to update your statistics on your tables once your data has loaded.

In general, there are two switches you can set to affect the performance of BCP; these are the network packet size (-a or -A) option and the batch size (-b).

Changing the size of the network packet will affect how efficiently you move data to the server. To determine the most effective packet size to use, you will need to have an understanding of your standard network packet size as well as any network load issues that apply to your site. A less time-consuming way of finding this out may be to create a simple table with a set number of records (for example, 100,000) and then change the network packet size to different values and see which BCP process works the quickest. Remember that your organization's network load at a given time will affect the performance information gathered here.

By changing the batch size, you will do two things: first, you will decrease the amount of log space consumed by the load since it will be able to incrementally clear the log as each batch is processed. However, for those of you who need an all-or-nothing approach with the loading, batching is not for you. Once a batch is loaded, it will not be rolled back if the BCP process fails prior to completion. Second, when there are a large number of records being loaded, it will reduce the length of the transaction, and this will ultimately affect the performance of the transaction. In some cases, you may find that by configuring the batch size to a percentage of the overall number of records to be loaded, like 10%, you may achieve improvements in performance. This percentage is affected by the size and configuration of your server.

Sybase SQL Server has additional performance features for BCP using parallel bulk copy, which can be done only on partitioned tables. This process allows you to split your BCP file into several smaller chunks and then load each chunk into a separate partition on that table. The table you are copying into must be partitioned. You can additionally specify different physical disks for each partition, which can also improve the performance of BCP. You may use the same source file as long as you specify different first and last rows on each BCP process. An example of this format of BCP is as follows:

```
bcp pubs..authors:1 in authors.txt ....
bcp pubs..authors:2 in authors2.txt ....
```

In this example, the authors table has been split into two partitions, and data is being loaded from two separate source files.

BCP Format Files

One of the most useful features of BCP is the ability to create format files. These files allow you to customize your input or output file to a certain extent and also allow you to manipulate the order of the data or exclude data by changing the format file. The format file is broken down into two sections:

header information
: The header contains two lines that detail the version of the BCP program being used and the number of columns described in this format file.

detail lines
: The detail section describes each column that is being either exported or imported. The structure of the detail line is as follows:

  Host file column order (HFCO)
  Host file data type (HFDT)
  Prefix length (PL)
  Host file data length (HFDL)
  Terminator (T)
  Server column order (SCO)
  Server column name (SCN)
  Column precision
  Column scale

Column precision and column scale are included only if the table column is a numeric or decimal.

A simple format file for the authors table may look similar to the following (note that the third line is not in the format file; it is just shown to relate the columns to their meanings):

```
6.0
9
{HFCO}   {HFDT}        {PL}{HFDL}  {T}     {SCO}    {SCN}
1        SQLCHAR       0    11     ","     1        au_id
2        SQLCHAR       0    40     ","     2        au_lname
3        SQLCHAR       0    20     ","     3        au_fname
4        SQLCHAR       0    12     ","     4        phone
5        SQLCHAR       0    40     ","     5        address
```

```
6       SQLCHAR     0   20      ","       6       city
7       SQLCHAR     0   2       ","       7       state
8       SQLCHAR     0   5       ","       8       zip
9       SQLBIT      0   1       "\r\n"    9       contract
```

This format file says that all columns will be separated by commas and that a carriage return line feed will be inserted between the rows. This specification applies to both exported and imported data. A sample of the generated data file is as follows:

```
172-32-1176,White,Johnson,408 496-7223,10932 Bigge Rd.,Menlo Park,CA,94025,1
213-46-8915,Green,Marjorie,415 986-7020,309 63rd St. #411,Oakland,CA,94618,1
238-95-7766,Carson,Cheryl,415 548-7723,589 Darwin Ln.,Berkeley,CA,94705,1
267-41-2394,O'Leary,Michael,408 286-2428,22 Cleveland Av. #14,
   San Jose,CA,95128,1
```

Formatting Data

You can use format files to customize the layout of your imported or exported data. For example, you can export a table with commas between certain fields and tabs between others by modifying the format file. You can also use this method to manipulate dissimilar datatypes. The next example illustrates how to create a comma-quote-delimited export file from the authors table:

```
6.0
9
1       SQLCHAR     0       11      ",\""       1       au_id
2       SQLCHAR     0       40      "\",\""     2       au_lname
3       SQLCHAR     0       20      "\",\""     3       au_fname
4       SQLCHAR     0       12      "\",\""     4       phone
5       SQLCHAR     0       40      "\",\""     5       address
6       SQLCHAR     0       20      "\",\""     6       city
7       SQLCHAR     0       2       "\",\""     7       state
8       SQLCHAR     0       5       "\","       8       zip
9       SQLBIT      0       1       "\r\n"      9       contract
```

Using this BCP format file would generate an output file similar to the following:

```
172-32-1176,"White","Johnson","408 496-7223","10932 Bigge Rd.","Menlo
   Park,"CA","94025",1
213-46-8915,"Green","Marjorie","415 986-7020","309 63rd St.
   #411","Oakland","CA","94618",1_
238-95-7766,"Carson","Cheryl","415 548-7723","589 Darwin
   Ln","Berkeley","CA","94705",1
267-41-2394,"O'Leary","Michael","408 286-2428","22 Cleveland Av. #14",
   "San Jose","CA","95128",1
. . .
```

Importing Data When Columns Are Transposed

You can use the format file to insert data into fields that are not necessarily in the same order as the data in the table. In order to do this, you will need to modify the format file and set the server column order (SCO) and server column name column (SCN) to reflect the destination columns. In the following example, the file that is being used to populate the authors table has the au_fname and the au_id columns transposed. The format file has been modified to BCP the data into the right columns by changing those columns to reflect their new order.

```
6.0
9
1    SQLCHAR    0    20    ","       3    au_fname
2    SQLCHAR    0    40    ","       2    au_lname
3    SQLCHAR    0    11    ","       1    au_id
4    SQLCHAR    0    12    ","       4    phone
5    SQLCHAR    0    40    ","       5    address
6    SQLCHAR    0    20    ","       6    city
7    SQLCHAR    0    2     ","       7    state
8    SQLCHAR    0    5     ","       8    zip
9    SQLBIT     0    1     "\r\n"    9    contract
```

Skipping Columns

You can also modify your format file to selectively import data from a text file. This allows you to ignore columns in an import file that may not be relevant. In order to do this, you need to set the server column order (SCO) field to 0. You can also change the server column name field to make the format file easier to read, as shown here for host file columns 5 and 8:

```
6.0
9
1     SQLCHAR    0    11    ","       1    au_id
2     SQLCHAR    0    40    ","       2    au_lname
3     SQLCHAR    0    20    ","       3    au_fname
4     SQLCHAR    0    12    ","       4    phone
5     SQLCHAR    0    12    ","       0    dummy
6     SQLCHAR    0    40    ","       5    address
7     SQLCHAR    0    20    ","       6    city
8     SQLCHAR    0    20    ","       0    dummy
9     SQLCHAR    0    2     ","       7    state
10    SQLCHAR    0    5     ","       8    zip
11    SQLBIT     0    1     "\r\n"    9    contract
```

Summary

This appendix described the BCP utility. BCP is a command-line utility that allows you to import data from files into database tables and export table data out into operating system files. The BCP format files allow you to manipulate the data being imported or exported.

Index

Symbols

Numbers

A

B

E

H

I

N

O

X

Z

About the Authors

Kevin Kline administers well over 100 SQL Server installations across the country for Deloitte & Touche LLP. When he's not pulling out his hair, he likes to spend time with his wife and kids, play classical guitar, restore his '66 Chevy truck, and write screenplays. Kevin is also the author of *Oracle CDE: Reference & User's Guide* (Butterworth-Heinemann) and a coauthor of *Professional SQL Server 6.5 Admin* (WROX Press). Kevin is also an instructor at Ziff-Davis University (*www.zdu.com*). He can be reached at *kekline@compuserve.com.*

Lee Gould is a principal consultant with Sybase Professional Services in New York where she works mainly in the financial services sector on Wall Street. She has been working with SQL Server since 1992 and has been involved in the computer industry for over ten years. She has published numerous articles in *Microsoft SQL Server Professional* (Pinnacle Publishing) and presented on a variety of topics at the International Sybase User Group and Powersoft conferences. Lee was born in Liverpool, England. She grew up in Johannesburg, South Africa where she attended the University of Witwatersrand and received her Bachelors of Commerce in Business Information Systems. Lee immigrated to America four years ago and is currently pursuing an MBA at Seton Hall University in New Jersey. Lee lives in North Brunswick, New Jersey, with her two cats Lady and Paganini. She can often be seen running, cycling, swimming, and horseriding while she trains for marathons and ultra triathlon events. When not immersed in sport, Lee is an avid fan of classical music, good wine, the piano, science fiction, and Terminator II. Her motto for life is "Carpe Diem," which she endeavors to follow regardless of where it leads her. Lee can be contacted at *lee_k_gould@hotmail.com* or *lee.gould@sybase.com.*

Andrew Zanevsky, an independent consultant and founder of AZ Databases, Inc., has been working with SQL Server since 1992. He writes a monthly column "Super Administrator," for *Microsoft SQL Server Professional* (Pinnacle Publishing) and has published more than 100 technical articles throughout his career. He immigrated to the United States from Minsk, Belarus in 1991. He started programming in 1982 and holds a degree from the Belarus State University of Informatics and Radioelectronics (equivalent to an M.S. in computer science). Andrew lives in a suburb of Chicago with his wife Katrin, son Anthony, and stepdaughter Esther. Katrin is also a SQL Server consultant. They work on some projects together and can talk about Transact-SQL at dinner. Andrew's daughter Nikkie lives in New York, wants to be a writer, and has won numerous awards in art contests. Andrew was the president of the Great Lakes SQL Server Users Group in Chicago from 1994 through 1997. He can be reached at *zanevsky@azdatabases.com.*

Colophon

Our look is the result of reader comments, our own experimentation, and feedback from distribution channels. Distinctive covers complement our distinctive approach to technical topics, breathing personality and life into potentially dry subjects.

The animals on the cover of *Transact-SQL Programming* are wallcreepers (*Tichodrama muraria)*, colorful nuthatches with two subspecies, whose habitat is the alpine regions from Eurasia to North Africa. The wallcreeper is a rock dweller, and seeks food by climbing in its native rocks and ravines—hence the name. Its hind toes have long claws with which the bird can grasp small protrusions. While climbing, wallcreepers flap their wings, showing brief glimpses of a red band of feathers; this coloring is intensified in males during mating season. An adult wallcreeper is about seven inches long. Its nests are built of feathers, moss, and other materials found in the rock cliffs.

Jeffrey Liggett was the production editor for *Transact-SQL Programming*; Sheryl Avruch was the production manager; Norma Emory was the copyeditor; Ellie Maden, Sarah Jane Shangraw, and Melanie Wang provided quality control. Robert Romano created the illustrations using Adobe Photoshop 5 and Macromedia FreeHand 8. Mike Sierra provided FrameMaker technical support. Ruth Rautenberg wrote the index.

Edie Freedman designed the cover of this book, using a 19th-century engraving from the Dover Pictorial Archive. The cover layout was produced with Quark XPress 3.32 using the ITC Garamond font. Hanna Dyer designed the CD label. Whenever possible, our books use RepKover™, a durable and flexible lay-flat binding. If the page count exceeds RepKover's limit, perfect binding is used.

The inside layout was designed by Nancy Priest and implemented in FrameMaker 5.5 by Mike Sierra. The text and heading fonts are ITC Garamond Light and Garamond Book. This colophon was written by Nancy Kotary.

More Titles from O'Reilly

Windows Programming

Access Database Design & Programming

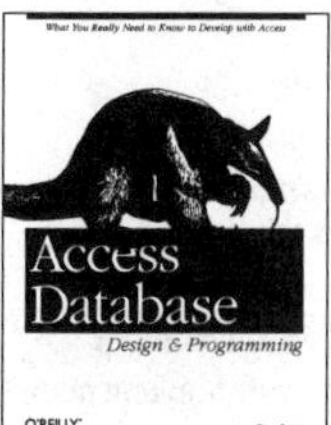

By Steven Roman
1st Edition June 1997
270 pages, ISBN 1-56592-297-2

This book provides experienced Access users who are novice programmers with frequently overlooked concepts and techniques necessary to create effective database applications. It focuses on designing effective tables in a multi-table application; using the Access interface or Access SQL to construct queries; and programming using the Data Access Object (DAO) and Microsoft Access object models.

VB & VBA in a Nutshell: The Languages

By Paul Lomax
1st Edition October 1998
656 pages, ISBN 1-56592-358-8

For Visual Basic and VBA programmers, this book boils down the essentials of the VB and VBA languages into a single volume, including undocumented and little documented areas essential to everyday programming. The convenient alphabetical reference to all functions, procedures, statements, and keywords allows VB and VBA programmers to use this book both as a standard reference guide to the language and as a tool for troubleshooting and identifying programming problems.

Learning VBScript

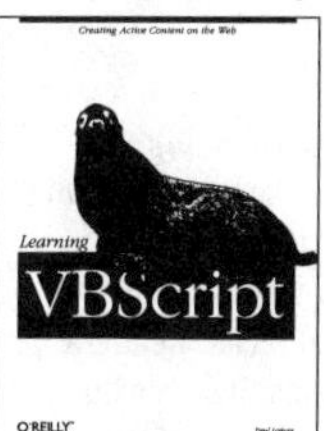

By Paul Lomax
1st Edition July 1997
616 pages, includes CD-ROM
ISBN 1-56592-247-6

This definitive guide shows web developers how to take full advantage of client-side scripting with the VBScript language. In addition to basic language features, it covers the Internet Explorer object model and discusses techniques for client-side scripting, like adding ActiveX controls to a web page or validating data before sending it to the server. Includes CD-ROM with over 170 code samples.

Visual Basic Controls in a Nutshell

By Evan S. Dictor
1st Edition June 1999 (est.)
720 pages (est.), ISBN 1-56592-294-8

This quick reference covers one of the crucial elements of Visual Basic: its controls, and their numerous properties, events, and methods. It provides a step-by-step list of procedures for using each major control and contains a detailed reference to all properties, methods, and events. Written by an experienced Visual Basic programmer, it helps to make painless what can sometimes be an arduous job of programming Visual Basic.

Learning Perl on Win32 Systems

By Randal L. Schwartz,
Erik Olson & Tom Christiansen
1st Edition August 1997
306 pages, ISBN 1-56592-324-3

In this carefully paced course, leading Perl trainers and a Windows NT practitioner teach you to program in the language that promises to emerge as the scripting language of choice on NT. Based on the "llama" book, this book features tips for PC users and new, NT-specific examples, along with a foreword by Larry Wall, the creator of Perl, and Dick Hardt, the creator of Perl for Win32.

Learning Word Programming

By Steven Roman
1st Edition October 1998
408 pages, ISBN 1-56592-524-6

This no-nonsense book delves into the core aspects of VBA programming, enabling users to increase their productivity and power over Microsoft Word. It takes the reader step-by-step through writing VBA macros and programs, illustrating how to generate tables of a particular format, manage shortcut keys, create FAX cover sheets, and reformat documents.

Windows Programming

Developing Windows Error Messages

By Ben Ezzell
1st Edition March 1998
254 pages, Includes CD-ROM
ISBN 1-56592-356-1

This book teaches C, C++, and Visual Basic programmers how to write effective error messages that notify the user of an error, clearly explain the error, and most important, offer a solution. The book also discusses methods for preventing and trapping errors before they occur and tells how to create flexible input and response routines to keep unnecessary errors from happening.

Inside the Windows 95 File System

By Stan Mitchell
1st Edition May 1997
378 pages, Includes diskette
ISBN 1-56592-200-X

In this book, Stan Mitchell describes the Windows 95 File System, as well as the new opportunities and challenges it brings for developers. Its "hands-on" approach will help developers become better equipped to make design decisions using the new Win95 File System features. Includes a diskette containing MULTIMON, a general-purpose monitor for examining Windows internals.

Win32 Multithreaded Programming

By Aaron Cohen & Mike Woodring
1st Edition December 1997
724 pages, Includes CD-ROM
ISBN 1-56592-296-4

This book clearly explains the concepts of multithreaded programs and shows developers how to construct efficient and complex applications. An important book for any developer, it illustrates all aspects of Win32 multithreaded programming, including what has previously been undocumented or poorly explained.

Windows NT File System Internals

By Rajeev Nagar
1st Edition September 1997
794 pages, Includes diskette
ISBN 1-56592-249-2

Windows NT File System Internals presents the details of the NT I/O Manager, the Cache Manager, and the Memory Manager from the perspective of a software developer writing a file system driver or implementing a kernel-mode filter driver. The book provides numerous code examples included on diskette, as well as the source for a complete, usable filter driver.

Windows NT SNMP

By James D. Murray
1st Edition January 1998
464 pages, Includes CD-ROM
ISBN 1-56592-338-3

This book describes the implementation of SNMP (the Simple Network Management Protocol) on Windows NT 3.51 and 4.0 (with a look ahead to NT 5.0) and Windows 95 systems. It covers SNMP and network basics and detailed information on developing SNMP management applications and extension agents. The book comes with a CD-ROM containing a wealth of additional information: standards documents, sample code from the book, and many third-party, SNMP-related software tools, libraries, and demos.

Developing Visual Basic Add-Ins

By Steven Roman
1st Edition December 1998
186 pages, ISBN 1-56592-527-0

A tutorial and reference guide in one, this book covers all the basics of creating useful VB add-ins to extend the IDE, allowing developers to work more productively with Visual Basic. Readers with even a modest acquaintance with VB will be developing add-ins in no time. Includes numerous simple code examples.

How to stay in touch with O'Reilly

1. Visit Our Award-Winning Web Site

http://www.oreilly.com/

★"Top 100 Sites on the Web" —*PC Magazine*
★"Top 5% Web sites" —*Point Communications*
★"3-Star site" —*The McKinley Group*

Our web site contains a library of comprehensive product information (including book excerpts and tables of contents), downloadable software, background articles, interviews with technology leaders, links to relevant sites, book cover art, and more. File us in your Bookmarks or Hotlist!

2. Join Our Email Mailing Lists

New Product Releases

To receive automatic email with brief descriptions of all new O'Reilly products as they are released, send email to:
listproc@online.oreilly.com
Put the following information in the first line of your message (*not* in the Subject field):
subscribe oreilly-news

O'Reilly Events

If you'd also like us to send information about trade show events, special promotions, and other O'Reilly events, send email to:
listproc@online.oreilly.com
Put the following information in the first line of your message (*not* in the Subject field):
subscribe oreilly-events

3. Get Examples from Our Books via FTP

There are two ways to access an archive of example files from our books:

Regular FTP

- ftp to:
  ftp.oreilly.com
  (login: anonymous
  password: your email address)
- Point your web browser to:
  ftp://ftp.oreilly.com/

FTPMAIL

- Send an email message to:
  ftpmail@online.oreilly.com
  (Write "help" in the message body)

4. Contact Us via Email

order@oreilly.com
To place a book or software order online. Good for North American and international customers.

subscriptions@oreilly.com
To place an order for any of our newsletters or periodicals.

books@oreilly.com
General questions about any of our books.

software@oreilly.com
For general questions and product information about our software. Check out O'Reilly Software Online at **http://software.oreilly.com/** for software and technical support information. Registered O'Reilly software users send your questions to: **website-support@oreilly.com**

cs@oreilly.com
For answers to problems regarding your order or our products.

booktech@oreilly.com
For book content technical questions or corrections.

proposals@oreilly.com
To submit new book or software proposals to our editors and product managers.

international@oreilly.com
For information about our international distributors or translation queries. For a list of our distributors outside of North America check out:
http://www.oreilly.com/www/order/country.html

O'Reilly & Associates, Inc.
101 Morris Street, Sebastopol, CA 95472 USA
TEL 707-829-0515 or 800-998-9938
(6am to 5pm PST)
FAX 707-829-0104

International Distributors

UK, Europe, Middle East and Africa (except France, Germany, Austria, Switzerland, Luxembourg, Liechtenstein, and Eastern Europe)

INQUIRIES
O'Reilly UK Limited
4 Castle Street
Farnham
Surrey, GU9 7HS
United Kingdom
Telephone: 44-1252-711776
Fax: 44-1252-734211
Email: josette@oreilly.com

ORDERS
Wiley Distribution Services Ltd.
1 Oldlands Way
Bognor Regis
West Sussex PO22 9SA
United Kingdom
Telephone: 44-1243-779777
Fax: 44-1243-820250
Email: cs-books@wiley.co.uk

France

Orders
GEODIF
61, Bd Saint-Germain
75240 Paris Cedex 05, France
Tel: 33-1-44-41-46-16 (French books)
Tel: 33-1-44-41-11-87 (English books)
Fax: 33-1-44-41-11-44
Email: distribution@eyrolles.com

Inquiries
Éditions O'Reilly
18 rue Séguier
75006 Paris, France
Tel: 33-1-40-51-52-30
Fax: 33-1-40-51-52-31
Email: france@editions-oreilly.fr

Germany, Switzerland, Austria, Eastern Europe, Luxembourg, and Liechtenstein

INQUIRIES & ORDERS
O'Reilly Verlag
Balthasarstr. 81
D-50670 Köln
Germany
Telephone: 49-221-973160-91
Fax: 49-221-973160-8
Email: anfragen@oreilly.de (inquiries)
Email: order@oreilly.de (orders)

Canada (French language books)

Les Éditions Flammarion ltée
375, Avenue Laurier Ouest
Montréal (Québec) H2V 2K3
Tel: 00-1-514-277-8807
Fax: 00-1-514-278-2085
Email: info@flammarion.qc.ca

Hong Kong

City Discount Subscription Service, Ltd.
Unit D, 3rd Floor, Yan's Tower
27 Wong Chuk Hang Road
Aberdeen, Hong Kong
Tel: 852-2580-3539
Fax: 852-2580-6463
Email: citydis@ppn.com.hk

Korea

Hanbit Media, Inc.
Sonyoung Bldg. 202
Yeksam-dong 736-36
Kangnam-ku
Seoul, Korea
Tel: 822-554-9610
Fax: 822-556-0363
Email: hant93@chollian.dacom.co.kr

Philippines

Mutual Books, Inc.
429-D Shaw Boulevard
Mandaluyong City, Metro
Manila, Philippines
Tel: 632-725-7538
Fax: 632-721-3056
Email: mbikikog@mnl.sequel.net

Taiwan

O'Reilly Taiwan
No. 3, Lane 131
Hang-Chow South Road
Section 1, Taipei, Taiwan
Tel: 886-2-23968990
Fax: 886-2-23968916
Email: benh@oreilly.com

China

O'Reilly Beijing
Room 2410
160, FuXingMenNeiDaJie
XiCheng District
Beijing, China PR 100031
Tel: 86-10-86631006
Fax: 86-10-86631007
Email: frederic@oreilly.com

India

Computer Bookshop (India) Pvt. Ltd.
190 Dr. D.N. Road, Fort
Bombay 400 001 India
Tel: 91-22-207-0989
Fax: 91-22-262-3551
Email: cbsbom@giasbm01.vsnl.net.in

Japan

O'Reilly Japan, Inc.
Kiyoshige Building 2F
12-Bancho, Sanei-cho
Shinjuku-ku
Tokyo 160-0008 Japan
Tel: 81-3-3356-5227
Fax: 81-3-3356-5261
Email: japan@oreilly.com

All Other Asian Countries

O'Reilly & Associates, Inc.
101 Morris Street
Sebastopol, CA 95472 USA
Tel: 707-829-0515
Fax: 707-829-0104
Email: order@oreilly.com

Australia

WoodsLane Pty., Ltd.
7/5 Vuko Place
Warriewood NSW 2102
Australia
Tel: 61-2-9970-5111
Fax: 61-2-9970-5002
Email: info@woodslane.com.au

New Zealand

Woodslane New Zealand, Ltd.
21 Cooks Street (P.O. Box 575)
Waganui, New Zealand
Tel: 64-6-347-6543
Fax: 64-6-345-4840
Email: info@woodslane.com.au

Latin America

McGraw-Hill Interamericana
Editores, S.A. de C.V.
Cedro No. 512
Col. Atlampa
06450, Mexico, D.F.
Tel: 52-5-547-6777
Fax: 52-5-547-3336
Email: mcgraw-hill@infosel.net.mx